FUNDAMENTALS
OF
PSYCHOLOGY

AN
INTRODUCTION

FUNDAMENTALS OF PSYCHOLOGY

AN
INTRODUCTION

Michael S. Gazzaniga
NEW YORK UNIVERSITY

Academic Press • New York and London

ACADEMIC PRESS, INC.
111 Fifth Avenue, New York, New York 10003

United Kingdom Edition published by
ACADEMIC PRESS, INC. (LONDON) LTD.
24/28 Oval Road, London NW1

LIBRARY OF CONGRESS CATALOG CARD NUMBER: 72-88364

PRINTED IN THE UNITED STATES OF AMERICA

**To all the girls
Linda, Marin, Anne, Kate, and
finally, Alexandra**

Contents

I. *Nature of the Organism*

II. *Developmental Processes*

7. PERCEPTUAL AND COGNITIVE DEVELOPMENT **139**

III. *Measuring Behavior*

8. STATISTICAL CONCEPTS IN PSYCHOLOGICAL RESEARCH **183**

9. PSYCHOLOGICAL METHODS OF INQUIRY **225**

IV. Sensation and Perception

10. VISUAL SENSITIVITY   245

11. THE PERCEPTION OF THINGS   267

12. PERCEPTION OF SPACE AND MOVEMENT   301

V.   *The Changing Organism*

VI. Personality and Social Behavior in Perspective

VII.   *The Mind of Man*

Preface

The behavioral sciences have tackled no less a problem than to come to a rational and scientific understanding of life. While the physicist continues to unearth new subatomic particles and to work out the subtle details of the inner workings of the atom, and the biologist, just having cracked the genetic code, labors on filling in the details of biochemical pathways, the psychologist takes on the most basic question of all: "What is the nature of man?" With knowledge accumulating at an incredible rate in the physical and biological sciences, the student of behavior is faced with the question of how all of this relates to conscious experience. Progress in understanding these issues has been dramatic. Yet, even though thousands upon thousands of men and women have contributed a wide variety of fascinating and intriguing observations on the problem, many of the fundamentals of behavioral science remain elusively mysterious.

The objective of this book is to center the study of psychology around issues that cut through the artificial barriers commonly established in the study of behavior. It is an organic view, one that builds upon what is known about the physical aspects of the nervous system and then proceeds to integrate the dynamic aspects of biological function with many of the psychological findings and theories about the development and overall maintenance of behavioral patterns. The challenge in tackling the problem in this way has been great, but then again, of course, so is the need. Perspective must be sought in the study of behavior. The subject demands that we understand how the different factors interrelate. We must realize that we live and work in a gloriously complex universe, and must assume from the start that the study of behavior will be no less complex than the world in which we live.

The nature–nurture theme appears throughout the book. At almost every level in the study of behavior we are faced with the problem of determining the extent to which behavior is influenced by environmental and genetic factors. Most often, of course, behavior is the result of an interaction between the two. It is a vastly important question because if we are to understand the determinants of behavior we must know which realm to investigate.

In writing an introductory book one discovers just how complex the science of psychology has become. When I undertook this enterprise, I thought I would write every word of the book, and indeed the book as it now appears was conceived as a whole with its special approach of trying to integrate structure with function, nature with nurture. It soon became clear, however, that with today's information explosion in the behavioral sciences, one must call upon specialists for advice and help. I was fortunate in obtaining the assistance of a number of extremely talented people whose enthusiasm for their topics was contagious. In being served by this group, the reader benefits because these people have specific, up-to-date knowledge in particular psychological disciplines.

I would like to thank the following people for writing several chapters. Their help has been essential.

Ethology: Stuart Dimond
Cardiff University, England

Language and Self-Control: Ann Premack
Santa Barbara, California

Cognitive Development: Richard Sanders
Columbia University, New York

Statistics and Measurement: Arthur Sandusky
University of California, Santa Barbara, California

Experimental Design: John Seamon
Wesleyan University, Connecticut

Perception: Lloyd Kaufmann
New York University, New York

Animal Learning: James Terhune
Stanford University, California

Information Processing: Geoffrey Loftus
University of Washington, Washington

Motivation: Edgar E. Coons
New York University, New York

Personality: Andrea Velletri Glass
New York University, New York

Social Psychology: Judith Rodin
Yale University, Connecticut

Social Problems: Sheldon Cohen
New York University, New York

These contributions—plus those of many reviewers, graduate students, and others—had to be integrated into a coherent book. As a result, there have frequently been numerous changes during the many stages of revision. Thus, I must take full responsibility for any existing errors.

In addition, I would like to extend my profound thanks to Robert Filbey, the book's illustrator. From his fascinating three-dimensional brain model at the end of the book to his illustrations depicting psychological problems, Filbey has given his every talent to the task of improving the art of communication.

I would also like to thank the many reviewers, including Colin Blakemore, Charles Harris, and Leo Goldberger for their helpful suggestions during revision. I will be forever grateful to Leon Festinger, the overall editorial consultant of the book. He brought to bear on his task an extraordinarily profound understanding of the problems of behavior, and was exceedingly generous in his aid. It was an exhilarating experience for me to work closely with him.

I have taken the liberty to reserve my own views and prejudices on the subject of psychology for the last chapter wherein I review much of my own research. The objective here is to outline for the student the organization of a general laboratory research program and to inform the reader that the variety of prejudices one has in research has, as much as is humanly possible, been channeled in this book into the last chapter.

Michael S. Gazzaniga

Acknowledgments

I would like to thank and acknowledge the kindness of the publishers and authors for the following permissions.

Figures 3-5, 3-6, 3-7	Tinbergen, N., *The study of instinct.* Oxford: The Clarendon Press, 1951.
Figure 3-10	Thorpe, W. H. *Bird song.* London & New York: Cambridge Univ. Press, 1961.
Figures 3-12, 3-13	Hess, E. H. Imprinting in animals. *Scientific American,* 1958, **198,** 81–86.
Tables 6-1, 6-2	Classification of English Consonants by Place and Manner of Articulation. Table 4-1 from Denes, Peter B., & Pinson, Elliot N. *The speech chain. The physics and biology of spoken language.* Copyright 1963 by the Bell Telephone Laboratories. Reprinted by permission.
Figure 7-14	Olver, R., & Hornsby, J. On equivalence. In J. Bruner, R. Olver, and P. Greenfield (Eds.), *Studies in cognitive growth.* New York: Wiley, 1966. Pp. 68–85. Copyright © 1966 by John Wiley and Sons, Inc. Reprinted by permission.
Figure 7-3	Five jars of liquid used by the child to make a yellow mixture. From Inhelder, J., & Piaget, B., *The growth of logical thinking from childhood to adolescence.* New York: Basic Books, 1958. P. 108.
Figure 7-6	A model of memory processes. Modified after a figure in Norman, D. A. *Memory and attention.* New York: Wiley, 1969. P. 90.
Figure 7-7	Haith, M. M., Developmental changes in visual information processing and short-term visual memory. *Human Development,* 1971, **14,** 249–261.

Figure 7-9

Visual scanning patterns. A composite of two figures in Vurpillot, E. Judging visual similarity: The development of scanning strategies and their relation to differentiation. *Journal of Experimental Child Psychology*, 1968, **6**, 632–650.

Figure 7-11

Belmont, J. M., & Butterfield, E. C. What the development of short-term memory is. *Human Development*, 1971, **14**, 236–248.

Figure 7-15

A collection of geometric shapes. From Inhelder, J., & Piaget, B. *The growth of logical thinking from childhood to adolescence.* New York: Basic Books, 1958. P. 108.

Quotation on page 205

Goddard, Henry. *The development of intelligence.* Baltimore, Maryland: Williams & Wilkins, 1916.

Figures 8-2, 8-3

Kinsey, A. C., Pomeroy, W. B., & Martin, C. E. *Sexual behavior in the human male.* Philadelphia, Pennsylvania: W. B. Saunders, 1948.

Figures 8-1, 8-4, 8-5

Kinsey, A. C., Pomeroy, W. B., Martin, C. E., & Gebhard, P. H. *Sexual behavior in the human female.* Philadelphia, Pennsylvania: W. B. Saunders, 1953.

Figure 8-6

Jensen, Arthur R. How much can we boost I.Q. and scholastic achievement? *Harvard Educational Review*, **39**, Winter 1969, p. 24. Copyright © 1969 by President and Fellows of Harvard College.

Figure 11-8

Cornsweet, T. N. Information processing in human visual system. *Stanford Research Institute Journal*, 1969, Feature issue No. 5.

Figures 11-2, 11-5, 12-2

Ratliff, Floyd. *Mach bands.* San Francisco, California: Holden-Day, 1965.

Figure 11-22

Blakemore, C., & Sutton, P. Size adaptation: A new aftereffect. *Science*, 10 October, 1966, **166**, 245–247. Copyright 1966 by the American Association for the Advancement of Science.

Figure 12-9

Gibson, J. J. *The perception of the visual world.* Boston, Massachusetts: Houghton-Mifflin, 1950.

Figure 12-36

Harris, Charles. Perceptual adaptation to inverted, reversed, and displaced vision. *Psychological Review*, 1965, **72**, 419–444. Copyright 1965 by the American Psychological Association and reproduced by permission.

Figure 16-7

Peterson, L., & Peterson, M. Short retention of individual items. *Journal of Experimental Psychology*, 1959, **58**, 193–198.

Figure 17-1

Kennedy, G. C. The hypothalamic control of food intake in rats. *Proceedings of the Royal Society, London, Series B*, 1950, **137**, 535–548.

Figure 17-2

Teitelbaum, Philip, & Epstein, A. N. The lateral hypothalamic syndrome: Recovery of feeding and drinking after lateral hypothalamic lesions. *Psychological Review*, 1962, **69**, 74–90. Copyright 1962 by the American Psychological Association and reproduced by permission

Figure 17-3

Anand, B. K., & Brobeck, J. R. Localization of a feeding center in the hypothalamus of the rat. *Proceedings of the Society for Experimental Biology and Medicine*, 1951, **77**, 323–324.

Figure 17-4   Teitelbaum, P. Sensory control of hypothalamic hyperphagia. *Journal of Comparative and Physiological Psychology*, 1955, **48,** 156–163. Copyright 1955 by the American Psychological Association and reproduced by permission.

Figure 17-5   Olds, J. Self-stimulation of the brain. *Science*, 14 February, 1958, **127,** 315–324.

Table 18-1   Shields, J. *Monozygotic twins*. London & New York: Oxford Univ. Press, 1962.

Table 18-2   Fuller, J. L., & Thompson, W. R. *Behavior genetics*. New York: Wiley, 1960. Copyright © 1960 by John Wiley and Sons, Inc. Reprinted by permission.

Figure 19-3   Rorschach Inkblot Test. Berne, Switzerland: Hans Huber.

Figure 19-4   Murray, Henry A. Thematic Apperception Test. Harvard University Press, Copyright 1943 by the President and Fellows of Harvard College; 1971 by Henry A. Murray.

Tables 20-1, 20-2, 20-3   Coleman, J. C. *Abnormal psychology and modern life* (3rd ed.). Glenview, Illinois: Scott, Foresman, 1964.

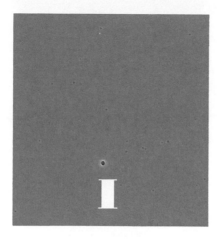

Nature
of the Organism

1

Physical Aspects of Behavior: Basic Neurology

On the night of August 2, 1958, Vernon Atchley went to the home of his wife, from whom he was separated, and shot her dead. He claimed she was behaving promiscuously.

Atchley was a borderline mental defective, with an I.Q. of only 60, and he could neither read nor write. However, he had an unusual talent for business for he was the owner of a used car lot, a number of rental properties, an 80-acre ranch, and a tavern, all in, or near, the prospering northern California town of Oroville. Nonetheless, his marriage had been a total failure. Both Atchley and his wife were alcoholics and they fought constantly. Their tavern companions grew weary of hearing them threatening to kill each other.

Atchley, then 44, was convicted of first-degree murder in Butte County Superior Court, the same county that had sentenced his brother to life imprisonment for another killing. Atchley was sentenced to die in the gas chamber on March 25, 1960, but was given a reprieve because the State Legislature was then considering the abolition of capital punishment. Subsequently, the Legislature chose not to outlaw the death penalty, and Atchley's date of execution was reset for August 23, 1961.

When Atchley's case was automatically reviewed by the State clemency secretary, it was noticed that a report from the San Quentin psychologist had indicated that Atchley had suffered a head injury in 1956, which had left him unconscious for the whole day. Since then Atchley had had "recurring

3

nightmares and headaches and could not sleep." The psychologist concluded, however, that Atchley's responses to certain tests gave no conclusive evidence of organic brain damage. This was also the opinion of the neuropsychiatric committee that had examined the condemned man.

However, the clemency secretary observed that Atchley had never been given an electroencephalogram, an electrical measurement of the brain waves that might confirm the psychologist's findings. He was finally given such a test in San Quentin just five days before he was to die and the results were startling. "Diagnosis: abnormal brain wave with bilateral slowing, spikes indicative of unseen and traumatic central nervous system residual." These brain waves tend to be present in people who have suffered from serious brain damage and who have a residual of increased sensitivity, emotional lability, and irritability. They are somewhat less able to control emotional situations and impulses. Because of this new evidence, the Atchley case fell under the Durham rule of the Federal Court, which declares that, if a criminal act is a product of a mental deficiency or disease, the act is not punishable. Atchley's sentence was commuted to life imprisonment.

Who is to blame for Vernon Achley's plight? Is society? Is his mother? His father? Or was he born with a genetically determined predisposition for violence? Or was it the residual of his head injury? This is the kind of general problem that continually faces the psychologist. How much of any piece of behavior is the product of the social or physical environment changing the natural tendencies of the organism? Or how much of our behavior is inborn? There is no more fundamental point in psychology; the question arises in every aspect of the study of behavior, from the mating behavior of bees to personality development.

The aim of this book is the study of behavior. Before one can proceed, however, we must understand something about the fundamental nature of the controlling organ of behavior—the brain. We must know what it is capable of, what normal development is, and how much of it is physically and genetically determined. Then we can approach one of the most crucial problems in psychology, namely, how and to what extent can the environment modify the predetermined capacities of an organism?

It may come as a surprise that these are proper questions for the psychologist. But it is so. Whether he studies behavior from a genetic, developmental, physiological, or experimental basis, the psychologist is continually trying to understand the basic issues raised in the heredity versus environment issue. Separating the causes and distinguishing data from inference is the job of the psychologist.

In this section of the book, our aim is to clearly establish many of the basic, locked-in physical and psychological characteristics of the organism.

Surprisingly, until recently, few psychologists have thought it important to consider the basic properties of the nervous system. It was long part of the American psychological dream that all brains are created equal. The idea has not held up, however, and the following discussions look at the evidence for and against equality in nervous systems. Generally, our aim is to outline the kinds of existing data that indicate what nervous systems can and cannot do. Only by understanding the physiological and psychological limits of the system can we gain insight into the nature of brain and mind.

NEUROLOGICAL ORGANIZATION OF CENTRAL NERVOUS SYSTEM

The Neuron

The basic unit or building block for the entire nervous system is a slimy, extraordinarily thin, long, and magnificently mysterious piece of protoplasm called the neuron (Figure 1-1). Its basic components are the dendrites, which receive information in a bioelectric form from other neurons. The information received at the dendrites is fed into a large cell body. This electrical information produces an action potential, which amounts to one unit of electrical information and which is subsequently propagated down a long cylindrical structure called the axon. The neuron can be microscopically small or up to five feet long, as in the sensory neurons that receive information from the leg in man.

Neurons come in a variety of shapes and sizes and consist of a grayish-colored cell body which houses the metabolic machinery and sustains the cell through all of its electrical activities. The complex chemical reactions occurring in the cell body that keep the neuron alive and functioning are understandable on their own terms, yet it remains quite mysterious how these metabolic activities support the electrical activity of the neuron.

The neuron is surrounded by a membrane that is semipermeable to a variety of chemicals. In the normal resting state, an active process is going on in the neuron that maintains a critical imbalance between certain of the chemical ions in and around the neuron. This imbalance produces an electrical charge across the neuronal membrane. When a nerve impulse occurs, there is a progressive change in electrical properties of the neuronal membrane, which results in the conduction of the nerve impulse down the axon. The energy involved in producing a nerve impulse is provided by the neuron itself. The input merely serves to trigger the neuron, which means that once fired the amplitude of the electrical impulse is constant as is the speed of conduction down most of the length of the neuron.

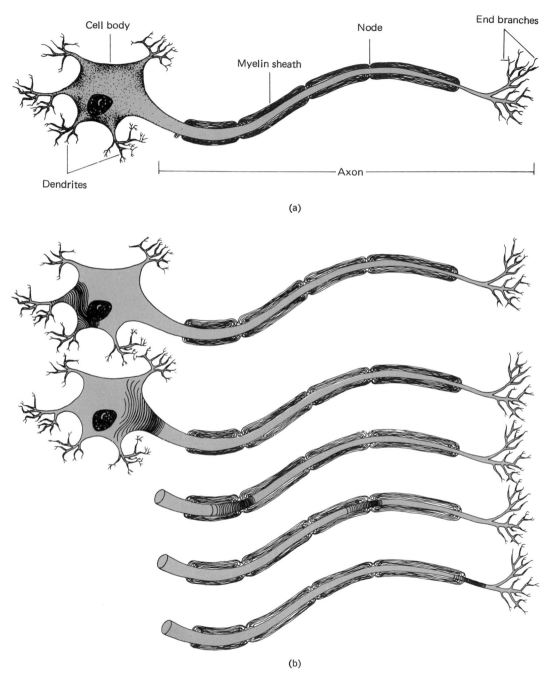

FIGURE 1-1   (a) The basic features of a neuron. (b) The propagation of the electrical impulse from the cell body to the axon terminal.

Another feature of neurons is that, after one has fired, there is a period of time within which it cannot fire again. This is called the absolute refractory period. Thus, two stimuli occurring extremely close together will probably result in a neuron firing only once.

There are many kinds of neurons. Each of them obeys the same laws for electrical propagation. There is, however, significant variation as to how they receive information at their receptor sites.

Some of the specialized neurons that receive information of a specific kind and quality are shown in Figure 1-2. For example, the olfactory neurons enable us to distinguish different smells. The mechanism of smell is fascinating and mysterious. In brief, odorous particles from the object being smelled must pass into the nose and the upper and posterior portions of the nasal cavity. There they come into contact with what is called the olfactory epithelium, which is a thin layer of tissue with many olfactory receptors embedded within. The odorous particle must dissolve in the solutions surrounding the epithelium. The resulting reaction somehow fires the olfactory receptor, which is part of the neural chain on the way into the brain. It is not at all clear how the process occurs or what characteristics the chemical stimulus must have in order to cause an olfactory response. Similar intriguing mechanisms are seen in the auditory system as well as the system that informs us of touch information on the surface of our bodies.

The Synapse

No matter what process is involved in precipitating an action potential, a neuron, once triggered, is irrevocably committed to sending the electrical impulse down its axon to the very tip. At that point it is either successful in firing the next neuron in sequence or it is not. Sir Charles Sherrington named this anatomical point a synapse (Figure 1-3), and was largely responsible for initiating the systematic exploration of synaptic mechanisms.

There are three basic kinds of synapses: one kind is excitatory, and the other two are inhibitory in nature. The excitatory synapse consists of an axon lying in direct proximity to a dendrite. The actual junction is made by the synaptic knob. Between the knob and dendrite of the receiving neuron is a space called the synaptic cleft. At present it is thought the knob secretes chemicals into the cleft, by having little tiny vesicles migrate through the knob and squirt their contents into the cleft. The postsynaptic membrane becomes affected by the secreted substance by lowering its threshold for triggering an impulse. If enough excitatory impulses are received, the neuron fires resulting in what is called an EPSP or excitatory postsynaptic potential.

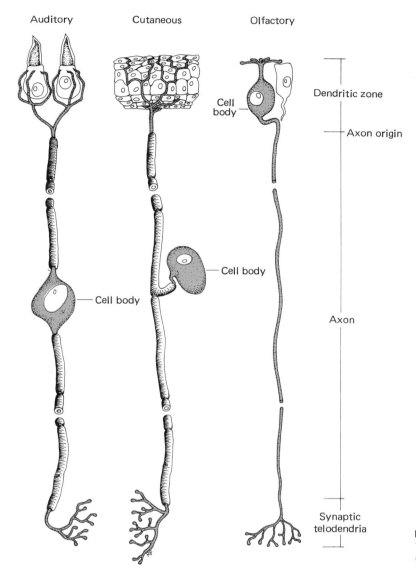

FIGURE 1-2
Three types of receptor neurons.

In addition to excitatory inputs to a neuron, there are also inhibitory inputs. These generally occur on the cell body, or soma, and are called axosomatic synapses. Anatomically, they look almost identical to excitatory synapses and the electrical potentials they produce. An inhibitory postsynaptic potential (IPSP) is the mirror image of an EPSP, that is, an inhibitory potential serves to make the internal charge of the neuron more negative, thereby decreasing the probability that it will discharge.

With these two more or less push-pull forces acting on a neuron, it is

Synaptic knobs

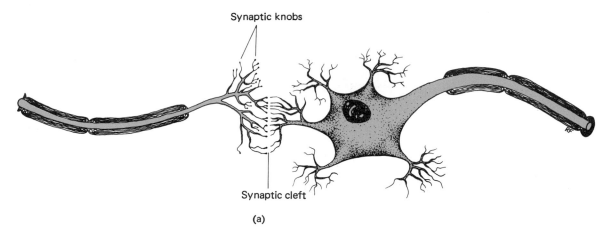

Synaptic cleft

(a)

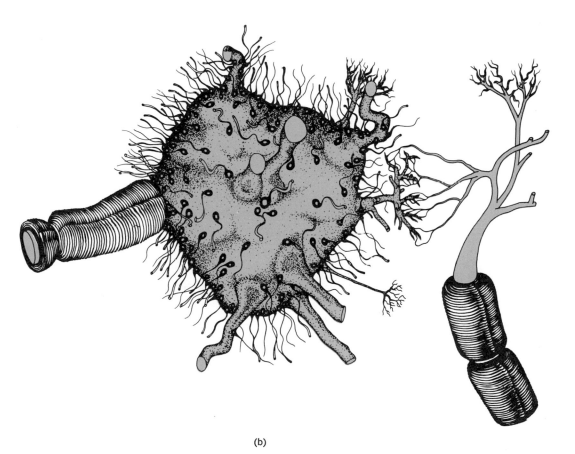

(b)

FIGURE 1-3   (a) An excitatory synapse. (b) The complexity of the synaptic connections on each neuron is apparent by noting the number of synaptic knobs.

a wonder to some that a series of neurons ever fires properly at all. Yet, the mechanism of action is quite simple. Each individual neuron simply adds up the excitatory and inhibitory influences impinging upon it. If enough excitatory influences are present to move the voltage to a state of depolarization of the membrane, an action potential is generated. If there are not enough excitatory forces, the neuron remains in its resting state.

A third kind of neural junction, seen in the central nervous system, is the axoaxonic synapse in which the axon makes functional contacts with the axon of another neuron. The kind of inhibitory influence exerted is called presynaptic inhibition. It is much more complicated than the other varieties, and it will suffice only to mention its existence.

The Organizational Principles of Nervous Tissues

Neurons are interesting and their mechanisms for action are intriguing, but to some extent the psychologist who is mainly interested in behavior only has to know that they work. A far more important question for the psychologist is "What are the laws governing neural development?" More generally, is the nervous system a fixed network of ten billion neural connections, or is it a loosely organized mass of tissue that is easily modified and changed in response to the environment? This is the most fundamental question the student of behavior can ask the student of biological systems.

In the 1920's, the predominant view was that nervous tissue grew at random and a diffuse unstructured equipotential network was established that "knew nothing" and could be altered and structured only by experience. The cry was that "function precedes form in the nervous system" and the scientific literature was replete with data to support the assertion. For example, the clinical condition of "crocodile tears" was reported to be eliminated by reeducation and practice. Here, following a facial injury severing peripheral nerves, normal regeneration frequently results in neurons, which normally innervate the salivary gland, finding their way to the tear or lacrymal gland. In such a case, when a patient saw a nice, big, juicy piece of meat, he would cry instead of salivating. With practice, however, it was maintained that he would quickly inhibit his bizarre response and everything would shift back to normal.

Alternatively in cases where nerve regeneration was impeded for one reason or another, the neurosurgeon would intervene and take a branch from the nerves normally growing out to the neck and shoulder muscles and shove it into a facial muscle. Initially, the patient's face would appear to twitch and shrug a bit, but here again it was maintained that with practice the problem corrected itself.

The dogma, then, was that the nervous system is not fixed in any way. Any particular pattern of response a neuron might have could be easily modified and changed by different environmental conditions. Today, this notion is considered totally incorrect and untenable. Yet, one can well imagine its authority in the 1920's when, at scientific meetings all across the country, biologists were telling psychologists about the wishy-washy nature of the central nervous system, and psychologists were enthralled because this went along with the view that an organism could be made into anything. "Give me," said J. B. Watson, the founder of American behaviorism, "any baby and I'll make him into anything." This apparently airtight physiological and psychological story plus wishful thinking explains why these views held up so long.

In the early 1940's, however, evidence to the contrary emerged. R. W. Sperry, in a stunning series of experiments, firmly established the dogma of neuronal specificity. He showed that each neuron in the central nervous system has its own chemical identity and is genetically predestined to hook up to a particular point in the brain. In short, a biochemical code is embedded in each individual neuron, which must, by virtue of this code, grow to a particular place.

This idea dramatically opposed the prevalent view of nonspecificity in random growth processes. But over a twenty-year period, with experiment after experiment confirming and elaborating his results, most scientists came to favor Sperry's position.

Some of the evidence for neurospecificity comes from fish (Figure 1-4). In higher organisms, however, this kind of recovery from injury is not possible. Consequently, the kind of evidence accumulated here on the question of neural wiring is of an opposite kind. It demonstrates how once the system is set it cannot be changed. In the rat, for example, the sensory nerve enervating the left leg can be surgically disconnected and stuck into the right leg. After recovery, stimulation of the right leg results in the left leg withdrawing! If reeducation and neural plasticity were possible, the rat would learn to withdraw the right leg, but it never does. This is because the wiring for this kind of behavior is fixed, and, no matter what kind of reeducation or how intense the environmental stimulus, the nervous system is never able to adapt to the change. The implications of neuronal specificity are profound. If a newborn baby has all its neural connections firmly established, then the main way for the environment significantly to modify the ultimate potential of the organism is by not providing critical stimulation to some of these prewired circuits at a particular point in development. Thus, if a cat does not see horizontal lines in its environment at an early age, there is a good chance it never will (Blakemore & Cooper, 1970). A cat is born with horizontal edge detectors, but they must be used. If they are not, they give away due to disuse or are

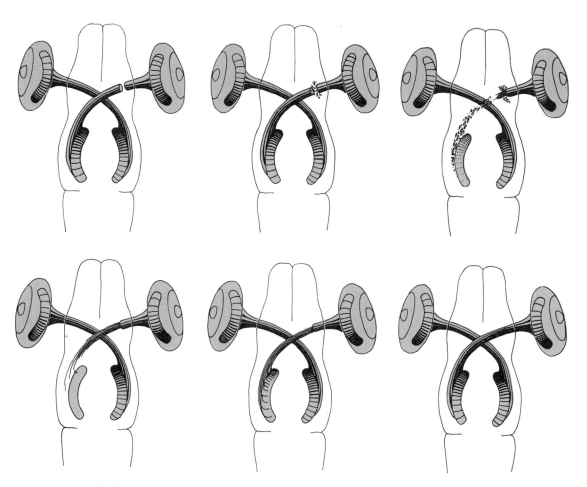

FIGURE 1-4   An ingenious experiment by Attardi and Sperry (1960). The optic tract of a fish, which is the nerve structure leading from the eye to the brain, was cut (top left). In the fish, unlike in man, the structure first degenerates (top right) then regenerates (bottom left to bottom right). What was discovered was that the growing optic tract pushes its way through all kinds of foreign nervous tissue until it finally makes contact with the visual part of the brain. Then it mysteriously stops growing and hooks up properly with the existing visual structures within the brain, with the result that the fish again sees normally.

perhaps modified for other duty (see Chapter 2). This process is not completely understood biologically, but the phenomenon does occur.

Still the matter is not closed. Given what is in the balance, the issue continues to receive major attention, and various experimental programs are constantly engaging in trying to specify the extent to which the wiring diagram is "fixed." Was, for example, Lee Harvey Oswald born a murderer, constitutionally predisposed to violence, or was he made into a criminal by the social forces of our contemporary society?

Or consider the matter of intelligence. Are you as smart as you are because of a particular neural wiring pattern in your brain, which was specifically constructed from the combined genetic information donated by your parents? Or are you bright by virtue of the training you received in both school and at home? Are nymphomaniacs predisposed to their particular interest because of neural wiring in combination with abnormal body chemistry? Or, are they people who have simply grown to love sexual intercourse?

Who knows? The answer, at present, is nobody. Yet, before we can unravel the complex forces that make an individual what he is, it is necessary to try to understand what his overall behavioral and biological constants are. What is it that is fixed about the individual? How is he constituted when delivered to this big, mad world?

These questions will be illuminated in Chapter 2 through studying the visual system. It is our most dominant sense, and it turns out to be one of the more extensively studied mechanisms. But first, a few generalities of brain development should be considered.

GENERAL FEATURES OF BRAIN DEVELOPMENT

The developing brain takes its form from a deepening neural groove appearing on the outer layer of the fertilized egg (Figure 1-5). The outer layer surges up and joins together, producing a neural tube underneath. It is this neural tube that develops into the brain and spinal cord. And, according to a strongly biased genetic view of man, it is already set that Oswald will kill.

Subsequently, the rostral end of the tube develops at a rapid rate, and, as can be seen from Figure 1-6, the 50-mm human embryo already has the general outlines of a baby. It is interesting to note that at the 3.5-mm stage, less than one month after fertilization, all eggs of vertebrates look alike. Only after this stage do the different specific features of an animal start to appear. Yet details about the human are still obscure, for embryological data on the human fetus have been tedious and slow to collect in the past. With the advent of legalized abortion, however, many of the mysterious features ought to be cleared up.

As the brain continues to develop, the neural tube divides into three main subdivisions: the forebrain, which becomes the cerebrum and thalamus; the midbrain; and the hindbrain, which becomes the pons, cerebellum, and medulla oblongata. The latter structures are not of primary concern to the psychologist, whereas the cerebrum absorbs much of our time.

The cerebrum, which does not follow the relatively simple development

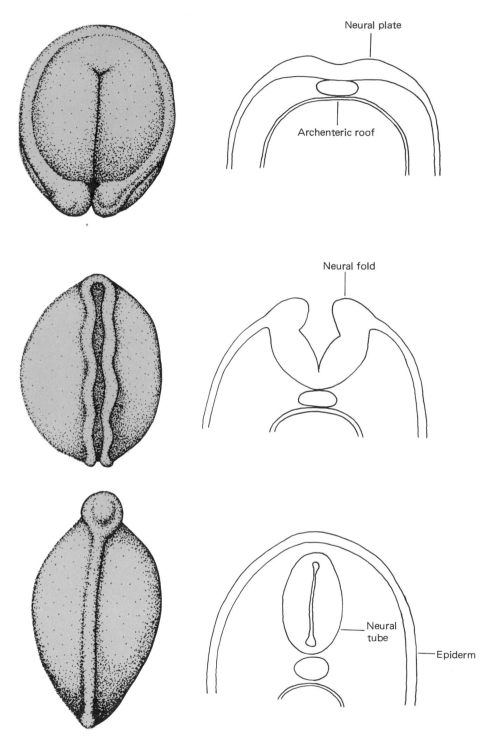

FIGURE 1-5 The fertilized zygote begins very early in establishing the neural groundwork for a complex central nervous system. Progressing downward, we see how the embryo organizes itself for development of the neural tube that eventually becomes the brain in the anterior portion of the zygote and the spinal cord in the more posterior regions.

14

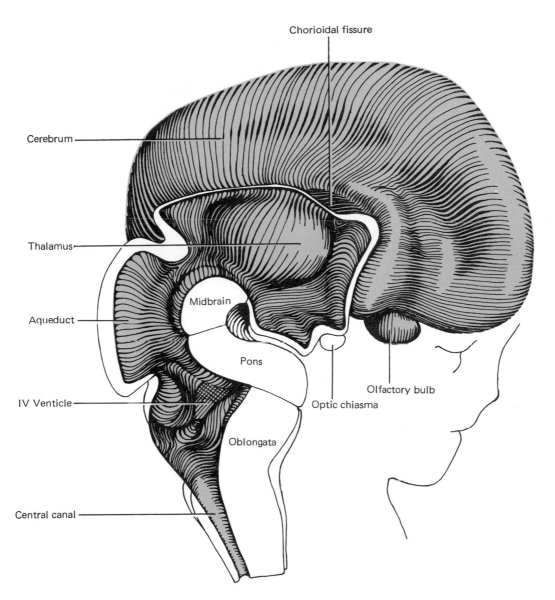

FIGURE 1-6   The developing embryo takes on human features in formation at an early age. The 50-mm embryo would not be able to exist separate from its mother. Indeed, it would be difficult to maintain that the embryo at this stage is "human," for none of its neurological system interacts in a way that would allow the subjective feeling we as humans enjoy.

plan of other brain areas, starts to balloon and grow like a tumor. Moreover, unlike the thalamus, for example, there is unequal development of the lateral walls or, more accurately, the cerebral cortex. This is the "stuff" of man. We have more of it than other animals, and it is largely responsible for getting us into and out of most of our predicaments.

Once started, the cerebrum grows at a faster rate than any other part of the brain. The cerebrum is prevented from growing forward indefinitely by the skull. Since it is genetically predisposed for bigger things in man, it must find space. Consequently, it starts a backward extension that eventually results in its covering thalamus, midbrain, and even cerebellum (see Figure 1-6).

As development continues, the various brain structures take on more enduring features and the individual neurons become myelinated. This is a process whereby a fatty protein sheath covers a neuron and makes it more efficient at electrical conduction. It is thought that before a neuronal system becomes functional, it must undergo myelination. Studying the relative time course of myelination in the central nervous system (CNS) reveals that myelination continues after birth. It is also clear that the cortical areas of the brain are the last to be myelinated.

It is generally believed that the motor areas of the brain are in operation before the sensory system. In the chicken embryo, for example, there is much activity before any of it is related to specific sensory stimulation. Killing the embryo and subjecting it to histological inspection reveals its motor system to be functional while the sensory system is not yet fully developed.

Early Brain Trauma

Nonetheless, the brain is very likely to be extremely fragile at or around birth. There are many scientists who feel the slightest injury to the brain at this time has disastrous consequences later on in life. Mental retardation, which is one of the saddest and most perplexing of human problems, may result, in part, from a momentarily insufficient oxygen supply to the brain because of traumatic delivery. Certainly, diminution in oxygen at a time when the cortical cells are insufficiently established could prove to be disastrous in later years.

Even after birth the brain is terribly fragile. D. O. Hebb has shown that children suffering a traumatic blow on the head during the first year of life tend to show mental impairments at maturity. Curiously, blows to the head after one year do not have such serious effects. It is as if the final touches of neural maturation are carried out during this time and an unnatural intervention with the dynamics of cerebral physiology impairs their normal course of development.

In the newborn monkey, 8–10 minutes of diminished oxygen can result in abnormal behavior in later years. The normal adult monkey is easily capable of learning which of two food wells has been loaded with a peanut and can retain the information for up to 15 seconds. In this test which psychologists call a "delayed response" test, the examiner, with the monkey watching, places a peanut under one of two cups. An opaque screen is then lowered between the monkey and the covered wells. Fifteen seconds later it is raised again and the monkey is free to respond. The normal monkey has little problem with the long delay, while the monkey who was asphixiated at birth responds appropriately only when no delay is imposed. It is completely baffled if only a 5-second delay is imposed. Thus, the slightest physiological manipulation at birth permanently affects the adult behavior of an organism. In this particular experiment the implication is that the deficit produced is strictly related to short-term memory processes. For, so long as all stimulus information is in view, the asphixiated monkey is as good as a normal one in carrying out any number of complex discriminations.

There are, of course, any number of other influences on a developing organism that may result in physical and mental deficiencies. In pregnancy, for example, a mother's diet that lacks sufficient protein may result in a premature birth and neural defects in the infant, since the fetus depends on the maternal blood supply for its nutrition. Drugs and overdoses of irradiation as a result of therapeutic procedures can all cause problems for the fetus. In one study, women irradiated heavily in hopes of controlling a cancer had a greater tendency to have babies with central nervous system abnormalities. Microcephaly, which is mental feebleness and which is associated with an abnormally small brain and pointed skull, is characteristically seen in these cases.

But finally the baby arrives, and the question is what is he like? What can he do? And how set is he in his ways? For some answers, as mentioned previously, we will look in the next chapter at what is known about the development of the visual system and closely inspect this mechanism.

SUMMARY

The brain is the organ of behavior; it is made up of neurons which are richly interconnected by a number of different kinds of synapses. Most, if not all, of the resulting nerve circuits are genetically determined, and many of these circuits give rise to specific behavior patterns. The brain is a very fragile organ and is highly susceptible to influences during its development, which can cause irrevocable effects on adult behavior.

SUGGESTED READINGS

CORNSWEET, T. N. *Visual perception.* New York: Academic Press, 1970.

CREUTZFELDT, O., & SAKMANN, B. Neurophysiology of vision. *Annual Review of Physiology,* 1969, **31**, 499–544.

SPERRY, R. W. Embryogenesis of behavioral nerve nets. In R. L. De Haan and H. Ursprung (Eds.), *Organogenesis.* New York: Holt, 1967. Pp. 161–186.

STEVENS, C. F. *Neurophysiology: A primer.* New York: Wiley, 1966.

2

The Course of Normal Development: The Visual System

In New Zealand, recently, a doctor injected some air into the vagina of a young pregnant mother, in order to position the placenta for a diagnostic x ray. That night she and her husband were awakened by loud crying. The wailing came from the baby in her womb. The next day the doctor explained that the air bubble must have lodged next to the baby's face causing it discomfort and making it cry. Ordinarily babies cry, he said, but no sound is heard because of the damping effect of the fluid-filled womb.

This case suggests some of the difficulties in defining what is normal. Have all newborn babies experienced the same amount of discomfort in the uterus? One would think not. Suppose baby X was uncomfortable and cried all the time and baby Y never was uncomfortable and never cried in the womb. What effect might this have on their reaction to the normal discomforts of everyday life? One could easily imagine that baby X after birth would put up with more discomfort. In the womb he cried and nobody "came to help," for nobody heard him. As a result, he began to cry less often when uncomfortable. The womb-comfortable baby, however, never tried crying until birth, whereupon he found out how rewarding it can be!

Of course, no one knows the answer to these problems as yet. Clearly, however, one can begin to see the multitude of forces working on the developing embryo. There are both physiological and environmental influences. Therefore, it becomes very difficult indeed to determine what is normal. In this chapter we will look at the visual system as exemplifying the problem of development. We will first examine how this brain system develops normally. Then we will see how changes in the environment can change the normal organization of the visual part of our brain.

THE DEVELOPING VISUAL SYSTEM

When a newborn chicken takes its first peck, it is right on target. If, prior to its first peck, a prism is placed in front of each eye, which skews the visual world approximately 10° to one side, the chicken pecks off center by 10° and continues to do so for as long as the prisms remain in place.

A variety of investigators have reported that the 6-month-old baby can discriminate depth. In an experiment using a "visual cliff," babies are placed on a walkway that straddles two different visual arenas (Figure 2-1). On one side, there is a shallow drop-off. On the other side, there appears to be a steep cliff. Since both sides are covered with clear glass, there is no way the baby can fall. From the start, babies avoid the cliff and become very agitated when placed over the deep side.

The strict empiricist will argue that the 6-month-old child has had sufficient time to develop the cerebral circuitry for such depth discriminations. While this kind of argument is always a problem, recent data on prelocomotor infants support the nativist view. Fifty-day-old infants who can, of course, neither walk nor crawl, when placed on the deep end of the cliff, responded with a faster heart rate than when they were placed on the shallow side. There were not, however, the concomitant agitation and attempts at escape seen in 6-month-old babies. Somehow the basic autonomic response (producing an increased heart rate) becomes translated into an emotion only later, sometime between 1 month and 6 months of age.

This behavioral evidence supports the view that such things as depth perception are inborn properties of the brain. In the following discussion of the basic features of the visual system of the brain, you will see there is a good fit between the neurophysiological data and the psychological data.

THE RETINA

The retina, an extraordinarily thin protuberance from the developing brain, develops into a most intricate light-sensitive mechanism (Figure 2-2). The

FIGURE 2-1   Newborn babies are able to discriminate the different distances represented in the "visual cliff" apparatus originally designed by J. J. Gibson. Between two visual fields, one indicating great depth and the other not, a 6-month-old baby crawls along a tight rope. Movement to the deep side would suggest that babies do not have depth perception, or if they have it, they do not know its meaning. The babies mainly choose the shallow side.

particular cells that respond to light are called rods and cones. Paradoxically, they are at the back of the retina, and in order for light to make its way to them it has to pass through a network of connecting cells.

The rods and cones are hooked up to bipolar cells, and from there they connect to ganglion cells, which then send their long axons out of the eye, leaving through a small area that is responsible for our blind spot. The axons travel all the way up to the middle part of the brain into a structure called the lateral geniculate nucleus before they make another synapse. On the way

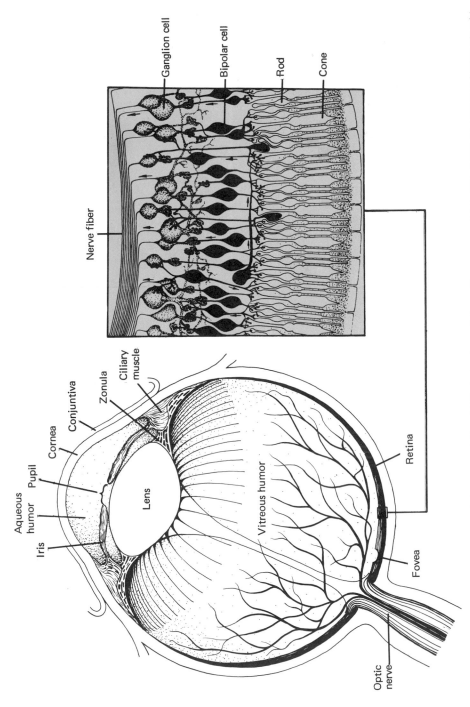

FIGURE 2-2 Both the gross structure of the eye and the detailed structure of the retina are seen here. The retina is arranged backwards with the light sensitive elements, the rods and cones, appearing at the back of the retina. The rods and cones pass the nerve impulse they generate to a bipolar cell that, in turn, connects with ganglion cells. It is the long axon of the ganglion cell that passes out of the eye back into the brain.

they cross at a point called the optic chiasma. It is here where half the neurons from one eye cross over and go up to the opposite side of the brain. The remaining half stay on the same side.

The cones are found in the greatest numbers in an area of the retina called the fovea. All rods are absent in this region, which is in the center of the retina. To get an idea of the power of resolution, the smallest cone receptor is only 2 microns in size, which is 2/100,000 of an inch.

Yet even though the cones are responsible for our great acuity, the rods are most sensitive to low levels of illumination. The rods are inherently about 100 to 1000 times more sensitive to light than the cones. An old trick used by astronomers when searching for a distant faint star was to look off to one side. As a result, the eye would be positioned to allow the light to fall on the rod part of the retina. The greater sensitivity of the rods is also partly due to a phenomenon called areal summation. This mechanism gathers light from all over the retina via rods. However, more than the response of one receptor is necessary to trigger a bipolar cell and finally a ganglion cell. Since several rods feed into one bipolar cell (whereas each cone has its own), there is a greater probability that the rod mechanism with areal summation will detect dim light scattered about the retina than will the cone system.

Photopigments

A major feature of a retina is the presence of photopigments. These are the chemicals responsible for translating light energy into neural activity. How this is done, no one knows. Yet, all of us have experienced the effects of staring at a light bulb. This action bleaches out the photopigments. When the eye shifts its gaze to a white background, it looks as though a dark or gray bulb is in view. This is called a negative afterimage. It results from the low sensitivity in the bleached area relative to the nonbleached surround. When our gaze is quickly cast on a dark background after fixating a light bulb, a positive afterimage is obtained. Here the light looks very bright. This is due to the continual firing of the stimulated portion of the retina relative to the unstimulated background.

The photopigments of rods are present in greater amounts than in cones, and visual purple, the chemical present in rods, is also more sensitive to light than the pigments found in cones. As a result, in the dark, when all receptors are given a chance to accumulate and build up their store of photopigments, the eye becomes extremely sensitive to light, with the rods being more sensitive than the cones.

In all, four photopigments have been discovered: one for rods and three for cones. All are differentially sensitive. Most color theories predict there should be three cone pigments. With three pigments, each with a different and appropriate spectral sensitivity (response to different colors or wavelengths of light), color vision in all of its variation can be easily explained. We will return to this later in Chapter 10.

Physiological Recording

The next question, of course, is how or in what way is the information from the retina transmitted to the brain (Figure 2-3). One obvious approach

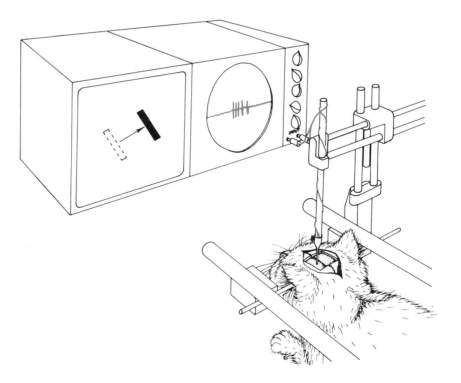

FIGURE 2-3   Most electrophysiological analysis of the brain's visual system is carried out using this type of setup. The animal is anesthetized and placed in a stereotaxic instrument, a device that locks the head into a fixed, measured position so that deep probing of the brain with an electrode along fixed coordinates will assure the experimenter that he is recording from a particular brain structure. The animal views a display screen with many kinds of moving targets. As a cell responds to the moving target, the electrode measures the small signal and sends it along to an amplifier that, in turn, sends the signal to a display oscilloscope. Here we see a neuron in the cat's visual cortex responding to a moving edge.

to this problem is to record from individual neurons leaving the retina to see how their discharge pattern varies with light stimulation of various kinds. The simple technique of recording from individual neurons is used throughout most areas of physiological psychology. In brief, an electrode with a very small tip is lowered into the brain structure being studied. It is completely insulated except for the tip. Therefore, it senses only the nervous tissue next to the extremely fine tip of the electrode. The electrode is connected to an amplifier, which magnifies the various slight electrical discharge of the neuron (.5–20mV) up to a manageable signal. This electronic signal is then displayed on an oscilloscope. Every time there is an electrical discharge, there is a corresponding deflection of the electron beam on the oscilloscope. In addition, the signal is fed through a high fidelity speaker so that when the neuron is firing one hears a "zat-zat-zat."

The original work on the electrophysiology of the visual system was done on the frog. Recordings were made from the optic nerve leaving the retina. In general, three kinds of fibers were discovered. There are "on fibers," which respond maximally at the onset of visual stimulation, "off fibers" which fire when lights go off, and "on-off fibers," which fire both at the onset and termination of illumination.

Similar findings were made in the cat. Imagine a cat looking at a projection screen. When a dot of light is moved about on the screen during a recording session, a place is reached where the neuron fires. By systematically moving the dot on and around this point, the visual field of that particular neuron in the optic nerve will reveal fields with a circular configuration. The neuron turns on when a light is in the middle and turns off when the light falls in an area adjacent to the excitatory region. This kind of field is said to have a "center surround" organization, where either the center can be excitatory and the surround inhibitory, or vice versa.

Since all this is occurring in the fibers just beyond the retina, it is safe to conclude that quite sophisticated processes are occurring at the most primitive level of the visual system. In other words, the brain does not receive raw visual information. It is already highly digested and organized into specific patterns by the time it leaves the retina.

The processes at the retina that allow for this kind of organization are largely due to lateral inhibitory effects. H. K. Hartline of Rockefeller University is largely responsible for detailing the exact mechanisms involved. Working on the horseshoe crab, which has several hundred receptors in a compound eye, he has determined precisely how stimulating one receptor influences the firing pattern of a neighboring receptor. He has found that each receptor (called an ommatidium) interconnects with other receptors and inhibits activity in these receptors in a systematic way (see Chapter 11).

Neural Activity and Light Intensity

The horseshoe crab is interesting for a variety of reasons. Unlike vertebrate eyes, its receptors are not upside down and each receptor is easily accessible to inspection by electrophysiological recording. Investigators have capitalized on this and have shown how physiological processes relate to actual perceptual phenomena. It has been determined that the rate of discharge of an optic neuron is directly related to the log of the intensity of the light stimulus (Figure 2-4). This is true for most intensities. With low levels of illumination, however, the relation does not hold. The reason is most interesting and is the key to a host of problems in the study of perception.

In brief, because the retina and the connecting optic nerve have their own spontaneous rate of discharge occurring at different set frequencies depending on the background illumination, the brain must be clever enough to detect a change in that frequency before it can make a judgement that a perceptual event occurred. To state it more simply, it is the signal to noise problem, or how does a system detect a signal over a background of activity? It means, of course, that there are lights in this world that are on, but we cannot see them. Our brains cannot distinguish how the light in question significantly alters the normal frequency of discharge of the optic nerve.

"Bug Detectors"

But perhaps the most spectacular experiments of all on the retina were the studies done by Lettvin and his colleagues at M.I.T. The experiments were among the first and are now considered classics. Lettvin sank an electrode into a frog's optic nerve. He then moved about a variety of stimuli in the frog's visual field. These stimuli included dots, lines, edges, and checkered patterns, as well as other curved and angular figures. The characteristics of numerous neurons were explored, and these neurons fell into roughly five categories. There are cells that only fire when (1) an edge of an object is in the visual field; (2) a small dark object is moved about within the field; (3) a dark or light object moves in a particular direction across the field; (4) lights dim or go off; and (5) lights are off entirely.

The retina of a frog has essentially performed all the operations on visual information received that the frog needs to live a normal life. The cells that respond only to small black objects moving about have been called "bug detectors." This suggests the frog sees bugs in his retina and not in his brain. This is amazing because studies in cat, monkey, and man show complex visual

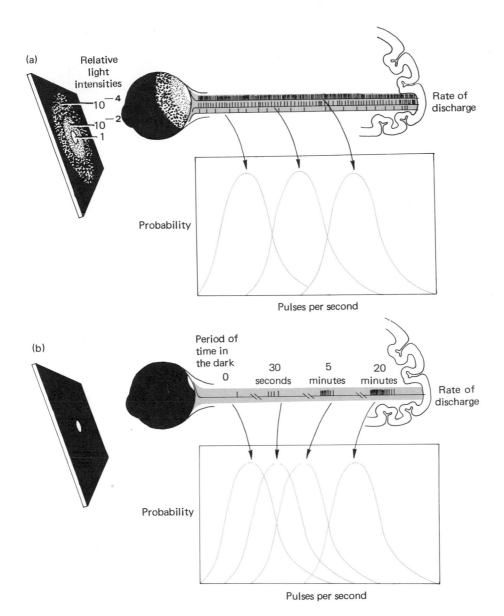

FIGURE 2-4   (a) The rate of neurons discharging in the optic nerve is related to the intensity of the light impinging on the eye. When a bright light is on, the neuron discharges at a fast rate, as can be seen in the top line. With the light a little dimmer, the neuron does not fire as fast. When the light is extremely dim, the neuron fires at a rate only very slightly higher than its normal spontaneous rate. (b) Being in the dark has a great effect on our perceptual capacity. A light of fixed intensity may only be just detected, if the eyes have not been in the dark. After five minutes in the dark, however, the same light will give a big discharge in the optic nerve, and it will appear to be very bright.

analysis deferred and carried out mostly in the visual cortex. No such "bug detectors" are to be found in your retina.

VISUAL PATHWAYS FROM THE RETINA TO THE BRAIN

When the electrical code makes its way out of the retina and starts up to the brain, it passes through the lateral geniculate nucleus (LGN) (Figure 2-5), a part of the midbrain or thalamus. Its name is derived from its position relative to other thalamic structures (lateral) and its knee-shaped organization (genu).

Many things occur in the LGN. It is, for example, the main visual structure that differentially responds to high doses of LSD. Some people think the bizarre and rich visual phenomenon experienced with LSD is due to its effects at this anatomical site. LSD inhibits the normal exchange of electrical information between the incoming optic nerve and the outgoing fibers to the visual cortex. These latter fibers are called geniculostriate fibers. (Quite frequently, neuroanatomical connections are named by considering the site of origin and termination. In this case, geniculo is for geniculate and striate refers to the visual cortex, a nickname due to the visual cortex's striped appearance under the microscope.)

The visual hallucinations are thought to result from the effects of the LGN being disengaged. Thus, the visual cortex would not receive its normal tonic input. As a result, bizarre visual phenomenon occur. Of course, the actual mechanism of why this should result in hallucinations is not known.

In addition to projecting to the LGN, the optic nerve sends some fibers to a structure called the superior colliculus, which is in the midbrain and is largely responsible for organizing basic optic reflexes. Indeed, much has been written in recent years suggesting that this part of the neurological system is responsible for the normal orienting we do toward the visual stimuli.

Take, for example, the everyday experience of "seeing something out of the corner of your eye." It is now claimed that the peripheral rods and cones pick up the information and relay it to the superior colliculus as well as to the cortex. The superior colliculus, in turn, organizes a response and directs the eyes to the target in question. From there, foveal visual processes come in and take over for the detailed analysis of the visual target.

Thus, we have two visual mechanisms, one involved in gross orientation and the other specialized for detail. It is the latter system that has received considerable attention by brain and behavior investigators.

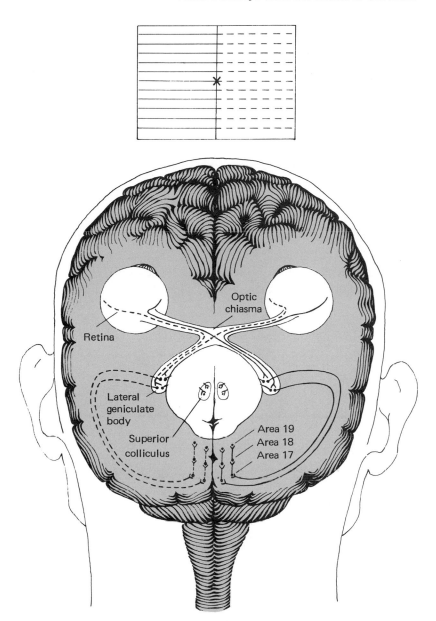

FIGURE 2-5   The anatomical organization of the human visual system. The optic nerves leave the eye and cross, sending half of their fibers to each half of the brain. After crossing, they immediately go to the lateral geniculate body. Here they form a synapse, and most subsequent fibers go to the rear of the head to the visual cortex. Some of the fibers leave the LGN and go to a midbrain structure called the superior colliculus. In man, as in animals, the visual cortex is subdivided into special areas, usually referred to as 17, 18, and 19. This is where visual responses described in the text occur.

THE VISUAL CORTEX

The part of the brain most concerned with visual processes is found at the rear of the head. It is called the occipital lobe and it receives its primary input from the LGN. The visual cortex is where extraordinarily complex analysis starts on the visual information originally presented to the retina.

If a bullet enters and exits at a particular trajectory at the rear of the skull, a very clean hole or lesion can be made in the visual cortex tissue (Figure 2-6). Such wounds are common enough during wartime, and the cooperating victim can often aid in our understanding of the visual system. Studies on such cases have confirmed a variety of animal studies that there exists a "point-to-point" representation between the eye and visual cortex, that is, a particular point on the retina is projected consistently within a given species to a particular point in the visual cortex. This idea had been confirmed

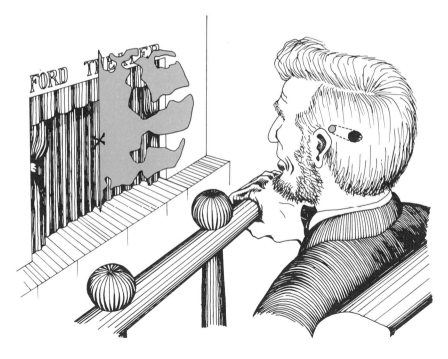

FIGURE 2-6   President Lincoln was shot on the left side of the head. The bullet's course through visual cortex would produce the kind of blind spot seen here. The left hemisphere processes visual information to the right of fixation. This kind of cleancut data has produced support for the notion that each part of the visual world we see has a physical correlate in the brain.

in animal studies, when a discrete lesion made in the visual cortex always results in a discrete degeneration or death of neurons in the LGN.

These findings received considerable attention from early psychologists who felt this gave support to their ideas of "psychophysical isomorphism." This million dollar word described a simple idea that when a person viewed a "triangle," the brain responded in kind by having a set of neurons respond that made a more or less exact duplicate of the actual triangle in neural activity!

The idea has been abandoned for several reasons. It has been shown in fact that the foveal region of the retina has a much larger exaggerated area for projection on the visual cortex than do other retinal sites. Accordingly, a triangle would appear disproportionately skewed and would look strange indeed.

But the real advance in understanding how the visual cortex handles visual information comes from the pioneering and truly remarkable series of studies by David Hubel and Torsten Weisel at Harvard Medical School. Their findings have major implications for any psychological theory of vision or behavior of any kind.

Hubel and Weisel (1962) studied the cat with the microelectrode technique described earlier. The cat was placed in front of a projection screen and an electrode was lowered into the visual cortex (Figure 2-7). The cortical cells just one synapse in from the LGN projections responded in one particular way. Their behavior has been called "simple." Their receptive fields have an oblong organization with excitatory responses juxtaposed to inhibitory responses. The border constitutes an edge and has the almost household name "line detectors" (Figure 2-8).

A little further along into the visual system, "complex" cells are found. These cells differ in their behavior in that the neuron fires no matter how the visual field is stimulated. (In the simple cell, the moving edge of the stimulus has to enter the field in a particular direction.)

As Hubel and Weisel proceeded further into the visual system, i.e., the anatomical areas beyond the primary visual cortex that receives the input from the LGN, even more complex kinds of responses were seen. In general, the rule is that the further one goes into the system the more exact the stimulus on the screen in front of the cat has to be before the neuron being examined responds. What one begins to see, of course, are the factual building blocks for a theory of visual perception. Simple line detector cells converge onto other cells giving it a complex behavior. Subsequently, a series of complex cells converge on a "hypercomplex" cell limiting it to a still further level of sophistication. This process has been called "convergence." Ultimately, the theory predicts there is a cell somewhere in our brain for such bizarre perceptions as a purple cow.

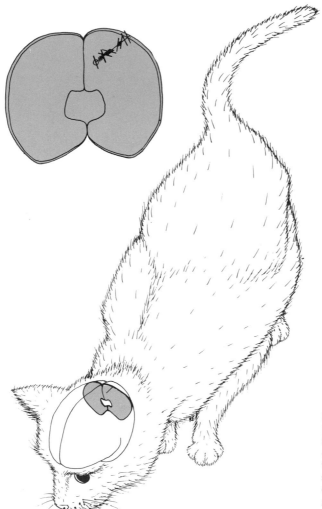

FIGURE 2-7   Hubel and Wiesel presented a line on the screen in front of the cat. The cutout of the brain shows the orientation that produced the maximum response recorded for each single cell. The anatomical features suggested are schematic.

CHANGING THE NORMAL BRAIN BY CHANGING THE ENVIRONMENT

In the summer of 1969, two British physiologists started a most remarkable experiment. They raised two newborn kittens in separate environments. From birth, the one kitten saw nothing except vertical white lines when it opened its eyes. The other kitten saw nothing except horizontal white lines. They endured these special conditions for almost 6 months. The experimenters wanted to know if the vertically deprived cats would be able to see vertical lines and if the horizontally deprived cats would be able to see horizontal

Visual   Evoked response   Visual   Evoked response   Visual   Evoked response from a single cell
stimulus   from a single cell   stimulus   from a single cell   stimulus

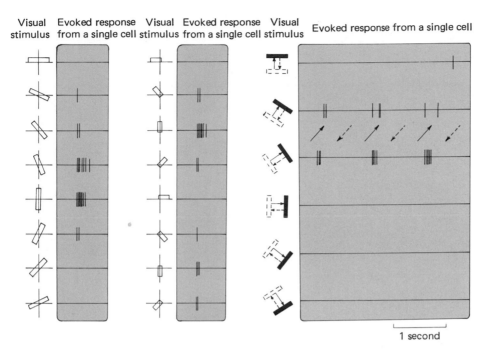

1 second

FIGURE 2-8   This figure shows how many brain scientists discovered the physical elements of visual perception. Here we first see how lines oriented in a particular direction trigger a vigorous response from a nerve cell. Lines oriented or positioned out of the optimum tend to produce less neural response.

lines. With these behavioral facts established, they then wondered what the corollary change in brain physiology would be.

They first took the vertically experienced, horizontally deprived cat and set him on a course through dangling white vertical stripes (Figure 2-9). The cat neatly avoided the obstacles. They then placed the cat in a field of horizontal stripes. Dramatically, the kitten forged ahead as if nothing were in the way and continually bumped into the horizontal obstacles. The other cat performed in the opposite manner and constantly bumped into the vertical barriers, but neatly avoided the horizontally placed obstacles!

Then these same kittens were anesthetized, their brains exposed, and the visual cortex analyzed in much the same fashion we have discussed earlier. The two physiologists, Blakemore and Cooper (1970), discovered that neurons in the vertically deprived cat essentially never responded to vertical edges as they would in a normally reared cat (Figure 2-10). At the same time, these same neurons would normally respond to horizontal edges. Not surprisingly, the horizontally deprived cat responded in opposite fashion.

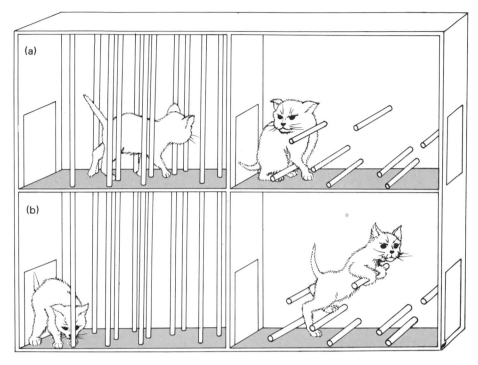

FIGURE 2-9 (a) This cat was raised in an environment with only vertical white lines appearing on a black background. (b) This cat only saw horizontal lines. After a few months, the horizontally deprived cat can only see and navigate around vertical obstacles. The converse is true for the vertically deprived cat.

Two American scientists, Helmut Hirsch and Nico Spinelli (1971), have found similar effects in cats reared with goggles that eliminated horizontal lines from one eye's view and vertical lines from the other. They too found the predicted physiological change in the cat's visual cortex. The effects on behavior, however, were not as striking.

These studies are among the first actually to correlate the extensive physiological studies delineating visual cortical mechanisms with actual behavior. However, they also neatly demonstrate how a change in the environment can produce a change in the basic neurological wiring of an organism. This extremely important point bears close scrutiny. Consider again what is at stake. In the foregoing, we have indicated that the central nervous system develops in a fixed way. Now we seem to be saying it can be changed with corollary behavioral changes if the environment is systematically manipulated. Does this mean that the brain can be either impaired or improved and that such personal aspects of our mental lives such as intelligence can be changed? More generally, does this suggest that personal traits like the ability to love

(a) Normal cat

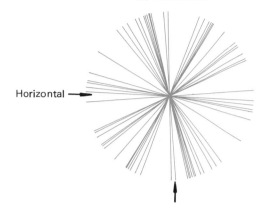

Horizontal ⟶

(b) Vertically deprived cat

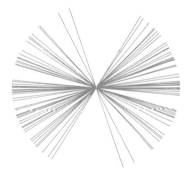

(c) Horizontally deprived cat

FIGURE 2-10   (a) The distribution of optimal orientation for 34 cortical cells from a normal cat. (b) The distribution of neuron responses in a cat brought up in a visual world containing only horizontal stripes. (c) Seventy-two cells recorded from a cat exposed to only vertical lines.

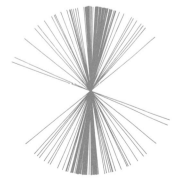

and to hate, each having a neurological substrate, can be taken away or enhanced in an organism by a change in the environment at an early age?

Answers to all these questions are being pursued in the behavioral sciences and we will be discussing them as we go along. But again let's explore some of the fundamentals. We will start by taking a close look at how changing the environment affects the developing visual system.

SOME CHARACTERISTICS OF NORMAL ADULT VISUAL ORGANIZATION

As described earlier the visual cortex of the cat responds in an orderly and particular way to light stimulation appearing in front and in full view. There are three general categories of receptor responses: simple, complex, and hypercomplex. In addition to these kinds of characteristic responses, it has been discovered that over 80% of the visual cells recorded from in the cat visual cortex respond to stimulation from both eyes. The remaining 20% of the cells respond to stimulation of only one eye or the other. There are many other general features of visual organization, but it is the last fact that Hubel and Wiesel were able to parlay into utterly fascinating experiments.

To begin with they first asked if the kind of organization seen in the adult is present at birth. To answer this question, they simply examined the responses of visual cortex in 8-day-old kittens. To the chagrin of most empiricists, they discovered most aspects of visual organization known to exist in the adult. While there is some question whether newborn kittens have neurons that show orientation specificity, most of the neurons are definitely binocular.

Visual Deprivation

With this experiment complete, the stage was set for examining the effects of depriving one eye of its normal visual input while leaving the other normally exposed. Would such an abnormal state of affairs affect the basic neurological wiring of the visual system?

The answer is now a matter of scientific history. The monocularly deprived cats were found to have a completely different distribution of responses when their visual cortex was analyzed. Instead of 80% of the cells responding to stimulation of both eyes, now most, if not all, cells responded only to stimulation of the nondeprived eye. Behaviorally, the eye deprived from vision from birth, when opened, would render the animal "blind." The electrophysiological observations substantiated these behavioral findings.

Hubel and Wiesel then ran the logical extension of this experiment. They examined the visual cortex of a cat that had been binocularly deprived. The expectation was that most of the visual cortex would not respond, for all input channels had now been tampered with. To almost everyone's surprise, the cells responded to stimulation of both eyes, and showed the normal kind of simple, complex, and hypercomplex responses. In short, total deprivation found the visual system more normal than if only one eye had been deprived.

These fascinating results suggested that the normal development of binocular interaction is a function of a certain kind of interdependence of the neuronal projections from the two eyes. In other words, what is important in proper neuronal development is not only physical proximity to proper points in the central nervous system, but also functional interaction with the various elements that eventually contribute to the overall organization of a neurological system.

In another experiment, which really nailed down this point, Hubel and Wiesel raised cats under conditions of alternating monocular deprivation. Here one eye would be deprived 1 day at a time, followed by the other. In this fashion, both eyes received the exact same visual experience. The effect on the neurological wiring, however, was dramatic. For the most part, the cells in the visual cortex only responded to monocular stimulation! In other words, normal binocular responses are produced by the timing of impulses arriving from each eye. The alternating monocular deprivation condition never allows this to happen.

Behavioral Studies

A most fascinating aspect of this experiment is the fact that Hubel and Wiesel reported these binocularly deprived cats were "blind." "As the kitten moved about the room, there were no indications that visual cues were used; placed in an unfamiliar room it frequently bumped into large obstacles in its path." This observation is of particular interest, because we have just seen that the binocularly deprived cat has a near normal visual cortex! At the time the original experiments were carried out, there was no good explanation offered for this seemingly grave paradox. Hubel and Wiesel, alarmed at the thought that the entire physiological story intricately built up over the years had little relation to behavior, could only suggest that the critical change produced by deprivation was to be found further along in the visual system.

Today, however, these findings are not so peculiar. First we saw at the beginning of the chapter, specific deprivation does produce specific effects in the visual cortex, that is, the known physiology does relate directly to behavioral processes. Second, other investigators have disclosed that, while binocularly deprived cats appear blind, they see quite well upon close examination Using a conditioning process that administers a shock through an animal's foot if it does not pull a lever when presented with one of two visual patterns, it has been found that deprived cats learn the task at a near normal rate. Third, the effects of deprivation on the organization of the visual system are time dependent. If deprivation procedures are started after a cat has reached 2–3 months of age, there is little or no effect on behavior. There is then a "critical period" in visual development, and at that moment the right state of affairs must exist for normal development. Recent studies have shown that the particular time conditions for normal development during the critical period are short. Cats need only 36 hours of exposure to vertical lines to produce the described effect, but the exposure must occur during the critical period.

IMPLICATIONS

An environmental influence of lid suturing was inflicted upon young kittens. As a result, there was a dramatic change in the role of responses in the cat's visual cortex. Does this mean an abnormal environment has produced a change in the neurological organization by influencing and redirecting neuronal growth? Or does the change observed simply reflect the effect of disuse? The former suggests that neurological growth can occur in response to environmental influences; the latter suggests that the environment can influence only indirectly by not allowing normally organized connections to develop. The first view is more optimistic about the effects of the environment on our ultimate performance, whereas the second position suggests that our upper limits are genetically determined and can only drift downward through the course of development. With this view, the environment plays the important role of offering critically needed stimulation for maximizing our innate neural circuits. If critical stimulation is not forthcoming, we may not be the person that we might have been. However, even the most enriched environment imaginable would not push the organism past its genetically determined upper limit.

At present, the evidence points in the direction of genetic determinacy with slight modifications possible at early stages of development. The earlier discussed work on neurospecificity and the experiments on visual deprivation support this view. In fact, all of Hubel and Wiesel's results could be easily explained by assuming the initial neurological organization present at birth undergoes no change. Instead deprivation results in the disuse of some neurons, which has the effect of changing the response characteristics of the general properties of cells in the cat cortex. Thus, if a cell normally responds if and only if it receives inputs from the two eyes in the right time sequence, then it ought not to fire after monocular deprivation. If this were the case, one would predict that recording from a monocularly deprived cat would show responses from cells that only require input from one eye. As we have already seen, this was indeed the case.

Yet, it is too soon to be completely sure. The Blakemore and Cooper experiment found no regions of silent cells when recording from the cat's cortex. All the neurons were quite normal in their firing patterns, which means half of them must have been modified, not just degenerated. With degeneration, they would have found great quiet areas in the cat's cortex. These results are exciting and pose fascinating questions concerning how the environment effects permanent change on the brain.

SUMMARY

We have seen how the visual system is organized, starting at the retina, going back to the LGN, and finally reaching the visual cortex. There is an intricate system of neural connections that produces and allows certain kinds of visual behavior.

Moreover, it is clear that during development the environment can effect changes on the developing brain. A variety of studies have now shown that systematic changes in the visual environment produce systematic changes in the visual organization of the brain.

SUGGESTED READINGS

HEBB, D. O. Hereditary and environment in mammalian behavior. *British Journal of Animal Behaviour*, 1953, **1**, 43–47.

HORN, C., & HINDE, R. A. *Short term changes in neural activity and behavior.* London & New York: Cambridge Univ. Press, 1971.

QUARTON, C. G., MELNECHUK, T., & SCHMITT, F. O. (Eds.) *The neurosciences.* New York: Rockefeller Univ. Press, 1967.

ROSENZWEIG, M. R., & LEIMAN, A. L. Brain functions. *Annual Review of Psychology*, 1968, **19**, 55–98.

THOMPSON, R. F. *Foundations of physiological psychology.* New York: Harper, 1967.

3

Fixed Patterns
of
Behavior

The brain of man is constructed in a certain way with certain materials. As a consequence of the way man is put together he must act as he does to an extent, just as a boomerang must return to the hand of the thrower because it is shaped in a certain way and constructed of certain materials. In this chapter, we will examine the degree to which there is machinery laid down in the brain and nervous system for complex behavior predetermined by the genetic code. Is the brain computerlike and capable of an infinite variety of responses or does it consist of patterns of an automatic kind predetermined by heredity? We know that much behavior, such as the reflex mechanisms of the vertebrate, is of the latter type. But are there inborn mechanisms that determine our more complicated behavior?

To begin with, instinctive behavior is thought to comprise patterns of behavior that are transmitted from one generation to the next. These patterns do not require individual learning; they are mapped on the genetic code in such a way that the behavior of the species is transmitted to each individual member. They are expressed irrespective of the experience of the individual or his capacity to learn. There is then a code of behavior of a complex kind, which is transmitted from one generation to the next. To some extent we share inheritance of predetermined behavioral mechanisms with our immediate ancestors or, for that matter, our more remote ancestors in the animal kingdom.

We will now look at some examples of inborn behavior. First we will consider the smiling behavior of infants.

INBORN BEHAVIOR

Smiling Behavior of Infants

Smiling usually occurs during the first few months of life. It appears spontaneously in sleep, in passing wind, in drinking, etc. Laughing, however, where the infant opens the mouth wide as distinct from smiling, is a pattern of behavior that occurs from the age of 4 months on. Smiling and laughing are behaviors that greatly strengthen the bond between the baby and his mother. Smiling is used also to communicate. The spontaneous smile is replaced in the normal child by an answering smile in which the child smiles at the mother and the mother smiles back. There is some evidence that the child smiles at first to a wide class of objects and does not always differentiate his mother or other human beings by their smiles. Spitz (1946) for example, obtained a smile from 3- to 6-month-old babies by presenting them with scarecrow faces and distorted grimaces as well as by letting them look at the normal face. Up until the second month of life, a cardboard model of a face painted with highly contrasting eye spots making them extremely prominent from the background will, in fact, elicit a greater amount of smiling than a realistically painted face.

If we ask to what extent the expression of these forms of behavior is dependent on the infant's experience, we then can gain some information by the study of children who are born blind (Figure 3-1). At first, smiling in these children is little different from the normal. However, normal children smile more and more as time goes on, but blind children smile less and less. Some kind of social feedback is necessary, and the child is dependent upon the response of others if the frequency of smiling is to be maintained or increased. Still, in the complete absence of normal stimuli, the child smiles in a completely normal way. A blind-born child will come to fixate upon the source of his mother's voice and laugh when she speaks to him. Interestingly, the continuous nystagmus, i.e., the rapid movement of the eyes from side to side, seen so frequently in the blind child, ceases during this time, even though, of course, the child cannot see the face.

Eibl-Eibesfeldt describes how patterns of smiling occur in children who are born both blind and deaf, but who otherwise have no mental impairment. The pattern of smiling corresponds exactly to that of normal children. Thus,

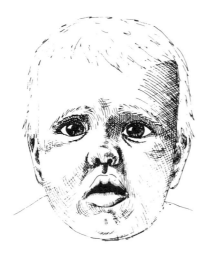

FIGURE 3-1   A 2-month-old baby born blind. The eyes in the normal child usually move around incessantly but not in the blind child. Yet the blind child is capable of a bright smile. After Eibl-Eibesfeldt (1970).

even in the absence of the customary knowledge gained through the eyes and the ears, the child still smiles. Clearly, children who are unable to learn through what we might suppose to be the customary means can develop patterns of muscular activity and can show expressive behavior.

There are a number of other examples that could be discussed. However, in humans the patterns of innate behavior are most frequently overlaid by learning, which interacts with them and makes it difficult to decide which patterns are inborn and which are learned. In the case of insects, the causation by inborn factors is much clearer. In this case, the scope for learning to modify behavior is reduced, and the inborn patterns are revealed to their full extent. The French naturalist Fabre describes, for example, the behavior of the larva of the capricorn beetle.

Insect Behavior

The larva of the capricorn beetle burrows its way through the heart of an oak tree, increasing meanwhile to the size of a small caterpillar. The larva is entombed within the tree because it is now too large to escape by way of the hole through which it entered. The tunnel also is blocked with wood pulp that the larva ate and passed through its body. Imprisoned in the tree, it is isolated totally from members of its own kind, and it can have no opportunity to learn patterns of behavior from them. The larva burrows continuously until, during the course of several years, it reaches the far side of the tree. At this time the animal seldom penetrates to the outside world. It leaves a thin cover of bark remaining between itself and the exterior. It retreats for a short distance into its burrow and then begins to excavate a large chamber far more spacious than for its present needs, but large enough to accommodate the adult beetle into which it will become transformed. Not only is this chamber large enough to contain the body of the adult beetle, but room has been provided for the action of its legs. The larva constructs a door to this chamber from a chalky cement disgorged from its stomach. The sides of the chamber are rasped to form a soft downy wood-wool, which is applied to the surface of the chamber to form a protective felt. The larva takes up a position with its head pointing towards the exit, in order that when it turns into the adult beetle it may escape. If, with its stiff horny structure, it were to emerge with its head towards the center, it would certainly die because it could not escape. Having completed preparations the larva is transformed into a pupa and then into the adult beetle. When the beetle is ready to emerge it needs only to break the wall of the chamber to escape to the outside world. Obviously, we have here a clear example of how a complicated behavioral sequence is under genetic control.

The Concept of Instinct

There is wider significance to inborn behavior than is obvious from the examples just described. It is frequently supposed that not only the patterns themselves are inborn but the motive forces that put them into operation also are inborn. In historical terms this brings us to the concept of instinct and what this means for the study of behavior.

Charles Darwin believed that an action is instinctive "when it is performed by an animal, more especially by a very young one without experience, and when performed by many individuals, without their knowing for what purpose it is performed." Darwin was aware that much of this is not entirely automatic for he states, "A little dose of judgment or reason often comes into play, even with animals low on the scale of nature." Darwin was one of the first, if not the first person, to point out the significance of patterns of innate behavior to evolution through natural selection. It is popularly called the principle of "the survival of the fittest." In his evolutionary theory, Darwin believed that small changes from one animal to another may on some occasions assist an animal to survive because they provide an advantage in competition with others. Because animals with this advantage are better able to survive, they are likely to pass this advantage on to their offspring.

Advantages often relate to physical features. A moth, for example, that lives in a smoke-blackened industrial area of a country is better able to survive if its own coloration is changed to a darker hue. Darwin not only realized that physical changes of this kind can provide an advantage, but also that changes in the pattern of an animal's behavior can provide it with a similar advantage in the race for survival. Insofar as these patterns of behavior are represented in the heredity mechanisms, these also can be transmitted from one generation to another. William James also supposed that instinctive actions are performed without a knowledge of their purpose. James defined instinct as "the faculty of acting in such a way as to produce certain ends without foresight of the ends and without previous education in the performance."

McDougall (1923) on the other hand, moved away from an emphasis on the biological aspect to that of the world of human experience and to the inner functions of the mind. McDougall supposed that there are inherited tendencies common to men of every race and age. These are the essential springs or motive powers. Human action is governed by primitive urges and not by any rational search for pleasure or the avoidance of pain. These irrational urges take the form of instincts. McDougall classified thirteen human instincts, including such obvious urges as curiosity, submission, sneezing, and coughing.

Freud called the inherited forces the id (see Chapter 21). The id contains everything that is inherited and remains fixed in the constitution; it represents the blind impulsive forces in the personality. Even as early as 1916, Freud had described the strivings of the id as largely sexual both in the narrower and wider sense. However, Freud supposed that not all instinctual forces are sexual in nature. The infant, for example, is required to adjust to external social forces, and some instinctual energy is bound up with this.

Freud's views about instinct in man developed through a number of stages. He supposed at first that there were two types of instinct: first, those which preserve the well-being of the individual, and, second, those which enable the continuation of the race. Schiller's antithesis between hunger and love would be examples of both types.

The second stage in the development of Freud's thought came about when he considered self-love or narcissism. He supposed that many of the instinctual forces are bound up with not only love of the self but also with an ideal picture as the person would like to be—the image that represents all that the person wishes he were, an ideal picture, an improvement on the real self.

At a later point Freud supposed that instincts are of two types: Eros, the life instinct, and Thanatos, the death instinct. Eros, the sustaining principle of life, serves the function of union and growth, the act of recreating, whereas Thanatos is represented in the neurotic manifestations of death wishes, sadism, and masochism, as well as the primitive instinct toward aggression, which could be turned outward toward the destruction of other individuals or inward toward the destruction of the self.

However, just as Molière's doctor said that "opium produced sleep because of its soporific qualities," so the instinct theorists were criticized because it was said that the use of the term "instinct" did not help in understanding behavior. For example, if we talk about the curiosity "instinct" instead of curiosity itself, we are no nearer to an explanation of this form of behavior, because in a sense curiosity becomes even more mysterious when described in this way.

Also, many human activities described as instinctive were in fact learned, and none of the so-called instincts proposed by these early theorists seem to escape the influence of learning. Opposition to the instinct view of human nature also arose from the cultural anthropologists who showed great diversity between one human culture and another. What had been assumed to be a fixed and unchanging characteristic of human behavior throughout the world was not always so.

ETHOLOGY

In spite of these difficulties, ideas about instinct had wide currency and exerted a powerful influence, which continues to this day in psychoanalytic thought. It was, however, left to the investigators of animal behavior to establish the concept of instinct as important in biological science. Arising from the study of instinctive patterns within a biological framework, a new discipline formed itself and was known as ethology.

The ethologists studied animal behavior usually in a natural context or one as natural as possible. They concentrated on instinct as opposed to learned patterns of behavior. They chose to call the behavior they studied innate behavior. This was behavior that (1) was determined by heredity; (2) formed part of the original constitution of the animal; (3) arose independently of the animals experience and environment; and (4) was distinct from acquired or learned behavior. Patterns of behavior such as these could be described and classified in an ethogram, which provided an account of all behavior patterns of the type that a particular animal species displays.

Fixed Action Patterns

It was well known to naturalists that different animal species may be distinguished not only by their external physical form or by their coloration, but also by their behavior. The ethologists suppose that each example of instinctive behavior contains "a hard core of relatively fixed and complex automatism, an inborn movement form."[1] These inborn fixed action patterns permit a distinction to be made between the behavior of an animal of one species and the behavior of that of another. For example, there are characteristic movements made during feeding, nest building, courtship, and rearing the young. These movements may be used to classify the animal species, to assess its evolutionary status, and to discover the relationship that it holds in terms of the evolutionary process to other animal groups.

Fixed action patterns occur most commonly in insects, fish, and birds. They were reported first in pigeons and ducks. For example, the male eider during courtship may show a pattern of head turning in which the bill is moved slowly from side to side through an angle of 90°. The head appears to move as if by clockwork, and a number of these movements are made in succession. The birds also exhibit a pattern known as the "cooing" movement. The head is suddenly lifted and thrown right back until the nape touches the back of the bird which simultaneously emits a cooing sound.

The work of Tinbergen (1951) on the behavior of the three-spined stickleback provides a classic example of fixed action patterns. In the spring, the full-grown male stickleback migrates to shallow water, where it lays claim to a territory. It then builds a tubular nest resting on the stream's bottom. The breast of the male turns bright red, and any other male entering the territory, easily recognized at this time by his bright coloration, is hastily and aggressively dispatched. The female who lacks this vivid coloration is greeted in quite a different way. Because she is pregnant, her abdomen is swollen and she swims with an uptilted posture. The male moves towards her in a zigzag fashion and then retreats slowly towards his nest. If the courtship has been successful, the female follows him. The male points to the nest with his nose, whereupon the female cautiously enters. The male quivers and prods her abdomen violently with his nose. He releases spermatozoa to fertilize the eggs as she spawns. From then on, the male takes charge of the eggs and fans them with his tail in order to adequately supply them with oxygen. After hatching, the young stickleback has contact only with the male who looks after the young or occasionally with other young. Yet, at maturity the stickleback displays the whole cycle of sexual behavior without prior experience.

These patterns are by no means confined to insects, fish, and birds. In recent years, a number of such patterns have been described for primate species. Gorillas, for example, display a typical pattern of threat behavior, which

---

[1] Ogden Nash expresses something of this concept when he states:

> The song of canaries
>   Never varies,
> And when they're moulting
> They're pretty revolting.

FIGURE 3-2   An example of play fighting in young gorillas. After a session of rough playing the "victor" drums with his hands on his chest while the loser climbs away. After Eibl-Eibesfeldt (1970).

is the pattern well known to viewers of Tarzan films as the pounding with clenched fists upon the chest (Figure 3-2). Chimpanzees also beat their chests as well as beating against special drumming trees or other resonating objects if they are in captivity.

By a study of the gestures and signs, particularly those of greeting, threat, and acceptance, it is possible for a human to penetrate to some extent the communication barrier between chimpanzees and man. Jane Goodall describes how, after an interpretive study of the chimpanzee's social ceremonies, she was able to use these signs herself to become accepted and greeted as another chimpanzee (Figure 3-3). Similar investigations are in progress with the behavior patterns of gorillas. Intrepid investigators of these animals have also become accepted as members of the group by the display of appropriate behavioral signs (Figure 3-4).

THE STIMULUS RELEASER.   The questions now arise as to how these fixed action patterns are initiated, and what is the relationship between the patterns

FIGURE 3-3   Young male inspecting the genital area of a new female in his group.

of muscle movement and the events or stimuli occurring in the world around the animal.

Tinbergen showed that the male three-spined stickleback welcomes females to his territory after having constructed a nest but that he drives other males away. In other words, he is able to differentiate between a pregnant female and an intruding male; they court the former and fight the latter.

The features that allow the animals to distinguish between males and females appear to be the uptilted posture of the pregnant female and, more importantly, the red coloration of the male. Tinbergen constructed a series of models which he presented to males that had already established their territories. Almost irrespective of the shape of the model, the fact that the belly portion was painted red was significant in releasing fighting in the territory

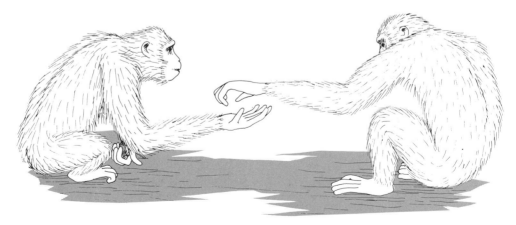

FIGURE 3-4   Gestures used by chimps when meeting. The lower ranking chimp holds hand out in begging fashion. After Eibl-Eibesfeldt (1970).

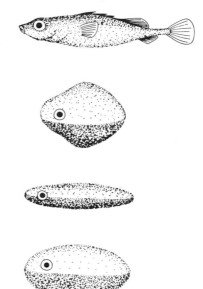

FIGURE 3-5   The critical stimulus is discovered for eliciting a particular kind of behavior. Here the four bottom figures all have a red belly, and regardless of shape they elicit aggression behavior in the three-spined stickleback. The upper model is ineffective. After Tinbergen (1951).

owner. Red belly coloration was thus said to be an important stimulus releaser (Figure 3-5).

The response occurred almost as a perceptual mistake or an errror, because response was made to only part of the environment, namely the red coloration of the belly. Its blind and uncomprehending behavior led it to ignore other aspects that may have been important.

Another example of a stimulus releaser can be found in the behavior of the herring gull chick. Parent gulls, noted for their scavenging, return to the nest and disgorge food for the benefit of the chick. The bill of the herring gull is yellowish in color, but it also contains a bright red spot on the lower mandible. As the parent's bill opens the chick pecks in the direction of the red spot and receives the food. The actions of the parents and the chick are thus coordinated in feeding. The chick normally pecks at the parent's bill, but it may also be induced to peck at models constructed to resemble, in different degrees, the bill of the parent. Chicks direct pecks towards the models, although they barely resemble the parent's bill in physical appearance, if the model has a red spot situated on it at a convenient pecking position (Figure 3-6). In the absence of the spot, pecking may not occur, although the model closely resembles the parent's bill in other respects. Clearly, the red spot acts as the trigger for the pecking response.

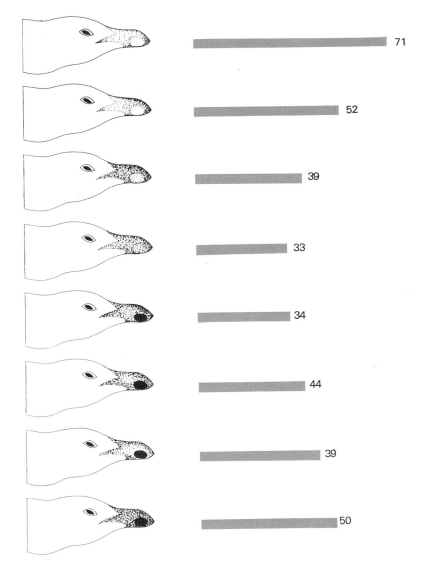

FIGURE 3-6   Young herring gulls will peck at a cardboard model of their mother so long as there is a red dot close to the mouth. With it gone, they will not peck even though the rest of the face looks normal. After Tinbergen (1951).

Another example of a stimulus releaser is the behavior shown in the visual cliff situation (see Chapter 2). It has been reported by a number of investigators that small chicks shortly after hatching show fear of a sharp decent such as that of a stair or the edge of a box. Although a sheet of clear plastic may be placed over the box, extending the surface on which the animal can walk, the animal nonetheless avoids the edge. This type of behavior is observed particularly strongly in kittiwakes, which are cliff-nesting birds. The mechanism that has evolved to avoid plunging over the cliff is a retreat with slow, shuffling, backward steps. As we have already seen, human babies show a somewhat similar response, and they too avoid visual cliffs of a similar type.

THE SUPERNORMAL RELEASING STIMULUS.   Occasionally models may be constructed that prove more effective than the real or actual stimulus occurring in nature. Plovers, for example, prefer to incubate a model egg painted black with white spots rather than their own egg which is a lightish brown with darker spots. Oyster catchers, when faced with a choice among their own egg, one twice the normal size, and one three times the normal size, choose the biggest one to incubate despite its large size and the discomfort of sitting astride such a large object (Figure 3-7).

This supernormal releasing effect is not confined to birds. Howard Smith showed the same effect in rats. Laboratory rats, for example, press a lever that enables them to open a window to view other rats. Plasticine models of rats with colored features are more effective as a stimulus in this viewing situation than a live rat placed in a similar position at the opposite side of the screen; that is, the colored features of the plasticine model lead to a higher response rate.

FACTORS HOLDING THE RELEASING MECHANISM IN CHECK.   The ethologists believe that each fixed action pattern is brought into a state of readiness because there is a buildup of energy associated with it. Konrad Lorenz, the Austrian zoologist, suggested the accumulation of this type of energy, when he observed that the grayleg goose occasionally performed the pattern of retrieving an egg and placing it back in the nest even when there was no egg to retrieve (Figure 3-8). This instinctive act pursued its course regardless of the adequacy of its function. Normally such a response would be held

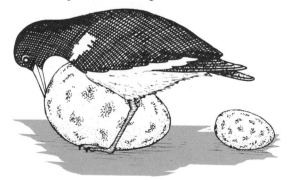

FIGURE 3-7   A stimulus controls the release of specific behaviors. An oyster catcher tries to roll a supernormal model of an egg into its nest. After Tinbergen (1951).

FIGURE 3-8   Egg rolling movement in the grayleg goose. Sometimes this entire sequence is triggered with no egg present After Tinbergen (1951).

in check, but apparently the energy for its expression had accumulated to such an extent that it could no longer be restrained.

Lorenz applied these concepts to the study of aggression. Aggression is widespread among animal species. For example, an ant which enters a strange nest is submitted to prolonged seizure and dragging. Strange individuals are often licked before being made the subject of attack by the home members of the colony. It may be that chemical signals are particularly important as the means by which the ant distinguishes members of its own colony from foreign individuals against whom it is necessary to initiate an attack.

Dogs also show aggressive behavior that is related to social rank. Even at the age of 6 weeks playful wrestling and biting is a common feature of the behavior of many types of domestic dog. True aggression normally appears at approximately the ninth week of life, and from then on, attacks by one animal upon another can have serious consequences. It is also at this time that one dog establishes dominance over another. The heavier dog has a considerable advantage when males are involved in encounters, but weight is less important in the case of females.

Lorenz drew attention to the submissive postures that dogs use to ward off attack when they occupy a low position in the hierarchy. These postures supposedly hold the aggression in check. In the absence of submission on the part of one animal, aggression appears in a full-fledged form in the other and usually terminates only when one of the contestants leaves the field. Lorenz believed that there was an instinctive urge to attack, which builds up in the potential aggressor, but, for the most part, is held in check by the submissive postures of other animals living in the social group (Figure 3-9). He believed that human aggression follows a similar pattern, supposing that the primitive instincts remain in an attenuated but essentially similar form. Man, like other animals, has an innate urge to be aggressive. Lorenz argued that there are prepotent mechanisms in the brain and that aggression comes about because of some form of internal urge to attack.

An individual does not wait to be provoked, but rather the urge to fight builds up even in the absence of provocation, until finally that individual seeks the opportunity for fighting and indulges in spontaneous aggression. However, we must be cautious in generalizing from animal behavior to human behavior.

First, there are clear differences between one animal species and another. Indeed, there are differences between man and the most closely related primate. Second, although mechanisms are apparently laid down in the brain, it by no means follows that such a mechanism induces a spontaneous buildup of the urge to attack. Finally, it is possible to point to aggression, whatever the nature of the stimulus conditions leading up to it, as potentially securing rewards that would otherwise be unobtainable. Stuart Dimond (1970), in his book *The social behavior of animals* suggested that aggression can be viewed as an instrumental act. Aggression is used to service the needs of man, and any hostile aggressive act that brought about satisfaction would increase in frequency.

THE DEVELOPMENT AND UNFOLDING OF INSTINCTIVE PATTERNS

If behavior patterns make an appearance at a certain time and seemingly bear little relationship to the developments which have gone before, then such behavior is generally attributed to maturation, i.e., behavior arising spontaneously as the result of growth and differentiation of the nervous system and which is not dependent for its origin on factors outside of the organism.

Often, however, there is a gradual transformation from infantile behavior patterns to the more integrated ones of the adult. Simple and undifferentiated responses develop to more complex sequences and chains of activity. Weiss (1939) in his book *Principles of development* stated

> The condition of the central nervous system at the time that it is first functionally activated can be compared to a ship at the time of its launching. While it still remains to be completely outfitted it is already capable of floating, moving, and being steered. In the same way the central nervous system, when activated can transmit impulses, coordinate them and can control the musculature in a general way.

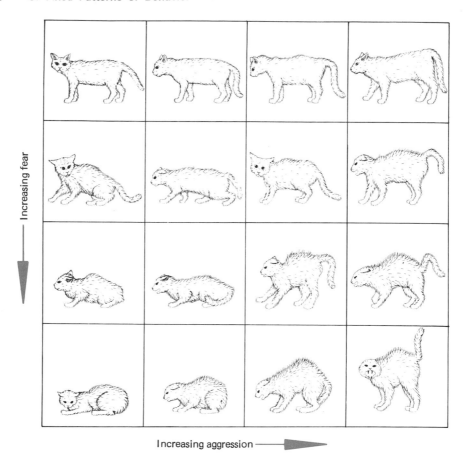

FIGURE 3-9   Threat and fear expressions in cats. In each row, fear increases downward and aggression increases from left to right. From Leyhausen (1956).

Clearly, many of the developments of the instinctive patterns take place out of the existing structure. In terms of the ship analogy, they represent the complete outfitting that makes the vessel something more than a hulk. They change it into a completely functioning unit, i.e., something geared to behave in a way closely related to the environment. One example illustrating the unfolding of instinctive patterns is the development of the adult song of the chaffinch from the infantile and juvenile forms.

The chaffinches begin the process of calling while they are in the egg. The calls at this time are extremely restricted and are most noticeable for distress calling, which occurs if the eggs are cooled slightly at a time just before they hatch. After hatching the nestling is equipped with a restricted range of calls. Again the most noticeable are those of distress, but contentment

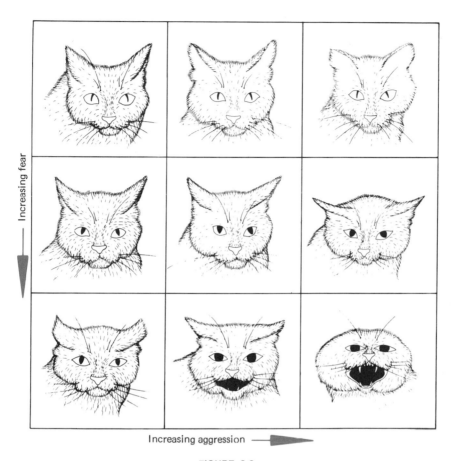

FIGURE 3-9

calls are also heard frequently. From the time the young become fledglings up until the time they reach sexual maturity they produce the juvenile or immature form of the song known as the subsong.

The simplest of these subsongs consists of a series of steady chirping notes which can be described by the word tchirp. These sounds are repeated and they fluctuate in pitch. Toward the end of the song, there may be an intense burst of sound called a rattle, although this is usually not in evidence at this time.

The subsong remains much the same throughout the first year of life, but, when the fledgling becomes sexually mature in the spring, the subsong undergoes a change. The male forms the full song out of the elements of the subsong when it enters the new territory in the spring. The change from the subsong to the full song is related to the circulation of sex hormones in the animal's blood stream. This is illustrated by the fact that the injection of sex hormones results in the appearance of the full song at an earlier time. However, these hormones are not the only factor leading to production. If the young are taken from the nest at 5 days of age and reared in auditory isolation, they produce a clear juvenile subsong; but when the time comes to replace this with the adult song, a simplified and debased form is produced (Figure 3-10). The song is not divided clearly into three phases, and it lacks the terminal flourish so characteristic of the normal song. While these songs are of the normal length and contain the right number of notes, the whole performance is at a low level. (Deafened birds also show this pattern.) Thorpe regards this performance as the blueprint of chaffinch song, i.e., the part that must be coded genetically.

The fact that some auditory input of the songs of other individuals is important to the development of full song is further illustrated by wild birds that are caught in their first autumn and raised from then on in auditory isolation until the next spring. The song of these birds resembles normal chaffinch song much more closely than that produced by birds raised in isolation from the first 5 days of life. This suggests that the auditory input from the songs of other birds has its influence chiefly during early youth. While the basic outlines of the song are inborn, stimulation from other individuals is also important in fully developing the song.

The capacity to modify song by listening to sounds has also been analyzed by playing tape-recordings to the animals during their isolation. However, isolated birds will not learn any pattern which they hear. For example, there is no modification of the song to an artificial pure tone sequence of sound, but the song is changed as the result of exposure to genuine recorded chaffinch song, even when played backwards or distorted by the rearrangement of the phrases.

Not all species are the same in the pattern of development of their song, but the picture is similar in a number of species, including chicken juncos. The important feature is the existence of a genetically coded blueprint for song that is filled out by later factors such as the concentration of sex hormones and the early experience of the song of other birds.

INBORN BEHAVIOR AND LEARNING

Inborn patterns of behavior form a kind of fabric that later learning overlays. The two become woven together in interlinking strands. This can be seen

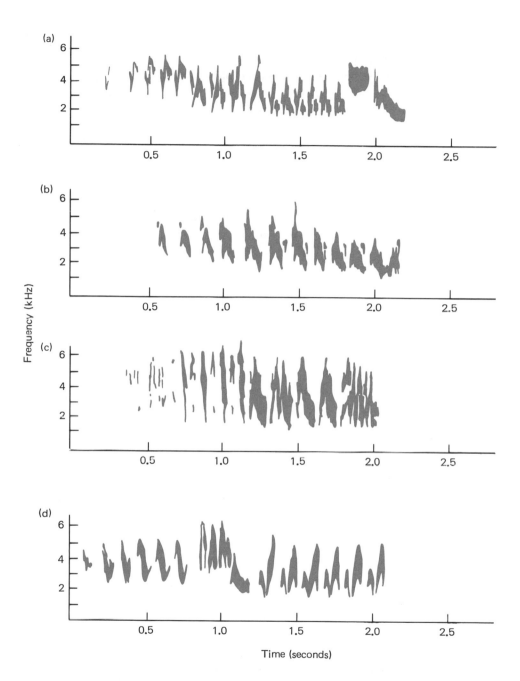

FIGURE 3-10   (a) The sound spectrograph of a normal chaffinch. (b) Song after being raised in isolation. (c) Song produced by an individual from a group raised in isolation. (d) The song from a bird reared in isolation after "tutoring" from an abnormal chaffinch song. After Thorpe, W. H. *Bird song*. London & New York: Cambridge Univ. Press, 1961.

in the nest-building behavior of birds. In the absence of opportunity to learn from previous generations, the birds construct nests, but, as in the study of the behavior of ravens, skill is acquired during the course of construction. Ravens learn to select only those twigs that can be manipulated and incorporated into the nest fabric. Also, many innate patterns are used to facilitate fresh learning. For example, chimpanzees retrieve a banana suspended by a string somewhat above their reach by stacking boxes one on top of the other. The animal stretches up, reaches its arms high in the air, and grasps the banana. Yet, chimpanzees pile objects one on top of the other and climb onto them as part of their normal pattern of play (Figure 3-11). It is as if the animal is performing this pattern in the learning situation and incorporates it into the task of reaching the banana. Thus many fixed action patterns can become interwoven with learned responses and used to solve problems that would otherwise present the animal with great difficulty.

IMPRINTING

Imprinting is a particular example of the situation where learned and innate factors interact. The term imprinting is derived from the German term, Prägung (coining or stamping). It was first used to refer to the tendency of newly hatched geese or ducks to respond by following the first large moving object encountered, very much in the same way as they would normally react to their parents.

Lorenz raised goslings on an estate near Vienna. Goslings hatched by the goose immediately followed their mother around the estate. Goslings hatched in an incubator, however, were denied the opportunity to see their mother. The first living being that these goslings saw was Lorenz. He acted as a substitute for the mother, and the goslings followed him around the estate. Lorenz now took the duck-imprinted and the human-imprinted ducklings and marked them to distinguish them from each other. He then placed all ducklings under a large box, while the mother looked on. When the box was lifted, the two groups of ducklings rushed headlong toward their respective parents, one group towards the duck and the other group towards Lorenz. The early experience of the animal had determined its social preference. Lorenz called this phenomenon imprinting. He was the first person to point out that imprinting: (1) occurred early in the life of the organism; (2) appeared to be confined to a brief period early in the life of the individual; (3) was irreversible once established; (4) occurred to a broad class of objects; and may be established long before it is evident in behavior.

FIGURE 3-11   Chimpanzees are capable of a wide variety of cognitive acts. Here they are seen putting sticks together and trying to reach a high piece of fruit by stacking boxes together and trying to fetch it with a stick. From Köhler (1925).

Lorenz also pointed out that this form of response may also be important in determining social choice, as occurs, for example, in sexual pairing later in life. Although the views of Lorenz stimulated much research, not all of this research has confirmed his view. For example, there is evidence that imprinting may be established to one object even after the animal has already become imprinted to another object. This suggests that imprinting can occur outside of the critical period and is not completely irreversible.

Human beings are not the only objects apart from the animal's mother to which a young chick or duckling will become imprinted. Hess (1959) reports

(a)

(b)

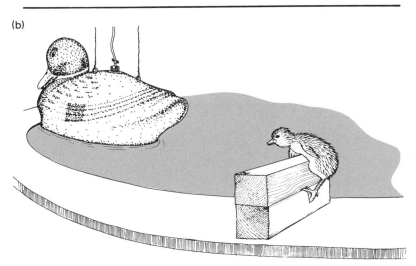

FIGURE 3-12 The imprinting process. (a) A young duckling is exposed to a male duck that emits a sound and subsequently follows it in preference to a duck emitting a different sound. (b) The strength of the imprinted response is related to the amount of effort made in following the original model. From "Imprinting in Animals" by E. H. Hess. Copyright © 1958 by Scientific American, Inc. All rights reserved.

how he began a study of imprinting in the laboratory. The imprinting object in this case was not a living being but a model of a male mallard duck (Figure 3-12). The subjects used in this experiment were young mallard ducklings. The eggs were collected from a nearby duckpond, and the animals were isolated from one another when they hatched. They were then exposed to the imprinting object at different ages to determine the age at which the imprinting experi-

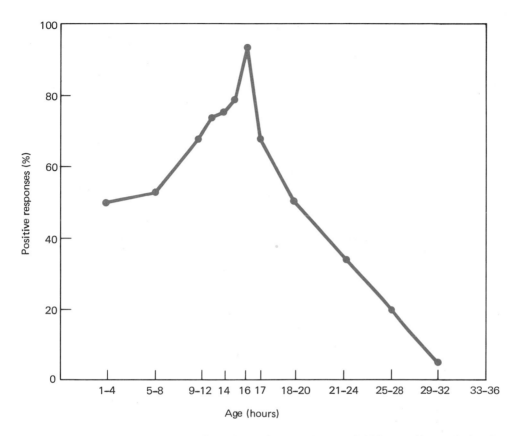

FIGURE 3-13   Ducklings are most effectively imprinted at the age of 16 hours. This is called their critical age. From "Imprinting in Animals" by E. H. Hess. Copyright © 1958 by Scientific American, Inc. All rights reserved.

ence is most effective. Some imprinting occurred immediately after hatching, but the ducklings were most ready to imprint to the object when they were exposed to it between 13 and 16 hours after hatching (Figure 3-13).

The behavior of following may occur to a variety of objects, including cardboard boxes, football bladders, balloons, and model railway trucks. However, it usually holds that the hatchling has a restricted experience of the world and usually only follows another object in the absence of its mother.

Other animals, in addition to birds, show imprinting. Guinea pigs follow moving objects in the same way that goslings do. It also has been suggested that imprinting-like processes operate in the attachment of the young to the mother in primates, and the question has arisen as to how far the attachment of the human infant to the mother is an imprinting-like process.

SUMMARY

In recent years, the work of the ethologists has provided a new spur to the study of instinct in man, not so much in terms of his mental makeup but regarding patterns of behavior viewed from within the framework of evolutionary theory. Man does not stand apart from the biological forces that have led to the shaping of the behavior of each species as it is today. In fact, the ethological viewpoint with its emphasis on instinctual patterns and innate behavior has significantly influenced the way we study human behavior.

Students of psychology, however, will need to be on their guard against some of the claims of popular ethologists. Desmond Morris, for example, supposes that because human beings are related in evolutionary terms to the other primates they share a common ancestry with them, and much that typifies the behavior of monkeys is a part of a common heritage. Human beings obviously form part of the evolutionary continuum, but it is a matter of argument as to how far man has moved along the evolutionary scale. There are differences between even closely related species in the animal kingdom and there are certainly major differences between man and the most closely related primates. Also, it is by no means clear that instinctive forces in human nature are as fixed and as unchanging as Lorenz has suggested. The capacity to learn assumes a more important status, which we will see in the next section on human development.

SUGGESTED READINGS

DIMOND, S. J. *The social behaviour of animals.* New York: Harper, 1970.

EIBL-EIBESFELDT, I. *Ethology: The biology of behaviour.* New York: Holt, 1970.

HINDE, R. A. *Animal behaviour.* (2nd ed.) New York: McGraw-Hill, 1971.

LORENZ, K. *On aggression.* London: Methuen, 1963.

TINBERGEN, N. *Study of instinct.* London & New York: Oxford Univ. Press, 1951.

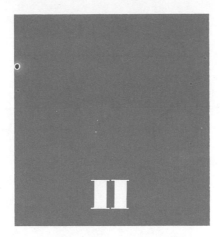

Developmental
Processes

4

Emotional
Behavior

———————————

The development of emotional behavior is both a fascinating and fragile process. We will discover that there are critical periods during development when an organism should be exposed to certain kinds of influences if it is to experience a normal adult emotional life. It frequently comes as a surprise to learn that depriving a rat or human child of the right kind of environmental stimuli at particular times during development has dramatic effects on subsequent behavior.

In addition, we will examine three basic aspects of emotional behavior: "love," "fear," and "aggression." An experimental analysis of "love," for example, has been carried out by Harry Harlow at the University of Wisconsin. The work was done on monkeys, but has wide implication. For the most part, Harlow studies the psychological consequences of depriving newborn monkeys of normal monkey interpersonal relations. But before starting, we should be clear on the body mechanism involved in emotional arousal.

BIOLOGICAL MECHANISMS

The most important physical mechanisms involved in emoting are the autonomic nervous system (sympathetic and parasympathetic) and the endocrine system. Both are complex systems that interact in the body to secrete

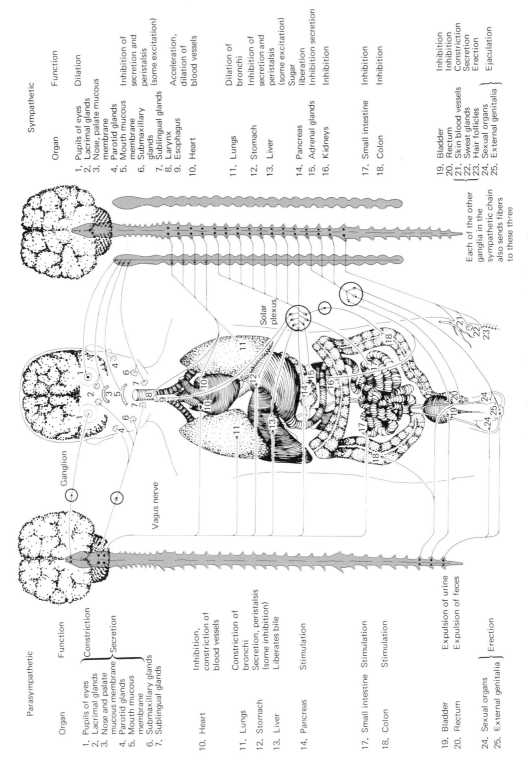

FIGURE 4-1 Sites and functions of autonomic nervous system innervation.

Sympathetic

	Organ	Function
1.	Pupils of eyes	Dilation
2.	Lacrimal glands	
3.	Nose, palate mucous membrane	
4.	Parotid glands	Inhibition of secretion and peristalsis (some excitation)
5.	Mouth mucous membrane	
6.	Submaxillary glands	
7.	Sublingual glands	
8.	Larynx	Acceleration, dilation of blood vessels
9.	Esophagus	
10.	Heart	
11.	Lungs	Dilation of bronchi
12.	Stomach	Inhibition of secretion and peristalsis (some excitation)
13.	Liver	Sugar liberation
14.	Pancreas	Inhibition secretion
15.	Adrenal glands	
16.	Kidneys	Inhibition
17.	Small intestine	Inhibition
18.	Colon	Inhibition
19.	Bladder	Inhibition
20.	Rectum	Inhibition
21.	Skin blood vessels	Constriction
22.	Sweat glands	Secretion
23.	Hair follicles	Erection
24.	Sexual organs	Ejaculation
25.	External genitalia	

Each of the other ganglia in the sympathetic chain also sends fibers to these three

Parasympathetic

	Organ	Function
1.	Pupils of eyes	Constriction
2.	Lacrimal glands	Secretion
3.	Nose and palate mucous membrane	
4.	Parotid glands	
5.	Mouth mucous membrane	
6.	Submaxillary glands	
7.	Sublingual glands	
10.	Heart	Inhibition, constriction of blood vessels
11.	Lungs	Constriction of bronchi
12.	Stomach	Secretion, peristalsis (some inhibition)
13.	Liver	Liberates bile
14.	Pancreas	Stimulation
17.	Small intestine	Stimulation
18.	Colon	Stimulation
19.	Bladder	Expulsion of urine
20.	Rectum	Expulsion of feces
24.	Sexual organs	Erection
25.	External genitalia	

Ganglion

Vagus nerve

Solar plexus

chemicals and neurally innervate (i.e., signal for action) many internal organs such as the heart, lungs, intestines, bladder, and sex organs (Figure 4-1).

In a typical stressing situation, for example, the normal rhythm of these systems will be disrupted as a result of innervation of the sympathetic division of the autonomic nervous system. The hypothalamus, a neural control center, will also be active as well as the pituitary, a gland at the base of the brain in charge of all endocrine functions. This gland secretes a chemical called ACTH (adrenocorticotrophic hormone), which travels by way of the blood stream to the adrenals, a set of glands near the kidneys. The outer segment or cortex of these glands responds to ACTH and, in turn, produces chemical hormones called steroids. These hormones again travel through the bloodstream and accelerate the metabolism of all tissues throughout the body.

The parasympathetic system is not as involved in excitatory behavior as is the sympathetic system. While the sympathetic system tends to trigger all systems it innervates at once, the parasympathetic system acts more specifically. Among its other functions, it is active in producing erections in men as well as expelling feces and urine.

EFFECTS OF STIMULATION IN INFANCY

How these biological mechanisms act in the development of emotional behavior can be seen from work done by Levine and Mullins (1966) at Stanford University. They made a most remarkable discovery concerning the effects of *not* handling young rats. The adult behavior of these rats deviates from the normals in that they appear terrified of new environments. Placed in a clear plexiglass box for the first time, these rats will cower in the corner, while a normally handled rat will run about exploring its new environment with enthusiasm.

Levine relates his work to the well-known fact that during stressing situations the pituitary and adrenals release several hormones with ACTH being the dominant one. He discovered both his deprived rats and handled rats secreted just as much when they were given a stressing test, but the pattern of response of the two was completely different. The deprived rats were slow in producing ACTH, but, once aroused, the ACTH level remained high for a long period of time. The normal rat's ACTH level rose and decreased quickly, being present only when it was needed. This latter kind of response, of course, has a greater survival value for the animal, while the slow and sustained response of the experimental group can cause an ulcer in the long run and eventually death by adrenal exhaustion.

It has also been noted that early stimulation and handling has the effect of accelerating the neural development of the CNS. Cholesterol, which is a chemical found in high concentration in growing white matter of the brain, is found in even higher concentration in the handled or stimulated rats compared to the unstimulated rats.

These telling experiments unhappily are confirmed by observation of the developmental rates of children living in institutional homes. The child raised in a foundling house tends to be retarded and is more susceptible to disease. He even takes a longer time to smile than the child raised in a family. Thus the effects of infrequent handling, a problem in institutional care, can be seen even in humans, and it has been suggested that the foregoing physio logical mechanisms are involved.

EMOTIONAL STATES

Heterosexual Affectional System

Harlow (1971) got the idea that there may be a heterosexual affectional system in animals from an observation his daughter made on their pet guinea pigs. It turns out the male guinea pig is very amorous. Upon introduction of a female into his cage, there is a steady development of a relation where the guinea pigs stare at each other, nuzzle, and cuddle one another. The final sexual act is not characterized by rape so much as by patience. The male starts by purring, nuzzling, licking, smelling, and brushing up against the new female who at first is quite frightened by the whole matter. The male, nonetheless, conquers. At this point, if a new female is introduced into the cage, the male approaches her in the same friendly way he did before. A previously seduced female becomes furious, however, at such activity and does not tolerate infidelity. Although the male will finally win, it is clear from these observations that there is a well-developed heterosexual affectional system in these guinea pigs.

Harlow has demonstrated a similar affectional system in the rhesus monkey with a series of stages. There is an infantile stage lasting through the first year. Here the monkeys partake in inappropriate and inadequate sexual play and posturing. This is followed by the preadolescent stage, which continues into the third year for the female and the fourth year for the male. Here the posture and sexual play is appropriate, but the animals are unable to complete the act. Then there is the adolescent and adult stage, which is like the foregoing, but reproduction is possible.

In the beginning we must have clearly in mind what are the normal sexual postures of the rhesus monkeys. In Figure 4-2, we see the sexual invitation when it is initiated by a female (a), the invitation by the male (b), and lastly the normal male–female sexual act (c). In the infantile stage as early as the second month of life, the males show earlier and more frequent sex behavior than do females. While the males almost never assume the female sex posture, the females frequently display the male sex posture. In general, frequency of sexual behavior increases progressively with age for both sexes.

From the start there are few threatening responses by females, whereas males continually threaten other males and females as they grow up. The differences are clearly seen. Also, females are much more likely to passively respond to a threat. They characteristically adopt a position of presenting to the male and then let events take their course. In addition, the grooming response, which is critical for monkey socialization, is almost exclusively a function of the female. This caressing is a very important part of the infant–infant affectional system that Harlow feels is essential to the normal development of adult sexual behavior.

The implications from these studies are clear. It is hard not to believe that many of the sexual differences that normally develop are a product of the genetic story. These basic primitive responses unfold in man as in the monkey and play a critical role in the overall development process that leads to sexual activities that we as adults enjoy.

Love

What is love? Usually such ephemeral questions as this are left to poets, philosophers, priests, and YMCA leaders. Psychologists as a rule have not tackled it because most experimentalists believe the subject is not approachable. Many psychologists think the concept itself is perhaps illusionary. Yet Harlow has unearthed a number of phenomena that can easily be thought of as love or at least represent the biological primitive of that behavioral state in man.

One approach to this problem was revealed in Harlow's now classic experiment. Instead of letting newborn monkeys be raised with their mothers, they were placed in cages that had cloth surrogate mothers or sometimes wire-framed mothers. Babies without a real mother would desperately cling to these frames. Harlow would then shake the frame violently in an effort to make the surrogate mother unappealing, only to find the baby monkeys clinging to the surrogate as tightly as ever. None of these monkeys so raised demonstrated neurotic behavior at this point. They were clearly devoted to their mother, which in this case proved to be nothing but a cloth-covered or wire surrogate.

It was only when a large number of monkeys, which had been raised in separate cages away from their normal mothers, grew up that a number

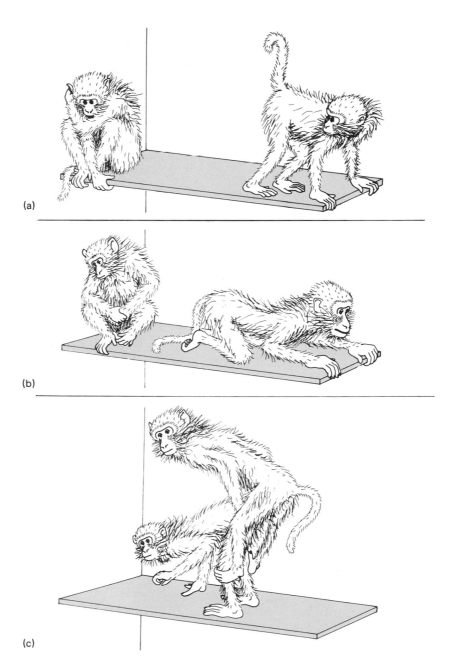

(a)

(b)

(c)

FIGURE 4-2 The normal sexual soliciting posture in the rhesus monkey. (a) The female wants the male. (b) The male is presenting himself to the female. (c) They get together in the normal sexual position.

of truly remarkable phenomena were seen. The older they became the less normal they became. In general they would sit in their cages staring off into space. They were completely mute and were indifferent to other monkeys and to people. (Monkeys are usually extremely volatile and reactive to people.) These neurotic monkeys had a tendency to bite themselves voraciously and also to adopt a number of strange behaviors such as clutching their head in both hands and rocking back and forth.

Harlow later placed a number of these monkeys in the same cage. When males and females were allowed to interact in this fashion, a normal sex act seldom occurred. Instead the monkeys almost had a platonic relation toward one another and would never violate the other's privacy. He then tried to push the matter and tried to see whether these abnormally raised animals could perform sexual acts.

> At this point we took the 17 oldest of our cage-raised animals, females showing consistent estrous cycles, and males obviously mature, and engaged in an intensive re-education program, pairing our females with our most experienced, patient, and gentle males, and our males with our most eager, amiable, and successful breeding females. When the laboratory bred females were smaller than the sophisticated males the girls would back away and sit down facing the males looking appealingly at these would-be consorts. Their hearts were in the right place but nothing else was. When the females were larger than the males we can only hope that they misunderstood the males intentions, for after a period of courtship they would attack and maul the ill-fated male [Harlow, 1962].

Curiously, the effects of social deprivation can be titrated to a rather fine degree. If newborn monkeys are not allowed to develop infant–infant normal affectional relations, they turn out to be social disasters as adults. They neither desire nor partake in sexual activity nor do they desire interpersonal relations. On the other hand, if an infant raised without a mother is allowed the normal peer group relations, normal sexual behavior is seen when they are adults. Yet, there is a striking difference. These motherless females, while able to reproduce, have no inkling as to how to treat their newborn baby (Figure 4-3). The motherless mother treats her own children in the most heartless way and is seemingly devoid of all feeling.

It would appear then that this kind of study argues for the view that there are certain biological primitive impulses that newborn organisms have. The clinging response of the neonatal monkey to the real mother produces the kind of information it will eventually need to be a mother. If the monkey

FIGURE 4-3   The response of a neurotic mother toward her young. It is as if the mother never learned how to behave toward children because she never had a mother to teach her.

clung to a wire surrogate, the primitive impulse in no way can be nurtured and developed along a normal course. Similarly, peer–peer interrelations are necessary for the normal development of sexual behavior. It would seem that without these interrelations the affectional system never properly develops in animals and perhaps also in man.

PSYCHOANALYTICAL VIEW OF SEXUAL DEVELOPMENT

Sigmund Freud, of course, tells the story of emotional development quite differently. After listening to hundreds of disturbed men and women, Freud set forth his theory of psychosexual development. It was not arrived at as the result of experimentation, but as a post hoc analysis of abnormal behavior.

In brief, Freud maintains the human child is born with an overpowering drive—the sexual drive. He called this the libido. If its normal course of development is ever frustrated, grave consequences would eventually occur. The libido was nourished by stimulation of various erogenous zones on the body. Indeed any "pleasurable impulses" are taken by Freud to reflect a link to sexuality.

Freud maintains that we advance through five sexual stages. If frustration at any stage occurs, fixation at that stage may take place whereby the person spends an abnormally long time at that level of psychosexual development. At times, regression or a return to an earlier stage of development occurs.

The first stage is the oral stage, which lasts through the second year. Here the body receives great pleasure from the sensation of sucking.

Next comes the anal stage. The critical erogenous zone has shifted to the anal region and the two- and three-year-old finds great pleasure in defecating. However, at this time the parents maintain that feces are a "no-no" and start to toilet train. As a result, according to Freud, a conflict arises. Whereas the child wants to take his pleasure anytime, the parents are trying to impose a schedule for this performance.

After the anal stage comes the phallic stage. The primary erogenous zone has now shifted to the genitals. The child discovers the genitals are capable of eliciting pleasures. This ushers in sexual awareness and the Oedipal conflict. Freud says that little boys fall head over heels in love with their mother and desire them sexually. This produces a conflict between the father and son, which is only resolved after the boy feels the mother has rejected his advances. At this point the boy is left with only his father, if he is to have the love of either parent, and consequently redefines him as "the greatest" and begins to identify with him completely. A similar series of events in the opposite direction occurs for girls.

Then comes the latency stage. Because the child has had to suppress his sexual desire *vis-à-vis* his parents, he suppresses all heterosexual impulses. As a result he becomes sexually inert for a period of time. Finally, the genital stage arrives at adolescence. There is a sexual rebirth with great interest in the opposite sex. This usually lasts until death.

So there it is. According to Freud, any tampering with the normal course of events such as frustration, punishment, or facilitation will increase the probability of abnormal sexual behavior. This basic design of development has produced most of Freud's psychoanalytic theory, a theory not easily neutralized by experimental data.

FEAR

Once again we must focus on the problem of the origin of a primitive emotion. Is fear innate or is it learned as a result of an interaction between the organism and the environment?

The problem has been carefully studied in the mallard duck by Ronald Melzack (1965) and his colleagues. It is well known that all gallinaceous birds and in particular the mallard duck are afraid of hawks. The simple movement of a cardboard hawk-shaped figure over a duck will produce a violent response.

In fact, the critical stimulus features of the paper hawk are the short neck and the long tail, characteristics of most predatory birds.

Melzack ran an experiment in which he raised young ducks from birth. Some experienced overflights of the hawk almost from birth, while other birds were raised in complete isolation. When tested at 25 days of age, the isolated ducks showed a tremendous response to the hawk, while the hawk-exposed ducks showed none. Yet, even in the deprived ducks, the violent response abated and disappeared completely in three days. The conclusion here is that there is certainly an innate component to the fear response, but that it can be modified by events in the environment.

In children the appearance of "fear" comes early. In the newborn any great shift of body position or posture seems to produce what J. B. Watson called a "fear" reaction, one of three basic reactions he felt newborns had. This, however, simply shows that the "idea" of fear is inborn, not that the fears we accumulate in a lifetime are present from the start. These fears are mostly acquired through a process of conditioning or other complex processes active in the inculcation of these very basic behavioral responses.

In a classic study by Watson and Rayner (1920), a young baby less than a year old by the name of Albert was conditioned to "fear" a rat. Everytime the child was in the presence of the rat, a piece of metal was struck near the child. Soon the child began to cry vigorously when the rat alone was presented.

Albert's "fear" reaction generalized to other stimuli that resembled the rat such as a rabbit, dog, cat, or simply a ball of wool. Other completely unrelated stimuli such as the ever-present examiner caused no such reaction.

Just as fear can be learned using standard conditioning procedures, fear reactions can be eliminated by the operant procedure of "fading in." Here the fearful stimulus is gradually introduced to the environment in a positive context as in the standard procedure used in handling fear of the dark. In one study, a child feared dark rooms. During the course of playing ball with a friend, the friend made sure the game moved toward a dark room. Finally and "accidentally" the ball rolled into the dark room. Almost without hesitation the child, in this positive context, went into the room for it. An hour before, the room held only terror for the child.

AGGRESSION

The problem of aggression is discussed more than it is understood. Every conceivable view on the subject is represented with authority, and more than one theory is in direct conflict with another. There are, on the one hand, theories that aggression is strictly inherited and exists outside the control of environment. On the other hand, there is the notion that all aggressive behavior is learned.

Aggression is a very difficult concept to define. Is it aggression when a cat kills a mouse for dinner? Or is it only aggression when a cat kills a mouse and chooses not to eat it? These are complex distinctions to make, and one can see from the start that the same piece of behavior can be variably defined. In man, this is a particularly profound problem. Is it aggression when a black ghetto teenager who has been repressed all his life robs Whitey's liquor store, or only aggression when he robs another black man's store? When he robs the white man he most likely defines the act as "getting even" and will receive large reward from his peers for his action. His act is interpreted as "just" and within the strict moral framework of his friends. If, however, he robs a black man's store, the act would be considered aggressive and antisocial by his own peers.

To take a more straightforward example, consider abortion. Up until June, 1970, it was a crime in New York and considered quite an act of aggression by both the doctor and the patient. Now it is legal and the "aggressive" aspect of the act has disappeared and been replaced with euphemisms such as "necessary," "intelligent," etc.

Clearly all organisms have a certain rate or level of aggression. If aggression is defined as the tendency to engage or challenge the environment, then one can view all activity on a continuum, with some responses viewed as more "aggressive" than others. The student who studies 10 hours a day is more aggressive than one who studies 5 hours. Without a certain minimum level of aggression, man and animals could not exist.

Ethological View

Most ethologists and general biologists feel the tendency for aggression is innate. It is not due to a bad or deprived environment. Rather, the aggression tendency can be turned into destructive behavior by a bad environment.

In the animal kingdom the predators who hunt and kill for food are not viewed as doing so out of fear, anger, or "meanness." Indeed, in the long run it would work to the predator's disadvantage to view all prey as objects to be killed since enough of his prey must survive to produce another generation so as to make more food. With respect to the prey animal, aggression is only a defense response. As a result most ethologists point to the basic survival value of aggressive behavior; it is a positive force, not a negative force.

What is difficult to explain by "survival value" is the intraspecies aggression commonly seen among animals. This is where animals of the same species engage in fighting each other. Konrad Lorenz (1963) maintains that most of the fighting in this category is ritualistic and never leads to killing or even serious fighting. It is a symbolic show of who's boss. It is this kind of data that has led many scientists to maintain man is the only species that kills his own. While this pure separation of responses is contested by other scientists, it would seem fair to say there is a trend in this direction.

In summary, the biological view is that the organism has a clear disposition for aggression. Without it, most organisms simply could not survive. The tendency only takes a violent and antisocial turn when the environment does not allow normal outlets for aggressive behavior.

Psychological View

Most psychological views build on the biological analysis. In general, psychological notions deal with aggression in the sense of violent, antisocial behavior, i.e., aggression gone sour.

Once defined in this light, there are many factors involved in aggressive behavior. Simple physical pain can lead to aggressive behavior. N. H. Azrin and his colleagues (1964) have shown how two monkeys calmly and peacefully sitting together one minute can be viciously fighting each other the next. By painfully stimulating one monkey through a set of electrodes, the pain-induced monkey goes crazy with rage and attacks the nearest object, which in this case is the peaceful monkey. This is like the husband coming home from work, throwing open the door, and saying "Hi, Honey," only to have a frying pan thrown in his face by an exhausted and exasperated wife and mother of five children. It is not too surprising that aggression often takes the form of violence.

Many psychologists have wondered whether the aggressive impulse can be channeled and the tensions released through nonviolent means. For instance, the exasperated wife may prefer to feed her husband the food she knows he likes least that evening, or she might say shame on you for allowing me to have five children.

Albert Bandura (1969) at Stanford University has shown that children easily and continually imitate the aggression they see on the part of adults around them. In one study, nursery school children watched a movie picture in which an adult behaved aggressively toward a toy clown. When the movie was over, some children watching the film tended to behave aggressively toward the same clown figure presented to them.

This same kind of reaction can be seen from a study by Sears (1961) on the effects of punishment on aggressive behavior of children. Mothers who were very punitive toward their children produced boys and girls who themselves tended to be extremely aggressive and violent toward others and their play objects around them. Less punitive mothers found their children to be far less aggressive and violent.

Most studies on aggression suggest that the normal aggressive impulse can be cultured and sent in a positive direction or can be frustrated and sent in a negative direction. The final outcome is clearly an interaction between the biological organism and its environment.

COGNITIVE CONTROL OF EMOTIONAL BEHAVIOR

We have briefly described but three of a wide range of emotions. By isolating them in this manner, we could mistakenly come to believe that the brain is organized in such a way as to similarly isolate them into specific brain circuits. This notion in fact has become widely accepted. However, it is also the basis of a considerable and fascinating controversy in psychology.

It was William James who first proposed a theory of emotional behavior. He stated quite simply that "the bodily changes follow directly the perception of the exciting fact and that our feeling of the same changes as they occur is the emotion [James, 1890, p. 449]." In other words, James felt our emotions are the direct result of visceral and other bodily changes that accompany a behavioral event.

This idea was directly attacked by Canon who pointed out that a total separation of the viscera from the central nervous system does not eliminate emotional behavior. He had also observed that the same visceral states occur in a wide variety of emotional states. His views gave rise to the idea that there were specific neural structures in the brain that were responsible for our emotions.

With these lines drawn, several psychologists have urged a hybrid view. The dominant idea today is that the cognitive state of a person is extremely important in emotional behavior. During an emotional response, there is first a general bodily arousal. Subsequently, the cognitive system interprets and gives affective meaning to the arousal. If an individual is in a positive social and psychological state, an arousing event will produce positive feelings. However, if the person is in a negative social and psychological setting, arousal will lead to negative feelings.

Much of the fascinating work that supports this cognitive–visceral inter-

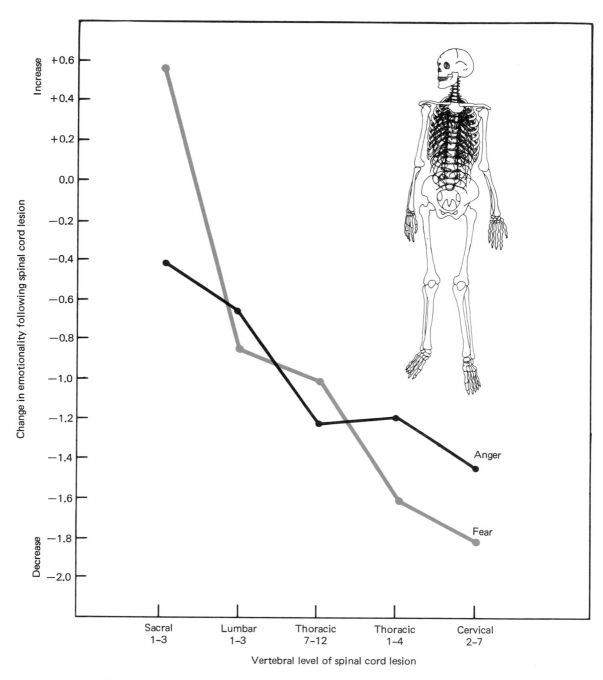

FIGURE 4-4   Changes in emotionality as related to level of spinal cord lesion. After Schachter and adapted from Hohmann (1966).

action view of emotion has been done by Schachter (1971) (see Chapter 21). He has recently reviewed a large body of data that demonstrates that visceral changes are important in emotional behavior. Schachter draws attention to a series of studies by Hohmann carried out with patients with spinal cord lesions occurring at various levels of the spinal cord. A striking effect on the patients emotional life has been found (Figure 4-4). The lower the lesion in the cord, the less damage there is to neuronal input from our viscera to the brain. With a higher lesion, the input to the brain from the viscera is almost completely eliminated.

Hohmann asked the subjects to compare an emotional event both before and after their lesion. The prediction was that with a higher spinal cord lesion the subjects would now feel less emotion. Hohmann found exactly this. The patients described themselves as acting emotionally but not feeling emotional. One patient said, "It is sort of a cold anger. Sometimes I act angry when I see some injustice. I yell and I cuss and I raise hell because if you don't do it sometimes I've learned people will take advantage of you. But it just doesn't have the heat to it that it used to. It is mental kind of anger." These results clearly support the cognitive–visceral interaction theory of emotional behavior.

SUMMARY

The wide range of emotions we experience daily is what gives us a sense of being alive. It colors our life, for without emotions humans would be automatons with each life event seemingly no different from any other. The general state of bodily arousal that is involved in emotional behavior is effected by the brain through the autonomic nervous system as well as the endocrine system. Whether an emotional system develops normally seems to depend on whether the proper social and environmental conditions are present during critical periods in early development.

SUGGESTED READINGS

FREUD, S. *New introductory lectures on psychoanalysis.* New York: Norton, 1933.

GLASS, D. C. *Neurophysiology and emotion.* New York: Rockefeller Univ. Press, 1967.

HARLOW, H. F. *Learning to love.* San Francisco: Albion Publ. Co., 1971.

HOPPE, R. A., MILTON, G. A., & SIMMEL, E. C. (Eds.) *Early experiences and the processes of socialization.* New York: Academic Press, 1970.

MOLTZ, H. *Ontogeny of vertebrate behavior.* New York: Academic Press, 1971.

5

Self-Control

———————

We have seen so far that man has a wide range of emotions and that there are rich genetic as well as environmental factors that are critically involved in the development of our emotional life. Emotions, of course, play an important role in motivation, and it is our motivation to do things that sometimes places us in behavioral patterns we would rather not be in. Need we be the victim of early emotional development or can we gain self-control of our behavior?

In this chapter, the question of self-control will be discussed. It is simultaneously one of the most fascinating and one of the least understood areas in psychology. In general terms, the problem of self-control has two meanings. It can refer to the process whereby an individual can control his behavior in the direct sense of showing great willpower by denying himself certain of life's pleasures. For example, the chain-smoker who decides he must quit smoking for health reasons and does so instantly is one with great self-control.

In addition to this meaning of self-control, the term has come to mean something else in the psychological literature. In a way it has come to mean what behavior a person must go through when he lacks the kind of self-control just described. Thus, the smoker who wants to quit but can't is a person who must evolve other behavior patterns in his effort to stop. We will describe such a case later, but first let us examine the case of the individual with great self-control, the man who can stop smoking at will. Those who study the problem in this form quickly find themselves dealing with the problem of inculcation of values and most usually of moral values. Through what psychological process do we acquire such values as "good health," "abstention," "moderation," "fair play," and the like? Clearly, when studying self-control of this kind we are dealing with a strong behavioral phenomenon. When a class B premed student who desperately wishes to get an "A" in his organic chemistry course does not cheat when given a foolproof opportunity, we are dealing with a strong value system. Why doesn't the "cheater" have the same value system?

INCULCATION OF MORAL VALUES

Since it is extremely difficult to study the primary inputs during development of how any aspect of our mental life arises, psychologists tend to analyze how, once in, it can be changed or manipulated in some systematic way. With knowledge gained here, hypotheses are easily generated on how moral values arise in the first place.

Much of the work done on this problem derives from the theory of cognitive dissonance, which is described in detail in Chapter 23. In brief, this is the notion that peoples' beliefs, attitudes, and values change as a consequence of their behavior if the behavior is in conflict with a value they hold. More specifically, when a person holds two different cognitions that are incompatible, dissonance is produced, and, because this state is psychologically incompatible, it forces the person to achieve consonance by changing one of his cognitions. This psychological process is very active in our internalization of values. A classic experiment by Aronson and Carlsmith (1963) illustrates these ideas.

Children were viewed through a one-way mirror as they played with five toys placed on a table. After a while, a preference hierarchy for the toys was established for each child. The experimenters then spaced four of the toys around the room leaving the second-ranking toy alone on a table. At this point, one of three experimental conditions was initiated. In what was called a "no threat" condition, the experimenter told the child he could play with any toy in the room while he was gone. He then took with him the second ranking toy on the table. In a "severe threat" condition, the second-ranking toy was left on the table and the child received the same instructions except he was told not to touch that toy at all or he would be severely punished. A "mild threat" condition was the same except here the punishment for touching the toy was to be mild.

Through the one-way mirror the experimenter watched the children for 10 minutes. None of the children in the severe and mild threat conditions touched the toy on the table even though they looked at it frequently. In the first condition, of course, the child had no opportunity to play with the toy. At this time the experimenter returned and asked the children to rank order the toys once again. The results are seen in Table 5-1. Clearly, the children were all affected by the experience. All children changed their preference for the second-ranking toy. In the control or no threat group it became more desired, which is to say we like the forbidden. But, more important, the preference for it also increased in the severe threat group where a strong punishment was forthcoming if the toy was touched. However, in the mild threat condition it actually decreased!

The authors explain these results as follows.

> The results clearly support the theory of cognitive dissonance. In the severe threat condition, an individual's cognition that he did not play with an attractive toy was consonant with his cognition that he would have been severely punished if he had played with the toy. There was no need for him to provide further justification for his abstinence. However, when he refrained from playing with the toy in the absence of a severe threat, he experienced dissonance. His cognition that he did not play with the toy was dissonant with his cognition that it was attractive. In order to reduce dissonance, he derogated the toy.

In this experiment, the cognition that gave way was the value placed on an external object. However, we are more interested in the attending consequences. As Festinger and Friedman (1964) point out, the process described here does not explain how these events affect our deeper moral values. It is easy to imagine how a robber might react to not stealing in the pressure of mild threat. The robber simply decides that the object of his initial desire really is not worth stealing. To find out whether changes in basic attitudes occur,

TABLE 5-1   Change in Preference for Forbidden Toy[a]

	Preference		
	Increased	Unchanged	Decreased
No threat ($N = 11$)	7	4	0
Severe threat ($N = 22$)	14	8	0
Mild threat ($N = 22$)	4	10	8

[a] From Aronson and Carlsmith (1963).

Mills (1958) conducted an experiment dealing with the attitudinal consequences of succumbing to or resisting temptation. The experimental design placed sixth-grade students into a situation where it would be either highly or barely rewarding to cheat. However, the students first answered a questionnaire on their views about cheating. Two days after the experiment they were questioned again and their attitudes were compared. With this experimental design, we can see how resisting the temptation to cheat in the presence or absence of reward affects one's moral position on cheating as well as how actually cheating affects one's personal attitudes on cheating.

The results of this experiment were clear. Those who were found to be cheaters in the presence of a high reward experienced little change in their attitude about cheating. Those who cheated with only a little reward at stake predictably viewed cheating even more leniently afterwards. The interpretation is that they have a cognitive or value about the "badness" of cheating. Since they cheated for a very small reward, they must rationalize that there is very little wrong with cheating. The noncheaters who maintain their "honesty" in the presence of great temptation wind up strongly opposed to cheating.

There are, of course, additional mechanisms involved in the inculcation of values. Other studies have shown that the simple frequency of saying something is effective in changing a person's attitudes about an idea or object. The point we wish to make here is that values are inculcated in a variety of ways, and, when they exist in strength, they can be responsible for much of our self-control. In the following section we will gain insights into how people control their behavior in the absence of this kind of self-control.

BEHAVIORAL THEORY AND TECHNIQUES USED IN GAINING SELF-CONTROL

Some years ago, a smoker, a woman in her thirties with three young children, received some frightening news concerning her chest x ray. A lesion about the size of a quarter was clearly visible on the upper right lobe of her lung. No one seemed to be quite sure what caused the lesion, but everyone was convinced that smoking was somehow involved. The woman, a devoted two-pack-a-day smoker, was panic stricken. Not only did life seem suddenly short, but, as a result of doctor's orders, her one source of release, smoking, was being denied. Believing herself incapable of an abrupt halt in smoking, she decided in favor of methods that would assist her in gradually reducing her cigarette consumption. Since smoking is often paired with other activities, e.g., smoking and reading, the woman decided that she would permit herself a cigarette whenever she wanted one, but with the stipulation that she must smoke it in the bathroom. At first, there were innumerable trips to that area, which led some of the members of her family to be a bit concerned. Two months later, smoking was reduced to about five cigarettes a day, but the woman found herself unable to either smoke less or quit altogether. When an x ray report revealed that the lesion had calcified and healed, the relieved patient returned immediately to smoking two packs of cigarettes a day.

The smoking habit has been particularly unyielding and, as we have just seen, rarely comes under self-control, even in the face of intense efforts by psychologists and others to devise methods to help eliminate this dangerous habit. The management of self-control techniques is essential for those who wish to stop smoking. These methods, developed in the laboratory, have succeeded in causing the reduction rather than the elimination of smoking among participating subjects.

Gaining self-control by behavioral techniques has been formalized by the well-known behaviorist, B. F. Skinner (1953). He has defined self-control in terms of reward and punishment. He maintained that all instances of self-control (or the lack of it) can be described in terms of variables of reward that we experience in everyday life. Since a great deal of research in self-control has utilized the application of both reward and punishment, we will define and give examples of these terms from a behaviorist point of view.

REINFORCEMENT AND PUNISHMENT

Reinforcement and punishment are considered the two fundamental determinants of behavior (Figure 5-1). Reinforcement increases the performance rate of a behavior, while punishment decreases performance rate. There are two types of reinforcers, positive and negative. Positive reinforcers are stimuli that, when introduced in an experimental situation, lead to an increase in the subject's responding. For example, a hungry rat, sitting in a box, will press an attached lever at a very low rate. However, if the rat receives a food pellet for every bar press, the rate of bar pressing will increase greatly. The food pellets are positive reinforcers, since they increase the output of another behavior. Negative reinforcers are essentially aversive stimuli, the removal of which increases responding. Electric shock, for instance, when removed from the rat's cage, would lead to an increase in bar pressing; thus, the shock is a negative reinforcer.

Punishment is a behavioral event that has the effect of decreasing a particular piece of behavior (Figure 5-2). The procedure can be utilized in two ways, again with negative and positive reinforcers. The clearest example of

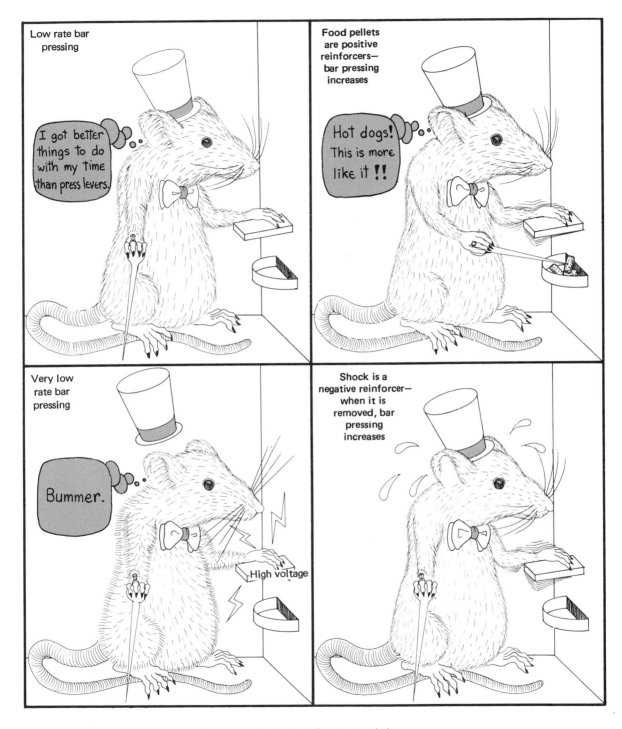

FIGURE 5-1   Skinner's analysis of reinforcement relations.

FIGURE 5-2   Skinner's formulation of punishment.

punishment is the introduction of shock, a negative reinforcer, while the rat is bar pressing for food pellets. Another example of punishment, though not classic in nature, is the removal of food pellets, the positive reinforcer, from the lever pressing situation. A rat will markedly decrease its lever pressing in both situations.

The most common procedures, used in self-control experiments carried out by behaviorists in real life situations, have involved the application of positive reinforcers for reinforcement, and negative reinforcers for punishment. Thus, watching television, reading magazines, and drinking coffee are used in contingencies to increase other behaviors, and are examples of reward. Shock, cleaning the toilet, and sweeping the walk are negative reinforcers that will decrease other behaviors when used in contingency situations and are forms of punishment.

SKINNER'S DEFINITION OF SELF-CONTROL

Skinner (1953) contends that, when a person practices self-control, he manipulates his own behavior variables in exactly the same way he manipulates those of another person. The use of reward and punishment in controlling the behavior of another person can be reversed and applied to oneself, so that one can both reward and punish oneself (Figure 5-3). We can apply pepper sauce to the tongue of a nail-biting friend every time we see him chewing his nails. We can promise and deliver an ice cream cone to a young boy for tidying up his room. These punishments and rewards are straightforward and easy enough to administer to oneself in a similar situation, but there are instances where self-reinforcement and self-punishment are elusive, unlikely, and inapplicable. Take the case of spanking, for instance. It is probably the oldest and most popular form of punishment, but is unlikely to be used by the adult in the control of his own behavior. But one can control his own "mental events," by saying positive or negative things about himself.

Skinner mainly views self-control as a procedure for decreasing an undesirable behavior for he wrote, "an organism may make the punished response less probable by altering the variables of which it is a function. Any behavior which succeeds in doing this will be automatically reinforced. We call such behaviors self-control." He lists several methods of self-control, consisting mainly of controlling responses (Figure 5-4). Placing a time-lock device on the door of the refrigerator to eliminate snacking between meals is a controlling response. For those who cannot resist shopping sprees, leaving credit cards

Punishment for nail biting   Reward for cleaning room

FIGURE 5-3   Methods of rewarding oneself.

or money at home would be a controlling response. The controlled responses, eating and spending, become less probable behaviors. The major feature of this procedure is the interruption of a behavior sequence at a very early stage.

SELF-CONTROL VIEWED AS BEHAVIORAL TECHNIQUES

The view of self-control as a series of behavioral techniques has resulted in a variety of methods for controlling certain kinds of behavior. Self-reinforcement, self-punishment, and stimulus control have all been found effective in changing behaviors. Eating, smoking, studying, and improving the self-image are some of the behaviors that have been subjected to behavioral techniques, involving principally those based on self-control. The following outlines the several methods used to create self-control using behavioral techniques.

FIGURE 5-4   Skinner's ideas on how to control responses.

Self-Reinforcement

Negative self-reinforcement, or the removal of aversive stimuli to increase responding, has been little used. The popular approach in human research has been the introduction of a positive reward as a self-reinforcer. This technique has been used to help students with dating problems, to relax children who behave disruptively in school, and to improve academic performance. Positive thoughts are also utilized in conjunction with behaviors that have a high rate of occurrence; the thoughts are designed to help improve an individual's self-esteem.

DIRECTED LEARNING PARADIGM.   This paradigm is the first of three main experimental paradigms utilizing self-reinforcement as its main technique. In the directed learning experiment, the subject is given a learning task and is reinforced by the experimenter only until the subject has achieved a low level of learning on the task. At this point, the subject is given control of the reinforcement, and can administer his own rewards on the basis of his subsequent performance.

Vicarious Learning Paradigm.   Vicarious learning, also referred to as modeling, consists of a subject, usually a child, who watches the performance of another individual. The model, or performer, plays a game of skill, in this case a miniature bowling game. Upon achieving a prearranged score, the model rewards himself by taking candy or tokens from a freely available source, while at the same time praising himself for his performance saying, for example, "I deserved that, that was a good shot!" The score that permits self-reinforcement is made explicit through the model's comments. When the model has completed his performance, the child, or viewer, is then offered the opportunity to play the game himself, and his self-reward pattern is monitored.

Temptation Paradigm.   The situation here involves the phenomenon of illegal self-reinforcement. Rewards are freely available to the subject; however, the experimenter instructs the subject concerning the standards that must be achieved in order to merit self-rewards. Though the rules are clearly given, no effort is made to enforce the rules subsequently, nor does the experimenter remain in the same room. The equipment used in such procedures automatically detects any undeserved self-rewards.

Self-Punishment

In this procedure, an individual presents negative consequences to himself in order to decrease the probability of engaging in a target behavior. The use of electric shock has been most heavily used in the lab as a punishment for smoking, drug addiction, hallucinations, and sexual disorders. The use of a self-imposed time-out procedure, in which a subject denies himself some positive reinforcement when he engages in an off-limits behavior, has been effective. For instance, if an individual smokes his forbidden cigarette, he must refrain (time-out) from reading the newspaper that evening (Figure 5-5). We assume that the subject is a devotee of the evening paper who will view his deprivation of the paper as a punishment procedure.

Auxilliary Techniques.   The emphasis in this experimental procedure is in gaining control over stimuli and their variables and introducing responses that are incompatible with the undesired response. In part, overeating is due to the visual availability of food. Therefore, by storing food out of sight, for instance, we can reduce eating. The same kind of procedure can be employed

Smoking forbidden cigarette

Denying self prerogative of
reading newspaper

FIGURE 5-5   Controlling responses by administering self-punishment.

where ability to concentrate needs to be strengthened. In this case the student's desk is cleared of all but essential items, so that the desk becomes a stimulus for study (Figure 5-6). Since it is difficult to eat and talk on the telephone at the same time, the latter would be considered incompatible with the undesired response, eating. Walking outdoors, playing tennis, and attending concerts would all be considered incompatible with eating and therefore highly desirable activities.

THE CONTROL OF OVEREATING

Since much behavior is heavily controlled by external stimulus conditions, the frequency of indulging in certain activities can be reduced by simple changes in stimulus conditions. Eating is less likely to occur, for instance, if food is stored out of sight. In 1971, Stanley Schachter demonstrated that overweight people are less responsive to internal hunger states than people

FIGURE 5-6   Controlling responses by eliminating stimuli. (a) Eating is reduced by removing food from sight. (b) Studying is improved by eliminating distractions.

FIGURE 5-7 Having alternative responses is a good way to control responses. These activities, which are incompatible with eating, would be helpful to those who want to lose weight.

of normal weight. The overweight group is controlled primarily by the sight of food.

In studying methods to overcome obesity, R. B. Stuart (1967) considered that three basic steps needed to be followed.

1. An assessment made of the variables that influenced eating

2. An examination of the manner in which the variables could be manipulated

3. Subject is reminded of the harmful effects of overeating

The control of eating activities was managed by the introduction of distracting behaviors that were, for the most part, mutually exclusive with eating (Figure 5-7). The behaviors involved such activities as calling a friend, taking a walk, etc. Stimulus control procedures were introduced. The subject was required to confine any eating activities to a specified chair, located in a specified room. He was not to pair his eating with any other activities such as watching television, reading, or drinking. In addition, imaginal procedures

FIGURE 5-8   Imaginal procedures are also effective in controlling behavior. A big eater is told to imagine awful things about his food.

were introduced in order to encourage a dislike for food. For example, the subject was instructed to relax and dream about being on the verge of devouring a luscious, gourmet meal. At this juncture, he was asked to interpose a highly aversive image of a rat emerging from the roast, flies struggling in the salad, or some other nauseous possibility (Figure 5-8). In this particular study, eight patients were followed in their application of self-control techniques for the period of a year. All subjects managed to adopt and maintain new eating habits as well as sustain a weight loss that ranged from 26 to 47 pounds.

THE CONTROL OF STUDYING

In 1962, L. Fox met with a group of students who complained of having ineffective study habits. The students spent initial meetings describing their course schedules, after which they carefully examined their study habits. The experimenter then gave explicit instructions to the students in the use of stimulus procedures to encourage study. Students were advised to clear their desks of all distracting objects, confine their studies to just that particular desk, and to leave the vicinity as soon as they felt their attention beginning to stray. In order to prolong study time, students were asked to read an extra paragraph or work out a simple problem prior to leaving the study area. Students reported studying more effectively for longer periods of time. These self-imposed stimulus control methods succeeded in minimizing the aversiveness of studying and maximizing the information retained while studying.

DELAY OF GRATIFICATION

Self-control programs ordinarily require the temporary sacrifice of certain immediate pleasures for the sake of more distant, fulfilling ones. Whatever factors enable a person to delay gratification should also facilitate self-control. W. Mischel and his co-workers (1966), viewing self-control as the ability to postpone gratification, conducted a series of experiments with young children on precisely this issue. Youngsters were encouraged to deny themselves an immediate, small reward in favor of a large, delayed reward.

DIDACTIC SELF-CONTROL

Behavior modification procedures have proved quite effective with institutionalized populations in state mental hospitals. The "token economy," in which members can increase their privileges by performing token-rewarded behaviors, is an active, lively institution compared to the usual state institution where torpor and hopelessness seem to grip the members. However, outside the institution, where environmental control is neither feasible nor possible, only self-control methods can be relied upon with any seriousness. In the behavioral approach to self-regulation, the relationship between the patient and the psychologist resembles that of a training or tutorial situation. In this case, the psychologist instructs the patient in behavior analysis and control, skills that can make a life more effective. In 1965, R. Goldiamond introduced a formal didactic course in behavioral analysis for his patients. Self-control methods were taught, starting with the appraisal of both the behavior and the environment of each individual in the group. Each subject was then instructed in the procedure for manipulating his own behavior, i.e., using the techniques we have already mentioned of self-reward, self-punishment, and stimulus control. This particular approach to handling problems is considered feasible for adults with high intelligence who nevertheless lack the techniques that can help them to change either their environment or their own behavior.

THE COVERANT AND AN ORIGINAL VIEW OF REINFORCEMENT

Several years ago, L. Homme (1965) introduced the term coverant and restored the "mind" to behaviorism. The term coverant is an abbreviated version of the terms covert (a hidden and unmeasurable behavior) and operant (a highly visible and measurable behavior). Early behaviorist systems refused to consider mental events on the grounds that they were of no importance; it was the behavior that counted. Homme proposed using thoughts as covert responses that could be modified. Homme had his subjects use positive statements about themselves whenever they engaged in a high rate of preferred behavior. These statements had virtually no currency in the subject's repertoire. For instance, a person with a negative self-image was instructed to think or say "I am a worthwhile person," or "I am the master of my fate," and to increase the frequency of the statement by using it prior to engaging in any preferred behavior such as eating or driving, etc. (Figure 5-9). The rationale for establishing the contingency of performing a low rate or nonpreferred behavior in order to perform a high rate or preferred behavior follows from the view that reinforcement is a relative rather than an absolute phenomenon (see Chapter 16). Any behavior will reinforce another, provided only that a higher rate behavior is made contingent upon a lower rate behavior. Homme utilized high rate behaviors in human beings in precisely the same manner. He required his subjects to make high rate behaviors contingent upon positive self statements. This approach was designed to increase positive as well as decrease negative self-evaluations.

FIGURE 5-9   The coverant response.

THE ROLE OF MODELING IN SELF-CONTROL

In a series of modeling studies, Albert Bandura (1962) at Stanford examined some of the variables that influenced children to reinforce themselves. In one study, children observed while an adult played a miniature bowling game. The adult adopted very high standards of self-reward, that is, he had to achieve a high score before reinforcing himself either with praise or with goodies. The performance standards were encouraged by other adults who were present in the experimental situation. Subsequently, when children played the game, they imposed the same high performance standards on themselves before engaging in self-praise or other self-reward. Models who were permissive and playful with children prior to the modeling procedure were not taken as examples, especially if high performance standards were set. Children who received a kind of nurturing, consisting of play and affection in this case, did not emulate their hard driving models in the performance situation, but tended instead to reinforce themselves for attaining low scores. The most austere pattern of self-reward was displayed (1) by children who had experienced a fairly cool relationship with the model; (2) when children were not exposed to conflicting standards, e.g., peer model who set lower standards for self-reinforcement than did the adult; and (3) when other adults encouraged the adult model for his standards in the presence of the child observer.

Surprisingly, the absence of the experimenter seems to have very little consequence to the subject in these modeling studies, for a subject who has adopted high standards of self-reward will continue to behave in the same fashion whether or not he is under surveillance. One of the problems with viewing modeling experiments of this type as being examples of self-control is that the child seems to model the adult's total performance, of which the self-reinforcement sequence is only one portion. It is simpler to assume that the child imitates the adult model rather accurately, including his reinforcement pattern; but it would be questionable to conclude that the child now has high standards because his self-reinforcement pattern is austere.

THE ROLE OF ANXIETY IN SELF-CONTROL

J. Aronfreed (1968) believes that the major goal in socialization of the child is the development of the conscience. The child is taught to internalize certain social sanctions such as the inhibition of aggressive and sexual behavior. Aronfreed views anxiety as playing an important part in self-control (Figure 5-10). Anxiety is acquired as a component of punishment during childhood, but it is aroused whenever a tempting situation arises and causes the individual intense discomfort. Self-critical behaviors inhibit action, reduce the anxiety, and relieve the discomfort. Aronfreed stresses the importance of self-control in reducing uncomfortable "states" that arise from childhood punishment anxieties. He later describes straight reward techniques that are used by families when children manage to inhibit certain kinds of behavior. It is not clear whether the child manages to inhibit certain kinds of behavior through self-criticism in order to reduce the anxiety of punishment, or because he receives both lavish praise or material rewards from adults when he does so.

A great deal of monitoring of the child's behavior takes place at home

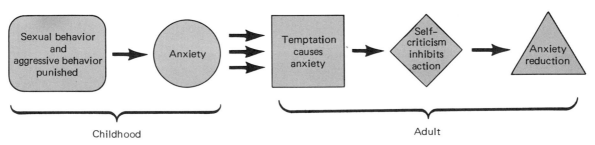

FIGURE 5-10   Aronfreed's concept of the role of anxiety in self-control.

by the parents. This monitoring is gradually shifted to self-monitoring, and the shift is produced by continuous guidance and reinforcement. Middle-class parents who are oriented toward a child's intentions rather than his actions are apt to use reason and explanation in order to establish an internal guide to action. Working-class parents respond to concrete actions; they use physical and direct punishment methods rather than verbal chastisement. One finds that self-regulatory behavior is reinforced in middle-class American families.

SUMMARY

Since most studies on self-control are viewed as a series of behavior techniques, specific methods for controlling certain kinds of behavior have resulted. Self-reward, self-punishment, and stimulus control have been the most frequently applied techniques for changing the frequency at which certain behaviors will occur.

The introduction of coverants as mental events that could be modified helped enlarge the view of behavior as something more than a series of motor events. Utilizing positive self-statements, such coverants were made in conjunction with preferred behaviors. The procedure helped to increase the self-estimation of subjects who had a low opinion of themselves.

There is a great deal of self-control that is practiced inadvertantly. People distract themselves from bothersome thoughts by watching television, engaging in hobbies, etc. The use of diversions are used casually by some, while others must be taught how to control their thought processes through instruction. Presently, instruction consists of the application of self-control methods to behaviors that need to be reduced or increased. The examination of the phenomenon known as self-control is still in its infancy, for most experimental results are suggestive rather than conclusive. Nevertheless, the procedures do have a short-term effect. The search is still on for techniques that will provide long-term or permanent changes in one's behavioral patterns.

SUGGESTED READINGS

Aronfreed, J. *Conduct and conscience.* New York: Academic Press, 1968.

Bandura, A. *Principles of behavior modification.* New York: Holt, 1969.

Hunt, W. A. *Learning mechanisms in smoking.* Aldine Publ. Co., 1970.

Kanfer, F., & Phillips, J. *Learning foundations of behavior therapy.* New York: Wiley, 1970.

Skinner, B. F. *Science and human behavior.* New York: Macmillan, 1953.

6

The Development of Language

Language is one of man's most complex behaviors. The subtlety and refinement that is possible in this extremely sophisticated and abstract communicative mechanism is overpowering. Where did it come from? How does it develop? Is the capacity inherent in the brain, with the environment only adding particular information to an already present form? These are but some of the questions that have fascinated so many students of behavior from anthropologists and linguists to psychologists and physiologists. Each science has approached language from its own perspective; from these efforts we have come to learn something about this extraordinary complex psychological capacity.

In the past linguists have traditionally given us a formal analysis of the properties of various languages. Their interest has been in dissecting a language into its constituent parts. For example, a linguist may analyze how many different words the Eskimo has for snow, or how many different ways one can say "I'm sorry." More recently, linguists have tried to specify certain unusual rules that underlie the structure of statements in various languages and have made formal statements about "rules of transformation," i.e., the rules for how one makes declarative, interrogative, active, or passive statements.

Today, psychology has united with linguistics in a new and vigorous science of psycholinguistics. Psycholinguists approach language from an experimental-psychological perspective. Given the linguist's "rules of transformation," for example, the psychologist may ask what is the psychological reality of these rules? If one does in fact go through a sequence of steps in transforming an active to a passive statement, does this mean it takes longer to "process" a passive statement than an active one? Or, since language involves memory, the psycholinguist asks what can be learned about human mechanisms of memory from language processing. Language and thought are also bound around one another. How does language relate to thought? What happens to thought without language? The physiologist asks if language is localized in a particular part of the brain or if it is a general cortical capacity. How is the brain related to language function? Which areas are crucial for speaking and which for understanding; how are they interrelated? These are the kinds of questions surrounding psycholinguistics, some of which will be discussed in this chapter. But, before starting with these problems we will first consider the great controversy that has arisen over the basis of language acquisition in the child.

This conflict has come to be called the empiricist versus nativist argument, and its chief spokesmen are B. F. Skinner, a psychologist on the side of empiricism, and Noam Chomsky, a linguist on the side of nativism. Skinner is a behaviorist who views language as verbal behavior that is reinforced. He believes that the sentence is an association of words. Chomsky is a rationalist who defines the sentence as a structure that is generated by a series of rules. Children listen to the language spoken, formulate hypotheses about language rules, and then produce sentences. Chomsky places great emphasis on the innate capacity of the child for language, and insists, moreover, that man is unique in this respect.

SKINNER'S VIEW OF LANGUAGE

Some years ago, while attending a dinner at the Society of Fellows at Harvard, B. F. Skinner happened to be seated next to Professor Whitehead, the famous logician. The two started an animated conversation on the topic of behaviorism with Skinner arguing vigorously, and Whitehead listening carefully. Finally, the logician agreed that a science of behavior might be successful in accounting for human behavior, but he doubted that such a science could handle verbal behavior. He insisted that in the arena of language something else must be at work. Finally, at the end of the exchange, Whitehead flung this challenge at Skinner: "Let me see you account for my behavior as I sit here saying, 'No black scorpion is falling on this table.' " At six in the morning of the following day, Skinner started his plans for a behavioral treatise of language.

Almost twenty years later he published *Verbal behavior* (1957). Though the account was not able to specify the stimulus for Whitehead's remark on the absence of a black scorpion on the table, the book did give a functional analysis of verbal behavior that remained an accepted analysis until Chomsky subjected Skinner's views of language to severe criticism.

Skinner defined language in strictly behavioral terms. Abstract notions of meaning and symbols were allied with nonbehavioral definitions of language and had no currency for a behaviorist. Skinner asserted that language was simply another form of behavior, a form he termed verbal behavior. In addition, he stated that predictions could be made about the kinds of verbal responses that occurred, quite as they were made for nonverbal responses. Of the two main types of responses, reflex responses and operant responses, the latter type was considered important in verbal behavior. Operant responses differ from reflex responses in that they occur freely. There are either no stimuli or no identifiable unconditioned stimuli that can account for operant responses.

Of the several verbal operants described by Skinner, three appear to have a great relevance for language development. If one wished to simplify language, one might say that children like to name what they see, to express their needs, and to mimic the sounds their parents make. In a nutshell, this is how Skinner viewed verbal operants. He proposed that the tact, the mand, and echoic response were the essentials of verbal development (Figure 6-1). The tact, probably the most important of the verbal operants, is also most closely allied to the traditional view of meaning. Tacts are verbal responses for which the cause, or discriminative stimulus as Skinner called it, is a particular stimulus in the environment. The child, toddling about a room full of objects, naming, TABLE, PUPPY, RED, PRETTY, LIGHT, is producing verbal responses called tacts. He is simply naming stimuli that he sees and knows.

Another factor that can produce verbal responses is some kind of deprivation condition. Loosely speaking, the child verbalizes a need. When he says COOKIE, he is not naming, he is expressing his hunger. This kind of verbal response is called a mand, a shortened form of the term demand. There are a number of deprivation conditions such as hunger, thirst, fatigue, etc., which are discriminative stimuli for such mands as COOKIE, MILK, or NITE-NITE.

Finally, the tendency to repeat, or echo sounds, results in verbal responses called echoic responses. Skinner considered that this tendency to mimic sounds was extremely important to the eventual production of the correct speech sounds made by children of a language community. The various types of verbal operants produced by children are reinforced by the members of the adult community. Attention, smiles, and the encouragement of correct gram-

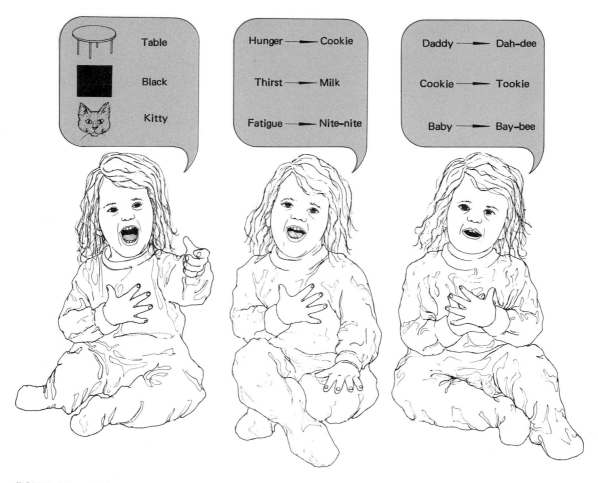

FIGURE 6-1   Skinner's major verbal operants in the language of the child. Examples of tacts (left), mands (center), and echoic responses (right).

matical statements are the means by which the adult language community assists the child in language acquisition.

Skinner's analysis of sentence structure was behavioral rather than linguistic (Figure 6-2). He did not define the sentence as a complete thought, nor as consisting of a subject and a predicate, but rather as a grammatical frame. Vocabulary items, that is, words, were placed in the frame in a sequential fashion. A person composing a sentence, gave nouns, verbs, and adjectives first priority. Later, articles, prepositions, tense words, etc., were added to the sentence frame. The sentence was viewed as proceeding by a series of intraverbal associations, in which every word influenced the choice of the

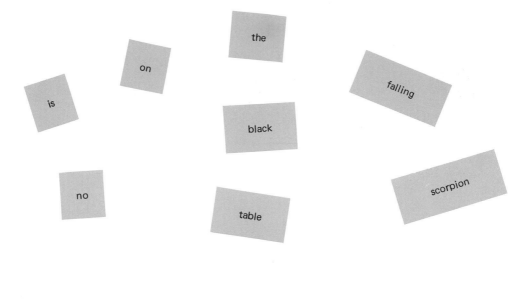

Frame 1

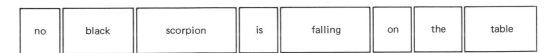

Frame 2

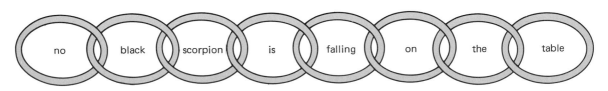

Chain of associations

FIGURE 6-2   Skinner's analysis of sentence structure.

next word in the sequence. Skinner's analysis, then, stated that every verbal operant in the sentence served as a stimulus for the next verbal response, so that the sentence was interpreted as a chain of associations.

INADEQUACY OF THE ASSOCIATIONISTIC MODEL

The associationistic model was not a radical proposal of Skinner, for it had its origins in the nineteenth century, long before modern behaviorism. Karl Lashley, a neuropsychologist, challenged the idea before Skinner had proposed his model of language development, because he felt that it was quite inadequate to describe the sentence as a stringing together of responses. He strongly disagreed with the view that a sentence was mainly under the control of external stimulation, which was later to be the essence of Skinner's emphasis on the importance of environmental stimuli. Lashley particularly disliked viewing the sentence as being constructed of a series of intraverbal associations. This was a far too superficial account of the sentence. Lashley (1951) believed that there were a vast number of integrative processes involved in the production of a sentence. These processes, however, could only be inferred by studying the final results. To clarify his position, he offered an example from music. He proposed that it was the melody that prompted the specific organization of notes and chords. The melody dictated the form. To assume that notes followed one another in an associationistic string was to ignore the reality of a melodic plan.

Analogously, the sounds of a language are quite unpredictable. One would be challenged, indeed, to try to predict the sound that might follow O---. Sounds are determined by words. Word sequences are similarly unpredictable since they, too, are determined by higher levels of organization such as the phrase. With this kind of reasoning, Lashley made clear that linear or sequential predictions were not possible. Predictions could only be made about one level of behavior by formulating assumptions about a higher level of behavior. He challenged traditional psychology by stating quite flatly that an associationistic model could not account for the kind of grammatical structure that exists in language. A psychology based on a theory that linked stimulus and response units into a learning chain could not deal with a topic that was obviously organized into classes, hierarchies, and structural patterns. Lashley argued the point vigorously and convincingly, and there were many who agreed with his views. Unfortunately, he was unable to formalize his proposal. The actual description of the sentence as a hierarchical structure was made not by a psychologist but by a linguist, Noam Chomsky.

CHOMSKY'S DESCRIPTION OF THE SENTENCE

In order to fully appreciate the kind of grammar a language user must have in order to generate or produce a sentence, let us examine this very simple sentence.

TIM ATE THE ORANGE

Let us approach the sentence in the hierarchical spirit as proposed by Lashley. English speakers will intuitively sense some type of structure in the sentence. We can say that the sentence consists of a series of relationships, in which the words THE and ORANGE, for instance, are siblings, but in which ATE and THE are barely kissing cousins. We can also say that the sentence consists of an actor, an action, and an object that is acted upon. Further, we can christen TIM, the actor, a noun (N); pronounce that the action ATE is a verb (V); and conclude that the object acted upon, ORANGE, is another noun (N), which is modified by an article (A), in this case, THE. In climbing up the hierarchical ladder, we come to view TIM as having the status of an initial noun phrase, even though, in this case, the phrase consists of only one word, a noun. The sequence ATE THE ORANGE is a verb phrase, which can be analyzed into the verb ATE, plus a final noun phrase, THE ORANGE. Breaking down a sentence into its parts in this way reveals the constituent structure of the sentence. This kind of analysis may lead to a hierarchical view of the sentence, such as is revealed in the "tree" diagrams.

Some linguists have not only been concerned with the constituent structure of given sentences, but they have analyzed how sentences are changed or transformed into many variations. The simple declarative sentence, for instance, may be changed to a question or the passive voice, to name just two alternatives. Generative grammar describes the rules for making these transformations.

In 1956, Chomsky contributed the kind of theory that Lashley could not himself provide. Chomsky proposed that a grammatical sentence could be generated by using a few basic terms, in conjunction with a few simple rules that would permit terms to be rewritten as other terms. Let us assign the letter S as the general description of a sentence (Figure 6-3). We then apply an obligatory rule that instructs us to rewrite the term S as a noun phrase plus a verb phrase. The next rule instructs us to rewrite verb phrase as a verb plus a noun phrase. Then, the rule stipulates that noun phrase may be rewritten as an article (A) plus a noun. You will notice that the rules

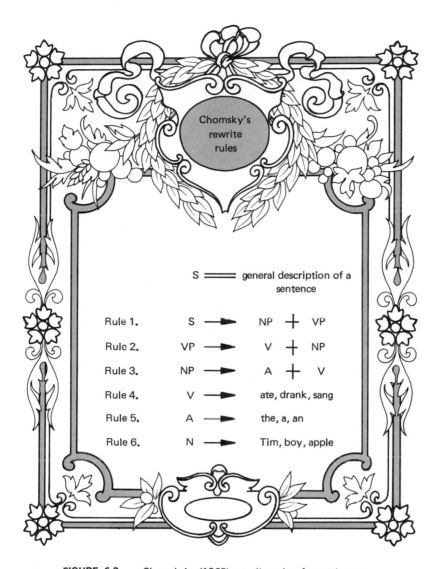

FIGURE 6-3   Chomsky's (1965) rewrite rules for sentences.

permit only one term to be rewritten at a time. Finally, the rules can also be demonstrated by a tree graph, which clarifies the idea of constituent structures. Our intuitions about the closeness of the relationship between certain words is nicely borne out in an examination of those branches that bifurcate from a parent branch (Figure 6-4).

The kind of grammar that we have been discussing is called a **phrase structure grammar**. This, however, is not the only kind of grammar that is

Tree diagram
The hierarchical organization of a sentence

FIGURE 6-4   Chomsky's tree diagram of the hierarchical organization of a sentence.

essential in the construction of sentences. There are different kinds of relations that exist among sentences.

TIM ATE THE ORANGE
THE ORANGE WAS EATEN BY TIM
TIM DID NOT EAT THE ORANGE
DID TIM EAT THE ORANGE?

These sentences have differences that could be described in a number of ways. Some theorists believe that individual sentence frames are learned separately, i.e., various types of sentences bear no relationship to one another. Others, while agreeing that there are no intrinsic relations between the types of sentences, insist that there are entirely too many types of sentence frames for the speaker to learn individually. They propose certain kinds of rules for producing the various sentence frames. They further consider that there is one set of rules for forming active-declarative-affirmative sentences such as TIM ATE THE ORANGE, another set of rules for forming passive-declarative-affirmative sentences such as THE ORANGE WAS EATEN BY TIM, and so on.

The third main group proposes describing the relations among sentences in terms of explicit rules of transformation. These transformational rules can turn a declarative sentence into an interrogative sentence, so that, TIM ATE THE ORANGE plus transformational rules for the question becomes DID TIM EAT THE ORANGE? An active sentence that contains a specific kind of verb, as well as an object, may be converted into a passive sentence in a fairly simple fashion. Using the reliable sentence TIM ATE THE ORANGE, we find that a passive sentence can be formed by the application of a transformational rule that converts active sentences into passive ones. In an active sentence the doer of the action comes first, next comes the action, and last comes the object acted upon. Thus, TIM ATE THE ORANGE is an active sentence. In a passive sentence the object acted upon comes first (the orange), then the verb to be in the past tense (was), and the past participle of the main verb (eaten), then the preposition (by), then the name of the actor or doer of the action (Tim). THE ORANGE WAS EATEN BY TIM is a passive sentence. The transformations we have just made on our active sentence follow the linguists rules of transformations, and are simply an economical and elegant statement of the formal relationships within the sentence.

The theory of generative grammar, besides describing the rewrite rules for producing a grammatical sentence, illustrates two very different types of sentence structure. Surface structure emphasizes the actual form of a sentence. Deep structure is seen as existing in the deep recesses of the generative process, and is much more in touch with meaning. The psychological actuality of both transformations and deep structure is open to question. Studies that examine the psychological reality of both of these concepts will now be considered.

PSYCHOLOGICAL REALITY OF THE TRANSFORMATION

Earlier we discussed the possibility of testing whether there is any psychological reality in the transformation idea. George Miller, a pioneer psycholinguist, reasoned that if a grammatical transformation involved a lot of steps on a formal level, it would also take longer to process. He argued that a simple transformation, one involving few formal steps, would take less time to process psychologically. He wished to test whether Chomsky's purely formal transformational rules could be translated into a measurable difference in speed of processing (Miller, 1962).

Subjects who took part in this language experiment were given a set of sentences to transform and were timed to see how long it took to process various kinds of sentence transformations. The test involved the use of 18 simple, declarative sentences. The sentences in the experiment contained the words JANE, JOE, or JOHN as the subject of the sentence; LIKED or WARNED as the verb; and THE SMALL BOY, THE OLD WOMAN, or THE YOUNG MAN as the object phrase. From the 18 sentences that could be constructed (from the various combination of nouns, verbs, and object phrases), negative, passive, and negative-passive sentence transformations were composed for each variation of declarative sentence.

Declarative sentence	JANE LIKED THE SMALL BOY
Negative sentence	JANE DID NOT LIKE THE SMALL BOY
Passive sentence	THE SMALL BOY WAS LIKED BY JANE
Negative-Passive sentence	THE SMALL BOY WAS NOT LIKED BY JANE

In one phase of the experiment, a test sheet consisting of a series of sentences was presented to subjects who were required to match passive sentences with their corresponding negative-passive sentences. For instance, a left-hand list of a mixture of passive and negative-passive sentences had to be matched with a right-hand list of similar sentences which were arranged in scrambled order.

—The old woman was warned by Joe   1. The small boy wasn't liked by Jane
—The small boy wasn't liked by John   2. The old woman was warned by Jane

—The young man was liked by John   3. The old woman wasn't warned by Joe

—The old woman wasn't warned by Jane   4. The young man wasn't liked by John

—The small boy was liked by Jane   5. The small boy was liked by John
—The young man wasn't liked by Joe   6. The young man was liked by Joe

The subject was instructed to read the sentence in the left column, perform the negative transform or its inverse, search for the proper sentence in the right hand column, and then place the correct sentence number in the blank space in the left-hand column. The results of this particular test series demonstrated that the simple negative transform list was completed in the shortest period of time. Thus, the test list containing such sentences as

JANE DID NOT LIKE THE SMALL BOY

was processed speedily. The list containing passive sentences such as

THE SMALL BOY WAS LIKED BY JANE

took slightly longer, and the negative-passive transform took the longest to complete. The study provided psychological evidence that a transformation process was involved, for the more difficult a transformation was on a formal level, the more time the transform took to process on a performance level. The results of the above experiment are hardly definitive, however. To assume that transformations take real time is to interpret transformational theory in a particular way. This assumption is not part of Chomsky's theory. Even in the view of the experimenter, the use of a speed measure to assess the reality of the transformation has a high degree of uncertainty about it.

Mechanisms of Sentence Recall

DEEP STRUCTURE MODEL.   Transformational generative grammar has spawned two main psychological models that describe the manner in which people recall sentences. One model suggests that the deep structure determines our memory for sentences. The deep structure idea received early support from a series of experiments that showed that phrases with simple deep structures were recalled more quickly than phrases with complicated deep structures. The deep structure idea also gained support from an interpretation of Chomsky's elusive concept of the kernel sentence. In brief, the kernel sentence is a formal arrangement of symbols upon which generative rules will work to produce a spoken sentence. This kernel sentence is a basic aspect of Chomsky's deep structure system. It has been maintained that people remember a nonkernel sentence such as a passive sentence by first transforming it into its kernel structure and then placing a tag on the sentence that specifies the transformation that must be applied to the kernel when the sentence has to be reproduced. To illustrate, THE STORY WAS TOLD BY ME would be translated into structural sequence that is more similar to that found in a declarative sentence. The kernel might look like noun (pronoun) + verb (past tense) + article + noun (common). The tag would then specify passive transformation. All this material

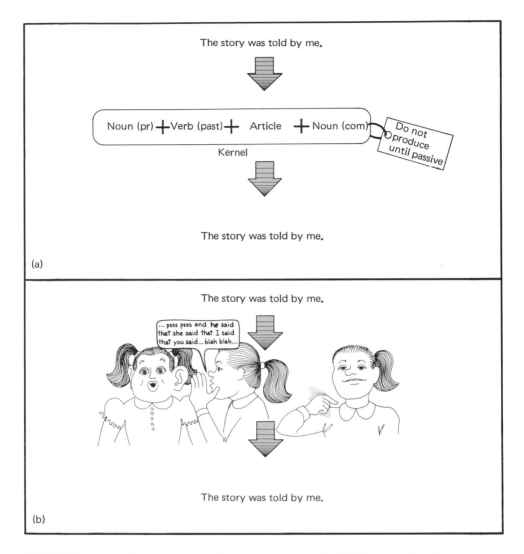

FIGURE 6-5   (a) Chomsky's model of sentence memory. (b) Paivio's model of sentence memory.

would be stored in this fashion until the time arrived for its reproduction, whereupon the transform would be applied to the kernel to yield THE STORY WAS TOLD BY ME [Figure 6-5(a)].

The assumption that sentences are stored in this way seems sensible enough. Kernels are far simpler in structure, and do not tax the memory load as severely as do nonkernel sentences. Early research on this hypothesis yielded supporting evidence, but several subsequent studies failed to verify the assumption.

IMAGERY MODEL.   The second model has been proposed by Allan Paivio, a Canadian psycholinguist who has found that one of the salient factors in "remembering" is the degree of imagery of the noun. Paivio decided to investigate whether it was the imagery value or the deep structure that enhanced recall. The possibility of explaining memory or ease of recall in terms of psychological processes (imagery) rather than with a linguistic concept (deep structure) was an enticing possibility.

Nouns have varying abilities to arouse sensory images, so that a "colorful" noun produces a more vivid image, and is subsequently more easily recalled. To clarify the issue of whether deep structure or noun imagery contributes the most to recall, subjects were asked to rate a number of nominalizations according to their imagery value. Rated high in imagery were such subject nominalizations as

> Dancing girls
> Migrating birds
> Staring eyes
> Wriggling tadpoles
> Baying hounds
> Falling stars

Rated low in imagery were the subject nominalizations

> Existing situations
> Persisting doubts
> Vibrating wires
> Thinking scientists
> Longing mothers
> Aspiring actors

Object nominalizations such as

> Changing tires
> Painting pictures
> Mowing lawns
> Mopping floors

were also rated for imagery value. Object nominals are considered identical with subject nominals in surface structure, but the object nominals are more complex in their deep structure. The extra elements in deep structure are not visible on the surface, of course. For instance, PAINTING PICTURES, an object nominal, implies that some agent paints pictures. There are other variations as well, so that the more complex deep structure is found in object nominals.

Noun imagery overshadowed all other linguistic devices as a predictor of recall. The experiments ruled out quite conclusively that the simplicity of deep structure facilitated recall. The better the imagery ratio on a nominalization, the better the recall. The object nominalization was as easy to recall as the subject nominal provided that the two were rated equally high on imagery value. The possibility exists, of course, that there is no such level as deep structure. Paivio (1971) questions the necessity for such a concept in psychology. Instead, Paivio proposes the view that words, phrases, and sentences are encoded as images during input. When output is intended, the images are decoded into original statements [Figure 6-5(b)].

HOW THE CHILD ACQUIRES LANGUAGE: CHOMSKY'S MODEL

In 1959, Chomsky wrote an extremely critical review of Skinner's book on verbal behavior. One of the deep and irreconcilable differences in the two

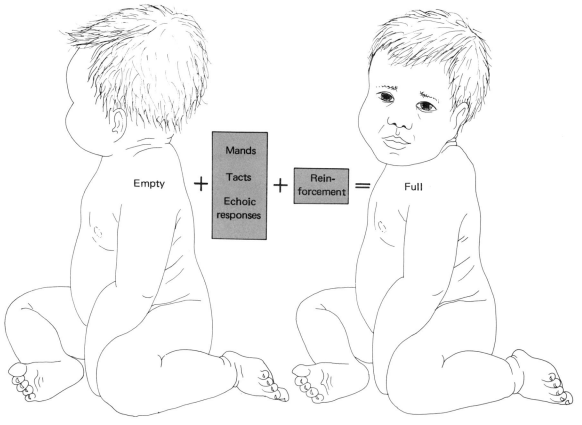

(a)

FIGURE 6-6   (a) Skinner's child acquires language.

points of view rests on the fact that Skinner is a behaviorist and believes in an essentially "empty organism," whereas Chomsky holds the view that the organism is filled with theories and hypotheses. Skinner's empty organism is replenished with large amounts of learning experiences. Chomsky's well-filled organism makes constant guesses and assumptions about his learning experiences. In Chomsky's view, the organism imposes his structure upon the environment, whereas Skinner envisions the environment as shaping and structuring the organism. These differences in view are most clearly expressed in their differing accounts of the acquisition of language by children (Figure 6-6).

Skinner claims that children learn language by the use of verbal operants such as mands, tacts, and echoic responses, all of which were reinforced by the language community. Chomsky states that the child must have a linguistic theory and a strategy for grammar selection in order to learn language. These prerequisites for language learning seem to be genetic givens, although the

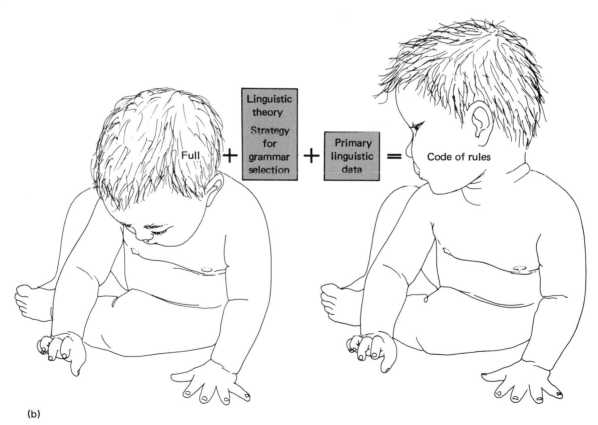

(b)

FIGURE 6-6   (b) Chomsky's child acquires language.

model does not indicate the specific nature of the prerequisites. The child is exposed to his family and other adults who speak to him. This exposure to language Chomsky calls the primary linguistic data. In other words, the child is so constituted that he can construct a theory of his language solely by being exposed to speaking adults. To make the assumption that a child can formulate a theory of language in this fashion, one must have a very strong belief in the innate capacity of the child for language. The element of "learning" in this model is virtually absent. Chomsky considers that the child "knows" a great deal more about language than he "learns."

The child, in Chomsky's view, is born with a store of possible grammars. His knowledge of language is far greater than that of the primary linguistic data to which he is exposed. One might almost say that linguistic data serves simply as a catalyst for activating the theoretical proclivities of the child. Exposed to examples of grammar in the language of his family, the child actively formulates or rejects theories about that grammar. He can, for instance, recognize grammatical sentences. In Chomsky's view, a child who has developed an internal code of rules that will guide him in the production of correct sentences can be said to have learned a language.

EXPERIMENTAL APPROACHES TO CHILD LANGUAGE

There has been a great change in the manner in which language development in children has been studied in the last few years. Vocabulary surveys and frequency counts of grammatical classes, a general sort of "count and classify" approach, was typical of the assessment that used to be made in the child's language development. Some years ago, child language was seen as an impoverished version of the adult model. Psychologists assumed that the adult grammar was the correct and only form, whereas the child's grammar was viewed as a kind of unsuccessful attempt to approximate the adult form. Recently, the psycholinguist has adopted an approach to child language that the anthropological or field linguist used in his study of exotic languages. They insisted that one could not apply the rules of English grammar to a language such as Mandarin. Mandarin has a system of grammatical rules that is pertinent to its own language structure, and grammatical rules for English are of no consequence except when applied to adult English grammar. When this insight was applied to child language, some extraordinary discoveries were made about the grammar of the child's first sentences. By assuming that the child speaks as foreign a language as Mandarin, psycholinguists uncovered a great deal of information about how the child learns a language. The present view states that the child is a fluent speaker of his own language rather than a producer of a telegraphic form of English. The rules that the child utilizes in constructing sentences are as law-abiding and unique as are the rules utilized by adult speakers of English, Catalan, or Mandarin.

DEVELOPMENT OF THE PHONOLOGICAL SYSTEM

Before dealing with the structure of early sentences produced by children, let us examine some of the early sounds as well as words that are found among children raised in an English speaking community. Phonology includes all the consonant and vowel sounds that are found in speech. Phonetics is the study of individual sounds, how they are produced by the vocal tract, and what they look like on a sound spectrogram (Figure 6-7). We are more interested, in this section, with the area of phonemics, which concerns itself with classes of sounds and how they differ (Table 6-1).

There are 46 phonemes in the English language, that is, 46 classes of sounds. To demonstrate what is meant by a class of sounds, let us examine the status of the sound P in the three words listed below.

(a)   (b)

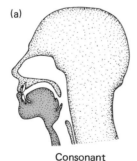 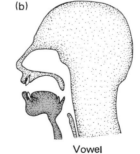

Consonant   Vowel

FIGURE 6-7   Development of the phonological system. (a) Variations in obstruction produce different consonants. Obstruction can occur at the mouth, teeth, tongue, or velum. In this case a bilabial (B or P) will be produced since the lips are touching. (b) A vowel is produced with no obstructions. Vowel sounds are determined mainly by jaw height.

TABLE 6-1   The Phonemes of General American English[a]

General American is the dialect of English spoken in midwestern and western areas of the United States and influences an increasing number of Americans. Certain phonemes of other regional dialects (e.g., Southern) can be different.

Vowels	Consonants	
ee as in heat	t as in tee	s as in see
i as in hit	p as in pea	sh as in shell
e as in head	k as in key	h as in he
ɔe as in had	b as in bee	v as in view
ah as in father	d as in dawn	th as in then
aw as in call	g as in go	z as in zoo
U as in put	m as in me	zh as in garage
oo as in cool	n as in no	l as in law
ʌ as in ton	ng as in sing	r as in red
uh as in the	f as in fee	y as in you
er as in bird	θ as in thin	w as in we
oi as in toil		
au as in shout		
ei as in take		
ou as in tone		
ai as in might		

[a] From Denes and Pinson (1963).

Though it may not seem so to the untrained ear, the three P's are quite different acoustically. In spite of the differences that exist, they all belong to the same phonemic class of sounds designated /p/. When two sounds differ so much that they designate a different meaning, the two sounds are considered different phonemes. PIT and BIT are words that differ in meaning. All the sounds in the words are the same except /p/ and /b/, and these sounds signal a difference in the message, so that /p/ and /b/ are considered separate phonemes.

At one time is was thought that the child learned the sounds of his language by practice. Repetition and drill helped the child to graduate from approximate to accurate linguistic sounds. Studies of the development of the child's phonology recently have shown that children learn sounds by noting maximal differences first. The first distinction that the child makes is the vowel versus consonant distinction. The vocal system differentiates vowel and consonant sounds very simply. Vowels are generally unobstructed sounds. Variations in the sounds of vowels are made by varying the height of the jaw. Consonant sounds are made by producing obstructions either at the level of the lips, teeth, tongue, or velum. Consonants are classified in English according to which of the speech organs are primarily involved in making the sound (place of articulation) and the movements involved in making the sound (manner of articulation). To get some idea of the classification of consonants, refer to Table 6-2. As you can see from the table, most consonants are plosives and fricatives. The names of the categories for consonants are simply descriptive of the sounds produced. Plosives are explosive sounds made by the sudden release of air; fricatives are sounds really made by the friction of air escape; liquids are flowing sounds as their name suggests; and nasal consonants are made through the nose.

The first group of consonant sounds that the child notes are labials. Labials are consonants that are formed by an obstruction at the level of the lips, and include such sounds as P, B, and M. Gleason (1961) wrote a rather clear account of the development of phoneme distinctions in his daughter's speech. At first, the girl distinguished between labial and nonlabial stops, that is, she distinguished between the labial stops P and B versus the nonlabial stops T, D, K, and G. Later, she noted the difference between voiced stops D and G versus the voiceless stops T and K. Voiced refers to the sound produced by the larynx. The young girl was unable to establish the difference in the sounds T versus K for a long time. For instance, her pronunciations of the word CAKE included KATE, TATE, TAKE, and sometimes, accidentally, even CAKE! Since the words TAKE, KATE, and TATE were also meaningful terms in her vocabulary, all of the words were confused with one another as well as with the word CAKE. When the child finally discovered the distinction between T and K, she proceeded to pronounce all the words correctly. Both T and K are voiceless stops, but T involves an obstruction between the tongue and the teeth, whereas K is formed by joining the velum to the soft palate.

TABLE 6-2   Classification of English Consonants by Place- and Manner-of-Articulation[a]

	Manner of articulation				
Place of articulation	Plosive	Fricative	Semi-vowel	Liquids (incl. laterals)	Nasal
Labial	p b		w		m
Labio-Dental		f v			
Dental		θ th			
Alveolar	t d	s z	y	l r	n
Palatal		sh zh			
Velar	k g				ng
Glottal		h			

[a] From Denes and Pinson (1963).

The first consonant sounds to develop in the speech of English-speaking children are the M of MAMA and the D of DADA, as any parent knows. Soon the labials P and B are added, followed by the dentals T and N. A little later, the velar sounds K and G appear, to be followed shortly by the semi-vowel W. Only much later do the difficult sounds R, Th, S, H appear (Figure 6-8).

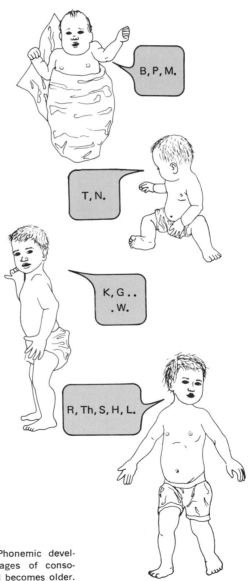

FIGURE 6-8   Phonemic development. Four stages of consonants as the child becomes older.

RELATIONSHIP OF BABBLING TO PHONOLOGY

It has been often said that out of babbling comes our first phonemes. Babbling reaches its peak at the age of 8–10 months, during which time the child produces a vast number of sounds that are not found in the parent language. Some psychologists theorize that the parents select and reinforce particular babbling sounds. Others believe that the child is rewarded simply by hearing himself produce sounds similar to those made by family members. He retains these sounds and automatically drops the others from his repertoire. However, some researchers, who are skeptical about the relationship between babbling and phonological development, assume instead that the two are entirely different developmental phenomena.

The skeptical group cites some evidence comparing the kinds of sounds produced in early babbling with those produced in the first words. Velars (e.g., K, G) and glottals (e.g., H) are the most frequent babbling sounds. These sounds are produced far back in the mouth near the throat. However, when first words are produced, the labials (e.g., P, B, M) and dentals (e.g., D, T, N) predominate as consonants. A cautious hypothesis of phonological development would include some interaction between speech and babbling. But it is doubtful that babbling sounds are reinforced into phonological sounds, since the child's first words are made with the lips rather than back in the throat. These findings, of course, make it difficult to accept Skinner's view of language development.

THE PIVOT-OPEN GRAMMAR; FIRST SENTENCES

Most children begin to form simple two- and three-word sentences between the ages of 18 and 24 months. Some of the early sentences consist of forms such as the following.

TWO BOOT
HEAR TRACTOR
SEE TRUCK MOMMY
PUT TRUCK WINDOW

Speech of this kind has been referred to as telegraphic, for it resembles the sort of sentence an adult devises to cut the costs of sending a telegram. In comparison to adult speech, the child leaves out articles, prepositions, inflections on verbs and nouns, and seems to indulge in ungrammatical combinations! In part, the short sentence may be the result of the limited memory span found in the child.

The child's vocabulary reaches the moderate number of 50–150 words when the child is between the ages of 18 and 24 months. At this stage, the child begins to join words in simple sentences for the first time. Several investigators discovered, at about the same time, that the first two-word sentences were not constructed in a random fashion, but had a marked and sensible structure. The child does not join arbitrary words together to form his sentences. He has two classes of words, one of which consists of few members, the other of which includes many words. The small group is called the pivot class; the large group, the open class. Martin Braine's (1963) terminology has been adopted since it has the greatest currency. The child's strategy for producing a sentence is to pair a word from the pivot class with one from the open class. There is very little overlap, as a rule, between the words in the two classes. For instance, members in the various classes, listed below, do not overlap.

Pivot Class	Open Class
ALLGONE	BOY
BYE-BYE	SOCK
BIG	BOAT
MORE	MILK
SEE	SHOE
	MOMMY
	DADDY, FAN, etc.

Early sentences consist of such constructions as

ALLGONE DADDY, ALLGONE MILK, ALLGONE BOAT
BYE BYE SOCK, BYE BYE MOMMY, BYE BYE DADDY
SEE SOCK, SEE SHOE, SEE BOY, etc.

In other words, a heavy reliance is placed on the pivot words to form an alliance with the varying and large number of words in the open category. Since many of the sentences are rather peculiar combinations in the opinion of the adult listener, it is assumed that the child is not imitating the adult sentence. The child has discovered a productive pattern for sentence formation. The first term to be used in the pivot position appears quite early. In a week or two, other pivot words are noted, until the pivot class contains quite a large number of words. In one child, out of a total of 240 two-word utterances, 62 began with the words ON or OFF, while 45 began with THIS and THAT.

Typical sentences were

> ON HORSEY, ON SOCK
> OFF HAT, OFF SHOE
> THIS BABY, THIS CHAIR
> THAT DADDY, THAT SOUP

When the pivot category of words increases, the child's sentence pattern becomes quite a bit more complicated. At this time, the child begins to differentiate between members belonging to the pivot class. The articles A and THE and the demonstrative pronouns THIS and THAT come to represent unique and separate classes. At this phase of development, the child's rules will tolerate only certain kinds of constructions. The child utilizes a formula which has been termed privileges of occurrence. A child may say

> THAT A MY CAR   or   THIS A HORSIE

The child gives the privilege to THIS and THAT to appear as first terms in a sentence, but his rule does not give the article the privilege of occurring before a demonstrative. For instance the child would not say

> A THAT MY CAR   or   A THIS HORSIE

About five months after the pivot grammar has appeared about five grammatical classes begin to emerge from the original pivot class. True grammatical classes such as articles, adjectives, demonstrative pronouns, and possessive pronouns arise from the mass of pivot terms.

GENERAL PRINCIPLES OF LANGUAGE ACQUISITION

There has been a vast increase, recently, in the knowledge of how English-speaking children acquire their native language. Fortunately, developmental psycholinguistics has become more universal in its interests. It has concerned itself with the acquisition data found in other language environments and with the consideration of the child's general cognitive development as well. At present, developmental data is available on at least thirty languages from ten major language families.

Appearance of Word Order

The verb–object relation is learned early. In English, where word order is important, the correct order of the verb and the object is demonstrated in the language of the child. In inflected languages, where there is an accusative inflection, this distinction is learned quite early by children. English sentences that contain a verb and an object run

Praise THE ANGEL
Beat THE DEVIL

Children have no trouble learning that the devil follows beat. If a language was less dependent on order, but marked the object with a special accusative inflection, say -TOO for masculine nouns, and -TOY for feminine nouns, such as

BEAT THE DEVILTOO
PRAISE THE ANGELTOY

children would hypothetically learn the -TOO, -TOY accusative distinction quite early.

The Negative Case

In Finnish, Latvian, and Russian, the accusative marker is the earliest distinction produced by children. In every language where data is available, one finds an early negation form that consists of a negative particle that is placed before the simple sentence the child wishes to negate.

| DADDY GO CAR | BABY GO BYE BYE | MAMA EAT COOKIE |
| NO DADDY GO CAR | NO BABY GO BYE BYE | NO MAMA EAT COOKIE |

Early yes/no questions, questions that require only a simple affirmative or negative answer, are formed by the use of a rising intonation patter. This particular pattern has been found in the speech of children from as diverse language backgrounds as English, Arabic, Czech, Latvian, Japanese, and Samoan!

Learning Word Place

A curious finding cropped up in the analysis of the speech of two young bilingual girls whose languages were Hungarian and Serbo-Croatian. The children learned the Hungarian inflections for location much earlier than those in Serbo-Croatian. Location terms such as IN, ON, INTO, ONTO, OUT OF, etc., were expressed early in Hungarian, but failed to be expressed in Serbo-Croatian. An examination of the grammatical structure of location indicated that the structure for expressing location was far simpler in Hungarian. For instance, the marker that indicated location is placed always at the end of a noun. Assuming that -FIN, -FAN, -FEN, -FUN and etc., are location markers, then

THE ASHTRAY SITS TABLEFIN
PUT THE ASHTRAY TABLEFIN
THE DOG SITS TABLEFEN
THE DOG CRAWLS TABLEFEN

The markers are unambiguous in that they indicate both position as well as motion into a position. An examination of the sentences shows that in spite of the verbs of motion such as PUT and CRAWL, the inflections on the following noun do not change. In contrast, the Serbo-Croatian locatives are true prepositions in that the term for location appears before the noun. Further, when location is expressed in terms of a position, a prepositional case marker appears after the noun. When motion into a position is indicated by the verb, the accusative inflection appears after the noun.

THE ASHTRAY SITS ON TABLEFIN	Location verb—preposition—prepositional inflection
PUT THE ASHTRAY ON TABLEFAN	Motion verb—preposition—accusative inflection
THE DOG SITS UNDER TABLEFEN	Location verb—preposition—prepositional inflection
THE DOG CRAWLS UNDER TABLEFUN	Motion verb—preposition—accusative-inflection

Those who have studied highly inflected languages such as Latin or Russian, are quite aware that inflectional systems are hardly as simple as those quasi-English examples. In the case of the Serbo-Croatian locative, the problem is complicated further by the fact that certain locative terms such as "through," or "between," require other types of inflections, all of which are quite arbitrary in nature.

The data on language development in children of various cultures have indicated that children attend to and quickly learn suffixes more easily than prefixes. The Hungarian locative, for example, is marked not by a preposition as in English, but by a simple suffix attached to the noun, and this ending is learned easily by Hungarian children. When playing word games, little children usually imitate the last syllable in words, not the beginning ones. Most observers of child language have found that prepositions (which stand alone before the noun), prefixes, and initial syllables are frequently ignored by children. In Czech, in spite of the fact that initial syllables of words are stressed, the final syllable is nevertheless the portion learned earliest by children. This kind of observation means, then, that inflections should be learned early, since they are placed at the end of words. If languages were organized to express locational ideas by means of inflections or postpositions, children would be able to acquire these verbal expressions more rapidly.

The processing or memory span of the child limits the number of words that he can use in an utterance. During the period when the two-word sentence is in evidence, the child can express such relations as agent–verb, verb–object or agent–object, but he cannot unite the items into the three-term utterance. In other words, the child can say

> MAMA EAT or
> EAT APPLE or
> MAMA APPLE, but cannot say
> MAMA EAT APPLE

Children in every linguistic environment engage in the analysis of language inputs in order to ascertain both the meaning and structure of what they hear. Apparently there may be some universal predispositions in the child's analysis of language input, but this hypothesis requires further study.

LANGUAGE IN ANIMALS

Language has long been viewed as a distinctly human ability, serving to separate man from beast. In recent years, psychologists have attempted to teach language to chimpanzees in particular, since these primates are very close to man on the evolutionary scale. Initial attempts emphasized the use of speech as proof of language ability, but later efforts adopted sign language as well as a written language as alternate means of communication. These nonvocal approaches to language uncovered the linguistic ability of the chimpanzee.

In 1884, Sir John Lubbock, a British naturalist, reported that he had taught his dog Van to identify a few written words. He printed the words FOOD, BONE, WATER, OUT, etc., on pieces of cardboard. The dog was trained to bring a card to his owner, and was subsequently given whatever item was designated on the card. In order to rule out the possibility that olfactory clues were being used, especially in the case of the FOOD card, a new FOOD card was replaced in the card set whenever Van brought a FOOD card. Lubbock assumed that, since the dog was given a small amount of food upon request, the FOOD card might easily retain a familiar and delightful odor. Consequently, a third party added a new FOOD card to the vocabulary set. Sometimes Van brought between 8 and 10 FOOD cards before his appetite was appeased. Whenever Sir John went for a walk, he invited his dog to come along. Van would hastily retrieve the OUT card, running enthusiastically to the front door with the card in his mouth. If Van inadvertently brought a card that specified something he did not want, in other words, if he made an error, he would return the incorrect card, and carefully study the remaining samples until he spotted the correct card. Sir John was quite convinced that his animal could not only distinguish perfectly between one word and another, but that he could also associate word with object.

This kind of word recognition has been reported for chimpanzees who are able to follow rather complicated vocal directions. Winthrop Kellogg (1933), a psychologist, and his cooperative wife adopted a $7\frac{1}{2}$ month old female chimpanzee, Gua, who served as a playmate for their son Donald, then 10 months old. The two young creatures were raised in as similar a manner as possible, with no special training afforded to Gua except that given to a child in her normal surroundings. At the age of $18\frac{1}{2}$ months, Donald had a comprehension vocabulary of 107 words, while Gua, at 16 months, comprehended 95 words. Some of the sentences to which Gua responded are listed below accompanied by a description of Gua's reactions to the statements.

NO–NO	Stops whatever she is doing
KISS–KISS	Gives a kiss
COME HERE!	Comes to the speaker
GUA!	Looks at the speaker
CHAIR–CHAIR	Sits on her potty chair
SHAKE HANDS	Extends her arm to a visitor
BYE–BYE	Runs over to her buggy and climbs in
WANT SOME MILK?	Emits a food bark
WANT SOME ORANGE?	Emits a food bark
SIT DOWN	Sits
OPEN YOUR MOUTH	Opens it
GET UP ON THE BED	Climbs onto the bed
LIE DOWN	Lies down
SHOW ME YOUR NOSE	Points to her nose (cannot identify any other facial part)
BLOW THE HORN	Presses the car horn with fervor

No doubt Gua as well as Donald were responding to mainly key words in each sentence, while ignoring other words. It is doubtful that they could distinguish the difference between the words YOUR and SOME, for instance. There were probably also a number of nonverbal cues that helped both child and chimp to comprehend what was being said. It is unfortunate that the verbal commands were not organized to distinguish minimally different instructions such as

WANT SOME MILK?	EAT THE ORANGE
OPEN SOME MILK	CUT THE ORANGE
DRINK SOME MILK	CUT THE APPLE

If instructions like these are carried out correctly, one is more easily convinced that all sentence terms are comprehended, rather than just individual key words in each sentence. The Kelloggs found that Gua was extremely responsive to tactile communication, for even the slightest touch would be correctly interpreted by Gua as a request to "Turn to the left," or "To the right," etc. Donald, however, showed a greater sensitivity to verbal instruction.

Cathy Hayes, a journalist, author of the book *The ape in our house* (1951), and her psychologist husband, Keith, taught their chimpanzee, Viki, to say the words MAMA, PAPA, and CUP. Viki did not use the words with their specific referents. For instance, she did not say MAMA in the presence of Kathy, or PAPA when trying to catch Keith's attention. She used the words as mands for desired objects. CUP was the only word that was reliably associated specifically with thirst. Viki was able to follow a number of simple spoken instructions, similar to those that Gua could comprehend. At the age of 5, Viki was tested intensively on concept development. Many psycholinguists believe that language can only proceed if certain cognitive distinctions can be made. Concepts such as sex, color, age, size, etc., must be developed before they can be expressed with language. Since animals do not have a language system, the assumption was that animals did not understand concepts. The Hayes designed a series of experiments to try to resolve the issue.

Viki was presented with a series of pairs of realistically colored pictures. One member of each pair represented an inanimate object; the other member, an animate object. Forty-one such pairs were shown to Viki. In one test series, the correct choice of card was the one depicting the category animate. On the animate cards, various types of animate creatures were depicted: six humans, several nonhuman mammals, a few birds, some insects, and one snake. The inanimate cards pictured mainly furniture, but included an automobile and a clock (both of which evidence motion). Viki was required to infer the categories under consideration from each paired presentation. For instance, if bird was the correct member of the first pair shown, and cow was the correct member of the second pair, Viki had to entertain something like the category ANIMATE in order to make the correct choices on the 39 remaining pairs. She was able to distinguish quite nicely between animate and inanimate. In other tests that examined such concepts as male humans versus female humans, red versus green, circles versus crosses, larger versus smaller, etc. Viki performed about as well as human children of the same age. The experiments indicated that the chimp is capable of a rudimentary understanding of concepts, a necessary precursor to language.

In June of 1966, two psychologists, Beatrice Gardner and her husband, began to train their chimpanzee Washoe in language. They decided to use a gestural medium, in this case, the American Sign Language, a system of gestural signs that is used by the deaf in North America. The American Sign Language is made up of two systems: the manual alphabet, and signs. The manual alphabet is a simple series of finger arrangements that correspond to the letters of the alphabet. Signs, however, are roughly analogous to words. The two systems are usually conjoined in the manual speech of the human signer; the manual alphabet being used mainly when the signer wants to use a specific word. Washoe was taught actual signs, rather than the manual alphabet (Gardner and Gardner, 1969).

American Sign Language has been analyzed into units called cheremes. Earlier in the chapter, we discussed the fact that spoken language is analyzed into phonemes, distinctive classes of sound that signal changes in word meaning. These changes in sound are, of course, produced by changes in the vocal apparatus. Cheremes are classes of hand configurations, locations, or actions. The configuration of a pointed hand located by the forehead, cheek, etc., denotes one series of meanings. A wholly new series of meanings is indicated when the hand moves away from these locations.

Since signs, as indicated above, are rather complicated, the most effective training procedure in introducing new signs to Washoe was to actually direct the chimp's hands through the desired motions. This guidance procedure was far more successful than trying to induce gestural mimicry. After the movement was jointly produced by the signer (instructor) and the student (chimpanzee), the signer performed the manual gesture in the presence of the object being named. In other words, after performing the motion, the signer indicated the gesture's meaning by associating the gesture and the object. At the end of approximately 3 years of training, Washoe had a reliable vocabulary of about 85 signs. Signs were used productively. In other words, the language did not involve a pattern of the signer performing the gestures, and the student following commands or directions. The student was actively producing gestures which named objects, requested objects, and so on. Nouns in Washoe's repertoire included such items as

TOOTHBRUSH
FLOWER
DOG
BIB
SHOES
CAT
BABY
CLOTHES

Proper nouns referred mainly to the Gardners and their additional trainers. Adjectives consisted of the three colors

RED
WHITE
GREEN

In the tenth month of the project, Washoe began to combine her signs for GIMMEE and SWEET to form the sentence

GIMMEE SWEET

She also took the separate COME and OPEN, linking them together as COME OPEN.

Later, Washoe's two-word combinations came to resemble the pivot and open class grammar found in child language, which marked the beginning of structural differentiation.

David Premack, a psychologist at the University of California, utilized a physically manipulable series of colored pieces of plastic in teaching language to Sarah, a chimpanzee from Sierra Leone. These plastographs varied in both color and shape, were metal-backed, and adhered to a magnetized slate that was attached to the wall. Each piece of plastic represented a word. Sentences consisted of a series of words arranged in vertical sequence on the slate. This particular arrangement, similar to Chinese, of a vertical sequence of columns that proceed from right to left, was initiated by Sarah herself.

Premack (1971) contended that before deciding whether or not an animal was capable of language, it was first necessary to analyze language into what he called exemplars. Exemplars of language, are, loosely, essential features of language, so that one exemplar would be word usage; another, sentence formulation; and so on. In addition to the list of exemplars, there was a list of strict training procedures for instructing the animal in the exemplars. Some of the main language exemplars which Sarah learned were

WORDS	Nouns, verbs, objects
SENTENCES	Rules for sequencing words
THE INTERROGATIVE	Question
THE CONDITIONAL	If–then relation
METALANGUAGE	Use of language to teach or learn language
DIMENSIONAL CONCEPT	Color, shape and size

In the formation of sentences, word order and the hierarchical organization of the sentence were examined in detail.

The initial training procedure involved a social transaction between the pupil (Sarah) and the trainer. The social transaction involves three essentials: a donor, an action and a receiver. Words were mapped onto these basic units of the transaction. One social transaction, the feeding routine, was an effective unit to use with the chimpanzee. An edible bit was placed between the trainer and Sarah, and, while the trainer looked on affectionately, Sarah ate the morsel. After the transaction began to take on the quality of a routine, a language element, the piece of colored plastic, was placed close to the chimp, while the edible slice of banana was moved out of Sarah's reach. In order to obtain the morsel of fruit now, Sarah was required to place the plastic word on the language board. Additional training consisted simply of making changes in the transaction with simultaneous changes making very clear to the chimp that there was a relationship between what was happening and the words for what was happening.

At first the correct name of the fruit was sufficient to obtain the fruit. But later, in order to obtain the fruit, Sarah was required to specify the donor as well. Now the two-word sentence, DONOR FRUIT was produced. A specific order in the words was desirable.

MARY

GIVE

APPLE

SARAH

was the target sentence. The target sentence was approached gradually, so that every change in a nonlanguage element was clearly mapped to a new language element. The training made it very clear that for the transaction to be completed all required sentence elements had to be arranged in a certain sequence.

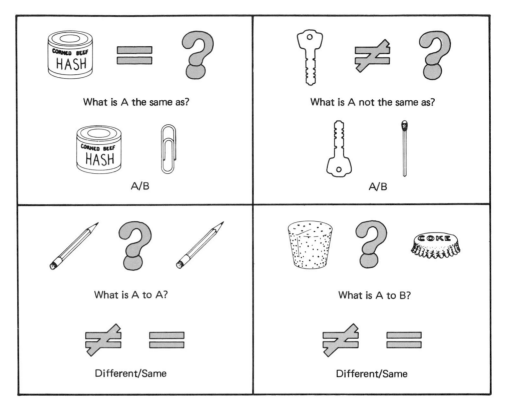

FIGURE 6-9   Four WHAT questions for the chimp based on the SAME/DIFFERENT distinction.

The use of the basic concepts SAME/DIFFERENT helped to introduce the INTERROGATIVE. A matching-to-sample type of game was used to determine Sarah's ability to pair SAME objects. Sarah was given a cup and a spoon; another cup was then introduced, and the animal was required to pair the two objects that were alike. Later, when presented with two similar objects, Sarah placed the plastograph meaning SAME between them, and the plastograph meaning DIFFERENT between dissimilar objects. To make clear that the procedure really represented a form of the interrogative, a plastograph meaning "?" was placed between the objects. Sarah removed the "?" and replaced it with SAME or DIFFERENT, whichever was appropriate. As can be seen from the drawings, both WHAT questions and YES/NO questions can be devised from the basic concept of SAME/DIFFERENT (Figures 6-9 and 6-10).

The language element APPLE was paired with the language element NAME OF, followed by the object, apple. This use of metalanguage was far faster as a method for naming items than the use of mapping in the social transaction. Sarah began to use the system productively, assigning names to foods that

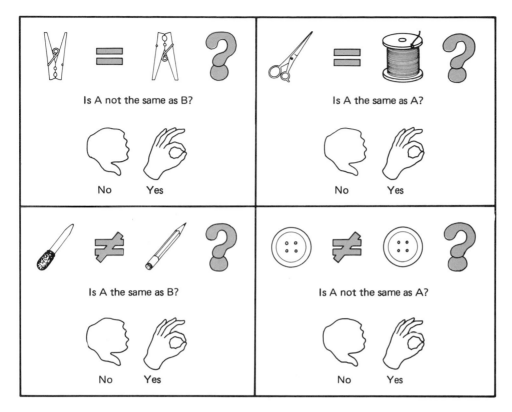

FIGURE 6-10   Four YES/NO questions based on the SAME/DIFFERENT concept.

had not already been named. The conditional IF–THEN was introduced by contingency training, that is, "If Sarah does X she'll get Y: If Sarah does A she'll not get Y." The sentences that Sarah had to process in order to receive her reward consisted of two columns, each containing about eight words!

Were someone to ask you to describe APPLE, you would describe the qualities of an actual apple. The word apple is not seen as a series of sounds but as a very real apple. Sarah's plastic words achieved a similar status for her. She described an apple as being red, round, and with a stem. When presented with the plastograph for APPLE (a small, blue triangle), she responded that it was red, round, and with a stem. She did not describe a small blue triangle. Dimensional classes proved no problem for Sarah; she learned and identified several colors, shapes, and sizes.

The compound sentence was of considerable importance, for it provided the answer to the question of whether an animal could understand the notion of constituent structure or the hierarchical organization of a sentence. To correctly interpret the sentence

SARAH

INSERT

BANANA

PAIL

APPLE

DISH

which translates as "Put the banana in the pail and the apple in the dish, Sarah," she must intuitively sense that banana and pail are more closely related than pail and apple and that insert, the verb, applies to both fruit. Further, she must understand that it is Sarah who performs the series of actions on the fruit. The interpretation of the sentence amounts to a tree diagram (an ideal diagram for a chimpanzee), in which the subject (S) is Sarah, the verb phrase branches into the verb (V) insert, and some noun phrases, etc. The tree diagram described for the sentence TIM ATE THE ORANGE is applicable to the sentence presented to and correctly interpreted by a chimpanzee. Thus, we see that the chimpanzee has a certain kind of language competence. Washoe comprehended and produced gestures, whereas in Sarah's case the plastic words were mainly controlled by the trainer. Sarah comprehended sentences of a complicated hierarchical structure and produced ordered sentences, while Washoe was inclined to string terms together in an arbitrary fashion. What Sarah does not have, Washoe seems to have, and vice versa. Perhaps these two creatures from the jungle may provide us with some beginning formulations that will relate mind and environment.

LANGUAGE AND THE BRAIN

In the preceding section we have given a formal account of language, discussed what is known about its development, and made some psychological statements about it. These are the psychological realities of linguistic behavior. Let us now take a neurological look at language and the brain. What part of the brain is involved in language? What happens to language if these cortical areas are destroyed? These are the questions the neurologist brings to bear on our discussion of language.

Cerebral Dominance

Of all psychological functions, language appears to be that which is most clearly localized in a single hemisphere. In most people, the left hemisphere is primarily responsible for their language behavior. Hemispheric localization of language, however, shows a peculiarity. It is related to an individual's handedness. About 93% of all people are thought to be right-handed; of these right-handers, over 99% of them have speech controlled by the left hemisphere. You will remember that the right half of the brain controls motor movements of the left side of the body, and the left half of the brain controls the right side of the body. In most people, then, preferred handedness and speech are controlled by the same hemisphere. This dominance of one hemisphere is what is called cerebral dominance. If most right-handed people have speech in the left hemisphere, it might be assumed that left-handed people have speech in the right hemisphere. However, of the 7% of the population that is left-handed, only 40% have speech in the right hemisphere.

Localization of Higher Cognitive Functions

What is meant when we say that speech or any other function is localized in a particular area of the brain? To begin with, we do not mean that that circumscribed area alone is responsible for a given function. The complex cortical and subcortical interconnections within the brain form systems or networks that subserve various functions. Within these circuits there may be crucial way stations or subsystems that take the information of a particular system and adapt it to produce a particular psychological function such as speech or language. If that way station is destroyed, the information cannot be so transformed, and the psychological function is impaired. It is in this spirit that one talks about localization of function and "speech centers."

Our knowledge of localization of function has come mostly from pathology. Cases of penetrating brain wounds in which the trajectory of the missile is known have been studied for psychological deficits. Tumor cases may also shed light on the localization question, although tumors generally distort the brain and have effects at a distance. Cortical excision or the removal of cortex for therapeutic purposes is another source of data. The major source of data, however, comes from stroke patients. A stroke is the occlusion of a blood vessel, which cuts off the blood supply to a particular area of the brain and causes the cells in that area to die. Brain wounds, tumors, cortical excision cases, and strokes all provide data on the role of various cortical areas in psychological functioning.

An impairment in language due to cortical damage is called aphasia. By studying the locus of the lesion (damage) that accompanies aphasia, one can discern those regions subserving the language function. The first such correlation between language disorder and brain lesion was made in the middle of the nineteenth century by a French neurologist, Pierre Paul Broca. Broca described two patients who had difficulty speaking but who could understand language well. Broca correlated this expressive aphasia, as it has come to be called, with lesions in the third frontal convolution (see model brain). This area is now called Broca's area. Some years after Broca, another neurologist, Carl Wernicke, found that damage to the association area immediately surrounding the primary auditory cortex appeared to be correlated with another kind of aphasia. These patients could speak relatively well, but they had severe impairment in understanding language, both spoken and written. The hearing of these patients, however, was intact. Wernicke called this sensory aphasia, and the area is now called Wernicke's area. Since there is hemispheric dominance for speech, the lesions producing aphasia need only be unilateral in that hemisphere subserving speech and language.

In order for a language impairment to be classified as an aphasia, the cause of the disturbance must be cortical and not peripheral impairment. Expressive aphasics, for instance, are able to move the speech musculature; their deficit resides in the cortical initiation of language production. Speech disturbances that originate from damage to the speech apparatus (tongue, vocal cords, etc.) or motor centers of the brain stem are qualitatively different from aphasic speech and are called dysarthria. Dysarthric speech is thick and slurred with disturbances in timing and intonation. The speech of the expressive aphasic, on the other hand, sounds normal in quality. Even the severe cases of expressive aphasia are able to say some words, though their use of these words may be reduced to an automatism. The patients vocabulary may be reduced to only a few words, such as "yes" and "no," or perhaps a phrase. These few words are used consistently by the patient to express all his ideas.

The verbal output of the expressive aphasic is greatly reduced, both in speed of speech and in number of incidences of speech initiation. Receptive aphasics, on the other hand, are frequently loquacious; their speech is often repetitious, roundabout, and longwinded.

Some aphasics show agrammatism, or the omission of the small "function" words in speech such as articles, prepositions, conjunctions, and so forth. This shortened form of communication resembles telegram messages, and is often called telegraphic speech.

A more severe breakdown in grammar is that encountered in syntactical aphasia, a term used by Henry Head. An example of the writing of such a patient is given by Penfield and Roberts (1959).

> Well, I thought thing I am going to the tell is about my operation and it is not about all I can tell is about the preparation the had was always the time was when they had me to get ready that is they shaved off all my hair was and a few odd parts of pencil they pr quive me in the fanny.

The grammatical breakdown in the above example is severe, but one can still discern the gist of the patients thoughts. The central problem does not seem to be a disordered thought process, but difficulty in the expression of those thoughts.

In another kind of aphasic disorder the patient has difficulty specifically in naming objects. Nominal aphasia is a particularly difficult disorder to understand, as the patient may use the noun spontaneously in conversation, but be unable to produce it in a specific naming situation. This kind of difficulty is often complicated by perseveration, as evidenced in the following example. A patient described by Braine was asked the name of the object before him. Although it was a pair of scissors, he called it a nail file. When his error was corrected by the examiner, the patient replied, "Yes, that's it! Of course it is not a nail file, it's a nail file." He seemed unable to produce the correct name.

Studies of aphasic patients have shown something about how language capacity can be broken down. Various investigators have attempted to correlate the kinds and severity of aphasic disturbance with particular areas of cortical damage, but these attempts, for the most part, have failed. There does seem to be a close correspondence between lesions in Broca's area of the frontal lobe with expressive disorders, and posterior lesions with receptive impairment, but even this correlation is not perfect. Disorders of expression through writing or speech can occur with either anterior or posterior lesions, as can difficulty with naming. In all but rare cases, however, comprehension deficits are associated with more posterior lesions. Although aphasic disturbances of language can be correlated with damage to various areas of the dominant hemisphere, specific symptoms cannot be perfectly predicted from the site of cortical damage.

SUMMARY

There are two main theories on how the child acquires language. The radical difference between them serves to illustrate the strong undercurrent of controversy between the nativists and the empiricists, a controversy that has been woven into the fabric of psychology. One emphasizes man's response repertoire, for responses can be measured and increased or decreased by environmental factors. The other has little use for responses per se. The child "knows" much more than he "learns," and it is this knowledge that a child organizes into language behavior. Loosely speaking, the nativist concerns himself with the organization of the mind, while the empiricist struggles with the environment.

Obviously, humans with minds grow up in environments, so that there is a considerable interplay between the two factors. Therefore, it would be most helpful to have a theory that describes how the mind interacts with the environment.

SUGGESTED READINGS

CHOMSKY, N. *Language and mind.* New York: Harcourt, 1972.

HAYES, C. *The ape in our house.* New York: Harper, 1951.

MILLER, G. A. Four philosophical problems of psycholinguistics. *Philosophy of Science*, 1970, **37**, 183–199.

NOTTENBOHM, F. Ontogeny of bird song. *Science*, 1970, **167**, 950–956.

PAIVIO, A. *Imagery and verbal processes.* New York: Holt, 1971.

SKINNER, B. F. *Verbal behavior.* New York: Appleton, 1957.

7

Perceptual and Cognitive Development

――――――――

Until recently, psychological thought and theory have been dominated by the view that the newborn baby is essentially a tabula rasa. The notion directly stems from the views of John B. Watson the famous behaviorist who, in 1924, wrote

> I should like to go one step further now and say, "Give me a dozen healthy infants, well-formed, and my own specialized world to bring them up in and I'll guarantee to take any one at random and train him to become any type of specialist I might select—doctor, lawyer, artist, merchant, chief, and yes, even beggarman and thief, regardless of his talents, penchants, tendencies, abilities, vocations and race of his ancestors." I am going beyond my facts and I admit it, but so have the advocates of the contrary and they have been doing it for many thousands of years.

One can easily see how a scientist with a talent for polemics like that had an important influence over the entire field of psychology. Today most students of behavior deny the field ever harbored the idea that genetic influences were small or inconsequential, yet the mood was pervasive and fit well with the American Dream. Indeed, the notion that the environment is all important in shaping behavior is still the majority view.

In the following, we will look at a variety of recent studies that examine how learning, memory, and conceptual processes develop in the normal child. We will begin by presenting the ideas of Jean Piaget on the nature of cognitive development.

COGNITIVE DEVELOPMENT

The study of cognitive development is the study of how an organism acquires the mental abilities found in the normal adult members of its species. An adequate account of cognitive development must include a description of the behavioral changes found in a growing organism as well as an account of the factors responsible for these changes. Theories that account for the changes in cognitive functioning during development include classical conditioning, instrumental conditioning with its emphasis on reinforcement of behavior, imitation of others' actions, and the reduction of discrepancies between beliefs and observations. Unfortunately our knowledge of the descriptive features of cognitive development is greater than our understanding of the causal factors responsible for change; therefore, our treatment here is heavily weighted in the direction of description.

THE PIAGETIAN VIEW OF COGNITIVE DEVELOPMENT

The work of the Swiss psychologist, Jean Piaget, is singular in its scope, for he has attempted to discover general principles of development that span the length and breadth of the growth of intelligent behavior. Cognitive development in the Piagetian system is a process of elaboration based on sensory input from the child's activities. The object of this elaboration is the structure of the child's acts which Piaget calls a schema (pl. schemata). For every set of actions that are equivalent from the child's point of view, one can describe the organization or the structure common to the actions. It is the generalized characteristics of these actions that constitute a schema. Early schemata include the actions of grasping, sucking, and looking. Each instance of grasping in the newborn, for example, will share certain features with other grasping acts because they are products of the same schema. But as the child grows, new structures will emerge from the differentiation of this basic schema. The behavioral consequences of this differentiation is that reflex grasping gives way to different kinds of grasping, e.g., repetitive clutching at blankets and bed clothes in the first months, grasping at toys, and later holding a bottle of milk.

Mechanisms of Schemata Development

Piaget's theory of how schemata are elaborated incorporates both the sensory input reaching the child as well as the child's actions on the input. Years of work attempting to describe relations between input stimuli and subsequent responses have convinced psychologists that it is not the external stimulus itself that is lawfully related to behavior, but rather it is the external stimulus as interpreted by the organism. Consider the picture in Figure 7-1. Would you place this in a class with pictures of vases or with pictures of social situations? Well, either would be an appropriate response because the picture can be seen either as a vase or as two individuals facing one another. Similar differences in the interpretation of sensory events are possible and frequent. A common cause of variable interpretation is selective attention, focusing one's analysis of an input on only a few features and ignoring others. Piaget has

FIGURE 7-1   An ambiguous picture that can be seen as a vase or as two faces looking at one another. Such stimuli point up the importance of individual interpretation of an event in determining what the effective stimuli are.

emphasized the role of the child's activity in determining which aspects of experience he will attend to.

Piaget's collaborator, Bärbel Inhelder (Inhelder, 1962), has identified two types of action that the child brings to bear on the elements of his experience. First there are the logicomathematical actions of bringing together, dissociating, counting, ordering, etc., which emphasize properties that are not inherent in the objects acted upon. The objects are merely supports for the actions. Second are the physical activities of exploration which are directed at extracting information from objects themselves about their color, size, form, function, etc. Through such activities, the schemata are progressively brought into line with physical reality. With each new encounter, the child likens his experience to the stored information of the schemata and attempts to categorize the incoming stimulation in terms of one or several familiar schemata. However, the input may contain information that is not present in the relevant stored information. In this case the schemata are accommodated to the new information, and, in so doing, a small step toward a more realistic construction of the physical world is achieved.

Stages of Development

Piaget has found evidence in his work of three major stages in the course of cognitive development: the sensorimotor stage (birth to 18 months), the stage of concrete operations (18 months to 11 years), and the stage of formal operations (from 11 years). In each stage there is a period of formation in which the child explores the characteristics of the physical world and is exposed to various inconsistencies between his beliefs about how things work and how they are actually experienced to work. As a result of these incongruent experiences, a period of attainment follows in which the child discovers new principles that can account for the inconsistencies and bring the schemata into a state of relative equilibrium with one another. The child's problem at these points of attainment is like that of a physicist who sets out to measure the distance between two cities. Having measured the distance in the winter's cold and in the summer's heat, he is faced with an incongruent bit of information. He had assumed that the distance between the cities would be a constant. But his measurements show that the distance is greater in the winter than in the summer. To resolve the discrepancy he must alter his beliefs about the nature of measurement and consider the possibility that his measuring instrument can change as a function of the temperature. As the temperature drops, the length of his measure decreases so more of its lengths are needed to go the distance between the cities.

SENSORIMOTOR STAGE.   In the sensorimotor period, the child masters some of the basic concepts and relations found in the physical world. The newborn begins postnatal life with a small number of reflex activities. His behavior is rigid and limited to a small number of situations in which there are releasing stimuli present to elicit the reflexes. But very soon, the newborn begins to stay awake for longer periods and makes rhythmic, repetitious movements on his own or in conjunction with objects around him. The sensorimotor period is a time in which the infant learns to coordinate his various sense modalities. Initially, the activities of grasping, reaching, looking, listening, and sucking are themselves uncoordinated and operate somewhat independently of one another. For instance, the visual system is slow to follow the path of a moving object, a sign of uncoordination internal to the visual motor system. But in addition, the infant does not look for the source of a voice he hears, nor does he reach for an object he sees. Some of these developments in the first 18 months, called sensorimotor coordinations, will be discussed later in this chapter.

For the present, we will consider another important development in this period, the development of the concept of the permanent object. As adults, we think of the physical world as being full of solid objects which exist in some place, i.e., occupy space, independent of our perceiving them or thinking of them. We can verify this in our actions toward objects, both verbal and nonverbal actions. We talk about objects in their absence and can speculate where absent objects may be before we have found them. Without speech, our nonverbal behavior shows that we expect objects to obey certain physical laws. If a newborn shared this appreciation of objects as permanent entities, we would expect his behavior to indicate this, just as our nonverbal behavior does.

Consider the behavior of a child around the age of 6 months. The child has learned to coordinate his movements with vision and is able to successfully reach for objects in his visual field. However, when the object a child has been reaching for disappears from view, e.g., a parent places his hand over it, the child does not search for the vanished object but moves to some new activity. We know that the child has the motor coordination to move his hand to the place where the object is hidden. Why, then, does he not do so? Piaget's explanation is that the child believes the object has ceased to exist, something like Lewis Carroll's Cheshire cat. It is as if the child feels that objects obey physical laws only so long as he perceives them. He learns of this error as he gains more experience with objects. He may grasp an object in the visual field, move it away, and then bring it back into view. Now he is faced with an object which has continued to exist tactually because it has remained in his grasp, but it has popped in and out of visual existence in the meantime.

Confronted with such conflicting data, the child reorganizes his schemata of objects so that objects are conceived to exist even when not immediately perceived.

The concept of the permanent object does not stabilize until the end of the sensorimotor period. Until that time, various complications will cause the child to again behave as if the hidden object has vanished. For example, we hide a toy beneath a pillow with the child watching, but then secretly place a cloth over the toy while it is hidden behind the pillow. The child responds by lifting the pillow in search of the toy, but, when he sees only the cloth, he will revert to the earlier type of reaction and abandon the search. It is as if the child believes that objects sometimes maintain permanence and sometimes do not.

By the end of the sensorimotor period, at around 18 months of age, the child has coordinated his various sense modalities with one another, has learned to adjust his goal-directed actions to the particular demands of the situation, and his behavior shows that he has some understanding of the laws of the physical world.

There is another important change in the child's activities that occurs at this time and signals the end of the sensorimotor period. That is the appearance of symbolic representation, the ability to represent objects and events in their absence by words, images, or actions. Prior to the appearance of this ability, most of the infant's activities are determined by the immediate context. But by 18 months, the child engages in a number of representational activities. He imitates a playmate's temper tantrum on the day after it has occurred. This is called deferred imitation and can be accomplished only if the child is acting upon some stored representation of the event in its absence. Other indications of representation are symbolic play where the child pretends to carry out events he recalls from past experience as part of his play, and a very important form, language use.

STAGE OF CONCRETE OPERATIONS.   With the development of symbolic representation, the child begins the second stage of development, the concrete operational period. This is an extremely long stage which spans the greatest part of preadult development. The concrete operations are schemata that have progressed a long way from the sensorimotor schemata. Evidence of the concrete operations in thought appears as early as the fifth year, but the most rapid period of development in this stage is somewhat later, around the eighth year.

The concrete operations are coordinated actions integrated into systems in which one action can compensate for another. A similar state of affairs existed at the end of the sensorimotor period on the plane of overt actions.

The concrete operations differ from those sensorimotor schemata in that the actions are covert actions of thought. They are marked by their generality, being applicable to a wide range of situations and found in all individuals who have reached the same mental level. In addition they share the feature of reversibility, the actions being organized in such a way that for every transformation of a stimulus there exists another transformation whose application would return the stimulus to its original state. Among the concrete operations, Piaget includes those of addition and subtraction, comparison (greater or less), multiplication and division, and conjunction and disjunction.

Preoperational thought is the name that has been given to the mental activities of the child who is beyond the sensorimotor period but has not yet attained the concrete operations. Piaget has used the same tests to explore the properties of preoperational and concrete operational thought in the child. Among these tests are classification and seriation, conservation, and other tests requiring verbal explanation of physical phenomena. The preoperational responses to these tasks are marked by several common features. The answers share an egocentric quality. An egocentric response is based only on the child's view of an event, ignoring other possible interpretations different viewers might have. In egocentric speech, for example, the preoperational child fails to consider the explicit information the listener will need in order to understand the child's message. There is an abundance of ambiguous pronouns used by the child (*This goes there on that thing*) and the words are used in special senses that may be difficult for the listener to understand. In fact, a preoperational child may be so oblivious to the informational needs of his listener that he may tell a blindfolded listener, "You *see* this thing goes here." Among the other characteristics of preoperational thought are the tendency to center attention on one striking feature of an event to the neglect of other important information and the ability to represent states of events but not the transformation from state to state.

THE DEVELOPMENT OF THE IDEA OF CONSERVATION.   Consider, for example, the reactions of a child in a conservation of quantity task as he passes through the preoperational and concrete operational levels of thinking about such a task. Typically, the child is shown two beakers of equal size containing water and is asked to add or take away whatever water he feels is needed to make it so that both beakers contain the same amount of water. Even preschool age children respond to the instruction by making the water levels the same height. Now a third beaker is introduced which is taller and thinner than the two standard beakers. The child is then asked where he thinks the water level will be if the water from one of the standard beakers is poured into the taller one, and whether he thinks there will be just as much water in the taller beaker as there was in the standard beakers. Finally, the water is poured into the third beaker and the child is again asked whether there is the same amount of water in the taller beaker as there is in the remaining standard beaker. These events are depicted in Figure 7-2 along with the answers representative of children at the preoperational and concrete levels as well as the interesting transitional level.

Successful performance on this task is reached only after the child has realized that water level is not an accurate measure of quantity when the width of a container is changed, and that the act of pouring water from one

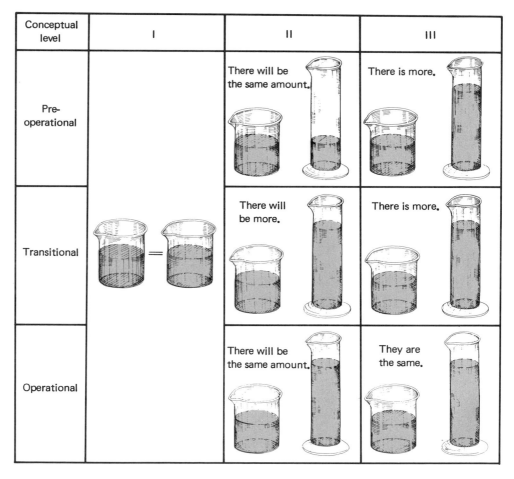

FIGURE 7-2   Three types of response to a conservation task. The water level that the child predicts will be obtained after pouring is depicted in the middle column along with the child's prediction about the amount of water. The last column presents the child's decision about the amount of water after seeing the results of pouring.

vessel to another is a transformation that does not alter the amount of water, although it does alter other characteristics of the liquid such as height and width. The preoperational child at first expects that the act of pouring will not alter the amount of liquid. And of course he is quite correct. But the stimulus by which he judges the amount of water is the level it reaches in the beaker, i.e., he predicts that the levels will be the same in the taller beaker and in the standard. Consequently, he is forced to reject his hypothesis of conservation in favor of a nonconserving interpretation when he sees that the water level in the taller beaker rises above the level in the standard. His error is caused by the failure to attend to both the height and width of the liquid when judging the amount in the beakers. The child's first resolution of this conflict between his expectations and his observations about the quantity of liquid is to abandon the conservation hypothesis and adopt the assumption that quantity is not conserved in the pouring transformation. In the transitional phase, then, we find the child predicts that the water level will indeed be higher in the taller beaker, and, because of his attention to height only, concludes that there will be more water after it is poured from the standard to the taller beaker.

The correct solution to the problem is finally achieved after the child begins to shift his attention between the height and width of the columns of water. At first he may center on the height one time, then on the width the next. Eventually he applies both to a single problem and then sees that the conclusion about the amount of water reached on the basis of the greater height of the water in the taller, thinner beaker is in conflict with the one he would reach on the basis of the smaller width of the column. He then concludes that the greater height must be compensated for by the lesser width and therefore the amount of water is not changed by pouring from one beaker to another.

When a child has truly understood the nature of the compensation and the act of pouring, his behavior toward the task changes. In particular, when the child is really convinced that the act of pouring does not affect the amount of a substance, but only certain of its dimensions, he will no longer examine the heights and widths of the columns of water in the beakers before making his decision about the amount held therein. Seeing that nothing has been done to the water other than pouring from one beaker to another, he is sure that no operation that would alter the amount has taken place. In reaching the solution, the child has decentered his attention from single aspects of the situation to multiple aspects and has come to consider the transformations of matter that link the different states of affairs. The act of pouring has come under the control of the concrete operations of addition and subtraction and is understood to change only superficial features of the substance operated upon.

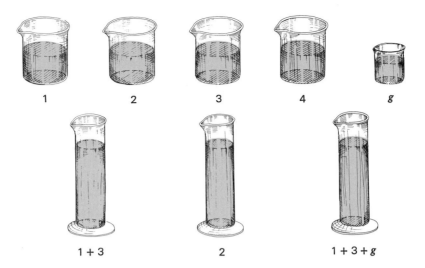

FIGURE 7-3   The five jars of colorless liquids from which a child must choose to produce a yellow mixture. To begin the task, a drop from *g* is added to unlabeled glasses of $1+3$ and 2. The $1+3+g$ combination is the correct mixture. From Inhelder and Piaget (1958).

Stage of Formal Operations.   The third and last of Piaget's stages of intellectual development is the stage of formal operations. Unlike previous stages, this stage may not be attained by all normal individuals. It deals with the most abstract activities of any of the stages, which we will call hypothetico-deductive thought (Inhelder, 1962). A person who has achieved the level of formal operations approaches certain tasks differently than one who has not. He may consider the various states of affairs that might occur in a situation and then test to see which of these actually occurs.

Piaget presents children with the following problem to demonstrate the differences in approach between children at the concrete operational level and children at the formal operational level. The child is given four flasks containing odorless, colorless liquids (numbered 1–4) and a bottle, *g*, with a dropper (Figure 7-3). The experimenter then shows the child two glasses which contain liquid from $1+3$ and 2, respectively, but does not tell the child this. The experimenter then drops some of the liquid from *g* into each glass. The $1+3+g$ combination turns yellow, while the $2+g$ combination remains colorless. The child's task is to then reproduce the color using any of the contents of the five flasks. $1+3+g$ is the simplest combination that will reproduce the color. Number 2 is only water and will not affect the color if added to the $1+3+g$ combination. Number 4, however, will bleach the color if added to $1+3+g$. Here are the reactions of a child at the concrete operational level of thought faced with this problem.

> REN (7;1) tries $4 \times g$, then $2 \times g$, $1 \times g$, and $3 \times g$: "*I think I did everything. . . . I tried them all.*"—"What else could you have done?"—"*I don't know.*" We give him the glasses again: he repeats $1 \times g$, etc.—"You took each bottle separately. What else could you have done?"— "*Take two bottles at the same time*" [he tries $1 \times 4 \times g$, then $2 \times 3 \times g$, thus failing to cross over between the two sets (of bottles), for example 1×2, 1×3, 2×4, and 3×4] (Inhelder & Piaget, 1958, p. 111).

First, the concrete operational child is prone to consider only four 1×1 combinations of elements without realizing that there are ten other combinations of more than one of the chemicals with g. Second, when it is suggested that he try some of these other combinations, he does so haphazardly, selecting only two possibilities in this example.

Now let us examine the response of a child who has attained the formal operational level of thought.

> ENG (14;6) begins with $2 \times g$; $1 \times g$; $3 \times g$; and $4 \times g$: "*No, it doesn't turn yellow. So you have to mix them.*" He goes on to the six two-by-two combinations and at last hits $1 \times 3 \times g$: "*This time I think it works.*"—"Why?"— "*It's 1 and 3 and some water.*" "You think it's water?"— "*Yes, no difference in odor. I think that it's water.*"—"Can you show me?"—He replaces g with some water: $1 \times 3 \times$ water. "*No, it's not water. It's a chemical product: it combines with 1 and 3 and then it turns into a yellow liquid* [he goes on to three-by-three combinations beginning with the replacement of g by 2 and by 4—i.e., $1 \times 3 \times 2$ and $1 \times 3 \times 4$]. *No, these two products aren't the same and the drops: they can't produce color with 1 and 3* (Inhelder & Piaget, 1958, p. 120).

The difference between this child and the first we presented is striking. The older child behaves as if he were systematically testing each of the possible combinations. In addition he is able to test the hypothesis that g is water by comparing its effect with the effect of tap water. Such willingness to consider the "what if" side of things comprises the essence of scientific reasoning and, for Piaget, the highest form of intellectual activity.

Piaget has contributed a wealth of data to the field of child development. His research is always opening new areas of interest to psychologists eager to explore further into the areas he has pioneered. Even those who disagree with his theoretical interpretations cannot dispute the importance of his discoveries. Before Piaget's demonstration, adults and even school teachers were not aware that a child believed that the quantity of a liquid could be altered by pouring. Parents who had not studied Piaget's work were upset to see their children "tricked" by a psychologist conducting such a conservation experiment with their child. We are indebted to theorists like Piaget for dispelling the erroneous belief that children's thought is qualitatively identical to adult thought, differing only in a quantitative way from the adult form.

Few psychologists working in the area of cognitive development have attempted to study development on the grand scale Piaget has undertaken. It is more common to examine the development of a particular cognitive function like perception, learning, memory, or conceptualization, or even to restrict attention to only one aspect of a function like classical conditioning or the development of depth perception. In the remainder of this chapter we will consider some of the findings that have emerged from these attempts to understand the development of specific cognitive functions.

LEARNING

The ability to learn is the ability to modify one's behavior in light of past experience. Even a very young child is capable of learning, although it may take many training sessions to teach a new response to the infant. In one study of learning in newborn infants (Papoušek, 1967), 3-day-olds were given access to a bottle of milk if they would turn their head to one side upon hearing the sound of a bell. On the average, it took them 177 trials to learn to respond regularly to the bell. If the same procedure is done with 20-week-old infants, the response is learned with an average of 27 trials. Studies of this type have demonstrated that there is a gradual decrease in the number of training trials required to produce learning as the chronological age of the subjects increases.

The ease of learning is also affected by other factors that are related to the level of maturation of the subject. For example, the sensitivity of the receptors (i.e., eyes, nose, ears) to the stimuli used in these studies has an effect on the speed with which an infant is able to learn. Russian work on infant learning indicates that auditory sensitivity is one of the earliest to appear and visual sensitivity is the last to appear (Brackbill, 1962). However, factors that normally play a role in adult learning, e.g., motivation, may not have an effect on some types of learning in the newborn. For example, in another study in which newborns were taught to turn their heads in order to get milk, it was found that it did not matter how hungry the infants were during training, at least within the ranges of deprivation used in the study. An infant who had been fed just an hour before training learned as quickly as one who had gone $2\frac{1}{2}$ hours without eating (Siqueland & Lipsitt, 1966).

Reflexes and Beyond

An infant uses this learning ability to organize the smooth functioning of the reflexes present at birth. Infants are sometimes very awkward in obtaining food during their first attempts at nursing. Often their mouth must be held against the nipple to prevent them from losing contact. During the first month of life, there is evidence of increasing coordination and flexibility in this nursing behavior. The child learns to search for the nipple on the basis of tactile cues. He comes to recognize the feel of the nipple before he has tasted any milk, whereas earlier he had to rely on taste to identify the nipple. These advances are characteristic of the acquisition of new responses to previously neutral stimuli, which has been demonstrated by observational studies of learning in the newborn (Piaget, 1952).

The effective functioning of reflexive activities indicates that information from the senses has been coordinated with the infant's movements. Much of this learning occurs during the first 18 months of life. Sharpening the reflexes is only the first sign of sensorimotor learning. At birth the various sensory systems and the impulsive movements of the newborn are only slightly coordinated. By the age of 6 months, the infant has mastered a major portion of the coordinations between the movements of arms, hands, and fingers, and the sensory information from the various receptors.

Visual–Motor Coordination

The development of visually directed reaching is a good example of the way in which sensorimotor coordinations are acquired (White, Castle, & Held, 1964). At 1 month of age, there is no attempt on the part of the infant to reach for an object presented in his field of vision. The infant stares at the object, but he makes no attempt to grab it. The first change in the infant's reaction comes at about $2\frac{1}{2}$ months, when the child begins to take swipes at the object, but his aim is poor and he may not grasp as he makes contact with the object. At 4 months, the infant uses a more effective strategy. He raises his hand toward the object until both are in the field of vision. Then he will look alternately at the object and his hand, gradually reducing the gap between the two, until he successfully touches the object.

This kind of reaction, in which each movement toward the goal is checked and altered on the basis of the result, is similar to the way an adult behaves in situations where new coordinations are required. For example, we can disrupt the association between visual stimuli and hand movements by having an adult wear glasses with prism lenses reversing the visual field. Now the visual counterpart of every movement in the visual field will be backward of what the person has learned to expect. In this case, the person spends much more time watching where his hand is going and makes corrections for errors in visually directed reaching by watching where each movement takes his hand in relation to the object. Because we can produce behavior similar to that observed in 4-month-old infants by distorting the hand–eye coordinations of the adult, we have reason to believe that the infant's behavior is due to the same causes, i.e., a lack of knowledge of the visual–motor coordinates.

As the adult wears the distorting glasses for a longer time, the hand movements in the visual field become faster and are made more smoothly (see Chapter 12). Interestingly, some of the subjects report that the world begins to look alright to them again. The same improvement in visually directed reaching occurs in the infant. By $5\frac{1}{2}$ months, the infant reaches and grasps an object in a smooth, efficient motion. It seems that, by practicing movements in the visual field, the infant learns to feel where his arm is in relation to the object and need no longer rely solely on visual information as he did $1\frac{1}{2}$ months earlier.

Practice is an important element in the acquisition of sensorimotor coordinations. Infants who are raised in institutions where there are few opportunities to look at and reach for attractive objects develop coordinated reaching later than $5\frac{1}{2}$ months. On the other hand, the presence of bright mobiles and the opportunity to reach for them may accelerate the acquisition by a month or more. Yet, regardless of the speed of acquisition of visually directed reaching, all children who learn to reach for objects in the visual field progress through the same stages of development.

The extent to which an infant's behavior can be influenced by the adults around him is surprising, especially to many parents who have been led to believe that a newborn has a sort of genetic "automatic pilot" that wisely directs his activities in the first months. Studies that have attempted to influence the infant's social behavior by using operant techniques have successfully increased the amount of vocalization in 3-month-old infants (Weisberg, 1963), and decreased the amount of crying in 6- to 20-week-olds, while at the same time increasing the amount of smiling by the selective use of reinforcement (Rheingold, *et al.*, 1959). The thoughtful use of social rewards can enable adults to exert a powerful influence over an infant's behavior.

PERCEPTUAL DEVELOPMENT

It is fascinating to speculate on what the newborn must think of the world, although reliable data on the matter are nonexistent. We cannot ask the newborn what he thinks about, but we can get information about the messages the infant receives about the world through his senses. Since much of the work has been concerned with the development of visual perception, those results will be emphasized here.

Emerging Visual Processes

The visual stimulus comes from light falling on the retina of the eye. The image is turned upside down by the lens. Because it must pass through the liquid and nerves inside the eye, this image is blurred. Our ability to see lines and edges is due to the action of the receptors in the retina. The image that is projected onto the retina from an object in our visual field seems too impoverished to provide us with the rich view of the world we experience. The retinal image is flat, that is, it seems to contain information about only two dimensions; yet, with no apparent effort, we see a world in depth. Also, the objects that we see stay the same size and shape as we move around them. But the visual image they cast on the retina may be changing erratically, as you can see if you walk around an object like the window in Figure 7-4. These abilities to see the world as it "really" is, rather than as it appears in the retinal image, require the integration of multiple sources of information.

Depth perception, the ability to judge the distance of an object from the eyes, draws on information from several sources. Some cues come from the image itself. For example, if one object blocks our view of another, then it is closer to the viewer than is the obscured object. This is called interposition (see Chapter 12). Motion parallax provides cues to depth when observing an object in motion. The speed with which nearby objects move across the visual field is much faster than with distant objects. The difference in rate can be used to judge relative depth. Other cues to depth come from the mechanical apparatus of the eye. As we look at an object, our eyes move together so that each eye is directed toward the stimulus. This is called convergence, and the amount of effort spent on pulling the eyes inward to view an object can be a cue to the distance of the object from the eyes. In addition, the lens of the eye is adjusted by ciliary muscles to bring the image of an object into focus. This adjustment is called accommodation. Information from the muscles involved may also tell us about the distance of the object being viewed.

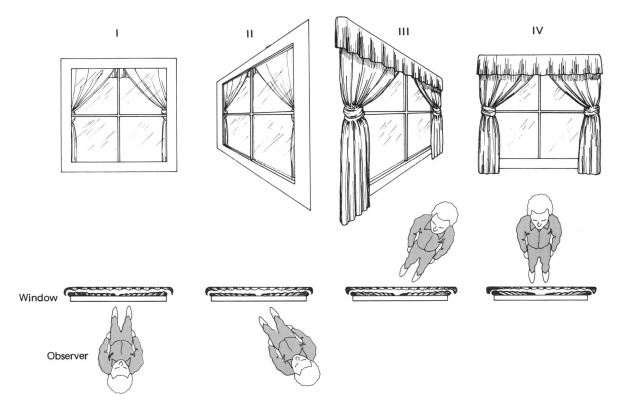

FIGURE 7-4   Four views of a window demonstrating changes in the visual form presented to the retina from a solid object viewed from different positions.

During the first weeks of life, some of these cues are not available to the infant. A newborn's eyes do not converge on an object in view, but rather they turn outward, or diverge (Wicklegren, 1967). Also, newborns do not accommodate the lens to the distance of an object until about 2 months of age. Only objects approximately 8 inches from the eye are seen in focus. It is not until 4 months that accommodative responses reach a mature level (Haynes, White, & Held, 1965).

During the second month, in addition to progress in accommodation, convergence for objects at different distances improves markedly. These changes in the visual system are accompanied by changes in the infant's reactions to objects at different distances. For instance, until 3 weeks of age, infants do not show any protective eyeblink reaction to a disk that is dropped from a height over the infant's head to within a short distance of its face. From 3 to 14 weeks, the regularity and vigor of the eyeblink response increases (White, 1968).

Size Constancy—Innate or Learned?

There is an inverse relationship between the distance of an object and the size of the image it casts on the retina. The retinal image of an object seen from 1 foot away is twice as large as the image of the same object seen from 2 feet away. If we had no information about the distance of an object from the eye, the object would appear to grow and shrink as we moved past it. However, adults do take the perceived distance of an object into account and see the object as remaining the same real size, despite changes in the size of the visual image. This ability is called size constancy. The development of size constancy may be closely related to the development of depth perception in the infant.

The experimental evidence bearing directly on early signs of size constancy is sparse. Many of the studies that have examined the infant's response to depth have not been able to convincingly demonstrate the presence of size constancy. For example, in one study (Cruikshank, 1941) infants were shown two rattles, a small one held 25 cm from the baby and a large one 3 times its size held 75 cm from the baby. Although the visual images of the two rattles were identical, older infants (6 months) reliably reached for the smaller rattle. This study is often cited as a demonstration of size constancy, because the infants were not reacting simply to the visual image. Actually the study tells us very little about the infants' perception of the rattles, since it is just as likely that depth perception alone was responsible for the infants' preference for the smaller, but nearer, rattle.

A more convincing demonstration of size constancy and depth perception in infants has been conducted based on the principal of stimulus generalization (Figure 7-5). Previous studies of learning in lower animals and man have found that, when an organism is trained to make a response in the presence of one stimulus, there is a tendency to make the same response to other stimuli resembling the training stimulus. The amount of responding decreases as the similarity of the stimuli decreases. When a complex training stimulus is used, e.g., a red circle with a black stripe down the center, an examination of the subject's tendency to generalize the response to different stimuli can tell us to what aspects of the training stimulus the subject was attending. If only the vertical stripe was noticed, then the response would be made to other stimuli with stripes. If only the shape was attended to, we would find generalization to other circular shapes, although they might be a different color and without a stripe.

This same idea was employed with infants from 40 to 85 days old, in order to determine whether they attended to the size of the retinal image,

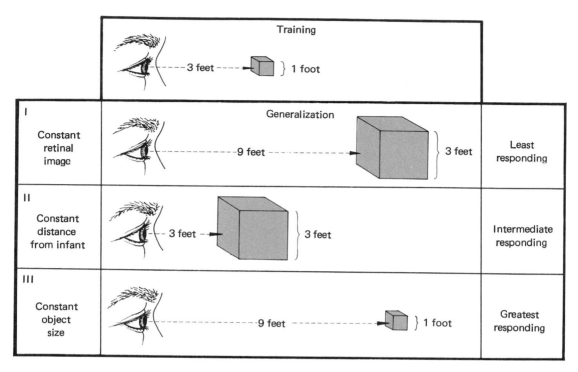

FIGURE 7-5 An experiment designed to study the infant's perception of depth and objective size by independently varying retinal size, object size, and object distance. After Bower (1965).

the actual size of the object, the distance of the object from the child, or some combination of these (Bower, 1965). The infants were first trained to turn their heads in the presence of a small cube placed 3 feet away. In subsequent generalization tests, the infants showed the greatest tendency to respond to the same cube placed 9 feet away. An intermediate amount of responding was made to a much larger cube placed 3 feet away from the child. The fewest responses were made to the large cube placed 9 feet away from the child.

To see what these results mean, it is necessary to consider what cues remained unchanged in each condition. If a cue is held constant, and if the infant attended to that cue during training, then there should be a relatively large amount of responding to that cue during the generalization test.

The least amount of responding was made in the presence of the large cube placed 9 feet away. This stimulus differed from the training stimulus in size (it was 3 times as large) and in distance (it was 3 times as far from the child), but the image of the stimulus on the retina was the same size as that of the training stimulus. The relatively small amount of responding to this stimulus indicates that the size of the visual image is not a critical feature of the infant's visual experience. The two remaining stimuli differed from the training stimulus either in size (a large cube seen from 3 feet away), or in distance (the small cube placed 9 feet away). If the infant attended to the distance of the training cube from him, generalized responding should occur to other stimuli at the same distance (3 feet). If he attended to the actual size of the training cube, he should generalize to that cube at other distances (9 feet). As early as 60 days of age, infants showed generalization to both types of stimuli, confirming the presence of both depth perception and size constancy in infant perception. However, the actual size of a stimulus was a more critical factor than its distance from the child, since there was a greater amount of generalization to the smaller training cube seen at a different distance.

There is conflicting evidence on the course of perceptual development in the visual system. Some studies have found that the ability to use certain visual cues continues to improve through childhood. Size constancy, for example, shows improvement up to the tenth year. When children between the ages of 2 and 10 years were tested, there was a gradual decrease in the tendency to use the size of the retinal image as the critical measure of objective size (Zeigler & Leibowitz, 1957). As we have seen in the Bower study, there is evidence that 60-day-old infants do not attend to the size of the retinal image, but rather focus on the real size of the object. It is difficult to understand why older children do not do so as well. One possibility is that the development of visual perception is completed during infancy, but that judgmental or other cognitive factors related to the particular task can interfere with the performance of the older children. Such task specific factors could explain the results of several apparently contrary findings. In one study (Smith & Smith, 1966), children ranging in age from 5 to 12 years and adults were asked to judge the distance of objects in a variety of tasks. When the judgments were made under normal viewing conditions, children reproduced the distances just as well as the adults did. However, when the objects were viewed under restricted conditions in which only some of the visual cues were available, there was improvement with age. An age trend has also been found with children and adults, 8 to 19 years of age, when they were asked to judge the distance of objects shown on stereograms during very brief exposures (Leyer, 1939). Such results may be due to changes in the subjects' ability to attend to rapidly presented material, since stereoscopic vision has been found to function in children as young as 2 years old when longer exposure durations are used (Johnson & Beck, 1941).

MEMORY

Memory, in some sense, is present at birth. As we have seen, 3-day-old infants are able to learn simple habits, implying that they have stored information about past experiences. No studies dealing specifically with memory in newborns are presently available. The information we do have about memory comes from studies of learning and habituation in infancy. There are major differences in the way children and adults deal with information from the senses, and there are also some surprising similarities.

Basic Memory Model

The sequence of processes that are believed involved in memory performance is presented in Figure 7-6. They include an afterimage of sensory trace that survives beyond the termination of the physical stimulus, an intermediate storage phase called short-term memory (STM), and a more permanent form of storage phase called long-term memory (LTM). These stages comprise the flow of information from a visual stimulus, which in Figure 7-6 is a 3 by 4 matrix of letters and numbers. To study these perceptual and memory processes, which occur very rapidly, the stimulus array is presented in a tachisto-

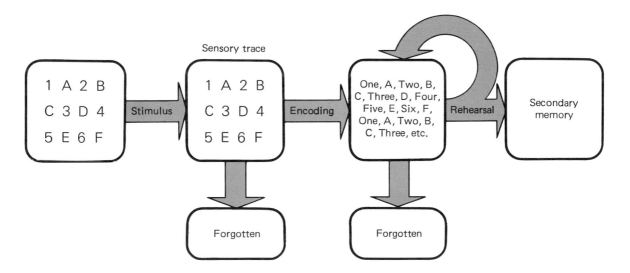

FIGURE 7-6   A model of memory processes. After Norman (1969).

scope, a device which presents visual stimuli at very brief durations. Durations of 50 to 500 milliseconds are commonly used.

When the visual stimulus is followed by a dim blank field, it leaves something like an afterimage, a visible trace estimated to last from 50 milliseconds to 1 second or more. The information in the sensory trace is uncoded, that is, it has not yet been identified in terms of its meaning. As a consequence, one cannot judge whether a letter is named, e.g., A or B, or whether it is a vowel or a consonant. Identification takes time (fractions of a second). The more abstract or superordinate a concept, the longer it takes to decide whether it applies to the input or not. It is believed that adults scan this visual trace just as if they were examining an actual stimulus. As we scan an item in the matrix, we establish its identity and encode it in a more permanent form of storage, short-term memory.

Short-term memory is an intermediate form of storage. The information in STM is forgotten in a number of seconds unless it is given further attention. Often, the information is verbal, particularly when the input is a word, letter, or number. However, when the input is not easily described verbally, or when a subject knows that he will have to use the visual information again shortly, the information in short-term memory may be visual rather than verbal. The way to prolong the life of information in short-term memory is through rehearsal. Without it, most information would be forgotten within 20 seconds.

Rehearsal of verbal information is usually thought of as talking to one's self, while rehearsal of visual information is likened to watching a film. The effects of rehearsal are twofold: (1) to prolong the life of the information in STM and (2) to transfer information from STM to LTM. First, rehearsal rejuvinates the decaying information in STM. It has been suggested that attending to an item in rehearsal is similar to reintroducing the item. In addition, each rehearsal increases the length of time the item can go unrehearsed before being forgotten. As this time increases we speak metaphorically of an item entering LTM. But how rehearsal has its effect on LTM is not yet understood. If we consider memory as a billboard exposed to the extremes of weather and the presentation of the physical stimulus and subsequent rehearsal as a fresh coat of paint, then each presentation or rehearsal increases the thickness of the paint, which, in turn, increases resistance to weathering. Just as we can only say one word at a time, we can only rehearse one word at a time. Because items in STM are forgotten in a few seconds if not rehearsed, the number of items we can hold in STM is limited by how fast we can rehearse them. If the list of items to be remembered is too long, the first members of the list will be forgotten while later ones are being rehearsed.

In recent years, researchers have investigated the development of this information processing system that serves human memory. Since studies of the sensory trace and encoding process require a good deal of cooperation from the subject, no data exist on these topics for children younger than 5 years old.

Short-Term Memory in Children

THE VISUAL TRACE.   By the age of 5, a child's sensory trace is comparable to that of an adult. To measure the number of items available in the visual trace, Sheingold (1971) presented an array like that in Figure 7-7 to 5-year-olds and adults for 100 milliseconds. Then, after a delay of from 0 to 1 seconds, a teardrop indicator was directed to one of eight positions. The subject's task was to report which item had occupied that position. Using this procedure, it is possible to estimate the number of items contained in the visual trace, by calculating the percent of correct responses. If a subject is correct on 100% of the trials, then we assume that 100% of the items are available in the visual trace. Sheingold's results are shown in Figure 7-8. The reports were judged to be based on the visual trace alone during the first 150 milliseconds. Beyond that time, other factors became operative. For the first 150 milliseconds, when children and adults are thought to use information in visual trace, the 5-year-olds were as accurate as the adults. It was estimated that both children and adults began with 7 items available in the visual trace.

Although children have as many items available in the visual trace as adults, 5-year-olds are not as competent in processing a complex stimulus trace. If the stimulus is a single item, there are no differences in the speed with which 5-year-olds and adults perceive the item. However, if the item is only

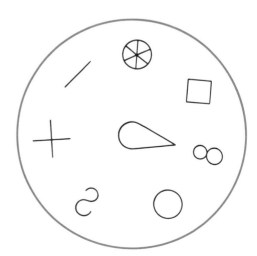

FIGURE 7-7   The stimulus array used by Sheingold (1971). To investigate memory encoding, the teardrop indicator in the center is presented after termination of the array. From Haith (1971).

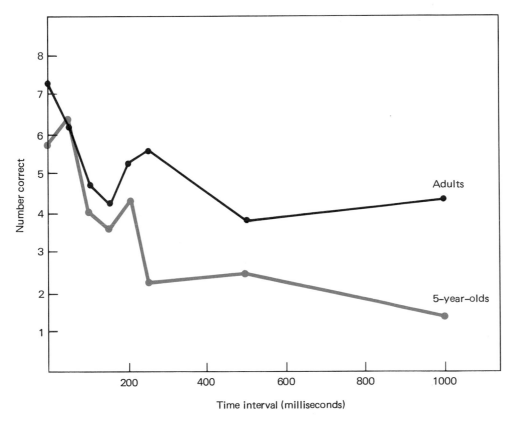

FIGURE 7-8   The number of items identified by 5-year-olds and adults after various delay intervals. From Sheingold (1971).

one of several presented in a compound array, 5-year-olds are much slower than either 10-year-olds or adults in perceiving the presence of the item. The difficulty is in encoding information when irrelevant information is present, not in the encoding process itself. As a consequence, 5-year-olds show a rapid loss of available information at the time the visual trace fades. Haith (1971) has suggested that young children do not know what portions of the array to attend to first. When the stimulus is a single item, or when the teardrop indicator is presented soon enough in the case of a complex stimulus to make the decision for the child, youngsters are as adept as adults.

IMPORTANCE OF EYE MOVEMENTS.   By studying how children look at real pictures, we can get some idea of why young children have trouble with compound arrays. In Figure 7-9 is a pair of pictures that was presented to children and adults who were to decide whether the pictures were the same or

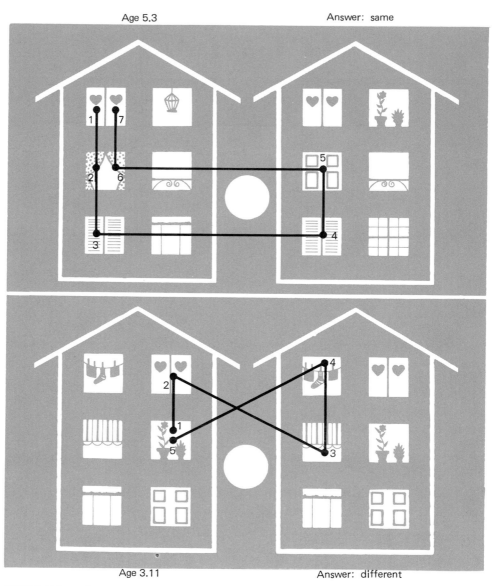

FIGURE 7-9   Examples of children's visual scanning patterns. The points on the scan lines are numbered in order of occurrence. The age of the child and his answer are given below each picture. Adapted from Vurpillot (1968).

not. The darker lines in the figure are typical scanning patterns of children. In order to decide, rather than guess, whether the two pictures are truly identical, it is necessary to examine all the windows. However, as the scanning patterns indicate, younger subjects frequently make their judgment on the basis of inadequate information. Similar immature scanning strategies may also underlie their failure to encode much information from tachistoscopic presentations of compound arrays.

From the Sheingold study, it appears that, after the visual trace has ended, a young child may remember the position of only one or two items in a seven-item array. Presumably, these items have been encoded and identified by the child. As a result of this processing, the items are more resistant to decay than they were in the visual trace, and they may be held as verbal labels rather than visual images. The latter possibility, however, has not yet been demonstrated within this type of task for children.

SHORT-TERM MEMORY CAPACITY.   One very common measure of memory ability is the immediate memory span, i.e., the greatest number of items that can be remembered from a list of items after having seen the list once. As shown in Table 7-1, the memory span is a function of the age of the subject and the nature of the items to be recalled. For a time, these figures were accepted as evidence that retention in STM increases with age. Recently however, it has been questioned whether the developmental improvement in memory span is due to increased retention or to development of acquisition processes like encoding and rehearsal.

Belmont and Butterfield (1971) attempted to determine the role of acquisition and retention factors in a large sample of the research that has been

TABLE 7-1   Development of the Memory Span: The Number of Words and Digits That Can Be Recalled in an Immediate Test at Different Ages[a]

Age (years)	Number of digits recalled	Number of words recalled
2	3	—
4	4	—
6	5	—
8	5	2.1
10	6	3.2
12	6	3.7
.		
.		
.		
18	7	4.7

[a] After Munn (1965).

done on memory development. They reasoned that a memory score is a function of the amount of information that is acquired from an event and the amount of the acquired information that is retained over the retention interval. Furthermore, they proposed that the effects of acquisition ought to be the same at any retention interval, thereby implying that acquisition is over by the time of immediate recall. Therefore, changes in the amount remembered at different retention intervals should reflect only retention factors, with the influence of acquisition factors being equal at all intervals. If one were to plot these data for children and adults, a true difference in retention ability would be reflected by a difference in the slopes of the two curves. An example of what such a graph would look like is presented in Figure 7-10.

From their survey, Belmont and Butterfield concluded that a sizable majority of the studies had failed to find any difference in the retentive ability of children and adults, although most studies did show poorer acquisition with children. Therefore, the development of STM is a reflection of changes in acquisition processes rather than retention factors. Belmont and Butterfield suggested that the acquisition process responsible for the lower scores of chil-

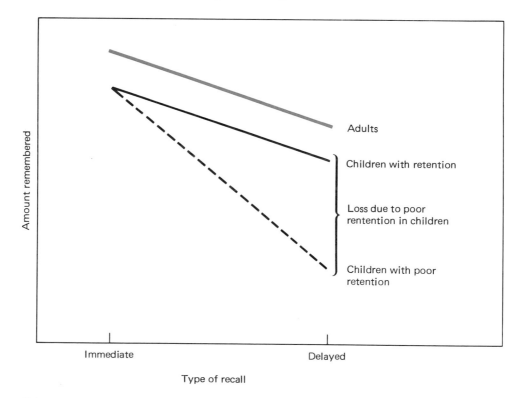

FIGURE 7-10   The hypothetical results of a study allowing separation of acquisition and retention factors. Differences in the slope indicate retention differences only.

dren was rehearsal and subsequent transfer strategies of items from STM to LTM.

THE APPEARANCE OF REHEARSAL MECHANISMS.   One of the major changes occurring in the course of memory development is the appearance of spontaneous rehearsal. When a subject verbally rehearses items in memory, he can often be observed to make lip movements or talk to himself. However, this type of behavior usually does not appear until the age of seven (Flavell, 1970), the same age at which subjects report they use rehearsal to remember items. The failure of children at younger ages to use verbal rehearsal is not due to an inability to do so. Indeed, it is possible to induce 5-year-olds to use verbal rehearsal in memory tasks, and, when they do, their memory scores improve. However, when the impetus to rehearse is removed, most of the children below the age of seven stop rehearsing. It appears that rehearsal can be thought of as a skill learned just as the sensorimotor skills are learned in infancy. There are two elements to acquiring the skill of rehearsal. The first is the problem solving aspect in which the child must discover that he is capable of influencing his own memory performance. This is accomplished at the time of the appearance of spontaneous rehearsal at age seven. The second aspect is the acquisition of specific rehearsal techniques and the ability to adjust the type of rehearsal to the type of task.

The development of specialized forms of rehearsal continues beyond the age at which spontaneous rehearsal appears. One way to study rehearsal is to examine how the subject chooses to distribute the appearance of the items in a list to be remembered. Pauses between items could be an indication of rehearsal of previously presented items. In one such study, 9- and 13-year-olds were given control over the exact time of presentation of each of six items in a list as well as control over the delay between the last item and the test (recall of the serial position of one of the items specified by the experimenter). The results revealed that only the older group responded to the increasing memory load by increasing the amount of rehearsal at later positions. As can be seen in Figure 7-11, the 13-year-olds take increasingly longer pauses between the items in the list. During the pauses, they repeat all exposed items to themselves before presenting the next item. The 9-year-olds use a different strategy, which seems designed to get through the items and on to the test as quickly as they can before all those numbers get confused in memory. The 9-year-olds are actually depending primarily on the brief persistence of unrehearsed items in STM to carry them through the test, but the 13-year-olds doggedly refuse to trust STM before turning to the test. In fact, many adult subjects find it unnecessary to rehearse the very last items much, because they will remain in STM if the test follows immediately. However, the 13-

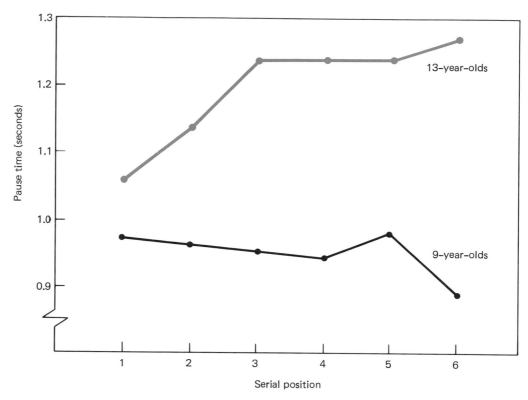

FIGURE 7-11   Average serial pause times for children 9 and 13 years of age. From Belmont and Butterfield (1971).

year-olds do not mix techniques; therefore, they rehearse the entire list after the last item.

Research on memory development has been of growing concern among psychologists. Indeed, most of the research that has been presented here was conducted in the last few years. Because the area is so new, many issues have yet to be resolved. However, there are some significant facts emerging from the recent work. Psychologists have found that an information processing model of memory, which is composed of several interconnected stages of representation, is a useful way of thinking about human memory. Within such a framework, we have seen that memory development occurs in only some of the stages. The sensory trace is mature by the age of five, and it has been suggested that retentiveness does not increase with age when other operations like rehearsal are ruled out (although it remains to be seen what retentiveness in this sense means in terms of the model). However, the processes of encoding from complex inputs, like a matrix of symbols, and the rehearsal of the encoded information show definite developmental improvement. Neither encoding of complex arrays nor spontaneous rehearsal of encoded items are mature at 5 years of age. Spontaneous rehearsal appears near age seven and continues to show refinements in style beyond that age.

CONCEPTUAL DEVELOPMENT

Concept is a psychological term referring to the apparent organization of sensory input on the basis of attributes shared by sensory events. Concepts are themselves organized into conceptual systems. Concepts of square, round, and triangular are considered subsets of the concept shape. Similarly, red, green, and blue are subsets of the concept color. And these concepts of shape and color are themselves subsets of the concept appearance. The world of the human adult is permeated with concepts. The words of his language are labels for many of the concepts an adult uses. Other concepts may have no word to identify them, although they may be communicated to some extent in a phrase or sentence.

The organization of experience reflected in a conceptual system has its effect on the way an organism deals with sensory inputs. A concept can enable us to respond to aspects of an event that are not present in the percept itself. For example, one of the attributes of the concept cup is its ability to contain things. We do not have to see the open end of something we recognize as a cup in order to appreciate this. In fact, we do not have to see a cup at all. Obviously, an organism, which has not learned that cuplike shapes have this property, could only react to it if the cup were present in the sensory input. The conceptual level used by the organism in dealing with experiences can determine its understanding of what has occurred. For example, as noted previously, preschool children generally do not have the concept of conservation, that is, they believe that the size, weight, and quantity of physical stimuli are changed simply by a change in the shape or arrangement of the physical stimulus. Adults on the other hand believe that these attributes can be altered only by addition or subtraction. As a consequence, the child interprets the change in a row of blocks, as shown in Figure 7-12, differently than the adult. The child, who agrees that top and bottom rows have the same number of blocks in (a), says that there are more on top after the rows are rearranged as in (b).

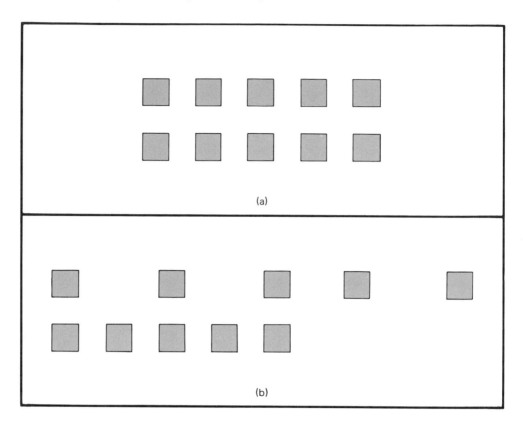

FIGURE 7-12   A conservation of number experiment demonstrating how conceptual organization can affect a subject's understanding of physical stimuli. In (a) children say that each row has same number of blocks, whereas in (b) they say that the top row has more blocks.

Critical Attributes in Concept Development

We infer the existence of a concept from an organism's behavior. An organism that makes a common or equivalent response to a variety of sensory events, all of which share certain attributes, is said to have the concept that is defined by those attributes. For example, laboratory rats have learned to select a triangular shape in preference to other shapes in order to gain access to food. From the common response made to the triangular shape, we might infer that these rats have the concept of triangularity. However, it would be an error to do so.

Care must be taken in establishing just what the critical attributes are, whether the subjects are rats or people. This example is instructive, for it highlights one of the errors that can occur if we do not take care in isolating the critical features of the stimulus. Indeed, the rats were responding conceptually, but further investigation revealed that the critical feature of the stimulus was not its triangularity but, rather, the shape of the lower part of the figure. As this example shows, equivalent responding need not reflect an underlying concept similar to that of the adult human. There are many analogous processes producing behaviors that are identical on their surface but that are actually due to quite different events. Very early in his life, a child shows signs of conceptual activity similar to that found in the adult, but the conceptual structures underlying the behavior are not similar at all.

The Development of Classification

A child's first concepts, i.e., categories of stimulus attributes that elicit equivalent responses, are closely tied to action and appearance. An infant develops many sensorimotor routines or schemes and applies them to different objects around him. Rocking, shaking, throwing, dropping, sucking, and eating are all activities the infant may use to classify an object. The infant is like a chemist trying to identify the elements of an unknown substance. Both go through a battery of tests and judge the novel element on the basis of the results. The difference is that the chemist can group substances on the basis of his results, but an infant 6 to 12 months of age shows no tendency to assemble objects into the categories he uses.

Infants also show preferences for certain visual stimuli like human faces. Such preferences may indicate early conceptual organization. As early as 12 months of age, an infant can separate a group of objects into two classes on the basis of perceptual attributes (Ricciuti, 1965). In a previously mentioned study of depth perception (Bower, 1964), infants younger than 6 months of age were apparently classifying objects in terms of real size and distance.

During the first 12 months of infancy, there is little or no evidence of perceptual and sensorimotor concepts in the absence of the objects to which they apply, that is, there is no evidence that the infant can make use of these modes of classification without real objects to apply them to. Yet, adults can easily work with conceptual categories and relations with no support from their physical referents. The difference is one of representation.

Symbolic Representation

We are able to represent sensory experiences to ourselves through imagery, e.g., visual, auditory, tactile, etc., or through language. The child does not develop these modes of representation until between 12 and 18 months of age. At that time, several changes in the child's behavior signal the appearance of symbolic representation. The first is deferred imitation. Piaget cites an incident with his daughter who observed a little boy having a temper tantrum in his playpen. On the next day the girl began stamping her feet, shouting, and trying to move her playpen, just as the boy had done a day earlier. This was unusual for the girl, who, as Piaget notes, had never witnessed such a scene before. Logically, the girl must have held some representation of the tantrum during the interval from its termination to her imitation of it, and was able to recall it without the presence of the original event. The second sign of representative activity is symbolic play. Here the child pretends that an object is something else. For example, the child treats a block of wood as if it were a car, pushing it around and making carlike noises. The third change is the appearance of language through which the child can express thoughts about past and future events or about conditions contrary to fact.

The Acquisition of Symbolic Behavior

Piaget (1962) attributes the absence of these types of activities at an earlier age to a representational deficit. It is his opinion that younger infants are capable of sensorimotor representation only, and that activation of sensorimotor representation is quite dependent on the presence of the physical referent or a context closely associated with the referent. The development of language and imagery in particular is linked to progress in sensorimotor representation in the following way. The infant's conceptual knowledge of the world is limited to his active experience with it. Through sensorimotor exploration in the form of grasping, sucking, rocking, tasting, looking, etc., the infant builds up categories of objects and actions. Having thus handled objects for almost a year, the infant can predict certain features of objects or actions before actually experiencing them. Because the visual–motor routines become so familiar, they can run off by themselves. What is not clear in Piaget's account is how the overlearned motor habits become symbolic images. This is a major difficulty, of course. Whatever the mechanism, there is independent evidence that well-learned motor habits can come to be represented as images. Mandler (1962) reported a study in which adult subjects learned to solve a complex maze of toggle switches without being able to see the maze itself. The training was continued for some time, even after the subjects had mastered the maze. Some of these adult subjects, who initially solved the maze by sequential motor habit, reported that they now had an image of the path through the maze that guided their movements. While this study does not provide an answer to how transfer takes place, it does demonstrate that transfer can occur.

Attributes and Class Formation

Even with the development of symbolic representation, the child continues to organize his experiences into categories based on action and appearance. For this reason, a child's concepts share a concreteness that adult concepts are able to transcend. In addition, the rules of classification (the formal structure of a class and its relation to other classes) are different for a child than for an adult. These discrepancies between child and adult, in the attributes selected when organizing objects and events into classes and in the rules that specify how attributes can be used to form classes, are seen most clearly when the type of classificatory activity that is presumed to underlie concept formation and organization is brought into the open. This has been possible through the use of sorting tasks that require subjects to group words, pictures, or objects into "groups that go together."

Using a sorting task with thirty-three objects (real and toy tools, silverware, a ball, a bicycle bell, etc.), Reichard, Schneider, and Rapaport (1944) traced the changes in the attributes of classes constructed by children between 4 and 14 years of age. The subjects constructed groups of their own and defined them in addition to groups constructed by the experimenters. At the youngest ages, children were found who defined groups in terms of concrete attributes of the objects, i.e., characteristics of the objects' appearance. A pear and a banana, for example, might be in the same class because they are both yellow. From 6 to 9 years of age, children used both functional, i.e., a pear can be eaten and so can a banana, and nominal-conceptual attributes, i.e., fruits. In terms of adult conceptual categories, only the last is an adequate definition. Banana and pear are logically related by their common feature, fruit. Color and use are only incidental to this semantic relation between them.

The same shift with increasing age from groups based on perceptual attributes to those based on functional attributes to those based on nominal-conceptual attributes was reported by Olver and Hornsby (1966). Their results (Figure 7-13) make it clear that, between the ages of 6 and 19, there are no abrupt changes from one type of definition to another. In fact, at all ages there was a preponderance of functional definitions. The greatest amount of perceptual grouping (30%) occurs with 6-year-olds and decreases thereafter, while the amount of verbal-conceptual grouping increases with age.

It should be emphasized here that the type of attribute used by a child is also affected by the nature of the task and the form of instruction he is given. Olver and Hornsby found that, at all ages tested, pictures were grouped on a concrete-perceptual level more often than were the words referring to the pictured objects. Conversely, words were grouped more often on a func-

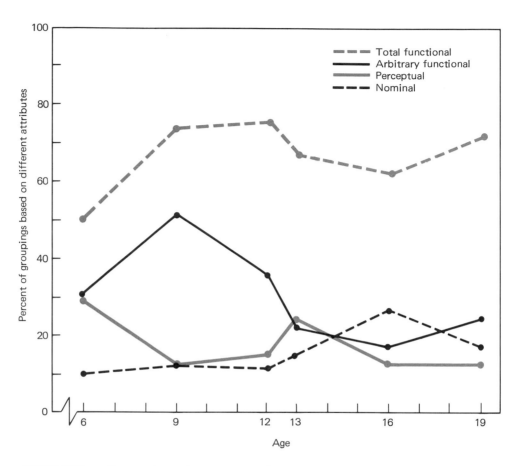

FIGURE 7-13   Percent of groupings based on different attributes. From Olver and Hornsby (1966).

tional level than were the pictures of their referents. As for instructions, In-helder and Piaget (1964) found that a young child (4 to 6 years of age) will group objects differently if told to "put together whatever is alike" than he will if told to "put together whatever goes together." "Whatever is alike" leads to groups based on physical similarity, whereas "whatever goes together" leads to functional groups based on shared contexts, e.g., a doll, cows, sheep, horses, and chickens belong together because "the woman [is] bringing in all the cows and the sheep and the horses and all the chickens."

Choosing Attributes: Three Rules

Children use attributes differently than adults in deciding what objects belong in a group and how that group is related to other groups. Olver and

Hornsby describe three types of rules used at different ages in forming groups: thematic, complexive, and superordinate.

THEMATIC GROUPING.   At the youngest ages, one of the common responses is thematic grouping. The child brings several objects together in a spontaneous, unconventional theme. The theme may be a story if the items are common objects, or it may be a design or pattern if the items are geometric shapes. The 4-year-old child who grouped cows, sheep, horses, chickens, and a doll together used a thematic rule. The doll was bringing in all the animals. In Figure 7-14, a symmetrical pattern and the construction of several houses are the thematic basis for a collection of geometric shapes made by a 5-year-old. The attributes that serve in the collection are both perceptual (symmetry) and functional (can be made into a house).

COMPLEXIVE GROUPING.   Along with thematic grouping, we find another type of organizing principle used by young children, called complexive grouping. The hallmark of a complexive group is the inconsistency with which a group is formed. The collection of shapes in Figure 7-14 has complexive elements about it in the sense that the child used several different attributes

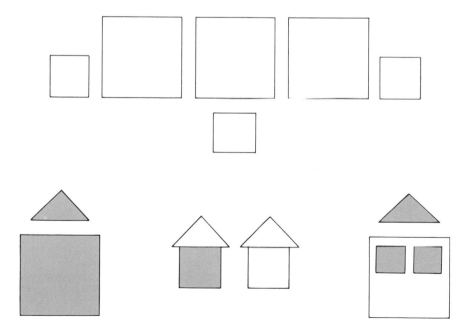

FIGURE 7-14   A collection of geometric shapes assembled by a 5-year-old. The collection has elements of thematic and complexive grouping based on both perceptual and functional attributes. After Olver and Hornsby (1966).

to make the collection: identity of color and shape in the upper portion, overall symmetry, and elements capable of forming a house in the lower portion. Another example of complexive grouping taken from Inhelder and Piaget (1964) is seen in Figure 7-15, which shows the steps in which a 3-year-old built up the final pattern. This child began by placing a yellow triangle next to a yellow square (color). He next placed a red triangle below the yellow triangle (shape). Finally, he placed a red square below the yellow square (shape, color, and symmetry). At this point the group looks very well planned, i.e., a 2 by 2 matrix based on color and form. But this apparently is not

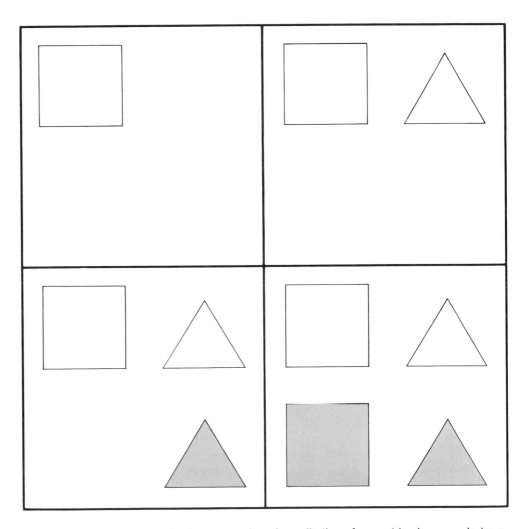

FIGURE 7-15   Four steps in the construction of a collection of geometric shapes made by a 3-year-old. After Inhelder and Piaget (1964).

what the child has in mind, because the red square is then removed and a blue one is put in its place (shape).

The thematic and complexive groupings reveal some of the shortcomings (from the adult's point of view) of a child's conceptual system. First, the child seems to lack any foresight for what kind of collection he is about to form. He proceeds step by step, changing from the criteria of shape to color to overall pattern as he moves along. A typical adult response would be to divide the geometric forms into groups all based on either color or form, and then to subdivide the groups thus constructed into subgroups on the basis of the remaining attribute, with the result being a matrix based on color and form. Second, the child's collections are often nonexhaustive, that is, the child fails to include in a group all the available objects that fill his definition of the group. Thus, he may construct a group of triangles and squares and leave several of these shapes unused in the pile from which he has been selecting the items. Third, the child is often inconsistent in the way he applies a critical attribute. He may put several squares in a group along with a single triangle, which may not be related to the other items at all or, if so, related in a different way.

SUPERORDINATE GROUPING.   Beginning around 5 years of age, according to Inhelder and Piaget (1964), there is a decrease in complexive and thematic sorting in favor of groups based on logical classes. This type of response is called superordinate grouping. It differs from earlier types of groups in that a group is composed of elements sharing one or more attributes, and all available elements possessing the critical attribute(s) are included in the group. In addition, the subgroups are themselves used as members of superordinate groups, which are defined by attributes common to all subgroups. Olver and Hornsby report that 50% of their 6-year-old subjects grouped items in this way and that the percentage increased to 100% by 19 years of age. This change in sorting has been attributed to the older child's understanding of a class as both a collection of elements and a defining attribute that these elements share.

The three types of rules for sorting, i.e., thematic, complexive, and superordinate, describe overt behaviors, but they also presumably are suggestive of the organization of the child's conceptual system. It is not so much that the preschool child actually has a stable concept of food items, for instance, based on the complexive rule "a banana is yellow, and a peach is red and yellow, . . . and a potato is light flesh, and meat is brown" as this definition from one of Olver and Hornsby's subjects would suggest. On the contrary, such a group and its definition are undoubtedly a spontaneous solution to the problem posed by the experimenter, a solution that might change in a matter of hours or days. The child has most likely never thought of how such a collection might be related before and may forget his answer soon afterward. The sorting task results are suggestive of conceptual organization of the youngest children only in so far as they provide an idea of how the children go about organizing their experiences when they have cause to. Any other interpretation of these results without additional supporting evidence would be unwarranted.

Concept Development: Is It Hierarchical?

Piaget presents an example of the discrepancy that may exist between the picture of the child's conceptual system inferred from sorting tasks and that inferred from other tasks. As we have said, beyond 5 years of age, a child may construct a collection consisting of groups defined by attributes shared by all members. These groups are exhaustive and appear to be hierarchically organized. However, according to Piaget, the hierarchical organization of collections made prior to 8 years of age or so is only apparent, not real. Not until 7 or 8 years of age does the child actually understand, in an abstract way, the relation between superordinate and subordinate classes. A younger child's appreciation that a class is the sum of its subclasses is very fragile and is easily suppressed. In fact, he may only be able to use this knowledge when aligning real objects. Anything that requires the 5- to 8-year-old to think about a set and its subsets in one operation will be difficult.

To demonstrate this difficulty with hierarchical relations, we simply need to ask the child to compare an entire class with one of its subclasses in some way. For example, we can show a 5-year-old an assortment of fruits consisting of four oranges, two apples, and a pear. Generally, it is easy to get the child to name each of the fruits and to refer to the entire collection as fruit. Furthermore, the child responds correctly to the instruction "Show me all the . . . (e.g., fruits)," and can count the number in each group (although such counting may be based on a simple routine rather than on an understanding of quantity). Up to this point, the 5-year-old appears to have a good grasp of what is going on. But simply ask him if there are more bananas or more fruit and the difficulty is revealed. He will answer that there are more bananas. What the child is doing is comparing the 4 bananas with the fruits that are not bananas, the two apples and one pear, and concludes that four is greater than three. Predictably, the same child will answer that there are more fruit if asked to compare all the fruit with the apples, because the two apples are less than the five other pieces of fruit. Although the child can think simultaneously about classes at the same level of organization, he must break up a superordinate group in order to consider a subgroup; therefore, he cannot reason about both in a single problem. To resolve the difficulty, the child interprets the question as a request to compare the named subset of fruits with the unnamed complementary subset.

Based on the developmental characteristics of classification revealed in the sorting tasks just discussed, we can make some predictions about the nature of concepts children of different ages use. In terms of attributes defining a concept, young children are strongly influenced by perceptual appearance and sensorimotor aspects of objects and activities. Color, shapes, sounds of objects, and typical actions or contexts in which an object is found are features that can bind an object to another in thought. Furthermore, the rules of organization are sublogical. A concept is not determined by a feature or features common to all members, but is defined in a complexive way so that one item may be included because of its color and another because it is commonly found near other members of the concept.

Concepts and the Appearance of Language

A child's first words, which are labels for some of his concepts, offer ample evidence of these characteristics. One child used the word "qua-qua" to refer to both ducks and water, a complexive rule combining both physical similarity between different ducks and between different instances of water, and shared context between ducks and water, which are usually found together. The word "afta" was used to mean drinking glass, pane of glass, window, as well as what was drunk from the glass (Werner, 1948). There is no simple, straightforward way to determine the basis on which the child assembled these disparate items under one name. However, physical similarity between drinking glass and pane of glass, and shared context between drinking glass and its contents, on the one hand, and between window and pane of glass, on the other hand, are possibilities. The strongest evidence for the use of perceptual-functional attributes and thematic-complexive organization in a young child's verbal concepts is not the accuracy of an individual interpretation of the meaning of the child's words. It is indeed difficult to establish a single interpretation. The strength of the argument comes instead from the fact that of all the reasonable interpretations of a word's meaning, so many of them are of a sublogical nature. For example, Piaget's daughter first used the onomatopoeic sound "tch-tch" to indicate a passing train seen from her window. Later, she used the sound for any moving thing (cars, carriages, people) seen from another window, then any noise from the street, and finally for Piaget himself when he played peek-a-boo with her (appearing and disappearing like the train) (Piaget, 1962, p. 216).

The Appearance of Logic

As a child's conceptual system develops and becomes more stable, there is an increased use of logical concepts as mediators of sensory input. The child is interpreting the information present in the input in terms of the concepts with which he is familiar. Also, when the particular instance of a concept does not quite match anything in the child's stored information, he can adapt the stored information to fit the new facts. These processes of assimilating sensory information in terms of the child's organization and accommodating that organization to account for new data are very general and probably play a role in the functioning of all organisms (Piaget, 1952). We shall examine just two studies in which the organization that a subject imposes on his experience influences the ease with which he can learn the solution to a problem, or the ease with which he can learn the solution to a new but related problem.

Sometime between the ages of 5 and 8 years, children learn the principle of transitivity. If a transitive relation exists between elements A and B and elements B and C, it follows necessarily that the same relation holds between the elements A and C. For example, if A is longer than B, and B is longer than C, then it follows that A is longer than C. Youniss and Furth (1965) have studied the influence of transitive relations on problem-solving with kindergarten, first grade, and third grade children. The task was to learn which of three balls would push one another off an inclined plane. In the experiment the balls were the same size but different colors. For some of the subjects, the relationship between the balls was transitive, i.e., one ball (A) could push both the others (B and C) off the incline, a second ball (B) could push one (C) but not the other (A) off, and the third ball (C) could push no ball off the incline. For the rest of the subjects, the relationship between the balls was intransitive, with the relation between A and C being reversed so that C pushed A off the incline.

Force, like length, conforms to a transitive principle, and an adult would expect such a relation to hold in this study as well. Seeing that A could move B, and B move C, an adult would expect that A also would move C. Therefore, it should be easier for someone who understands and uses the principle of transitivity to solve the transitive task than to solve the intransitive one.

The results were that the older subjects (first and third graders), who were expected to have a grasp of transitivity, did, in fact, learn the transitive problem faster than the intransitive problem. However, this type of relation had no effect on problem difficulty for the kindergarten subjects, presumably because they either did not or could not use intuitions about transitivity in reaching the solution. The Youniss and Furth task is simple and the results are clear. In processing sensory information, the way in which the information is organized depends in part on the organization of the subjects' conceptual system.

SUMMARY

We have seen some of the general developmental changes that characterize the growth of the child. In order to form a concept, for example, it is necessary to perceive and abstract attributes of a stimulus and to notice some equivalence between various sensory events. In the infant, the common attributes are aspects of physical appearance and action or function. Although it was not mentioned, it should be clear that many of the concepts a child will acquire in the course of development will be shaped by adults around him and may be found only in the culture in which he lives. The attributes that define these concepts may not be so apparent or accessible to the child as the attributes he uses to form his first concepts. Some degree of perceptual learning, i.e., learning to attend to critical attributes of a stimulus not immediately apparent, will be a prerequisite for the acquisition of these concepts. Language and vocabulary growth are a primary factor in the development of cultural concepts. A child's first attempts at verbal reference (using words) may be formed around diffuse concepts, which an adult would not ordinarily use. Presumably, as a child begins to use words that sound approximately like those of his language, his elders begin to guide him in the proper referential use and, in so doing, teach him which attributes are critical to the definition of particular words. As a child learns to look for those conventional attributes, his conceptual system becomes culturally standardized. This is reflected in the age-related changes in the sorting tasks from idiosyncratic to superordinate groupings.

SUGGESTED READINGS

LAVATELLI, C. S., & STENDLER, F. (Eds.) *Readings in child behavior and development.* (3rd ed.) New York: Harcourt, 1972.

MUSSEN, P. H., CONGER, J. J., & Kagan, J. *Child development and personality.* (3rd ed.) New York: Harper, 1969.

PIAGET, J., & INHELDER, B. *The psychology of the child.* New York: Basic Books, 1969.

REESE, H. W., & LIPSITT, L. P. *Experimental child psychology.* New York: Academic Press, 1970.

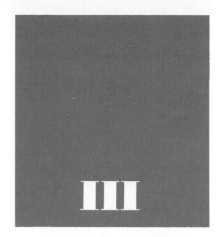

Measuring
Behavior

8

Statistical
Concepts in
Psychological
Research

In 1927, Zeigarnik, a student of the eminent social theorist Kurt Lewin, tested an idea predicated on Lewin's concept of "valences," that is, positive and negative forces in an individual's cognitive life space. She suggested that a task begun by an individual but left incompleted would generate a negative "valence," creating psychological tension relative to that task and consequently elevating its level of availability in memory. To test her notions she set up twenty elementary tasks and instructed her subjects to complete these within certain time limits. For each subject, she selected ten tasks for which the subject was given enough time to complete and ten that were interrupted before completion. After this part of the experiment, the subjects were asked to recall the various tasks they had attempted. Ziegarnik expected that the incomplete tasks would be selected out for retention. She then calculated the I/C ratio, where I is the number of incompleted tasks recalled by the subject and C is the number of completed tasks recalled. Since the average I/C score for her subjects was numerically greater than one, she concluded that the tension theory had been confirmed because the ratio of number of incompleted tasks to completed tasks recalled exceeded one. Consider the data for two hypothetical subjects in this experiment. Subject A recalled two I tasks and four C tasks, with $I/C = 0.5$. Subject

B recalled four I tasks and two C tasks with $I/C = 2.0$. The average I/C ratio is then $(2 + 1/2)2 = 1.25$ which is greater than one.

Subject	I	C	I/C
A	2	4	0.5
B	4	2	2.0
Average			1.25

Consider this same experiment from the point of view of a modern reinforcement theorist. He would assert that completion of a task would be a positive reinforcing event; therefore, the completed task would be more likely to be recalled than a nonreinforcing incompleted task. Consequently he would assert that the proper measure for the results would be the C/I ratio rather than the I/C ratio. If the average C/I ratio for a group of subjects proved to be greater than one, then this reinforcement theory would be confirmed. Suppose he uses this new measure on the same data from our two hypothetical subjects. For Subject A, $C/I = 4/2 = 2$; for Subject B, $C/I = 0.5$. The average C/I ratio is then $(2.0 + 0.5)/2 = 1.25$.

Subject	I	C	C/I
A	2	4	2.0
B	4	2	0.5
Average			1.25

Thus, using the very same data, he has proved the opposite theory.

How can a simple change in the way the same data is analyzed cause it simultaneously to support two opposite theories at once? The error in this case arises from the erroneous measures I/C and C/I. The proper measure to use is a difference score, $I - C$. If this is positive, the result favors Zeigarnik; if negative, the reinforcement theorist. By this measure, neither theory receives support from our hypothetical subjects.

Subject	I	C	I − C
A	2	4	−2
B	4	2	+2
Average			0

In reality, when Zeigarnik's data were analyzed using the proper measure $I - C$, rather than the improper measure I/C, the effect was still shown to exist. Nevertheless, it should be clear from this example that the selection of the proper measure and appropriate statistical treatment plays a most important role in interpreting the results of our experiments. Statistical methods are vital tools for psychologists, but these tools must be used skillfully.

BEYOND COMMON SENSE

How does the psychologist advance our understanding of the nature of man? He must have ideas, theories, and educated guesses to guide his investigations, but so must the artist, the author, and the philosopher. What distinguishes the psychologist from these other investigators of man's thought and action are the criteria he maintains for determining what is fact.

For many years, psychological inquiry was an armchair enterprise, with common sense dictating belief. But in the last hundred years, psychologists have moved out of their armchairs and into the world, or they have brought the world into their laboratories by observing carefully controlled experiments. Hopefully, our understanding of ourselves can advance beyond the level of common sense by developing theories in the light of observed fact; however, this is not easily done.

A fact should be objective. How then can man's view of himself be objective? Other sciences have developed an objective viewpoint by creating a system of measurement. Indeed, the sciences of physics, astronomy, and chemistry could never have developed to their current high level of knowledge without developing extensive measuring systems. However, for the psychologist, measurement is an art. Physical dimensions, e.g., distance, time, weight, seem naturally suited for measurement, but what are the dimensions of the mind? Or should we ask what constitutes an act of behavior? These fundamental questions are still matters of controversy. Consequently, measurement in psychology can hardly be considered systematical. Each area and subarea have developed their own measurements with new ones continually arising. But, in general, it is widely accepted that, in order to get beyond a common sense description of man's behavior, we must be able to define meaningful and objective measurements. Therefore, we must critically evaluate the numbers that psychologists collect in their research.

THREE AREAS OF MEASUREMENT

The descriptive measurements made by psychologists vary widely, and the types of statistical analyses applied to them depend upon the type of measurement. We will consider three different levels of behavioral studies and their associated statistical considerations. These three areas have been chosen because the measurements and statistical methods are representative of the problems encountered in most psychological research.

Group Differences

The first of these is the interview study of the characteristics and differences of large groups. This kind of study is exemplified by the well-known Gallup political opinion polls, the Neilson television preference surveys, and numerous consumer surveys. The measurements taken in these studies are simple countings of responses such as "yes" and "no," "Democrat" and "Republican," or in some instances quasi numerical responses such as "never," "occasionally," and "often." The results of such surveys are used to predict the successful candidate, guide the development of products, or assess the current practices and beliefs of different groups. They can also be misused to promote self-serving ideas; therefore, they require critical evaluation.

Individual Differences

A second level of psychological measurement is in the applied area of individual differences. These may be differences in personality as measured by the Minnesota Multiphasic Personality Inventory (MMPI), a paper and pencil inventory which is taken to reflect pathology, or the well-known Rorschach Inkblot Test, a projective test of personality.

Tests such as the Scholastic Aptitude Test or the Stanford-Binet Intelligence Test may also measure differences in ability. These tests examine the individual's behavior in a microcosm of the world of activity to which the tests are intended to apply. Intelligence tests pose a series of intellectual problems that require cleverness to solve. The problems are usually contentless, like the puzzle games sold in novelty stores. Their solution depends not so much on learned skills and abilities as they do on pure cleverness and problem-solving ability. The results from these tests are numerical scores, which are used to compare the individual's skills or traits to those of others.

These comparisons are used to determine a future course of action such as selecting a type of therapy or determining psychological fitness for some job, position, or training level. For example, the Graduate Record Exam is used to help determine the fitness of a candidate for graduate school; and an intelligence test is used to group students by ability.

Individual Processes

The third level of behavioral study concerns psychological processes within individuals. Studies of these processes comprise most of what is called experimental psychology. These involve the study of processes that are assumed to be characteristic of all individuals, e.g., attending, perceiving, learning, remembering. The primary method used is controlled experimentation. The method at this level of behavioral observation differs from the two previously described in that the scientist is no longer a passive observer, but acts to manipulate behavior before observing the results.

The experimenter may ask a person to learn a list of words and then see what type of intervening activity will interfere with his recall of the list. He may stimulate the eye of a cat and note the activity in a nerve in some part of the eye or brain. He may ask how strongly a person agrees with certain statements of attitudes and then present persuasive messages to alter these attitudes. A man traveling to the moon might even try to project his thought images over thousands of miles and see if a counterpart on earth can correctly identify the images. An experiment of this type was attempted with some success by Edgar Mitchell, one of the U.S. Astronauts, on a recent trip to the moon according to *Time*.

> *A-O.K., ESP*
>
> While there are still plenty of people who associate extrasensory perception with science fiction movies and low laughs from nightclub comics, there is also a growing number of scientists who believe that ESP is as worthwhile as reaching for the stars. Among these Astronaut Edgar Mitchell, U.S.N., reported last week on his ESP experiments conducted during the flight of Apollo 14 last February.
>
> Mitchell made pre-flight arrangements with four people to beam them, telepathically, various symbols in random sequence. He attempted transmission during four rest periods on the flight, then had the results checked after his return.
>
> By normative statistical measurements the findings were

significant. Mitchell scored 51 hits on his recipients' consciousness out of 200, where chance allows for only 40. According to the laws of probability, the odds against such a score are 20 to 1. Still, it is rather discomforting to think of a space-age Lamont Cranston peering into the minds of earthlings as he sails among the stars [*Time*, July 5, 1971].

EVALUATION OF PSYCHOLOGICAL MEASUREMENT

Prior Considerations: When Do Numbers Count?

Psychological numbers are easy to get, but intuitively they do not have the same status as inches, pounds, or other physical measurements. The quantities the numbers are supposed to represent are illusive. They are difficult to grasp between the finger and thumb, and warrant careful investigation before we can trust them.

Whom do you know who actually watches the television shows with the highest Neilson ratings? What have consumer surveys provided us with besides the Edsel? And why are you studying to be a psychologist when the preference test scores show that you ought to like being a mechanic or draftsman? Consider the slick magazine personality tests on such topics as "Can your marriage succeed?" or "How do you rate as a lover?". You answer the fifty or so questions, tabulate the number for your score, and check the description or rating category into which you fall. Then, in disappointment, you may well ask whether the test is any good or not. Why should you believe the results? Closer to home, you take a multiple choice exam that proports to measure the knowledge of the subject matter presented in an introductory psychology course. Again you may disappointedly ask, "Who made up those lousy questions?" You feel you know the material, but the test was unfair. Somehow there was a failure to measure what was supposed to be measured.

These same doubts can be expressed for any type of psychological measurement, and there has to be some means of systematically evaluating psychological scores. Hopefully the material that follows will put these means at your disposal.

Reliability

Consider first the assertion about the psychology exam questions. What would your score have been if someone else had made up different questions or if a different type of measurement, e.g., an essay exam had been used? Your exam score would probably be different from the one you got. But just how different would it be? One or two points wouldn't make much difference, but maybe it would vary by one or two grades.

The basic question posed by these considerations is one concerning the reliability of the measurement. A measurement can be of little value if, upon repeated testing of the same element, a widely differing score is obtained. All measurements, e.g., survey questionnaires, psychological tests, scores indicating performance in an experimental task, should yield similar scores on remeasurement. Certainly if the gas gauge on your car indicates empty one minute and full the next and then empty again, it would not be a very useful index of the internal state of the gas tank. Nor would you be able to tell when you are about to run out of gasoline. To be useful, a measure must have reasonable consistency. If it does not, then it cannot be measuring anything.

Of course, in psychological measurement, the retesting procedure must be subtle and take account of the effects of prior measurement. For example, there exist several alternate forms of the Stanford-Binet Intelligence Test, different sets of questions that attempt to measure the same ability. If all were administered to the same person, they should yield similar I.Q. scores; if not, the test cannot be measuring intelligence. Similarly, if you broke down your introductory psychology test into two parts, you could consider them as alternative forms of the test. Tabulating the score you would get on odd-numbered questions ought to produce reasonably similar scores or the test is not reliably measuring your knowledge.

Validity

Reliability is necessary, but it is not enough to satisfy our doubts about psychological measurements. To be useful, the scores must measure what they purport to measure. In other words, they must have validity. For example, your gas gauge may give a consistent measurement, always reading full. But if the needle is shorted out, then the measure is useless for fuel information. It may only indicate that the battery is still charged. Similarly, an I.Q. score might repeatedly yield the same score for you upon retesting, but does it really measure intellectual ability? The Nielsen ratings may be consistent, but are people really watching those shows?

The election pollster is perhaps most lucky in the matter of determining the validity of his measurements. When the vote is actually taken, he can directly assess the validity of his predictions. The problem of determining the validity of a measurement or an experimental result is a harder one, but it is basic to the determination of what is fact and what is fiction. For tests, validity is determined usually by the usefulness of the measure in predicting success or failure in some future course of action. For experimentation, the validity of the measure used relates to whether what is being measured is what the experiment was designed to measure. For example, the ability to learn or recall a list of words may depend less on pure memory, which is supposedly what is being measured, and more on previous familiarity with the items.

To determine the validity of a measure, there must be some criterion external to the measure by which we can gauge its usefulness. Persons successfully engaged in intellectual vocations should have higher I.Q.'s on the average than others, and high I.Q. persons should do better in school work where intellect is presumably required. Persons who are advanced in the field of psychology should do well on introductory psychology exams.

SAMPLES AND POPULATIONS: WHOM DO YOU MEASURE?

All psychological studies involve measurements taken from a relatively few individuals. These results are then used to make general statements about a large number of individuals.

Surveys usually reach about 1000 persons and are used to infer the needs, beliefs, viewing habits, and voting intentions of millions. Most personality tests were developed from the responses of a few thousand persons. In the experimental lab, studies in perception or learning and memory typically use twenty or thirty subjects and often only one or two.

The people used in these tests are chosen to be representative of some larger group, which is called a population. Populations are usually so large in size that it is not feasible to measure everyone. Only a part of the population is measured, and this part is called a sample.

Samples should be representative of a population. Surprisingly, the best way to ensure representativeness is to choose the subjects by a completely random selection procedure. Each individual is assigned a number, and then a set of random numbers is used to select the individuals actually measured. Random sampling ensures that every element in the population has an equal chance of being selected. More importantly, it assures that a systematic unrepresentativeness, a biased selection, does not occur. However, this ideal is rarely achieved. Even though pollsters are highly trained, they will often decide to call at a neatly kept house rather than at a run-down house across the street. If no one is at home, they sometimes call next door. It is easy to see how a biased report can result. Gallup is aware that a systematic conservative bias creeps into his political polls, and the results must be corrected because of it.

·The worst extreme of sampling methods is the volunteer or handy sample. It is easy to imagine how representative the findings of a sex survey would be if only volunteers were sampled. Yet this approach is often taken. Before any measurements are considered valid enough to be generalized to a population, a careful examination of the sampling method is required.

Most experimental studies use handy samples, usually students in beginning psychology courses. But the experimenter manipulates the conditions of measurement and usually includes a condition called a control group, which establishes a base line for measurement of the experimental effect. As long as the subjects in his handy sample are assigned at random to the conditions, experimental or control, no systematic bias between conditions should exist. Ideally the only systematic difference between the groups is the experimental manipulation and is presumably the cause of any systematic differences in the observed measures. This special logic permits a cautious generalization from a handy sample in experimental work.

SAMPLING VARIABILITY

Individual results from samples are, in a sense, historical accidents and of little interest per se. If a study were repeated, a completely different sample might well be chosen, and a somewhat different result might be obtained. If a test were readministered, different scores might well result. What we would like to have is measurement of an entire population. We would like to know the "true" I.Q. score for every individual. Since this ideal is usually denied through expense or impossibility, we are forced to estimate the population values from the few measurements we make in the sample. It is for this reason that statistical properties of samples are considered.

Of course, the larger the sample size the better our estimates of these measures will be. But how large is large enough? As we said, the Nielsen ratings try to determine the viewing habits of many millions of people with a sample size of only 1000. Surprisingly, we will find that this sample is large enough to give reliable estimates.

THE KINSEY REPORT: A SURVEY OF GROUP CHARACTERISTICS AND DIFFERENCES

There are then three basic questions to ask about the measurements taken in any psychological study: (1) Are the measurements reliable? (2) Are they valid? (3) Is the sample representative and of sufficient size to warrant meaningful generalization? These questions will be considered in a discussion of the famous Kinsey Report, a report which once both shocked and titillated the nation, but which serves here as a vehicle for studying the difficulties encountered in measuring behavior.

> This is a study of sexual behavior in certain groups of human species, *Homo sapiens*. It is obviously not a study of the sexual behavior of all cultures and of all races of man. At its best, the present volume can pretend to report behavior which may be typical of no more than a portion, although probably not an inconsiderable portion, of the white females living within the boundaries of the United States. Neither the title of our first volume on the male, nor the title of this volume on the female, should be taken to imply that the authors are unaware of the diversity which exists in patterns of sexual behavior in other parts of the world [Kinsey *et al.*, 1953].

Sexual behavior in the human female, popularly known as the Kinsey Report, begins with this disclaimer of its scope, yet it is perhaps the largest and most thorough study of its kind ever undertaken. The work spanned fifteen years until the eventual publication of the male and female reports, which were received with a furor of criticism and praise. Extravagantly it was said that "the Kinsey Report has done for sex what Columbus did for geography," and alternately it was reviled with assertions that, "there should be a law against doing research dealing exclusively with sex."

The facts that Kinsey revealed shocked the nation. Geddes, in *An analysis of the Kinsey report* (1954), summarized some of the more startling facts in the male report.

> To begin with, he completely explodes the idea that sex interest and activity begins with marriage. More completely he annihilates the idea that sex is or can be sublimated until marriage. . .
>
> Masturbation is one thing that few males will admit to family and friends that they have ever done; yet Kinsey finds that more than 90% of American males do masturbate at one time or another.

As to homosexuality, Kinsey finds that more than one-third of all American males have had experience of this sort resulting in orgasm, at least once in their lives.

Of the so-called animal contacts, these—while constituting man's most infrequent outlet—take place in sufficient quantity to make statistical measurement possible.

One of the most startling revelations made in this most revealing study is the fact that the height of the sex drive in the male comes between the ages of sixteen and twenty. This fact is most amply illustrated by figures which show that for this age group more than 70% of American boys and young men are involved in premarital intercourse.

Kinsey began his work in response to numerous questions about human sexual behavior from his biology students. He felt that the general ignorance that existed as to what constitutes normal practices on a subject of such vital interest demanded some illuminating data. It was indeed a difficult and treacherous task to undertake an investigation that would eventually detail the intimate sexual practices of over 8000 males and 8000 females.

The Sample

The population considered by the report included all white nonimprisoned females within the boundaries of the United States. Minority races were interviewed, but the sample for these groups was considered too small to be reliable. Selecting the sample was no mean task and much criticism has been levied at the work on this account. The problems involved in randomly selecting 8000 females and sending out interviewers across America to ask them about their sex lives are numerous. Many would undoubtedly refuse to comply and the random sample would then be reduced to a volunteer sample. Imagine the followup contact of a housewife who initially refused to cooperate. Day after day, the man from the Sex Institute returns to ask those impertinent questions until he is arrested or is severely beaten by the woman's husband. To avoid a volunteer sample in the face of the impossibility of a random sample, Kinsey devised an ingenious solution. He and his associates entered a community and contacted many of the existing social organizations, e.g., churches, fraternities, church groups, clubs, etc. His co-workers addressed these groups to gain their confidence and respect and then urged that every member contribute his sexual history to the scientists. These groups were fairly amenable to the 100% cooperation approach, thus greatly alleviating the problem of numerous refusals.

Refusals were diligently followed up by recontacts, and the data for those

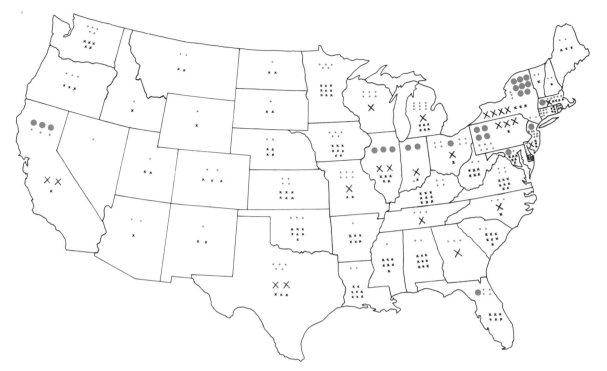

FIGURE 8-1   Geographic distribution of the sample from the Kinsey Report on females. Each small dot represents 25 females in the sample who had lived at least one year in the state; each large dot represents 250 females. Each small x represents approximately 160,000 females living in the state according to the 1940 census; each large X represents 1,600,000 females. From Kinsey *et al.* (1953).

who initially refused are carefully compared to the cases where the initial contact was successful. The differences were slight, but those who consistently refused remained an unknown quantity.

The sample included just about every occupational, socioeconomic, and religious group from the then forty-eight states. The spatial distribution over states of the female sample is not exactly proportionate to the population, but it appears to be reasonably representative (Figure 8-1). Kinsey even detailed the segments of the population that were underrepresented, including the lower educational level groups, females over fifty, laboring groups, etc.

Interviews

The interviewers had to be carefully trained to handle each case in a manner that would develop rapport in a face-to-face interview. They had to develop the skills that would lead to truthful and accurate data without offending the person in any way and assuring absolute confidentiality. Any differences in language or attitude could lead to grossly different results for the different interviewers.

> Vocabularies differ in different parts of the United States and there are differences among individuals belonging to different generations. Sexual vocabularies may differ among persons in different portions of a single city, depending upon their social levels, occupational backgrounds, racial origins, religious and educational backgrounds, and still other factors.
>
> For instance, one has to learn that a person in a lower level community may live common-law, although he does not enter into a common-law marriage with a common-law wife. As we have noted in our volume on the male (1948:52), we have had to learn that a lower level individual is never ill or injured although he may be sick or hurt; he may not wish to do a thing although he may want to do it; he does not perceive although he may see; he may not be acquainted with a person although he may know him. Syphilis may be rare in such a community, although bad blood may be more common. At such a level an individual may not yet have learned about a particular type of sexual activity although he may have heard about it and even observed it many times; but he considers that he does not know about it until he has had experience. Such an individual does not understand our question about seeing a burlesque although he can tell you about the burlesque show which he saw. The existence of prostitutes in the community may be denied, although it may be common knowledge that there are some females and males who are hustling. Inquiries about the frequency with which a prostitute robs her clients may not bring any admission that such a thing ever happens, although she may admit that she rolls some of her tricks. But the use of such terms with an upper level subject would leave him mystified or offended. At every level, inquiries about the circulation of pornographic literature might elicit very little information, although most teen-age boys may have seen eight-pagers. The adaptation of one's vocabulary in an interview thus not only contributes to the establishment of rapport, but brings out information which would be completely missed on a standardized questionnaire [Kinsey *et al.*, 1953, pp. 61–62].

The reliability between different interviewers was checked by the simple expediency of comparing their results. Some 80% of the interviews were conducted by Kinsey and the second author, Pomeroy. Their results were strikingly in accord. A second check on the reliability of each interviewer's report was made by comparing the results from a single interviewer over successive periods of the study. These comparisons will be examined after detailing some of the descriptive statistics used in the study.

Descriptive Statistics

PROPORTIONS.   A statistic is simply a summarizing measure on the sample that is intended to reflect some characteristics of the population. The descriptive statistics compiled were of two basic kinds: yes/no data to questions of the type "do you now . . ." and numerical responses to questions of the type "how many times do you . . . ?" The yes/no or incidence data are reported as the number of yes answers divided by the total number of respondents asked. Not all questions were asked of all respondents.

The proportion of males with an eighth grade level of education who at a particular age had ever performed a particular act show that about 90% had experienced intercourse by age twenty. There is very little difference between the two incidence curves for the two interviewers (Figure 8-2).

CENTRAL TENDENCY AND FREQUENCY DISTRIBUTIONS.   In order to get some feel for the average response to the "how often" or frequency questions, two common measures of central tendency were chosen. One was the familiar mean response used in calculating grade point averages. In Kinsey studies, frequencies were added up for all respondents and the total was divided by the number of respondents. The second measure of central tendency was the median. The median response is found by ordering all the responses from smallest to largest. The median is the response that is just greater than half of the responses.

The mean and median will be approximately equal to each other for symmetric distributions of scores. There are several types of symmetric distributions, the most common being the normal distribution for which most of the values fall in the middle of the range with a few extreme low and high scores. Many psychological variables, including most test scores, are normally distributed in the population.

The curve for males comparing the case histories reported separately by Kinsey and Pomeroy for ever having had intercourse is approximately a cumulative normal distribution (Figure 8-2). If the curve were uncumulated, to

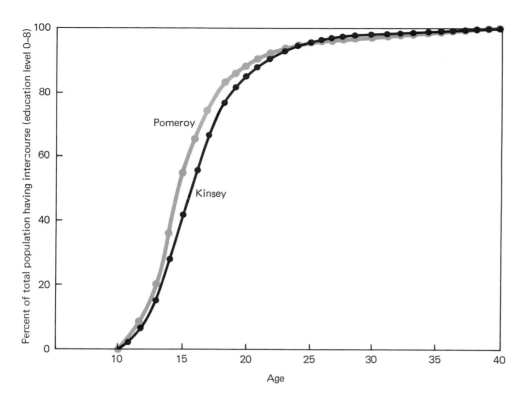

FIGURE 8-2   A comparison of accumulative incidence data obtained by different interviewers for data on intercourse of any kind for males with an eighth grade education or less. From Kinsey *et al.* (1948).

show the frequency distribution of age of first experience, it would be approximately normal in form (Figure 8-3). The median age for first intercourse for the males with less than an eighth grade education is approximately 15 years of age with a very similar mean age. In other words, approximately 50% of the males in this sample reported having had intercourse before 15 years of age.

In positively skewed distributions, most of the cases fall in the lower end of the range. This would mean there would be a median score smaller than the mean. Many of the frequency distributions in the Kinsey report are positively skewed. For example, the frequency of experience in marital coitus shows an increasing positive skew with increasing age groups (Figure 8-4). For the 21 to 25 age group, the distribution is more normally distributed, while the distribution for age group 51 to 55 is extremely positively skewed.

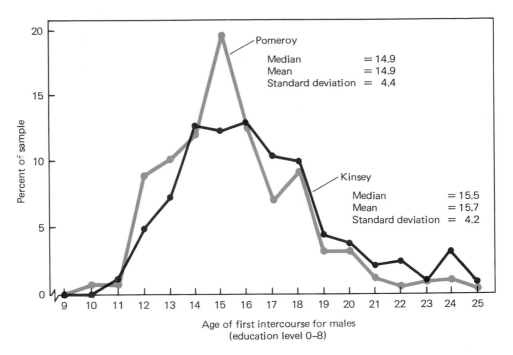

FIGURE 8-3   The distribution of age of first intercourse for males with an eighth grade education or less. The curves comparing the results obtained by Kinsey and Pomeroy are approximately normal in form. Data derived from Kinsey *et al.* (1948), p. 138.

In negatively skewed distributions, most of the scores fall in the high end of the range. It is a much more rarely encountered distribution than the normal or positive skew and has a median score larger than the mean score. Obviously the statistical average reported, the mean or the median, can be used to slant reported results. For example, according to the 1970 census, the median family income in the U.S. was $9,800, while the mean family income was $10,100. Obviously the distribution of income is positively skewed.

VARIABILITY.   Measures of central tendency are often reported as statistics summarizing the data as a whole, yet they can be misleading as to the actual state of affairs. The amount of variability between individuals does not affect the value of the mean or the median. Consider two cities that have the same annual mean temperature, say 65°. Sounds like a fine climate. In fact, many cities in the world have the annual mean temperatures in the 60's. However, some vary in temperature during the year from −10° below zero to 120° above, while others vary from 45° to 95°. This is quite a difference in climate!

If summary statistics are given, some measure of the variability of the scores should be reported, otherwise they may be quite meaningless. One measure of variability that could be reported is the range, the difference between the largest score and the smallest score. However, this measure depends on only two scores and does not necessarily give an accurate picture of their consistency. A single oddball score could greatly affect the range.

A more representative summary measure of variability has been developed by statisticians to reflect the consistency of scores in a distribution. This somewhat complicated number, called the standard deviation (σ), takes into account the magnitude of discrepancy of all the scores from their mean value. It is calculated by subtracting the mean from each score, squaring the result (which removes all the negative signs), and then finding the mean of the squared discrepancies. Finally, the square root of the result is taken as the standard deviation. The squaring procedure is carried out for complicated reasons that are beyond the scope of our present discussion.

It is more important to understand the usefulness of the standard deviation than to be able to calculate it. As the variability measured by standard deviation increases, the sample mean will more poorly reflect the true population mean, unless this variability is compensated for by a larger sample size. Also, as the sample size increases, the sample mean will more closely, on the average, reflect the true population mean. Thus, the effect of sample size and the standard deviation work together in determining the accuracy of the sample estimate of the population mean.

Estimating the precision of a sample mean depends fairly strictly on the assumption that the sampling method employed is random. If it is not, then any systematic bias in the selection of the sample will cause a degree of distortion in the results that we are usually unable to estimate.

Statisticians have shown that the precision of estimate of a sample mean depends not on the sample size, but on the square root of the sample size. Doubling the precision of a sample estimate of a mean requires a fourfold increase in the sample size. There is, then, a law of diminishing returns in sampling. However, the precision of estimate does not depend on the size of a large population but on the sample size.

These statistics are used throughout the Kinsey Report to summarize the enormous mass of data collected by the researchers. After we have evaluated the possibility of bias in these measures due to the sample selection and inter-interviewer reliability, we are still left with a possible major source of distortion that could invalidate the results. This is in the basic reliability of the subject's own report of his behavior. Human memory is fallible, and honesty in the face of social embarrassment is tenuous. However sensitive the interviewer may be or however good the rapport, social pressures of acceptability are likely

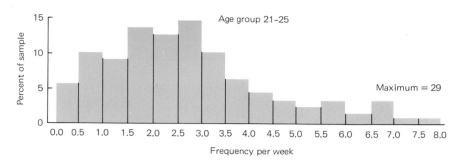

Age group 21-25

Maximum = 29

Frequency per week

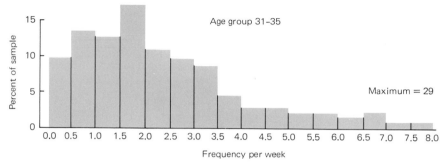

Age group 31-35

Maximum = 29

Frequency per week

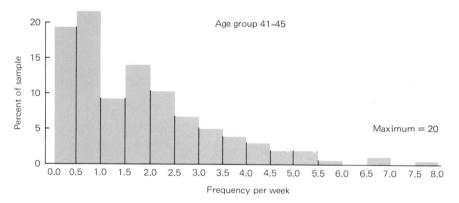

Age group 41-45

Maximum = 20

Frequency per week

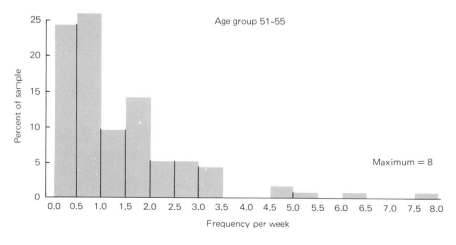

Age group 51-55

Maximum = 8

Frequency per week

to cause distortions. Pluralistic ignorance is the name given to the phenomenon of "everybody's doing it, but nobody's talking about it."

Reliability of the Histories

The statistical challenge to Kinsey was to evaluate the reliability of the subject's own report. He used the simple expediency of reinterviewing a small subsample and comparing their "retake" responses with their original responses. The retakes were obtained long after the original histories with a median time lapse of 33 months for the female subjects. If the subjects were purposefully distorting their responses to sensitive questions, then they would, in all likelihood, show little consistency upon remeasurement. The original distortions would have long been forgotten and different distortions would be invented. Of course, another problem is that the memory is not infallible, and some inconsistency is bound to occur. Consequently, it was necessary to establish some baseline for simple memory distortions using questions that were not of a sensitive nature, e.g., age of the subject, educational level, age at marriage.

Incidence data on sexual matters proves to be quite reliable with agreement between original history and retake being in the 90–100% range (Figure 8-5). Frequency data is somewhat more fallible, but is still reasonably good. Average frequency of total outlet (combined sexual activities) shows agreement to within once a week for 63% of the histories and frequency of extramarital coitus shows agreement for 91% to within one-tenth of a time per week. The reliabilities are quite similar for vital statistics, with age at marriage showing 58% agreement to within one year and the reported age of the subject agreeing for 88% of the cases to within one year.

These reported reliability data give one a feeling for the probable overall consistency of the reported data. In addition to the retake data, Kinsey reports the appropriate statistics from previous sex surveys conducted by other researchers, and shows that, where comparable statistics exist, they are in surprisingly good agreement with his own data.

Validity of the Histories

Even though the retakes indicate a reasonable degree of reliability for the data, we are still in doubt about their validity. We would like to know

FIGURE 8-4   Individual variation in frequency of experience in marital coitus from the Kinsey Report on females. The distribution for the 21–25 age group is approximately normally distributed while that for the 51–55 age group is highly positively skewed.

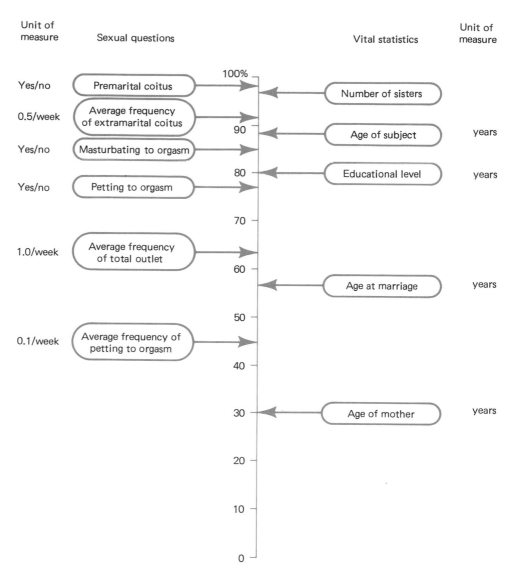

FIGURE 8-5   Comparisons of data reported on original histories and retakes of 124 females from the Kinsey Report. Incidence or yes-no data show the highest overall reliability. Data are compared to nonsexually oriented questions.

what the sexual practices of U.S. females and males really are. We only know what they have told us. The fact that they gave us more or less the same history after a few years may simply indicate that the same social pressures were effective in distorting the record. The problem is to determine to what extent the responses accurately reflect behavior.

To do this, Kinsey compared the responses given by pairs of individuals engaged in sexual behavior together, namely, the responses of husbands and wives. If both members were reporting exactly what occurred sexually in the marital relationship, their incidence and frequency data should concur exactly. However, since the data for a single individual reporting on his own behavior is less than perfectly reliable, we cannot expect perfect concordance.

Nevertheless, the agreement for incidence data for paired spouses is quite high. For example, accord on accumulative incidence for coital foreplay and coital techniques is for the most part in the region of high 80 to 90% agreement. Agreement on accumulative incidence of coital positions ranges from 82 to 99% and on techniques from 89 to 98%. For frequency data, the average frequency of coitus at the age of the report agreed to within once a week for 67% of the cases and within twice a week for 85% of the cases. However, reports on vital statistics such as the number of years of marriage agree to within one year for 84% of the cases. The time lapse until the first child birth agrees to within six months for 72% of the cases and to within one year for 88% of the cases. The overall spouse agreement, though far from perfect, tends to lend credence to the validity of the report. Nevertheless, it is possible that both parties are distorting their behavioral reports in the same direction. Both are, in all probability, subject to the same or similar social pressures, which would cause them to give similar false reports to the interviewers. Though helpful in establishing credibility, this evidence does not cinch the case.

Kinsey does report an instance where such pressures would produce distortion in reports that could be checked by external information. In one case, his co-workers interviewed a prison population of 350 men. A male acquainted with the prison indicated 32 prisoners among those interviewed with whom he had had relations or whom he had seen having homosexual relations. For this subgroup, there would be strong pressure to deny such activities to the interviewers in fear of reprisals by prison authorities. Of these 32 cases, 27 admitted such practices to the Kinsey group on first interview and three more did so on reinterview (the remaining two had left prison). This high level of validity indicates an excellent level of interviewer-subject rapport.

As mentioned previously, the validity of the evidence is much more difficult to establish than its reliability, and in the case of the Kinsey report only peripheral evidence can be gathered. Since direct evidence is impossible, the exact level of validity remains unknown, although the evidence presented suggests that it is quite high.

INTELLIGENCE: TESTS OF INDIVIDUAL DIFFERENCES

Development of I.Q. Testing

Writers of science fiction novels have suggested the utopian future in which every citizen, through careful psychological testing, will be placed in his just and fitting position in the society. The idea of such calculated placement sits poorly with most of us. It suggests a determinism of abilities that denies us the freedom to choose to improve ourselves.

How just can a psychological test be? Can it really determine our abilities and propensities to succeed? We all have heard the popular tales of the 50 I.Q. child who becomes a genius concert pianist.

> *Boy with I.Q. of 55*
> *Is Genius at Piano*
>
> LOS ANGELES (UPI)—When Rickey Ponce de Leon sat down to play, the audience hushed then listened in awe to the impressive organ rendition he pounded out with fingers of a musical virtuoso.
>
> The teen-ager is mentally retarded with an IQ of 55. Yet the Filipino youth was the featured soloist at the 25th-anniversary banquet of the Exceptional Children's Foundation here.
>
> Considered a musical genius, de Leon can play about 1,000 songs from memory, is adept with seven instruments and composes excellent music—yet displays a retardate's poor muscle coordination when he is away from his music.
>
> Robert Shushan, local director of foundation, introduced the youth as a "gifted, retarded individual" who is an "exceptional example" showing that mental retardates can perform well under the right conditions.
>
> ". . . when he seats himself at the console of an electronic organ a miracle happens," said Mr. Shusan, "poor coordination disappears, replaced by excellent independence in the use of all four limbs, playing keyboard and pedal board [*The New York Times*, August 6, 1971].

Are the limits of our abilities fixed? Part of the American credo asserts that anyone who tries hard enough can succeed at whatever he wants, regardless of almost anything else. These days we are environmentalists, almost to a man. But what are the facts?

Let us consider the applications and implications of the most widely used and most successful test of ability, the Stanford-Binet I.Q. test. When the list of important contributions of psychology to society is drawn up, intelligence testing often heads the list. How did it all begin?

One of Napoleon's gifts to France was the creation of a national educational system. One of the educational problems that evolved from this system was to determine which children could profit from regular instruction and which required some form of remedial training. To this end, Alfred Binet, a French psychologist, was commissioned in 1904 by the Minister of Public Instruction in Paris to devise a test of intellectual ability.

Binet was a most suitable choice. He had published his work on the experimental study of intelligence, much of which he had carried out with his own two daughters, and was convinced of the value of objective measures of intelligence.

> What importance can be attached to public statistics of different countries concerning the percentage of backward children if the definition for backward children is not the same in all countries? How will it be possible to keep a record of the intelligence of pupils who are treated and instructed in a school, if the terms applied to them, feeble-minded, retarded, imbecile, idiot, vary in meaning according to the doctor who examines them? The absence of a common measure prevents comparison of statistics, and makes one lose all interest in investigations which may have been very laborious. But a still more serious fact is that, because of lack of methods, it is impossible to solve those essential questions concerning the afflicted, whose solution presents the greatest interest; for example, the real results gained by the treatment of inferior states of intelligence by doctor and educator; the educative value of one pedagogical method compared with another; the degree of curability of incomplete idiocy, etc. It is not by means of *a priori* reasonings, of vague considerations, of oratorical displays, that these questions can be solved; but by minute investigation, entering into the details of fact, and considering the effects of the treatment for each particular child. There is but one means of knowing if a child, who has passed six years in a hospital or in a special class, has profited from that stay, and to what degree he has profited; and that is to compare his certificate of entrance with his certificate of dismissal, and by that means ascertain if he shows a special amelioration of his condition beyond that which might be credited simply to the considerations of growth. But experience has shown how imprudent it would be to place confidence in this comparison, when the two certificates come from

different doctors, who do not judge in exactly the same
way, or who use different words to characterize the mental
status of patients [Binet & Simon, 1905].

Other scientists, notably Francis Galton, a brilliant cousin of Charles Darwin,
had worked on the measurement of intelligence partly in hope of establishing the mental components of the Darwinian notions of evolution. Galton's
analytic approach was to measure abilities of sensory discrimination, reaction time, and dexterity, which are skills presently not at all associated
with intelligence testing. Binet was audacious enough to attack the problem
directly and use questions that dealt with intellectual skills as a means of
measuring intelligence. In 1905, he published the first metrical scale of intelligence. His questions tested memory, judgment, and decision making abilities.
It was a "dirty" test in the sense that there was no particular theory of intelligence behind its construction. It was a crude but practical approach.

The developmental nature of the tests through successive school grades
led to a rather natural way of defining intelligence. Each succeeding question,
or "stunt" as Binet named them, was more difficult than the preceding questions.
The older the child, the more stunts he could perform. An item was defined
as normal for a particular age group if 60% of the children at that age could
answer it satisfactorily. A child's mental age (M.A.) was defined as equivalent to the age level for which he showed mastery of the items. The intelligence
quotient was defined as the child's mental age divided by his chronological
age and multiplied by 100.

$$\text{I.Q.} = \frac{\text{M.A.}}{\text{C.A.}} \times 100$$

This makes I.Q. a relative measure, one that measures by comparing the performance of a child to the norm for his age group. The distribution of I.Q.
scores is approximately normal or bell-shaped, defined to have a mean of
100 and a standard deviation of 15.

Normal Distributions

Since the normal distribution is so common in psychological measurement
its properties deserve special note. The distribution is symmetric with the mean
equal to the median. Consequently, 50% of the scores lie below the mean
and 50% lie above. The effective range of scores is about six standard deviations. Most of the scores lie near the mean with fewer scores in the extremes
(Figure 8-6). About 68% of the scores fall within one standard deviation

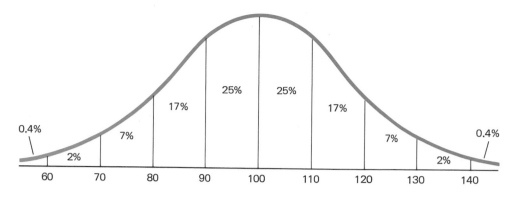

FIGURE 8-6   The normal distribution of I.Q.'s, showing the expected percentages of the population in each I.Q. range. Except at the extremes (below 70 and above 130) these percentages are very close to actual population values. (The percentage figures total slightly more than 100% because of rounding.) From Jensen (1969).

of the mean, and 96% fall within two standard deviations of the mean. If your I.Q. is 100, you are "average" with 50% of the population scoring below you. If your I.Q. is 115, 84% score more poorly, and, if your I.Q. is 130, 98% score below you.

Test-Retest Reliability

DEFINITION.   How good is the I.Q. test? It appears to be objective in its measurement, since the score does not depend on anyone's subjective assessment. It is standardized by comparing the scores to well-established norms. Since its inception, the Binet scale of intelligence has undergone many revisions. Items that did not sharply discriminate for a particular age group were replaced and several equivalent alternate forms of the test were also developed as its use became more common. The question then is how reliable is the measure.

Suppose we measure your I.Q. today with Form L of the test and remeasure tomorrow with Form M. Chances are we would not get the same score. The average absolute difference in the score would be about three points, pretty good given the broad range of I.Q. scores in the population. What we need is a summary index of the similarity of scores obtained by making two measurements, test and retest, on the same individuals.

A measure of the test-retest reliability that takes account of the difference in the test score for remeasurement of the same individual is called the coefficient of reliability. This statistic is a particular instance of the use of the more general statistical procedure called the correlation. A correlation is an index of the closeness of association between any two measures taken on a common element.

CORRELATION.   In physics, relationships between variables such as force, distance, and time are usually found to be functional in character, and simple equations describing these functions can be written. But in biology, genetics, or psychology, relationships are not so perfect. For example, one could assert a possible genetic connection between the heights of fathers and the heights of their sons, if a systematic relationship could be shown to exist. But you

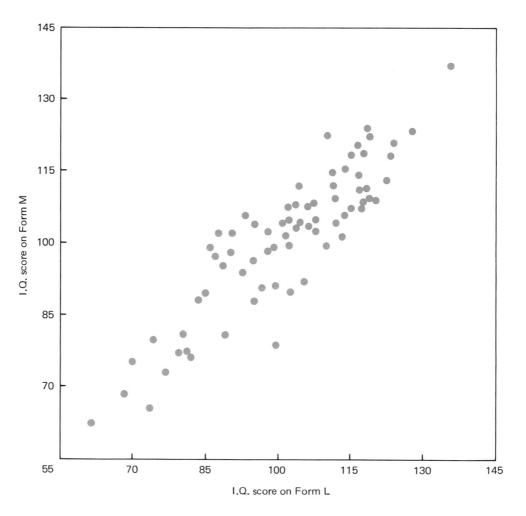

FIGURE 8-7   Hypothetical test-retest scatter plot for the Stanford-Binet intelligence test. The correlation is .90.

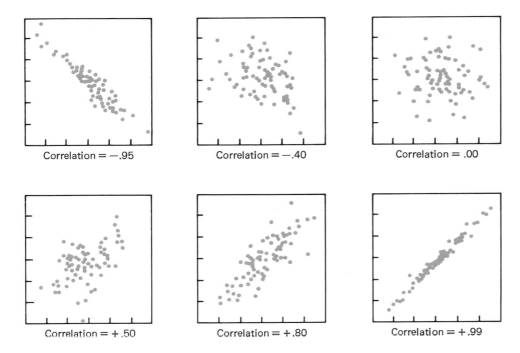

FIGURE 8-8   Hypothetical scatter plots for different correlations.

cannot write a simple equation for this relationship, because a father who is 6 feet tall may have a son either 2 inches taller or shorter. In general, however, the taller the father, the taller the son. To describe this imperfect but systematic linear relationship, the correlation, r, was developed by Galton and his student Karl Pearson.

To get a better picture of a correlational relationship, it is usually helpful to plot the values of one measurement against the values of the related measurement in a scatter plot. Consider the result of administering the Stanford-Binet I.Q. test to 100 persons and then giving these same persons an alternate form of the test as a remeasurement. If we plot the I.Q. scores from test Form L against the scores for the same individuals from test Form M, and if there were a perfect (functional) linear relationship between the measures, they would all lie on a straight line. The actual result is not a perfect line but a closely grouped scatter of points (Figure 8-7). If the relationship were perfect, the correlation would have the value 1.0. The actual test-retest correlation for the Stanford-Binet test is better than .90. This is an excellent reliability coefficient and indicates that the test is a consistent measure.

Correlations can range in value from +1.0, a perfect positive correlation, to 0.0, indicating no relationship between the measures, to −1.0, a perfect negative correlation (Figure 8-8). A negative correlation indicates an inverse relationship. As the value of one measure (grade point average) goes up, the value of another measure for the same individual (hours spent in leisure activity) goes down.

CALCULATION OF THE RANK ORDER CORRELATION.   Alhough the Pearson (1903) *r* correlation is somewhat complicated to calculate, the rank order correlation, ρ, is not, and, for many purposes, it is a reasonably close approximation to *r*. Say for example, you wanted to estimate the reliability coefficient of a multiple-choice examination given in an introductory psychology course. Since you would not ordinarily have an alternate form of the exam available, you could create an equivalent measure by considering the score you would receive if you only counted the odd-numbered items on the test as one measure and the score you would receive if you counted only the even-numbered items on the test as another measure. By comparing these measures, you would be considering the odd-even test reliability.

Of course, your two scores alone will not be sufficient to calculate a correlation of reliability. You would have to get similar odd-even scores for about twenty other class members. To be fair, these scores should span the range of overall test scores from the best to the worst. If all the scores are high ones, you will get an erroneously low correlation because of the restriction of the range. This would be similar to determining the father-son height correlation using only fathers over six feet tall.

Next, you would rank order the obtained scores for the odd test items, assigning the lowest score a value of 1 and the highest score a value of 20. Any ties in the ranks would all be assigned the average value of the tied ranks. For example, if three scores are tied for the first three places (1, 2, and 3) then all three scores would be assigned the average rank value $[(1+2+3)/3]$ of 2.0.

In a similar fashion, assign the appropriate rank values from 1 to 20 for the even test scores. Now you have two rank scores for each person, one for the rank of the odd test item score and one for the even test item score. How similar are these rankings? To determine this, subtract the difference in rank value for the pairs of scores, square these differences, and add them all up. This sum is indicated by Sum D^2 in the following equation.

$$\rho = 1 - \frac{6(\text{Sum } D^2)}{N(N^2 - 1)}$$

In this equation ρ is the rank order correlation, N is the number of pairs of scores, and 6 is a constant multiplier, always used, which does not depend on the number of scores (see example in Table 8-1).

TABLE 8-1   Calculation of a Rank Order Correlation, ρ, from Ten Pairs of Odd-Even Test Scores

50 Odd items	50 Even items	Odd rank	Even rank	D	D²
25	27	4	6	−2	4
28	15	6	3	3	9
42	38	10	9	−1	1
31	33	7.5	8	−.5	.25
31	30	7.5	7	.5	.25
14	11	2	1	−1	1
8	20	1	4	3	9
27	26	5	5	0	0
19	12	3	2	1	1
35	45	9	10	1	1
					26.5

$$\rho = 1 - \frac{6 \times 26.5}{10 \times 99} = 1 - \frac{159}{990} = .84$$

The odd-even reliability coefficient you calculate will be somewhat smaller than the true test reliability, since you reduced the length of the test by one half by using only odd or even items. If the test is a long one, this will not matter much. But if you have only 100 or less items, the reduction in the calculated correlation may be significant. However, even for this test length the odd-even reliability coefficient should be above .50; otherwise, the test cannot be measuring your knowledge of psychology.

Test Validity

As we have pointed out, if a measure is not reliable, it cannot have any validity. But if it is reliable, it may or may not be valid. Test validity requires additional investigation to be established. An I.Q. test may appear on the face of it to require intelligence for the solution of questions posed, but this face validity does not insure that it is in fact measuring what we ordinarily mean by intelligence as distinct from acquired knowledge or learned skills. In order to establish the validity of a test, we must be able to predict behavior on some other external, objective criterion.

The I.Q. test was originally developed to separate those who can profit from education from those who cannot. Consequently, one criterion we can use to establish the validity of the I.Q. test is to compare success in school as measured by the grade point average. Those who have higher I.Q.'s ought to have higher GPAs.

To evaluate the predictability of GPAs from I.Q. scores, we again turn to the statistical correlational technique. In this instance, the correlation between GPA and I.Q. is called a coefficient of validity since one measure, GPA, is being used to validate a different measure, I.Q. In this case, it would be unreasonable to expect a perfect prediction since GPAs depend on many things other than intelligence. They depend on student motivation to perform, emotional stability, and often on the teacher's subjective judgment of the student's ability, which may be colored by many factors other than objective performance. The approximate correlation between I.Q. and college GPA is about .5, a fairly good validity coefficient. This means that about 25% (r^2) of the variation in college GPAs can be accounted for by the I.Q. measure.

Consider as further evidence that persons who graduate from high school have a mean I.Q. of approximately 110 while those who graduate from college have a mean I.Q. of 125. Those who earn doctorates of psychology have a mean I.Q. of 130 or 140 depending on whether they are in a professional field or in scientific research. Success in the more intellectually demanding academic tasks apparently correlates with high I.Q.'s.

Intelligence testing is now widely used by educational systems, industry, and the military for ability grouping and placement. Perhaps the most extensive application was by the military in testing millions of men upon entrance into the armed services, especially in World War II. As a result, mean Army General Classification Test scores were obtained for many occupational groups and confirmed in most instances that the more intellectually demanding fields show the higher mean I.Q.'s. Accountants register a mean of 128; lawyers, 127; chemists, 125; and teachers, 123. On the other hand, cooks and bakers showed a mean I.Q. of 97; truck drivers, 96; farmers, 93; and miners, 91. Interestingly, the standard deviations for the higher I.Q. occupations all range around 10 while those for the lower I.Q. occupational groups are twice as large, indicating considerably greater individual differences.

While such data tend to establish the validity of I.Q. tests as a predictive device, there is always the possibility that the test is measuring the effects of the superior background of individuals who reach the higher educational levels. Is the I.Q. test a measure of innate, genetically inherited ability or does it strongly reflect the cultural and socioeconomic environment in which the children are raised? We cannot conclusively answer this question to date, but there is a good deal of interesting data concerning this point.

Some writers argue that the heritability of I.Q. is an irrelevant question. They assert that we should devote our time to raising ability levels by training. Yet, this begs the question. How effective can training be in altering academic abilities and the success to which these abilities lead? As surely as severe undernourishment will stunt growth, conditions can exist that greatly inhibit intellectual development. But as nourishment can only go so far in establishing height, so may there be stringent limits to the extent to which we can raise I.Q.

The argument for establishing the degree of heritability of I.Q. goes something like this. The I.Q. that we measure is a phenotypic I.Q. Underlying this measure are a number of environmental factors, a number of genetic factors, and possible interactions between the two. Although the genetic contribution to I.Q. is fixed, the rest may vary as a function of the environment. The point to be established is what proportion of the observed variations in I.Q. for the population of interest is determined by heredity and what proportion by environmental interactions. We know, for example, that parental I.Q.'s have a .5 correlation with the I.Q.'s of their children. But this fails to answer the question, since parents contribute both to the hereditary and the environmental influences.

HERITABILITY OF I.Q.

The principal means of investigating this question has been to find the I.Q. correlation for groups of varying genetic and environmental relationships ranging from unrelated children brought up together to identical twins reared separately. A number of twin studies have been conducted, and the reported results are fairly consistent. Some of these studies were compiled by Jensen (1969). Recently, however, these data have come under severe criticism as not being reliable (Kamin, 1972). For present purposes we will take the reported data at face value and evaluate the relative contributions of heredity and environment.

The heritability analysis must try to separate these factors by considering the differences in I.Q. correlations between individuals who differ in their genetic similarity under conditions in which the environment is more or less the same and under conditions in which the environment substantially differs. As a baseline for evaluation, consider the correlation between children randomly selected from the population and paired at random. The I.Q. correlation would of course be zero. What if these pairs are raised together in the same family, as in the case of foster children? The observed correlation for these cases is a significant .24. Is this an effect of the environment? Possibly, but it may be confounded with the attempt to place brighter foster children in homes with brighter parents. The correlation between foster parent and child is about .20.

What about siblings raised in separate environments? Studies of these cases show a median I.Q. correlation of .47, as we might expect from the closer genetic relationship. When siblings are raised together in the same household, the correlation between I.Q.'s is .55, not much different from the separately raised siblings. Dizygotic twins (siblings born at the same time but from different ova and sperm) show results quite comparable to siblings, as would be expected from their equivalent genetic relationship.

Now consider the case for which two individuals have the closest possible hereditary similarity, monozygotic twins. These are siblings who have developed from a single ovum and a single sperm cell. Their genetic makeup is essentially identical. This type of twin has been most extensively studied,

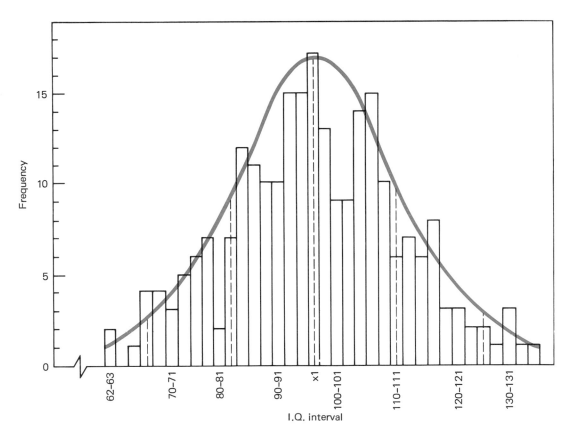

FIGURE 8-9   I.Q. distribution of 244 monozygotic twins reared apart, from four studies. The superimposed normal distribution was constructed using a mean of 97 and a standard deviation of 14. Adapted from Jensen (1969).

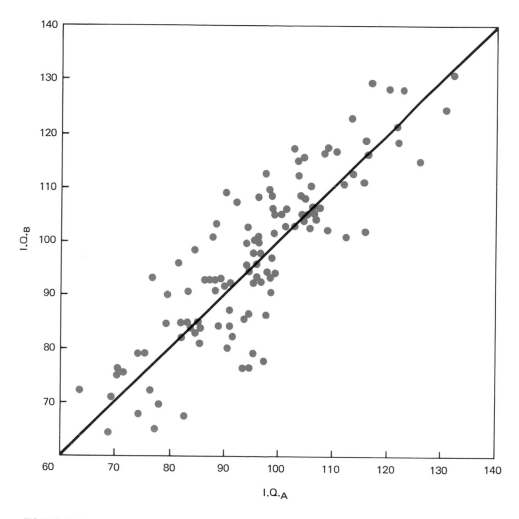

FIGURE 8-10   Scatter plot between I.Q.'s of 122 sets of monozygotic twins. The obtained correlation is .82. The diagonal line represents perfect correlation (r = 1.00). Adapted from Jensen (1969).

since, when these children happen to be raised in different environments, we have a case of identical hereditary makeup with different environmental conditions, effectively separating the two influences. Four studies of identical twins were combined to produce 244 monozygotic twins who were reared apart from each other. The I.Q. distribution for these twins is very nearly normal with a mean of 97 and a standard deviation of 14 (Figure 8-9). The correlation for twin I.Q.'s is .82, astonishingly high (Figure 8-10). For monozygotic twins reared together, the I.Q. correlation has been shown to be .92, which was as high as the test-retest reliability of the test permitted (Burt, 1966). In a sense, when monozygotic twins take the I.Q. test, the scores are equivalent to the same person taking two alternate forms of the I.Q. test.

These results are indeed a powerful argument for the strong role of heredity in the determination of I.Q. A number of researchers, on the basis of this type of data and with a good deal of statistical work that we cannot consider here, have concluded that, for the cases studied, about 80% of the variability can be attributed to hereditary influences and the rest to environmental interactions.

The height and weight of individuals also show about the same degree of genetic determination. For the identical twins reared apart, the correlations are .94 and .88 for height and weight, respectively. While most of us are ready to concede height and weight are largely determined by heredity, fewer would, without the data, concede a similar role in the determination of I.Q.

A word of caution is necessary here. These data do not relate to racial differences in intelligence. Although some writers have unwisely jumped to the conclusion that, since a 15 point median difference in the I.Q.'s of whites and blacks has been consistently found, this difference is hereditary. Such conclusions are unwarranted. The data simply do not include blacks and can take no account of any cultural differences between the races. In addition, there are many ways in which environmental influences can be missed by the type of data presented. How different were the environments for the separated twins? Could there be overall effects of the environment that tend to raise or lower I.Q.'s of large cultural groups? What is the effect of neonatal experience on the child? Has the right kind of intelligence been measured? These are only some of the questions that can be raised concerning this work. Nevertheless, the question of intellectual heritability is a vital one for the course of future educational policy, with enormous consequences for society. It is a question that demands our best statistical and theoretical skills as psychologists.

PERILS OF CORRELATION

Consider a rank order correlation between two simple measures, the number of residents who are over 65 years old in different cities and the number of forcible rapes committed in these cities.

City	Rank no. over 65	Rank no. of forcible rapes
New York	5	5
Los Angeles	4	4
Philadelphia	3	3
Pittsburgh	2	2
Poughkeepsie	1	1

For these data, r is 1.0, a perfect correlation. Would anyone infer that the old codgers were feeling their oats too much? No one would impute any causal relationship between these two perfectly correlated variables because it is clear that a third variable, factor X, the different size of the city populations, readily accounts for the correlation. Furthermore, on a priori grounds, the causal relationship between old folks and rape, whichever way it works, seems absurd. However, what if we had shown a similar ranking between the number of destitute residents and the number of burglaries committed in these cities with a similar 1.0 correlation? Some persons might buy a causal relationship. Yet clearly on the basis of such a correlation, it is improper to conclude that any causality exists, since a third factor, city size, could easily account for the observed correlation.

Whether or not a third variable, factor X, can be specified, in no case can a correlational relationship be taken to demonstrate a causal relationship. Yet, this type of false conclusion is one of the most common errors committed by trained psychologists and laymen alike. Consider the reported conclusion that schizophrenia, a catchall psychosis category, produces disassociative thinking. This conclusion is based on a comparison between schizophrenics and "normals" on verbal association tests.

When I say "white," what is the first verbal associate that comes to mind? Most college students would say "black." When I say "window," they say "door." This is the normal response. Associative norms are collected for a large number of words using college students and this becomes a verbal associations test. Unusual or disassociative responses occur occasionally for college students, but they are quite common for schizophrenics. If the severity of schizophrenia is defined by the length of time the schizophrenic has been hospitalized, then, the more severe the schizophrenia, the more severely dissociative is the patient. When I say "white," the schizophrenic says "nurse." When I say "window," he says "bars."

A perfect correlational result has been shown. Normal college students give normal associate A, and schizophrenics give abnormal associate Z. Therefore, schizophrenia causes verbal dissociation. Or could it be that these schizophrenics have lived for years in a different environment, a hospital, with different patterns of association. The point is that a correlational relationship does not ever confirm a causal relationship.

Is this a mistake you would never make? What about the conclusion that cigarette smoking causes cancer because smokers get cancer more often than nonsmokers, with a substantial degree of correlation. Is factor X a genetic predisposition? What about the conclusion that watching television violence causes aggressive behavior in children, because children who watch the greatest number of hours of television violence test out to be the most aggressive. What is factor X in this instance?

ESP: A CASE OF EXPERIMENTAL ANALYSIS

Logic of the Analysis of Experiments

Unlike observational studies or psychological testing, the experiment allows an active manipulation of the conditions under which interesting behavioral phenomena are exhibited. The conception of most experiments is based on a complex set of psychological premises by which the scientist believes he can systematically influence the behavior of his experimental subjects. What he has to do is prove that he has influenced their behavior in a meaningful way to his satisfaction and ours.

Edgar Mitchell supposed that he could influence the responses of his subjects on earth by means of telepathy as he traveled to the moon on Apollo 14. He attempted to project an image of one of five symbols which his earthbound counterparts were expected to identify. Experiments of this type were frequently carried out by E. B. Rhine and his students at Duke University. Using a deck of cards, each of which contains one of five symbols, a star, a plus, a circle, a square, or wavy lines (Figure 8-11), these researchers attempted to define the conditions under which the receiver could determine which card the sender was contemplating. Presumably, some form of mental telepathy would enable the receiver to accurately name the cards over a series of test trials. Of course, receivers are never perfectly accurate, but they must be able to perform at better than a chance level.

The standard against which performance is measured is a proportion of correct responses that could be obtained if the receiver were only guessing.

If there are five different possible events that can occur, then one could be correct by chance about one-fifth of the time over a long series of trials. However, it is possible to be lucky in a short series of trials and get them all correct by chance.

FIGURE 8-11   The five symbols of the Rhine deck used in ESP experiments. The back of one of these symbols was used for the card in the lower right corner. Can you guess which one?*
(Courtesy of J. B. Rhine.)

* Answer: the plus sign.

To simplify, assume that the card deck Rhine used had only two different figures, a plus sign, "+", and a circle, "O". Say that you arrange five plus cards and five circle cards in some order and go through the deck attempting to telepathize the cards to a friend. How could we decide whether or not you had shown that you actually had some influence over his answers? If he were only guessing, he would get about half of them correct. In fact, the odds of getting exactly half correct by chance are about 1 in 4. He might even get all of them correct by chance! In other words, any outcome from 0 to 10 out of 10 correct is possible by chance, and mathematicians have developed the laws of chance to determine the probability of each different outcome (Table 8-2). Much of this work was inspired by gamblers who wanted to be able to calculate the odds on different types of bets.

According to these calculations, the chances of getting all ten correct by luck are about 1 in 1000 tries—possible, but quite unlikely. In fact, you could get 9 or better correct only 1 in 93 tries. However, you could get 8 or better 1 in eighteen tries, and 7 or better 1 in 6 tries.

Consider one other possibility. What if you miss them all? That is just as unlikely to occur by chance as getting them all correct! If our receiver missed them all, he might have ESP with crossed signals.

When we observe the actual outcome of the experiment, we will have to decide whether or not we choose to believe that the receiver actually has ESP capabilities. Although we can never be 100% positive, because anything

TABLE 8-2   The Probability for Each Possible Number of Correct Guesses in Ten Trials Assuming the Probability of a Correct Guess is One-Half.

Number correct	Probability (p) Decimal	Ratio
0	.001	1:1000
1	.01	1:100
2	.04	1:25
3	.125	1:8
4	.20	1:5
5	.25	1:4
6	.20	1:5
7	.125	1:8
8	.04	1:25
9	.01	1:100
10	.001	1:1000

is possible by chance, we will feel more certain about some results than others, depending on the probability that they could have occurred by chance.

Which results should lead us to decide in favor of ESP and which will lead us to consider that only chance guessing may have been operating? Although this is somewhat a personal decision, psychologists have come to accept results that could be equaled or bettered by chance only 1 in every 20 tries. For more novel or extraordinary findings psychologists demand a more stringent criterion of 1 in 100 tries be met. Assume that our receiver gets all 10 correct or misses them all. The odds of one or the other of these two events occurring when he has no ESP are 1 in 500 tries and should convince the skeptic that the receiver does have ESP. The odds for getting 9 or more, or 1 or less, by chance are 1 in 45 tries and so might suit the less demanding criterion. Any poorer performance, i.e., one closer to half correct, could occur too often by chance alone to convince anyone that ESP ability has been shown.

Our formal decision rule then is to credit ESP to 0, 1, 9, or 10 correct and to be disinterested in any other outcome. Whatever we decide, we might be wrong, but by our careful logic we try to minimize the decision errors. If we rule that he does have ESP for 0, 1, 9, or 10 correct, we will be wrong and chance will be at work in less than one out of twenty times that we use this rule, a pretty good bet. Of course, if we find ESP only one in twenty experiments, on the average, then we have good reason to suspect that these are nothing more then decision errors.

If we fail to decide in favor of ESP, we could also be wrong. In that case, we might try to use a greater number of trials. Mathematicians have shown that if we use a greater number of trials, our decision rules will be more sensitive in discovering very small nonchance effects. Using something like the Rhine deck, astronaut Mitchell's receivers on earth correctly identified 51 out of 200 cards. With five different symbols, the odds against a result this good or better occurring by chance alone are not quite 1 in 20 tries, a rare enough event to convince *Time,* but not the skeptic, that such an extraordinary phenomenon has been demonstrated.

In most psychological experiments the researcher decides that he can manipulate behavior in a meaningful way. Bluma Ziegarnic (1955) believed that a task would be better remembered if it was not completed, for our procrastinations nag us, while our accomplishments are soon forgotten (even by ourselves). After devising a suitable way of measuring the behavior, she had to consider which of the possible outcomes could be readily obtained by chance and which were rare enough to warrant a rejection of chance as an explanation. For example, she might have noted for 10 hypothetical subjects, how many remembered more interrupted (I) than completed (C) tasks (a positive instance), and how many remembered more C than I tasks (a negative instance).

On the basis of random or chance remembering, we would expect that the subjects would remember more I than C tasks half the time on the average. If 9 or 10 subjects remembered more I tasks than C tasks, then this is good news for Bluma, since the odds are 1 in 20 against the assumption that only chance is operating. If 0 or 1 subjects remember more C than I tasks, then the reinforcement theorist can take heart. Any other outcome would be unworthy as news and would not be published.

You now know how to perform a statistical test, the sign test (positive instances, +; negative instances, −). The exact decision rule depends on the assumed chance probability and the number of trials, but the logic remains the same. Most statistics books contain tables for the sign test, or binomial test as it is sometimes called, in which the odds or probabilities of different results are listed. These tables should be used in any ESP experiment.

Reliability of Experimental Results

When we ask if the results of an experiment are reliable, we want to know whether or not a similar result would be found, if the experiment were performed over again with no major changes in the procedure. This is called a replication of an experiment. Many experiments are expensive and time consuming to perform. Consequently, only indirect evidence is usually given for their reliability. When an observed result is very rare as compared to expectations based on chance alone, it is assumed that a replication will very probably produce the same effect. In fact, if an experiment produces a result which could occur by chance with odds exactly 1 in 20 times, it can be shown that only half of the replications will be successful. Certainly, this fact should not disuade us from the truth of the matter. Behavior is notoriously variable, and a 50% successful replication rate is no grounds for dismissing a finding.

There are cases, however, where an extremely novel finding has been published with 1 in 2 odds, which has proven to be totally unreplicable. One such case showed that when mice had been trained to approach a light and certain chemicals extracted from their brains were injected into other mice, these mice also would approach a light—a case of chemical transmission of memory! Scientists from several major laboratories in the country were unable to replicate this finding and published the fact in *Science,* a major journal of scientific reporting. Unfortunately, spurious findings tend to remain in the popular folklore long after they are expunged from the scientific record. When you startle the world of science you must be sure that your result is replicable by performing other similar experiments. Happily, these unfortunate instances are rare.

Validity of Experimental Results

As in all the other cases of behavioral study, the validity of the experiment, once the result has been shown to be reliable, is the most difficult and most important concern. When the logic of the experimental design proves faulty, it is most often because of a contaminating effect called confounding. The experimenter tries to vary one experimental manipulation or variable independently of other variables that may also cause the observed effect.

If the sender and receiver are in the same room and can view each other, the sender may deliver extremely subtle visual cues to the identification of the symbol on the card without even being aware of this himself. The story of clever Hans is a most revealing case of such unconscious communication. Mr. von Osten in Germany in 1904 had a horse called Hans who could perform such fantastic feats of arithmetic as to convince his owner and many others that he had a horse of rare intelligence. He willingly subjected himself and his horse to the scientific scrutiny of Oskar Pfungst (1965) who discovered that the horse who tapped out his answers with his hoof was receiving extraordinarily subtle cues from his master or even from an expectant audience as to when to begin and end his tappings. Slight leaning forward in anticipation of the answer began the tapping, and relaxing back at the correct moment stopped the tapping. It was a case of unexpected sensitivity on the part of animals but not a case of mathematical ability.

The means of escaping such subtle confounding demand the greatest attention of the careful investigator. Generally, what is done is to try to randomize all contaminating variables. It would be most foolish of Ziegarnic to have assigned a fixed set of tasks to be interrupted and a fixed set to be completed. It could have been quite possible that the tasks chosen to be interrupted were also easier to remember. In that case, task memorability would be confounded with its completability. The trick is to randomly assign the task as an I or C task differently for each subject. If a task is more memorable, it is as likely to wind up as an I or a C task and thus "unconfound" this variable.

Evaluation of Results from Experiments

It should be remembered that the technical use of the term significant in a statistical context is not to be confused with the importance of the finding. If it is significant, then it is assumed to be a reliable enough finding to warrant discussion of its importance. Quite often, it is concluded that a finding is significant but unimportant. The experiment which produced the result also must have a sound structure to permit the inference of causation, being free from a variety of possible confounding variables, including stimulus and subject-confounding.

SUMMARY

Have we made the task of psychological inquiry sound difficult and fraught with peril? Well, if so, we have succeeded to some extent in convincing you of the profoundity of the enterprise. Hopefully, you will not read this as a pessimistic view, but rather as a testimony to the diligence and integrity of the psychological researchers. Criticism of error comes more easily than the recognition of the innovative technique and the appreciation of the advancement of understanding. We can provide no simple statistical tools to aid you on this account. The task of psychology is as complex as the nature of human behavior itself.

SUGGESTED READINGS

BROAD, C. D. *Lectures on psychical research.* Humanities Press, 1962.

EYSENCK, H. J. *Know your own IQ.* Baltimore: Penguin Books, 1962.

HUFF, D. *How to lie with statistics.* New York: Norton, 1954.

KINSEY, A. C., POMEROY, W. B., MARTIN, C. E., & GEBHARD, P. H. *Sexual behavior in the human female.* New York: Pocket Books, 1965.

WALLIS, W. A., & ROBERTS, H. V. *The nature of statistics.* New York: Free Press, 1965.

9

Psychological
Methods of
Inquiry

In a recent report on school financing, a startling announcement was made. It was reported that higher expenditures per pupil resulted in smaller class size and lower pupil achievements, while lower expenditures resulted in larger class size and higher achievement levels. The relationship between expenditures per pupil and class size was not surprising. A wealthy school system can afford to hire more teachers and may thus have a smaller number of pupils per class than a poorer school district. However, the relationship between expenditures and achievement is contrary to our intuition. Clearly, we would expect that more money would result in a beneficial, rather than a detrimental effect. Could the report be true?

The study was conducted in several large cities throughout the United States. School districts were separated on the basis of their average expenditures per pupil. Schools that spent more than $1100 per pupil were designated as high-expenditure schools, while those that spent less than $600 per pupil were termed low-expenditure schools. The overwhelming majority of the schools examined were between these extremes and were not included in the analysis. Also many of the high expenditure schools were in urban areas like New York where educational expenditures have beeen steadily increasing at an astounding rate and student achievement has been decreasing.

Looking at just the high- and low-expenditure schools, the researchers were able to determine the average class size for each. The teacher to student ratio was approximately 1:12 in the high-expenditure schools and 1:25 in the low-expenditure districts. A review of reading skills, however, showed that students in high-expenditure, small-class schools performed below grade level, while students from low-expenditure, large-class schools read above their grade level.

We must be cautious of accepting "facts" at face value. If this study was done appropriately, we would be correct in concluding that money is detrimental to the educational process. However, in fact, it was not done correctly. The researchers who performed this study failed to take note of several significant factors in analyzing their data. In particular, city school children are, for the most part, very different from suburban school children. The low achievement level of many city children may reflect the influence of an inadequate social environment outside of the classroom. The fact that educational achievement has been decreasing over recent years in city schools may not be attributable to the funds spent on these children, but instead to changes in the makeup of the city school population. The percentage of middle-class children has decreased, while that for children of poorer families has increased. At this point, we really do not know the relationship between school financing and pupil achievement. It may be that even though cities spend more for educating disadvantaged students than for others, they are not spending enough. Alternatively, additional funding for needy schools may not be enough to offset the tragic consequences of growing up in a ghetto.

The purpose of this chapter is to examine the methods that man has available for observing generalities in nature. The methods of inquiry are basically the same in all areas of science. What differentiates psychology from other disciplines is its subject matter. Scientific methodology provides a way of posing a question of nature and observing her answer. The experimental methods may thus be thought of as a program for thinking about problems in a systematic way. They provide a means for asking a question and evaluating a reply.

CURIOSITY AND IDEAS

While this chapter concerns itself with experimental methods, it is necessary that the student realize that the methods go hand in hand with the original idea or problem of interest. Neither can be emphasized in isolation. An original idea may not be fully developed without a proper methodological approach, and a poor idea may simply produce trivial results. Hence, the first problem we are faced with is that of the source of researchable ideas. Where do ideas come from? Do ideas simply strike us as a bolt from the blue?

For the introductory student of research, the first thing we must do is attempt to define our interests. Everyone has a certain amount of native curiosity about life. The range of questions one could raise are virtually endless, even within a discipline such as psychology. Consider, for example, the following questions: What do we know about dreams? How do we remember past events? Why do people have phobias? Why do people not help others in an emergency? Given that we can state our interests and formulate them, however vaguely, the next step would appear to be to acquire background information on the subject. This will tell us what other people who have thought about the problem in the past have observed. Very few ideas occur *de novo*. Familiarization with our subject will indicate what is known about the problem and what is still unanswered.

Let's review one of the questions raised. What do we know about dreams? This is an extremely general question, which can include such queries as, Does everyone dream? How frequently do we dream? How long does a dream last? Is there a relationship between external and internal stimuli and the content of our dreams?

Research on dreams, aside from psychoanalytic studies of dream content, is fairly recent. It began during the 1950's with the discovery of an appropriate objective method for observing dreams. It was found that sleep consisted of a number of levels or stages through which a person fluctuated during the night, and that dreaming tended to occur only during a particular stage, which is characterized by specific brain waves as measured on an electroencephalogram (EEG). Further, within this stage of sleep it was found that people frequently engage in rapid eye movements (REMs). These REMs are highly correlated with periods of dreaming. People awakened during periods of REMs are much more likely to report that they were dreaming than people awakened at other times. By recording brain waves and REMs and getting verbal reports from subjects it is possible to study dreaming. Kleitman (1960) provides a review of this work.

Some of the more interesting findings to date suggest that everyone dreams. Some people report that they do not dream, but this may be due to forgetting. In fact, people have an average of three or four dream periods each night. Kleitman says that the probability of a person recalling his dream decreases as the length of time from the REM period to awakening increases. Most interestingly, when people were deprived of their dream periods by being awakened as soon as they began to occur, people tended to make up for these lost periods by dreaming more on successive nights. Continued dream deprivation produced anxiety, irritability, and weight gain in these subjects. Similar effects were not observed in other subjects awakened as frequently, but during nondream periods.

Additional research has shown that dreams last from 10 to 30 minutes with the total time spent in dreaming each night approximately 1 or 2 hours. This is at variance with the common notion that dreams occur in the twinkling of an eye. Also, dreams seem to be unaffected by external or internal stimuli. Subjects deprived of water for long periods before sleep do not report dreaming about water. Similarly, ringing bells while a person is dreaming does not appear to intrude into the content of the dream.

The picture that emerges from the study of dreams is that dreaming is a type of thinking that occurs during a particular stage of sleep. This thinking differs from that done while awake in that it need not be rational. What is interesting, and as yet unanswered, is the apparent need in each person for this type of activity while asleep.

REAL LIFE APPROACHES TO RESEARCH

For many types of questions it is either impractical or impossible to do controlled laboratory research. We might want to study mating behavior in a tribe of primitive people, or the social order of a colony of wild monkeys. In both cases, the researcher must go to his subjects and record his observations. The experimenter may go as a journalist and simply record events as they occur, or he may take an active part in trying to arrange conditions to observe particular behaviors.

Another way to study behavior patterns is to use the survey. People are continually queried on an endless variety of topics. Consider educational differences among people. We might wish to determine how people with a high school education differ from those with a college education. By questioning large numbers of people from each group we may find that the groups differ on such dimensions as type of employment, affluence, geographical location, mobility, etc. Knowing how these groups differ, however, does not tell us why the groups differ. For example, are affluent people more highly educated because they can better afford an education, or is their affluence in part the outcome of their education? We have no way of knowing in this approach.

These methods are illustrative of research conducted under "real life" settings. Data collected by these methods frequently have a degree of imprecision not found in controlled laboratory research. Results tend to be more suggestive than conclusive.

THE SCIENTIFIC METHOD: A SIMPLE EXPERIMENT

In its simplest terms, the scientific method is a means by which a problem is studied by an experiment. The method may be thought of as a guide or a system of rules for observing behavioral phenomena. An experiment is undertaken to determine which factors influence the behavior under study and how these factors produce their effect. Let us say that we are interested in the effect of food deprivation on the behavior of rats. B. F. Skinner has demonstrated that rats can be taught to make simple responses, such as pressing a bar to obtain a food pellet. Using an apparatus like the Skinner box we may observe if deprivation can influence the rat's behavior. We are observing the effect of one variable, deprivation, upon another variable, behavior. The former is termed an independent variable because the experimenter is free to select the type or amount of which he chooses to study. The latter is called a dependent variable as its value is determined by the independent variable. We always manipulate an independent variable and measure a dependent variable.

Before starting our experiment, we must be more concrete in our terminology. Deprivation and behavior must be more specifically defined. What is needed is an operational definition. Deprivation could be defined in terms of the number of hours since the rat last ate.

The dependent variable of behavior is also much too global to be of practical use. What is required is some response that can be counted or measured over time. The Skinner box is excellent for this task, since it was designed to record the number of bar presses that the rat makes per unit of time. In restating our simple experiment, we will now observe the effect of some number of hours of food deprivation upon the rate of bar pressing in the rat.

The independent variable of hours of food deprivation must have at least two levels for our example to actually be considered an experiment. We want to manipulate the amount of food deprivation and measure bar pressing. Therefore, we need a minimum of two levels of deprivation to see if the variable has an effect. One group of rats might be deprived for 5 hours before the experiment, and another group might be deprived for 25 hours. We would then put each rat individually into a Skinner box and observe how often it presses the bar for a food pellet over a fixed period of time. Clearly, our hypothesis or expectation would be that rats deprived for 25 hours will bar press more frequently than rats deprived for only 5 hours. The results of the experiment will show whether the independent variable has an effect upon the dependent variable, and, if so, in what direction the effect is.

If there is no difference in the rate of bar pressing in our two groups of rats, we may conclude that 5 to 25 hours of food deprivation did not have a discriminably different effect on bar pressing.

In setting up an experiment, it is essential that only the independent variable be allowed to vary between the two groups. Assume we ran our experiment and found the hypothetical results shown in Figure 9-1. However, due to the method employed for assigning subjects to groups, all the rats in the group deprived for 5 hours were females, while all the rats deprived for 25 hours were males. What does this mean? Does it mean that the second group bar pressed more because it was deprived of food longer, or because it was composed of males, or both? We have no way of knowing in this instance as there are really two independent variables that are confounded, hours of deprivation and sex. Either or both could have produced the effect. Sex must not differentiate the groups, if we are only interested in hunger. To eliminate sex as a confounding variable, we would run all males or all females in both groups, or assign males and females to both groups randomly.

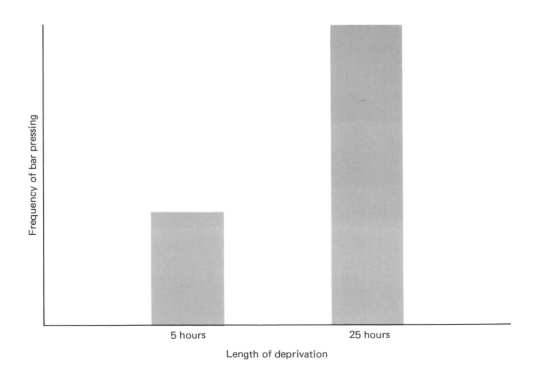

FIGURE 9-1   Bar pressing in rats as a function of the length of food deprivation before the experiment.

GENERALIZATION

If we did control all irrelevant variables and found that rats deprived for 25 hours bar pressed more than those deprived for 5 hours, can we generalize from this experiment? It may certainly be said that rats deprived for 25 hours will under the same conditions bar press more than rats deprived for 5 hours. But this is not too interesting for science. We are after general truths. Can we say that bar pressing is a monotonic function of hunger, that is, the more the rat is food-deprived, the more it will bar press? Our results are certainly in this direction, but the possibility exists that this conclusion would represent an overgeneralization, an overextension of the experimental results. We would probably want to run a few more groups of rats deprived for longer amounts of time to see if the relationship holds.

In addition, there is the consideration of the generalization of the results to other rats. We did not run just one rat in each condition, as one rat may perform better than another on any given day for a number of reasons. We used groups of rats. But will we obtain the same results with other rats? If our rats had been assigned to the groups in a nonsystematic, random fashion, then our results should be true of the entire population of rats of which we have selected a sample. Further, there is the problem of generalization to other species, most notably man. Is our observation limited to rats or is it true of higher species as well? We would probably want to test some higher species to see if the same results are obtained before claiming a general finding.

CONTROL GROUP

The concept of a control group is most easily grasped by an example. Let us leave our rats for the time being and move up the phylogenetic scale to the college student. We are now interested in knowing whether drug-taking can effect performance on a final exam. More specifically, we want to know if taking a stimulant such as caffeine (No-Doz) will improve our test score. We may on a given occasion have taken a stimulant before an exam and felt that our high score on the exam was, in part, due to the drug. This is not, however, scientific evidence about a particular drug's effects. Rather, it is no more than a hunch. Any number of things could have caused us to get a higher than average score on a particular exam. We might have studied harder, the material might have been easier, or the test might have been graded more leniently. Other possibilities also exist. Thus, we may not be sure that our improved performance was due to the drug. We need an experiment.

We cannot simply give the drug to a group of students and observe their performance on an exam for the same reasons as given above. What we need is a comparison group, a group of students who are like the other students in all important respects, but who do not take the drug before the exam. This comparison group is called a control group. The independent variable that we are manipulating in this experiment is whether or not a student takes caffeine before the exam; the dependent variable is the student's test score. The independent variable differs from that used in the previous experiment with rats, where each group had different amounts of the independent variable; now the groups differ in terms of whether the variable is applied.

There are only three possible outcomes that can occur: no difference between the groups indicating that the drug was not effective, superior performance by the experimental group indicating that the drug was beneficial, or superior performance by the control group suggesting that the drug was harmful.

While this experiment seems very simple, in reality, it is not. If the experimental group does better than the control group, can we be sure that the effect is due to the drug? Remember that the groups should differ only in terms of the independent variable; all else must be constant to eliminate the possibility of confounding. In our example, there is something else that varies between groups. One group goes through the act of taking a pill and the other does not. We want our groups to differ only in that the experimental group takes caffeine and the control group does not. Why is this important? Some people will not drink coffee before going to bed for fear that it will keep them awake. This expectancy may be enough to actually keep them up. The same thing could happen in our experiment. Taking a drug might change behavior simply by what the student thinks it will do. Thus, if we are interested in the effects of the drug per se, this factor must be controlled. One possibility is to give both groups a pill before the exam. The experimental group's pill contains the stimulant, while the control group's pill is a placebo, which is composed of an inert substance that has no behavioral effects. Only now can we look at test performance to see the effect of the drug.

As another example, we may want to know how important suggestion is. In this event, we would give our experimental group a placebo pill and our control group nothing. Test performance would now be measured as a function of whether or not a pill was ingested. If our experimental group did better or poorer than the control group, then expectancy is a potent variable.

SIMPLE VERSUS COMPLEX DESIGNS

Up until now we have been discussing simple experiments in which there is only one independent variable and one dependent variable. Furthermore, there were always just two levels of the independent variable. More complex experiments are generally the rule in psychology, and we will consider some of these designs briefly now. There are essentially two ways of making a simple experiment complex: by adding more levels of the independent variable or by adding more independent variables. There are advantages for each approach.

Factorial Designs

Use of more than two levels of food deprivation in the rat experiment would permit us to more clearly observe if bar pressing is monotonically related to hunger. The use of only two levels could lead to an erroneous interpretation of the behavior under study. Figure 9-2 illustrates this point. Assume that the plotted function represents the true relationship between bar pressing and hunger in the rat. If we had selected 5 and 45 hours of food deprivation for our two groups of rats, we would find no effect on our dependent variable of bar pressing and thus might wrongly conclude that bar pressing was un-affected by hunger over the range of deprivation tested. This would be an error of interpolation by the experimenter, assuming that values of the inde-pendent variable between 5 and 45 hours of deprivation, for example, 15, 20, and 25 hours, all have the same effect. Note, however, if we had selected 5 and 25 hours or 25 and 45 hours for our two groups, we would also obtain an inaccurate picture. In the first instance, we might conclude that bar pressing increases with length of food deprivation and in the second that it decreases. Both of these interpretations would represent errors of extrapolation by our extending the finding beyond the range of levels used.

Although there is no fixed rule for selecting the number of levels of an independent variable, we should use enough levels to try to get an accurate representation of the functional relationship for the variable, but, at the same time, we should keep the number of levels few enough so that the experiment is feasible to perform. The original idea for the experiment should specify to some extent the range of possible levels we consider reasonable to examine.

The same reasoning could be applied to the drug experiment discussed earlier. We could apply different amounts of the drug to be compared with the control group, or we could compare different drugs. In the first case we

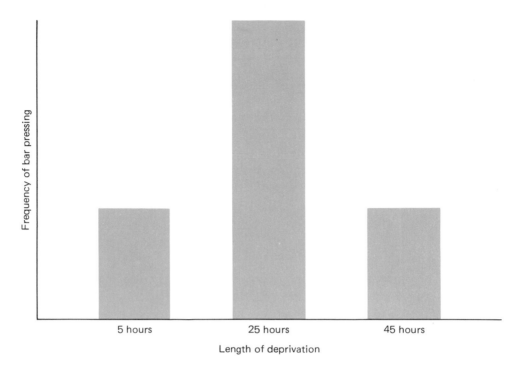

FIGURE 9-2   Bar pressing in rats as a function of length of food deprivation before the experiment.

are treating the drug as a quantitative variable. Each group of students would get a different amount of the same drug with the control group receiving a zero dosage.

Subjects	Group 1	Group 2	Group 3
Dosage	0 gms	2 gms	4 gms

In the second instance we are treating drugs as a qualitative variable, and each group would receive a different type of dosage.

Subjects	Group 1	Group 2	Group 3
Dosage	Placebo	Stimulant	Depressant

We could add as many levels as considered necessary for both types of independent variables.

The second way of making a simple experiment more complex is to add one or more independent variables. Using our basic experiment again, we may now want to study hunger and sex simultaneously. This may be represented by a 2×2 table.

		Hunger	
		5 hours deprived	25 hours deprived
Sex	Male	Group 1	Group 2
	Female	Group 3	Group 4

Note that this is procedurally the same as doing two simple experiments simultaneously. If we add Groups 1 and 3 and 2 and 4 together we have our original experiment on the effect of hunger on bar pressing, whereas, if we collapse Groups 1 and 2 and 3 and 4, we have another simple experiment with sex as the independent variable.

What advantage is there to doing two simple experiments simultaneously? The answer to this question is that examining the effects of two independent variables on a dependent variable enables us to observe a possible interaction. An interaction exists when two variables have differential effects at different levels. Consider the fictional data displayed in Figure 9-3. First, at either level of food deprivation, males bar pressed more than females. Second, for both males and females, rats bar pressed more when deprived for 25 hours than for 5 hours. Simple experiments with sex and hunger as independent variables would provide the same information. What the simple experiments would fail to show, however, is the interaction of sex with hunger. As food deprivation increases, the difference between males and females increases. Females increase their rate of bar pressing, while males radically alter their bar pressing behavior. This observation could not be made with simple experiments. In addition, the interaction can take any one of a number of different forms. For example, the difference between both groups could decrease as the number of hours of deprivation increased, or the groups themselves might have behaved differently at each level with females bar pressing more than males at 5 hours, but males superior at 25 hours. These examples would all constitute an interaction.

Repeated Measure Design

The above designs have all used different groups of subjects for each level of an independent variable. The design that uses the same subjects under

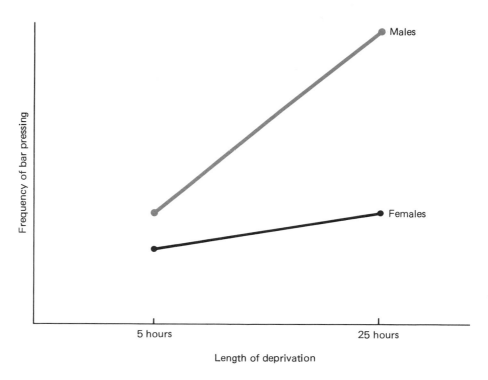

FIGURE 9-3   Bar pressing in rats as a function of sex of subject and length of food deprivation before the experiment.

all conditions is called a repeated measures design, since we are taking repeated measurements on the same subjects. An advantage of this design is that it can be employed with relatively few subjects. Instead of running a different group of subjects under each condition, we run the same subjects under all conditions. Differences between treatment conditions due to individual differences in subjects is eliminated, and the number of subjects necessary to get the same number of observations is less than before.

Suppose, for example, we were interested in determining if students perform better on short-answer or essay exams, and we have only six students available for testing. We may give each student both exams and see which type of test students perform better on. Our independent variable is the type of exam and our dependent variable is the exam score.

There is one potential problem with the repeated measures design that must be avoided. This concerns possible order effects. If one test type is always given before the other test, e.g., short answer before essay, the students may do better on the second test because of a practice effect of test taking, or conversely, they may do poorer because of fatigue or boredom. Differences between the tests could result from factors other than the test type itself. Although we cannot eliminate practice effects or fatigue, we can distribute these effects to both exams by a method called counterbalancing. This is simply giving the short-answer test first to half of the students, and the essay exam first to the other students. Now, differences between the tests may more accurately reflect differences due to test type.

This concludes our brief discussion of experimental design. It was intended to give the reader a flavor of design approaches and not meant to be all-inclusive. Other more complex designs, which build on the models presented here, are possible, but are best saved for a more advanced course.

PROBLEMS IN RESEARCH: EXPERIMENTER EFFECTS AND SELF-FULFILLING PROPHECY

Several years ago, Robert Rosenthal (1963) performed an interesting and troublesome experiment with rats. The task was simple enough. Rosenthal asked his assistants to teach a group of rats to run a maze. Rosenthal was not interested in whether rats could learn mazes, for this was determined long ago. Rather, Rosenthal was interested in determining if the experimenter can unknowingly influence the results of his experiment. He did this by giving each of twelve experimenters a group of rats to test in a maze learning task. Half of the experimenters were told that their rats were specially bred for maze learning and were labeled maze-bright. The other experimenters were told that their animals were maze-dull. In reality, there was no difference between the rats assigned to both groups of experimenters. The results most surprisingly show that the maze-brights learned faster than the maze-dulls. This suggests that the experimenter exerted an influence on their subjects to alter the outcome of the experiment to fit their expectancy.

Experimenter effects have been found with human subjects as well as rats. Rosenthal has observed that sex, age, and race of an experimenter can influence the results of an experiment. By viewing films of an experiment, it has been shown that male experimenters smile more and are generally more attentive to female subjects than male subjects. While this may be intuitively obvious, it is troublesome from the standpoint of methodology as male and female subjects are being treated differently. The only thing that should vary is the independent variable.

The seriousness of this discovery was fully revealed in research done by Rosenthal and Jacobson in several school systems across the country. In their book *Pygmalion in the classroom*, Rosenthal and Jacobson (1968) describe the experiment. They visited classrooms and administered standard I.Q. tests to the children along with a fictional test for "intellectual blooming." Rosenthal and Jacobson reported the results to the teachers, but distorted upward the scores for intellectual blooming for 20% of the students in each class. The teachers were told that these children, who were selected at random, would show much intellectual growth over the course of the school year. Of course, the only difference between these children and the rest of the class was the expectancy the teacher had for each.

At the end of the year Rosenthal and Jacobson returned and repeated the I.Q. test. The results were impressive. The experimental group, the intellectual bloomers, gained an average of 4 I.Q. points more than the other students in their classroom. This finding was true of children of all ability levels. Improving teacher expectations improved intellectual development.

Rosenthal and Jacobson also asked the teachers to rate their students on classroom behavior. The teachers rated the bloomers as happier, more curious, and more interesting. In each classroom, there were also children who were not designated as bloomers, but who showed I.Q. gains nonetheless. Interestingly, the teachers rated these children negatively. They were judged less-well-adjusted and less interesting. Apparently the teachers were pleased when their expectations were confirmed and upset when contrary, although positive, changes were evident. Rosenthal has labeled this effect the self-fulfilling prophecy.

The implication of Rosenthal's work is quite important. If our goal is to maximize the development of each individual in our school system, it is necessary for teachers to realize the potential for growth and for harm that they possess. Rosenthal and Jacobson did not show that teachers could retard the development of a child, as it would have been unfair to the child so selected, but the results of the experiments with rats indicate that "experimenters" can achieve results in either direction.

How are experimenter effects communicated? In the case of the student and teacher it may be in the form of extra attention, kind words, or even a smile from the teacher to the student. We do not completely understand how people communicate without words, but we do so everyday by such nonverbal forms of expression as tone of voice and body movements and posture.

Similar nonverbal forms of communication may be involved in animal experiments when experimenter effects have been demonstrated. It may be that maze-bright rats were handled more often and more gently than maze-dulls. It has been reported that rats, like dogs, enjoy being petted. This might be one way of an experimenter communicating to his subject.

As experimenters, we must guard against experimenter effect unknowingly influencing our data. Rosenthal suggests that one answer might be automation. Some experimenters have resorted to this in part by keeping themselves physically removed from their subjects during testing and having instructions read over a tape recorder so that all subjects receive the same input. Another technique, if assistants are available, is to use experimenters who are uninformed of the expected results.

There is probably a significant message that runs through all of Rosenthal's research beyond that which is directly relevant to experimental psychology. One realizes, especially after reading about the children in the classroom studies, that our expectations and feelings about other people can have serious consequences. It is important that people sensitize themselves to this fact and treat each other accordingly.

ETHICAL CONSIDERATIONS

Before leaving the topic of research we should consider the proper relationship between the experimenter and his subjects. There are rules for dealing with subjects, whether rat or man, that have been formalized by the American Psychological Association. Further, directives have been issued by the Surgeon General regarding the use of human subjects. In general, subjects are to be treated humanely and not exposed to harmful procedures. The researcher should have a fundamental respect for life in whatever form he finds it. The guidelines are, however, broad; they leave much to the interpretation of the individual scientist. For expository purposes, we will consider some examples of research with human subjects that may have infringed on people's rights. The examples were provided by a perceptive paper written by Herbert Kelman in 1967. In each of the studies, the subjects were systematically deceived about the true purpose of the experiment.

Mulder and Stemerding (1963) wanted to study the effect of threat on group attraction and the need for strong leadership. They informed small food merchants in a number of towns that a large organization was planning to open supermarkets in their area. The experimenters wanted to observe the shopkeepers behavior to this threat of possible business competition. The shopkeepers were not told that it was an experiment, since this would have eliminated the effect of the threat. The question we should ask ourselves is whether researchers have the right to infringe on the lives of other people for the purpose of collecting data. It is the issue of means and ends.

College students were involved in a study employing deception by Bergin

(1962). Students of both sexes took a battery of psychological tests and were later given erroneous information regarding their level of masculinity or femininity. While the students were debriefed after the experiment, it may be that some regarded the debriefing as a lie and interpreted it as an attempt to make them feel better.

Perhaps the most well-known research involving deception is the study of obedience by Milgram (1963). In this experiment, the subject believed he was in a learning task. He was instructed to deliver increasingly severe electrical shocks to another person in an adjoining room, if that person did not perform as required. In reality, no shocks were delivered and the person in the adjoining room was an accomplice of the experimenter. Milgram found that a sizable number of students followed his instructions to shock the other person and did so up to a level described to the subjects as extremely painful. This work, perhaps more than any other, has served to raise the issue of ethical standards of research. Milgram reported that his subjects revealed a great deal of stress in this situation, both subjects who obeyed and those who defied his command.

It is reasonable to assume that many of the subjects who were obedient came out of this experiment with a lowered sense of self-esteem knowing that they had been willing to administer pain to another human being simply because it was demanded of them. Milgram has argued that his experiment provided a unique opportunity for people to learn something about themselves. This may be true, but it was certainly not the intent of the subjects to obtain this self-knowledge when they entered the experiment.

The above review of the uses of deception is by no means exhaustive, but is only intended to give some idea of the type of problem encountered in the acquisition of knowledge about man. In each instance we must ask if there is some ethical standard that has been violated by the experimenter. Does the experimenter have the right to study whatever he wants and under any conditions he feels appropriate? And, if so, at whose expense? There is a fundamental issue at stake here. It is to some extent unanswered, but must be faced nonetheless. What are people for? Kelman (1967) thoughtfully attempted to deal with this issue.

> The broader ethical problem brought into play by the very use of deception becomes even more important when we view it in the light of present historical forces. We are living in an age of mass societies in which the transformation of man into an object to be manipulated at will occurs on a mass scale, in a systematic way, and under the aegis of specialized institutions deliberately assigned to this task. In institutionalizing the use of deception in psycho-

logical experiments, we are, then, contributing to a historical trend that threatens values most of us cherish.

Most people would agree that honesty is more appropriate than dishonesty
and, as such, we should not try to manipulate other people. But the tragic
events at My Lai have a direct bearing on this issue. Is My Lai not a direct
parallel to Milgram's study of obedience? Given that some people do obey
orders, perhaps we should now seek to determine the factors or variables that
influence obedience. This might be studied in the same way that propaganda
methods were examined in the hope that an awareness of the techniques might
permit the individual to more adequately determine his own course of action.
Thus, the issue of ethical considerations for the rights of subjects is not entirely
resolvable. Individual rights must be preserved. However, knowledge about
human behavior must be obtained, if we are to better the human condition.

SUMMARY

In research, a question is turned into a researchable idea by restating the
question in a form that may be answered by an experiment. This involves
manipulating an independent variable and observing its effect upon a dependent variable. Rules for manipulating variables and measuring their consequences have been described by the different experimental designs, with special
attention given to possible sources of confounding within each design. The
approach has sought to demonstrate the complexities involved in pursuing
research and provide a framework with which to interpret data from widely
different sources. General research problems concerning experimenter effects
and the place of others in research have also been reviewed.

SUGGESTED READINGS

ANDERSON, B. F. *The psychological experiment*. Belmont, California: Brooks, Cole, 1969.
BACHRACH, A. J. *Psychological research: An introduction*. New York: Random House, 1962.
HYMAN, R. *The nature of psychological inquiry*. Englewood Cliffs, New Jersey: Prentice-Hall,
    1964.
UNDERWOOD, B. J. *Psychological research*. New York: Appleton, 1957.

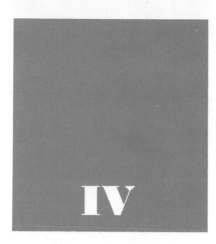

Sensation
and
Perception

10

Visual Sensitivity

On June 30, 1956, the sky over the Grand Canyon was perfectly clear. The sun was shining and the pilot, James Snyder, was pointing out the canyon to his passengers as they flew over it. Suddenly, without any warning, the DC-7 collided with a Lockheed Constellation. All 128 people on the two aircraft fell to their deaths in the worst airline disaster in history.

This was not a unique incident. In April, 1958, the visibility over Las Vegas was 35 miles. Yet an F-100 aircraft flew into another DC-7 at 21,000 feet. Elsewhere, two Norsemen aircraft collided over the airport at Kenora at 10:30 in the morning despite the fact that visibility was unlimited. The conclusion of the investigators was that both pilots failed to maintain an adequate lookout. In 1959, there were two collisions, one over Cheyenne and another over Philadelphia. Here again, the visibility was good in both cases, yet the expert crash investigators had to conclude that the pilots failed to see each other.

One might think that if the sky is clear and the light levels are high enough it should be easy to see another aircraft. A number of facts make this assumption questionable however. First, when landing at a major airport, say the John F. Kennedy airport in New York, rarely do you see more than one or two other aircraft during the landing approach. Yet, there are dozens of aircraft aloft at the same time in the vicinity of such a busy air terminal. Even if you concentrate on looking for other aircraft, you are unlikely to see more than two or three. The reason for this lies in the limitations of our sense of sight.

If two aircraft travel towards each other at speeds of 300 mph it will take only 30 seconds to close a distance of 5 miles. If the aircraft should be traveling at greater speeds, which is more likely, then the time to collision would be proportionately less. This leaves precious little time for a pilot to detect and recognize another aircraft, determine if it is on a collision course, and then execute a maneuver to avoid the collision. If one considers that the pilot may have to spend the entire day on the alert for intruding aircraft, and that he must detect these intruders while they are still far enough away for it to do some good, then one can easily appreciate how critical vision is. The next three chapters will be concerned with vision and how it is used in detecting, recognizing, and evaluating a variety of events in our world.

THE PROBLEM OF DETECTING

What conditions are necessary to ensure that an observer will visually detect an object? In actuality, there is no single answer. The fact that an object may be detected by the eye under some circumstances does not insure that it will be detected under slightly different circumstances. Consider the case of a person looking straight ahead at a screen. Subsequently, a very dim spot of light is projected onto that screen so that it falls directly in the path of gaze. If the spot is dim enough, the subject will not be able to see it. However, if the spot gradually increases in brightness or intensity it will ultimately become bright enough to see. A physical measurement of how much light is needed in order to just see the spot is called the threshold, a term that we will define more accurately later.

Let us now suppose that one wants to measure the threshold level of the light. This could be done by painting a ring onto the screen and asking the subject to stare into the center of the ring using the right eye, while keeping the left eye closed. Then the spot is introduced into the center of the ring and gradually made brighter until the subject reports seeing it. Conversely, the light could have started out as very bright and gradually become dimmer until the subject says it disappears. If these trials are repeated over and over again, an average intensity at which the spot was just visible can be calculated. If the spot is much brighter than the threshold level, it is very likely to be seen; if it is much dimmer than the threshold level, it is highly unlikely it would be seen.

Now, consider what would happen if the light is moved outside the ring, while the subject still stares at the center of the ring. The subject is told to continue to stare into the ring but that the spot may appear either inside the ring or outside of it. If the same procedure as before is repeated, a higher light intensity will be needed in order to see the spot outside the ring. The threshold level is higher. As a matter of fact, this entire experiment could be done very systematically by plotting the threshold level for spot detection as a function of distance from the center of the ring. Figure 10-1 illustrates what this plot might look like. It is apparent from the figure that we cannot detect an object with equal ability at different places in the visual field. As the object moves away from the center of gaze, it becomes more difficult to

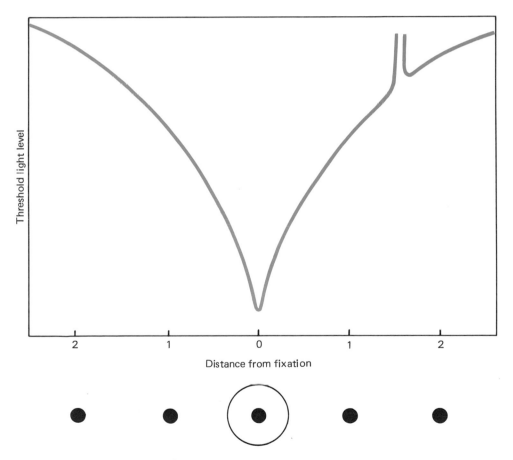

FIGURE 10-1   As the spot is moved from position zero (inside the ring) to more distant positions on either side of the ring, much more light intensity is required to detect it. In one region to the right of the zero or fixation point, the threshold light level reaches infinity. This is the blind spot.

see it. That is why a pilot, for example, must continually scan the sky if he is to detect an intruding aircraft.

STRUCTURE AND FUNCTION

Why is it that it is harder to see an object when it is somewhat off to the side than when the object coincides with the direction of gaze? The answer to this question stems from a consideration of the structure of the eye itself.

The back of the living eye is usually examined with an ophthalmoscope, a device used by doctors to see the fine structure of the retina, which is the surface that lines the interior of the eye. The retina contains nerve endings (as discussed in Chapter 2) that are sensitive to light. When light rays reflected by an object enter the eye, an image of the object may be formed by the lens on the retinal surface (Figure 10-2). The light within the image excites the specialized nerve endings, causing them to send nerve impulses ultimately to the brain.

The fine structure of the retina is depicted in Figure 2-6 of Chapter 2. There are two kinds of nerve endings in the retina that are sensitive to light: the rods and the cones. We shall have more to say about these later on.

The optic disc, which represents the place of entry of the optic nerve, is a portion of the retina that is free of rods and cones. Consequently, one should be incapable of seeing objects whose images are formed on the optic disc or blind spot (Figure 10-3). This explains why Figure 10-1 indicates that no amount of light is sufficient to produce detection of the spot at one particular position in the visual field. In that position, the spot falls within the blind spot of the right eye.

Fovea

There is a second disc on the retina, which is called the fovea. When an object is fixated by looking directly at it, its retinal image falls within the fovea. The fovea is richly supplied with cones. As a matter of fact, the very center of the fovea, the small spot in the middle of the fovea in Figure 10-2, is entirely comprised of cones. This small spot is actually the shape of a small shallow pit in the retina. It is aimed at objects being attended to. Thus, when looking at something, the eyes will turn so that the image of the object is formed on the center of the fovea. The reason for this is that the abundance of tiny cones permits very sharp vision. Visual acuity in the central fovea is many times better than it is in the more peripheral

(a)

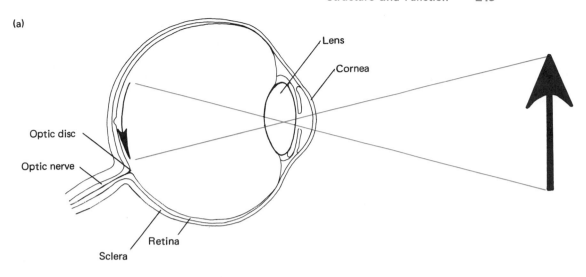

(b)

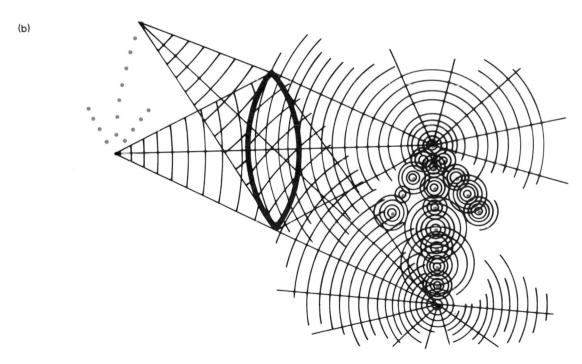

FIGURE 10-2   (a) A schematic diagram of the eye showing the formation of an image on the retina. The mechanism of image formation is illustrated by (b) where the arrow is depicted as a collection of points. Each point emits or reflects light in all directions. Bundles of rays from each point intercept the lens. The lens bends these rays so that they converge to points on the retina. It will be observed that the resulting image on the retina is upside down.

Z

FIGURE 10-3   The blind spot. If you close your left eye and stare fixedly (or fixate) the X while keeping the page about 10 inches from your eye, the Z will disappear. It may be necessary to move the page slightly toward and away from you in order to get the distance from the eye just right. When the Z does disappear, its image is within the zone of the blind spot or optic disc. While keeping the X in the center of vision, you may then open the left eye. The Z will then be visible, since the left eye's blind spot is on the opposite side of the eye. This is one reason why the blind spot is not detected in normal binocular vision. The blind spot in the right eye is offset by good visual sensitivity in the left eye and vice versa. You may find the left eye's blind spot by fixating the Z with the left eye and noticing the disappearance of the X.

portions of the retina. Less light is needed to detect the spot in the central field of vision, in the fovea, than in the more peripheral field of vision (Figure 10-1).

There is one important qualification that must be made with respect to the foregoing. Visual sensitivity is better in the fovea than in the periphery under daylight conditions. However, it is not necessarily better in the dark. This is due to the fact (described in Chapter 2) that rods, which are numerous in the periphery, are suited for seeing in very dim light, whereas cones are more suited for seeing in the daylight.

Adapting to the Dark

The different functions of rods and cones are inferred, in part, from the phenomenon of dark adaptation. This phenomenon is commonly experienced by going from bright daylight into a darkened movie theatre. Upon first entering the theatre, one feels virtually blind. The seats are hard to find. Occasionally, a person may try to sit in someone's lap. After a while, however, sight comes back and large objects are quite easily seen. After some more time, say 40 minutes or so, even a bar of candy can be seen after it has fallen to the floor. In other words, the eye becomes more and more sensitive to light as it spends time in the dark. When this increase in sensitivity was subjected to scientific investigation, the findings suggested that rods and cones work differently and have different roles in vision.

An observer, in a typical experiment on dark adaptation, would spend a few minutes in the dark after being exposed to a very bright light. After the prescribed period in the dark, he would be asked if he could detect a very dim spot of light, as in the first experiment on detection discussed in this chapter. The intensity of light in the spot would be slowly increased until the observer reported seeing the spot. The average level of light leading to detection could then be plotted as a function of time spent in the dark. The curve in Figure 10-4 shows what a typical plot might look like.

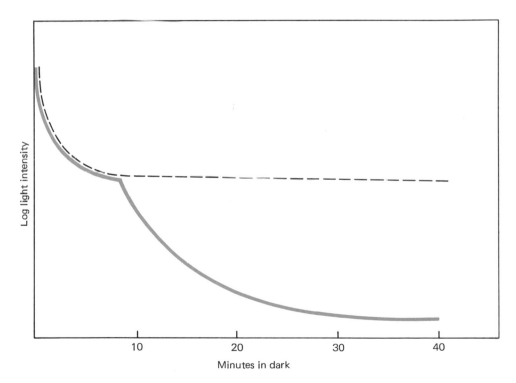

FIGURE 10-4   The dark adaptation curve. This curve shows how much light is necessary to detect a target as a function of time in the dark after looking at a very bright field. The log of light intensity is used for the ordinate so that the curve would fit onto the page. If a simple plot of light intensity were used, the ordinate would have to be at least 10,000 times larger. This gives some idea of how sensitivity to light improves with time in the dark.

The interesting thing about the dark adaptation curve is the very abrupt change in its direction near the 10-minute point on the abcissa. However, people who are night-blind, those who do not see well in the dark, give a dark adaptation curve resembling only the upper limb of the curve in Figure 10-4. This is sketched into Figure 10-4 as the upper dotted line. As a matter of fact, when the dark adaptation experiment is done very carefully with the test target located at different positions in the visual field, the solid curve of Figure 10-4 is obtained when the target is slightly to one side of fixation. When the target is centered in the fovea, something very much like the dotted curve is obtained. Moreover, with the target well off to one side of fixation, the resulting curve resembles only the lower limb of the solid curve.

Such results fit some well-established anatomical facts that were described in Chapter 2. The cones are numerous in the fovea, and, as was pointed out above, rods are not present. As we go into the periphery of the retina, we find an increasing number of rods and decreasing number of cones. What the curves reveal, then, is that cones become somewhat more sensitive in the dark, perhaps ten times more sensitive, and then remain at that level of sensitivity regardless of how much longer the eye remains in darkness. The rods, on the other hand, continue to become more sensitive with time in the dark, although at a slower and slower rate so that finally, after 30 or 40 minutes, they may be as much as 1000 times more sensitive to light than they were right after exposure to a bright light.

Let us return now to the statement that the center of the retina, the fovea, is more sensitive to light than is the periphery. We can see now that this is true only when the eye is adapted to a high light level. When the eye is dark adapted by being kept in darkness for several minutes, then the fovea may actually be less sensitive to light than the periphery. It is for this reason that lookouts aboard ships during World War II were taught to be alert for targets appearing in peripheral vision at night. Since the fovea may be less sensitive than the periphery, it was considered possible that targets would be less likely to be seen when looked at directly than when they are imaged somewhat off the axis of the line of sight. Often a dim star can be seen by looking to one side of its real position.

SELECTIVE SENSITIVITY OF RECEPTORS

One trick used by people who must maintain good night vision is the wearing of red goggles when in a lighted place and removing them when going into a dimly lit place. This is particularly true aboard ships when an officer must go from a lighted room, e.g., a radio shack, to the deck without time to dark adapt. The reason why red goggles preserve dark adaptation is that the rods are very insensitive to red light. To the rods, wearing red goggles is just like being in the dark. Thus, through dark adaptation the rods can attain their maximum sensitivity to other kinds of light. As soon as the goggles are removed, the rods are ready for night vision. In the meantime the cones, which are quite responsive to red light, allow the goggle wearer adequate vision in well-lighted surroundings.

Light and Color

When Sir Isaac Newton placed a prism in the path of a beam of sunlight he found that the prism caused the beam of white light to break up into a spectrum of colors. Then Newton took a lens and placed it so that it would intercept the spectrum of colors, and found that he could recombine them into a beam of white light. It was from this experiment that Newton inferred that white light is actually made up of light of many different colors. Today, we know that this means the spectral colors differ from each other in wavelength, and that sunlight is made up of a broad range of wavelengths.

Light is but a small segment of the entire electromagnetic spectrum, which ranges from cosmic rays to long wavelength radio waves. We cannot see radio waves nor can we see x rays or cosmic rays. Broadcast radio waves are very long. The crest-to-crest distance of a radio wave may be as long as one kilometer. Cosmic rays, however, are at the other extreme of wavelength. The wavelength here is on the order of 10^{-12} centimeters. Visible light is well between these two extremes. Ranging from violet at one end to red at the other, the visible spectrum includes electromagnetic radiation of from 400 to about 700 nanometers (billionths of a meter). But even within this 300 nanometer range of wavelengths, the eye is not equally sensitive to all of them. We can understand this with another hypothetical experiment.

Suppose we follow Newton's example, but, instead of using a beam of sunlight, we use a tungsten bulb as a white light source. If we mount the bulb in front of a slit and place the prism behind the slit, we can form a spectrum of colors on a screen (Figure 10-5; see page 265). If the screen itself contains a narrow movable slit, we can move the slit back and forth across the spectrum and thereby select any one of the colors for presentation to an observer. Moreover, by placing a variable neutral filter in front of the observer's eye, we can adjust the brightness of the colored light. An apparatus like this, known as a monochromator, makes it possible to measure the sensitivity of the eye to lights of different wavelengths. If we now use colored light coming from the slit in the monochromator and measure the amount of light energy necessary for detection, it will be found that lights of different wavelengths must be at different intensity levels if they are to be detected. Thus, more energy is needed to detect a pure red or a blue light than to see a green light.

Retinal Sensitivity

If the experiment is done with a light adapted eye and the colored test light is imaged on the fovea, then the curve depicted in Figure 10-6 is obtained. This relationship between wavelength and sensitivity of the light-adapted eye

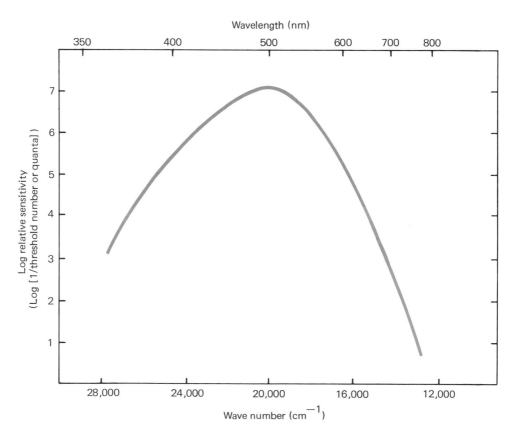

FIGURE 10-6   Photopic luminosity function. Shows how sensitivity of the eye varies with wavelength of the stimulus. Sensitivity is greater for yellows and greens than it is for reds and blues. Sensitivity is defined as the reciprocal of the threshold light level. Thus, where less light is needed to just detect a particular color, we say that the eye is more sensitive to that color.

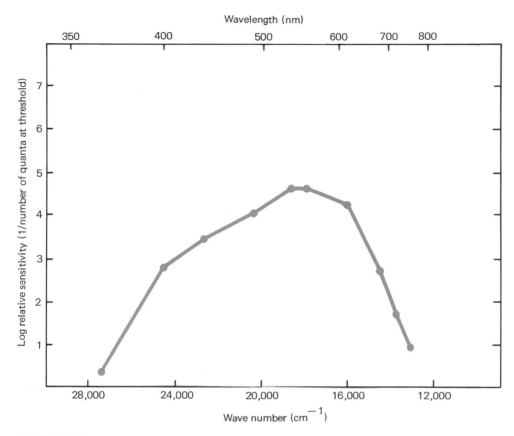

FIGURE 10-7   Scotopic luminosity function. Sensitivity of the dark adapted eye to light of different wavelengths. This is an empirical curve where points represent actual data obtained from a subject.

is known as the photopic luminosity function (from the Greek *photos*, light) (Figure 10-6). The same sort of curve may be obtained for the dark adapted eye. After a long period in darkness, a very dim colored light can be shown to an observer and its intensity slowly increased until he just detects it. Then he would be dark adapted again, and the same procedure repeated for another wavelength of light. This long and laborious experiment would yield a relationship called the scotopic luminosity function (from the Greek *skotos*, darkness) (Figure 10-7). The scotopic luminosity function is similar, but not identical, to the photopic luminosity function.

The difference between the photopic and scotopic luminosity functions is thought to be due to the differential sensitivities of rods and cones to different wavelengths of light. The rods, which are quite insensitive to red (>650 nm), are active in the dark adapted eye, and cones are active in the light adapted eye.

COLOR VISION

Though we have been discussing the differential sensitivity of the eye to light of various wavelengths, nothing has yet been said about the perception of color. It is true that we have used the terms "yellow light" and "red light," but this has really been a convenient but somewhat inaccurate way of saying that a light with a wavelength of 660 nanometers ("red") was used in an experiment or that light of 580 nanometers ("yellow") was employed. Our observer could have detected both of these lights as lights without any awareness at all that one was colored red and the other yellow.

As a matter of fact, colored objects are often perceived as colorless. People often react merely to light intensity differences rather than the color itself. This occurs, for example, when night is about to fall. Imagine walking on a summer evening. Though the grass may be green and the houses you pass surrounded by colorful flowers, in the twilight one is usually aware only of relative lightness rather than the color itself. The red roses may look black (remember that the rods are insensitive to red), and the pale yellow house may look white. At twilight, the eye is becoming dark adapted, and vision under these circumstances is mediated to a great extent by the rods. Though the rods are differentially sensitive to lights of different wavelengths, they do not give the impression of qualitative color differences. It is the cones that mediate color perception. There is an important difference between detecting lights of different wavelengths and actually seeing the different colors of these wavelengths.

In actuality, the relationship between wavelength and perceived color is not that clear-cut. It is commonly asserted that, if a light is perceived as red, then it must be comprised largely of light within a particular band of wavelengths, i.e., between 600 and 700 nanometers. This is not true. White light composed of all wavelengths may appear colored under a number of different circumstances. We might, for example, surround a neutral gray patch with a green field (Figure 10-8; see page 265). Although the light coming from the gray patch contains the same wavelengths with or without the green surroundings, it looks distinctly reddish against the green. The important point here is that neutral or white light can give the impression of color.

Yet another way to produce the impression of red with white light is simply to reduce the amount of green light in the original beam of white light. This leaves all the wavelengths except green in the beam of light. Despite the fact that red wavelengths do not predominate in the beam, it still looks reddish. Therefore, we must conclude that the color of a light or of a surface is not related in a one-to-one manner with the predominant wavelength of light.

A beginning to an understanding of color perception may be achieved with an experiment. An array of colored pieces of paper is presented (Figure 10-9; see page 265 for Figures 10-9 to 10-12). There is a very wide array of seemingly randomly related colors, such as green, red, orange, blue, purple, yellow, and brown. To do the experiment, imagine placing the patches in some order.

What you might have done is place the red patch near an orange patch, the orange near a yellow, the yellow near a green, and so on. In addition, the ones set out side-by-side, perhaps as shown in Figure 10-10, have the greater purity. This would leave out the very pale yellows and the pinks.

Most people make a continuum ranging from blue at one end to a deep red at the other (Figure 10-11). But what is to be done with the purple? The purple looks as much like the blue as it does like the red. One elegant solution to this problem is to abandon the linear ordering and create a circular ordering (Figure 10-12). The resulting pattern places the purple as near the red as it is near the blue. Yet, the relations among all the other colors are preserved.

But what about the shades and tints of the colors and the patches that are not so pure? These can be handled by adding another dimension. Instead of considering only the side-by-side relations among the colors, the lighter patches could be placed above the more similar original colors and the darker ones below.

Still other colors are not simply shades or tints of some other colors, but seem to vary in purity. These can be placed inside the circle so that the less pure, but equally bright colors are near to the center. If this is done carefully, the classical color solid illustrated is produced (Figure 10-13).

The Color Solid

The color solid is a way of representing many of the dimensions of perceived color. As we go around its periphery, we have a representation of the

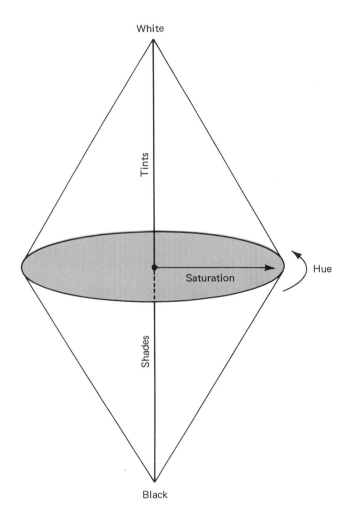

FIGURE 10-13   The color solid.

different hues ordered in terms of their similarity to each other. This is the color circle. As we move from the periphery toward the center, the colored patches becomes less saturated or less pure. Going up or down, we get the shades and tints of the various colors.

All of these things can be observed for any one of the colors by taking a slice out of the double cone color solid. Such a slice is called the color triangle (Figure 10-14; see page 265). All of this has to do with colors as they appear in daily life; it has nothing at all to do with wavelength per se. We could construct a color solid even if we were ignorant of the wave nature of light and had never seen Newton's spectrum of colors.

The difference between the physical spectrum and the psychological continuum of colors becomes apparent when you consider the color purple. This color is not represented by any single wavelength of light. Red is associated with a particular band of wavelengths. So, too, is blue at the opposite end of the physical spectrum. Purple, however, can only be perceived if both red and blue are present and mixed together. There is no purple wavelength, yet purple is just as much a color as red or blue.

The color purple is not the only place at which hues in the color solid lack a one-to-one correspondence with the spectral colors or single-wavelength colors. There are also the metameric colors, which are perceptually indistinguishable from spectral colors but are compounded of spectral colors of different wavelengths. Thus, red and green lights may be added together to produce a yellow light.

Color Mixture

The mixing of colors by adding them together to form other colors is a well-known phenomenon. What is not so well known is that there are actually two kinds of color mixture, additive and subtractive. Subtractive color mixture is what is involved when an artist mixes pigments on his palette to produce new colors. Additive mixture occurs when two spotlights covered with two different colored filters are aimed so that their beams of light are superimposed on a common point on a screen. This basic method of adding up two or three beams of light to obtain metameric matches to other spectral lights is also the favored method of the visual scientist.

It is possible to produce a very pure spectral light by passing a beam of white light through a special colored filter. If two such colored beams of light are projected onto a white screen, they will mix to form another color. That pale yellow is produced by adding red and green light can be predicted from the color circle we described earlier (Figure 10-15; see page 265). If three colors were to be added together in different amounts, it is possible to produce the impression of any color in the color circle. This fact is the basis for the trichromatic theory of color perception, which will be considered later.

Subtractive color mixture is the basis for mixing pigments to produce colors in painting. A given artist's color, e.g., ultramarine blue, appears blue because the pigment absorbs all but blue wavelengths of light. When white light falls on this paint, its blue wavelengths are reflected back to the eye of the observer, while the red, green, and yellow wavelengths are largely absorbed. Similarly, the yellow paints absorb blue, red, and green light and reflect yellow wavelengths back to the eye. These pigments are not perfect absorbers. Some red and green and yellow may well be reflected along with the blue light by the ultramarine pigment. However, the blue does predominate.

When blue and yellow paints are mixed it is common for them to produce the color green, which is not what we would predict in a straightforward way from the color circle. This occurs because the mixed yellow and blue paint absorbs both yellow and blue, the yellow pigment absorbing the blue light reflected by the ultramarine paint and the ultramarine pigment absorbing the yellow light reflected by the yellow pigment. The predominant remaining wavelength turns out to be greenish, although somewhat muddy and not nearly so brilliant as the colors reflected by the original pigments taken alone. Various nuances in color mixture may be elicited by making use of the fact that pigments of different types reflect light other than that which gives them their names. Alizarin crimson, for example, reflects a substantial amount of blue light as well as red light. Therefore, mixing other pigments with this paint will yield different results than would occur if they were mixed with other red paints, e.g., cadmium red, which reflect substantial amounts of yellow light.

THEORIES OF COLOR VISION

In a very real sense, there are no theories of color vision. What most people mean when they use the phrase "theories of color vision" is that they are concerned with the problem of explaining color mixture. Color sensations per se are usually treated simply as primitive conditions for more complex phenomena. The experience of redness, for example, is just accepted as given. The most that one might want to say about this is that a particular subset of cells in the brain may fire when the observer says that he sees "red." Any further explanation gets into the mind-body problem and is generally dismissed as too speculative or philosophical an issue for scientific concern. However, when red and greenish lights add up to give the impression of a yellow color, we can make a theory relating the reaction of the organism to superimposed red and green light to its reactions to the metameric yellow light that it matches.

There are two basic theories of color vision that account in a satisfactory way for the facts of color mixture. These are the trichromatic theory, which was mentioned above, and the opponent-process theory.

Trichromatic Theory

The trichromatic theory was first proposed by Thomas Young and was then rediscovered by Helmholtz in the nineteenth century. Hence, the theory is sometimes called the Young-Helmholtz theory. It is based upon the fact that any three colors from the color circle may be mixed in various proportions to give a match to any other color on the circle. To explain this, it was proposed that there are three pigments in the human eye. Each of these pigments absorbs different wavelengths of light (Figure 10-16). Thus, there may be one pigment that absorbs largely red light and relatively less of other wavelengths, another pigment that absorbs green light, and another that absorbs mostly blue or violet light. These pigments are presumed to reside in different cones. When a cone containing the red sensitive pigment is stimulated, it will send a signal saying "red" to the brain.

Since each of these pigments is somewhat responsive to wavelengths other than those to which they are maximally responsive, a red-responding cone

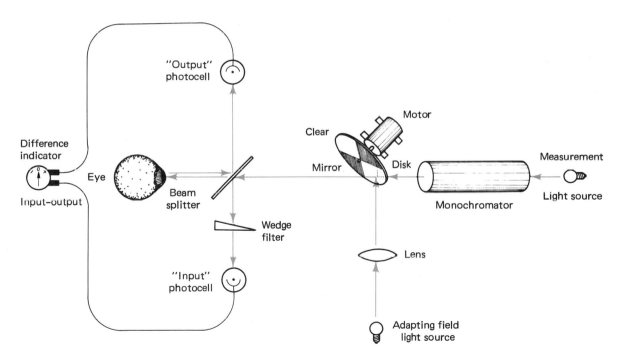

FIGURE 10-16   Diagram of apparatus used to measure the change in light absorption by retinal pigments in the human eye. This was originally done by Campbell and Rushton (1955). In brief a very sensitive electronic system measures the difference in the light projected into the eye from that reflected back out and the difference reflects how much light quanta were adsorped by the visual pigments. Adapted from Cornsweet (1970).

might be excited to some slight extent by a blue wavelength light. As a matter of fact, if a light of pure color, e.g., red, is very intense, it may appear yellowish. This is because the red pigment absorbs as much light as it can, and the remaining light excites the pigments most responsive to green light. We might presume that this phenomenon, called the Bezold-Brucke effect, is consistent with the fact that a very intense colored light may excite cones that, otherwise, are responsive to other colors only.

If a light containing complementary green and red wavelengths enters the eye, it will excite the receptors that respond to red light and those that respond to green light. Yellow light also affects these same two types of receptor, since the red-responding pigment reacts also to yellow light as does the green-responding pigment (Figure 10-17; see page 265). In fact, the trichromatic theory proposes that there is no single yellow-sensitive receptor. The meaning of yellow, by this theory, is the simultaneous excitation of the red- and green-responding pigments by yellow light. The trichromatic theory has been given strong support by the brilliant experiments of Rushton (1962) who was able to measure the absorption spectra of pigments in the living human eye. Moreover, direct physiological evidence indicates that there are receptors for three different though overlapping spectra of wavelengths in the retina. However, direct physiological evidence indicates that there are cells at higher levels in the nervous system that respond to light in a manner that is consistent with an opponent process theory.

Opponent Process Theory

The opponent colors theory is based upon the fact that some colors have a unitary subjective appearance, while others look like they are in fact a mixture of other colors. Thus, orange looks like it is made up of red and yellow light, while yellow, the product of mixture in the trichromatic theory, looks single and pure. This theory proposes that there are receptors that are excited both negatively and positively. Thus, blue light could cause a receptor to become active, while yellow light would tend to turn that receptor off. Also, some receptors could be turned on by yellow light and off by blue. Blue and yellow light presented simultaneously would therefore tend to cancel each other out, thereby producing the impression of a neutral or achromatic light. Similarly, red and green are envisioned as opponent colors, since these too are complementary. A green light, which is tinged with yellow wavelengths, when mixed with red light, would balance out the effect of the red light in the red-green receptor, thus leaving the residual yellow wavelengths to turn the blue-yellow receptors on, thereby leading to the perception of a pale yellow. As indicated, there are cells in the central nervous system that are turned on by red light and off by green, on by blue and off by yellow, etc. Some writers have thus been led to the conclusion that both theories, the trichromatic and the opponent colors, are true, with one of them being appropriate to the more peripheral nervous system and the other to the higher nervous centers. However, a more accurate view is probably that the two theories are not so much complementary as they are deducible from each other and therefore essentially equivalent.

SUMMARY

We have come a long way in this chapter on visual sensitivity. We have ranged from midair collisions of aircraft through visual detection as a function of target brightness, the distinction between rod and cone mechanisms, differential sensitivity of the eye to different colors, and, finally, color perception itself. All of this, however is terribly simple. It does not even begin to make us aware of how we perceive and recognize more complex sensory phenomena. The next chapter will be concerned with the perception of contour and form. We shall see there how the visual apparatus enables us to perceive two dimensional objects and patterns. After that, we shall turn to the problem of space perception.

SUGGESTED READINGS

Cornsweet, T. N. *Visual perception.* New York: Academic Press, 1970.

DeValois, R. L., & Jacobs, G. H. Primate color vision. *Science* 1968, **162**, 533–540.

Dowling, J. E., & Boycott, B. B. Organization of the primate retina: Electron microscopy. *Proc. Roy. Soc., Ser. B.,* 1966, **166**, 80–111.

Pirenne, M. H. *Vision and the eye.* (2nd ed.) London: Associated Book Publishers, 1967.

Wyszecki, G. W., & Stills, W. S. *Color science, concepts and methods, quantitative data and formulas.* New York: Wiley, 1967.

LEGENDS FOR COLOR FIGURES

FIGURE 10-5   Selecting pure colors for a visual detection experiment. The prism breaks the white light up into a spectrum of colors. The observer sees but one color at a time through the slit in the opaque screen. The particular color that he sees depends upon the position of the slit. A filter placed between the slit and the observer's eye makes it possible for the experimenter to adjust the intensity of the colored light.

FIGURE 10-8   Induction of color by contrast. The neutral gray patch is surrounded by a green field. Though the gray reflects white light to the eye, it takes on a reddish cast because of the presence of the green.

FIGURE 10-9   Patches of color. (See text for explanation.)

FIGURE 10-10   Subset of ordered colors.

FIGURE 10-11   Linear ordering of saturated colors. What shall we do with the purple patch?

FIGURE 10-12   The color circle.

FIGURE 10-14   The color triangle. The color triangle is a slice out of the color solid. It enables us to see how any particular color can vary in saturation and in shade with the purest color located at the right hand vertex of the triangle and the least pure on the vertical axis. As the color is mixed with more and more white light, it becomes less and less saturated until, finally, it is white, gray, or black, and is therefore placed on the vertical axis. As it becomes lighter or darker in shade, it is located above or below the horizontal axis of the triangle. The maximally saturated or purest color has a very narrow range of shades and tints while relatively unsaturated colors can take on many such shades.

FIGURE 10-15   Additive color mixing produces colors at intermediate positions on the color circle. The line connecting a pure red with a point on the circle near green produces a pale or desaturated yellow. This corresponds to the place where the midpoint of the line falls within the color circle. Similarly, the line connecting red and blue produces a less desaturated purple. The horizontal line connecting the pure red and the pure green crosses the exact center of the circle and therefore produces a neutral or gray color. This is why red and green and blue and yellow are called complementary pairs of colors.

FIGURE 10-17   Wright's (1947) empirical absorption response curves for the red, green, and blue pigments. These curves are similar to those predicted by Helmholtz.

FIGURE 11-1   The phenomenon of contrast. The gray square is exact same shade in all squares.

FIGURE 11-21   The McCollough effect.

FIGURE 12-23   The green figures represent the images in the left eye and the red figures the images of the right eye when the doorknob is fixated. The finger in the foreground exhibits the greater disparity. The box between the finger and the wall exhibits a lesser disparity. When this figure is viewed through stereo spectacles, with the green filter held over the left eye, the images in the two eyes will be relatively segregated from each other, as in a real scene. This will cause the finger to be seen as elevated above the page, the box to be seen as somewhat less elevated, and the door is behind the page.

FIGURE 12-25   The Wheatstone stereogram. Wheatstone observed that when C_L is shown to left eye and C_R to right eye, the line on the right in the combined binocular view is behind line on left. This can be seen looking through stereo spectacles with the green lens over the left eye.

FIGURE 12-28   Rivaling stereograms. The oppositely oriented contours in the two eyes exhibit complete binocular rivalry when the two fields are viewed separately in a stereoscope. When viewed through the stereo spectacles, the rivalry is weaker since each eye also sees something of the other eye's view. In both cases, when viewed with a stereoscope or through the spectacles with the green lens over the right eye, the inner square is seen to float above the background. This occurs even though the contours are not perceived as fusing. After Kaufman, Bacon, and Burroso (1972).

FIGURE 12-30   The Ponzo illusion. (a) The more distant log appears to be larger than the nearer log because it appears to be farther away. In actuality, both logs are of the same length. (b) A stereogram of the same situation. The only difference is that the disparities are arranged so that when the stereo spectacles are worn the roadway appears to recede into the distance, while the logs are seen floating above the road and in the same plane. This causes the illusion to fail since now the logs appear to be of equal length. To achieve this effect, the green lens should be held before the left eye.

FIGURE 12-31   The Ehrenstein illusion. The square appears to be trapezoidal in shape. It has been suggested that this illusion occurs because the upper horizontal line of the square appears to be farther away than the lower horizontal line. This is presumed to be due to the perspective cue inherent in the converging background lines. However, this theory is erroneous because, when the pattern is viewed with the stereo spectacles, the illusion persists even though the square is seen as elevated above the plane of the background lines that now slant into depth.

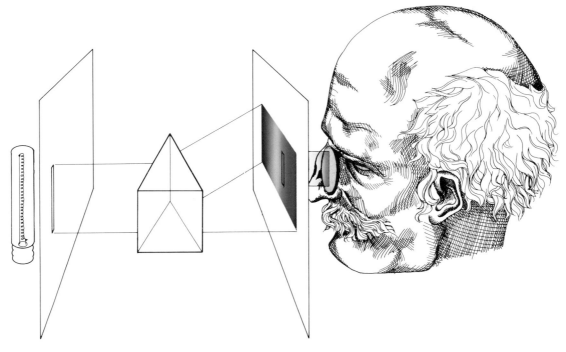

FIGURE 10-5

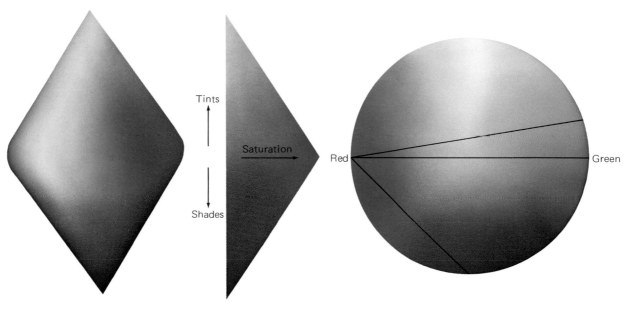

FIGURE 10-14

Tints

Saturation

Shades

Red

Green

FIGURE 10-15

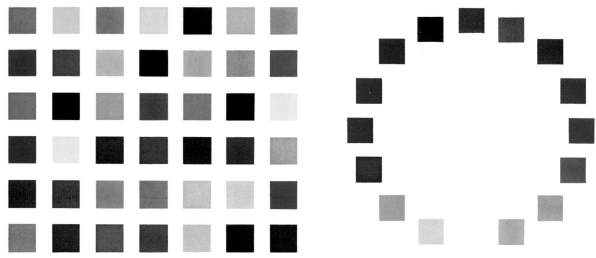

FIGURE 10-9

FIGURE 10-12

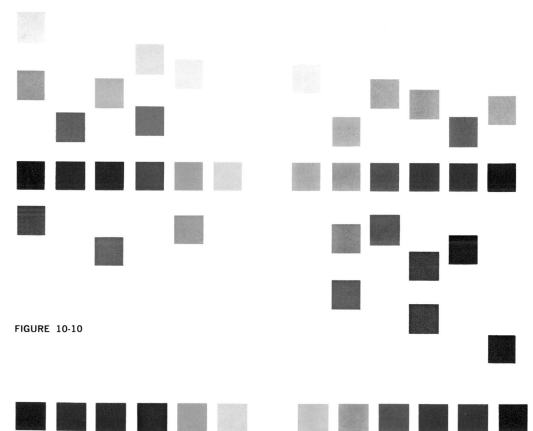

FIGURE 10-10

FIGURE 10-11

FIGURE 10-8

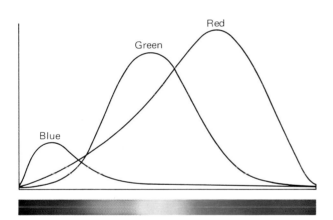

Blue

Green

Red

FIGURE 10-17

FIGURE 11-1

(a)

(b)

(c)

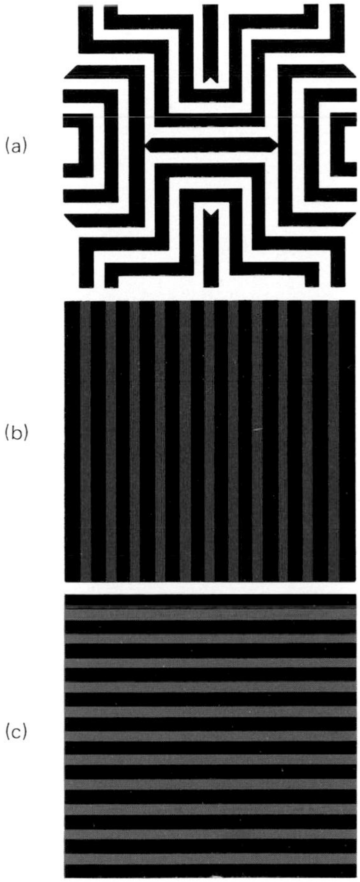

FIGURE 11-21

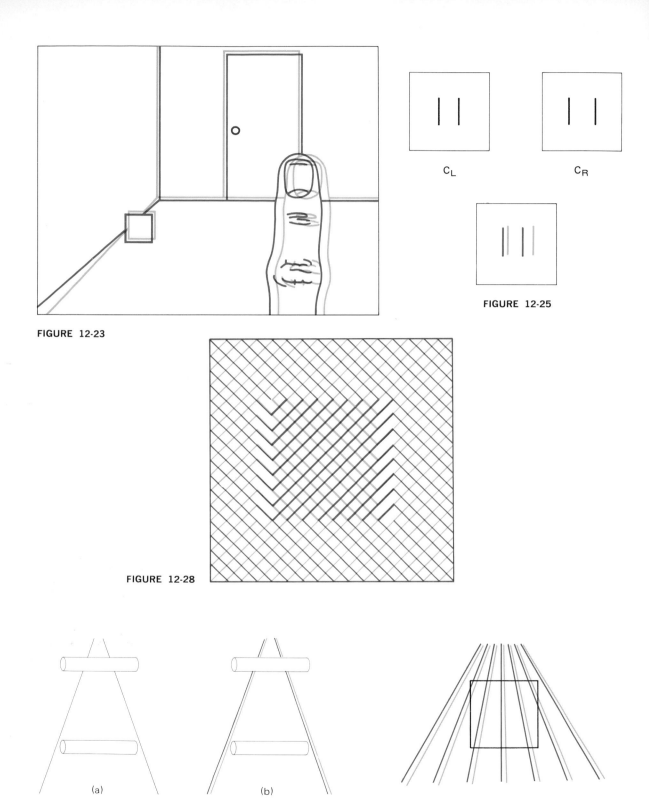

FIGURE 12-23

C_L C_R

FIGURE 12-25

FIGURE 12-28

(a)   (b)

FIGURE 12-30

FIGURE 12-31

11

The Perception
of Things

On November 28, 1943, a Mosquito aircraft took off from Leuchars, England, to fly a photographic reconnaissance mission over Berlin. Since the sky was overcast, the pilot, Squadron Leader John Merifield, decided to turn north to photograph various secondary objectives. Almost as an afterthought, the Mosquito flew over Peenemünde and took a few photographs before returning to England.

Three days later, Section Officer Constance Babbington Smith was looking at the first of Merifield's photographs. Suddenly, she noticed something new. There, on a ramp leading right up to the shores of the Baltic, was a small aircraft with stubby wings. It proved to be the pilotless aircraft or flying bomb, which Britons came later to call the "buzz bomb." This moment of recognition explained a great deal to the puzzled and anxious British intelligence establishment.

The recognition of the flying bomb seemed to occur in an instant. Yet, years of intelligence gathering were required to make that recognition possible. The first hints of German efforts to develop pilotless bombs and rockets came to the British in 1939. Aerial reconnaissance missions over Peenemünde in 1942 revealed strange circular earthworks, which seemed to have no apparent function. Concrete structures, which reminded one observer of skis laid out on their sides, were noticed in photographs of France and Holland. Finally, the ramp on which Constance Babbington Smith saw the flying bomb was also observed, but its function was not recognized. The bombs themselves had been seen too, but they were thought to be conventional aircraft. The interpretation of all of these data was hindered by other expectations. Some people thought that the Germans were trying to build rockets. It was only later that they discovered that the Germans were building both rockets and pilotless aircraft. Moreover, some prominent scientists, including Churchill's science advisor Lord Cherwell, believed that the rockets had to be powered with cordite. This would require an enormous rocket, which would carry a very large warhead if it were to be launched economically. Therefore, many intelligence workers were busy looking for large rockets, perhaps 60 feet in length. They simply had not reckoned on the use of liquid fuels, which would permit the construction of the much smaller V-2 rocket that subsequently fell on London. These false expectancies led to confusion concerning the objects actually seen on the ground. It was only when the small buzz bomb was actually recognized that everything fell into place, and the purpose of over 90 German "ski sites" was apparent.

Many factors delayed the ultimate recognition of the flying bombs. In some photographs of Peenemünde, the aircraft were flying too high to get sharp pictures. The resolution was too poor and image size too small. Hence, the targets in the photographs were simply not above the detection threshold of the human eye. Nor could color differences be used to aid detection; in the days of World War II color film was too slow to use for reconnaissance purposes. But even more important than the factors discussed in the last chapter, which affect visual sensitivity in simple situations, more complicated perceptual processes were involved in hiding the buzz bombs. Camouflage, both man-made and that naturally provided by complex surroundings, can make an object invisible, even when it is well above the threshold for detection. We will see examples of this when considering the Gestalt laws of organization in this chapter. In addition, mistaken expectations doubtless inhibited the identification of some of the things that actually were seen. Bruner and Potter (1964) have shown that a premature guess, based on a blurred image, can severely impair correct recognition of a much sharper picture of the same scene. They projected somewhat blurry slides of a pile of bricks, a dog standing on grass, and the like. Observers were able to correctly identify them 73% of the time. However, another group of observers, shown slides just as well focused but only after viewing very blurry versions of the same slides, were correct just 25% of the time.

In the last chapter, no consideration was given to such facts. However, in daily life most of the things we detect and recognize are complex objects, objects with which we are usually quite familiar. A very distant aircraft in a clear sky is more like a simple dot than it is like a complex object such as a human face or a deer you are stalking in the woods. Such objects have form and texture and are embedded in equally complicated backgrounds. Simple statements about light intensity and wavelength do not do them justice. In this chapter, we shall work our way from the consideration of simple perceptual events like contrast and contour formation up to the perception of complex objects in three-dimensional space.

BRIGHTNESS CONTRAST

One illustration of the difference between simple and complex visual display is the phenomenon of contrast. In the last chapter, we spoke of apparent brightness depending on the intensity of light, and color depending on its wavelength. There we were talking about a single small area of light in a dark room. As soon as the visual scene becomes richer than that, we find that the perceived brightness and color of an area depend on more than just the light coming from that area. In Figure 11-1 (see page 265), all four squares are precisely the same shade of gray. The light reaching your eyes from each square is identical. Nevertheless, the four squares look noticeably different. The one on the white background looks darker than the one on the black background; the one on red looks greener than the one on green.

The amount of contrast in Figure 11-1 is not very great, because of the limited range of intensities available on a printed page, and because there are other visual regions, such as the rest of the page, that affect all four squares equally instead of adding to the contrast. In other situations, contrast can be much more powerful.

Suppose a disk of light is projected on a screen in a darkened room and, with another projector, the disk is surrounded with a ring of light whose intensity can be varied. By making the ring 20 times more intense than the disk, the disk appears jet back. If instead the ring is made much less intense than the disk, the disk will appear white or luminous. Any intermediate shade of gray can be obtained by suitably adjusting the intensity of the ring.

The Structuralist's Explanation

How does this come about? How can the ring, which is imaged on one set of receptors in the retina, have such a powerful influence on the disk, which is stimulating a totally different set of receptors? Such an influence was a problem for early psychologists. The so-called structuralists believed that a perception is the sum of many simple mental events or sensations. They believed that sensations were independent of each other and could therefore be analyzed or examined through the process of introspection, a careful looking inward on one's own experience; for example, the analysis of the perception of some surface as a combination of sensations of light intensity, hue, and size. These same sensations could appear in other contexts to produce perceptions of different objects. However, it was assumed that, through training, a good observer could isolate these same sensations from each other in any context.

This view of psychology had no room for a fundamental change in the sensation of brightness, depending on surroundings. That would mean that sensations could lose their identities and thus become unavailable to introspection. A necessary concomitant of this view is that events that occur within some pathways in the nervous system are independent of events that occur within other pathways. Thus, a red patch at one place on the retina should not affect the sensation of a gray patch that originates at some other place. As we have seen, interactions between different patches of retinal excitation do occur. In recent years, a physiological mechanism that can produce such interactions has been uncovered.

Physiological Mechanism

In his Nobel Prize winning research on the eye of the horseshoe crab, *Limulus*, H. K. Hartline (1942) discovered that the response of one receptor unit is indeed affected by the activity of another. This particular animal has what is known as a compound eye (see Figure 11-2).

The eye is similar to the familiar insect eye. Each facet or ommatidium in the eye funnels light down to a receptor cell. In this way, the compound eye builds up a mosaic picture of the world. However, Hartline found that the receptor is not independent of what happens at another receptor. In fact, the presence of light on one receptor can decrease the response of another nearby receptor to light (Figure 11-3). This lateral inhibition could account for perceptual brightness contrast. Consider what happens when a disk is surrounded by a very bright ring. The disk appears less bright than it does when the ring is of moderate brightness. This is just what should occur, if there is suppression of firing of the receptors stimulated by the disk whenever the ring stimulates nearby receptors. Thus, the same principle which operates in the lowly horseshoe crab, may operate also in the more complex human retina.

There is an interesting effect of lateral inhibition on the firing rate of

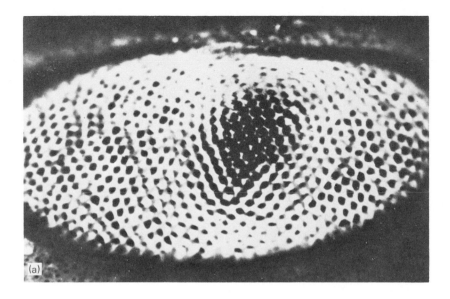

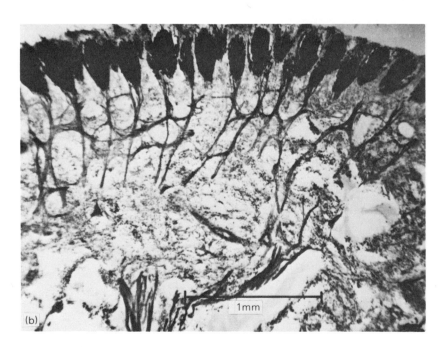

FIGURE 11-2   The compound eye of *Limulus*, the horseshoe crab. (a) Note the multifaceted appearance of the eye. (b) Each facet is an ommatidium, which funnels light down to a photo-sensitive cell. Each of these cells sends a fiber down into the animal's optic nerve. The fibers are interconnected just beneath the ommatidia by a set of horizontal fibers known as the lateral plexus. From Ratliff (1965).

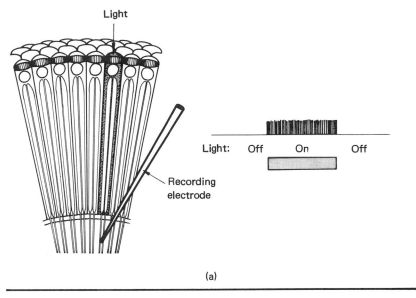

(a)

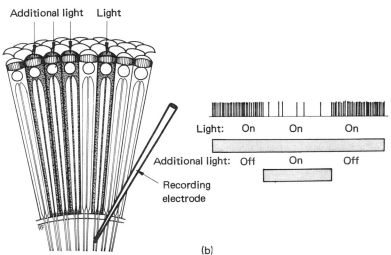

(b)

FIGURE 11-3   Lateral inhibition of steady firing of ommatidium by other cells. (a) Light in ommatidium causes fiber to fire continuously as indicated by oscillographic record shown on right. (b) When additional ommatidia are illuminated, the original ommatidium becomes inhibited.

a single receptor, when a pattern divided by a contour into a lighter and darker half is used (Figure 11-4). The pattern is first placed so that its lighter side stimulates the receptor, and the rate at which the receptor fiber fires is measured. Then the pattern is moved to another position, so that a region nearer the contour stimulates the receptor, and the firing rate is measured again. This is done for many different positions of the pattern, yielding a graph of firing rate as a function of the position in the stimulus. As the contour approaches the receptor on the lighter side, the firing rate increases; as the contour moves away from the receptor on the darker side, assuming that the pattern is moved from left to right, the firing rate is depressed and then gains a bit as the receptor gets farther into the darker side. There is an "overshoot." On the light side of the contour, the receptor fires more than it should, if it were influenced by the incident light alone, and it fires less than it should on the darker side. When the receptor is on the darker side of the contour, its activity is depressed or inhibited by neighboring receptors on the lighter side. The opposite situation occurs when the receptor is on the lighter side. The result is an accentuation of the difference between the two sides and the contour between them.

This phenomenon has its counterpart in human vision too. Ernst Mach, whose name is used in the Mach number of space flight, discovered that an

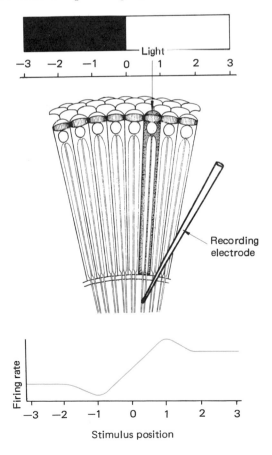

FIGURE 11-4   The firing rate of ommatidium as a function of its position with respect to a complex stimulus.

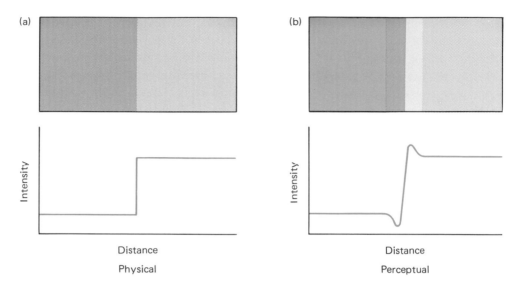

FIGURE 11-5   Mach bands. (a) The physical distribution of brightness on a surface is that of a uniform dark region that changes abruptly to a uniform white region. (b) The eye sees instead a darkening on the dark side of the contour and a brighter band on the lighter side of the contour even though these bands are not present in the physical stimulus. [The bands are not seen in (a) because the contrast on a printed page is not great enough.]

abrupt change in brightness from a dark region to a lighter region causes a strip on the lighter side of a contour to appear lighter than it should and a strip on the darker side of the contour to appear darker than it should (Figure 11-5). Mach suggested that lateral inhibition of the sort measured much later by Hartline was the basis for this phenomenon.

BRIGHTNESS CONSTANCY

When a white shirt is worn in a poorly illuminated room, it still looks white even though it reflects much less light to the eye than it does out of doors in bright sunlight. Similarly, a piece of coal in the bright sunlight looks black even though it actually reflects more light to the eye than does the white shirt in the dimly illuminated room. The tendency for the apparent brightness of an object to remain constant when the overall illumination changes is called brightness constancy. Constancy is obviously a worthwhile phenomenon. Imagine having to worry about your white shirt looking black whenever you go indoors!

For many years, brightness constancy was also a very puzzling phenomenon. How can the shirt retain its whiteness despite such vast changes in the intensity of the light that it reflects to the eye? You might be tempted to answer, "Because the shirt is white, no matter how much light is falling on it." But the brain has no way of directly ascertaining that the shirt really is white; the only available information comes by way of the receptor activity evoked by light reflected by the shirt. You do not simply remember the color of the shirt, having once seen it in good illumination, because when your friend arrives wearing a new shirt, you have no trouble immediately seeing it as white (or whatever color it happens to be).

The great nineteenth-century German scientist, Hermann von Helmholtz, proposed that you see the shirt as white because you make an allowance for the brightness of the illumination in the room. A physicist would determine the shirt's color by measuring the light hitting it and the light reflected from it. The ratio of the two specifies the shirt's reflectance, what we would call its "true brightness." Similarly, Helmholtz argued that we sense the intensity of the overall illumination and of the light reflected from the shirt. We then perform a rapid mental calculation. This calculation is done automatically, without any effort or awareness. Helmholtz called it an unconscious inference, and he used the same sort of notion to explain many other perceptual phenomena.

The Gelb Effect

A noteworthy demonstration by Gelb, in 1929, seems to support Helmholtz's idea. Gelb placed a black paper disk in a spotlight beam (Figure 11-6). The disk was located near a doorway so that stray light went into a large second room and was not visible to the observer. Hence, only the disk was illuminated and the rest of the room was dark. To an observer, the disk appeared silvery white or luminous, much like the moon when it is high in a very dark sky. In agreement with Helmholtz's idea, the perception matched the very bright retinal image when the observer had no way of knowing that the spotlight was providing extra illumination. Now Gelb placed a small piece of white paper just in front of the disk, so that both it and the disk were illuminated. Suddenly, the disk appeared black.

Again, this is what Helmholtz would have expected. The white paper revealed the presence of the strong spotlight illumination, and the unconscious inference was revised to allow for it. Gelb's next step, though, gave a more unexpected result. When the white paper was removed, the disk appeared silvery white again. In order for the disk to appear black, both the disk and the white paper had to be in view simultaneously. Could it be that the unconscious inference, which so cleverly allows for illumination when the white paper is present, "forgets" the illumination as soon as the paper is out of sight?

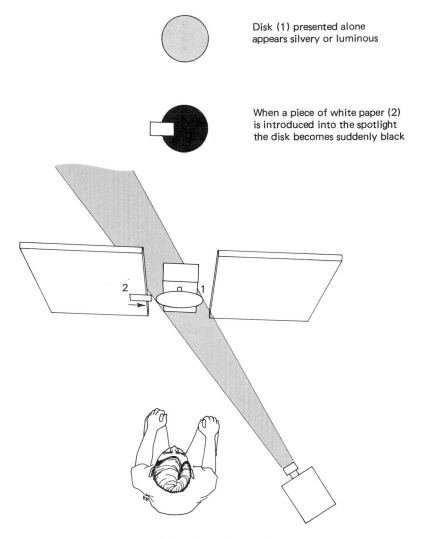

Disk (1) presented alone
appears silvery or luminous

When a piece of white paper (2)
is introduced into the spotlight
the disk becomes suddenly black

FIGURE 11-6   The Gelb experiment.

Contrast and Constancy: A Synthesis

The need for simultaneous presence of the white and black areas suggests
some form of interaction, like the lateral inhibition and contrast discussed
in the preceding section. In fact, Hans Wallach (1948) has proposed that brightness constancy (that great aid to accurate perception) and brightness contrast
(which produces perceptions that are distorted) stem from the same mechanism. He based his proposal on a more elaborate version of the experiment

described on page 269. Using four projectors in a dark room, he displayed two disks, each surrounded by a light ring (Figure 11-7).

First the two disks were adjusted to two different intensities, for example 1 and 10; then the left ring was adjusted until the left disk appeared dark gray, a setting of 10. When observers were asked to adjust the right ring to make the right disk look the same shade of gray as the left disk, they set it at about 100. In other words, the observer saw the two disks as equally bright when they had the same ratio of intensity to the rings surrounding them, even though one disk was actually twice as intense as the other. So far, this is just a more precise demonstration of interaction and contrast, presumably based on lateral inhibition. But Wallach went on to point out that, when a comparable situation occurs in the real world, the result is not called contrast but constancy.

The white shirt in the dimly illuminated room has relatively little light falling upon it and, therefore, reflects relatively little light to the eye. Similarly, the background of the shirt, the walls and other objects in the room, also has little light falling on it. Now, if the intensity of illumination were to be increased, more light would be reflected from the shirt to the eye. However, there would be a proportionate increase in the light reflected by the walls and other objects in the background. The ratio of light from shirt and background would remain constant. Therefore, as in Wallach's experiment, the perceived whiteness of the shirt should remain constant too.

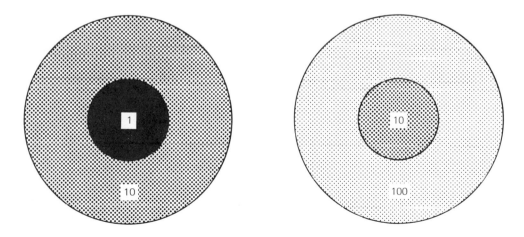

FIGURE 11-7   The Wallach ring-disk experiment. A ring-disk pair was set on either end of a darkened room. The observer had to adjust the brightness of one disk until it appeared to match that of the other disk on the other side of the room. The ring intensities were left constant, one having 10 units of light intensity, for example, and the other 100 units. Under this condition, the observer felt he had a good match when the disk on the right was made 10 times more intense than the disk on the left.

Apparent brightness is not determined strictly by ratio under all conditions. If the intensities of the lights are much lighter or much darker than those employed in Wallach's experiment, then a given ratio may produce a somewhat different apparent brightness than for intermediate intensity levels. Also, brightnesses with more complex surroundings cannot be predicted accurately from simple ratios. Nevertheless, it is clear that relationships between intensities play a major role in our perception of brightness.

STEADY-STATE STIMULATION

It was discovered some years ago that a totally uniform visual field leads to the cessation of accurate perception. In more recent years, Julian Hochberg (1951) verified these results in an extraordinarily simple and clever experiment. He fitted half of a ping pong ball over the eye of a subject and illuminated it evenly with colored light. In a relatively short time, the observer noticed that the colors faded and became neutral gray. Also, he lost the impression of seeing a surface and saw instead a bulky fog just as in the original experiments in Germany about 20 years previously.

This "Ganzfeld" or empty field experiment reminds us of "whiteout," a much feared set of visual symptoms encountered by flying over the snow or while climbing snow-covered mountains. An associated condition is snow blindness, which occurs when the eyes are exposed for a long time to the extremely high intensities of sunlight reflected by very white snow. This latter problem is an organic condition, which can be treated only by resting the eyes. Whiteout, however, is not the same as snow blindness. It is the simple failure of the visual system when the stimulus is entirely unchanging. Impaired vision also occurs when a pilot is looking into an empty sky. He may not realize it, but his eyes become myopic. They are focused only for near objects and therefore distant objects such as other aircraft may not be seen. This condition, known as empty field myopia, was studied extensively by the British who demonstrated that, even if you try to see clearly into the distance, your eye may well be suited for seeing objects clearly if they are about 6 feet away. As we shall see later, when a stimulus is unchanging, it conveys no information to the observer. In the absence of change or information, vision becomes impaired.

Troxler's Effect

Such effects of an empty field on vision can be experienced by the reader. Take a sheet of blue paper and place a number of small white pieces of paper upon it. With the reading lights somewhat dim, fixate one piece of white paper and take care not to move your eyes. In a short time, the white pieces of paper in the periphery will start to disappear. As time goes by, objects even closer will also disappear until finally only the fixated paper may be visible. This phenomenon is known as Troxler's effect. It also illustrates that, when the visual input is relatively unchanging, visual efficiency is impaired.

The same kind of phenomenon can be seen in Figure 11-8. Here it is seen that, when no part of the retina undergoes fast changes in illumination, a perceptual blindness will result. In other words the visual system is insensitive to low frequency targets. Another example of this phenomenon occurs when

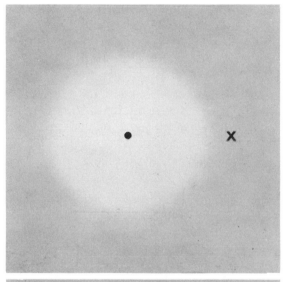

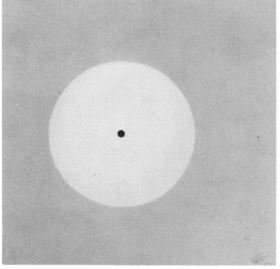

FIGURE 11-8   Fixate the dot in the top circle. After a time, this circle will disappear, but it will reappear if you shift your gaze to the cross. The circle at the bottom does not disappear when the dot is fixated. From Cornsweet (1969).

a faintly luminous object is presented to the eye in the dark. With constant fixation, parts of the object disappear. This fragmentation can be offset by moving the eye about.

Stabilized Images

Observations such as these led some scientists to suspect that eye movements play a vital role in normal perception. At about the same time, two groups of researchers, one group in England and the other in the United States, attempted to prevent eye movements from affecting the perception of an object. The image of an object formed on the retina changes its position on the retina whenever the eye moves. Thus, you may be looking at this word on this page. As your eye moved from the word "word" to the word "page," the retinal image of the word "word" shifted from the center of vision toward one side of the retina. In jumping from word to word, the images of the words are always exciting new sets of retinal receptors.

Even finer eye movements may occur. It may be that the eye drifts slightly while attempting to maintain fixation and then corrects its position by jumping back to central fixation. Even with slight movements, then, the eye will always cause images of objects to excite new receptors. In attempting to prevent this shifting of the retinal image from one set of receptors to another, the two research teams used the principle of the optical lever (Figure 11-9).

This heroic method for stabilizing the retinal image led to the discovery that, unless receptors are turned on and off, either by causing the image to move on the retina through eye movements or by flickering the intensity of a stabilized image, vision will cease. Images projected in the stabilized image system just disappear.

The Role of Eye Movements in Perception

The use of a mirror affixed to a contact lens makes it possible to measure eye movements. The beam of light reflected by the mirror can be used to write onto a moving strip of film. Hence the track left by the light beam enables one to tell how often the eye moves and by how far. Using these methods, it has been discovered that the eye is in a constant state of movement. It may shift back and forth by a very small amount as often as 100 times per second.

The eye also tends to drift away from a point upon which the observer feels he is fixating. It does this very slowly, and, after a while, the observer will cause his eye to flick or jump back to correct for the drift.

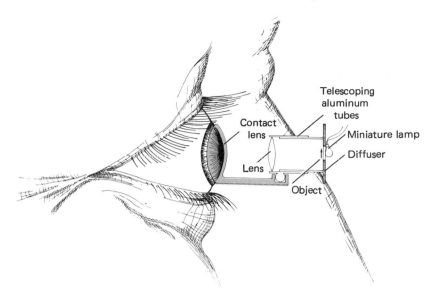

FIGURE 11-9   A stabilized image system. An image, the "object," in the telescope is focused sharply on the retina. When the eye moves, the image remains fixed on the retina because the telescope is carried along with the eye.

The eye also jumps when it reads and when it moves very fast from fixation to fixation in scanning the outline of some object. These jumping movements are called saccadic eye movements. Saccades occur in reading. The eye does not move smoothly from place to place on a page, but jumps so that it gets a stationary glimpse of small clusters of words. As a matter of fact, during the saccade or jump, the sensitivity of the eye is severely curtailed. For reasons that are not fully understood, the eye is relatively insensitive to stimulation during the saccade. This probably serves the purpose of enabling the brain to build up a picture of the world based upon a series of relatively sharp glimpses. Otherwise, it would have to work on the severely blurred images that would be formed during eye movements.

Massive Sensory Deprivation

In general, the visual system reacts to change more strongly than it does to steady-state conditions. This is true not only of the visual system. In the sensory deprivation experiments pioneered at McGill University, subjects were deprived of all possible changes in sensory input. Eye shades, ear plugs, and quiet rooms were used. Subjects were even isolated so far as possible from pressure against the skin. These subjects tended to hallucinate, lose track of time, and otherwise display symptoms reminiscent of psychopathology. Once again, the lack of change or information impairs perception.

THE PERCEPTION OF PATTERN

Although the eyes must be in motion relative to the retinal image if vision is to be possible, it is evident that eye movements alone do not suffice for pattern perception. The problem of how we see things organized as patterns is one of the most difficult problems in the psychology of visual perception.

At its most primitive level the problem of pattern perception is concerned with why we see things as organized into groups. The dots in Figure 11-10 are perceived as arranged in couplets or pairs. This patterning of pairs of dots is not readily understood to be a problem for the visual sciences. One might think that the pairing is due solely to the fact that the pairs actually exist in the physical world, and observers simply report their existence, with the nature of the observer not contributing in any way to the appearance of the pattern. However, Koffka (1928), the famous Gestalt psychologist, proposed that things look as they do because the organism responds to them in a unique way. Stimuli produce effects within the nervous system that become organized into patterns in accordance with certain laws. If it were not for the existence of these laws of organization, the dots in Figure 11-10 might just as well be perceived as triplets or quadruplets instead of couplets. The next example might make this clear.

Figure 11-11 is a rectangular matrix of dots whose horizontal separations are equal to their vertical separations. After staring at this pattern for a while, one has the experience similar to that often encountered while gazing idly at the tiles on a bathroom floor. The tiles seem to organize themselves into rows and columns and, sometimes, even diagonal patterns. This same sort of fluctuating organization may be encountered in Figure 11-11. Staring at the pattern for several minutes produces the impressions of rows or columns. Since the dots are equally spaced in both horizontal and vertical dimensions, the organizations seen must be due to some characteristic of one's own nervous system.

●● ●● ●● ●● ●● ●● ●● ●● ●● ●● ●● ●● ●● ●● ●● ●● ●●

FIGURE 11-10   A row of dots that appears to be patterned as a set of couplets.

FIGURE 11-11   Dots are evenly spaced.

To reinforce this point we can perform an experiment. Consider Figure 11-12. The dots in this figure are closer together horizontally than they are vertically. This greater proximity in the horizontal direction causes the dots to be perceived as rows rather than as columns. This illustrates the Gestalt law of proximity, which also underlies the appearance of couplets in Figure 11-10. Now stare attentively at Figure 11-12 for at least one minute, moving eyes slowly back and forth and up and down within the pattern while staring at it. At the end of the minute, look back to Figure 11-11, the evenly spaced rectangular matrix of dots. The pattern no longer shifts its organization from rows to columns, but appears as a stable set of columns.

The aftereffect of staring at Figure 11-12 will persist for a long time. One way to reverse the effect is to repeat the experiment by staring once again at Figure 11-12, after rotating the book through a 90° angle. Now columns are seen instead of rows. After two minutes or so, look at Figure 11-11. Most likely, the evenly spaced matrix will appear almost immediately to be com-

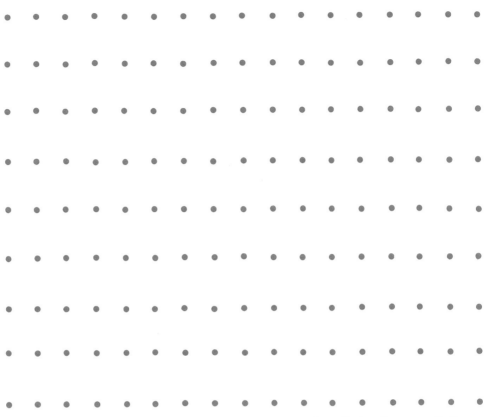

FIGURE 11-12   Rows of dots. Dots are closer together horizontally than they are vertically.

prised of rows. This is the reverse of the organization encountered when the experiment was first tried.

Both of these aftereffects prove that characteristics of the nervous system condition or contribute to the patterning we see in the world. We shall try to explain such aftereffects later, but first let us consider further some of the laws of organization.

The Gestalt Laws

The laws in question were first proposed by the founder of the Gestalt school of psychology, Max Wertheimer. Some of the laws he formulated can be given a relatively precise definition. An example of this is the law of proximity, which we encountered previously. According to this law, elements that are relatively closer in space will be more likely to be perceived as being in a group than are elements that are relatively farther apart.

LAW OF SIMILARITY.   Another law, one which is less simple and less easily quantified, is the law of similarity. According to this law, things that are alike will tend to be seen as belonging to each other. Thus, the open circles in Figure 11-13 are more similar to each other than they are to the dots in the figure. Therefore, the open circles are perceived as the vertices of a triangle.

As originally formulated by Wertheimer, some of the Gestalt laws are very ambiguous. They seem to point in the direction of basic principles, but they do not lend themselves readily to clear definition as, for example, does the law of proximity. Even the law of similarity is somewhat unclear. It is not possible to define the term "similarity" in a rigorous manner. As a matter of fact, the criterion of whether or not two things are similar may be thought of as a psychological response on the part of the experimenter. He decides on the basis of his own experience if two items are more similar than two

FIGURE 11-13   The open circles are perceived as vertices of triangles. This organization is done to differentiate similarity.

other items. Therefore, we cannot be sure that similarity stands for a definable attribute of a set of stimuli.

LAW OF GOOD FIGURE.   One of these more ambiguous laws is the law of good figure or good continuation, which holds, for example, that a continuous line is more likely to be perceived as a unit than a discontinuous or bent line (Figure 11-14). Also, circles are perceived more readily in very brief exposures than are polygons. The reason given is that a circle is a "better" figure than a polygon.

Some hint of why a circle should be a "good" figure may be derived from how the Gestalt psychologists explained the laws of organization. As was pointed out earlier, the Gestalt psychologists believed that events that occurred at different places in the nervous system can influence each other. In those early days of modern psychology, scientists had a rather unclear idea of how the brain was actually structured. The most widely accepted model of brain function was based upon knowledge of peripheral nerves. These were thought of as being similar to cables or telephone lines passing information into and out of a central switchboard, the cerebral cortex. The messages were

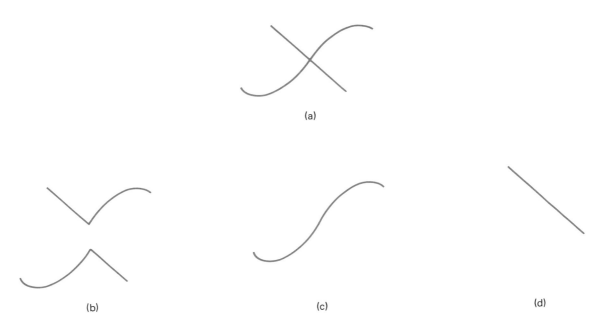

(a)

(b)   (c)   (d)

FIGURE 11-14   Pattern (a) is more likely to be perceived as consisting of superimposed lines (c) and (d) than the two figures in (b). This illustrates the role of good figure or good continuation in perceptual organization.

supposed to be kept apart throughout the system. This reflex arc was the physiological analog of the independence of sensations from each other. Now, in view of their notion that sensory events interact, the Gestaltists felt obliged to seek an alternative to the "telephone line" model of the brain. Therefore, they proposed that the cortex has properties of a physical field that enables action to occur across a distance. Since electric fields, magnetic fields, and gravitational fields all enable things to attract and sometimes repel each other across empty space, the Gestaltists proposed that the brain has similar properties. Thus, two dots placed in the field of view will attract each other. Moreover, the closer the dots are to each other, the stronger will be the attractive force between them. Hence, the law of proximity may be "explained" in terms of field forces.

Events within the hypothetical field have self-organizing properties. If an array of equally spaced dots (Figure 11-11) is presented to the eye, then fluctuations of the attractive forces within the field will cause the observer to see columns, rows, or diagonals. Similarly, circles create a better balance of these forces, since all points on the circle are equidistant from its center. This is not true of polygons.

The field theory of Gestalt psychology is no longer accepted by psychologists. Experiments in which gold foil was implanted into the brain to short-circuit the postulated field showed no effect on pattern vision in monkeys. Also, mica slices, which impede the direct current flows presumed to be associated with the field, had no effect on pattern vision. Moreover, the new knowledge we have about the extraordinary branching and interconnections of the fine structure of the cerebral cortex indicates that the brain can exhibit some fieldlike properties. These properties are sufficient to account for interactions among spatially separated events without the postulation of an electric field.

Despite these shortcomings of Gestalt psychology, its theory did point to a number of phenomena in pattern vision which psychology was otherwise unable to deal with. There have been a number of recent efforts to handle these phenomena without referring to the hypothetical field.

SIMPLICITY, INFORMATION THEORY, AND PATTERN PERCEPTION

The Gestalt laws are basically qualitative. Is there a way to make them more precise and quantitative? Are there some objective measures that can be applied to stimuli that can tell us how likely an ambiguous pattern is to be perceived in a certain way? Hochberg and McAlister (1953) and Attneave (1954) proposed similar approaches to this problem. The basic principle was that the more information it takes to describe a given perception, the less likely that perception will occur. Figure 11-14(a) for example, can be described either as "two intersecting lines, one straight and one curved," or as "two v-shaped figures, each with one straight and one curved side, joined at their apexes." Obviously, the first description is briefer than the second, and that is how we tend to perceive Fig. 11-14(a).

Simplicity of description tells us the same thing as the law of good con-

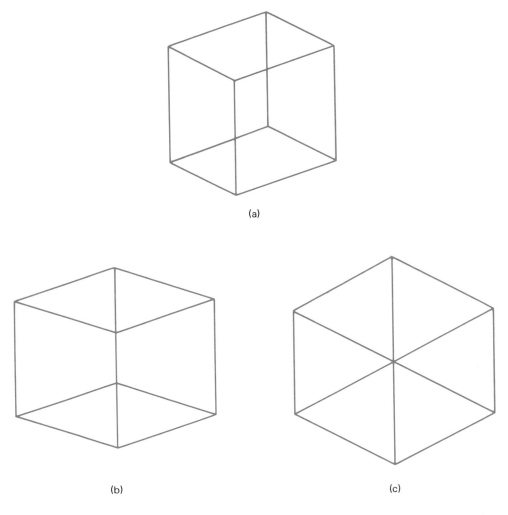

(a)

(b)   (c)

FIGURE 11-15 The simplicity principle. After Hochberg and McAlister (1953). (See text for explanation.)

FIGURE 11-16   Two sketches of a kitten. The line drawing provides sufficient information for perception.

tinuation. Each of the three patterns in Figure 11-15 can, in principle, be perceived either as a flat geometrical pattern or as a drawing of a three-dimensional cube. Yet, it is difficult to see Figure 11-15(c) as a cube and very hard to see Fig. 11-15(a) as a meaningless two-dimensional design. How can this be derived from the simplicity principle? A cube has 12 edges and 24 right angles forming its 6 squares faces. Viewed as two-dimensional designs, however, Figures 11-15(a–c) have 16, 13, and 12 lines and 25, 19, and 17 angles, respectively. Thus, Figure 11-15(a) has fewer lines and angles as a cube than as a two-dimensional pattern. The reverse is true for Figure 11-15(c). Once again, perception tends to embody the smallest possible number of elements.

A related approach to unambiguous pictures is illustrated in Figure 11-16, which shows a detailed drawing of a kitten and a line drawing. Although the one sketch contains much more detail, i.e., shadows, texture, curved lines, than the other, the simple line drawing is easily recognizable as a kitten. Attneave has pointed out that the "corners" or sharp changes in direction of a contour tell the most about a shape. The lines themselves convey little additional information. If the lines were thrown away and the corners retained, the picture would still be easy to recognize. There is a parallel here with a sequences of numbers such as 00101110010 or 000000011111111. The first sequence is much harder to describe than the second. The transitions from 0 to 1 or 1 to 0 in the sequences are similar to the corners in a broken line. This similarity was expressed more precisely when psychologists such as Attneave (1954) and Miller (1956) began to apply "information theory" to psychological research. Information theory was originally developed to provide a quantitative measure of the efficiency of communication channels such as telephone lines.

In its simplest form, information theory can be thought of as asking how many 0's or 1's would have to be transmitted in order to convey a certain message in code. If both parties know in advance what the set of possible messages is, it is easy to see that more information must be sent for a larger set. For a set of two code messages, one digit will do: 0 means the first message, 1 the second. For a set of four, two digits will be needed: 00, 01, 10, and 11 would signal each of the four. Eight messages would take three digits, and so on. Since we are talking only about two digits, a given number of digits, N, can code 2^N different messages. This N is defined in information theory as the number of "bits" of information needed to convey a message from the set.

The number of bits and other more complex equations from information theory provided one way of summarizing the results of certain psychological experiments. In fact, information theory actually inspired a large number of experiments that attempted to measure the human being's capacity for transmitting information, in much the same way as one would ask the same question about a telephone line. It was found that for various stimulus dimensions, e.g., pitch, loudness, and position of points on a line, subjects could reliably distinguish only four to ten different stimuli, if those stimuli were presented one at a time. That means they could transmit two to three bits of information. As the set size increased, they tended to confuse the stimuli and identify one with the label appropriate for another.

THE NATURE-NURTURE QUESTION

Does a newborn baby see the world in much the same way as an adult sees it? Or is the newborn's visual world a hopelessly jumbled, disorganized, meaningless hodgepodge of colors, which he must learn to see as definite shapes? This is a fundamental question to raise about pattern perception, and one that we will come to again in the chapter on space perception.

The laws of organization were considered by the Gestalt psychologists to be inherent properties of the brain. The laws were presumed to operate automatically, without the necessity for any learning or prior experiences, resulting in the perception of unified figures with definite shapes. There is obvious survival value in being able to see stable, identifiable shapes instead of a confusing disorder of colored patches. Therefore, it would not be surprising if the brain has evolved to perform this function at birth.

An alternative view is that one must learn to see forms. This is a rather old idea. The British associationists, for example, held that various elementary sensations are combined or associated through past experience to become the objects that we perceive. Thus, as Hartley put it in 1740, by the frequency of their repetition together, sensations become associated so that, when one of them occurs, the memories of others are recalled. James Mill took these ideas up in 1869, and also taught that complex objects are made up of simpler sensations. Thus, a house is a mental compound made up of less complex "ideas" such as the ideas of brick and mortar. It is easy to see how such views developed into those of the structuralists. Bishop Berkeley added a different dimension to this kind of analysis. He felt that the sense of touch is more basic than the sense of sight. Thus, we come to know that an object is at a given distance from the eye because of reaching for it repeatedly. Thus, most of the time, perception seems so immediate and automatic that it is hard to imagine that things could look any other way than they now do, or that it could require any learning in order to be able to see.

Aftereffects

Yet, it is easy to demonstrate that our past experience can change the way we see the same visual pattern. Look at Figure 11-17(a) and then at Figure 11-17(b). You probably see the same young lady, facing away from you, in both figures (though the latter drawing may seem a little sloppier). Now look at Figure 11-17(c) and look again at Figure 11-17(b). Chances are that it will now look quite different, like an old woman instead of a young one. Having seen both Figures 11-17(a) and 11-17(b) you can probably, at

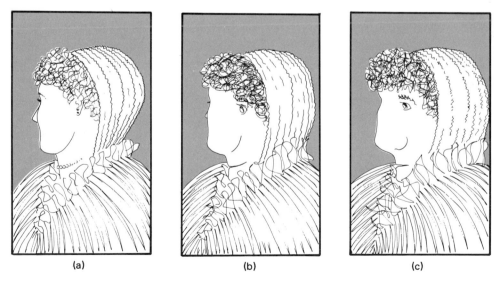

| | | |
| (a) | (b) | (c) |

FIGURE 11-17   Leeper's (1935) ambiguous wife.

will, see the ambiguous Figure 11-17(b) as young or old. But imagine two people, one who had seen only Figure 11-17(a) and one only Figure 11-17(c). Chances are, each would see Figure 11-17(b) quite differently, yet each would be convinced that he was seeing the picture as it really is, automatically and immediately. That is what Leeper found, using similar drawings. Past experiences or psychological set can affect the way we see the world.

There are other aftereffects that alter perception. One of these is the figural aftereffect of Wolfgang Kohler and Hans Wallach; another is the related curvature aftereffect of James Gibson (Figure 11-18). These aftereffects are local in the sense that staring at the inspection target of Figure 11-18 will produce an aftereffect only when the test target is viewed with appropriated fixation. Nevertheless, such phenomena illustrate that the quality of visual experience may be altered by prior visual experiences.

The Role of Experience in Perception: Hebb's Theory

If particular experiences can influences what an adult perceives, then perhaps certain sorts of experience are necessary before the infant can perceive anything other than blobs of light and dark. This theory is proposed by the Canadian psychologist, D. O. Hebb (1949). The theory starts with the assumption that contours attract the eye. Thus, if a single straight line were presented to a child, the child's eye would be attracted to it. Moreover, the eye would tend to scan along the length of the line. With a bent line, as in a geometrical figure, the eye will tend to hesitate at each corner before changing direction to move along the next side. These scanning movements of the eye along contours tend to trace out the shape of the object. There is some evidence that this does happen. Observations of infants' eye movements indicate that, when presented with rather large outline forms, they do tend to look at the contours of the forms.

Eye movements serve two related functions in Hebb's theory. First, by tracing out the shape of the object, they give the infant nonvisual information about that shape, much like tracing around the object with a fingertip. As in Berkeley's theory of touch educating vision, eye movements could give shape to visual perceptions. More important to Hebb, these eye movements insure that the corners of an object will often be imaged on the fovea of the eye in rapid succession. Each corner tends to activate a different set of cells in the brain, and those sets get activated one after the other, over and over. Hebb assumes that, whenever cells fire almost simultaneously, additional neural connections grow between them. This means that activation of one cell is more likely to cause activation of the other cell. The net result is that

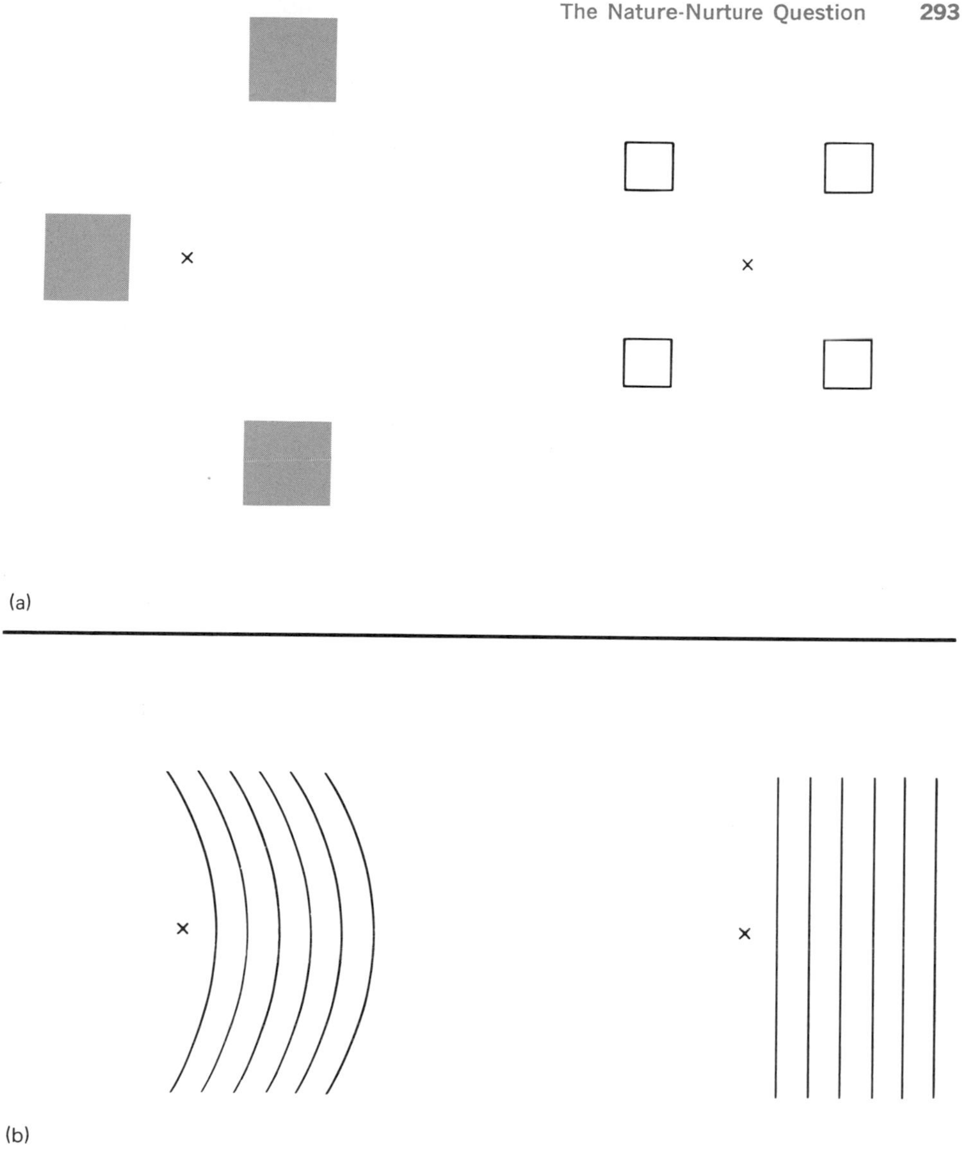

(a)

(b)

FIGURE 11-18   (a) The figural aftereffect of Kohler and Wallach. (b) The curvature aftereffect of Gibson. Study the fixation point in the left figure, and then switch to the fixation point on the right. What do you see?

all of the cells stimulated by the corners of the triangle become connected into a "cell assembly," which tends to work as a unit. Once this happens, it is no longer necessary to actually make eye movements to each corner. A mere glimpse is enough to activate the whole set of cells, which now represents a whole triangle.

Hebb's theory was inspired by a number of facts. For example, Riesen (1965) had found that monkeys raised in the dark from birth had great trouble in discriminating a square from a circle. Similarly, people who are born blind and whose sight is later restored through a cataract operation have trouble naming objects by sight, although they can immediately recognize them by touch. It seems that when monkeys and people are deprived of the opportunity to learn to see shapes, they are unable to see them. Moreover, in line with Hebb's assumptions about the importance of eye movements, newly sighted people sometimes identify shapes by laboriously moving their eyes from place to place, counting corners. As one final bit of support for the theory, the disappearance of stabilized retinal images shows that, when eye movements are prevented from having their usual effect, perception deteriorates even for the adult.

Pertinent to Hebb's theory are the data of Hubel and Weisel, which were described in Chapter 2. They found that lines in certain orientations are capable of exciting specific cortical cells even in very young kittens. Hence, learning theories such as the one proposed by Hebb may be better applied to very complex forms, since common simple forms conceivably involve very few cortical analyzer units, thereby eliminating the need for scanning movement of the eye.

One of the major conclusions that must be drawn from this discussion is that, if past experience plays a significant role in the ability to perceive forms, then the nature of this role is still somewhat obscure. The Street figure (Figure 11-19) may help to make this point. This figure is comprised of irregular blobs of ink. At first, one is hard pressed to identify the form that is portrayed. After some time, however, one may recognize it as a tricycle. If one tried to describe the figure both before and after recognition took place,

FIGURE 11-19   The Street figure. What do you see? Turn the book upside down.

the descriptions do not really differ in any significant way. Yet, the figure looks quite different after it is recognized.

CORTICAL ANALYZERS AND FORM PERCEPTION

The discovery of feature detectors or analyzer units in the visual systems of frogs, cats, and monkeys has encouraged some new ways of thinking about pattern perception. As previously described, certain cells in the visual cortex are activated best by lines in a certain orientation, while other cells respond best to some other orientation. Similarly, some cells are most sensitive to contours moving in one direction; others to movement in some other direction. Such properties as these have not only offered new explanations for old perceptual phenomena, but have also led to the discovery of new phenomena. Conversely, certain perceptual effects provide some evidence for the existence of such feature detectors in human beings. Otherwise, one would have to insert microelectrodes into a person's brain to obtain this evidence.

First, let us consider some of the older observations that fit with the idea of feature detectors. Consider a cell that responds best to a vertical line. We can presume that this cell, when stimulated, sends a message signifying "vertical line" to some cells farther along in the brain. Although this cell responds best to a straight vertical line, it can also be excited by single spots of light. It can be excited even more strongly by a row of spots that lie in its preferred orientation, that is, that all fall within the excitatory strip in its receptive field. Here, then, is a possible mechanism for the law of proximity: dots that are close together appear to be an organized whole, such as a line, because they excite the same specialized cortical detector.

As a second example, consider the puzzle of how we can recognize a triangle regardless of where it falls on the retina. Two triangles imaged on different retinal regions may be stimulating totally different sets of retinal rods and cones, yet we have no trouble recognizing that their shapes are identical. It was observations like this that led the Gestalt psychologists to postulate that it does not much matter which retinal receptors are excited; rather, the shape of the resulting fields of electrical activity in the brain is crucial. Hebb, on the other hand, was led to assume that straight contours evoke eye movements that are the same for a triangle on any part of the retina, and this equivalence of eye movements eventually makes certain retinal patterns perceptually equivalent. Hubel and Wiesel's findings (1962) offer another view. They found that "complex cells" require a straight line in a certain orientation, but the

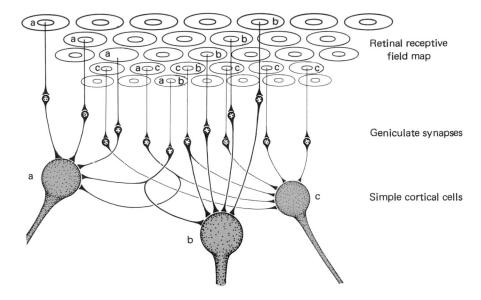

FIGURE 11-20   Schematic representation of Hubel and Wiesel's interpretation of their physio-logical results. Cells in the midbrain's lateral geniculate feed into the first cortical analyzer the "simple cell." The simple cell (a), (b), or (c) responds to a dot of light presented anywhere along the diagonal line. Simple cells feed into a cell still further into the visual system called a "complex cell." If a complex cell received inputs from simple cells responding to the same orientation, the receptive field for the complex cell would cover a larger retinal area.

line can fall anywhere on the retina (within the cell's receptive field) and still excite the cell. Thus, it could be that two triangles imaged on different retinal regions could activate the same set of three cells (one for each side of the triangle) (Figure 11-20).

If a sensory cell is stimulated for a prolonged period, its response tends to diminish even if the stimulus remains the same. We say that the cell becomes fatigued or adapted. If this is also true of cortical detectors, some novel experiments are suggested. Suppose we look at stripes moving constantly toward the left. This could fatigue the cells that respond to leftward movement without affecting those responsive to rightward motion. Suppose we now try to see some very dimly illuminated stripes. It should be easier to see them if they are moving to the right, thereby stimulating the unfatigued rightward-movement detectors, than if they are moving to the left. This is indeed what happens. The threshold is raised for test stripes that move in the same direction as the adapting stripes, while remaining unchanged for stripes that move in the opposite direction (Sekuler & Ganz, 1963). Likewise, if we stare at vertical stripes our threshold for seeing dim vertical stripes is raised, with no change in the threshold for horizontal stripes (Gilinsky, 1968). Cortical cells have receptive fields with different widths, so we might expect to be able to use wide bars to adapt only cells with wide fields. That too can be done; after viewing wide stripes, it is harder to see dim wide stripes than to see narrow ones.

In general, it seems that, for any property of cortical detectors, it is possible to raise the threshold for seeing that property under difficult or ambiguous conditions. It could be argued, though, that such threshold experiments do not really tell us anything about everyday perceptions, where the stimulus is well above threshold and seen clearly and distinctly. Other experiments inspired by the discovery of feature detectors do deal with above-threshold perceptions.

McCollough Effect

The first such phenomenon was discovered by Celeste McCollough in 1965. She reasoned that feature detectors in the human ought to be sensitive not only to orientation, as in the cat, but also to color. Perhaps, then, one could produce adaptation linked to both color and orientation. Figure 11-21 (see page 265) gives a demonstration of what she found. Spend 3 or 4 minutes looking alternately at the green horizontal stripes and the red vertical ones, spending 5 or 10 seconds on each. Then look at the black and white pattern. You will probably see a definite tinge of pink on the horizontally striped portions and perhaps also a greenish tint on the verticals. If you tip the page or your head, the colors will change places, since they depend on the orientation of the stripes on your retina. Although McCollough's experiment was prompted by physiological discoveries, it was not until several years later that a possible physiological base for her phenomenon was found, when Hubel and Wiesel found cells in the monkey brain that were sensitive to both color and orientation.

Another striking demonstration of the possible role of feature detectors in perception is offered in Figure 11-22. After moving your eyes along the little bar between the two striped areas in (a), quickly transfer your gaze to the dot in (b). For a few seconds, you will probably notice that the stripes on top appear quite a bit wider than those below, although they are actually equal. Again the supposition is that the top part of (a) adapts the narrow-stripe detectors in the upper part of your retina so that medium-width stripes (which normally have small but equal effects on narrow- and wide-stripe detectors) get less response from them than from the wide-stripe detectors.

Returning to the demonstration in Figure 11-11, we can now propose an explanation without recourse to hypothetical electrical fields or Gestalt laws of organization. The regularly spaced dots excite both horizontal and vertical line detectors. As these diverse units are excited for some time, some of them will tend to become fatigued. This will cause the opposite kinds of

(a)   (b)

FIGURE 11-22   A demonstration of how feature detectors are active in perception. After Blakemore and Sutton (1966).

detectors to predominate until they too become fatigued. By then, the original detectors may have recovered and a different organization or pattern will result.

Such fatigue notions underlie some theories of aftereffects. Thus, staring at Figure 11-12, which has horizontal organization, tends to fatigue horizontal slope detectors. When the observer then looks to Figure 11-11, which is theoretically equally likely to excite both vertical and horizontal slope detectors, the fatigued horizontal detectors are not excited to the same degree or in the same numbers as are the relatively unfatigued vertical slope detectors. This leads to the aftereffect.

It is obvious, then, that the notion of the cortical feature detector is fairly powerful. It helps to explain a number of phenomena in a reasonable manner. As we shall see in the next chapter, the fact that both eyes are capable of exciting the same cortical units may be very helpful in explaining three-dimensional space perception.

Do these phenomena prove conclusively that feature detectors of the sort found in lower animals are at work in human beings? As with any other theory that seems to fit some psychological data, we have to be cautious and search for other possible explanations, especially simpler ones, and other informative experiments. As an example, consider the McCollough colored-line effect demonstrated in Figure 11-21 (see page 266). Although it seems like direct evidence for colored-edge detectors, could it instead be due to some simpler visual mechanism, such as adaptation of receptors in the retina? Gibson and Harris (1968) claimed that perhaps it could. Whenever a subject looks at one of the green horizontal stripes in Figure 11-21(c), some of the retinal cones become adapted to green. The only cones so adapted are those on which a green stripe is focused. Hence, horizontal strips of the retina are adapted to green, making those retinal strips more sensitive to red than to green, as in a negative afterimage. When the subject then looks at a white horizontal stripe in Figure 11-21(a), it falls on a green-adapted strip of retina and therefore looks reddish. Similarly, the red vertical stripes in Figure 11-21(b) adapt vertical strips of the retina, making the vertical stripes in Figure 11-21(a) look greenish. Thus we have explained the illusory colors seen on Figure 11-21(a) without ever mentioning colored-edge detectors in the cortex. Only individual retinal cones have been adapted. The McCollough aftereffect colors appear on vertical or horizontal stripes only because those stripes fall on appropriately adapted regions of the retina.

This explanation was put to the test by alternately projecting colored patterns like Figures 11-21(b and c) on a screen, shifting them from place too rapidly for the subject's eyes to follow. The rapid shifting prevented any retinal region from being adapted differently from any other region. Nevertheless, the subjects saw McCollough aftereffect colors when they looked at a test pattern. The conclusion is that the McCollough effect does not arise solely from adaptation of individual cones, after all. It may indeed depend on cortical colored-edge detectors.

Several of the other phenomena discussed in this section may also be vulnerable to the same sort of reasoning. Rather than stemming from cortical detectors, these phenomena may depend on simpler mechanisms, such as localized retinal adaptation. In these cases, however, the crucial experiments have not yet been done.

SUMMARY

In this chapter, we have reviewed some of what is known about how we see objects, that is, how we distinguish figure from background. In recent years, the physiologists have contributed much information on how edges and contours are encoded in neural activity. In addition, a major aspect of all perceptual systems has been revealed. The perceptual system seems to respond to changes in stimulation. With steady-state stimulation, the perceptual system falters almost completely. These and other facts on the perception of pattern raise crucial questions on how much of our perceptual apparatus develops through experience. The answer to this crucial aspect of perceptual life remains open.

SUGGESTED READINGS

GRAHAM, C. H. (Ed.) *Vision and visual perception.* New York: Wiley, 1965.

GREGORY, R. *The eye and brain.* New York: McGraw-Hill, 1966.

HARTLINE, H. K., WAGNER, H. G., & RATLIFF, F. Inhibition in the eye of *Limulus. Journal of General Physiology*, 1965, **3**, 651–673.

HOCHBERG, J. *Perception.* Englewood Cliffs, N. J.: Prentice-Hall, 1964.

RATLIFF, F. *Mach bands.* San Francisco: Holden-Day, 1965.

12

Perception of Space and Movement

One of the classical problems of psychology is how three-dimensional space is perceived despite the fact that the retinal image is flat. Motion perception forms another problem for psychology. How fast must an object move in order for it to be perceived as moving? How fast does it move before it appears blurred? How can movement be perceived when the image on the retina is stationary, as when gazing at a moving object? Still another problem area is that of perceived size. How is the size of an object perceived, when its retinal image may be large or small, depending on how far away the object is? These topics of size, depth, and movement perception will be examined in the present chapter.

THE CONSTANCY OF PERCEIVED SIZE

As an object moves farther and farther away from an observer, its retinal image becomes smaller and smaller. Figure 12-1 illustrates the fact that the "visual angle," formed by lines between two ends of the object and the eye of an observer, will vary together with the size of the image on the retina. The farther away the object is, the smaller its angular size and the size of the image it forms on the retina.

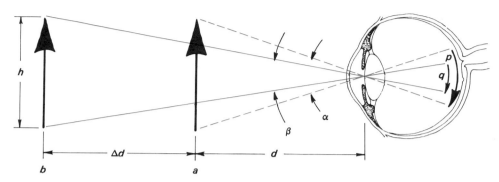

FIGURE 12-1   Euclid's law. The angular size of an object is inversely proportional to its distance. The arrow at *a* subtends an angle α at the observer's eye. The arrow at *b* is exactly the same length *h* as is the arrow at *a*. Yet it subtends an angle β, which is smaller than the angle α. The visual angle subtended by the arrow *a* at the eye may be computed from the formula tan $\alpha = h/d$. The angle subtended by the arrow *b* may be computed from tan $\beta = h/(d + \Delta d)$. Since $d + \Delta d > d$, β must be proportionately smaller than α. The sizes of the images of the arrows *a* and *b* formed on the retina are in the same ratio as the angles subtended by the arrows at the entrance to the eye. Thus $p/q = \alpha/\beta$. This relates image size to angular size.

If an object is first seen at a distance of 10 feet from the eye and then moves to double that distance, its image size will shrink to half the size; at triple the distance, 30 feet, the image will be one-third the size, and so on. The fact that both the image size and the angular size of the object vary inversely with the distance of the object from the eye is called Euclid's law.

It is surprisingly difficult to perceive things in accordance with Euclid's law. Artists trying to draw objects in a landscape, know this problem well. At first, objects in the distance are drawn too large, and nearby objects too small. The reason is that generally one perceives objects in terms of their physical sizes, their heights and widths as measured with a yardstick, whereas an accurate drawing must be in terms of their angular sizes. A man who is 6 feet tall looks about the same height whether you see him across a room or nearby, even though the image on your retina may be three or four times as large when he is nearby. This tendency to perceive his size as the same, in spite of different image sizes, is referred to as size constancy. Just as with brightness constancy (page 274), our perceptions match the real world rather than the retinal image.

In order to get around size constancy (so useful in everyday life but such an impediment to a realistic painter), Leonardo da Vinci suggested that the art student look at the scene through a plate of glass. He could then trace the main outlines of objects at various distances onto the glass. This would enable him to get the angular ratios correct before trying to paint them onto his canvas. The painter who measures objects against his thumb is also trying to get a good estimate of angular sizes.

Angular Size

How do we manage to perceive size correctly? An experiment by Holway and Boring (1941) suggests some answers. A luminous disk was placed in a corridor and an observer viewed it from a corner in the same corridor, as shown in Figure 12-2. A second luminous disk was placed around the bend in the corridor. This second disk could be adjusted in size by the observer, while the first disk could be moved by the experimenter to any distance from the observer. The observer's task was to make the adjustable disk appear to be the same size as the movable one. If the adjustment was based upon the perception of physical size, then regardless of the distance of disk 1, the subject would make the diameter of disk 2 equal to the diameter of disk 1. Moreover, he would do this regardless of the position of disk 1 in the corridor. This would be perfect size constancy, as shown in Figure 12-3. If the observer instead matched the angular sizes of the disks, the diameter of disk 2 would be equal to that of disk 1 only when they were both equally far from his eye. With disk 2 nearer than disk 1, the nearby disk 2 would have to be smaller than disk 1 to

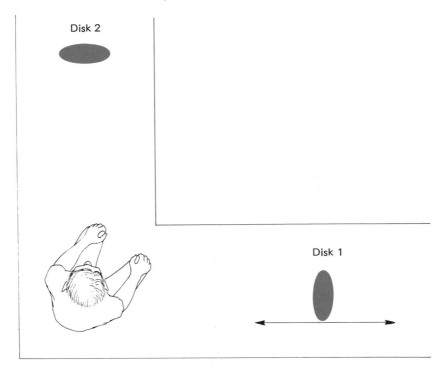

FIGURE 12-2   The size constancy experiment of Holway and Boring. Disk 2 is adjusted in size to match the apparent size of disk 1 when disk 1 is placed at different points along the corridor. Disk 2 remains fixed in place.

get a good match. As the distance of disk 1 changes, the diameter of disk 2 would have to be changed.

What actually happened? When the disks were viewed in illuminated corridors with both eyes able to see them, subjects gave a fairly good approximation to the size constancy function. They saw the disk as having its true physical size regardless of the distance.

The more informative part of the experiment is what happened when the experimenters systematically reduced the amount of information about the distance of disk 1. This was done in steps. In one condition, the ceiling lights were simply turned off and the corridor could not be seen very well. This caused the function to shift (Figure 12-4). As the target disk was placed farther and farther away, there was an increasing tendency to see it grow smaller with distance, i.e., disk 2 was made smaller to match disk 1. When the subject then closed one eye, there was an even greater falloff in perceived size as distance was increased. Finally, the subject viewed the scene through an artificial pupil, a tiny peephole. An artificial pupil keeps images in focus regardless of distance of an object; therefore, the eye does not change the accommodation of its lens when the distance of the target changes. Under this condition, the subject responded almost completely to the size of the retinal image, or angular size.

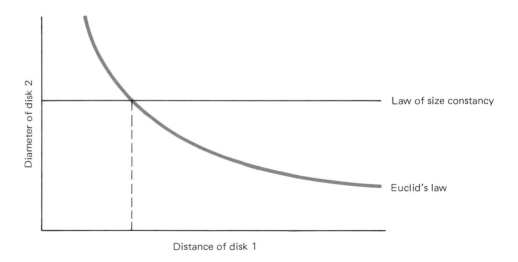

FIGURE 12-3   Two theoretical curves illustrating the law of size constancy and Euclid's law. The abcissa represents the distance of disk 1 from the eye. The ordinate represents the diameter of disk 2 in inches accepted by an observer as equal to the perceived size of disk 1. The dotted line intercepts the abcissa at the point where disk 1 is equal to the distance of disk 2. Both functions intersect at this distance showing that either law will give the same size match. The point on the ordinate intercepted by the size constancy function is the 12 inch diameter of disk 1.

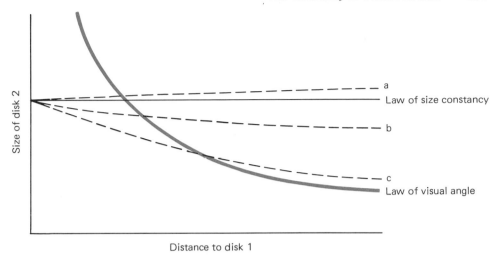

FIGURE 12-4   Empirical data obtained by Holway and Boring in a size constancy experience. Curve a shows how the diameter of disk 2 was adjusted to match that of disk 1 when disk 1 was placed at various distances in a lighted corridor. As distance increased, the size became somewhat too large but still approximated the theoretical law of size constancy. Curve b illustrates what happened to size judgments when the corridor was darkened and one eye was closed. Curve c illustrates the effect of further reduction of distance cues by use of an artificial pupil placed before the open eye. The function approximates the law of visual angle.

The Importance of Textured Surfaces

Since this work of Holway and Boring, which is about 30 years old, there have been significant additions to our knowledge of size perception. J. J. Gibson (1950) has pointed to the fact that the normal everyday visual world is comprised of textured surfaces. The density of the texture varies with distance from the eye. Thus, a pebbly surface will appear to be more densely textured as it recedes from the eye. Gibson observed that the amount of texture covered by an object on a uniformly textured surface remains constant regardless of how far the object is from the eye (Figure 12-5). This may well be an important cue to the subject when he makes size judgments.

Other Factors

Rock and Ebenholtz (1959) observed that the apparent size of an object can be affected by its frame of reference (Figure 12-6). Also, as we shall see in the discussion of the cues to depth, the convergence of the eyes may also contribute to size constancy. It has been shown by Heineman, Tulving, and

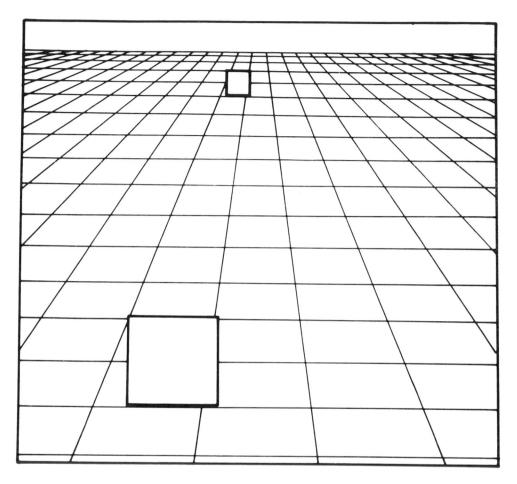

FIGURE 12-5   Gibson (1950) pointed out the importance of the density of textured surfaces in size perception.

Nachmias (1959), that convergence can strongly affect relative size judgments when all other cues are eliminated.

Instructing the Subject

Another very important factor in size judgments is the instruction given to the subject. Gilinsky (1955) had subjects adjust the size of one object at one distance until it appeared to match the size of another similar object at another distance. When the distances involved are very large then the measurements obtained from a subject will vary according to how he is instructed.

Thus, when Gilinsky encouraged her subjects to make matches in terms of visual angle, they showed very little tendency toward constancy. When they were told to match in terms of "yardstick" size, then, under the same physical circumstances, subjects exhibited strong size constancy. The effects of instructions, however, seem to be less strong when the stimuli are all close to the observer. Then, there is a much stronger tendency to exhibit size constancy and less ability to make visual angle judgments. This may be inferred from the work of Ono (1969) who observed that subjects can learn to give judgments consistent with size constancy quite easily in a visual field that is rich in cues to distance. Also, other subjects easily could learn to give judgments in terms of visual angle when the field is poorly endowed with cues to distance.

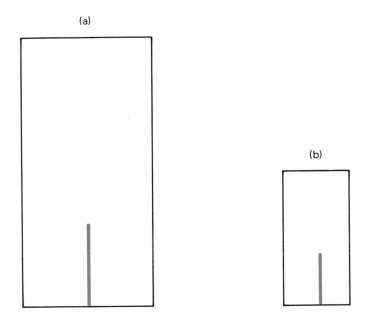

(a)

(b)

FIGURE 12-6   Rock and Ebenholtz showed that a frame of reference may affect perceived size. Luminous frames were presented in a darkened room. One frame contained a line segment of constant height, similar to that shown in frame (a) in the figure. The other frame was of a different size. It too contained a line but the line was of variable height. The subject was required to adjust the length of the line in this fixed smaller frame (b) to match the length of the line in the larger frame. Subjects rarely made perfect matches of the lines. Instead there was a strong tendency to adjust the line in frame (b) so that it would fill a proportionate amount of the height of the frame. Thus, as in frame (a), if the standard line was one-third of the frame height the subject would adjust the line in frame (b) so that it too was one-third of the frame height. Though this effect has been shown to be very substantial, it is not large enough by itself to account for the nearly perfect size constancy that may be encountered in a richer visual environment.

THE PERCEPTION OF DISTANCE

The size constancy observed in daily life is clearly dependent upon the ability of the observer to sense the distances of objects from his eye. Both animate and inanimate objects normally appear to have stable sizes. This probably has some adaptive value. However, as Holway and Boring have show, in order to perceive things as having a constant size, one must use the information concerning the distances of objects.

There are several classes of distance information. Each such class of information is called a cue. These cues were not immediately obvious; they had to be discovered, and the first discoverers of cues to depth or distance were the artists.

Pictorial Cues

The pictorial cues are used by artists in conveying the impression of distance or depth (Figure 12-7). Though the pictures are painted onto flat surfaces, observers feel as though they are peering into the distance and experi-

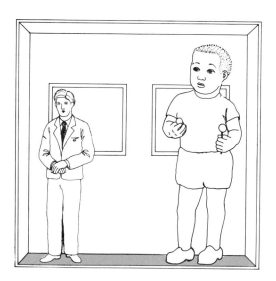 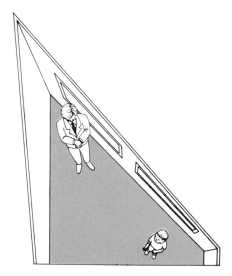

FIGURE 12-7   A distorted room. The man looks smaller than the boy, because, although he is actually farther away, the pictorial cues convey the impression that he is at the same distance. The cue of perspective and interposition coupled with an assumption that rectangles in the picture plane are "really" rectangular windows offsets the knowledge that men are larger than boys.

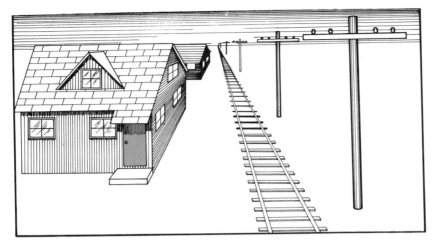

FIGURE 12-8   A drawing illustrating linear perspective.

encing the solidity of the portrayed objects. This occurs because the artist succeeds in capturing those features of the world that enable one to see it in depth with one eye closed and from a stationary position.

The most important of these pictorial cues is perspective. Today, we speak about two kinds of perspective: linear perspective and detail perspective.

LINEAR PERSPECTIVE.   The main outlines of objects appear to converge as they recede into the distance. This well-known convergence (Figure 12-8) is an instance of Euclid's law. Two points on the rails of Figure 12-8 have a constant lineal separation regardless of their distance from the observer since the rails are parallel, i.e., by definition parallel lines are always the same distance apart. However, at one distance the rails have a given angular separation which will apparently grow smaller as the distance from the eye increases. This angle becomes infinitely small at very great distances. The artist in drawing his figure makes the assumption that the world is flat. Moreover, he also assumes that the horizon is at infinity. On this endless and flat Euclidean plane, parallel lines would have to seem to converge at infinity when viewed by an observer. The place of convergence in a picture is the so-called vanishing point. It is the reference point at the horizon to which all lines converge in constructing a perspective drawing. Thus, you will notice that even the contours of the house shown alongside the railroad tracks in Figure 12-8 tend to converge. If these lines were to be extended, they would meet at infinity.

The artist does not do violence to the facts by making his simplifying assumption that the world is an infinite flat plane. Though the world is round, it is sufficiently large so that these assumptions do not noticeably distort the actual picture.

DETAIL PERSPECTIVE.   We live in a textured world. Objects with sharp and well-defined outlines do not abound in nature. They are most common in man-

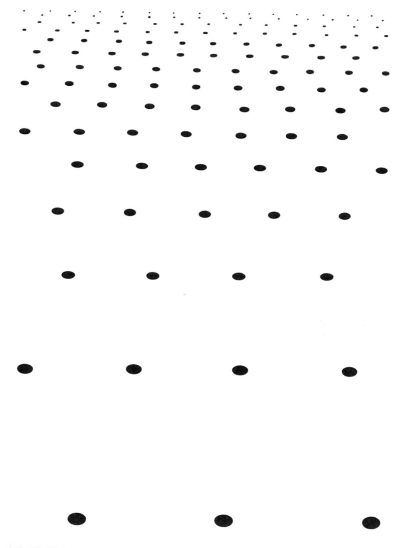

FIGURE 12-9   A textured field. Although there are no main lines or contours in this field, there is still a good impression of distance. This occurs because textural density becomes greater with distance. James Gibson identified this textural perspective as an important means for conveying the impression of depth. Adapted from Gibson (1950).

made cities, railroads, and highways. Nevertheless, one gets good depth information in grassy fields and on sandy or rock-strewn beaches, because the textural densities of such surfaces also vary in accord with Euclid's law. Thus, in a uniformly textured field, a constant visual angle includes more textural elements as distance increases (Figure 12-9).

RELATIVE SIZE.   As has already been noted several times, the angular and retinal sizes of an object diminish as the object moves into the distance. If two similar familiar objects are portrayed in a picture, and if one of these objects should be made small, the picture would be an imitation of what occurs on the retina when two such objects are seen at different distances in a real scene. This cue is illustrated in Figure 12-10, which shows two playing cards of different size.

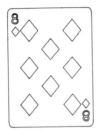

FIGURE 12-10   The cue of relative size. Which playing card is nearer? Although there are no other cues to distance, the smaller card appears to be farther away.

If this page were to be turned upside down, the depth effect produced by the size difference in Figure 12-10 is not nearly so pronounced. Hence, position in space may well be part of a complex situation that is identified by the term "relative size cue."

INTERPOSITION.   An idea that arose in connection with the attempted application of information theoretic concepts to the study of perception is relevant to the cue of interposition. Interposition occurs when one object covers a portion of another object. Referring to Figure 12-11, it will be observed that a square is simpler than a six-sided figure, i.e., the six-sided figure has six corners and a square has only four corners.

AERIAL PERSPECTIVE.   Objects become less sharp and tend to be bluish in color as distance increases. This cue was utilized by the artists of the Italian Rennaissance in conveying the impression of great depth in backgrounds to their portraits.

Kinetic Cues

In addition to pictorial cues, kinetic cues have also been studied by psychologists. Kinetic cues arise when the observer moves relative to the scene. Since these sources of information concerning the three-dimensional layout of objects depend on the observer moving about, they cannot be used in pictures, which permit only the representation of cues for a stationary observer. Kinetic cues were studied by Helmholtz (1962).

Some of his contemporaries considered Hermann von Helmholtz to be the greatest scientist of the nineteenth century. He was credited with the first formal statement of the law of the conservation of energy. Helmholtz also invented the opthalmoscope, and was the first to measure the speed of the nerve impulse. There are even reasons to believe that Helmholtz's doctrine of unconscious inference, which we shall discuss later, had a rather direct impact on Freud, especially in terms of his notions of psychological determinism (see Chapter 21).

MOTION PARALLAX.   Helmholtz's work in perception is detailed in his classical *Treatise on physiological optics*. He reported that movements of the body may yield information concerning the different distances to objects in the field of view. These body movements result in what has come to be known as motion parallax. As an observer moves about, objects at different distances produce images on the retina that change their positions at different rates.

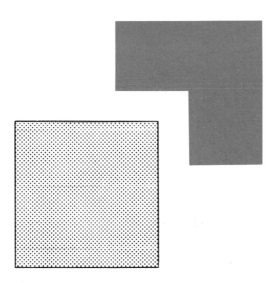

FIGURE 12-11   The cue of interposition. The lower square is perceived as nearer than the upper square, because the upper outline figure is identified as a square. It might just as well be perceived as a six-sided figure, as illustrated below.

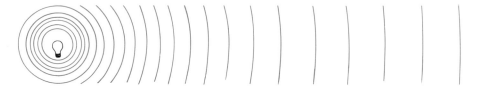

FIGURE 12-12   Waves of light emanating from a luminous body. As the distance from the luminous body becomes very great the diameters of the waves grow so very large that the wavefront appears to be planar.

Every child becomes aware that, as he moves about, the very distant objects, such as the moon and stars, will appear to move with him. This occurs because, as the distance to a luminous source of light becomes very great, the circular waves will have extremely large diameters (Figure 12-12). Thus,

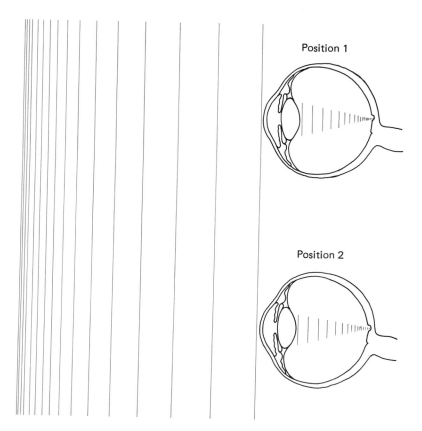

FIGURE 12-13   Plane wavefronts cast images on the same part of the retina regardless of the lateral position of the eye.

a wave of light reflected by a point on the surface of the moon will have a diameter of about 240,000 miles by the time it reaches the eye of an observer. It is just not possible to detect the curve in a wave with such a large diameter. For all practical purposes, the wavefront is planar at the observer's eye. Thus, by the time the wavefront reaches the observer, the information he can get about the point of origin is the same no matter where he stands (Figure 12-13). The image formed in the back of the eye by a point that is very far away will be in the same part of the retina whether the eye is in position 1, position 2, or any other parallel position in Figure 12-13.

Very near objects, however, generate or reflect light waves that still have considerable curvature when they reach the eye (Figure 12-14).

When the eye is displaced laterally from position 1 to position 2 in Figure 12-14, the curved wavefront first intercepts the lens at a different point. Due to the curvature of the lens itself, this causes the wavefront to be bent so

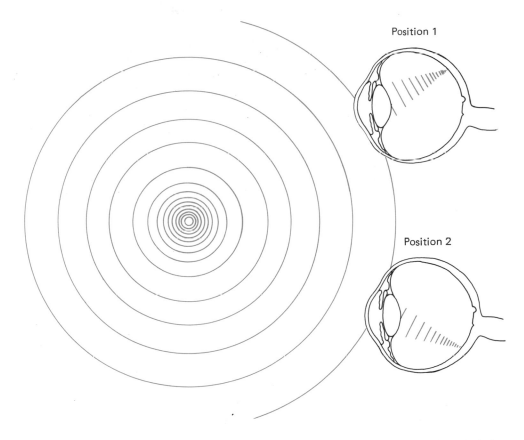

Position 1

Position 2

FIGURE 12-14   Curvilinear wave fronts are refracted to different positions when the eye is in different positions because they intercept the lens of the eye at different points.

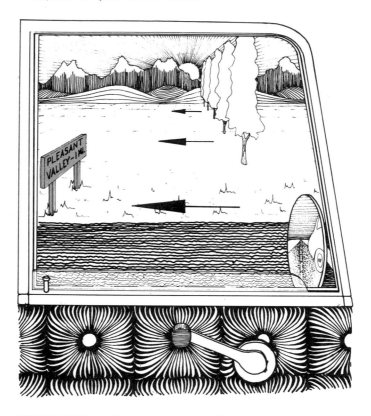

FIGURE 12-15   The gradient of velocities of points on the terrain as you ride along with gaze fixed at the horizon. Note that the vectors indicate how fast points on the terrain recede behind your line of sight. This gradient of velocities is an instance of motion parallax.

that an image is formed at a different place in the back of the eye. Thus, the image of the nearby point shifts on the retina when the eye is displaced.

The difference between very distant and very near objects becomes quite apparent when riding in an automobile. Nearby objects appear to race past while looking forward along the road, while very distant objects, such as hills and trees, usually appear to be riding along. Thus, when looking out the side window of a car and gazing at some point on the horizon, all objects between you and the horizon appear to recede away with a continuously diminishing velocity (Figure 12-15).

Helmholtz reported that, when he stood very still in a forest with one eye closed, he could only see a mass of undifferentiated greenery. However, as soon as he moved his head from side to side, the limbs of the trees and the bushes sprang into sharp relief.

MOTION PERSPECTIVE.   Motion parallax applies to any situation in which points are at different distances from the eye. Thus, two luminous points at different distances from the eye in a darkened laboratory can exhibit this same phenomenon when the head is moved. However, James Gibson (1966) found that this simple type of visual stimulus was not sufficient to give good depth perception. Instead, whole gradients of velocities, such as those illustrated in Figure 12-15, were necessary. He termed this cue motion perspective to distinguish it from motion parallax, which would include stimuli such as the two dots.

KINETIC DEPTH EFFECT.   Wallach and O'Connell (1953) discovered a related phenomenon which they termed the kinetic depth effect (KDE). The KDE occurs when a solid object is viewed with one eye and the head of the observer is moved relative to the object. Wallach and his associates investigated the KDE using a shadowgraph (Figure 12-16). They found that the contours of an object must change in both length and direction if the object is to be seen

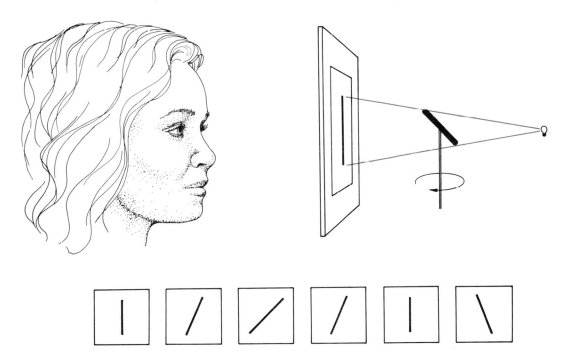

FIGURE 12-16   The kinetic depth effect. A small point source casts a sharp shadow of the tilted rod onto a ground glass screen. The tilted rod is rotated. The resulting shadow of the rod changes in both length and direction as it is rotated. It was found that, if either length or direction did not change, the depth perception was ambiguous. Insets show shadows of the rod in various positions. Rotation causes these shadows to be perceived as a rigid object in depth.

in depth. Moreover, they found that exposure to such a stimulus generalized so that similar stimuli could be perceived as three-dimensional even when they were stationary, provided that the original stimulus had been seen in motion previously. They called this the memory effect of the KDE and speculated that it could explain why congenitally monocular people may have good depth perception.

Physiological Cues

The kinetic cues described above cannot be incorporated in the flat and stationary scenes portrayed on canvas. There is still another class of spatial information that must also be left out by the artist. This information results from the changes that occur within the organism when it is confronted with an actual depthful scene.

ACCOMMODATION.   The curvature of the lens of the eye serves to bend waves of light to form a sharp image on the retina. Any particular degree of curvature is suitable for a given range of distances. Objects outside of this range are blurred. Blurred images are perceived as being at a different distance than sharp images. The curvature of the lens may change to cause the blurred images to become sharp. This changing of curvature is called accommodation.

Accommodation may be likened to the focusing of an image by a camera (Figure 12-17). The eye differs from the camera in that the distance between the lens and the retina cannot be changed. However, a similar focusing function is performed in the eye by causing the shape of the lens to change. If the lens is very curved, it will form clear images of nearby objects on the retina, leaving very distant objects as blurred images. With the lens stretched out or relatively flattened, the more distant objects will yield sharp images. Many experiments have demonstrated that, when all other cues are eliminated save for the ability of the eye to alter its accommodation, an observer may still be able to tell that one object is at a distance other than that of another object.

CONVERGENCE.   The angle formed by the lines of sight of the two eyes can be altered, depending upon the distance to a fixated object (Figure 12-18). This convergence is normally related intimately to accommodation. As an object moves into the distance, the lens becomes flatter. Moreover, at very great distances, the head may be shifted laterally without disturbing the position of the retinal image. The reasons for this phenomenon also explain why

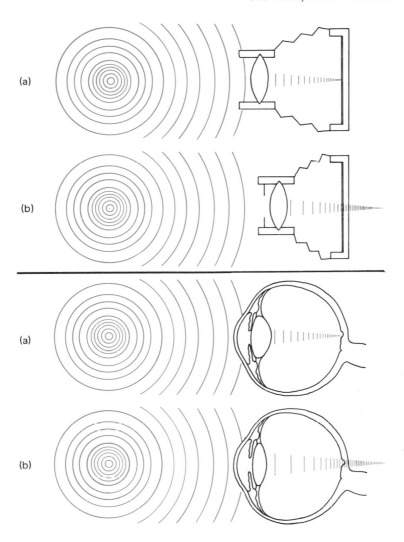

FIGURE 12-17   The focusing of an image by a camera. (a) If the lens of the camera is the correct distance from the film, it will bend the incoming waves of light to form a sharp image on the film. (b) However, if the lens is too close to the film, the waves will be bent so that, if the film did not block their progress, the image would be formed somewhat behind the plane of the film. This corresponds to shortsightedness or myopia in humans, where images are formed ''behind'' the retina. Since the film is in the way of the waves of light, they are picked up and recorded as a blurred picture of the object being photographed. The same is true for the eye.

the lines of sight for the two eyes are parallel for very distant objects. The plane wavefront produced by a very distant object will intercept the lenses of the two eyes at the same angles if and only if the lines of sight of the

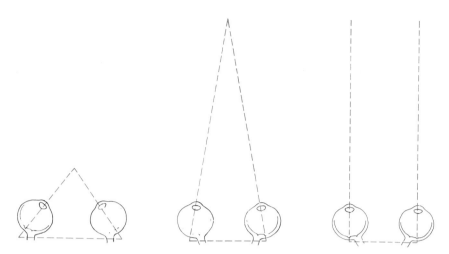

FIGURE 12-18 The convergence of the eyes. As the fixated object moves out into the distance, the angle formed between the lines of sight and the baseline connecting the two eyes becomes less and less pronounced. As the object becomes very distant, the lines of sight tend to become parallel if the images of the object are to remain within the central foveas.

two eyes are parallel. Similarly, the more curved wavefronts of nearby objects can also intercept the two lenses at the same angle if the eyes are tilted toward each other (Figure 12-19).

Accommodation is related to convergence in still another way. When an object attracts attention, the lenses of the two eyes must change their curvature in order for the object to produce sharp images. These changes in accommodation are associated with corresponding changes in the convergence angle of the eyes.

If the eyes are not properly converged, the wavefronts will not intercept the lenses at similar angles. In this case, the images in the two eyes will occupy noncorresponding places. This can be observed by pointing quickly with one finger towards some distant object, e.g., a doorknob or light switch. Keeping the finger in place and closing and opening the two eyes alternately will reveal that the finger seen by the left eye points in a different direction than the finger seen by the right eye. This observation reveals that the images of the two eyes are formed at disparate or noncorresponding retinal sites. This condition of double images is pervasive; in fact, anything outside the plane of visual fixation is seen as double. When attention is shifted from a nearby object to a distant one, two things happen. First, as we have seen, the lenses in both eyes will tend to become flatter so that the images in the two eyes will be sharper. Second, the eyes will change their positions by diverging from the angle most suitable for seeing a nearby object to an angle more suitable for a distant object, that is, the positions of the two images on the two retinas will be shifted so that they occupy corresponding retinal sites. The object is then seen as single.

The convergence angle, which is necessary to allow the eyes to see an object as single, assists in perceiving the distance to that object. Surveyors, for example, utilize the well-known method of triangulation after sighting along two different lines to determine the distance to an object. The trigonometric calculations are quite simple, and it was suspected as long ago as the seventeenth

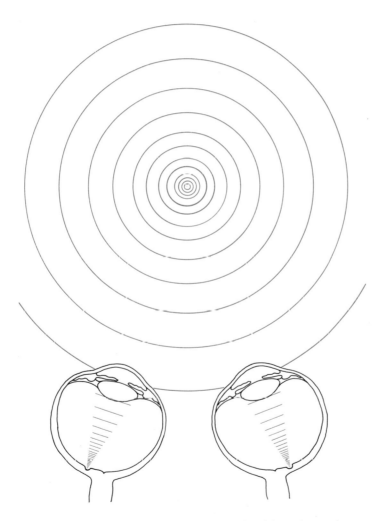

FIGURE 12-19   The eyes must be converged to intercept curved wavefronts emanating from a nearby source of light at a similar angle. If the eyes were converged for an inappropriate distance, the images would be formed at noncorresponding retinal places.

century that the brain may well make a similar computation. However, when one changes the angle of convergence while looking at some target, the target's size is often perceived as changing while its distance may be reported unreliably. Figure 12-20 depicts an experiment that permits one to see a target simply at two different convergence angles. The angular size of the target is the same, regardless of the convergence angle. When convergence must be increased in order to see the target as single, the target appears to become smaller. Likewise, when convergence is decreased the target appears to grow larger.

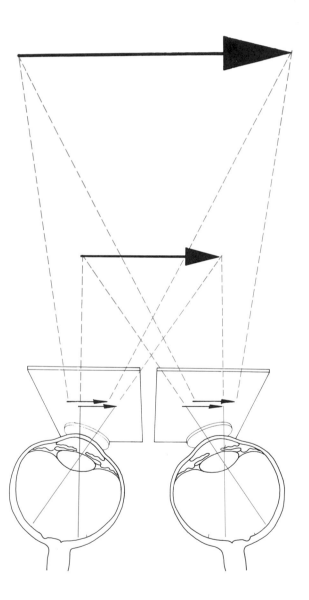

FIGURE 12-20 The effect of convergence on size. When two arrows are presented, one to each eye, the eyes may converge so that a single arrow is seen. The convergence angle needed to see the black arrows as single is greater than that needed to see the blue arrows as single. Subjects report that the blue arrow is larger than the black arrow when these are viewed at different times.

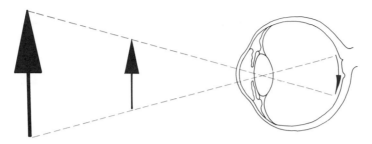

FIGURE 12-21   Emmert's law. The apparent size is related to the apparent distance. The critical cue comes via the convergence system of the eyes.

EMMERT'S LAW.   Figure 12-21 shows what would have to happen to the apparent lineal size of a target if it were perceived to be at different distances. If the target were localized at a greater distance, as with decreased convergence, it would grow larger. Similarly, as with increased convergence, if the target were perceived to be closer, it would be experienced as being of a smaller lineal size. This illustrates Emmert's law, which states that the apparent size of an object of constant angular size is proportional to its apparent distance.

This law can be illustrated with an imaginary experiment. Instead of assuming that the arrows in Figure 12-21 are real physical objects, which happen to subtend the same angle at the eye, imagine that a picture of an arrow is literally painted onto the retina. Also, imagine that this arrow may be seen by an observer. In this type of situation, which is similar to the after-image experienced after looking at a bright light, the image painted onto the retina is perceived as being out in space. Moreover, it appears to be on the surface at which one is looking. Thus, if one looked at a wall that is 10 feet away, the image will have an apparent size that can be measured against a yardstick mounted onto the wall. If the gaze was shifted to a wall that is 20 feet away, the apparent size of the image will appear to have grown. If a yardstick is also mounted on this second wall, its retinal image will be smaller than that of the yardstick on the first wall. By contrast, the size of the painted image remains constant and is therefore seen as proportionally larger.

CONVERGENCE AND PERCEIVED DISTANCE.   The changes in size produced by the experiment in Figure 12-20 are not surprising. Greater distance is associated with less convergence. This, in turn, may well be associated with greater target size. However, when subjects are asked how far such a target is from the eye, they report that it has become closer—not farther, as expected.

This surprising result usually occurs when other cues are absent. With accommodation paralyzed by means of drugs, and the scene devoid of all stimuli other than the targets, subjects say that an object that appears to grow larger is getting closer and one that appears to grow smaller is receding into the distance. The size changes are as expected from associated changes in ostensive cues to distance, i.e., convergence, but the distance judgments are inconsistent with the cue.

Helmholtz's doctrine of unconscious inference explains this seemingly paradoxical situation by assuming that the convergence does, in fact, operate as a cue to distance, but at an unconscious level. The computation of distance based upon the convergence angle affects the apparent size of the target in the predicted manner. However, once the size of the target is established, it, in turn, affects the subject's judgment of distance. Subjects have a great deal of experience with situations in which normal objects subtend larger retinal angles as they draw closer. Therefore, since the target grows larger

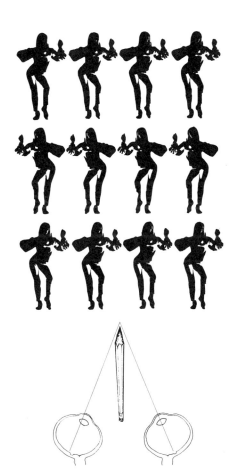

FIGURE 12-22   The wallpaper illusion. When the pattern is viewed with slightly crossed eyes so that the images in the right eye are fused with the images in the left eye, the girls appear smaller and closer. Crossing the eyes can be aided by holding a pencil up between the eyes and the page and fixating the pencil point. Moving the pencil back and forth enables the viewer to achieve proper fixation.

with decreased convergence, the subject is likely to decide that it has drawn closer.

This conflict does not occur, however, in situations where other cues are present. In the case of the so-called wallpaper illusion, increased convergence causes images to grow smaller and, at the same time, produces the impression of their drawing closer (Figure 12-22). So, at least in conjunction with other cues, convergence appears to affect the ability to perceive distance.

Binocular Stereopsis

The disparity that occurs when one is not converged at the distance of some object can, by itself, affect the perception of depth. Depth based solely upon disparity is termed binocular stereopsis or stereoscopic depth perception.

Once again the reader should point quickly toward a fixated point some distance away. As before, when the two eyes are opened and closed alternately, it becomes apparent that the left eye's image of the finger lies in a different direction as compared to the apparent direction of the right eye's finger (Figure 12-23; see page 265). The box, which lies between the door and the finger, exhibits somewhat less disparity than does the finger relative to the door. These differential disparities arise because the two eyes view the world from slightly different positions. The disparities can serve as a stimulus to actuate a change in convergence. However, convergence per se is fixed for the distance of the doorknob in this scene, and triangulation can tell us only about the distance of the doorknob. Nevertheless, the finger, box, and door are all seen as being at different distances even when the eyes do not change convergence. These disparities can reveal depth. This can be demonstrated by looking at Figure 12-23 through stereo spectacles. (To see these effects, it is necessary to cover the left eye with a piece of green cellophane and the right eye with red cellophane.)

STEREOSCOPE.   George Wheatstone was the first scientist to make use of the well-known fact that the two eyes get different views of three-dimensional scenes. He did this by inventing the stereoscope, a device that presents different pictures to each eye. The principle underlying Wheatstone's stereoscope is illustrated in Figure 12-24. Today, we have vastly improved stereoscopes, which include lenses and prisms to make viewing more natural. (One of these improved stereoscopes was invented by Oliver Wendell Holmes.)

An early Wheatstone stereogram is shown in Figure 12-25 (see page 265). When images are viewed in accordance with the directions provided, the right-hand line will appear farther away than the left-hand line. If the viewer

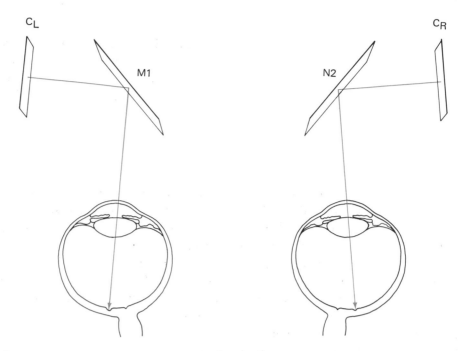

FIGURE 12-24   The Wheatstone stereoscope. A picture intended for the left eye (C_L) is reflected by a mirror (M_1) into the left eye. Similarly, the right eye's picture (C_R) is reflected by a mirror (N_2) into the right eye.

reverses the spectacles, so that the red lens is held over the left eye, the opposite depth effect occurs; the left-hand line appears behind the right hand line. In the nineteenth century, Dove viewed such a stereogram by means of an electrical spark, which lasted for a very tiny fraction of a second. Although the eyes did not have time to change convergence, the stereo effect was present.

Figure 12-26 illustrates how two objects in space are represented in a stereogram. This picture corresponds with having the image C_L in the left eye and C_R in the right. The reader may reverse this relationship and try to construct his own picture of the two objects in space that would yield the opposite depth effect.

FUSION THEORY.   A very old theory, one which has been repeatedly redis-covered in the history of psychology, proposed that disparate images fuse in the nervous system to produce the depth effect (Figure 12-27).

The fusion theory infers that the binocular images resulting from stereo-scopic viewing are the product of a fusing or combining of the original monoc-ular images. It is a very powerful theory because it predicts many phenomena.

Furthermore, this theory is not inconsistent with the finding that inputs to the two eyes do seem to combine in cells in area 18 of the monkey's visual cortex (see Chapter 2). Indeed, recent electrophysiological work on the cat showed that some cortical cells respond specifically to points of stimulation in three-dimensional space (Barlow *et al.*, 1967).

Still this view of stereopsis has been questioned in recent years. First, disparities may be large enough for one to be aware of his double images

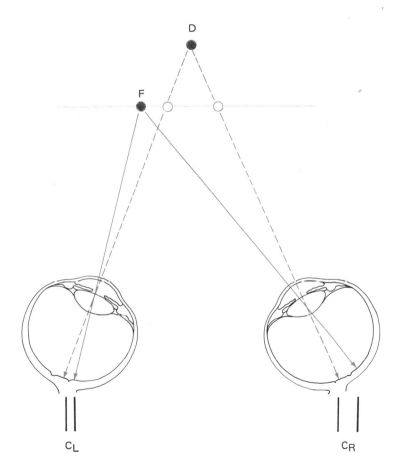

FIGURE 12-26   Binocular disparity in a real situation. Two objects, F and D are at different distances from the observer. The left eye's image C_L of F and D differs from the right eye's image C_R. The space between F and D is greater in C_R. F is the fixated object and its images fall on corresponding places. D falls on noncorresponding or disparate places. Lines of sight to D pass through the plane of fixation at different places. We are aware of these "half images," the two open circles on the plane of fixation, when the eyes are opened and closed alternately. A stereogram of this scene may be constructed by drawing a picture of C_L and another of C_R for presentation in a stereoscope.

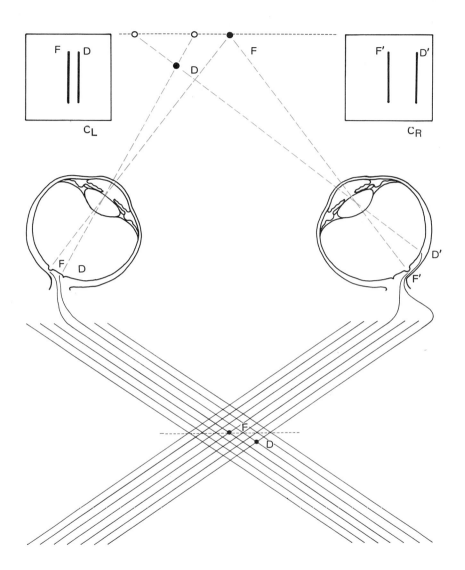

FIGURE 12-27 The fusion theory of stereopsis. Images of the lines F and D may be formed in the eyes by means of two objects in three-dimensional space or with the stereo pair C_L and C_R. In either case, the left eye sees F and D and the right eye F' and D'. The latter pair of lines is more widely separated than the former. This causes them to send signals along more widely separated pathways in the brain. These signals combine with corresponding signals arising from F and D in the left eye. The combining or fusion occurs at the intersections of the lines that represent neural pathways. The intersections themselves represent cell bodies onto which incoming axons converge. This model implies that, for depth to occur, the signals arising in the two eyes combine or fuse to form a representation of three-dimensional space in the brain. It also implies that the images from the two eyes must literally fuse if unambiguous depth is to occur.

and stereopsis will still occur. Therefore, apparent fusion or combining is not necessary for stereopsis to occur. Second, stereograms devised by Kaufman show that images that cannot appear as fused may still exhibit a depth effect (Figure 12-28; see page 266).

BINOCULAR RIVALRY. The stereogram in Figure 12-28 also illustrates a phenomenon that many have considered to be the antithesis of fusion, i.e., binocular rivalry. This occurs when oppositely oriented contours are presented to the two eyes. Instead of combining, the contours shift in predominance. Sometimes one sees the images in the left eye and sometimes the oppositely oriented images in the right eye. Most theorists in the past would have held that stereopsis cannot occur with rivaling stimuli because they do not fuse.

One view of the processes underlying binocular stereopsis depends upon a very important distinction, that is, fusion may be thought of as a phenomenal or perceptual occurrence or it may be thought of as a computation that occurs without the awareness of the subject. Phenomenal fusion might occur when disparities are very small or entirely absent. Here the images from the two eyes are essentially superimposed and indistinguishable from each other. Therefore, we can say that they appear to combine. Alternatively, when disparities are large so that double images are visible or when the objects in the two eyes are very dissimilar, apparent fusion does not occur. Despite the fact that these dissimilar and widely disparate images may exhibit binocular rivalry, they do have certain features in common. Thus, the central squares in Figure 12-28 are, on the average, darker than their backgrounds. This region, which is differentiated by an average brightness increment relative to the background, exhibits disparity. After discriminating the brightness-differentiated patches in the two eyes, the nervous system could then compute the disparity. However, this matching operation, performed below the level of awareness, results in a modification of a binocular image that is itself developed in a different neural network. This binocular image need not produce the appearance of fusion and may even exhibit binocular rivalry.

SPACE AND ILLUSIONS

All of the cues described in this chapter may play a role in size perception. In the Holway and Boring experiment on size constancy, the cues were reduced in effectiveness by occluding one eye, thus eliminating possible effects of binocular disparity. The artificial pupil destroyed the effectiveness of accommodation and convergence, and darkening the room eliminated perspective. At each successive stage, the removal of cues produced less accurate lineal size perception. A number of interesting illusions illustrate the importance of distance information in the perception of size.

The Moon Illusion

It has been known since ancient times that the moon may appear much larger over the horizon than it does in the zenith. Photographs of the moon do not reveal any significant difference in the angular size of the moon as it moves across the sky. Since the physical or angular size of the moon remains constant, the apparent changes in its size are referred to as an illusion.

There have been many theories to explain this illusion. Holway and Boring, for example, proposed that the moon in the zenith shrinks because it is viewed with the eyes elevated in the head. They found that, when an observer adjusts the size of a nearby disk to match the size of the moon, the obtained match will be small if the moon is viewed with elevated eyes. However, as we shall see, when the moon illusion is measured by different means, the magnitude of the eye elevation effect is about 3%, which is much smaller than estimates of the actual moon illusion.

PTOLEMAIC THEORY.   An alternative to the eye elevation theory is the apparent distance theory of Ptolemy (Figure 12-29), which holds that the moon at the zenith is perceived as closer than the moon on the horizon. Since it appears to be closer, and since the angle it subtends at the eye is the same as that measured when the moon is on the horizon, the zenith moon must appear as smaller. This same reasoning applied to the observed size changes accompanying convergence. A corollary to this theory is that the horizon sky and moon appear to be farther away because of the presence of many cues to distance. The zenith moon, which is seen in a relatively empty field with few distance cues, appears nearer.

To test the applicability of this theory to the moon illusion, two artificial moons were presented and were perceived by observers as located in the sky (Kaufman & Rock, 1962). One of these moons was presented on the horizon and the other at the zenith. The observers could adjust the size of one moon until it appeared to match the size of the other moon. In one experiment using this technique the horizon moon was projected to the sky over two different visible horizons. One of these horizons was perceptibly much closer than the other. When the horizon moon was seen over the nearer horizon, the magnitude

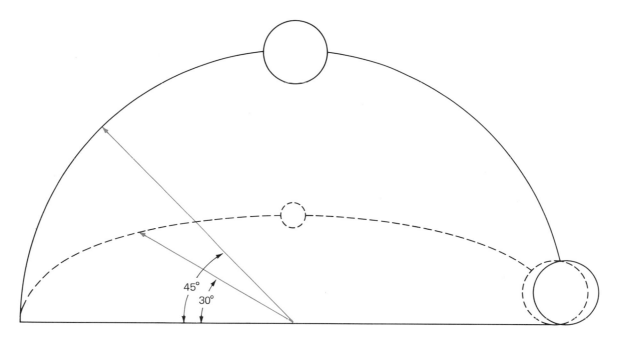

FIGURE 12-29   Ptolemaic theory of the moon illusion. The moon moves along a circular path since it is always at approximately the same distance from the eye of an observer. (Actually the distance of the moon varies somewhat because it travels on a circular path with respect to the center of the earth. Hence, the variation in distance to the moon is on the order of the size of the radius of the earth. However, this radial variation is of insignificant proportions.) Since the distance to the moon is constant, its angular size is also constant. This is illustrated by showing the moon on a circular path on the right side of the figure. According to the Ptolemaic theory, an object seen through filled space is perceived as more distant than an object seen through unfilled space. This causes the sky to appear to be flattened and the moon to appear to be closer when at the zenith. Since the moon is perceived as closer at the zenith, and since its angular size is the same as when it is on the horizon, then, by Emmert's law, it must be perceived as smaller. The fact that the sky is also perceived as ellipsoidal with the major axis in the horizontal direction is proven by the half-arc-angle experiment illustrated on the left side of the figure. If an observer is asked to point to a spot on the sky that appeared to bisect the arc between the horizon and the zenith, the angle his line of sight makes with respect to the ground is indicative of the degree of flattening of the sky. If the sky is perceived as a circle, the line of sight would form an angle of 45° with respect to the ground. If the sky appears as flattened, then the angle would be less. A typical measure obtained in experiments is 30°, which represents a severe apparent flattening of the sky.

of the illusion was substantially less than when it was over the more distant horizon.

In another experiment, the moons were presented on different days when the amount of cloud coverage varied. In general, it was found that the illusion was greatest when the cloud coverage was heavy and was smallest when the sky was completely clear. This result is consistent with half-arc-angle measures similar to those described in Figure 12-29. These measures have shown that the sky is flatter when the cloud coverage is greater. The greater flattening of the sky results in a greater difference in apparent distance between the zenith and horizon moons.

These and other experiments are consistent with an apparent distance theory of the moon illusion. The measured illusions were from 30% to more than 50%. The eye elevation effect, using the projected moons, contributed only about 3–5% of the total illusion magnitude.

Other Distance Dependent Illusions

When depth cues suggest that two objects of equal angular size are at different distances, they will appear to be of unequal linear sizes. The Ponzo illusion (Figure 12-30; see page 266) typifies illusions that are dependent upon this principle. Hence, this illusion is in the same class as the moon illusion and is consistent with Emmert's law.

Richard Gregory (1966) has proposed that many illusions are produced by the depth cues inherent in the patterns. The Ehrenstein illusion (Figure 12-31; see page 266) is not due to the same factors that produced the Ponzo illusion. Stereo viewing destroys the Ponzo illusion, but it has no noticeable effect on the Ehrenstein illusion. Obviously, factors other than distance cues may produce visual illusions.

THE NATURE-NURTURE QUESTION AGAIN

As with pattern perception, we can ask whether the infant learns space perception or whether it is innate. For example, we know that the image on the retina is upside down. Does this mean that the newborn only gradually learns to interpret the inverted retinal image as signifying an upright scene?

Adjusting to Visual Distortion

A classic experiment by George M. Stratton (1896, 1897) seemed to display an amazing flexibility in the visual system. Stratton wore a lens system over his eye that caused the world to appear upside down. In one experiment, he wore the lens system for several days and took it off only at night in a darkened room. At first, he was considerably disoriented. When he reached for objects he found that his hand ended up in the wrong place. Also, he had difficulty dressing, walking, and eating. With time, however, he became more and more expert at getting about. Based upon these reports, various interpreters of Stratton's experiments concluded that he came to perceive the world as right-side-up even though his retinal image was inverted with respect to its normal orientation. More to the point, he began to feel more and more at home in the inverted visual world and encountered fewer and fewer surprises. Finally, at times, the world appeared to be "in normal position" or "right-side-up" even though the lenses were still putting his retinal images in an abnormal position. Stratton was confident that if he had worn the lenses for more than a week, the world would eventually have looked upright again.

A similar conclusion about visual learning was reached by Ivo Kohler (1962) in Innsbruck, Austria. He had a subject wear an optical apparatus that interchanged top and bottom but not left and right. Thus, the sky appeared to be below eye level and the ground above it while the left hand of the subject still appeared to be toward the left. This subject claimed that after several days the world appeared to be right side up. He was even able to ski.

With less extreme optical disruptions, adaptation may be both complete and rapid. Over a century ago, Helmholtz tried looking through a glass prism that displaced images to his right. If he first looked through the prism at some object and then closed his eye before reaching for it, he would reach in the wrong direction (Figure 12-32). After some practice, he was able to correctly reach for objects seen through the prism after closing his eyes. Upon removal of the prism, this procedure would cause Helmholtz to reach too far in the opposite direction for the same object when his eyes were closed.

THE ROLE OF SELF-PRODUCED MOVEMENT.   Richard Held (1965) and his associates came to the conclusion that one must move his arm voluntarily when practicing with the prism, if a strong aftereffect is to be produced. Simply seeing one's arm moved by somebody else does not produce the "perceptual learning" involved in this experiment. Although some disagreement has emerged as to the importance of self-produced movements compared to the simple pickup of visual information in the course of adaptation experiments, it is obvious that one must associate what he actually does with what he intends to do, i.e., one must get some feedback if adaptation is to occur (Figures 12-33 and 12-34).

ADAPTATION: A VISUAL OR PROPRIOCEPTIVE CHANGE?   In the face of all of these demonstrations of extreme flexibility in the interpretation of retinal images, some recent research has suggested that, at least in some of these cases, there is no change at all in the visual system. Charles Hamilton (1964a) tried the Helmholtz prism experiment on monkeys that had had the connec-

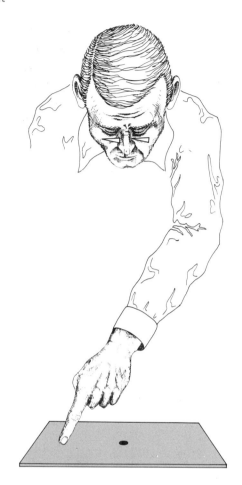

FIGURE 12-32   A prism adaptation experiment. The subject looks through prisms that deviate the world to the right. When he first tries to point to the dot, his hand points to the right. Quickly, however, he "adapts" and points to the dot.

tions between the two halves of their brains cut ("split-brain monkeys," see page 590). Just like human subjects, the monkeys quickly adapted and behaved as if they were seeing the world correctly despite the prismatic displacement. But, further testing produced some surprises. In other experiments on split-brain monkeys (see page 591), it is typically found that any visual learning, e.g., form discrimination, acquired through one eye is restricted to the hemisphere that that eye feeds into. If that eye is covered, forcing the monkey to use the other eye, he shows no evidence of having seen the forms before. However, with the trained eye open, he can use either hand to make his response to the visual stimulus.

When Hamilton tested his split-brain monkeys that had adapted to prism goggles, he found just the opposite. If the monkeys had one eye covered and used only one hand while wearing the goggles, they showed an adjustment

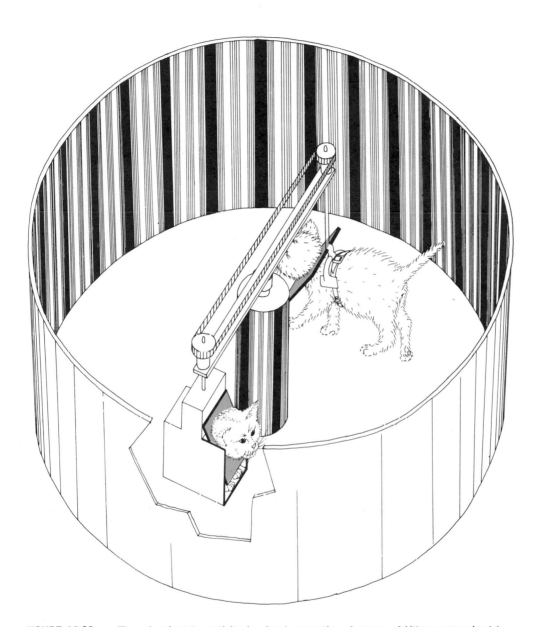

FIGURE 12-33   The role of motor activity in visual perception. A group of kittens was raised by Held and Hein (1963) under special stimulus motor conditions. From birth to 12 weeks of age they were allowed to view a patterned visual environment for 1 hour each day. The rest of the day was spent in the dark. One group of kittens was allowed to explore the patterned environment on their own four feet, while the other, tied to the first by means of the gondola's set of pulleys, viewed the same scene passively. After 12 weeks, each group was tested on a variety of perceptual tasks. The kittens who got the "free ride" were essentially perceptually blind, while the other kittens performed all visual tasks normally. These studies show that visual perception develops normally ony when the visual stimulation is accompanied by voluntary motor activity.

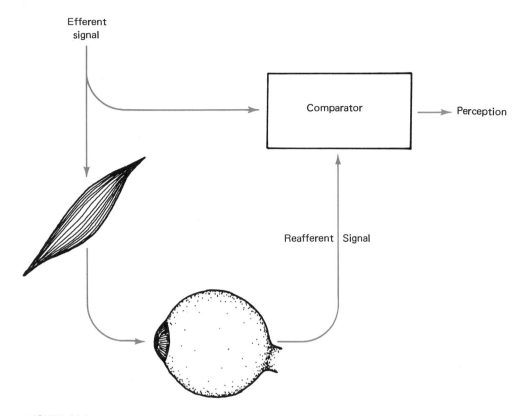

**Efferent
signal**

Comparator

Perception

Reafferent | Signal

FIGURE 12-34   Von Holst's (1954) reafference theory. When one's eyeball is moved by pressing on the lid of the eye, the world appears to jump. This is in contrast to what happens when the eye is moved voluntarily, thereby bringing the normal extraocular musculature into play. In the latter case, the world appears to be stationary despite the fact that the image moves across the retina. Von Holst suggested that a copy of the signal to the muscles of the eye is sent to a comparator. The visual signal from the retina is also sent to the comparator. This signal reflects the fact that the eye is in motion. When it is compared with the efferent copy in the comparator, it is found to be consistent with what is expected to follow from the efferent copy. Hence, the resulting perception is stable. If the visual signal reflects motion, however, and the efferent copy is inconsistent with this, as when the eyeball is pushed by the finger, then the world is seen to jump. Held (1965) suggested that this expectation may be altered by continual exposure to an originally anomalous situation, e.g., when wearing prisms. The signal from the eye is termed the reafferent signal because it provides feedback as to the consequences of eye movements.

in reaching for targets seen with either eye, but only when they used the practiced hand. In other words, adapting to prisms was nothing like learning a new visual discrimination. In fact, there was no change in the monkeys' visual perception at all, because, if there were, the monkey would have reached in the same way with either hand. Hamilton (1964b) repeated the same experiment with normal human subjects and found the same striking result. If a subject used only one hand while wearing prisms, only that hand manifested any adjustment to the prisms. Hamilton concluded that, rather than any change in vision, there was a change in the position sense of one arm. The subject's nonvisual perception of his arm was recalibrated to agree more closely with the shifted visual image of it as seen through prisms.

In his first experiment with human subjects, Hamilton had the prisms attached to a box, so that, when the subject looked through them, there was little head movement possible. When the prisms were instead mounted in goggles, so that the subject could move his head freely, the outcome was somewhat different. This time, adjustment was evident not only in the practiced arm, but in the other arm as well, just as should happen if the subject's visual perception had changed. But Hamilton proposed another explanation, consistent with what had occurred in his first experiment. Possibly, there is a change in position sense of whatever part of the body is moved while wearing prisms. In the second experiment, that would include the neck. Any change in the subject's perception of which way his head was pointing, relative to his torso, would of course affect which way he judges a visual object to be relative to his torso. Thus, as Hamilton found, a change in position sense of the neck would affect reaching with either arm.

CHANGES IN THE PERCEIVED POSITION OF BODY PARTS.   Harris (1966) confirmed and extended Hamilton's conclusion that it is the position sense for body parts, not vision per se, that is altered in these experiments. He found that allowing a subject to view one hand through prisms led to changes in pointing at targets other than visual ones. The error was the same whether subjects pointed at visual targets (after removing the prisms), or closed their eyes and pointed at a sound source or straight ahead. As in Hamilton's first experiment, there was virtually no error in pointing at anything with the other hand. Harris demonstrated that, even with such a drastic optical disruption as mirror reversal, a person's kinesthetic perception of his arm may be recalibrated to match the backward vision (Rock & Harris, 1967). After subjects had watched their moving arms through reversing goggles for an hour, they were blindfolded and asked to print various letters and numbers (Figure 12-35). Immediately after being blindfolded, subjects often wrote a letter backward but said that it felt correct. Just as often, they wrote the letter correctly (such as the "e" in the third column) but said that it felt backward!

If seeing one arm through reversing goggles can reverse its position sense, could it be that, after wearing such goggles for many days, the position sense for the entire body might change? Figure 12-36 shows Harris' conception of how such adaptation to reversal might proceed. If the subject's visual perception remains reversed, he will continue to see writing as mirror writing (until he has seen so much mirror writing that it, too, looks "normal" to him, though still different from preexperimental writing). However, if he sees a car apparently on the left (which means that it is really on his right), he sees it near where he now feels his right hand to be, due to its recalibrated position sense. So he might well say, "I see the car on my right-hand side."

Even with goggles that turn the whole scene upside down, similar changes in position sense may occur. In the diary that he kept during his 1896 experiment, Stratton wrote that after a few days, "the limbs began actually to feel in the place where the new visual perception (the inverted scene produced by the goggles) reported them to be. . . . I could at length *feel* my feet strike against the *seen* floor, although the floor was seen on the opposite side of the field of vision from that to which at the beginning of the experiment I had referred these tactual sensations." As Harris noted, if Stratton felt his feet pressing down on the floor in that new visual location, he must have

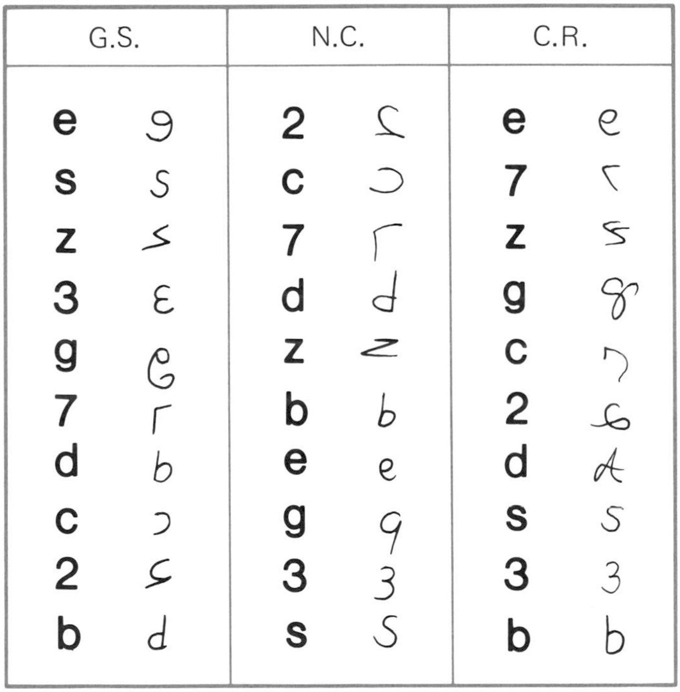

G.S.		N.C.		C.R.	
e	ꟼ	2	ꞔ	e	e
s	ꙅ	c	ꭎ	7	⸦
z	ꙅ	7	ſ	z	ꙅ
3	ε	d	�	g	℘
g	ꭆ	z	ꙁ	c	ꭆ
7	ſ	b	b	2	ℒ
d	b	e	e	d	ꓮ
c	ꜿ	g	ꝗ	s	ꙅ
2	ꙅ	3	3	3	3
b	d	s	ꙅ	b	b

FIGURE 12-35 Examples of results from an experiment in which subjects wore right-left reversing goggles for a total of 1 hour. During that time, they looked at their hands while doodling on a pad. They were then blindfolded and asked to write letters and numbers that the experimenter dictated. Subjects often wrote a letter backward but said that it felt correct. From Harris and Harris (1965).

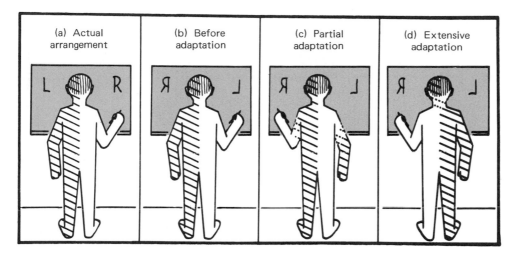

FIGURE 12-36   One interpretation of long-term adaptation to reversing goggles. When the subject first puts on reversing goggles, he sees the blackboard reversed (b). When he holds up his right hand, he sees it on the left. His position sense changes so that he eventually feels that his right hand really is in that visual position (c). After many days, the felt locations of the subject's torso and legs are also reversed (d). According to this interpretation, there is never any change in the subject's visual perception. From Harris (1965).

felt that that direction was "downward" and hence must have judged that the room was upright.

If this interpretation is correct, it seems that instead of the sense of touch educating vision and bringing it into line with reality, just the reverse occurs. This effect of vision on touch can be overwhelming and immediate. A straight bar seen through prisms that make it appear curved actually feels curved to the touch (Gibson, 1933). A plastic square seen through a lens that enlarges it feels larger; when seen through a lens that makes it look rectangular, it feels rectangular (Rock & Harris, 1967). The evidence that at first seemed to provide convincing testimony to the flexibility of visual perception now seems to show that changes in the perceptual world occur more readily in the proprioceptive system than in the visual system.

THE PERCEPTION OF MOVEMENT

The Waterfall Illusion

Illusions are not limited to static situations, but can be contingent upon movement. The waterfall illusion (Figure 12-37) is an aftereffect that is similar to the figural aftereffects described in Chapter 11. One theory proposes that there

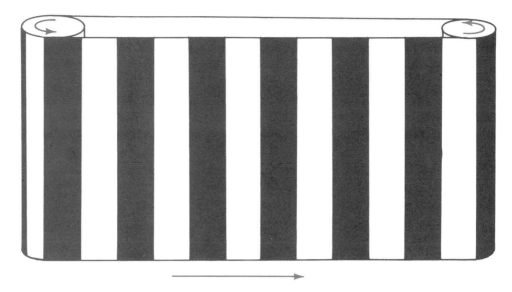

FIGURE 12-37   The waterfall illusion. A pattern of horizontal stripes is made to move down-wards in the visual field. The observer stares at the moving pattern for one or two minutes. Afterward the observer is instructed to look at a textured surface, such as a page of print. The new stationary surface now appears to move upward in the field.

are cells in the brain that are specially tuned to respond to moving visual stimuli. Some of the cells detect downward vertical movements, other cells detect upward vertical movements, and so on. According to the theory, these cells are all spontaneously active in a stationary visual situation. The movement signals provided in these circumstances tend to cancel each other out. When the eye is confronted with a continually moving scene, the cells responding to that class of movement become relatively fatigued. As a result, these previously stimulated cells are relatively quiescent when the movement has actually stopped. The other cells, however, the ones specialized for other directions of movement, tend to remain spontaneously active. The net result of this activity is the perception of movement in the opposite direction.

Other theories of this illusion have used the observation that the eyes tend to follow the moving bars. This fatigues the eye muscles. The fatigue causes the eyes to tend to wander upward when viewing the stationary pattern. The brain sends orders to the eye muscles to prevent the eyes from moving upward. These counterbalancing "eyes down" orders are also sent out when the eyes are tracking the bars. Now, however, the bars are stationary while the orders are being sent out. This stationary pattern in the presence of signals to move downward is interpreted by the brain as moving upward.

Although this approach cannot be ruled out entirely, there are two things wrong with it. First, Sekuler and Ganz (1963) were able to obtain a movement aftereffect even when the eyes could not follow the moving pattern. Second, similar illusions occur when two sets of bars moving in opposite directions are presented simultaneously. It is unlikely that the eye can move in two directions at once, so the continued presence of the aftereffect argues against a theory based on eye movement.

Induced Movement

The bars used to demonstrate the waterfall illusion are perceived as moving, while the framework around the bars is perceived as stationary. How do we perceive one object as moving, while we perceive a nearby object as stationary? Why is motion ascribed to some things and not others? This last question is significant when one realizes that all motion is relative. In physics, motion is defined in terms of relative displacement. It is only in perception that some things have the attribute of motion while others appear to be stationary.

Imagine a small luminous point that may be seen in an otherwise dark and empty space. This point is moved very slowly from one position to the next, and there is, of course, a threshold for the detection of movement. The hour hand on a watch moves so slowly that one may only infer that its motion exists because at one time it points to one position and at another time it points to another position. When confronted with such evidence, one may want to say that it had moved. Similarly, the luminous point may move so slowly that one cannot see it move. Therefore, its rate of displacement may have to be increased if movement is to be seen. A rate of the order of 3 minutes of arc per second is needed before one can say with some degree of certainty that the spot is moving. If a second, physically stationary spot is introduced when the first spot is at a near-threshold rate, it is extremely difficult to say which of the two spots is actually in motion. This ambiguous situation prompted Karl Duncker (1938) to define perceived movement in terms of relative displacement. The problem left unsolved by this definition was why the movement is unambiguous under some circumstances, i.e., one can determine which of the two objects is moving.

Duncker's resolution to this problem is explained by another experiment. In this case, he moved the first spot at a rate so slow that the observer could not be sure that it was moving. Now, when a luminous line was introduced instead of a second spot, the observer saw the first spot as moving. Moreover, there was no ambiguity about this. The spot moved and the line was stationary. It may be concluded that the line formed a frame of reference for the spot.

In yet another experiment, the spot was enclosed with a luminous rectangular framework. But now the framework was displaced at the slow rate rather than the spot. Duncker found that subjects reported that the spot was moving and the framework was stationary. An enclosed object is seen as moving, while the enclosing object or frame of reference is perceived as stationary. The frame of reference induces movement in the enclosed object.

An instance of induced movement occurs in everyday life when one feels himself as moving even though he is sitting on a stationary railroad train. The stationary observer experiences himself as moving because an adjacent train starts to move on the next track. This induced movement of the self occurs when the nearby train becomes a frame of reference for one's self.

Real Movement

Returning to the luminous spot in the darkened room, it is apparent that there are very slow rates of displacement that are below the threshold for movement detection. When an object moves more slowly than these threshold rates, movement can only be inferred from other evidence. Above this threshold is real movement, i.e., the movement that is perceived when an object moves physically from one retinal point to another.

Several conditions affect the threshold of real movement perception. When a spot is seen alone in the dark, it may be seen as moving when it displaces at the rate of about 3 minutes of arc per second. (This is roughly equivalent to having an object move through a distance of about 0.02 inches in 1 second when the object is 20 inches from the eye.) It is particularly difficult to make this threshold measurement in a psychophysical experiment, because a stationary dot in the dark may be seen as moving. This spontaneous illusory movement is known as the autokinetic effect. The occurrence of this phenomenon is related to the tension of the muscles that produce eye movements. However, the autokinetic effect can be eliminated by providing a frame of reference for the dot. When the frame of reference is absent, it is necessary to use dot exposures of fairly short duration in order to obtain comparable threshold data. Otherwise, the dot must move much faster in order to obtain reliable movement perception reports.

Unlike the mere detection of luminous spots (see Chapter 10), there are actually two thresholds of movement perception. The lower threshold concerns the minimum velocity at which movement is perceived. The so-called upper threshold concerns the maximum velocity. If a target moves fast enough, it will blur out and become a streak. At this velocity, one cannot be sure whether it is a target in motion or a stationary line. Depending upon the brightness of the target and the degree to which the eye is stationary while viewing the target, this upper threshold is between 12 and 32 degrees of arc per second.

(A target 20 inches from the eye may be perceived as a streak if it moves across a space of approximately 10 inches in 1 second.)

Apparent Movement

The image of an object need not move continuously across the retina to permit movement perception. Actually, if a spot of light at one place is turned off and a second spot at another place is turned on somewhat later, one may see the first spot jump across the gap to the position of the second spot. This is known as apparent movement to distinguish it from the real movement. However, the distinction between these two kinds of movement is, perhaps, a misnomer, because all perceived movement is apparent. Yet, we will remain within this tradition and continue to use the two different names, because there are, in fact, some definite differences between the two kinds of motion.

Max Wertheimer (1961), one of the founders of Gestalt psychology, conducted some very important experiments involving apparent movement. Using two spots that could be turned on and off alternately, he found that, when the time between the two spots was very short (even though they came on at different times), they were perceived as flashing on and off simultaneously. As this off time became longer, subjects reported that the first spot jumped across the gap to become the second spot. This movement was called beta motion. It refers to the common stroboscopic motion seen in advertising signs. The object actually appears to move. With still longer off times, Wertheimer's subjects reported the presence of a disembodied motion, i.e., when the first spot was turned off, it did not appear to jump the gap, but a sensation of movement occurred anyway. This disembodied movement was called phi motion. The Gestalt psychologists referred to a pure phi movement that was supposed to represent the forces existing in the brain between representations of the two spots. This concept became a cornerstone of Gestalt psychology.

Rock and Ebenholtz (1962) questioned the assumption that two points must excite different retinal locations successively if apparent movement, phi or beta, is to occur. They suggested, instead, that, if the same retinal locations were to be excited at different times with the eye in different positions at these times, apparent movement would also occur.

On the basis of their experiment (Figure 12-38), Rock and Ebenholtz concluded that excitation of two different retinal points is not necessary for movement perception. The results were explained with the notion that the observer realizes that his eye is pointing to different spatial locations at different times. Since the light is seen successively in these two locations, this results in a change in the position of the light's perceived location. They considered this

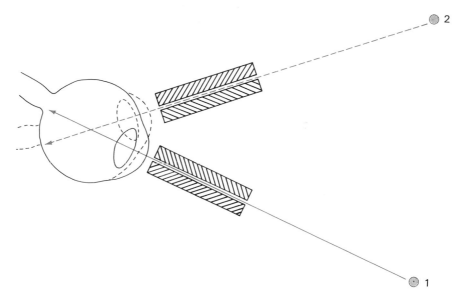

FIGURE 12-38   This figure shows the eye in two different positions looking through a very narrow tube at a light source. Positions 1 and 2 occur successively. As the eye looks back and forth from light 1 to light 2, the two lights blink on and off in step with the change in position of the eye. This results in stimulation of the same retinal place even though the eye assumes two different positons. Observers report that they see the light in motion.

change in perceived location to be basic to the occurrence of apparent movement. Regardless of the adequacy of their theory, it is apparent that one can no longer postulate that forces between different points of cortical excitation are basic to the occurrence of apparent movement.

Another issue to consider in the study of apparent movement is whether movement is based upon the same underlying neural mechanisms as real movement. One might think, for example, that the movement detectors of Hubel and Weisel may be excited by a target in real movement and also by the successive excitation of two retinal points by stationary targets. Before such a theory can be viable, however, one must be sure that the two phenomena are comparable.

One approach to this problem examines the comparability of the transit times or velocities over which real movement may be seen and the off times allowing the perception of apparent movement. Thus, we know that real movement occurs when the target velocity is less than about 12 degrees of arc per second. At higher velocities the target may appear blurred. In the case of apparent movement, the off time corresponds to the transit time of real movement. Thus, if the time between the offset of the first spot and the onset of the second spot is, as is typical, about 0.1 seconds, and if the two spots are separated by about 2 degrees of visual angle, then the equivalent transit time would be 20 degrees of arc per second. (If a spot in real movement were to move across the gap of 2 degrees at a rate which corresponds to the offtime of the spots in apparent movement, it would have to move at 20 degrees of arc per second to be seen as moving as fast.) Now, this velocity is in the vicinity of the upper threshold for real movement. These approximate theoretical calculations suggest that apparent movement occurs in very rapid jumps and does not really correspond to the slow and smooth movements associated with perceptible real motion.

To test these ideas, Kaufman and his associates experimentally compared apparent movement and real movement (Figure 12-39). The results of their

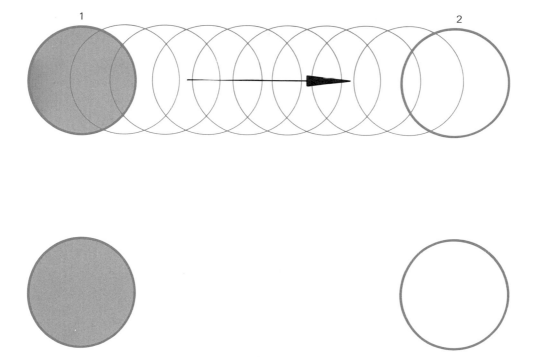

FIGURE 12-39   A comparison of real and apparent movement. A spot starting at position 1 could be moved physically across the field (arrow) to produce real movement, or it could be turned off and then turned on again at position 2. The transit times for the upper spots could be compared directly to the off times of the lower spots. It was found that the spot began to blur when the spots were moved at the rate of about 10° of arc per second. Complete streaking occurred at about 13° of arc per second. When the off times of the lower spots corresponded to these velocities, the subjects reported good apparent movement. When the offtimes corresponded to velocities of about 25° of arc per second, the spots appeared to flash on and off simultaneously. At off times corresponding to velocities lower than about 9° of arc per second, the spots came on and off successively and did not exhibit apparent movement.

experiment indicated that apparent movement does not parallel real movement. Apparent movement occurred with off times that corresponded to velocities at which objects in real movement began to streak (Kaufman *et al.*, 1971). It may be inferred real movement and apparent movement are complementary rather than parallel phenomena. Apparent movement may occur in order to extend the range of useful movement perception, even though the retinal image of a moving target becomes blurred due to the slow recovery time of photopigments.

SUMMARY

This chapter has considered many perceptual problems in the history of psychology. Even though the retinal image is flat, we see a three-dimensional world. In addition, an object is seen as moving although the eye may move, thereby keeping the object on the same place on the retina. Obviously, the world we experience is not a simple reflection of the physical relationships among retinal events. In assessing any visual stimulus, an organism actively takes into account its own state. But, the organism is also adaptive, and its perception of relations may change as a result of prior exposure.

SUGGESTED READINGS

BISHOP, P. O., & HENRY, G. N. Spatial vision. *Annual Review of Psychology*, 1971, **22**, 119–160.
HABER, R. N. (Ed.) *Contemporary theory and research in visual perception*. New York: Holt, 1968.
HELD, R. Plasticity in sensory-motor systems. *Scientific American*, 1965, **213**, 84–94.
JULEZ, B. *Foundations of cyclopean perception*. Chicago: Univ. of Chicago Press, 1971.
TEUBER, H. L. Perception. In H. W. Magoun & V. E. Hall (Eds.), *Handbook of physiology*. Sect. 1. Neurophysiology. Vol. III. Baltimore: Williams & Wilkins, 1960.

13

The Auditory Stimulus

PHYSICAL PROPERTIES

The stimulus for hearing is normally a change in the pressure exerted by air on the ear drum. The physical nature of this stimulus can be made clear by imagining what happens to a person sitting inside the cylinder of an enormous bicycle pump (Figure 13-1). With an increase in the force exerted on the pistons, the air within the pump becomes compressed. This increases the air pressure on the walls of the cylinder and also on our victim. If the piston is held in a constant position, say halfway down, the pressure will be much greater than normal but it would be unchanging. This steady-state pressure does not produce an auditory sensation. The ear is relatively insensitive to steady-state stimulation just as the eye refuses to respond to continually unchanging retinal stimuli.

Frequency and Amplitude

If the pump moves smoothly up and down once or twice in a second, the person would still not hear any sounds. However, if the pump moves up and down at a very rapid rate, the air pressure on the ear drum would

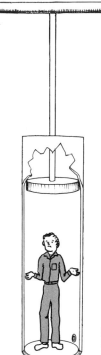

FIGURE 13-1   An illustration of how sound waves affect auditory processes.

change at an equally rapid rate and the sounds would be heard. If the pump moves up and down at least 20 times in a second, a very deep tone would be heard. As the rate of pumping increases up to, say, 1000 times per second, the pitch of the tone would grow higher. In fact, we are capable of hearing tones when the air pressure changes as infrequently as about 20 times per second and, perhaps, as frequently as about 20,000 times per second. (At still higher frequencies the sound would not be heard by humans but would be by a dog.) Thus, rapid changes in air pressure with respect to time can create the sensations of sound. The unit of frequency is the Hertz (Hz), named for the physicist Heinrich Hertz. A 20,000 Hz tone is one with a frequency of 20,000 cycles per second.

The piston in this example was capable of moving only halfway into the cylinder. It is intuitively obvious that the increase of pressure as the piston descends into the cylinder is related to the magnitude of the descent. So if the piston were to descend only one quarter of the length of the cylinder, the pressure change would be less. In principle, then, there is a frequency aspect of the sound stimulus, which in our example is related to the number of pumps per second, and an amplitude aspect of the sound or sound pressure level, which is related to the depth of pumping. These two parameters, frequency and amplitude, are characteristics of sine waves.

Figure 13-2 shows a number of different sinusoidal waves, which have various frequencies and amplitudes. Waves may differ in both amplitude and frequency, be the same in amplitude but differ in frequency, and be the same in frequency but differ in amplitude. Amplitude is always measured relative to the mean air pressure, which is determined by the altitude of the measuring

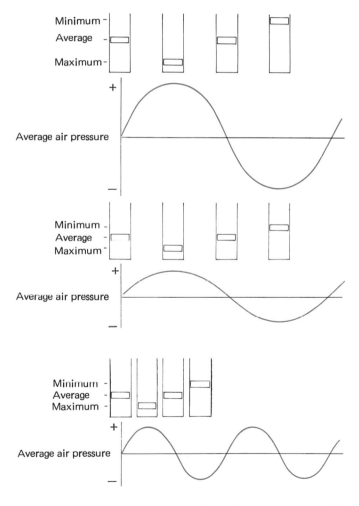

FIGURE 13-2   Sinusoidal waves. Three sine waves representing changes in air pressure as a function of time. The first two waves are identical in frequency but differ in amplitude. The third wave has a higher frequency but the same amplitude as the second wave.

instrument and other atmospheric conditions. Thus, at sea level the atmospheric pressure is higher than it is in the mountains.

Measuring and Producing Harmonic Oscillations

In simple harmonic oscillation, the increase in the air pressure is exactly equal though opposite to the decrease in air pressure, as when the piston rises in the cylinder. Hence when describing such sine waves, two equivalent measures of amplitude are possible. In the one case, we may simply measure the difference in pressure between the average air pressure, say air pressure at sea level, and the pressure at one of the peaks. This is called the peak amplitude of the wave. Alternatively, we may measure the so called peak-to-peak amplitude, which is exactly twice the value of the peak amplitude.

Air pressure is made to oscillate at the ear drum by means of vibrating objects. One such vibrating object is the tuning fork, a bent piece of steel that vibrates when it is struck with a sharp blow. A similar object is a simple water glass. This too will vibrate when it is struck. The reader may try an experiment by himself. He can take a water glass and strike it sharply with his fingernail. This will cause the glass to emit a tone of relatively high pitch. When the glass is partially filled with water, the tone has a lower pitch than when the glass is empty. The particular tone emitted by an object such as a tuning fork or a water glass is known as its resonance frequency. Substances like glass and steel have a tendency to bend away from an impact. After bending away, the molecules comprising the substance tend to resist deformation. Therefore, they exert an elastic force that pushes the object back in the direction of the initiating force. Inertia then serves to cause the object to continue to bend beyond the initial position of rest. Then the elastic force takes over once again and pushes the object back towards the initial position. Inertia then carries it beyond the initial point and the whole process continues

FIGURE 13-3 Damped sinusoid. The tuning fork is made to vibrate up and down by an initiating blow. As it oscillates, the amplitude of vibration is slowly diminished until it slowly fades away.

until frictional forces gradually cause the amplitude of excursion to diminish to zero (Figure 13-3).

Sound Waves

When a tuning fork is struck so that it vibrates back and forth, the vibrating steel will push against molecules of air. These molecules will collide with other molecules. Meanwhile, as the tuning fork moves away from its maximum amplitude excursion and swings back toward and through the initial position, it pushes molecules in the opposite direction. The first swing causes a condensation of molecules and the opposite swing causes the condensation to be followed by a rarefication or relative lack of molecules. This alternating condensation and rarefication of air is propagated as a wave, which is very similar to the waves set up by a pebble dropped into a pond. The major difference is that the waves in air are spherical, since they are propagated in all directions from the source of sound. When such waves enter the ear, they serve to produce audible sounds.

The wave motions of air produced by an object like a tuning fork are relatively simple harmonic oscillations, which may be described as simple sine waves. However, most of the sounds we hear are not such "pure" tones, but are rather complicated wave structures.

Figure 13-4 shows how a complex wave may be thought of as comprised of several simpler waves or harmonic oscillations. In this case, the wave at (a) is actually comprised of a sine wave shown at (b) and another wave shown at (c), which has precisely twice the frequency of the wave at (b). When two waves have frequencies that are related as integer multiples, the two waves are called harmonics of each other. Thus, the wave at (c) is the second harmonic of the wave at (b), because its frequency is two times the frequency of (b). Since (b) is the lowest frequency wave in (a), it is termed the fundamental component of (a). The French mathematician Fourier showed that any periodic or repeating complex wave may be analyzed into a number of simple sinusoids of different amplitudes, frequencies, and phases.

Beats

If two tones are close together in frequency, then from time to time their peaks get into phase with each other. Also, at other times the peak of one of the waves becomes coincident with the trough of the other. This results in a waxing and waning of the composite wave and results in the production

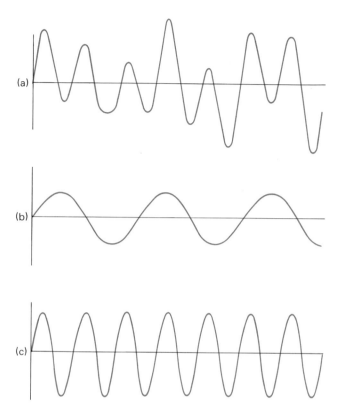

FIGURE 13-4 A complex sound wave and its constituent parts. (a) The complex sound wave repeats itself over and over again. This wave may be analyzed into the two simple harmonic oscillations shown at (b) and (c). When waves (b) and (c) are added together they will produce the complex wave (a).

of beats, a phenomenon commonly encountered when adjacent keys on the piano are struck at the same time.

Combination Tones

Still another result of playing two tones simultaneously is the production of the so-called combination tones. Suppose that two tones are played and they are sufficiently far apart in frequency so that they do not produce beats. The simple superpositioning of these tones does not account for what may be heard. Thus, a 1000 Hz tone together with a 1600 Hz tone very often produce the impression of the presence of other tones as well. It has been shown that sometimes when such stimuli are presented then the observer can also hear a tone at 2600 Hz and another tone at 600 Hz. These are the sum and difference of the original input frequencies. They are known to be produced by an action of the observer's ear. This action partially multiplies the two incoming tones. This mathematical operation can be shown to produce the combination tones. However, beats and combination tones are not necessarily mutually exclusive.

THE EAR

The ear has a very complicated inner structure (Figure 13-5). The external ear or the pinna collects sound waves from the air. This sets a column of air vibrating in the canal called the external auditory meatus. At the end of this canal is the tympanic membrane, which is commonly known as the ear drum. The ear drum is set into vibration by the oscillating column of air in the external auditory meatus. As the ear drum vibrates it sets into motion a set of bones or ossicles known as the incus (hammer), maleus (anvil), and stapes (stirrup). The ossicles are linked together and carry the vibrations to the cochlea, a snail-like bony structure that forms a portion of the so-called inner ear. Although it is coiled like a snail shell the cochlea may be thought of as a tube. At one end of the tube is the oval window, a membrane to

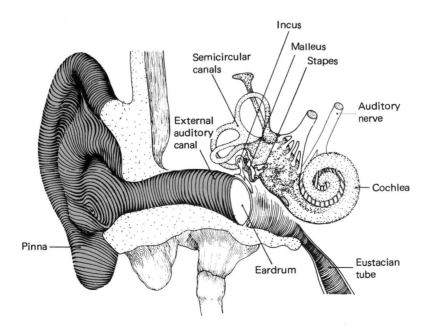

FIGURE 13-5   The inner structure of the ear.

which the stapes is attached. Hence, the mechanical vibrations carried by the ossicles are conveyed into the cochlea by vibration of the oval window. The cochlea itself is filled with a fluid. It requires much more force to transmit vibrations through a dense fluid than it does through air. The ear drum is about 20 times bigger than the round window. This disparity in size makes it possible to concentrate much more energy on the oval window than would be possible if air were impinged directly onto the entry to the cochlea. Thus, it becomes possible for the vibrations to be transmitted into the fluids within the cochlea.

From Sound Waves to Neural Impulses

The interior of the cochlea is a complicated structure (Figure 13-6). For our purposes, the most important structures are the basilar membrane

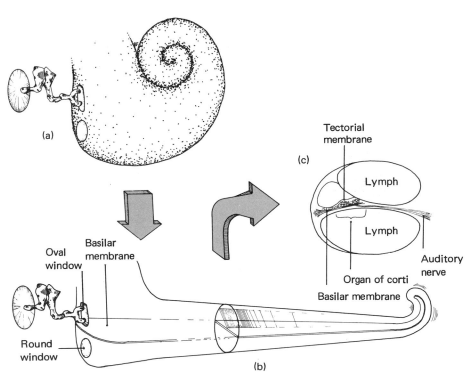

FIGURE 13-6   Sound waves are turned into neural activity. (a) The ear drum connects through the ossicles to the oval window. (b) The waves travel down to the cochlea, causing movements in the fluid of the canals. (c) These movements, in turn, trigger the hair cells in the organ of Corti, which rests on the basilar membrane. The movements of the hair cells then produce neural activity in the auditory nerve, which projects to both hemispheres.

and the organ of Corti. The organ of Corti contains about 17,000 specialized neurons or hair cells. These hair cells are mechanoreceptors that transmit impulses up the auditory nerve when stimulated.

As indicated, the fluid within the cochlea is started in motion by a sound applied through the ossicles to the oval window. The resulting wave in the fluid is carried to the apex of the cochlea and then around to the lower half of the cochlea on the underside of the basilar membrane. Since the fluid is not compressible, the round window serves to relieve the resulting pressure. The fluid motion causes a traveling wave to be propagated along the basilar membrane. This wave is similar to the one that travels along a length of rope when you flip one of its ends. Since the basilar membrane is stiffer at the end nearest the oval window, the wave is at its maximum in different places on the membrane depending upon the input sound frequency. Thus, high frequency tones cause large amplitude excursions nearer to the base of the membrane than do low frequency tones. This has been observed directly by Georg von Békésey (1960), the Nobel laureate. It is now widely believed that pitch discrimination depends, in part, upon the place of maximum displacement of the membrane. However, it is also acknowledged that this so-called place theory is not a complete account of the auditory mechanisms mediating pitch perception.

THE PERCEPTION OF SOUND

Pitch

The perception of sound is a complex affair. As in the case of light, sounds have quality or pitch and intensity or loudness. The psychological quality of pitch is affected by two of the dimensions of the stimulus, frequency and intensity. Sounds between 20 and 20,000 Hz may be detected by the young and healthy ear. As one grows older, the higher frequencies are not heard. As the intensity of a low frequency tone is raised, it appears to become still lower in pitch. Also, as the intensity of a high frequency tone is increased, it tends to appear to grow higher in pitch.

In the case of musical instruments, tone quality does not appear to change too much whether they are played softly or loudly. This is due to the presence of harmonics in the complex sounds emitted by musical instruments. These harmonics or overtones can be in the region of 2000 to 4000 Hz where the ear is maximally sensitive. Tones of these frequencies are not as susceptible to the effects of intensity changes as are pure lower and higher frequency tones.

Loudness

Two tones of equal energy but of different frequency will not sound equally loud. This is because the ear is not equally sensitive to all frequencies, just as the eye is not equally sensitive to different colors.

At any given frequency, loudness depends upon the amplitude of the sound wave. It is commonly measured on a decibel scale. The decibel is one-tenth of a bel. The bel is the logarithm (to the base 10) of the ratio of the sound pressure level of the tone being measured to the threshold sound pressure level of the same tone. Thus, if the threshold for a tone were .0002 dynes/cm^2, this value could serve as a reference intensity. If a tone of the same frequency were 10,000 times that of the threshold level, the intensity of the tone in bels would be 4, which is the logarithm of the ratio 10,000/1. The value in dB or decibels would be 40. Painful sounds are on the order of 130 dB, and ordinary speech is at about 60 dB.

Stereophonic Sound

When an observer wears headphones, the sounds that he hears are quite independent of the position of his head. If the headphones present tones to the two ears that are exactly alike, the observer would hear the sound as though it were localized in the center of his head. If a phase difference is introduced so that the crest of a sound wave reaches one ear somewhat earlier than the other ear, the position of the sound appears to shift. Similarly, increasing one ear's sound level will cause the observer to think that the sound originated in that ear. These differences in lateralization are differences in the apparent position of a sound heard in the head.

Sound Localization

When headphones are not worn but the sound is produced by means of a remote loudspeaker, we speak of sound localization. In this case, the sound is heard as originating outside the observer's body. Here, too, sound intensity and phase difference play a role. If a sound source is off to one side of the observer, the sound level reaching one ear is higher than the level at the more distant ear. This intensity difference, slight though it may be, helps the observer localize sound. Similarly, since a sound wave may reach one ear earlier than the other, there can be phase differences between the trains of sound waves as they reach the two ears. It has been found that binaural phase differences of 3 degrees for a 100 Hz tone can be detected. This corresponds to a time delay between the two ears of about 83 microseconds. Other factors that play a role in localization include the shadow cast by the head in the sound waves and the movements of the head.

Hans Wallach demonstrated that head movements allow us to perceive a sound as being external to our bodies. He also showed that a sound coming from directly overhead cannot be perceived as being external to the body unless the head is moved. Rotation of the head in the horizontal plane does not affect the levels or phases of the inputs to the two ears, but tilting of the head allows the observer to determine that the sound is overhead.

Dichotic Stimulation

In binaural stimulation, the sounds going to the two ears are largely alike, since they differ only in intensity or phase. Such sounds fuse or combine to give the impression of a single sound. This is not true when totally different sounds are applied to the two ears. Dichotic experiments in which the speech of two speakers is applied separately to the two ears have been performed. Generally, the listener is able to pay attention to one or the other and need not confuse them. This is especially true when the speakers differ in sex, when they speak different languages, or when their speech differs strongly in frequency content. However, if the same speaker transmits different messages to the two ears, confusion will occur depending upon how similar the contents of the messages may be.

Experiments of this sort have played a central role in the study of attention. Some investigators believe that there is a preliminary "filtering" process in which speech with certain physical characteristics is attenuated in the listener's nervous system. Although attenuated, it is analyzed in a preliminary way so that if something significant is said, like the listeners name, he may switch attention to listen to the speaker. An example of this in daily life is the so-called cocktail party effect. Here, one listens to one person despite many simultaneous conversations. However, if somebody on the other side of the room should mention the name of the listener's boyfriend, she might then switch her attention immediately, even though she may not previously have been aware that the new speaker had been carrying on a conversation.

SUMMARY

There are many parallels between vision and audition. Just as wavelength is a correlate of color, so is frequency one of the determinants of pitch. Also, some wavelengths of electromagnetic energy do not affect the visual system, for example, cosmic rays. Audition is similarly bounded to a limited range of frequencies. However, there are differences between audition and vision. There is the obvious difference that sounds have a very different quality from lights. We do hear sounds as emanating from visual objects such as faces and bells. But sounds are not spread out in space as are objects; instead, they seem to emanate from a point in space. Nevertheless, there is a considerable degree of coordination between the information we get about the world from light and the information we get from sounds. The way in which this coordination comes about is not well understood as yet. As we shall see in the next chapter, measurements of sensitivity show that the organism responds to different kinds of sensory information in different ways.

SUGGESTED READINGS

GULICK, W. *Hearing physiology and psychophysics*. London & New York: Oxford Univ. Press, 1971.

TRIESMAN, A. M. Strategies and models of selective attention. *Psychological Review*, 1969, **76**, 282–299.

VON BÉKÉSY, G. *Sensory inhibition*. Princeton, N. J.: Princeton Univ. Press, 1967.

WEAVER, E. G. *Theory of hearing*. New York: Dover, 1970.

WHITFIELD, I. C. *The auditory pathway*. London: Arnold, 1961.

14

The
Measurement
of Sensitivity

————————

Up to this point we have been discussing the concepts of sensitivity and threshold as though everybody agreed about their meanings. In the chapter on visual sensitivity, for example, we simply assumed that it takes some mimimum amount of light energy to make a person say that he sees a spot of light. Similarly, in discussing hearing in the preceding chapter, we noted that the observer is not equally "sensitive" to all sound frequencies. It is now necessary to become more specific about the meanings of the terms threshold and sensitivity.

ABSOLUTE THRESHOLD

How do we find out how faint a sound a person can hear, i.e, his absolute threshold for hearing? One commonly used procedure is to fit the person with headphones and tell him that from time to time a faint sound will be played. A warning signal, such as a brief flash of light, will precede each sound so that he will know just when to try to hear the sound. Immediately after each trial (warning signal plus sound), he is to say either "Yes, I heard it" or "No, I didn't hear it." The sounds could cover a wide range of intensities, from too faint for anyone ever to hear, up to loud enough for anyone with normal hearing to hear easily. More likely, though, mostly low-intensity tones would be used.

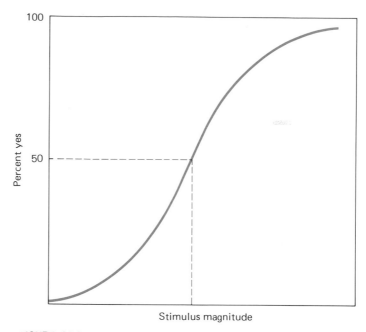

FIGURE 14-1 The probability of detection versus stimulus magnitude. The stimulus magnitude that is detected on 50% of its presentations is the nominal threshold value.

After the subject has undergone a fair number of trials, saying "yes" or "no" each time, the experimenter can count up the number of times the subject said "yes" for each different sound intensity. Perhaps the subject said "yes" 100% of the time when the loudest sound was presented, and only 5% of the time when the weakest stimulus was presented. For some intermediate intensity, he said "yes" 50% of the time, and so on. A graph of the probability of saying "yes" for each stimulus intensity usually yields an S-shaped curve (Figure 14-1). Psychologists customarily refer to the stimulus intensity to which the subject says yes to 50% of the time as the absolute threshold. This provides a single, standard number that can be compared for various kinds of stimuli in various conditions. In this example, the stimuli were sounds, but the same procedure applies equally well to other stimuli, such as lights. Thus, we can determine that a person's absolute threshold for light decreases when he spends more time in the dark (page 251). A less and less intense flash is needed to make him say "Yes, I saw it" 50% of the time.

DIFFERENCE THRESHOLDS AND WEBER'S LAW

Another kind of threshold is the so-called difference threshold, which is a just noticeable difference between two stimuli. Suppose that one side of a one inch square postage stamp could be increased in size. The task of the subject would be to determine when the postage stamp which he is looking at is not a true square, i.e., when the stamp is a rectangle. In this experiment it might be found that the subject can discriminate a square from a rectangle when one side of the stamp is only one-tenth of an inch longer than the other side. We might conclude from this that linear sizes differing by only one-tenth of an inch may be discriminated from each other. But the elongation of one side of a large billboard by one-tenth of an inch will not be noticeable. However, if the billboard is originally a 10-foot square, perhaps a 1-foot increase in the length of one side would be visible. This is, in fact, what E. Weber, the nineteenth-century German psychologist, found, i.e., generally, detectable differences are always a constant percentage of the magnitude of the original stimulus. Thus, a 50-gram weight can be reliably discriminated from a 51-gram weight but not from a 50.9-gram weight. Also, a 500 gram weight can be reliably discriminated from a 510-gram weight but not from a 509-gram weight. In both cases, increasing the weight by one-fiftieth made a just noticeable difference, no matter what the original weight was.

Weber's law can be expressed by the equation

$$\Delta I/I = k$$

where ΔI is the size of the just noticeable increase; I is the magnitude of the stimulus that you started with, and k is a constant (1/50 in our weight example).

We no longer accept the idea that there is a fixed difference threshold or just noticeable difference (JND). All thresholds are statistical in nature. Thus, though on the average an observer may say that when a length is increased by 10% he can tell that it is larger, sometimes he will make the same judgment when the length is increased by only 5% or by as much as 15%. To get an estimate of the statistical JND, a psychophysical experiment may be performed.

Two tones might be presented in sequence to an observer. The first tone could be of a fixed or standard loudness while the second tone might be more or less intense than the first. This second or variable tone would be responded to with the forced decision that it is louder or that it is fainter. In this "forced choice" procedure, the observer is not permitted to say that the two tones are equal. Even if they appear to be equal, he has to say whether the second tone is louder or softer than the first. In a typical experiment, the second or variable tone might have one of five or six different intensities, ranging from much softer than the standard through equality to much louder than the standard, some of the tones would differ only slightly from the standard in intensity. Following the same procedure used in constructing the absolute threshold curve, plotting the proportion of louder judgments against the mag-

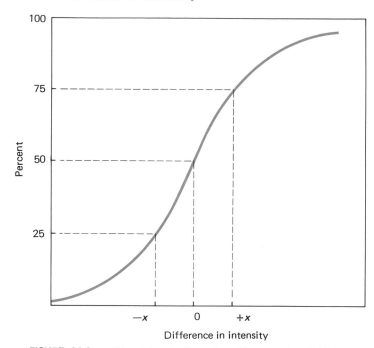

FIGURE 14-2   The determination of a difference threshold from a psychophysical function. This curve shows how the probability of detecting the difference between two stimuli varies as a function of the physical magnitude of the difference. The differences —x and x which are respectively adjudged to be "louder" on 25% of the trials and 75% of the trials determine the boundaries of the difference threshold. The difference threshold is, by convention, taken to be one half of the differences between the values —x and x.

nitude of the difference between the variable and standard stimuli results in an ogive (Figure 14-2). Clearly, the kind of relations coming out of this task would vary as a function of how willing a particular individual would be to say "yes" as opposed to "no" on a trial that was perceptually ambiguous.

FECHNER'S LAW

Gustave Fechner took Weber's law very seriously, and assumed that all JNDs were equal in psychological magnitude. Thus, the one-tenth of an inch added to the postage stamp must be considered psychologically equal to the 1 foot added to the billboard. Although the two physical magnitudes might differ, they are equal psychologically. If we further assume that all magnitudes consist of little increments that are psychologically equal JNDs, a number of interesting implications arise. For example, in the case of brightness, the JND or Weber fraction is about 1/60 or 0.17. Accordingly, any light would have to be increased by at least as much as 1/60 of its intensity if it is to be seen as brighter. Starting at the absolute threshold, an increase of 1/60 would represent a very small physical increment indeed. This first step above the absolute threshold would be the first detectably different increment in brightness. The next step in increasing brightness noticeably would be to add 1/60 of the new intensity. This new value physically is slightly larger than the first added increment, but it is psychologically equal to it.

Vision has an enormous dynamic range. We may appreciate light intensities that range from a few quanta up to the extraordinary brightnesses obtained when sunlight falls on a snow-covered field. Thus, by the time we get to these higher brightnesses, a truly large increment would be necessary to get still another JND increase in brightness. If we plot these JNDs versus the brightness increments necessary to achieve them, a curve similar to that shown in Figure 14-3 is obtained.

When drawing such a curve, it is sometimes necessary to plot it on special graph paper. This paper would represent the JNDs on the y-axis as equally separated increments, just as they are in Figure 14-3. However, the x-axis would have to be compressed so that all of the data could be represented in the graph, thereby avoiding the gap shown in Figure 14-3. A common method

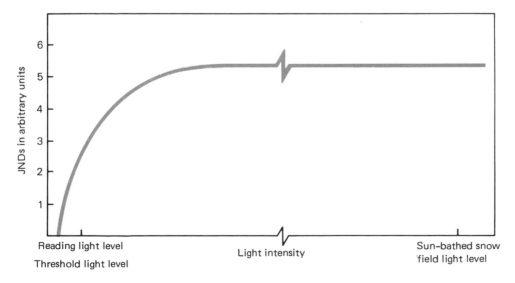

FIGURE 14-3   A plot of physical light level versus JNDs. This curve shows the way in which physical light intensity grows relative to the increase in number of JNDs.

for doing this is to employ a logarithmic scale on the x-axis. As we all know, such a scale would allow intervals to be increased by powers of 10. Thus, a light level of one arbitrary unit of brightness could be represented as the point 10^0 or, in logarithmic terms, 0. The next point on the axis would be 10 units of light intensity, which would be represented as 1 since the log of 10^1 is 1. The next increment would be 10^2, the next 10^3, and so on. Each of these points on the graph would be equally spaced, therby allowing a gradual compression of points along the x-axis. A very interesting thing occurs when this is done for data such as ours. The typical plot of JNDs versus log stimulus magnitude gives a straight line function. Thus, one might conclude that sensation magnitude (JND) varies in proportion to the logarithm of the physical stimulus magnitude. This has been formalized as Fechner's law which has the common form

$$S = k \log I/A$$

where S is the sensation magnitude; I is the stimulus intensity; A is the absolute threshold; and k is a proportionality constant, which varies with the sense modality involved.*

A number of objections have been raised with regard to both Fechner's and Weber's laws. With regard to the latter, it has been found that it simply does not apply to many data, particularly when the stimulus intensities are either very large or very faint. The major criticism of Fechner's law is that it is probably incorrect to assume that JNDs are additive. In addition to these criticisms, S. S. Stevens, a Harvard psychologist, has obtained quite different results using other psychophysical methods.

STEVENS' POWER LAW

Suppose that a subject was confronted with a series of tones of the same frequency. He may be told that, starting with one tone, he is to adjust the loudness of another tone so that it is noticeably greater than that of the first tone. Then, upon being given a third tone, the subject might be instructed to adjust its loudness so that it is as much louder than the second as the second is louder than the first. This procedure could be continued until many levels of loudness, which differ by equal amounts from their nearest neighbors, had been produced. Stevens (1966) reasoned that such an empirically determined set of loudnesses should correspond to the theoretical curve resulting from the sum-

* As originally derived, Fechner's law was expressed in terms of $\log_e$ for mathematical reasons.

mation of JNDs. As it turns out, if something like this experiment is performed, the resulting function relating perceived sensory magnitude to sound pressure level is not what Fechner's law predicts.

In actuality, this experiment was not done. Instead, Stevens simply presented subjects with a series of tones of the same frequency but different intensities. The subject was told to apply a number, say 10, to one of the tones. He was then told that all other tones should be judged against the reference number 10. If a particular tone, for example, was perceived as half as loud as the reference tone, it should be given the number 5. Similarly, if a tone was judged to be 1.5 times the loudness of the reference tone, it would be given the number 15, and so on. This method of magnitude estimation is similar to actually adjusting tones to provide equal sounding differences in intensity and it is more convenient to use.

The curves resulting from estimating magnitudes of differences among stimuli when the stimuli are lights, sounds, and electric shocks of different intensities are shown in Figure 14-4. When these curves are plotted on log

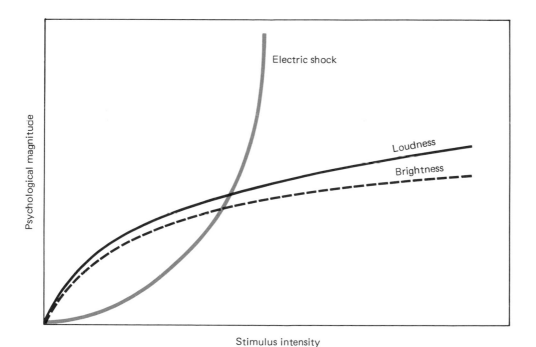

FIGURE 14-4   Functions relating psychological magnitude to stimulus intensity. These functions were derived using the direct magnitude estimation method of Stevens.

paper, the resulting lines are not straight, as would be expected from Fechner's law. However, it has been found that all of these curves, as well as many others obtained in magnitude estimation experiments, can be fit to a single equation

$$\psi = k\phi^n$$

where ψ is the psychological magnitude of the stimulus, ϕ is the physical intensity of the stimulus, and k and n are empirical constants.

These functions are commonly called power functions because they say that the psychological magnitude of a stimulus is equal to the intensity of the stimulus when it is raised to the proper power. Hence, it is now common to discuss the so-called power law of psychophysics. It turns out that the exponent n is equal to 0.33 when the stimulus is a spot of white light with a 5° visual angle. When the stimulus is an 800-Hz tone presented to both ears, n is about 0.6. In the case of small electric shocks, n is about 3.5. This says that, as electric shocks grow stronger, they have an accelerating impact on the organism. Small increments of relatively strong shocks have a greater effect than small increments of a weaker shock. This makes sense because the organism would be well advised to retreat quickly from a noxious stimulus. In the case of light and sound, however, one would expect that, as the light or sound levels get stronger, the organism need not be so sensitive to small changes in the levels of these stimuli.

THEORY OF SIGNAL DETECTION

Stevens' power law may be thought of as a revision of classical psychophysics. It holds that Fechner's law is an imperfect description of the magnitudes of sensory experiences. Yet another recent revision of classical psychophysics is the theory of signal detection, which takes issue with the concept of absolute threshold, the idea that a stimulus must exceed some minimal intensity in order for a person to perceive it.

The theory of signal detection grew out of research conducted during World War II. The aim of the research was to find ways of making sure that enemy airplanes and submarines were correctly identified by radar and sonar systems. The problem is that when sonar or radar waves are bounced off a target, the sonar or radar receiver picks up not only waves reflected from the target but also other "noise." In the case of sonar, the noise could come from the motions of water, the engines of one's own ship, the barking of porpoises, and slight fluctuations in the electronic sonar circuitry. The sonar operator may mistake one of these noises for an actual target, or he may overlook a target when it is accompanied by much background noise.

How can the operator decide what is noise and what is target? In some extreme cases, it is easy. In a properly designed sonar system, a very intense reading (with the appropriate delay) almost always indicates the presence of a large object. A very weak reading (with moderate delay) must be noise or, at most, a small and uninteresting object. But even for a given sized target at a given distance, the sonar reading will not always have exactly the same strength. Water currents may sometimes weaken it; other noises that happen to occur at the same time sometimes strengthen it. Thus, the reading from a target is sometimes stronger or weaker than usual as shown in Figure 14-5(a).

Similarly, although the reading is generally weak when there is no target present, it too can vary in strength as shown in Figure 14-5(b). If we combine Figures 14-5(a) and 14-5(b) to form Figure 14-5(c), it is easy to see that the sonar operator can be sure of detecting all targets if he reports a sighting

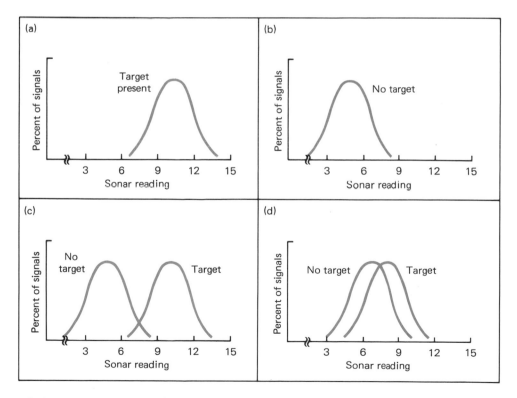

FIGURE 14-5   Various signal conditions for a sonar operator. With a background of noise, detecting a signal is difficult.

whenever the reading is stronger than 6. And he will only rarely give a "false alarm," since he will rarely get a signal of strength 6 when there's no target. But the problem is that the situation is usually not as clear-cut as in Figure 14-5(c). He wants to detect the target when it is still distant. That means that the reading is usually rather small. In fact, it often is no larger than signals he receives when there is no target present, as in Figure 14-5(d). What can he do? If he says "target" whenever the sonar signal is above 3, he will catch all of the targets, but he will be giving a huge number of false alarms. If, instead, he waits for signals above 6 before saying "target," he will miss many of the targets. Obviously, then, his criterion for saying "target" should depend on two considerations: how bothersome a false alarm is, and how important it is to spot targets at a great distance. The theory of signal detection provided mathematical procedures for determining the best criterion to use, given the "cost" of false alarms and the "payoff" for target detections.

A person in a psychophysical experiment is in much the same predicament as the sonar operator, according to Tanner, Swets, and Green (see Green & Swets, 1966; Swets, 1961; Tanner & Swets, 1954). In an experiment on the auditory absolute threshold, for example, the subject is trying to say whether or not he hears a very faint sound, knowing that on some "catch trials" there is no sound presented. But as anyone who has ever stayed in an empty house knows, one is always hearing various faint sounds. Even in a totally soundproof room, one hears not only one's breathing and heartbeat, but other barely perceptible noises. The spontaneous firing of neurons in the auditory system may produce experiences just like those produced by real sound. Such experiences can be thought of as "internal noise." (Sitting in a pitch black room, one soon notices various faint light patterns; there can be visual internal noise too.) How can the subject decide whether, on a given trial, he actually heard the faint sound that the experiment meant him to hear, or instead heard only a bit of external or internal noise? He is faced with a situation just like the one in Figure 14-5.

Now, if he simply says "yes" on every trial, he will always be right whenever the sound is actually presented. Since that tells the experimenter nothing, the experimenter usually penalizes the subject for false alarms. Either he urges the subject not to make mistakes or, in a more effective procedure, he deducts some amount from the payoff the subject gets for correct "hits" (yes with sound present). As soon as there is a penalty for false alarms, the subject raises his criterion for saying "Yes, I hear the sound." Just like the sonar operator, he waits for a higher "reading" in his auditory system. That reduces the number of false alarms, but it also somewhat reduces the number of hits. A larger penalty for false alarms leads to a still higher criterion and a still lower hit rate.

Since the absolute threshold was defined as the intensity for which the subject says "Yes, I hear it" 50% of the time, the measured threshold obviously is going to change whenever the subject changes his criterion. With a bigger penalty for false alarms, he says yes less often, and so his threshold is higher. But we do not want to say that a higher penalty makes him hear less well. The theory of signal detection offers a way out of this dilemma, by providing methods for assessing the subject's true sensitivity to the stimulus even though his criterion may be varying.

The ROC Curve

Suppose we deliberately encourage the subject to vary his criterion by making big changes in the penalty for false alarms. (We can accomplish the same thing by changing the proportion of trials on which there is no sound presented. If there are many no-sound trials, the subject will be less likely to say yes.) We can then graph, for each penalty, the number of correct hits versus the number of false alarms. This yields the so-called receiver operating characteristic, or ROC curve (Figure 14-6).

Suppose a sound is presented on half of the trials. If the subject cannot

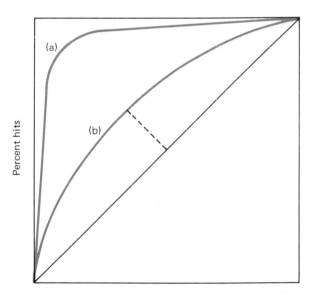

Percent false alarms

FIGURE 14-6 ROC (receiver operator characteristics) curves vary for individuals. The threshold sensitivity can be seen for a particular criterion.

tell sound from noise and just guesses, he will tend to have as many false alarms as hits. With a high criterion, he will have very few of each, because he never says "yes"; with a low criterion, he will have many of both, because he says yes so often. Therefore, his ROC curve will lie along the 45° line.

If, instead, he can discriminate sounds from noise very well, then his false alarms will be rather rare even with a moderately low criterion. Only when his criterion is so low that he says "yes" almost all the time will he make many false alarms. His ROC curve would be like curve (a) in Figure 14-6. In the typical case, though, he will be somewhere between these extremes, as in curve (b).

d'.   The theory of signal detection does a number of remarkable things with these curves. It is a detailed mathematical theory whose assumptions and equations are beyond the scope of this book, but some of the basic ideas can be presented. First, by measuring how far the subjects's ROC curve lies from the 45° line, we can calculate a number (usually called d') that measures the subject's sensitivity. This d' not only corresponds to the distance of the ROC curve from the 45° line, but also to the distance between the peaks of the two curves in Figures 14-5(c) and (d). In the sonar case, when the target was easy to detect, these two curves were far apart. When the target was hard to discriminate from noise, the curves were close together. By analogy, we can say that if a subject has a large d', his two curves are far apart. What he hears when a sound is presented is most often louder than the noise he hears when there is no sound presented by the experimenter. Unlike the absolute threshold measure, the d' measure is unaffected by the subject's criterion. Hence, d' does not change when the penalties and payoffs or the subject's motivation and alertness vary. Moreover, several quite different experimental procedures will produce a measure of the criterion (usually called β) for a given situation that reflects the subject's motivational and judgmental state or bias.

ATTENTION AND DETECTION.   The concepts and procedures of signal detection theory are applicable not only to traditional psychophysical questions, but also to other problems in perception, learning, and memory. For example, subjects were asked to listen for a faint tone of a certain pitch that was presented to one ear on some trials. This task was made more difficult by two complications: on each trial, a burst of noise was presented to that ear, and a set of 6 digits was presented to the other ear. In one part of the experiment, the subjects were told to ignore the digits, whereas in another part they had to say what they were. In both cases, though, they had to tell whether they heard the test tone in the other ear. As you might expect, subjects heard the test tone more often when they ignored the digits and could devote their full attention to the test tone ear.

There are two possible reasons for this effect of attention on detection. The first explanation is that attention is divided between digits and tone, or the same information about the tone reaches the brain, but the subjects are reluctant to say for sure that they hear it. In other words, because their attention is divided, perhaps they set a high criterion. The other possibility is that dividing one's attention somehow makes the tone weaker. A signal detection analysis answered this question. Making subjects pay attention to both ears instead of just one led to a decrease in d′, not an increase in β. Thus, the effect is indeed on the effective strength of the tone, not on the subject's criterion (Broadbent and Gregory, 1963).

SUMMARY

We have come a long way from our discussion in the beginning of this section on perception. A simpleminded notion of visual sensitivity has given way to a more sophisticated set of notions about psychophysical functions and the nature of sensitivity itself. It is obvious that psychology is now equipped with powerful tools with which to explore the workings of the nervous system. The theory of signal detectability, with its emphasis on the criteria used by observers, shows that even psychophysics is not terribly far removed from concern with human issues. The rapid growth of our understanding of the complexities of space, form, color, and sound perception suggests that a useful and meaningful science of human behavior is upon us.

SUGGESTED READINGS

GREEN, D. M., & SWETS J. A. *Signal detection theory and psychophysics.* New York: Wiley, 1966.

STEVENS, S. S. On the operation known as judgment. *American Scientist*, 1966, **54**, 385–401.

SWETS, J. A. (Ed.) *Signal detection and recognition by human observers.* New York: Wiley, 1964.

The Changing Organism

15

Learning and Motivation Theory

All of us are continuously involved in the learning process. From birth to death, we are besieged with information from the environment. We retain much of it, but also forget a great deal of what we have learned. Clearly, there is no more basic and important mechanism to understand than the process of learning. Psychologists have studied it for years. In this chapter, we will primarily deal with work that has been carried out on animals. In a subsequent chapter, we will examine how learning and memory processes are studied in man.

BASIC ISSUES IN LEARNING

Is it possible to learn a response or an act simply by engaging in it, or does it seem that in order for a response to be learned it must have some personal consequence? Perhaps the question is not a meaningful one, as it may not be possible to engage in behavior without the responses involved having consequences. After all, the mere fact that the response is completed is a consequence. But is this consequence sufficient to cause the response to be learned? In attempting to answer such questions as these, we may find it difficult to distinguish those consequences that are rewarding from those that are nonrewarding, because humans possess the cognitive capacity to see almost any consequence as a reward regardless of whether or not it actually is a reward. Therefore, we shall abandon humans for the time being and consider an organism that is, presumably, somewhat inferior to the human in terms of cognitive capacity, i.e., the white rat. Revised to accommodate the rat, the question now asks whether or not is it possible for the rat to learn a response or sequence of responses simply by performing it, even though it is not followed by a reward? Many experiments have been conducted in an attempt to answer this and similar questions. The following is one of the first such experiments (Tolman & Honzik, 1930).

The rat's task in this experiment was to find its way to the end of a maze. Every day, for 17 days, each rat was taken from its home cage and placed at the entrance to the maze. When it reached the end of the maze, it was removed and returned to its home cage. However, not all rats were removed immediately. They were divided into three groups. Group 1 found food awaiting them at the end of the maze, i.e., they were rewarded for running the maze. Group 2 rats also found food, but not until the eleventh day. For the first 10 days, they simply worked their way to the end of the maze. The rats in Group 3 were even less fortunate than those in Group 2; they never received food for running the maze.

The average number of errors made by each group was taken as the measure of learning, i.e., as the dependent variable. As we might expect, Group 1 made fewer and fewer errors as the experiment progressed (Figure 15-1). The rats in the unrewarded groups, Group 2 and Group 3, showed some improvement over the first 4 of 5 days, but their performance leveled at that point and remained fairly constant until food was introduced to Group 2 on the eleventh day. As can be seen from the graph, the performance of Group 2 improved dramatically when food was introduced, and they continued to make even fewer errors than the rats that had been rewarded all along. The performance of Group 3 remained constant throughout the remainder of the study, thus discounting the unlikely possibility that the sudden improvement seen in Group 2 was an accident or coincidence. It is as if the rats in Group 2 really knew what to do all along, but were not compelled to do it until they were rewarded.

The results of this study and similar studies have been interpreted in various ways. One interpretation is that reward simply is not necessary for learning. Others have cautioned against such an interpretation on grounds that we cannot be sure that exploring the maze (or some other unknown variable) was not rewarding to the animal. In any case, the experiment seems to indicate that a distinction should be drawn between the effect of reward on learning and its effect on performance. It appears that reward directly

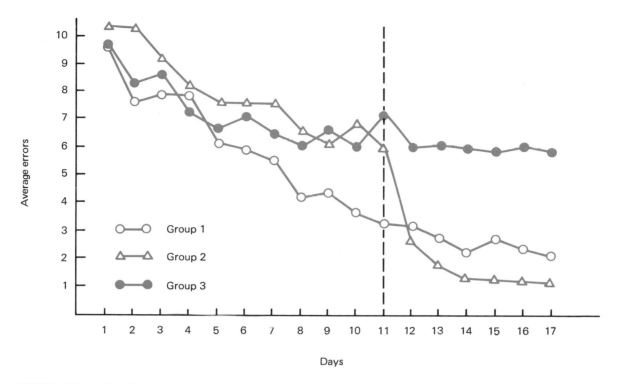

FIGURE 15-1   Data from two latent learning experiment by Tolman and Honzik (1930). Group 1 received food reward throughout the study. Group 2 did not receive food reward until the eleventh day. Group 3 received no food reward throughout the study.

influences more what an animal does than what it learns. Many basic issues such as this one have received the attention of experimental psychologists interested in the phenomona of learning and motivation, and have played a major role in the development of theories of learning and motivation. We will examine some of these theories but before we do, perhaps we should ask what exactly is meant by the terms learning and motivation.

What Is Learning?

We all have a reasonably good idea of what it means to say that something has been learned. Loosely speaking, it means that a rather permanent and nonphysiologically traumatic change has taken place with respect to an organism's behavior or thinking. The change would have to be "permanent" in order to rule out such temporary changes in behavior as those that occur when the organism is hungry. The behavior change must also be "nonphysiologically traumatic" to exclude changes that might result from gross physiological alterations of the organism. For example, loss of vision would certainly produce a permanent and dramatic change in behavior, but we would not say that such a change is the result of learning. Nor does our definition refer strictly to changes that are adaptive or beneficial to the organism. Many learned responses and habits carry no benefits for the organism over an extended duration, and still others, e.g., smoking in humans, are definitely detrimental to the health of the organism.

What Is Motivation?

Perhaps we would find it slightly more difficult to define the term motivation than to define learning, but, if pressed, we might decide that motivation refers to the organism's tendency to behave. When an organism is highly motivated, we say that it has a high tendency or likelihood of behaving, or we say that the probability of a response is relatively great. Conversely, when an organism is relatively unmotivated, the likelihood of a response is low. Unlike our definition of learning, the definition of motivation makes no reference to any sort of permanent change in the tendency to respond, simply because we do not want to exclude such temporary changes as those that might be brought about by hunger or thirst. We should say that a hungry organism is motivated to eat, but the exact manner in which it does eat, or the manner in which it places itself in a position to eat (such as pressing a lever in an experimental chamber or opening a refrigerator door) is probably learned. Once it has eaten sufficiently, the organism should no longer be in a state of specific motivation for food, but may be motivated to perform some other response such as drinking.

GENERAL DISCUSSION

While these general definitions of learning and motivation might satisfy most laymen and some psychologists, many of the psychologists interested in the scientific study of these phenomena would object on the grounds that the definitions are much too imprecise, inaccurate, or that they lack any kind of predictive insight. For example, an objection would no doubt be raised to the use of a change in "thinking" as a part of the definition of learning. It could easily be argued that one organism can never know for sure what another organism is thinking—only what the organism is doing, or how it responds. It would be, therefore, scientifically fruitless to include thinking in our definition, for no empirical measurements can be made of the thoughts of others, and reliable empirical measurement is intrinsic to systematic scientific inquiry.

Even though we know personally that we can learn something without providing a behavioral index of our having done so, this criticism is somewhat justified. One might be able to measure changes in one's own thinking, but the obtained measurements cannot be objectively compared with changes in the thoughts of other people, and therefore, any insight gained cannot legitimately be generalized to the thinking of other humans.

A similar objection might be raised against our definition of motivation. One might argue that it is perfectly possible to be "motivated" in an inner sense, without performing responses which reveal that motivation. For example, a student might be highly motivated to eat during a lecture and still not eat.

Whether or not we wish to accept these arguments is unimportant for the present, but they suffice to illustrate that psychologists tend to disagree on many of the questions that seem basic to the understanding of the learning and motivation phenomena. This realization is a source of frustration to many students beginning the study of learning and motivation, but it need not be. For although learning and motivation may be easily defined as subjective concepts, it is a far more demanding task to construct and empirically verify a list of the critical physical and relational attributes of learning and motivation as processes. This is the task of the theorist-researcher. How is learning represented neurophysiologically? What environmental situations are necessary and/or sufficient conditions for learning to take place? What can we discover about motivation that will allow us to make meaningful predictions about behavior?

If we wish to better understand the complex and somewhat abstract processes of learning and motivation, it will serve us well to briefly examine a few of the theoretical positions under which research has been conducted. Before we proceed, however, a brief glossary of terms and concepts frequently encountered in theoretical discussions of learning and motivation will be discussed. Some of the definitions will conform with common usage, but others will not be as familiar.

VOCABULARY OF LEARNING THEORY

Stimulus

Although there are almost as many different definitions of stimulus as there are theories of learning, it will be safe, for our purposes, to refer to a stimulus as a physical aspect of the environment that is capable of exciting an organism's sense organs. A simple stimulus might be a red light, a hot iron, a fragrant breeze, etc. However, a complex set of environmental aspects is often called a stimulus. For example, a classroom might be referred to as a stimulus, even though the classroom could conceivably be reduced to a multitude of simple stimuli. Nor are stimuli confined to the external environment; they may arise from within the organism as well. For example, when an organism is hungry, the gastrointestinal changes that take place may be stimuli.

Response

When an organism responds, it engages in an overt act or movement. Behavior ranging from minute movements of the vocal cords to complete behavior such as swimming or running all fall within the domain of responses, depending on the particular theoretical viewpoint being considered. The word response often refers to behavior that is not only measurable, but behavior that is potentially measurable.

Responses are sometimes said to have a certain response strength or a certain probability or likelihood of occurrence. Two popular measures of this are the frequency and the rate with which the response occurs, e.g., the number of lever presses per minute, etc. (Figure 15-2). Therefore, the term response-strength is encountered; it typically denotes some measure of the vigor and/or duration of responding.

S-R Connectionism

A concept that pervades most theoretical thinking on the subject of learning is the notion of stimulus response connectionism, or sometimes simply S-R learning. S-R theorists believe that, in its simplest form, learning consists of the actual or symbolic "hooking-up" of certain responses to the perceptions of specific stimuli, so that, whenever a particular stimulus impinges upon the organism, it will respond in a particular way, because the response has been attached to that stimulus via learning.

Conditioning

Some simple learning is called conditioning. Classical conditioning and instrumental conditioning are the two traditional experimental procedures whereby conditioning is brought about.

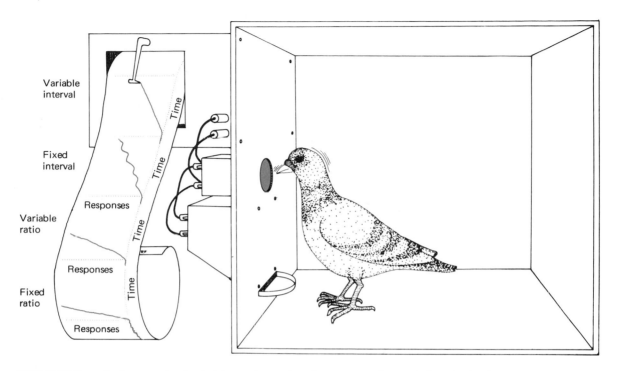

FIGURE 15-2   Basic apparatus for training and recording the response characteristics of animals. By pecking the blue screen, the pigeon can receive a food pellet in the trough below. In this particular training box (sometimes referred to as a Skinner box), a pigeon shows how his response rate can be manipulated by the kind of reward contingency that is used. The highest rate of responding is achieved by a fixed ratio (FR) schedule when an animal is rewarded after a set amount of lever presses (1 reward for 2, 4, 6, . . . 200 lever presses). Making the reward ratio variable changes the ratio of responding very little. When a fixed interval (FI) is used, that is, a reward is available only after so much time has elapsed after the last reward, one sees by the flatness of the curves that the animal essentially stops responding until the next reward is potentially available. When a variable interval (VI) is used the animal keeps responding at a low rate but more consistently eliminating the "scallop" (flat periods on the curve) seen with the fixed interval schedule.

Classical Conditioning

Ivan Petrovich Pavlov (1849–1936) studied a type of learning which has become known in the United States as classical conditioning. The major elements of the classical conditioning procedure can be taken from a description of a typical Pavlovian experiment (Figure 15-3).

A dog, held firmly in a harness, is presented with a morsel of food, and a bell is sounded at the same time. An experimenter then observes and measures the amount of saliva that flows from a fistula attached to one of the dogs salivary glands and leading through a small opening in the dog's cheek to a glass jar. After a number of such food-bell pairings, presentation of the

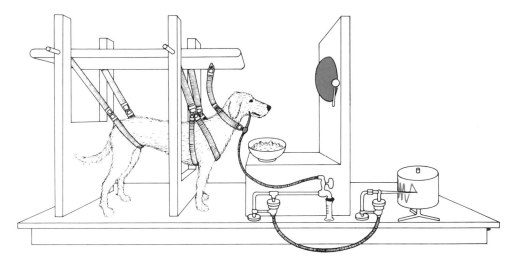

FIGURE 15-3   Pavlov trained his dogs in a similar apparatus. When the bell sounds, prior to training, the dog does not salivate. During training, a plate of food is presented when the bell sounds. Subsequent to the experience, the dog salivates when the bell is rung and the food is not presented.

food is discontinued and only the bell is sounded. Again, the experimenter's job is to measure the amount of saliva that flows as a result of the bell being presented alone. Although prior to pairings, the bell alone elicited no salivation, it is now found that the sound of the bell has acquired the ability to elicit almost as much saliva as the food. If the experimenter were to further present the bell unaccompanied by food, he would also discover that the saliva flow diminishes with continued presentations, until it finally elicits no saliva at all. This process is called extinction.

There are a number of new terms and concepts presented in this idealized Pavlovian experiment. The food is called an unconditioned stimulus (US), and the salivation elicited by the food is called the unconditioned response (UR). The previously neutral stimulus, the bell, is called a conditioned stimulus (CS), and the salivation to the bell is called a conditioned response (CR). Unconditioned stimuli are any stimuli that, independent of conditioning, elicit a particular response from the organism (Figure 15-4).

Instrumental Conditioning

Another procedure used in conditioning is called instrumental conditioning. If we borrow Pavlov's hungry dog with its flexible leg and supply of food, we can arrange an instrumental conditioning situation by simply making the presentation of food contingent upon a leg flexion. Leg flexion is still considered a conditioned response, but this time it is instrumental in bringing about the food. No specific stimulus is applied to elicit the first leg flexion. The experimenter simply waits until a flexion occurs and then rewards the dog with food.

What differences exist between the classical and instrumental conditioning procedures? First, as has been mentioned, there is no apparent specific stimulus that elicits the first response. In the classical conditioning situation, some particular response (the UR) that closely resembles the conditioned response is elicited each time the US is presented. However, in the instrumental conditioning situation no such specific eliciting stimulus can be identified; the conditioned response must occur spontaneously. The distinction is sometimes emphasized by saying that the classically conditioned response is first elicited and the instrumentally conditioned response is first emitted by the organism. The second major distinction is, of course, that reinforcement in the instrumental situation depends upon the occurrence of the conditioned response, or ultimately upon the organism's behavior, whereas reinforcement in the classical conditioning situation is independent of the organism's behavior.

Shaping

The entire process of selectively reinforcing responses that approximate the desired response to an increasingly greater degree is called shaping. It is easy to see the practicality of shaping as a method for modifying behavior.

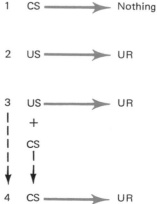

FIGURE 15-4   This diagram traces the progress of a classical conditioning experiment. (1) The CS (conditioned stimulus) is a neutral stimulus that, when presented, produces no significant response. (2) The US (unconditioned stimulus) elicits an unconditioned response (UR). (3) Pairing the US with the CS enables the CS to elicit a response of its own, the CR (conditioned response), which is very similar to the UR.

Discrimination Learning

Suppose that a rat has successfully been shaped to press a lever for food, and that we now wish to introduce a red and green light into the situation and further modify the rat's behavior so that responding only occurs when a green light is on and no responding occurs when the red light is on. Simply by periodically switching one of the lights on and reinforcing only in the presence of the green light, the rat will eventually confine all responses to the period of green light. This differential reinforcement of responding under specific stimulus conditions is called discrimination learning (Figure 15-5).

Punishment, Escape, and Avoidance

Three additional concepts that we should be familiar with are punishment, escape, and avoidance. Punishment causes a decrease in response strength by arranging a contingency such that a noxious or annoying stimulus is contingent upon the response.

Just as the name implies, escape refers to the response whereby an organism removes itself from, or terminates contact with a noxious stimulus. For example, a rat might learn to press a lever or run a maze in order to terminate an electric shock to its feet.

There are two main types of avoidance procedures. The simplest form is often called signaled avoidance. For example, a tone is turned on 5 seconds before a shock, so that during the first 5 seconds of its presence it serves to signal the immanence of the shock. By arranging a situation so that a lever press occurring within the 5-second preshock time signaled by the presence of the tone will cause the shock not to occur, we have set the requirements for avoidance conditioning.

Unsignaled avoidance occurs when a short, unsignaled shock is presented every 60 seconds. Although escape from the shock by pressing a level is not permitted, the duration of the shock is, in fact, so short that it is impossible to react in time to escape. However, a contingency can be arranged such that, if, at any time other than when the shock is being delivered, a lever press occurs, the shock will be postponed for 2 minutes. Obviously, by pressing frequently, the shock could be completely avoided.

In both signaled and unsignaled avoidance, then, it is possible for the organism to behave in such a way as to never receive the noxious stimulus, i.e., the noxious stimulus can be avoided.

(a)

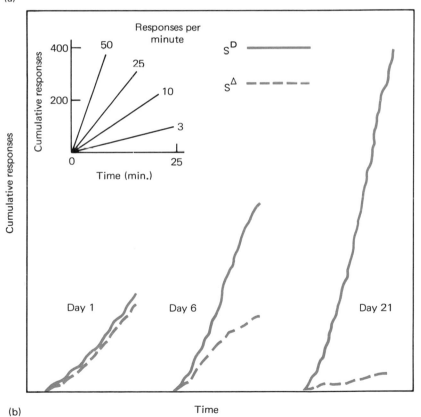

(b)

FIGURE 15-5 (a) Pigeon is seen working in a discrimination training set up. The "+" stimulus is called the positive discrimination stimulus (S^D) and the "O" is called the negative discrimination stimulus (S^Δ). The stimuli are presented in random order and the bird quickly learns that pecking the S^D is followed by a reward. (b) The cumulative response curves obtained in discrimination training.

THEORIES OF LEARNING

The main classical theories of learning and motivation will be presented. Many of them date back many years, but they still outline problems of great interest. All theories deal with the role of reward in learning. In a sense, the history of learning theory is really the history of the problem of reward.

Contiguity

The term contiguity comes from the idea of Edwin R. Guthrie that the only condition necessary for a response to become connected to a set of stimuli is for the response to be temporarily associated with the sitmuli, i.e., to be contiguous with the stimuli. A stimulus and a response become attached to each other simply by merit of having occurred close together in time.

RECENCY ASSUMPTION.   In addition to the contiguity principle, Guthrie provided the recency assumption. Suppose an organism finds itself in a stimulus situation where there is ample time to perform several responses. According to the contiguity principle, all of the responses should become attached to the situation and, to some extent, they do. But, the response that occurred last in the situation is the response that will enjoy a greater tendency to occur again if the same stimulus situation is again encountered. The usefulness of the recency assumption is most obvious in an escape situation.

Guthrie and Horton (1946) provided us with an example of a cat in a puzzle box. The cat was hungry and food was placed outside the box, the door of which could be opened by moving a lever located in the center of the floor (Figure 15-6). When first placed in the box, the cat engaged in a number of behaviors such as vocalization, chewing at protrusions, sniffing and pawing at corners, grooming, etc., but it eventually bumped into the lever, thereby opening the door. Now, which response has the highest tendency to occur again when the cat is returned to the stimulus situation, i.e., replaced in the box? According to the recency assumption, the response that occurred last in the situation is the one that will have the greatest tendency to reoccur. The results supported this assumption. On succeeding trials, the arbitrary (non-lever pressing) responses tended to drop from the cat's behavior and the appropriate escape response tended to occur more and more quickly.

FIGURE 15-6   Guthrie used a box like this to train cats. Moving the lever in any direction caused the door to open.

LEARNING: ALL-OR-NONE.   Guthrie proposed a third principle, which appears to contradict the description of the cat's behavior in the puzzle box. He assumed that, if a connection is to be found between a stimulus situation and response, it will be formed on a single contiguous pairing of the stimulus and response, i.e., learning takes place on an all-or-none basis. However, the cat learned to escape the puzzle box only gradually. In fact, most learning seems to take place gradually. How can learning take place in an all-or-none fashion and still appear to take place gradually? Guthrie resolved this problem by drawing a distinction between acts and movements. An act is an aggregate of many small movements, and these individual movements become conditioned on an all-or-none basis. However, all of the movements, which comprise an act, do not become conditioned on one trial. A few more become conditioned on each succeeding trial, so that the act as a whole is learned gradually over a number of trials. Thus, whereas the acquisition of a complex act may seem to take place gradually, the connections between the stimulus situation and the movements comprising the act usually are either formed on a particular trial, or they are not formed. The fact that many stimulus-movement connections must be formed before an entire act is learned gives the impression that the act is learned gradually.

PRINCPLE OF RESPONSE REPLACEMENT.   Since reinforcement is not a part of the Guthrian theory, the theory cannot account for extinction in terms of the removal of reinforcement. For Guthrie, when a response is extinguished, it simply means that a new, different, response or a number of different responses have been learned in connection with the stimulus situation. The old response is replaced by a new response or a number of new responses. To help illustrate this response replacement principle, imagine a cat in its box. After the escape response has been well learned, we will disconnect the lever so that it will no longer open the door. Eventually the perplexed cat will quit the lever and begin engaging in what appears to be the same arbitrary behaviors that were engaged in before the response was established. According to Guthrie's response replacement principle, what we have witnessed is the following. Prior to extinction, the lever press was always the last response to occur in the closed box, but, when the press was rendered ineffective, it is no longer the last response to occur. Therefore, a whole host of other responses are eligible to be connected through contiguity conditioning with the "box plus hunger" stimulus situation; and, according to Guthrie, they are connected.

PUNISHMENT.   When an organism responds in a particular way to a stimulus (call this stimulus and response S_1 and R_1, respectively), and a second stimulus (S_2), which is aversive, is applied to R_1, the S_1-R_1 connection is not directly weakened. Instead, any reduction in R_1 is due to the new response (R_2) that is elicited by S_2 and incompatible with R_1. If a rat has been trained to press a lever in response to a light, and is subsequently shocked for pressing the lever, the incidence of lever pressing will decrease. But, according to Guthrie, the reduction is attributable to the incompatibility of the lever pressing response and the natural skeletal responses to electric shock, e.g., crouching, freezing, jumping. If the light-lever press-shock sequence is repeated frequently, the rat learns to crouch, etc., as a response to the light; that is, the lever press is replaced by a new response or set of responses.

If Guthrie is correct in assuming that the effectiveness of punishment depends upon the type of response brought about by the punishing stimulus, one can easily see how an unwise choice of punishing stimuli could facilitate rather than decrease an unwanted response. If a rat's natural response to a mild shock on the tail is to run forward, then it would not be prudent to try to eliminate the rat's running by shocking it on the tail when it runs.

Rather, if a shock to the forepaw causes the rat to rear on its hind feet, such a shock would serve as a much more efficient punishing stimulus since rearing is incompatible with running.

CRITICISM OF GUTHRIE'S THEORY.   In spite of its apparent simplicity and generality, Guthrie's theory has not received a great deal of research attention in recent years. Critics of the theory point most vehemently to its lack of precision in defining terms and critical variables (such as stimulus and response!), which is directly attributable to Guthrie's anecdotal method of writing. They claim that his simple, intuitively appealing principles are not at all as parsimonious as they seem. For example, his notion that the stimulus-response connection is made in an "all-or-none" fashion does not lend itself to direct test because of the microminiature level of responding at which movements are assumed to occur. How does one go about distinguishing and measuring tiny movements, which supposedly comprise an act and which become conditioned to a particular stimulus?

Reward

Another staunch S-R connectionist was E. L. Thorndike (1886–1959). Thorndike was not as reluctant as Guthrie and the strict associationists to include the notion of reward in his theory. In fact, it was primarily Thorndike's faith in the concept of reward and his research on the phenomenon that place reinforcement in the position of relative research importance that it enjoys today. One of his first such experiments consisted of observing cats escape from a puzzle box. The box was equipped with a loop of string suspended from the top of the cage which, when pulled, released the door and permitted the cat access to a piece of food. Like Guthrie, Thorndike noted that the cats exhibited a number of random movements before the string happened to be pulled for the first time. Thorndike also noted that learning did not occur immediately, but that acquisition of an efficient string-pulling response required many trials. Unlike Guthrie, however, he did not assume that a few additional tiny movements were being learned on each trial; instead, he hypothesized that what was occurring was a gradual "stamping in" of the connection between the stimulus (in this case the box) and the response.

LAW OF EFFECT.   The law of effect, as it was first presented, consisted of two similar but separate laws called the positive and the negative laws of effect. The positive law of effect was

> When a modifiable connection between a situation and
> a response is made and is accompanied or followed by
> a satisfying state of affairs, that connection's strength is
> increased.

Similarly, the law's negative counterpart was

> When . . . the modifiable connection between a situation
> and a response is . . . made and accompanied by an an-
> noying state of affairs, its strength is decreased [Thorndike,
> 1911, pp. 4–5].

The future probabilities of a response depend upon what environmental
"effect" that response has; hence, the law of effect.

A satisfying state of affairs, "is one which the animal does nothing to
avoid, often doing such things as attain and preserve it." An annoying state
of affairs is, "one which the animal avoids or changes."

PUNISHMENT AND THE S-R CONNECTION.   The first major blow to the
law came in the 1930's and was, oddly enough, administered by Thorndike
himself. In 1932, he published a series of experiments on humans and animals
that led him to the conclusion that, while reinforcement was very effective
in strengthening the S-R connection, punishment did little or nothing at all
to weaken such a connection.

A typical human experiment involved presenting subjects with a list of
words. They were instructed to respond to each word with a number from
1 to 10. Each response was either "rewarded" by the experimenter saying
"right," or was punished by him saying "wrong." Controls were, of course,
included in which the experimenter said nothing at all. Thorndike found that,
in addition to an expected increased tendency to repeat the rewarded response
on a later test trial, there was a slight but definite tendency to repeat those
responses which were accompanied by the supposedly punishing stimulus
"wrong."

Similarly, in a study using chicks in a simple maze, he found that, while
rewarding the choice of a particular path with "freedom, food and company,"
i.e., an open compartment containing other chicks and food, resulted in an
increase in the tendency to make that choice on subsequent trials, punishing
another choice of paths by 30 second confinement did not reduce the tendency
to make that choice on subsequent trials. These experiments led Thorndike

to decrease support for the negative law of effect, and concurrently increase support for the positive side of the law.

Rejection of the negative law did not go unchallenged. The most obvious criticism of Thorndike's experiments involve his choice of "punishers." Certainly the word "wrong," or 30 seconds of confinement can be conceived as punishers, but they do not fit the traditional notion of a punisher being a very unpleasant or noxious stimulus such as electric shock.

As the issue now stands, there seems to be ample evidence to accept the position that punishment can serve as an efficient behavior control, at least in infrahumans. It should be mentioned that, so strong were the arguments against punishment as a means of behavior control, an unqualified reacceptance of Thorndike's negative law of effect was not again seriously suggested until recently (Rachlin and Herrnstein, 1970).

However, the issue as it now stands is more a behavioral issue, that is, the proponents of punishment claim that it effectively reduces the occurrences of a response, and little is said about its effect on the connections that have already been learned. The point of this strictly behavioristic position is that, if the occurrence of a response is suppressed or eliminated by punishment, there is no need to discuss "unlearning." Unlearning a stimulus-response connection is closely analogous to forgetting, but few punishment theories today would make the claim that punishment directly produces forgetting; instead, it merely reduces the likelihood of responding.

Drive Theory

Hull followed Thorndike in ascribing ultimate importance to the principle of reinforcement, although Hull's notion of reinforcement was not exactly that of Thorndike. Unlike previous S-R connectionists, Hull (1943) was very specific about how the connection was formed and maintained. The very formal manner in which Hull's theory was developed is represented in Figure 15-7.

INTERVENING VARIABLES.   The concept of an intervening variable is often used in connection with Hull's theory. It refers to the symbolic constructs that relate a stimulus presented to an organism to the response produced by the stimulus. In the vernacular, the closest we might come to an analogy to this variable is simply "behavior." The excitatory potential, represented as S^ER, symbolizes the organism's tendency to respond. The S^ER takes on a specific value in a given situation, according to the combination of values of three other variables: habit strength, drive, and incentive.

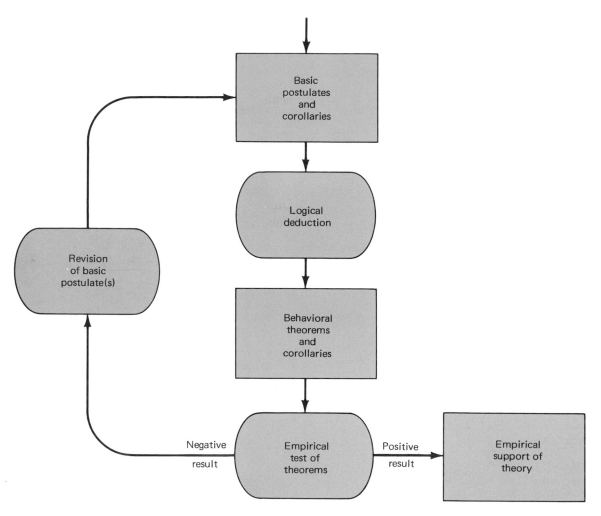

FIGURE 15-7   Clark Hull recommended these procedures for establishing fact from fiction in learning theory. If a particular therom failed a test, then the postulate could not hold and would have to be revised.

HABIT STRENGTH.   The intervening variable that most closely resembles what we would call learning in Hull's theory is habit strength. Habit strength is strength of the connection formed between a stimulus and a response (notice the S^HR symbol). The particular value of S^HR at any given time depends upon the reinforcement history of the S-R combination. S^HR for a particular stimulus and particular response increases each time a temporal association of the stimulus and response is reinforced. In this respect then, Hull's model closely resembles Thorndike's theory. The connection between S and R (Hull's S^HR)

gets "stamped in" by reinforcement. Reinforcing an S-R association serves to strengthen the connection, but nonreinforcement has no effect upon the strength of the connection. Also, the size of a reward does not vary its effectiveness. S^HR is increased by a constant amount regardless of whether the S-R association is followed by one or a dozen pellets. The specific drives can be divided into two categories on the basis of whether they are primary drives or secondary drives. Primary drives consist of the drives for food, water, sex, etc. and are drives that can be thought of as being innate to the organism.

Drive states are aversive to the organism, so that any response leading to a reduction in drive will be reinforced. Specifically, suppose that an organism is hungry. If it is, assume that the state of being hungry is aversive; it is easy to see how any response that reduces hunger by allowing the animal to eat, e.g., pressing a lever for food, would be reinforced.

In an abstract sense, this connection between drive and reinforcement, i.e., that drive reduction is reinforcing, may be appealing, but, when the specific situation is examined more closely, legitimate questions may be raised. For example, suppose the hungry rat presses its lever for a food reward, receives the reward, and ingests it. The reinforced response is obviously the lever press, but exactly how does that response coincide with the reduction of the hunger drive? The actual digestion of food does not take place in any significant amount until as long as several minutes after the food is ingested and may continue to be digested for several hours. It would seem, then, that it is not so much the lever press that accompanies the reduction in the hunger drive, but all of those responses that occur during digestion. Hull's theory handles problems such as these by assuming the existence of the drive stimulus.

DRIVE STIMULI.   Drive stimuli are stimuli in the organism's environment that are produced by or accompany a primary drive. These stimuli are usually, but not necessarily, in the organism's internal environment.

INCENTIVE.   In order to complete our equation for behavior, we need one more intervening variable. Remember that reinforcing a response to a stimulus serves to strengthen the S-R connection regardless of the size of the reward. This leaves us in the position of deducing, for example, that a rat would perform a response as well for one pellet as for twelve pellets, or that a rat trained to press a lever for 12 pellets would continue to press with the same vigor and frequency if the number of pellets were suddenly reduced to one. Such a prediction is not only counterintuitive, but runs counter to experimental evidence. The model requires another intervening variable, incentive (K). The value that K assumes is directly related to the magnitude of reward.

K would be greater in a situation where 12 pellets were received for lever pressing than in the situation where one pellet was received. If drive is analogous to the organism's need for a particular kind of reward, then K can best be described as the desirability of the particular reward.

COMPLETED MODEL.   Now our Hullian model or equation for behavior is complete. It will be assumed that the values of the three intervening variables, drive, habit strength and incentive, combine multiplicatively to produce a value for the organism's tendency to respond. Thus

$$S^E R = S^H R \times d \times K$$

In brief, the organism's tendency to emit a particular response (R) when presented with a specific stimulus (S) is equivalent to $S^H R$, or the strength of the S-R connection (which, in turn depends upon R's history of reinforcement in the presence of S), in combination with d, or the degree to which the reward is needed, and in combination with K, or the degree to which the particular reward is desired.

Cognitive Theory

As the name stimulus-response implies, learning to an S-R connectionist entails the learning of responses or movements. For Hull, for example, the rat learning its way through a maze actually learns a series of movements, each of which is a partial segment of the integrated maze-running response. Since the real action of learning is assumed to occur at such an elementary level, this type of theory is often called a molecular theory.

Tolman (1886–1959) approached learning from a quite different direction. His was not a molecular theory but a molar theory interested only in the complete behavioral act—not its constituent parts. He believed that an integrated act, such as driving a car, is different from the sum of its elementary parts or movements. Whereas Hull believed that the rat learning a maze actually learns a pattern of movements, Tolman believed that the rat learns a route. What is learned, according to Tolman, is not a response or series of responses, but the knowledge of what leads to what. Tolman provided animals with a cognitive capacity, i.e., the ability to acquire "knowledge." In this respect, then, Tolman's theory probably views the learning phenomenon in a fashion much more closely related to the intuitive notions on the subject with which this chapter began.

EXPECTANCIES.   A number of experiments have been conducted that were designed to show that animals form expectancies. One of the earliest experiments of this type was done by Tinklepaugh (1928). Two containers were placed in front of a monkey so that it could observe the experimenter placing food in one of the containers, but could not reach them. Later, the containers were made available to the monkey so that a choice could be made between them. The correct response, i.e., choosing the container holding food, was learned readily. The monkey was then permitted to view the experimenter placing in one of the containers a preferred food, e.g., a banana, that the experimenter, unseen by the monkey, later replaced with a lettuce leaf. Lettuce is also eaten by monkeys, but is not preferred to bananas. When the monkey was finally allowed to make its choice, it chose the container which had previously held a banana but now contained lettuce. Apparently disappointed that its expectancy was not fulfilled, the monkey refused to eat the lettuce and engaged in definite searching behavior. Other more rigidly controlled experiments have lent support to the notion that animals form a kind of reward expectancy. Expectancy is a cognitive concept and, needless to say, holds no prominent place in S-R connectionist theories.

THE ROLE OF SPECIFIC MOVEMENTS.   The belief that organisms learn a series of movements was not compatible with Tolman's belief that organisms learn what response leads to what consequence. These two divergent opinions sparked a good deal of research. In one experiment, Macfarlane (1930) demonstrated that rats do not exclusively learn a set of responses when running a maze. In this experiment, rats initially learned to wade through a maze partially filled with water. Later, more water was added and the rats were required to swim instead of wade, but they retained their previously learned ability to travel through the maze. That is, since the movements used in wading were definitely not the same movements used in swimming, a pure connectionist theory might stipulate the necessity of retraining. However, no retraining was necessary.

PLACE LEARNING.   Another type of experiment, which attempted to show that animals learn not a response or series of responses but a place to go, is exemplified by an experiment conducted by Tolman, Ritchie, and Kalish (1946). In a maze similar to the one shown in Figure 15-8, two groups of rats were trained to run to food in the goal boxes. Group P ("place learners") received food in the same goal box on each trial, e.g., always in goal box 1, regardless of whether they were started from start box 1 or start box 2. They were started alternately from each of the boxes. Group R rats were

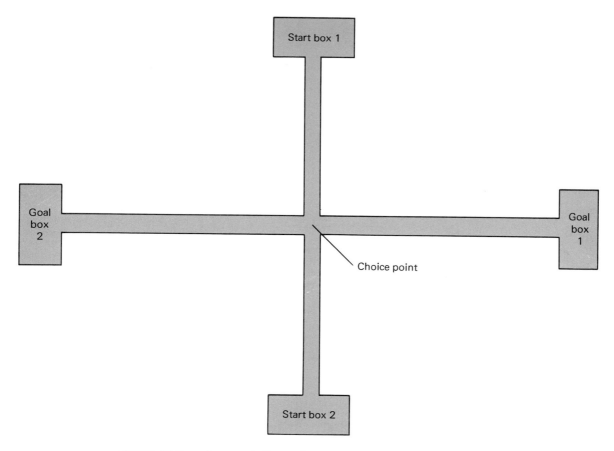

FIGURE 15-8   A maze similar to the one used by Tolman *et al.* (1946) to test whether or not place learning is easier than response learning.

"response learners." Their task was to always make the same response at the choice point, that is, when they were started in start box 1, they received food in goal box 1, so that they had to learn to turn left at the choice point. On alternate trials, when they started in start box 2, they were fed in goal box 2, which again meant making a left turn at the choice point. If responses are learned, Group R should learn faster (perform better); if places are learned, Group P should learn faster. The results indicated that place learning is the easier task.

REINFORCEMENT.   Another important type of experiment that was part of the Tolman legacy is the latent learning experiment, which served to under-score the distinction between learning and responding and to suggest that reinforcement does not play the same role in one as it does in the other. It was not true, however, that Tolman assigned no importance to reinforcement in learning. He thought that reinforcement served to call attention to the relevant dimensions of a stimulus in a learning situation and to confirm hypotheses that organisms form concerning which response is the correct response. He did not believe, however, that reinforcement increased the tendency of a response to occur, as the S-R connectionists did.

This leads to a major problem in Tolman's theory. If reinforcement does not increase an organism's tendency to respond, what does? While Tolman provided the organism with ample mechanisms for knowing what to perform, he left it bereft of a method for performing. In the final analysis, Tolman demonstrated that cognitive laws would account for much of learning, in some respects, even more than could be accounted for by S-R theories. However, he did not develop his laws enough to permit formal predictions and empirical testing.

Skinner's Approach

One of the most famous psychologists of our time has spent years urging against man's propensity to theorize. Skinner (1938) rejects theories of learning per se and insists one should be interested in studying only those variables that affect overt behavior. Consequently, Skinner concentrates on determining what events in the environment either sustain or control responding. Skinner does not find the complexities and subtleties of "intervening variables" helpful in explaining behavior. He maintains that, if we know what the reinforcers of behavior are, we will understand behavior. There is, however, no a priori definition of what a reinforcer is. For Skinner, it is the event that changes the probability of a response.

Skinner, on an operational level, has made profound contributions to training and teaching. Some of the procedures that he and his colleagues have developed are shown in Figure 15-9. In addition, Skinner's ideas on the control of behavior have been applied to self-control (see Chapter 5) and behavior modification (see Chapter 21).

The Relativity of Reinforcement

How can we recognize a reinforcer? Thorndike's definition of a reinforcer as a "satisfying state of affairs" suggests that we can only recognize what is a reinforcer for an organism by observing it in a learning situation. There is an inherent circularity in this definition. Reinforcement is the increase in

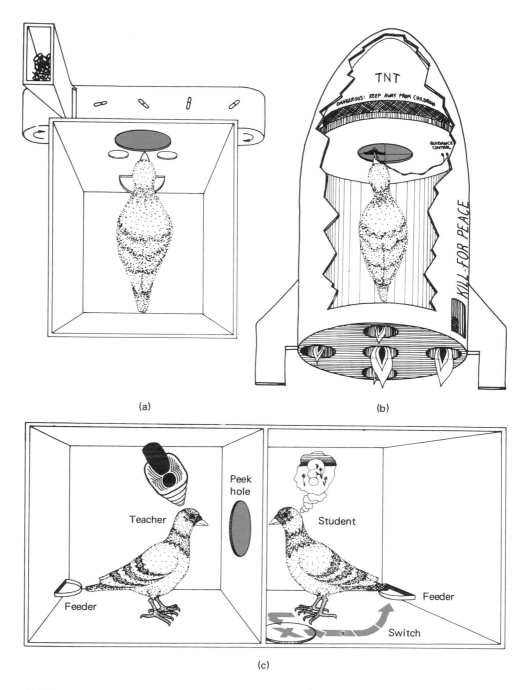

(a)

(b)

(c)

FIGURE 15-9   Skinner and his colleagues have devised a number of ingenious procedures for showing how animals could be trained to do a man's job. (a) A pigeon is trained to take the place of an inspector of pills. The pigeon presses one button if an imperfect one comes

probability of a response brought about by making a reinforcer contingent upon that response, and a reinforcer is that which brings about an increase in the probability of a response. Thus, as Thorndike, Skinner, and others would have it, the concept of reinforcement is relieved of any predictive empirical content. In order to determine whether or not a particular response, such as eating peanuts, will increase the probability of lever pressing, the opportunity to eat peanuts must be made contingent upon lever pressing and the results noted.

Meehl (1950) admitted that, in order to identify a reinforcer, it must be tested in a reinforcement situation, but he contended that this fact did not necessarily deny the reinforcement concept its empirical content. Once it is determined that a particular response can increase the probability of a second response through a contingency and in a particular situation, then it can be assumed that that response will reinforce any other reinforceable response in different situations.

Work by Premack (1965) has questioned this, for he has demonstrated that two responses, which tradition would have considered members of the class of reinforcers, could each serve as either a reinforcer or a "neutral" response with respect to the other, depending on their independent probabilities of occurrence. First, a group of rats, accustomed to running in an activity wheel and drinking water from a tube, were deprived of access to the activity wheel in their home cages for a few days and placed in an experimental situation in which an opportunity to run was contingent upon drinking. This procedure produced an increment in each rat's drinking behavior, i.e., running reinforced drinking. Then the situation was reversed. Free access to the wheel was reinstated in their home cages, but they were deprived of water, with access to water in the experimental chamber being contingent upon running (Figure 15-10). Predictably, drinking reinforced running.

PREDICTING THE REINFORCEMENT RELATIONSHIP.   From Premack's own theoretical point of view, if we wish to predict which of two responses (response

---

down the line and by doing so gets a reward. After a while they can work with 99% accuracy. (b) Pigeons were trained to commit hara-kiri. The pigeons were placed in the nose cones of missiles and were trained to peck the center of a target that was projected on a screen. A gold electrode was attached to the beak and, whenever the pigeons pecked, the point would be electronically sensed. If the target was not in the center of the screen, orders were issued to the missile guidance system for a corrected course. (c) R. Hernstein showed how pigeons could be shaped up to mutually reinforce each other. In this "teacher-student" experiment, the two birds could see each other through a window, and when the teacher pecked his screen food was delivered to the student. When the student was standing in a certain part of the cage at the moment the teacher pecked, both get food. With time it was seen that the teacher "shaped" the student by pecking as the student approached the "hot spot" in the cage.

A and response B) will reinforce the other, it is sufficient to know which of the two is more valuable to the organism. The important question is, of course, how does one obtain a measure of the subjective value of a particular response?

The answer is straightforward. The commensurable measuring device is the clock. Suppose, again, that we wish to know which of the two anatomically different responses A or B will reinforce, or be reinforced by, the other in a contingency. By making A freely available to the organism for a fixed duration, we can easily record the amount of time spent engaged in A, and by dividing this "time spent in A" by the total duration that A was available we arrive at a number that is called the probability of engaging in response A or simply the "probability of A." We can then apply the same methods and obtain a similar ratio for the probability of B. If the probability of A turned out to be greater than the probability of B, then we would predict that, if A were made contingent upon B, A would reinforce B.

If three responses are now considered: A, B, and C, where A is more probable than B which is more probable than C, then A will reinforce both B and C, but will not be reinforced by B or C. B can serve to reinforce C,

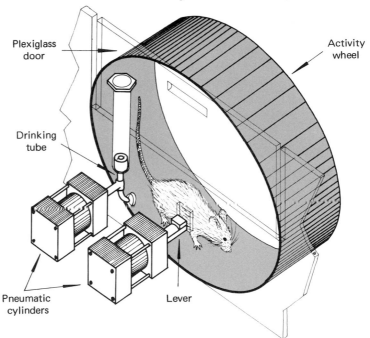

FIGURE 15-10   This training device measures the response probability of two separate behaviors, running and drinking. If running is more probable than the other, then the least probable behavior (drinking) can be reinforced by making running contingent on it. In this case, the animal drinks to run. After Premack (1965).

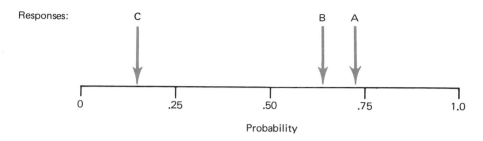

Probability

FIGURE 15-11   Of the three responses A, B, and C, falling along a probability continuum, A will reinforce both B and C, B will reinforce C, and C will reinforce neither A nor B.

but will not reinforce A, while C is incapable of reinforcing either A or B (Figure 15-11).

So we see that reinforcement is not an absolute matter, i.e., there is not a strict class of reinforcers, which themselves cannot be reinforced, and a strict class of neutral responses, which cannot serve as reinforcers. What is a reinforcer is a relative matter. We have also seen that the reinforcement relationship is reversible, that is, if the relative position of two responses reverse on the probability continuum, then the reinforcement relationship also reverses. This is exactly what was done in the experiment where running first reinforced drinking and then drinking reinforced running. At first, running was more probable than drinking and then, through manipulation of deprivation schedules, drinking was made to be more probable than running.

The data also very strongly suggests that the amount of increase in B that will be brought about by making a more probable response A contingent upon B depends upon the size of the difference in probability of the two responses, i.e., the distance that separates the two responses on the probability continuum. The greater the difference, the more B will be reinforced.

Stimulus Sampling Theory

If any one theory bridges the gap between the older general theories of learning and the more recent and usually more quantitative specific models, it is the stimulus sampling theory of W. K. Estes (1964). There are several parallels between the basic ideas that were first encountered in Guthrie's contiguity theory and the underlying assumptions of stimulus sampling theory. However, in most respects, Estes' theory is much more precise and easier to test experimentally than Guthrie's.

Since its inception, stimulus sampling theory has become less of a theory and more of a general guide for building various models of specific problems of learning. The assumptions of the theory include such entities as responses and stimulus elements and processes such as sampling and reinforcement, yet are very nonspecific about exactly to what these entities and processes refer. Their abstractness provides the flexibility and the power of the theory, i.e., its ability to cope with many diverse topics. The precision of the theory, on the other hand, comes from the exact manner in which the abstract entities and processes are said to interact.

THE IMPORTANCE OF THE RESPONSE.   A basic aspect of stimulus sampling theory is the response. Instead of defining movements as the basic unit of response, Estes simply divides responses into categories according to whether or not the response brings about a particular end. One response occurs on each experimental trial. In fact, the occurrence of a response often defines a trial. Two response classes will be needed: those responses that are successful or reinforced (response class R) and those responses that are not successful or not reinforced (response class O). Obviously, all possible responses fall under either R or O. It is important to notice that responses are successful or unsuccessful according to the experimenter's criteria, not necessarily according to the subject's criteria. Thus, a rat in a lever box may not divide its behavioral universe into lever pressing and not lever pressing, but a stimulus sampling theorist is likely to so divide the rat's universe.

THE ROLE OF THE STIMULUS.   The concept of stimulus undergoes considerably more abstracting in stimulus sampling theory than does the concept of response. All of the stimulus aspects present in a given situation are divided into an unspecified number (N) of elements. Also at any point in time, a particular stimulus element is functionally connected to only one of the possible responses. In our case, it will be assumed that each of the N stimulus elements is either connected to R or to O. By "functionally connected," it is meant that the stimulus element is conditioned to the particular response, or that the "function" of the element is to elicit the particular response. No claim of any sort of actual physical or neurophysiological connection between the element and its associate response is offered. These connections between stimulus elements and responses can be changed, and it is such change that, according to Estes, represents learning.

In order to describe the process of changing the connections between stimulus elements and responses, a few more basic assumptions will be needed. It is assumed that, out of the set of N total stimulus elements present on any given trial, only a subset (s) of these are effective, or "sampled." On a particular trial, the subject randomly selects a sample of size s of the N possible stimulus elements to attend to, and the response given on that trial depends upon which elements are sampled. Each element has an equal probability of being sampled, s/N, which is represented by O.

In the model that we are to consider, we will assume that the size of the sample s is fixed at some number greater than one and does not vary from trial to trial. The response actually given by a subject on a particular trial cannot be known for certain, but the probability that any particular response will occur can be known. It is equal to the proportion of elements in s that are conditioned to that response. If s = 100, and the number of R-connected elements in s is 40, the chances that an R will occur on that trial are 40/100, or the probability of an R occurring is 0.4. This is also statistically equivalent to the probability that any randomly selected element will be R-connected.

Now, how does learning occur, i.e., how do the changes in element-response connections occur? The answer is very straightforward. (a) If a reinforced response occurs on a given trial, all of the stimulus elements comprising the sample for that trial become connected to that response. Of course, if they were already connected to the reinforced response, they remain so connected, but if they were previously connected to the nonreinforced response, the connection changes. (b) If a nonreinforced response occurs on a given trial, no changes take place; the element-response connections remain just as they were when sampled. So the change in element-response connection depends upon the result of the response given. With each successive trial, more and more R-connected elements are established, and the probability that an R-connected element will be sampled on each successive trial is increased each time a reinforced response occurs.[1]

There are several important properties of this and related models derived from the general assumption of stimulus sampling theory. First, on any given trial, it cannot be known for certain what the outcome of the trial will be; it can only be predicted probabilistically. This is not to be considered a limitation of the model, because, on the whole, it fares better than any of the theories considered thus far. Second, learning, the switching of element-response connections, takes place on an all-or-none basis, just as Guthrie suggested. Third, as reinforced responding continues, the probability of a correct response approaches an asymptote of 1.0, that is, if reinforcement is continued, the theory predicts that ultimately R responses will be made on every trial.

---

[1] The general equation is $P_{n+1} = P_n(1 - P_n)$, where P_n is the probability that an R-connected element is selected on trial n (i.e., the probability of an R on trial n), and P_{n+1} is the probability that an R-connected element will be selected on trial $n + 1$.

ADDITIONAL THEORIES

There is a definite trend in learning theory away from general theories and toward theories and research applied to narrower problems. It is well beyond the scope of this chapter to discuss all of the various areas of specialization that have appeared in the last few years, but in order to acquaint the student with the type of specialization of interest that has occurred, a few selected topics will be discussed briefly.

Discrimination Learning

Discrimination learning has received a great deal of attention recently. Discrimination learning refers to the process by which an organism comes to discriminate (or, under perfect conditions to respond differently to) two or more distinct stimulus situations. The questions in this subfield are not so much directed at what stimuli organisms can be induced to discriminate successfully, but how the ability to demonstrate discrimination is achieved and what variables enhance or inhibit such learnings. One of the more frequently investigated variables in discrimination learning is the role played by "attention." For example, how does the organism come to attend to relevant stimulus dimensions or are redundant relevant stimulus dimensions effective in enhancing learning? Several models or theories of attention have been offered (Lovejoy, 1966; Sutherland, 1964).

Yet, the basic notion in discrimination learning was first put forth by Spence (1936). He felt all could be explained by the simple fact that as the positive stimulus of a discrimination (S+) was reinforced it gained in response strength. Similarly, the fact that the negative stimulus (S-) was not reinforced gave rise to conditioned inhibition. Once responses to S+ and S- were clearly established, Spence felt they would generalize to similar stimuli more readily than to dissimilar stimuli. This incredibly simple formulation correctly describes much of the work in discrimination learning.

In depth investigation of a subarea of learning such as discrimination learning often results in the discovery of very interesting new phenomena, which, in turn, often create a new "sub-subdiscipline" of research and theoretical endeavor. Two such phenomena that have turned up in discrimination learning situations are behavioral contrast and errorless discrimination learning.

Behavioral Contrast

The first systematic work on behavioral contrast can be attributed to Reynolds (1961). Briefly the phenomenon referred to is a reliable change in an organism's steady state instrumental responding under one stimulus condition induced by changes in the rate or size of reinforcement for concurrent instrumental responding under separate stimulus condition (Figure 15-12). This phenomenon has proved extremely reliable and runs counter to the predic-

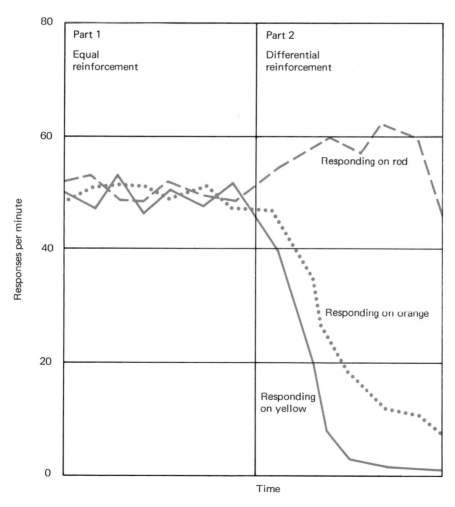

FIGURE 15-12   The results of a typical experiment in behavior contrast. With equal reinforcement available for all three color stimuli, the rate of responding was equal. However, when the reward rate was diminished for two of the three colors, the rate of responding on the third color increased even though there was no possibility of more reward.

tions of discrimination theories, which would assume that a change in the rate of reinforcement for one stimulus would affect rate of responding for only that stimulus. The inductive effect of the responding rate of an animal toward another stimulus when the actual rate of reward of that stimulus is not changed is shown to last for a long period of time. This has led many theorists to believe that the phenomenon may be due to simple frustration or emotional effects accompanying changes in reward rate of the one stimulus. The dominant idea today is that there has been a change in the "adaptation level" of the animal's view of the overall reward situation. In short, this notion claims that an animal makes a judgment on the level of reward of stimulus A in relation to the reward rate of stimulus B. If the level of B is dropped, the animal's view of the level of A is that there is now more reward value forthcoming with each response.

Errorless Discrimination

It will be recalled that the main idea in discrimination learning is that responses to S^- are extinguished. Terrace (1963) has shown the idea to be in error by the successful training of pigeons in a discrimination paradigm in which they never experienced an error. A pigeon was gradually presented with S^-, before S^+ was completely learned, but it was never allowed to respond to S^-. In addition, S^- was introduced for only brief periods during the training of S^+. The pigeons quickly and easily learned to press in the presence of only S^+ and never pecked at S^-, even when it was eventually left on for the same amounts of time as the positive stimulus.

The learning acquired with errorless discrimination learning seems different in kind to that seen when errors are allowed, which is the usual case in discrimination learning. The level of correct discrimination is far superior after errorless training. There is no emotional reaction to the negative stimulus as there is in training where errors are allowed. Such features obviously make the learning experience more appealing and several psychologists are trying to discover how similar methods could be used to upgrade general educative procedures for children.

SUMMARY

We have reviewed the major theoretical notions on the nature of learning mechanisms. We have extensively reviewed the famous theories of Guthrie,

Thorndike, Hull, Pavlov, Skinner, Premack, Estes, and others. Today, the field of learning is alive with a variety of exciting new discoveries that are frequently innovative and extend the earlier observations a great deal. Yet, for the introductory student, it seems wise to have clearly in mind that the major questions asked by the early theorists are as alive today as ever before.

SUGGESTED READINGS

Estes, W. *Learning theory and mental development.* New York: Academic Press, 1970.

Goldstein, H., Krantz, D. L., & Rains, J. D. (Eds.) *Controversial issues in learning.* New York: Appleton, 1965.

Hilgard, E. R., & Bower, G. H. *Theories of learning.* New York: Appleton, 1966.

Logan, F. *Fundamentals of learning and motivation.* Dubuque, Iowa: W. C. Brown, 1970.

Skinner, B. F. *The behavior of organisms.* New York: Appleton, 1938.

16

The Organism
as an
Information
Processor

In Montreal, Canada, some years ago a neurosurgeon stimulated the brain of conscious patients during the course of a necessary operative procedure on epileptics. Penfield and Roberts (1959) startled the world with their findings of what he called "psychical responses" to electrical probing of the temporal lobe.

The patients claimed to have experienced a flashback. They seemed to relive some past event, while being conscious of the present. Upon being stimulated, one patient exclaimed, "Oh, a familiar memory—in an office somewhere. I could see the desks. I was there and someone was calling to me—a man leaning on a desk with a pencil in his hand." Another patient recalled a scene from a play. Still another recalled the sound of her son playing and the honking of traffic. The patients reported seeing and hearing the sounds of the past event very vividly. A curious thing about these "memories" that were revived was that, for the most part, they were not events of monumental significance or high emotion; they were mostly unimportant events in the patient's life. These flashback experiences were not stagnant frames, but proceeded like a strip of film running forward in the order of the past event.

In the last chapter, we discussed how learning principles are derived from animal work. Today, the human counterpart to these studies is the study of memory mechanisms. In this chapter, we will examine how the phenomenon of memory, which ranks as one of the most puzzling and fascinating questions we confront in psychology, is studied by psychologists. Penfield's dramatic findings on the nature of the physical basis of human memory offers but a glimpse of the memory mechanism.

THE EXPERIMENTAL ANALYSIS OF MEMORY

Many chapters of this book have viewed man and his behavior primarily from a biological point of view. However, another way to conceptualize a number of psychological phenomena and, in particular, phenomena having to do with memory, is in terms of information. Psychologists who view man as an information processor generally think in terms of computers; the old cliche that a computer is a "giant brain" is turned around and the brain is thought of as a "compact computer." As we know, computers accept information from the outside world, process the information, make decisions on the basis of it, and then generate whatever it is that the computer user wishes to know. Similarly, human beings accept information from the outside world through their eyes and ears, act upon this information to produce appropriate responses, and thereby interact with the environment.

PSYCHOLOGICAL CODING.   The same information may be represented in a variety of different ways. Suppose, for example, one wants to convey the configuration of checkers on a checkerboard. One way to do this would be to write down on a list all 64 squares, noting what piece was on each square. Another way would be to draw a diagram of the board with X's in the squares that contained black checkers and O's in the squares that contained white checkers. Either of these representations of the board could be used to produce the other. Such a transformation of information from one form to another is called recoding, a very important concept in many theories of how people process information. Recoding may preserve all the original information, as in this example, or some information may get lost in the process. If in the checkerboard problem the recoding had taken the form "there are eight white checkers and ten black checkers on the board," a good deal of the original information, namely, the position of the checkers, would be lost.

Many psychologists take the view that, in a human being, information about the environment is constantly being taken in through the senses and is then successively recoded and stored for varying periods of time in a series of stages. Stop for a moment and without looking back try to remember what was said in the first few sentences of this chapter. Perhaps you can recollect that it had something to do with physiological as opposed to informational views of man. But notice a number of things: first, rather than seeing the words in your "mind's eye" you probably, if anything, heard them in your "minds ear." This means that information which was originally visual (words printed on a page) somewhere along the line got recoded into acoustic information. Notice also that you can't remember the exact words of the sentences, but rather you can only remember the gist. This means that, at some stage, a good deal of the information got lost. The general questions dealt with by information processing theories are the following. (a) What information from the environment does a person take in? (b) What are the stages within the person through which the information passes? (c) How is the information represented in these various stages? (d) How much and what kind of information is lost when it is transferred from stage to stage?

We have been using the expression "stage" very loosely. In physiological terms, stages may be defined with reference to specific parts of the nervous system, e.g., one stage might correspond to the retina, one to the lateral geniculate body, etc. In information-processing terms, however, a stage is thought of somewhat differently. It is conceptual rather than physical. Stages through which information passes do not necessarily have physiological referents. As will be seen in the next section, they are most conveniently thought of as stages of memory.

We know that people have memory because we can convey some information to them, and, later on, they are able to report back at least some of the information. During the intervening time, the information must have been stored somehow inside the person. This is what is meant by memory.

Short- and Long-Term Memory

Intuitively, it seems that there is more than one kind of memory. If someone reads you a telephone number and then asks you to repeat it back, you can generally do it. You must have had the number stored in memory for a few seconds, but were you using the same kind of memory in which your own telephone number is stored? You probably were not. William James, in the nineteenth century proposed two distinct memories. He defined "primary memory" as containing the information that has never left consciousness, and "secondary memory" as containing information that is stored more or less permanently, e.g., our names, our ability to speak a language, the multiplication table, etc. Thus, we can intuit at least these two types of memory, which are in current jargon short-term memory (STM) and long-term (LTM). The former is a transient sort of memory, the latter much more permanent. Later empirical evidence will be presented in support of this dichotomization of memory. First, however, there is one other kind of memory to deal with.

The Iconic Store

Suppose a subject in an experiment is shown an array of ten letters for a very brief period of time (50 milliseconds) and is then required to write down all the letters he can remember. Typically, people can only report four or five of the letters; interestingly, however, subjects in such an experiment generally claim that they can actually remember much more than that. They say they have a visual image of the array of letters, but that this image fades away as they are making their report, so that, as soon as they have reported the first few letters, the image of the rest has disappeared. In fact, naive subjects believe that the physical stimulus is actually fading away when in reality it is no longer present. These introspective reports suggest that immediately after a visual stimulus is presented, there is an extremely brief memory of it, and that this memory, while it is there, contains all the information in the original stimulus. This possibility was tested in a series of experiments by Sperling (1960).

AVAILABLE INFORMATION IN ICONIC STORE.   Sperling asked how much information is available to a subject immediately after the stimulus is turned off, and how does this information decay with time? To get at this, Sperling devised a very clever technique called partial report. The stimuli used were arrays of letters presented for 50 milliseconds (Figure 16-1). The twist was that subjects were only required to report the contents of one row of letters rather than having to report the entire array; however, they were not told which row to report until after the stimulus had disappeared. This was achieved by playing the subject a high, medium, or low frequency tone immediately after the stimulus was turned off. A high frequency tone meant that the subject was to report the contents of the top row; similarly, a medium or low frequency tone signaled that a report of the middle or bottom row was to be made.

Almost invariably, subjects were able to report back almost all the letters of the appropriate row. But since a subject did not know, at the time the stimulus was on, which row he was to report, this must mean that he must have had almost all the letters of the array at his disposal when the stimulus disappeared. Apparently, immediately after a visual stimulus is terminated,

FIGURE 16-1   An example of the kind of stimuli used in the experiments of Sperling (1960).

a memory remains containing all the information of the stimulus. We shall call this memory the iconic store, using the terminology of Neisser (1967). (Sperling called it visual information store and others call it the sensory register.)

Duration of Iconic Store.   We know that this memory is very brief, since, as we said above, if subjects are asked to report the whole array, the best they can do is about four or five letters. Thus, in the short time it takes to report these four or five letters, the iconic store has faded away. Exactly how long does the iconic store last? Using Sperling's technique, this was an easy question to answer. All it requires is that the interval between the offset of the stimulus and the onset of the signaling tone be varied. Presumably, the longer this interval is, the more the iconic store will have faded away, and the poorer will be the report.

The results of such an experiment are shown in Figure 16-2. The estimated total letters available to the subject is obtained by simply multiplying the

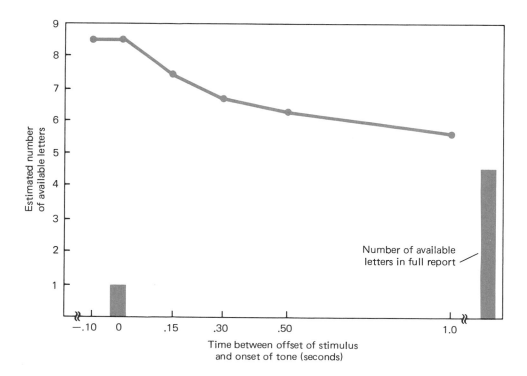

FIGURE 16-2   The estimated amount of information (letters) available to the subject at varying intervals after the stimulus has been turned off.

number of remembered letters per row by the number of rows. When the interval is zero, almost all letters are available; this is the result described above. However, after about a second, there are only about five letters available, which is the number that can be reported when the subject is asked to give back the entire array. Evidently, in this experiment iconic store fades away completely in a second. (Other experiments have placed this value at about one-quarter of a second.) In a later section, we will consider what happens to the information that had been in the store.

To reiterate, we have enumerated three types of memory: the iconic store, STM, and LTM. Other types of memory, e.g., intermediate-term memory, have been postulated by various investigators, but these three constitute the general bases of most integrated theories of memory (for example, Atkinson & Shiffrin, 1968; Waugh & Norman, 1965). The remainder of this chapter will be aimed at describing the characteristics of these types of memory in somewhat more detail.

For both STM and LTM a number of questions must be answered. How is information stored? In what form is the information stored? How is the information retrieved? How is the information lost?

SHORT-TERM MEMORY

Before presenting a detailed description of STM, we are compelled to face the question, does it really exist? Or, to be more precise, why include it as part of a model of memory? Ten years ago, the majority of memory theorists considered the postulation of STM to be an unnecessary frill in any theory of memory and claimed that existing data could be handled just as well, and more parsimoniously, by a theory that postulated a unitary memory. Today, however, this viewpoint is no longer viable. There are many results that can only be explained by assuming two separate and distinct types of memory. For the present, we shall describe two results that provide support for such a dual memory theory.

Neuropsychological Evidence

The first type of evidence is clinical. Brenda Milner, a McGill University neuropsychologist, has worked with several patients who have a rather strange disorder. Originally these patients were epileptic. As a means of stopping their seizures, certain types of lesions (bilateral hippocampal) were made in their brains. At first, it seemed that these operations had had no adverse effects on memory. The patients were able to remember things that had happened to them in the past, and performed normally on several types of memory tests such as digit span, e.g., they had no trouble remembering telephone numbers. However, a serious deficit soon became apparent. These patients could not learn anything new! If a new doctor came in to talk with such a patient, the two could converse normally. However, if the doctor left the room for five minutes, the patient would have no memory of every having seen him before, when he returned.

This syndrome can easily be explained in terms of a dual process theory of memory. It need only be assumed that the lesions had been made in that region of the brain involved in transferring information from STM to LTM. As we pointed out, STM and LTM themselves were quite normal for these patients. The patients could retrieve things from LTM such as their names, the multiplication table, childhood events, i.e., everything they had learned and stored in LTM prior to the operation. Similarly, situations that only involve the use of STM caused no difficulty. The patients could remember small amounts of information for a short time, or they could rehearse information and keep it available indefinitely. The difficulty was that no new information could be transferred to LTM. Once the information left STM, it was lost forever, for it had nowhere else to go.

Free Recall: Experimental Evidence

An experimental paradigm that is very useful for studying memory phenomena is free recall. A free recall task goes as follows. A list of words (say twenty words) is presented to a subject, one word at a time. The subject is then required to repeat back as many of the words as possible. One result, which invariably shows up, is known as the serial position effect. Suppose we plot the probability of a word's being recalled as a function of its serial input position, that is, the position of the word on the list that was presented to the subject. The resulting curve looks like that shown in Figure 16-3. The first and last few words presented are remembered best, while the words in the middle of the list are remembered the poorest. The reasons why the first few words are remembered so well are fairly complex and will be discussed in a later section.

For the moment, consider why the subject is so good at remembering the last few words. Proponents of a single-memory theory would make the following argument. Items which were presented most recently are remembered the best. Therefore, the last word, which was presented most recently,

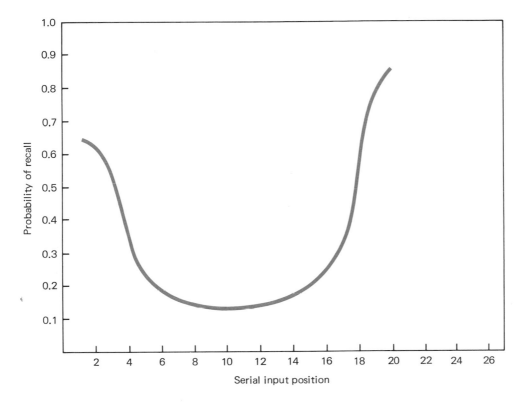

FIGURE 16-3   The probability of a word being recalled as a function of its serial input position in a free recall paradigm.

will have the highest probability of being recalled; the second-to-last word presented will have the second highest probability; and so on. However, those arguing in favor of two separate memories would say the following. Words in STM are recalled perfectly, whereas words not in STM, but only in LTM (if they were stored at all), have a much lower probability of being recalled. The closer a word is to the end of the list, i.e., the more recently it was presented, the higher the probability that it is still in STM, and, therefore, the higher its probability of being recalled.

A simple experiment can be run to distinguish these two hypotheses. Suppose that after the subject has been presented the list, but, before he recalls it, he is required to perform some complex mental activity such as a difficult arithmetic task. A single-memory theory would say that, after this activity, the last words in the list should still be remembered the best, since, after all, they still were the most recently presented words. Figure 16-4(a) shows what the serial position curve of the experiment should be according to this

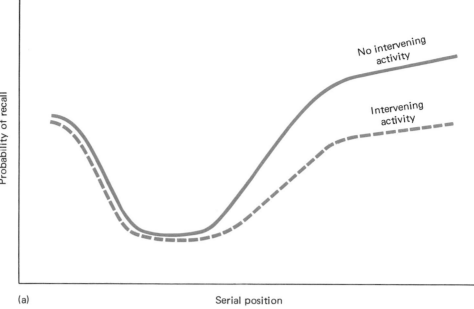

(a)

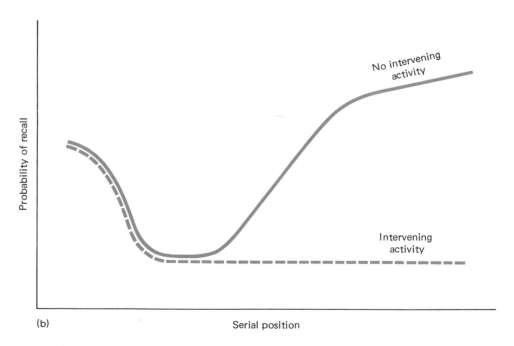

(b)

FIGURE 16-4   Hypothesized outcomes of the intervening activity experiment according to (a) single-memory theory and (b) dual-memory theory.

hypothesis. However, a dual trace theory would predict that the mental activity would clear STM of the words in the list; thus, when the subject recalls the list, everything would be recalled from LTM and the probability of recalling the last few words should be no greater than the probability of recalling words from the middle of the list. Figure 16-4(b) shows what the serial position curve would look like according to a dual-memory hypothesis.

This experiment was performed independently in two different laboratories at the same time (Glanzer & Cunitz, 1966; Postman & Phillips, 1965). The results are clear-cut and look like those depicted in Figure 16-4(b). Again, strong support was given for hypothesizing a STM that is separate from and independent of LTM.

We now have fairly strong experimental evidence that there exists at least two separate memory stores. A very large body of research has been aimed at making a detailed examination of the characteristics of these stores.

Storage of Information in STM: Transfer from Iconic Store

It will be recalled that Sperling performed experiments to demonstrate the existence of the iconic store. Sperling did not stop there, however, and he next attacked the question of how information is transferred from iconic store to STM. The first question was: at what rate is information transferred? This, of course, is an extremely important question reflecting on man's basic ability to handle information. Much information from the outside world impinges initially upon the sense organs. The capacity of a human being to informationally interact with the environment is thus initially limited by the rate at which he can extract information from iconic store and enter it into STM. To examine the transfer rate, an obvious experiment suggests itself: information is presented (say arrays of letters as in Sperling's experiments) for varying periods of time and the amount of information that can be reported is measured. Since the information has to be transferred to STM before it can be reported, we can infer from such an experiment how much information per unit time gets transferred.

Suppose, for example, that when an array of letters is presented for 20 milliseconds, two letters can be reported, and that, when the array is presented for 30 milliseconds, three letters can be reported. It could then be assumed that one letter gets transferred to STM every 10 milliseconds. However, this experiment has an obvious difficulty. A major characteristic of ionic store is that it lasts longer than 250 milliseconds, and there seems to be no way to present information for less than this time. Fortunately, there is a solution to this dilemma. It turns out that any bright stimulus, flashed to a subject, destroys the current contents of iconic store. Thus, if the array of letters is presented for 30 milliseconds and is immediately followed with some other bright visual stimulus (called a "masking stimulus"), we can be sure that the letters were available to the subject for only the 30 milliseconds.

The following experiment was then performed. Letter arrays were presented for periods of time varying from 5 to 60 milliseconds. As soon as the array was turned off, it was followed with a masking stimulus (for various reasons, Sperling used a field of bits and pieces of broken letters as a masking stimulus). Now we know that any letters reported by the subject must have been transferred to STM, and, furthermore, we know exactly how long he had to transfer them. The results of the experiment are shown in Figure 16-5. One letter can be transferred to STM for every 10 milliseconds the

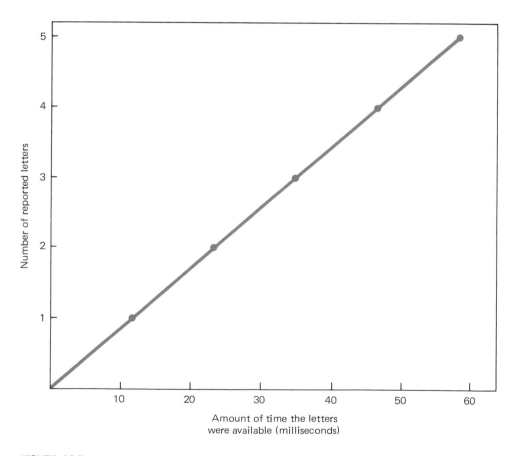

FIGURE 16-5   Number of letters transferred from the iconic store to STM as a function of the amount of time the letters were available. About one letter is transferred every 10 milliseconds. These are idealized results.

stimulus was on, up to about four letters. Apparently, then, STM is filled up from iconic store at the rate of about one letter every 10 milliseconds. Why does the number of reported letters level off at about four? STM has a very limited capacity, and it seems that in this experiment its capacity was about four letters.

So far, our discussions of iconic store have concerned visual memory. What about iconic stores or their analogs in other modalities? There may be such stores, but relatively little is known about them. Some work has been done (Crowder, personal communication; Moray, 1959) showing the existence of such a store in the auditory store.

Form of Information Storage in STM

In what form is information stored in STM? The information in iconic store is visual, faithfully reflecting the original stimulus. However, the situation is quite different in STM. There is considerable evidence that, while information is being transferred to STM, it is also being recoded into acoustic form, and that the representation of information in STM is acoustic, or verbal, in nature.

Evidence for this contention comes from studies of STM in which strings of letters are visually presented to a subject who is required to repeat them back. These letter strings are either acoustically distinct, e.g., ENXWQHM, or acoustically confusing, e.g., ETVPDZCG. Subjects remember the acoustically distinct lists considerably better than the acoustically confusing ones (Conrad & Hull, 1964). Other evidence for acoustic encoding in STM comes from an examination of errors in short-term recall. Both Conrad (1964) and Sperling and Speelman (1970) have pointed out that, when a subject makes an error in a short-term recall task, his response is likely to sound like (as opposed, for example, to look like) the correct response. Thus, if the subject is trying to remember the letter B, he is much more likely to erroneously respond T, which sounds like but does not look like B, than R, which looks like but does not sound like B. This was the case even when the original presentation of the letters was visual.

Capacity of Short-Term Memory

Throughout this chapter, it has implicitly been assumed that STM is of limited capacity. But how limited is limited? Just what is the capacity of STM? Before we can measure capacity, however, it is necessary to consider what actually goes into STM, that is, we cannot determine how many things we can put into STM without first knowing what those things are. In measuring the capacity of a bathtub, thimble, or cement truck, we can express the result of our measurement in quarts, cubic centimeters, or whatever. Unfortunately, as we shall see, finding such a unit of measurement for memory capacity is not such an easy task.

THE LIMITATIONS OF INFORMATION THEORY.   At first glance, the solution seems straightforward. We have been claiming that information is the stuff that fills up memory, and information has a unit of measurement, namely a bit (see Chapter 11). A good hypothesis, then, would be that the capacity of STM is some constant number of bits. However, an experiment that provided conclusive evidence that STM capacity cannot be measured in bits was carried out by Hayes (1957) and replicated by Pollack (1954). The experiment was simple. Consider a task in which a list of things is read to a subject whose job it is to simply remember and report as many of them as he can. This is called a memory span experiment, and, if you have ever taken an I.Q. test, your memory span has probably been measured. Of interest is the number of such things that the subject can remember. Now consider what the "things" may be. They can be binary numbers, i.e., ones and zeros or they may be letters of the alphabet. These classes of things differ in the amount of information that each member of the class contains. Each binary number contains one bit of information, whereas a letter contains about 4.7 bits of information. It follows that if STM capacity is constant in terms of information, then a subject should be able to remember 4.7 times as many binary numbers as letters.

Suppose that the capacity of STM were 9.4 bits. Then it should be able to hold two letters, at 4.7 bits per letter, or 9.4 binary numbers at one bit per binary number. However, this was not the case (Figure 16-6). As can be seen, approximately the same number of items was retained no matter how much information was contained in each item. (Although the curve drops slightly, it is not even in the same ballpark as a result that would support a constant-information hypothesis.) The main point of the experiment is that a person can retain on the order of about seven (plus or minus two) things, whether the things are binary numbers, decimal numbers, letters, or words. Thus, a person retaining seven binary numbers is retaining seven bits of information, whereas a person retaining seven letters is retaining about 38 bits of information. Clearly, STM capacity is not a constant number of bits.

CHUNKING.   It may therefore be argued that STM capacity is constant, but it is constant in a paradoxical sort of way, i.e., it can retain about seven of anything! George Miller coined the word "chunk" in referring to that

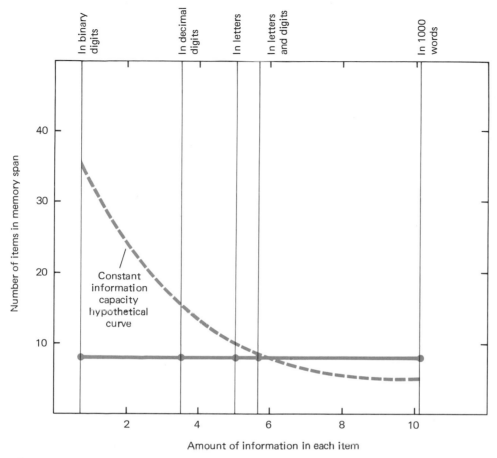

FIGURE 16-6   Number of items in the memory span as a function of amount of information per item. The observed curve is fairly flat at about seven items. The dashed curve depicts the kind of prediction a constant-information capacity hypothesis would make. Adapted from Hayes (1952).

which STM can hold about seven of. A chunk can contain a highly variable amount of information ranging from one bit, if the chunk is a binary number, to many bits, if the chunk is a letter or a word.

This finding is paradoxical because, by appropriate recoding schemes, it must be possible to increase the number of low-information chunks one can retain. A possible recoding scheme would be the following. Suppose you are given a series of binary numbers to remember. Suppose further that you had decided beforehand that any particular string of four binary numbers would correspond to a particular letter, as shown in Table 16-1. Now as you are presented with the binary numbers, you simply take each sequential group of four and recode them into the appropriate letters. Now how many binary

TABLE 16-1   A possible recording scheme for remembering strings of binary numbers. The recording scheme is memorized and then each string of four binary numbers is recoded into a letter.

String of binary numbers	Letter
0000	A
0001	B
0010	C
0011	D
0100	E
0101	F
0110	G
0111	H
1000	I
1001	J
1010	K
1011	L
1100	M
1101	N
1110	O
1111	P

numbers can you retain? You can retain seven letters, and each letter corresponds to four binary numbers, so you can retain a total of 28 binary digits, which is quite an improvement over seven. That this can indeed be done was shown in a demonstration by Smith (described in Miller, 1956) who, using recoding schemes such as the one described above, was able to remember up to 40 binary numbers. These types of schemes are also used by professional "memory experts" and are taught in the "memory improvement schemes" that are often seen advertised in Sunday newspapers.

Recoding schemes are used in everyday life to remember words. Assume that you are being presented strings of words to remember. As we know, the number of words you can remember is about seven. Suppose now that each word is five letters long. If asked to spell the words as you were recalling them, you could probably do so. But then you would be remembering 35 letters. How can this be reconciled with the notion that only seven letters can be remembered? The answer is that only seven letters can be recalled when the letters are unrelated. When the letters are organized into words, then we are recoding the letters into chunks which are informationally richer. We can do this, however, only because we have already learned the recoding scheme, for example, the letters C, L, O, W, and N can be recoded into the word CLOWN and then remembered as one word rather than as five separate letters. This is no different from the recoding scheme described above where the numbers 1, 0, 0, and 1 are recoded into the letter "J" and remembered as one letter rather than as four separate binary numbers.

Thus, the "capacity" of STM is an elusive quantity. We say that it can hold seven chunks; however, this is a loose and qualitative specification, since a chunk is so ill-defined. The issue of STM capacity is confused due to the fact that what we are remembering out of STM is combined with recoding schemes, which we have learned in the past and have stored in LTM. Hopefully these processes can, at some point, be unconfounded and STM will be specifiable in informational terms.

A computer analogy may be helpful in understanding the distinction between "pure" STM capacity and capacity that is enhanced by recoding schemes built in LTM. Consider a computer that has a large amount of memory but that has seven special words of its memory reserved and designated as STM. If we are going to use only those seven words then the amount of information that we can put into them is limited and is exactly specified (in fact, in bits, it is seven times the number of bits per word). But now assume that we can use the rest of memory as well. We can then fill up our seven slots of STM with addresses in LTM, and at those addresses might be found arrays of words, which, depending on the lengths of the arrays, contain an indefinite amount of information.

Thus, by using the seven slots of STM as pointers to other information (as opposed to containing the information proper), we can greatly increase the amount of information that these slots can contain. If we are trying to remember seven binary digits, we could have in each of the seven slots of STM a pointer to a location in LTM that would contain either the information "one" or "zero." If we are trying to remember seven words, each of the STM slots could point to a location in LTM that would specify the word. This scheme can be pushed to any length. Suppose we are asked to remember seven Shakespeare soliloquies. We could put in each STM slot an address that could point to a place in LTM where a particular Shakespeare soliloquy is stored. However, this scheme depends on having the other information already carefully organized in LTM. For most people, words are already stored as units. If we really wanted to see a case where people could remember seven Shakespeare solliquies in STM, we would have to choose people who had already memorized all of Shakespeare and thus had each soliloquy stored as a unit.

Forgetting from STM

Another basic characteristic of STM is that unrehearsed information decays away from it very rapidly. An experiment that showed exactly how fast this decay actually is was performed by Peterson and Peterson (1959). Their procedure was quite simple (Figure 16-7). First, a three-consonant trigram (such as BZQ) was presented to a subject for 2 seconds. Then at intervals ranging from 0 to 32 seconds later, the subject was asked to recall the trigram. A problem in this experiment was to prevent the subject from rehearsing the trigram during the forgetting interval. To accomplish this, a three-digit number was read to the subject immediately after he had studied the trigram, and he was asked to begin counting backward by threes from that number.

Figure 16-8 depicts the probability of correctly recalling a trigram as a function of the interval during which the memory of the trigram had been allowed to decay. This probability is over .90 when zero time has elapsed, then drops to about .15 after 15 seconds. After 15 seconds, recall probability is about constant, at least up to 32 seconds. The recall probability does not decay to zero because there is a little information about the trigram that has been transferred into LTM and remains indefinitely. This information can be used for responding if the short-term memory has decayed away. Thus, the point at which this forgetting function reaches an asymptote, about 15 seconds, is probably the point at which the STM traces of the information have completely disappeared.

This experiment thus provides a rather clearcut view of the time course of information decay from STM. The experiment has been replicated many times, and the function is always very close to that shown in Figure 16-8. A replication by Murdock (1961) used triads of words rather than trigrams of letters, and he still found the same phenomenon. This result provides evidence that not only are the Peterson and Peterson findings very stable, but

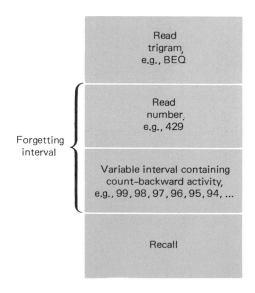

FIGURE 16-7   The basic design of the type of experiment used by Peterson and Peterson (1959).

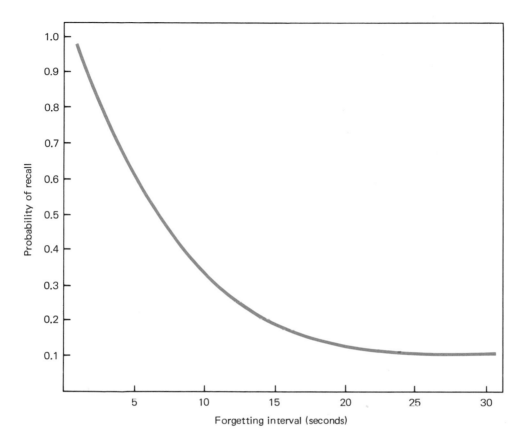

FIGURE 16-8   Results showing the Peterson and Peterson phenomenon. The trigram is forgotten very quickly as the forgetting interval increases up to 15 seconds. The asymptote of the curve represents long-term memory strength.

they fit in very nicely with the chunking notion of STM capacity discussed in the last section.

Mechanisms of STM Decay

What caused decay of information from STM? Two basic hypotheses, the decay hypothesis and the interference hypothesis, have been postulated. The decay hypothesis states that any information in STM that is not rehearsed will decay away of its own accord, much the same way as a swing will stop swinging if it is not pushed or otherwise propelled. The alternative hypothesis maintains that forgetting is a by-product of the limited capacity of STM. According to this hypothesis, information is only lost from STM because it gets shoved out, so to speak, by other information. The interference notion would explain the Peterson and Peterson results by assuming that the count-backward task caused new information to be entered into STM that eventually displaced the information necessary to displace the trigram.

A clever experiment to distinguish between these two hypotheses was performed by Reitman (1971). Reitman used a Peterson and Peterson task. She reasoned, however, that instead of counting backward during the forgetting interval, some kind of intervening task was needed that prevented rehearsal, but that did not cause new information to enter STM. One such task is called a signal detection task (see Chapter 14). Throughout the forgetting interval, from zero to five tones were played to the subject through earphones. The subject's job was to push a button each time he heard one. The tones were so soft that the subject could only detect them about half the time. The task was thus very difficult, requiring sufficient concentration that any other activity, such as rehearsing the trigram, was effectively prevented. However, this task does not require entering any new information into STM, as does a count-backward task.

What predictions do the two forgetting hypotheses make about the outcome of this experiment? The decay hypothesis would say that since rehearsal has been prevented, the information should decay away as usual and the forgetting curve should be no different from that obtained by Peterson and Peterson. However, the prediction of the interference hypothesis would be quite different. It would state that, since no new information has been entered into STM during the forgetting interval, no forgetting should take place.

The results of the experiment were dramatic: after 15 seconds, median recall was 98%. The information had not been at all degraded after an interval during which a count-backward task reduced recall to 15%. The subjects reported that during the interval, in which they were concentrating on the detection task, they were not rehearsing and were not thinking of the trigram they were supposed to remember, but that, when they were asked to recall it, it was "just right there, hanging around." Apparently, there is no such thing as "autonomous decay" from STM. Forgetting takes place simply because information is lost from STM when other, new information is entered in.

Retrieval from STM

Earlier, it was asserted that information from STM is retrieved rapidly and completely. Several questions now arise about the retrieval process. First, how fast *is* retrieval? Second, what is the nature of the process? In particular, suppose we have information in STM and we wish to retrieve some part of it. Can the desired information be simply "plucked out" or is it necessary to perform some kind of a search to find what we are looking for? If the latter turns out to be the case, what kind of search is made? A series of experiments by Saul Sternberg (1970) provides some provocative answers to these questions.

Sternberg used the following general task. A set of from one to six digits, called the memory set, is first presented to a subject for a few seconds and is entered into STM. Shortly thereafter, a single digit, the test digit, is presented. The task of the subject is to decide whether or not the test digit was a member of the memory set, and to respond by pulling one lever if the answer is "yes" and another lever if the answer is "no." Subjects are urged to respond as rapidly as possible without making errors. In practice, the error rate is very low; the subject pulls the wrong lever only about 2% of the time. The main dependent variable is the reaction time (RT) measured from the onset of the test digit to the subject's response.

Typical results for this kind of experiment are shown in Figure 16-9. The reaction time to make either a "yes" or a "no" response is related in a very systematic way to the size of the memory set, that is, the function

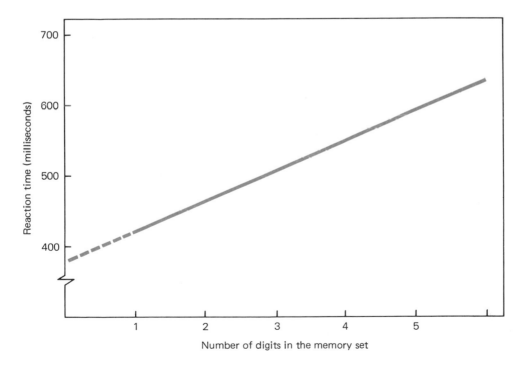

FIGURE 16-9   Reaction time to say "yes" or "no" to a test as a function of the size of the number of digits in the memory set.

is linear. For each additional member of the memory set, RT is about 38 milliseconds longer. Thus when the memory set size is one, RT is about 435 milliseconds; when the set size is two, RT is $435 + 38 = 473$ milliseconds; when set size is three, RT is $473 + 38 = 511$ milliseconds; and so on. This result suggests that a specific process is taking place during retrieval from STM, namely, that the test digit is being sequentially compared to each member of the memory set and that each comparison takes the same amount of time.

Sternberg postulated that the total reaction time is the sum of times taken by a series of information-processing stages, and he attempted to define these stages and determine how long each one takes.

Stage 1   The test digit is read and encoded into some suitable form. Assume this takes a seconds.

Stage 2   The encoded form of the digit is compared sequentially with each of the members of the memory set. Assume that this comparison time (per member) is c. Thus, if there are n members of the memory set, the total time for comparison will be cn.

Stage 3   A decision is made to say "yes" or "no" depending upon whether any of the comparisons yields a match. Assume that the decision takes d milliseconds.

Stage 4   A response is made. Assume that this takes r milliseconds.

Thus, the total reaction time can be expressed as the sum of all the individual times. When there are n members of the memory set,

$$RT = cn + a + d + r \tag{1}$$

Remember from algebra that when we have a function of the form $y = ax + b$, we obtain a straight line if we plot y as a function of x, where a is the slope of the line, and b is the y-intercept. If we lump together stages 1, 3, and 4 and call this time b, where, of course, $b = a + d + r$, we have

$$RT = cn + b \tag{2}$$

Consider again, the straight line function shown in Figure 16-9. Remember, this is a graph of RT as a function of n, the memory set size. The slope of this function is 38 milliseconds, and the intercept is 397 milliseconds. Thus,

$$RT = 38n + 397 \tag{3}$$

According to Sternberg's results, it takes 397 milliseconds for stages 1, 3, and 4 (encoding the test digit, making a decision, and outputing a response) and 38 milliseconds to make one comparison of the test digit with a member of the memory set.

A question arises concerning Sternberg's findings. Why are the functions relating RT to memory set size the same for "yes" and "no" responses? The reason why this question arises is that one might wish to make the following argument: When the answer is "no," the subject must search through all the n digits in the memory set. He therefore must make n separate comparisons, and the slope of the functions should be the average time per comparison, or c as stated above. Consider, however, a "yes" response. If the subject searches through the memory set until he finds the target digit and then immediately responds, fewer than n comparisons will have to be made, since, in general, the target digit will be in the middle of the list somewhere. In fact, since, on the average, the target will be in the middle of the list, the average number of comparisons made will be $n/2$. The slope of the function relating RT to n will then be $c/2$ rather than c, i.e., the slope of the "yes" function should be only half that of the "no" function.

Since the yes and no slopes are the same, we must conclude that, even when the subject finds the target somewhere in the middle of the list, he continues scanning until the end of the list before making a response. Why do subjects use this seemingly inefficient strategy? It may be that making a decision about whether a particular member of the memory set is or is not the target is a separate process from actually making a comparison of the two. If decision time were very long relative to comparison time, then it might be more efficient to make n comparisons followed by one decision, rather than to make both a comparison and a decision for each member of the memory set. This post hoc explanation is tentative and must be tested directly.

Sternberg's basic experiment has been replicated many times under varying conditions and using different types of test material. In all cases, the same qualitative result has been found, i.e., a linear function relates RT to memory set size. For most types of material, the time to compare a test stimulus to a member of the memory set is about constant, ranging from 30 to 50 milliseconds. Again, there is a certain degree of consistency regarding short term memory. Capacity is fairly constant around seven chunks, and, in addition, the time to compare two chunks to see if they are the same is constant at around 30–50 milliseconds.

SHORT-TERM MEMORY: A BRIEF RECAPITULATION

Before moving on to a discussion of long-term memory, let us summarize what is known about STM.

1. First, short-term memory is still basically conceptualized in terms used

by William James, that is, it is a limited-capacity store, used in a transient way to hold information.

2. Information enters STM from a high-capacity sensory store, and information can be read in very quickly, in some cases, at the rate of one letter every 10 milliseconds, up to about four or five letters.

3. The maximum amount of information that can be held in STM is around seven chunks, where a "chunk" is anything that is organized as a whole in long-term memory, e.g., a digit, a letter, a word, etc. Thus, in general, it is a poor idea to think of STM as a box in which "real" information is stored; rather it is probably better to conceptualize it as a box containing a list of directions to the places in which the real information is stored.

4. It is usually the case that unrehearsed information is forgotten from STM. However, the reason for this forgetting is that nonrehearsal of information is, in general, accompanied by the entrance of new information into STM. It is this displacement of the old information by the new that causes forgetting.

5. When information is retrieved from STM, it is retrieved in a very systematic fashion. All the information in STM is searched through in a serial order. Thus, the more information resident in STM, the longer the process of retrieval.

LONG-TERM MEMORY

Long-term memory, our repository of permanent or semipermanent information is, of course, a *sine qua non* of our existence. Without LTM, we would be unable to learn anything and unable to interact in any kind of dynamic way with our environment. In this section, we shall systematically examine the properties of LTM, inquiring how information gets there, how it is stored and forgotten, and how it is retrieved.

Entry of Information into LTM: Rehearsal

Atkinson and Shiffrin (1968) have proposed a theory of memory that places a heavy emphasis on the process of rehearsal. Rehearsal of information simply means repeating the information over and over again in STM. Rehearsal maintains information in STM for an indefinite period of time and serves as a process by which information is transferred from short- to long-term memory, i.e., the amount of information in LTM is some monotonic function of the number of times it was rehearsed while resident in STM. At the present time, there is a good deal of evidence to support this notion of rehearsal as an information-transfer mechanism.

The first study to demonstrate directly the relationship between rehearsal and LTM strength was performed by Hellyer (1962). Hellyer used a Peterson and Peterson task (Figure 16-7) with the following innovation. When the trigram was first presented for study, the number of times the subject was allowed to rehearse it was controlled. Either one, two, four, or eight repetitions of the word were allowed. The results of Hellyer's experiment are shown in Figure 16-10. Forgetting still takes place; however, the asymptote is higher the greater the number of rehearsals allotted the trigram. What does this mean? Remember that the asymptote of the forgetting curve is thought of as representing the amount of long-term memory strength that has accrued about the trigram. Thus, Hellyer's results suggest that more rehearsal leads to more information in LTM.

A similar result was found by Hebb (1961). In Hebb's experiment, subjects were read a series of nine-digit numbers, and after hearing a number

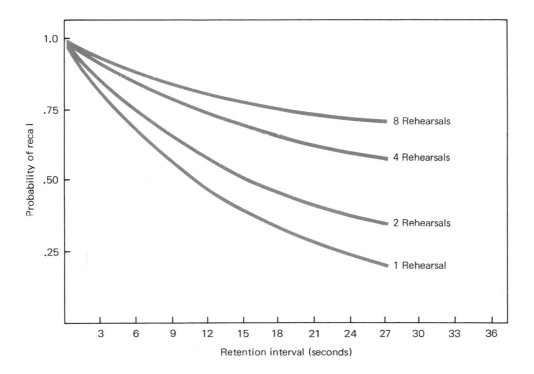

FIGURE 16-10   Retention as a function of forgetting interval for items rehearsed 1, 2, 4, or 8 times. Adapted from Hellyer (1962).

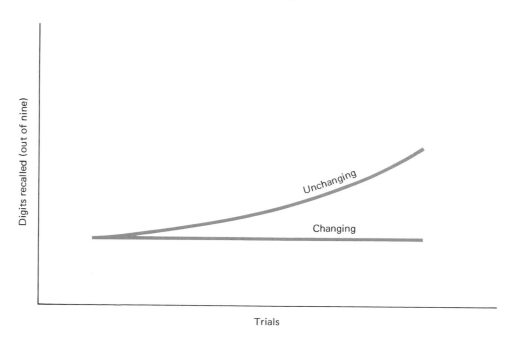

FIGURE 16-11   The kind of results seen in Hebb's (1961) experiment. A series of nine-digit numbers was read to the subject whose task was to repeat them back. Every third number was the same, thus dividing the numbers into unchanging and changing numbers. Over trials, the amount of information recalled from the changing numbers remained constant, whereas the amount recalled from the unchanging digits increased.

were required to repeat back as many of the digits in the number as they could remember. Unbeknown to the subjects, every third number was the same. Over trials, the number of digits remembered from the unrepeated changing lists remained constant, whereas the amount remembered from the repeated lists gradually increased (Figure 16-11). This result implies that, each time that a number is presented, some information about that number is transfered to LTM. If the number is presented and tested again, this LTM information is useful; thus, the increase in performance for the repeated numbers. Naturally, if a number is never tested again, then the information about it available in LTM is of no value.

REHEARSAL AND LTM STRENGTH.   Recently, Rundus (1971) has performed a series of experiments that provides major evidence concerning the relationship between rehearsal and long-term memory strength. Rundus used a free-recall paradigm. Twenty-word lists were shown to a subject at about one word every 5 seconds, and the subject recalled as many of the words in the list as he could, in any order. Rundus' innovation was that, during the time the words were being presented, subjects were required to rehearse aloud any words they wanted from the list they were currently studying, and this overt rehearsal was tape-recorded. Figure 16-12 shows a typical protocol of a subject's rehearsal. Thus, for a given word, Rundus obtained (1) the number of times it was rehearsed and (2) its probability of being recalled. It was therefore possible to plot the latter as a function of the former; this function is labeled "recall" in Figure 16-13. This result demonstrates that the number of rehearsals given a word is a very strong predictor of the long-term memory strength for the word, giving substantive support to the assumption of Atkinson and Shiffrin (1968). In an extension of this result, subjects from the Rundus experiment were called back 3 weeks later and given a recognition test for all the words they had studied. The curve labeled "recognition" in Figure 16-13 shows that recognition probability for a word is also greater the more times a word is rehearsed.

FIGURE 16-12   Words presented in a list from Rundus' (1971) experiment and a typical rehearsal protocol for the first seven words.

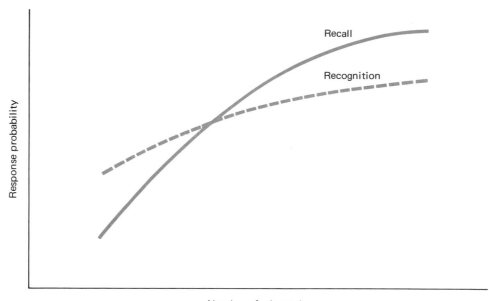

FIGURE 16-13   Probability of recall and of delayed recognition as a function of the number of times a word was rehearsed. After Rundus, Loftus, and Atkinson (1970).

THE PRIMARY EFFECT.   In addition to underlining the importance of re-hearsal in transferring information from short- to long-term store, Rundus helped to clarify several hitherto murky phenomena. Consider, for example, the serial position curve shown in Figure 16-3. We have already seen that the recency (right-hand) portion of the curve is due to the fact that the most recent items have the highest probability of being in STM. However, what causes the primary effect? Why are the first few items presented remembered so well?

Atkinson and Shiffrin (1968), in discussing the phenomenon, suggested that it may be a rehearsal effect (see Figure 16-12). Suppose that you can re-hearse four or five words at once. When the first word of a list is presented to you, it is all you have to rehearse, and it will get your undivided attention and will be rehearsed many times. However, when the second word of the list is presented, it will be rehearsed along with the first word. Thus, it will not get your undivided attention, but rather it will get your divided attention and will not be rehearsed as much as the first word. Similarly, the third word in the list will have to compete with the first and second words for attention, and will not be rehearsed as much as either of them. This process of diminishing attention (rehearsal) for each succeeding word will continue until the fourth or fifth word when the rehearsal buffer will be full, and some kind of a "steady state" will have been achieved.

With Rundus' procedure, this hypothesis can be tested directly. Figure 16-14 shows recall probability and the number of rehearsals for a word as a function of the word's serial input position. As can be seen from Figure 16-11 and 16-13, the first few words do indeed receive more rehearsals, and the rehearsal curve nicely reflects the recall probability curve, up to the recency portion. Apparently then, the primacy effect can be at least partially explained by the fact that the first few words are simply rehearsed more. Can the primacy effect be fully explained by rehearsal, that is, is there anything else about the first few words that makes them easier to remember? It turns out that words from the middle of the list that happened to receive the same number of rehearsals as words at the beginning of the list were remembered just as well. The implication of this result is that the primacy effect is due only to the fact that the initial words are rehearsed more. Other free recall phenomena were similarly accounted for by rehearsal (Rundus, 1971).

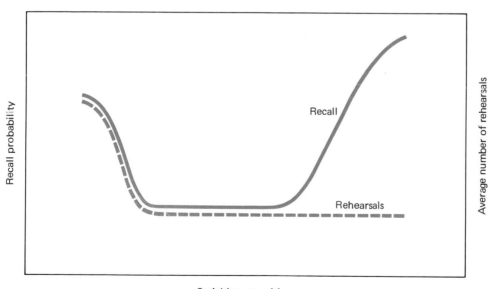

Serial input position

FIGURE 16-14   Recall probability (solid curve, left-hand ordinate) and average number of rehearsals (dashed curve, right-hand ordinate) as a function of serial input position. Up until the recency portion, the two curves are exceedingly similar, indicating that the primary effect is due, at least in part, to rehearsal factors.

Entry of Information into LTM: Organization of Memory

The notion that the transfer of information from short- to long-term memory depends only on the number of rehearsals is undoubtedly oversimplified *vis-à-vis* everyday life. People do not, in general, go around rehearsing information aloud, and other factors that, on the surface, have little to do with rehearsal can be shown to be very important in generating long-term information. For example, several investigators have stressed the organization of verbal material.

Most of the work done on organization has been in the context of free-recall experiments and has stressed a chunking notion. Suppose that a list of words is presented several times in a study–free-recall sequence, that is, a list is studied and then recalled, studied and recalled again, and so on for several trials. Over successive trials, more and more words are recalled, as might be expected. Work by Mandler (1967) and Tulving (1968) have investigated the question of why there is this increase in recalled words. The gist of their findings is that subjects, using some (unspecified) scheme, manage to set up groupings of words in the list.

The organizational principle used to remember more words consists of adding more and more words to the basic groupings. Retrieval is accomplished by recalling what a particular grouping is, and then reporting the words in the grouping. Several lines of evidence are offered in support of this hypothesis. First, Tulving has examined the order in which subjects report words in a multitrial free-recall experiment. Such an examination revealed the presence of groupings that are either remembered *in toto* or not at all. As the trials progressed it turned out that, in fact, each grouping incorporated successively larger numbers of words.

To bring the phenomenon under greater experimental control, a free-recall list may be so constructed as to consist of instances of taxonomic categories. Thus, for example, a thirty-word list might consist of six birds, six metals, six fruits, six cities, and six flowers. Tulving and Pearlstone (1966) presented such lists to subjects and varied two things: (1) the length of the list was either 12, 24, or 48 words and (2) subjects were either tested normally or in the presence of the category names as recall cues. Two major results were found.

First, the presentation of the category names as retrieval cues affected only the number of accessible categories, but not the number of words within accessible categories. Thus, given that the subject could recall at least one word from a category, the number of additional words recalled

for that category was the same regardless of whether he
remembered the category on his own or was reminded
of it. Second, the number of accessible categories was considerably greater for the 48-word list than for the 24-word
lists, but again, the number of words within accessible
categories was identical for both list lengths [Tulving,
1968, p. 28].

Thus the groupings of words seem to be the critical thing and were remembered
in an all-or-none fashion.

THE IMPORTANCE OF CATEGORIES.   Mandler (1967) has performed the following experiment. First, a list of unrelated words was presented to a subject
who simply had to sort the words into as many categories as he wished. After
the first sorting, the words were reshuffled and another sort was required.
This continued until the subject was sorting consistently, that is, until he
produced two identical sorts in a row. Then, a free-recall test was given on
the words. Mandler's finding was that the number of words recalled was a
linear function of the number of categories into which the words had been
sorted. The more categories there were, the better the recall. Although these
results are correlational, they support the notion that organization of memory
into categories is instrumental in recall.

THE IMPORTANCE OF ORGANIZATION ON REHEARSAL.   Evidence for memory organization of a somewhat different sort has been adduced by Bower
(1970). Bower presented 12-digit number strings for recall in a Hebb paradigm. However, instead of simply reading the digits one-by-one, a string would
be grouped; thus, for example, the string 271828182890 might be read as
"two seventy one, eighty-two, eight-thousand one hundred eighty-two, eight,
ninety." As would be expected from Hebb's results, when strings were repeated,
their probability of being recalled increased over trials. However, for some
of the strings, the grouping changed over trials. Thus, the above string might
be read as "two, seven hundred eighteen, twenty-eight, two eighty-one, eight-
thousand two hundred eighty-nine, zero" the second time it was presented.
For these "same-sequence-but-changed-organization" strings, recall did not improve over trials. Once again, organization appears to be a primary determinant
of memory performance.

WHICH THEORY IS CORRECT?   We have discussed two ways of conceptualizing the transfer of information from short- to long-term memory. The
first emphasized rehearsal, while the second stressed organization. Is it possible

to ascertain which, if either, of these conceptualizations is the correct one? Or could they both amount to the same thing? Although organization explains a good deal of data, rehearsal, which also explains much of the data in memory experiments, is a considerably simpler concept. Since it is a goal of science to find simple mechanisms underlying more complicated principles, rehearsal is a more useful concept, although perhaps both concepts could be explained in still simpler terms.

The Information Stored in Long-Term Memory

SEMANTIC ENCODING.   The nature of information stored in short-term memory is thought to be mostly acoustic, that is, when errors are made, the errors are likely to sound like the correct response. Furthermore, this information had been recoded from information in the iconic store that was basically visual in nature. What about long-term memory? When information is transferred from STM to LTM, what kind of recoding does it go through? What kind of information eventually is stored in LTM? A popular view has been that LTM information is basically semantic, that is, when a person is presented with words to remember, he takes the acoustic representation in STM, extracts information having to do with the meaning of the word, and transfers this information to LTM. As we shall presently see, this view is a bit too simple to be tenable, but first let us briefly examine the evidence for semantic encoding in LTM.

Like the studies showing acoustic encoding in STM, an examination of the errors that people make has led to the postulation of semantic encoding in LTM. A series of studies has indicated that errors made in LTM are more likely to be semantically related to the correct information than, for example, acoustically related. Suppose, for example, that you are searching for the word CAR, which is the correct response to some query of an experimenter. If you make an error, you are more likely to say something like AUTO, PORSCHE VEHICLE, or MOTORCYCLE, words that have some connection in meaning, than BAR or STAR, which sound like the correct answer but which are semantically unrelated to it (Anisfeld & Knapp, 1968; Baddely, 1966).

STORAGE IN LTM: ACOUSTIC SAVINGS.   Lately, however, a variety of work has demonstrated that somewhat more than semantic information is stored in LTM. Posner (1971) has raised the logical question, "If, only semantic information were stored in LTM, how would we ever learn to recognize accents?" Also, an ingenious series of studies by Thomas Nelson, (Nelson, 1971; Nelson & Fehling, 1972; Nelson & Rothbart, 1972) has provided an apt demonstration that many kinds of information are stored in LTM. Nelson was basically concerned with forgetting from LTM, and he asked if when some information is stored in LTM and then forgotten, is all of the original information lost or does some remain? Nelson's results indicate that some information is not lost in an all-or-none fashion. In itself, this finding, known as the "savings effect," is not particularly earthshaking. But Nelson also found that some of the remaining information is acoustic. If there is acoustic savings, acoustic information must have been originally stored.

An experiment (Nelson & Rothbart, 1972) illustrating the existence of acoustic savings used the following paradigm. Information is originally learned in a paired-associate task. (In a paired-associate task, a list of stimuli is paired with a list of responses. Nelson used two-digit numbers as stimuli and nouns as responses. So, for example, the stimulus "37" might be paired with the response DOE, 19 might be paired with EGG, and so on. The subject first studies the pairing and then is required to produce the response when given the stimulus.) Nelson and Rothbart had their subjects learn the list until all pairings were stored in LTM. The subjects then left, only to be asked to return 4 weeks later for the second half of the experiment. At this time, the subject first went through the list of stimuli once and tried to remember the responses. Some of the responses had, of course, been forgotten. The stimuli from these forgotten pairings were re-paired with new responses that bore one of two relationships with the old (forgotten) responses. In the first or experimental condition, the new responses were acoustically similar to the old responses, i.e., the new responses were homophones. If the forgotten pair had been 37-DOE, the new pairing might be 37-DOUGH. In the second or control condition, the new responses had no acoustic similarity to the old response. Thus in this condition, 37 might be re-paired with KETCHUP. The subject was then required to relearn these new pairings. Nelson and Rothbart reasoned that, if there is acoustic information about the old response remaining in LTM, the acoustically similar re-pairings should be easier to relearn than the acoustically unrelated re-pairings. The experimental evidence supported this view. When the new response was acoustically similar to the old, subjects were about 50% correct on the relearning trials, as compared to about 10% correct for the acoustically unrelated re-pairings. Therefore, the information stored in LTM is at least partially acoustic.

Using this paradigm, Nelson conducted a detailed investigation of the exact nature of semantic information stored in LTM. For example, it has been discovered (Nelson & Fehling, 1972) that superordinate information is stored about words, that is, if a subject has to remember a paired-associate such as 22-BUICK, part of the information that is stored is that a Buick is a car. Research is still under way to discover what other kinds of semantic information, e.g., synonymity, antonymy, etc., are stored. All findings indicate that the information stored in LTM is semantic, partly acoustic, and possibly partly visual. Even when this information is "forgotten" a good deal of it apparently remains.

Retrieval from Long-Term Memory

Sternberg's findings on retrieval from STM have sparked considerable interest in how information and, in particular, semantic information, are retrieved from LTM. Is the serial scanning process used for items in STM also used for LTM? That is, if you are asked to retrieve information from your long-term memory, to what extent do you consult successive items in your quest for the desired information? It seems pretty safe to assume that people do not randomly search through all of their memory when retrieving information. If I ask you for your mother's name, you do not, in the process of finding it come up with the information that Paris is the capital of France (unless you have a very strange mother). It might, however, be plausible that you have stored in LTM, a category called "family names," and that you scan through this information to produce the desired fact.

The major problem in studying how semantic information is retrieved from LTM is that the experimenter has no control over how the information gets into LTM. In order to postulate a retrieval scheme, it is necessary to also postulate a structure for LTM. To see why this is so, imagine trying to retrieve a subway token from a woman's pocketbook and trying to retrieve a book from a library. In the former case, the contents of the pocketbook are apt to be arranged somewhat randomly. A reasonable search strategy might thus be to go systematically from one side of the pocketbook to the other. In the latter case, however, books are rather well organized in a library. The general subject matter of the book for which you were looking would tell you the approximate location where it would be. Thus, whatever structure one postulates for long-term memory determines, to a large extent, what a reasonable retrieval scheme would be.

Therefore, several researchers have postulated both an information retrieval scheme and a structure for LTM. To the extent that experimentation supports the theory, it supports both the structure and the retrieval scheme. However, if experiments do not support the theory, it is impossible to judge which component is at fault.

Hierarchical Organization.   A popular conceptualization of long-term memory structure is that it is hierarchical. An example of a hierarchical struc-

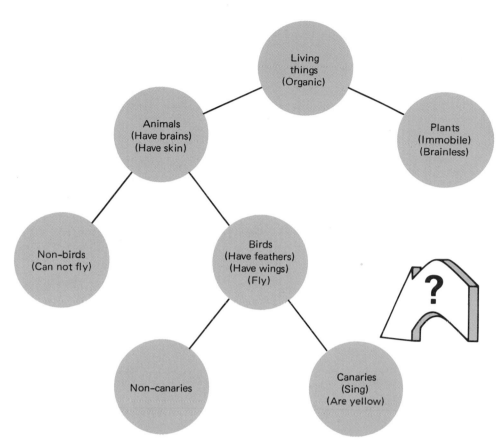

FIGURE 16-15   Part of a hierarchically organized memory structure. Collins and Quillian assume that information about particular classes is stored only at the level of that class. After Collins and Quillian (1969).

ture is shown in Figure 16-15. Basic to the memory structure postulated by Collins and Quillian (1969) is the assumption that information germain to a particular class of things is stored only at the level of the hierarchy corresponding to that class. Consider the part of the hierarchy involving "animals," "birds," and "canaries." Collins and Quillian assume that with "animals" is stored information common to all animals such as "drinks," "eats," and so on. Similarly, with "birds" is stored information relevant to all birds such as "has feathers" and "flys." Finally, at the level of "canary," there is information relevant to all canaries, such as "is yellow" and "sings." Suppose we perform an experiment in which a statement is made about canaries, and the subject has to respond "yes" or "no" as quickly as possible according to whether the statement is true or false. Now consider these three types of statements: (1) A canary is yellow; (2) A canary has wings; and (3) A canary has skin. What kinds of information processing are involved in deciding whether these statements are true? Collins and Quillian postulate the following retrieval scheme. When information is required about a noun (such as canary), the subject commences a search for memory. The search consists of entering the place in the hierarchy where information about the noun is stored, and, from there, whatever searching necessary to retrieve the desired information is carried out. Thus, to answer the first question, the subject would enter the place in memory corresponding to "canary," where he immediately would find the information that "canaries are yellow." He therefore should be able to produce the response "yes" rather quickly. To answer the second question, the subject will go to the "canary" location, but will find no information there that is relevant to whether canaries have wings. Instead, he will have to move up one location and interrogate "birds." There, he will find that birds have wings and, since a canary is a bird, he will then be able to make the correct response. Similarly, for the third question, the subject will have to start at canary and then go up two levels in the hierarchy to determine that a canary, which is a bird, which is an animal, has skin. To

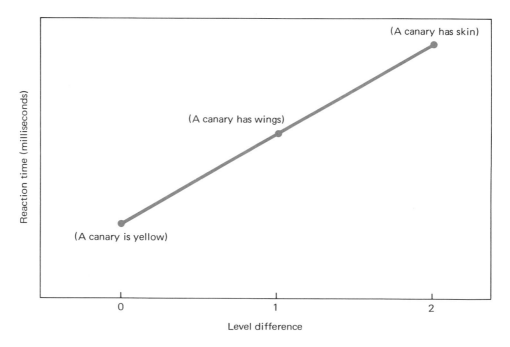

FIGURE 16-16   The reaction time taken to answer various questions about nouns. The abscissa indicates how far from the noun (in hierarchical levels) the necessary information is stored.

the extent that moving around in the hierarchy has to take place during retrieval, the process will take more time.

The results of this experiment support Collins and Quillian's memory-structure retrieval scheme (Figure 16-16). Reaction time to respond to "a canary has skin" is about 90 milliseconds longer than RT to respond to "a canary has wings," which, in turn, is about 90 milliseconds longer than the response to "a canary is yellow." According to Collins and Quillian's model and data, then, it takes a little under one-tenth of a second to move from one level of a semantic hierarchy to another.

LONG-TERM MEMORY: A RECAPITULATION

1. LTM is a reasonable permanent repository of the information that we need to survive in our environment. The capacity of LTM is very large; in fact, no limit has yet been found on the amount of information that can be stored.

2. Information is put into LTM from STM. Although there are many ways of describing STM—LTM information transfer, e.g., organization, imagery, etc., it appears that a simple theory using only the concept of rehearsal provides the best, most parsimonious account of such transfer.

3. Information in LTM is coded in many ways: semantically, acoustically, and probably visually.

4. A good description of LTM structure is that it is hierarchical. Retrieval of information consists of entering the hierarchy in some appropriate place and casting about from there for the desired information.

SUGGESTED READINGS

Bower, G. H. Analysis of a mnemonic device. *American Scientist*, 1970, **58**, 496–510.

Neisser, U. *Cognitive psychology*. New York: Appleton, 1967.

Normon, D. *Memory and attention*. New York: Wiley, 1968.

Penfield, W., & Roberts, L. *Speech and brain mechanisms*. Princeton, N. J.: Princeton Univ. Press, 1959.

Tulving, E., & Donaldson, W. (Eds.) *Organization of memory*. New York: Academic Press, 1972.

17

Motivation and Evolution

This chapter will explicitly examine the survival needs of organisms and how, through selection of the fittest, these have led to the development of motivational mechanisms by which an organism can recognize its needs and react appropriately to its environment. Accordingly, the emphasis here will be on the broad biological issues regarding the nature of motivation and the various motivational systems that have evolved in higher animals and man.

MOTIVATION REVISITED

It is important to know exactly what is meant by motivation. In common parlance one hears, "Suzie is smart enough to get an A, but she just isn't motivated," with the implication that, if her inner state or attitude could only be changed or heightened, she would then be predisposed to attend more assiduously to her studies. In the laboratory, after depriving a rat of food for a day, it more vigorously performs a previously learned response of pressing a bar for food. The rat is said to be motivated by hunger. If the rat is allowed free access to food and becomes satiated, its performance rate on the bar will greatly decrease. When a puff of food powder into the mouth of a dog was used as a UCS to elicit the UCR of salivating in Pavlov's experiments, the saliva flow was great only if the dog was hungry. Success in associating this UCR to an immediately preceding neutral stimulus such as a bell also depended on the dog being hungry.

From these examples, it is recognized that, on separate occasions, the same organism may react quite differently to the same stimuli. Numerous experiments have shown that a large part of this variation in behavior can be accounted for in terms of whether or not some other very specific stimulus or set of stimuli is also present in the environment. These stimuli largely determine the motivational state that affects how the organism responds to the test stimuli.

To say that there are predisposing stimuli governing how we react to other stimuli is one thing; to identify what these are is another. What is the stimulus governing our reaction to the odor of freshly baked bread? Only one thing is plain. After some hours without food, the odor that was previously resistible becomes irresistible. Yet nothing in the external environment has changed. In this case, the stimuli arise from the internal body environment in response to deprivation. The psychologists have spent years searching for the stimuli that the body uses to signal hunger to the brain and how the brain recognizes and converts these signals into effective action.

Fear can also affect motivation. A rat that initially prefers to be in a black rather than a white box will, after a series of painful electric shock experiences in the black box, reverse his preference. Even many trials or days after the shock has been discontinued, the rat will learn any new response that allows him to escape into the white box. Here the situation appears simpler. The rat has acquired a fear of blackness because of its learned association with the pain induced by an electric shock of external origin. However, once learning has occurred, this shock need not remain physically present in the outside environment in order to continue to predispose the escape reaction to the black box. Its presence has become internalized as a memory somewhere in the brain.

As with the cases of hunger and fear just described, most of the other predisposing stimuli governing motivated behavior seem either to arise from within the organism or to become internalized where they are much less accessible for study. For this reason, behavioral scientists are as yet relatively unclear not only as to the nature but even as to the number of these stimuli. In accounting for the behaviors that are somewhat mysteriously driven from within by these stimuli, arguments have arisen as to how many separate drives they are. Obviously, there is a hunger drive, for example, but is the drive unitary? Might there be different kinds of hunger for salt, sweetness, calories, etc? There are obviously sex drives, but should there be a separate drive category established for affections that are nonsexual? Is one justified in labeling as a drive something as primitive as the compulsion to scratch where it itches? Are there even separate drives for each of such higher mental endeavors as listening for the thematic developments in a symphony or working a crossword puzzle?

At this point in our proliferation of motivations, it should be remembered that the selection pressures for survival do not, in general, permit the successful evolution of structures and mechanisms that serve no function in meeting the needs of the organism. By keeping this rule in mind, ethologists and behavioral psychologists have been able to come to a fair notion of the types of motivational systems that most likely must exist for individuals and species to survive, and what sensory and response functions have probably evolved to serve these systems. In the following discussion of the basic requirements for biological existence, the emphasis will be on how the need to satisfy these requirements might have shaped the evolution of form and behavior (Coons, 1973).

FUNCTIONAL EVOLUTION: A PERSPECTIVE

In this universe everything, be it an entity as small as a molecule or as large as a galaxy, has an arrangement or form. Is it possible that any form from its inception can resist the so-called bludgeonings of chance with unbroken continuity? Yes, provided the following basic survival needs of replication and protection are met.

The form in question should confer on the entity representing it the ability to reproduce itself exactly. For this to occur, the appropriate building blocks necessary to construct the replication must be present in the environment. Also any entity replicating itself needs, on the average, to be shielded from accidents long enough for the rate of replication to at least match, if not exceed, the rate of accidental breakdown. If these two needs are always met, a form can remain in continuous existence because the entities representing it are recreated as fast or faster than they are destroyed.

ASPECTS OF CELL DEVELOPMENT AND PHYSIOLOGY

In the course of the evolutionary process, some of the mutations in form conferred on the template molecules (which are responsible for replication) the ability to construct protective skins or membranes about themselves that warded off some of the deleterious environmental influences. With this advantage, however, came a disadvantage that had enormous repercussions. The same membrane that tended to keep bad things away also tended to isolate its owner from ready access to the good things needed for replication. Obviously, the only mutations that could survive solved this conflict of needs between protection and replication by conferring on the membrane an ability to distinguish between noxious and benevolent elements and selectively exclude the former and incorporate the latter. To do this optimally, specialized receptor and response structures developed. These, however, tended further to separate the inside template molecules from the outside world and, hence, to strain the lines of supply. In response, digestive and circulatory structures slowly evolved, but these and the other structures required energy to run. This energy, in turn, yielded waste products requiring energy-consuming excretory structures to extrude them from the organism. Many of these structures that were constructed under directives from the template molecules lay between a central nucleus of such molecules and the surface membrane in a region known as cytoplasm. Thus, by these or similar steps, the repercussions stemming from the creation of a membrane culminated in what can now be called a cell. But perhaps more importantly, while this cell freed the inner template molecules, the continual turnover in energy required to sustain its upkeep imposed a third basic need for survival, that is, renewal of the substance of the individual as distinguished from the replication of the species.

Thermal Regulation

As the demands on upkeep functions escalated in the course of organisms becoming many-celled, large, and, finally, land-going, it became imperative that these functions operate extremely efficiently. This necessitated holding the body temperature constantly at just that level where enzyme reactions involved in metabolism would proceed most effectively. It was important that any drift either above or below that level be countered quickly by a homeostatic mechanism operating on the principle of negative feedback to drive the temperature back to its optimum. Due to the successful chance evolution of such a thermal regulatory mechanism, the template molecules sequestered within the cells of mammals and birds are much freer than in other animals to move from cold to hot climates in search of their needs for replication, protection, and renewal of their host.

Osmolar Regulation

A somewhat similar story can be told concerning the evolution of homeostatic osmolar mechanisms controlling the salt/water ratio in the body. Again, the upkeep metabolism of the body demands that the fluids bathing the cells be maintained at a salinity of 0.9%. In the external environment, the unavailability of either water or salt can eventually seriously upset this ratio in the body. When organisms emerged from the ocean onto dry land, such problems became very real, and internal mechanisms had to evolve in order to handle them. These mechanisms as they now exist counter water deficits, on the one hand, by having the pituitary gland release an antidiuretic hormone (ADH) into the blood that causes the kidney to reabsorb some of the water in which impurities are flushed from the blood, thereby resulting in a more concentrated urine, which helps to conserve the salt/water balance. These mechanisms counter salt deficiencies, on the other hand, by having the adrenal glands release aldosterone, which prompts the kidney to reabsorb some of the salt that is normally secreted in the urine.

Competition of Regulatory Systems

From the osmolar and thermal cases just described, it is apparent that if any animals and the template molecules they harbor are to survive and thrive, for example, in a dry climate having great variations in temperature, they must be responsive to a derivative need, i.e., the need for close regulation of the internal environment in highly specified ways. Such regulation may be relatively simple, as in the illustrations already given, or it may become quite complex, as when several separate homeostatic mechanisms come into conflict so that there arises a higher order need to judge which one has first priority in carrying out its regulation. As a case in point, each of us can recall that, at times when we were both hungry and thirsty, the desire for food played second fiddle to the desire for water. Some adjudicative regulatory mechanism recognized that the digestive process necessarily draws fluid from the rest of the body into the gut when food is eaten. If the body is already depleted of water, to eat is to add insult to injury. Therefore, the adjudicative mechanism decided to inhibit hunger until after thirst was slaked.

ORIGINS OF THE BEHAVIORAL RESPONSE

The homeostatic mechanisms in most of the foregoing examples use internal solutions that depend upon neural or hormonal intercommunication and coordination among internal need receptors and internal organs. However, these mechanisms can also utilize external solutions and they are frequently forced to do so by a failure of the internal solution. The activation of a perspiratory mecha-

nism in the tropics or a shivering one in the Arctic may be insufficient to maintain thermal homeostasis, so that the more externally oriented behaviors of
seeking the shade or a fire, respectively, must be called into play. Food-seeking
when the internal energy stores dwindle is another example. In these examples,
successful homeostasis again depends upon neural or hormonal intercommunication and coordination, but between internal need receptors and muscle tissue
developed to position the organism toward its external environment in various
ways. It is often true that if the more ancient and nonhomeostatic needs of
replication and protection are to be met successfully by action taken in the
outside world, they must be aided by some adjustments in the internal environment. For example, the sight of some feared object causes the release of epinephrine internally to mobilize the energy stores optimally for the emergency
exertions involved in sudden, rapid flight. Here, the intercommunication and
coordination is between an external need receptor and internal response
mechanisms.

From what has already been presented, it should now be very clear that
the variety of surviving life forms are the ones whose arrangements relative
to their environments have permitted solutions to the basic needs for replication
and protection. For many types of organisms, the solutions to their needs
to replicate, protect, and renew have had to involve, in addition to the regulatory solutions already discussed, a much more outgoing engagement with the
external world. These are the creatures of special interest to psychologists
because they exhibit a very measurable behavior.

Movement Systems

At some point, organisms became endowed with contractile structures
(muscles) having the ability to move the organism in response to any event
associated with a need. Though this movement was undirected and random,
its mere occurrence when the organism was in an unsatisfactory environmental
locale meant that, on the average, its net effect was to navigate the organism
away from that unfavorable locale and into another, and usually more favorable, position. This resulted in an increased survival for such an organism.
However, the movement response, called a kinesis by ethologists, could only
work if the organism also possessed sensory receptors to detect the event signaling need. This kinesis operated for as long as the need signal persisted and
ceased only when the need condition ceased.

Such kineses are still a part of the behavioral repetoire of many organisms.
They may be redescribed as simple go mechanisms, which are motivated by
needs but take no other sensory information into account in determining when

and where to operate. They only stop functioning when they have removed the source of motivation that drives them. In the Rocky Mountain tick, for example, a thermal homeostatic mechanism signals a condition of regulatory need when the temperature is either above or below 30°C. When many ticks are placed on a horizontal sheet of paper over a light bulb, they will at first engage in random movement, but most of them soon will be found resting in an area ringing the bulb at just that distance where the temperature is approximately ideal.

The present use of the steering mechanism to guide animals behaviorally to the solution of their needs varies from species to species. In insects and birds, behavior toward a goal fairly typically consists of a linking together of many complex but highly stereotyped behavioral subunits called fixed action patterns (see Chapter 3). Each of these is differentially triggered by some sign stimulus that turns out to be one of only a limited number of alternatives to which the immediately preceding behavioral subunit could have led. For such organisms, the steering mechanism can function as deterministically as it does because the demands of their existence remain highly invariant over generations and within the lifetime of the individual, even though a highly precise sequencing of behavior is required. Because of this, it was possible and even desirable to program the contingency rules for behavior genetically rather than depending on learning.

PRIMITIVE BEHAVIORAL PATTERNS IN MAN

For mammals, and particularly man, the steering mechanism is used quite differently, because the conditions of existence leading to the solution of needs vary too much from one generation to the next for wholesale programming of behavioral contingencies to succeed at the genetic level. There are, nevertheless, a number of such innate stimulus-response connections in mammals. The behavioral units involved are usually so short and simple as to be termed reflexes rather than fixed action patterns. They are more in evidence during infancy than in adulthood. This is just what one would expect, since infancy is a period during which the organism is necessarily without benefit of learning to guide him. Well-known examples are the sucking reflex and the visual-cliff withdrawal reflex (see Chapter 2).

In higher mammals, there are steering mechanisms to provide for getting the organism to the goals necessary for survival. In these animals, the same UCS that elicits the reflex consummatory behavior has assumed the added property of being a reinforcer, that is, it somehow permits learning to occur between the stimuli and the responses that precede the UCS. The result is that these stimuli, if presented again, now themselves act like elicitors in that they tend to call forth the responses that immediately followed them when the reinforcer originally occurred. It is by this more plactic principle of steering by reinforcement that the higher organism can learn any sequence of stimuli and responses that leads to reinforcers. This ability to learn, which is itself genetically determined, succeeds only because, in the lifetime of such organisms, a route that has once proven successful in arriving at a solution will generally prove successful again.

It is important to remember, however, that a stimulus that is a reinforcer on one occasion is not necessarily a reinforcer on all occasions; it depends upon whether or not the appropriate drive states (or predisposing stimuli) are also present. Since the reinforcement principle is designed to steer organisms so that they can successfully reduce their drive, the operation of a stimulus as a reinforcer is self-limiting in a way similar to the feedback operation of a kinesis, in that its reinforcing quality abates as the drive is reduced. In fact, the reinforcing quality of the stimulus is so intimately determined by the strength of the drive, and the strength of the drive is so much a function of how repeatedly the organism is exposed to the stimulus that it has been theorized until recently that reinforcement may arise ultimately from primary drive reduction itself. This drive reduction theory of reinforcement, though still useful in predicting and explaining most instances of behavior, is less popular than it once was because of results that are difficult to reconcile with it.

In addition to reinforcement, certain other mechanisms have evolved that free higher organisms to survive in ecological niches not available to animals whose behavior is too strictly keyed to the actual onsets and offsets of drives. A stimulus may, in some instances, cease having a reinforcing quality even before the absolute reduction of a drive is achieved. An example of this is eating driven by low blood sugar. Since in a large animal the conversion of food into blood sugar is a lengthy digestive process, it would not only be impractical but fatal for the animal to continue to eat until the blood sugar rises to normal; its stomach would have burst before then. Thus, some mechanism is necessary to turn off the eating well before true satiety in the blood is reached, but at a point when enough food has been eaten to produce this satiety eventually. This is accomplished by the brain monitoring the sensations produced by food passing through the mouth, down the throat, and into the stomach. Information from the UCS used in this way functions as more than a reinforcer for behavior; it becomes a metering signal by which the organism can detect in advance when the solution to a need has in effect been found and when, thus, the seeking behavior can be terminated.

The foregoing example illustrates that for some drives, particularly hunger, sensory information can be used by higher organisms to anticipate the reduction of a need. Sensory information can also sometimes be used to anticipate the inception of a need so as to avoid its onset. For example, as a result of being paired with pain, a neutral stimulus subsequently acquires the ability to elicit a fear reaction even though no pain is at that time actually present. Escape from the fear stimulus even acts as a reinforcer. The ability to·anticipate a primary drive has resulted in a learned drive. Not all primary drives, however, can form the basis for learned drives.

REGULATORY DRIVES

As stated earlier, renewal of the individual represents one of the basic needs and almost always also involves regulation and adjudication. All three needs arise from within the organism and are the basis for the drives of hunger, thirst, and temperature control. As an illustrative sample of how these operate we shall consider hunger.

The body continually requires energy (calories) and certain special substances such as vitamins, salts, etc., in order to renew itself. A variety of mechanisms has evolved by which the requirements can be attained and maintained at the appropriate level. The efficient operation of these mechanisms has depended upon the development of sensory systems to monitor the internal environment for those changes signaling when the needs to renew arise. In response to such signals the body may (1) release the necessary substances from special internal stores it had accumulated in times of excess, (2) insititute certain conservational measures, or (3) instruct the brain to send the whole organism in search of whatever stores of the necessary substance may be located in the external world.

The signals of change which the body uses to trigger the regulatory mechanisms are not well understood. Take the need for calories which is satisfied most usually by the presence and metabolism of carbohydrates (glucose) and less frequently by the metabolism of lipids (fats). When more calories are needed, to what signals is the body sensitive? Some evidence suggest that there are receptors that fire when the level and utilization rate of glucose in the blood falls too low. This monitoring system operates, thus, as a glucostat. Other evidence suggests that there are receptors that fire when the fat deposits and lipid levels in the blood diminish too greatly. This monitoring system could be termed a lipostat. Other systems may operate upon the basis of the amount of heat the body has the energy to generate (a thermostat) or upon whether, in the time since the last meal, the stomach has emptied itself enough to terminate the activation of stretch receptors that are inhibitory to hunger.

Not all of the food objects with which an organism comes in contact during its search will necessarily supply it with the exact substance it may need. What mechanisms, then, have evolved that allow it to make the proper selections? The simplest of these mechanisms seem to operate like a kinesis as follows. Rats having a thiamine vitamin deficiency become much more attracted to novel foods than before. If none of these novel foods happen to contain the necessary thiamine, the deficiency continues and the animal moves on to other novel foods since the ones just tried soon become familiar. Eventually, the laws of chance favor the rat sampling a food with the right thiamine content, after which the fascination with novelty fades, leaving the rat with just that food appropriate to its health. The yen that pregnant women sometimes suddenly exhibit for an exotic food may be caused by a similar mechanism.

INNATENESS OF TASTE PREFERENCE

The organism is guided to the solution of its needs by a positive preference for a particular taste that is innate, rather than learned, and which only expresses itself when the need is present. To date, only a few tastes have been shown to be of this type; saltiness is one of them. To prove that the preference for salty tastes in the presence of a salt need are innate, Krieckhaus (1970) performed the following experiment.

Rats were raised from infancy with an overabundance of salt in their diet so that they never developed a salt drive to render the taste of salt reinforcing. These rats were deprived of water and trained to run to either arm of a T maze to drink. One arm contained pure water, the other arm slightly salted water. The rats, when given a choice, preferred the arm with the pure water. Then they were deprived of salt until they developed, for the first time, a salt drive. Subsequently, they were retested in the T maze to see if they had acquired a memory for the whereabouts of salt in the past that they could use now to guide them in their search for salt. Of course, in the retest, both the pure and salty water had been removed, so that the present reinforcing effect of finding salt could not contaminate the memory of salt. The results showed that the rats, when salt deprived, now remembered and preferred the arm where salt had been, even though at the time of original training they had no experience with a drive for salt. Evidently, salt is so important to all rats that they have been genetically programmed to register the location of salt in their memories automatically and to find salt or its memory innately rewarding on their first experience with a salt need.

Aside from the innate palatability of a salt taste and a few others, the acceptability of most tastes must be learned in terms of what tastes are followed by some unpleasant state such as nausea. The delay by which the consequences can follow the injestion of the taste substance and still modify the palatability of the substance is quite long, of the order of several hours, as compared to the $\frac{1}{2}$-second optimum interval for classical conditioning. Such a long interval is, of course, adapted to the workings of the digestive system where the consequences of ingestion, necessarily, take a long time to express themselves.

Changing Taste Preference

Both the long delay of reinforcement and the modifiableness of taste acceptance have been elegantly demonstrated by Garcia and his colleagues (1961). In one experiment, vitamin-deprived rats were fed a flavored water and then some hours later were injected with the missing vitamin that made them feel better. As a result, these rats soon developed a preference for that particular flavor of water. In another experiment, rats that had been fed a particular type of food were then exposed to x rays that made them sick. Later, these rats were "bait shy" of all tastes similar to that of the meal that preceded their radiation treatment.

Palatableness and Hunger

The more palatable a food, the less hungry an organism must be in order to be tempted by it. For example, after a meal that we say has completely filled us up, there is often still room for dessert. Conversely, less palatable foods become more acceptable the greater the hunger. This was once attributed to an increase in the sensitivity of the taste receptor. However, no changes in this sensitivity have been found to accompany changes in food deprivation (Pfaffman & Bare, 1950). Consequently, it is now thought that hunger must facilitate the central connections between sensory and response systems concerned with food seeking and eating. This central arrangement is more reasonable, since it would seem important to survival for the ability to detect and gather information to be unaffected by changes in motivational state. The site within the brain at which hunger can exert its facilitative effect on palatableness is not known for certain, although portions of the amygdala may play a role. Electrical stimulation there can reduce an animal's liking for the type of food present at the time; that food, then, continues to remain undesirable for several weeks therafter (Fonberg & Delgado, 1961).

THE PHYSICAL BASIS OF HUNGER

In an effort to understand how the needs for food are apprehended and translated into appropriate action, the behavioral effects of experimentally manipulating the nervous system in various ways have been studied. For example, by electrically burning out the medial core of the hypothalamus, it was discovered that mammals would now overeat until they became quite fat, a phenomenon labeled hyperphagia (Figure 17-1). Since it was an increase in meal size rather than in number of meals per day that accounted for this hyperphagia, it was concluded that what was destroyed was the usual ability to judge from stomach stretch-receptor signals just when an appropriate amount of food had been eaten (Figure 17-2). In other words, a satiety-brake metering mechanism had been impaired so that the body's conception of its appropriate size was adjusted to some more sluggish and higher homeostatic set-point.

Hyperphagia and Palatableness

Other effects, however, complicate the simplicity of this interpretation. Rats made obese by this technique of destroying the medial hypothalamus, in particular the ventromedial nucleus, became much more finicky about what constituted a palatable food. As compared to normal rats, they would overeat when presented with delectable foods but undereat when given substandard fare. It is as if they had been left much more to the hedonistic mercies of their external sensory receptors in judging what they should eat and much less to the pragmatic mercies of internal need state receptors in making these decisions. In other words, without their ventromedial nuclei, animals can only exhibit appetitive behavior at either end of the food acceptance-rejection spectrum; they have lost the ability to modulate their behavior over intermediate points. It is interesting to note that Schachter and his collegues have shown that normally obese human subjects behave in much the same way (see Chapter 22).

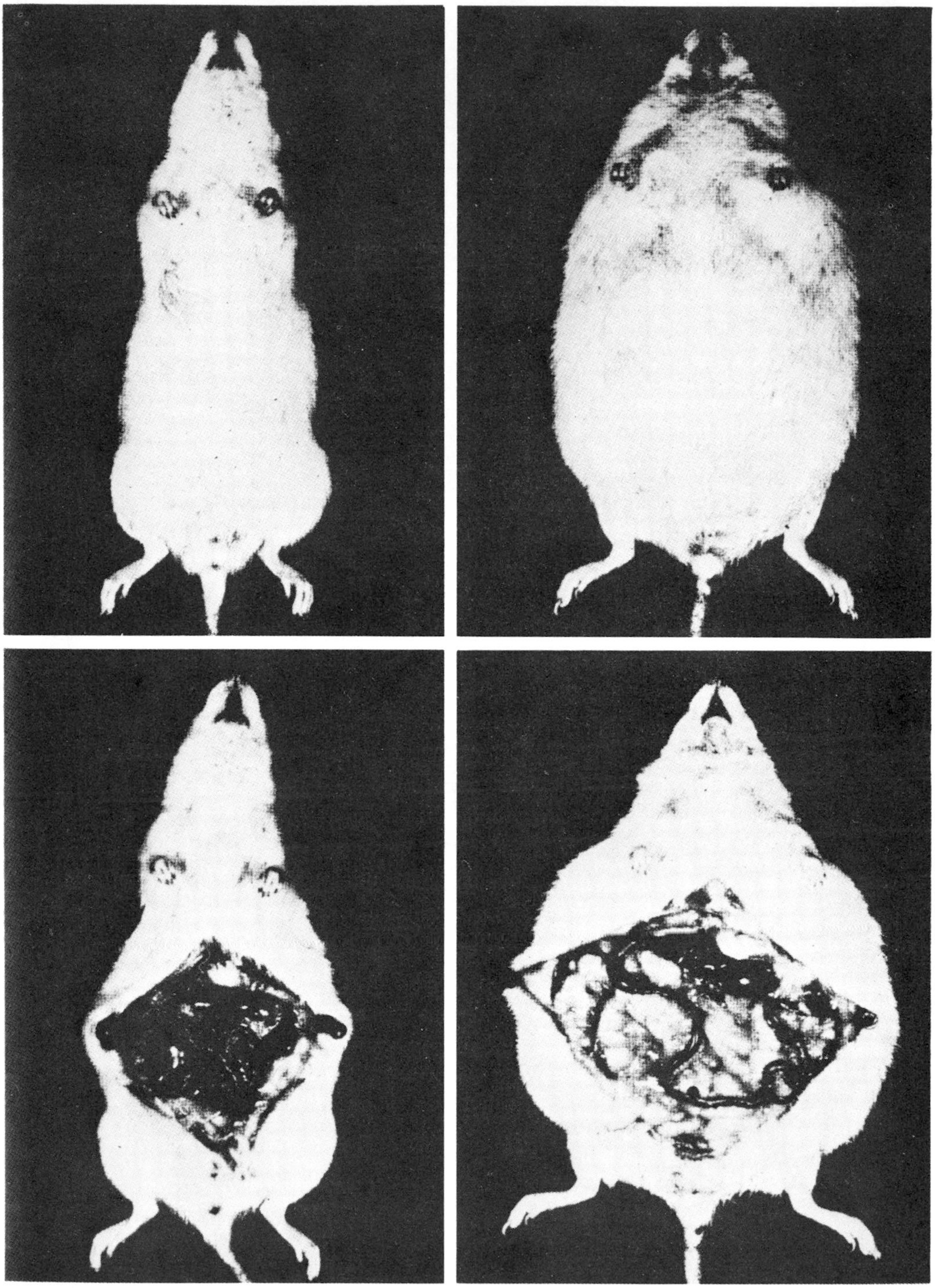

FIGURE 17-1   A comparison of a normal rat and one with ventromedial lesions of the hypothalamus. From Kennedy (1950).

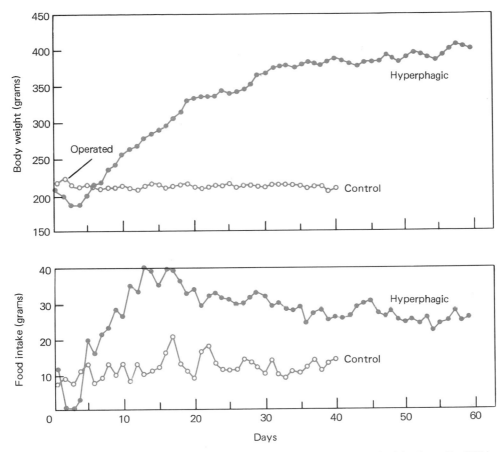

FIGURE 17-2 The amount of real weight put on by a hyperphagic animal is dramatic. Within a month, the rat doubles in size. From Teitelbaum (1955).

Aphagia: The Loss of Apetite

Destruction of the lateral hypothalamus on either side of the ventromedial nucleus produces animals that temporarily are aphagic in that they starve themselves (Figure 17-3). Much more drastically, however, the animals are adipsic, that is, they will not drink water. Since an animal long without water will not eat, the effect is to produce an extended aphagia that is seen to be only secondary if the animal is kept well supplied with water by tube feeding.

Recovery from primary aphagia usually occurs within a few days, but the recovery from adipsia is much more prolonged and may never be complete if the area of destruction is too large (Figure 17-4). Even after apparent recovery, however, the animal may regulate its water intake in a different way than normal. The drinking response to suddenly overloading a rat with salt or to depleting its body of fluid volume may not be normal. It may only successfully regulate by taking water with meals; if food is removed, the rat may fail to drink. It is as if the rat had learned to rely on dry-mouth cues associated with food-intake as the only way to successfully steer an approach to water. Evidently some, but not all, of the receptors for thirst or the pathways leading from these receptors to the regulatory response mechanisms have been destroyed by lateral hypothalamic damage.

Latent deficits other than those of water regulation remain after recovery from lateral hypothalamic destruction. The usual feeding response to injections of insulin may not occur, suggesting that there has been damage to some insulin receptor or some receptor sensitive to the drop in blood sugar produced by insulin. Abilities to regulate heat production are also often impaired.

Brain Stimulation and Hunger

Another experimental approach to studying the role of central neural structures in mediating hunger is to implant animals with electrodes in various parts of their brain and then to observe the effects of electrical stimulation of these regions on the animals' behavior. For example Coons, Levak, and Miller (1965) observed that rats electrically stimulated in their lateral hypothalamus

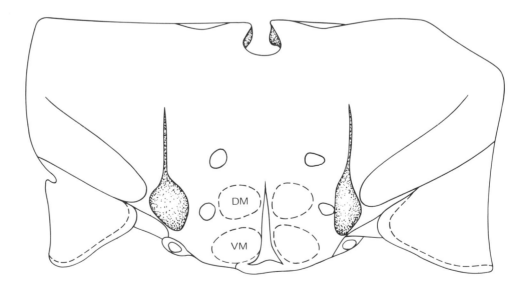

FIGURE 17-3   A schematic cross section of a rat's hypothalamus. The heavily shaded regions represent lesions in the lateral hypothalamic area that produce aphagia and adipsia. DM, Dorsomedial nucleus; VM, ventromedial nucleus. From Anand and Brobeck (1951).

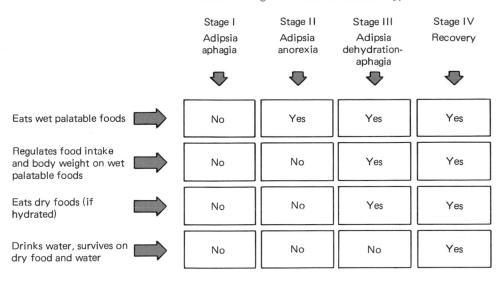

	Stage I Adipsia aphagia	Stage II Adipsia anorexia	Stage III Adipsia dehydration- aphagia	Stage IV Recovery
Eats wet palatable foods	No	Yes	Yes	Yes
Regulates food intake and body weight on wet palatable foods	No	No	Yes	Yes
Eats dry foods (if hydrated)	No	No	Yes	Yes
Drinks water, survives on dry food and water	No	No	No	Yes

FIGURE 17-4   The stages of recovery following lesions in the lateral hypothalamus. It is still unknown where compensation occurs in the brain. From Teitelbaum and Epstein (1962).

often would immediately start engaging in food-seeking and eating behavior, even though entirely satiated beforehand. This behavior was stimulus-bound in that it, generally, would terminate immediatealy with the offset of electrical current. The eating behavior elicited had most or all of the characteristics associated with normal hunger according to a battery of motivational tests. For example, while being stimulated, a normally satiated animal would readily learn a bar pressing response if it led to the receipt of food pellets.

Since destruction of the lateral hypothalamus produces decreased food intake while stimulation there produced stimulus-bound eating, one might then on the basis of symmetry predict that, since destruction of the ventromedial region produces increased food intake, stimulation there should stop a normally hungry animal from eating presumably by eliciting satiety. This is, indeed, what happens, although one might quibble with the interpretation as to why, since the stimulation may be merely detraction in some way. However, the fact that ventromedial stimulation in normally satiated rats is followed upon its termination by a brief "rebound" eating effect strengthens this argument.

EVIDENCE AGAINST DRIVE-REDUCTION HYPOTHESIS

The technique of stimulating the lateral hypothalamus to induce hunger motivation was also used to ask the question whether the offset of "hunger" stimulation would be rewarding as predicted by the drive-reduction hypothesis of reinforcement. Contrary to this prediction, it was found that, at low intensities of stimulation just capable of eliciting food-seeking behavior and eating, rats would avoid making a response that terminated stimulation. Furthermore, the rats would even press a bar to turn on this current, which again is not what one would expect from the drive-reduction hypothesis. Obviously, simple reduction of the hunger drive itself is not rewarding, although the taste of the food leading to this drive reduction is.

Just as with lateral hypothalamic destruction, electrical stimulation in that region produces more than one kind of goal-oriented behavior. For example, drinking, hoarding, nest building, and sexual behavior can also be elicited. This conglomeration of effect is what one would expect from an area importantly concerned with the adjudication of priority among a number of needs systems whose operation might otherwise interfere with one another. However, the eliciting of so many behaviors from this region raises the question as to whether there are separate pathways running through this region to serve each behavior or whether the same pathway can be plastically molded toward the expression of one or another of these behaviors, depending on what goal objects are at hand in the external environment to act as reinforcers. Valenstein and co-workers (1966) have successfully weaned rats from displaying eating when stimulated to displaying drinking by the simple expedient of removing food from their test cage and substituting a water tube. However, since many neural pathways run throughout the lateral hypothalamus and since electrical stimulation probably spreads to all of these structures, the question of whether or not there is specificity of function remains open.

EVIDENCE FOR BEHAVIORAL SPECIFICITY IN HYPOTHALAMIC FUNCTIONING

The studies using very small electrodes with little current spread or employing chemical stimulation through an implanted cannula (a hyperdermic needle) strongly suggest that there is much greater behavioral specificity than was hitherto measurable. For example, Grossman (1960) found that hypothalamic injections of a chemical closely related to acetylcholine, a neurotransmitter agent mediating conduction of a message, produced drinking in the rat. A different neurotransmitter agent, norepinephrine, produced eating when injected through the same cannula. Leibowitz (1970) has further amplified the work showing that specificity in the neural mediation of motivated behaviors may be chemically coded by demonstrating the presence in the hypothalamus of two different neurotransmitter receptors, alpha and beta, which respond differently to norepinephrine (a brain neurotransmitter) by signaling hunger and satiety, respectively.

From the preceding discussion, it might seem that the hypothalamus is the only structure that is involved in mediating the behavioral signals to regulate food intake. However, many other regions, though not as well studied, are certainly also involved.

BRAIN STIMULATION AND REWARD

In the early 1950's, Olds and Milner (1954), two psychologists at McGill University, discovered that there were places in the brain where electrical stimulation through a permanently implanted electrode was so reinforcing that the animal would actually learn and vigorously perform a response to self-deliver the current (Figure 17-5). Later research has shown that the most

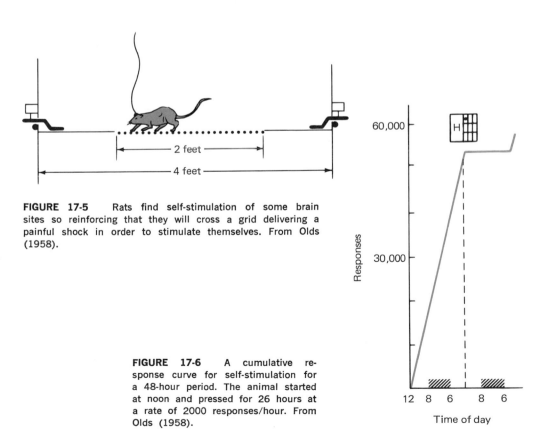

FIGURE 17-5   Rats find self-stimulation of some brain sites so reinforcing that they will cross a grid delivering a painful shock in order to stimulate themselves. From Olds (1958).

FIGURE 17-6   A cumulative response curve for self-stimulation for a 48-hour period. The animal started at noon and pressed for 26 hours at a rate of 2000 responses/hour. From Olds (1958).

highly reinforcing region is the lateral hypothalamus, which is also a region from which a great variety of drives including hunger can be electrically aroused (Figure 17-6). Is it just fortuitous then that a rat who repeatedly presses a bar to receive each time a brief burst of self-rewarding current to this region is also a rat who may drink, nest-build, ejaculate, etc., to longer bursts of this same stimulation? The implication is not only that drive and reinforcement are intimately interrelated, but also that there might be something to learn about the nature of this relationship by studying the hypothalamic mechanisms of self-stimulation.

Deutsch (1960) and others have theorized that self-stimulation is reinforcing because the stimulation jointly activates a neural pathway, producing a drive for a particular goal object, and a neighboring neural pathway, which reports back sensory information if the goal object appropriate to that drive has, indeed, been encountered. Only when both pathways are activated, does a set of neurons, onto which they converge, react. The reaction, in turn, facilitates and preserves in memory whatever responses and stimulus-response connections are present and are, thus, possibly the factors instrumental in bringing the organism in contact with the goal object.

As a deduction from this theory, it follows that, if the electrical stimulation could somehow be limited to activating only the drive pathways, the animal would not find it rewarding to press a lever for self-stimulation. In fact, this deduction has been tested. Rats that show the electrically motivated eating effect will also self-stimulate, but only at higher current intensities. With lower current intensities, no self-stimulation occurs, thereby suggesting that only the hunger drive pathway is excited. However, if food, the appropriate goal, is placed in a dish by the lever, the rat will self-stimulate at a low current intensity, provided the duration of current delivered for each lever press is long enough for the rat to bend its head down to the food dish and eat.

SUMMARY

Understanding the biological foundations of motivated behavior is a fascinating yet complex problem. Insight can only be achieved by first considering the broad evolutionary history of living matter. From this vantage point one can imagine how natural selection shaped tissue first into cell units and then into multicelled complex organisms. Regulation of function in life systems is certainly the keystone upon which much of our motivated behavior builds.

SUGGESTED READINGS

MILNER, P. *Physiological psychology*. New York: Holt, 1970.

OLDS, J., & OLDS, M. Drives, rewards, and the brain. In F. Barron *et al.* (Eds.), *New directions in psychology*. Vol. 2. New York: Holt, 1965. Pp. 327–410.

TEITLEBAUM, P. The biology of drive. In G. C. Quarton, T. Melnechuk, & F. O. Schmidt (Eds.), *The neurosciences*. New York: Rockefeller Univ. Press, 1967.

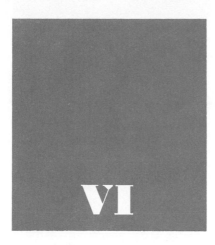

Personality and Social Behavior in Perspective

18

Biological Aspects of Personality

————————

Franco and Tony are identical twins born to a poor young woman in a small Italian town. Aware that she can never provide for both boys, the mother decides to raise one boy herself and let a wealthy American couple adopt the other boy and take him to America. Franco's adopted parents raise him with all the advantages and luxuries of an upper-middle-class home. They are achievement oriented, and push him to excel in everything, providing him with music lessions, tennis lessons, camp, and progressive schools. Tony, however, lives in another world, psychologically as well as geographically. His mother's poverty allows her to give him only the barest essentials and little attention. He shifts for himself most of the time and is given little guidance or coddling. At age 18, both boys are seeking psychological help. A comparison of their personality assessments, based on a series of personality tests and inventories show both boys to be strikingly similar: passive dependent personality, little initiative, low energy level, shy, latent aggression masked by defenses.

Franco has been going through long periods of depression over his repeated academic and social failures. He finds himself psychologically unable to take advantage of the myriad of opportunities at his disposal. His introversion and lack of competitiveness contributed to his series of failures and present state of depression.

Tony is also seeking psychological help because he cannot cope with his problems, but his objective situation is far different from that of his twin brother. Tony blames society for the fact that he has no job and could not keep those that he had in the past. He claims that only influence buys success in Italy, and his poverty has always precluded his becoming anything. While Tony's financial situation was indeed tough, he fails to mention that a number of people were interested in helping him because achievement tests showed him to be a bright boy. A more accurate description of Tony's situation would include the fact that he showed little initiative, was generally passive and withdrawn, and displayed little of the fighting spirit necessary to overcome his background of hardship.

The homes in which these boys grew up were radically different. They were exposed to very different value systems, peers, and social experiences. Although the worlds in which they played out their personalities were radically different, both boys displayed basically the same behavior patterns. Their emotional reactions to conflict, frustration, and discipline were highly similar. Can we conclude that, since their genetic makeup is their only apparent commonality, it must be responsible for their behavioral similarity? This problem, faced by those who wish to answer the question of genetic contributions to personality, is both the most basic and the most elusive question in the science of behavior.

GENETIC FACTORS

The extent to which genetic factors contribute to the development of personality is still an open question. Early theorists sought an answer to the "nature-nurture" question in terms of the extremes; some argued that nature was predominantly responsible for human behavior while others hypothesized a tabula rasa upon which experience could determine the fate of an individual. Such a dichotomous view is currently obsolete. Given that there are both genetic and experiential influences determining behavior, the question has been reformulated to determine the extent to which genetic factors contribute, the manner in which they contribute, and the extent to which they can be mitigated by experience.

Each man inherits a unique body and nervous system through which he interacts with the world. His perception of and response toward the world are to some extent dependent upon his body. Equally unique are each man's experiences. No two people have ever led exactly the same life, and even if they could (which they can not), their perceptions of events would be different since they differ physically. Assuming we hold the factor of experience constant, we still have to deal with biological differences such as, for example, the reactions of the autonomic nervous system. Jack may get the cold shakes when he is under tension to perform well, while Harold under equal pressure may sail through with dry hands, calm heart, and stable knees. To some extent, these differences are not due to psychological variables but physiological ones that are biologically determined.

If we are to unravel the mystery of our behavior, we must seek out clues both in the biological and psychological spheres. In Chapters 1–3, we looked at some of what is known about the relationship between the nervous system and behavior. Now let us turn to the question of how much of behavior is a product of learning, i.e., experience. Is one too shy, timid, and withdrawn because of some unique configuration of his parents' genes, or because one learns to respond to the world that way? Is it possible to inherit emotionality? These are the questions to answer, and the evidence thus far has only been indirect; it has come from research with animals, observations of infant behavior, and studies of twins, the nearest we can come to human genetic similarity.

Animal Studies

Researchers have been able to successfully inbreed strains of animals for various factors of temperament. By mating rats who were rated as highly emotional, offspring were produced who were also highly emotional; this has also been done for low emotionality (Hall, 1941).

Aggressiveness has likewise been inbred in animals (Scott, 1958). It is not known, however, exactly what information the appropriate genes carry. The genetic endowment may not be for emotionality or aggressiveness per se. It may be that the genes merely dictate the functioning of various key organs involved in controlling these factors. For example, the more emotional and active strains of rats were found to have larger adrenal, thyroid, and pituitary glands. The endocrine functioning of these glands is known to play an important role in emotionality. Thus, an animal may inherit specific biological predispositions that cause temperamental characteristics. In other words, there may be inherited differences in thresholds for sensory stimulation, different patterns of autonomic reactivity, differences in size and responsivity of various glands, and a host of other variables that do not predetermine but, rather, predispose an organism to respond in specific ways.

The interaction between heredity predisposition and experience was clearly illustrated in a study with mice. Four different strains of infant mice were chosen for the study. Half of each strain was subjected to a loud noxious auditory stimulus for 4 days. The other half of each group did not experience the noise. All the animals were tested for emotionality in the same and different situations both before the noise experience and after it, when they were 30, 70, and 100 days of age. The effect of the traumatic experience was evident in the increased emotionality of those animals that were subjected to the noise experience. Emotionality was thus influenced by the experience of these infant mice. The second finding of the study, however, showed a genetic component. There were marked differences in emotionality across strains of mice, regardless of whether or not they had experienced the aversive noise (Lindzey, Lykken, & Winston, 1960). This study showed that both genetic and environmental variables can influence emotional responding in animals.

Studies on Child Development

Research in child development has also shown how genetic factors play an important role in human behavior. It has been observed that marked differences in behavior exist from early infancy. Since infants have had a minimum of opportunity for learning, these differences may be seen as behaviors whose roots are primarily genetic. Caution is needed here, however, for the womb does not completely seal the neonate off from all environmental influences.

Newborn babies have been shown to differ in the amount and vigour of motor activity. They are differentially irritable, some crying easily and some not so easily. They cry for different periods of time; some babies cry for long periods at a time, while others cry in short bursts. Babies also differ in perceptual sensitivity, that is, the amount of stimulus change necessary to make them orient to the stimulus. Stimuli frequently used in studies are auditory and visual. With some infants, the slightest change will cause them to turn to the source of the sound or light, while with others a bigger change is necessary to evoke their attention. At the same time, babies cease to respond or pay attention to a stimulus at different rates. This is measured by how long they spend looking at a single object or toy before changing their gaze. There is some indication that this variable may be correlated with the amount of time they later spend engaged in a single activity (Janis, Mahl, Kagan, & Holt, 1969).

Patterns of physiological reactivity to stress, e.g., hunger, are different in different infants. Respiratory, cardiovascular, and gastrointestinal changes are not uniform for all children. Some also show elevations in skin temperature, some vomit, and some develop a skin rash. The stress responses are quite varied. Adults also respond to stress differently, developing stomach ulcers, high blood pressure, skin rashes, or respiratory ailments. Such ailments are said to be psychosomatic and it may be that these differences that babies display in their responses to stress may be related to the particular types of responses, like these psychosomatic ones, which they will later display in their adult lives.

PRENATAL INFLUENCES.   Scientists now realize that a fetus is subject to a great many intrauterine influences. The state of the infant at birth, therefore, is a product of both his genetic makeup and intrauterine environment. The womb is a relatively stable place that is conducive to the growth of the fetus. It is during this period that the organism's capacity to respond to stimulation develops.

The uterus, however, is not sealed off from the outer world. It has been demonstrated that it is possible to prenatally condition a fetus. Using the techniques of classical conditioning, unborn infants were conditioned to respond to a neutral stimulus that was paired with loud noise (Sarason, 1966). It was also discovered that fetuses differed in conditionability, which may be an important factor in personality development.

MATERNAL INFLUENCES.   The emotional states of the mother during pregnancy might also influence her child. When the mother experiences some emotion, autonomic changes occur in her body and cause the release of various substances into her blood, which can, in turn, pass on to the child via the placenta. The exact functional significance of this fact is not known, but it is hard to believe that these conditions would have no effect on the developing organism. Sontag (1944) has observed that body movements of the fetus increase several hundred percent while the mother is under emotional stress. In fact, some researchers believe that prolonged maternal emotional stress may have long range effects on the child (Sontag, 1944). One study showed that children whose mothers were under extreme stress during pregnancy were hyperactive and irritable. They cried a lot, had persistent feeding problems, defecated often, spit up their feedings frequently, and, in general appeared to be neurotic individuals even at birth (Sontag, 1944). Thus, an individual is not safe from stresses even in the womb.

The process of birth itself, as pointed out by Freud, has been considered traumatic. The normal stress of birth is augmented when the birth is premature, and researchers have looked at prematurity and its effect on subsequent development. In one study by Knoblock, Rider, Harper, and Pasamanick (1956), 1000 babies were examined. They found that the lighter the birth weight of the premature baby, the greater the probability of mental or neurological defect, although most of the defects were motor dysfunctions. Another study focusing on personality variables found that premature babies later showed various difficulties such as shyness, awkwardness, poor coordination, speech difficulties, and either hyperactivity or sluggishness (Shirley, 1939). These difficulties, however, may be due to parental overprotection of a child whom they consider to be frail and weak.

All of the above considerations serve to emphasize the fact that the behavior of an infant at birth is a product both of genetic makeup and of prenatal factors such as maternal emotional state, intrauterine conditions, and time of birth. To assume that behavior at birth is purely reflective of hereditary factors would be to ignore the contribution of environmental modifications that begin to take place not at birth, but at conception. If we are to control for these prenatal influences we must study twins.

Twin Studies

An important source of data on genetic contributions to personality comes from studies on siblings and twins. Identical twins are the nearest we can come to genetic identity, since identical twins develop from the same egg. For this reason they are called monozygotic (MZ). Fraternal twins are really siblings born at the same time. They develop from two different eggs, and are called dizygotic (DZ) twins. Identical twins, then, have the same genetic makeup; fraternal twins do not. Both kinds of twins, however, share the same uterine environment.

Twins afford us a near perfect opportunity to investigate genetic influences on behavior. If a given factor is genetic, it must be shown that, as individuals resemble each other more closely genetically, they also are more and more alike on the factor we are correlating. There must be a high correlation between MZ twins, a lesser correlation between DZ twins and siblings, and the least correlation between unrelated pairs of people. Since the turn of the century, various researchers have studied the personalities of siblings and twins; unfortunately, the data have been all but clear-cut.

Pearson (1903) studied the physical and personality traits of a group of siblings and found the correlation for traits like vivacity and temperament to be .52, the same as the correlation for physical traits. He concluded that there is an inheritance of some psychological as well as physical attributes. Other researchers, however, have not been able to find such a correlation for psychological factors. In one study, concordance between identical twins on factors of personality and temperament was no higher than that for fraternal twins (Newman, Freeman, & Holzinger, 1937).

Whether or not one obtains significant results, however, may be a function of those factors one chooses to measure. In a relatively recent study (Gottesman, 1963), two standard personality tests, the Minnesota Multiphasic Personality Inventory (MMPI) and Cattell's Highschool Personality Questionnaire (HSPQ), were given to pairs of fraternal and identical same sex twins. On the MMPI, 5 of the 10 traits or personality predispositions showed heredity played a role. On the other scores, environmental influences were predominant. The HSPQ six scales showed significant contribution by heredity, though, here again, environment predominated. The scales were submissiveness versus dominance, shy versus sensitive versus adventurous, and liking group action versus fastidiously individualistic. Even in these studies using twins, it is very difficult to disregard the factor of environment; and although some of the scales showed a heavy genetic contribution, environmental factors still predominated.

A classic study of the interaction of heredity and personality was done by Shields (1962) who studied twins who were reared apart and twins who were reared together. He used a total of 88 identical twins, half of whom were separated at an early age, and 32 pairs of fraternal twins, 11 of whom were reared apart. Here was a situation in which both genetic and environmental factors could be simultaneously manipulated. Shields found that, regardless of whether or not they were reared together, identical twins were more alike in their responses to a self-rating questionnaire than were fraternal twins. The correlations that Shields obtained are presented in Table 18-1. Identical twins showed higher correlations than fraternal twins on all dimensions, regardless of where they were raised. He also found that on the dimensions of extraversion and neuroticism the identical twins reared apart were more alike than those reared together. This finding seems to bolster the conclusion that, at least for those factors measured, genetic endowment is a larger contributor than social factors.

Although Shields seems to present strong data, there are studies reporting contradictory results, which must be explained. The lack of agreement in

TABLE 18-1   Intraclass Correlation Coefficient[a]

	MZ (together)	MZ (apart)	DZ
Height	.94	.82	.44
Weight	.81	.37	.56
Dominoes	.71	.76	−.05
Mill hill	.74	.74	.38
Comb. I.Q.	.76	.77	.51
Extraversion	.42	.61	−.17
Neuroticism	.38	.53	.11

[a] From Shields (1962).

these studies points to the difficulty of carrying out a carefully controlled study on so complicated a question, and the difficulty in integrating all the studies, which draw their conclusions from the measurement of different behaviors using different tests.

One criticism of twin studies, which presume that concordance between identical twins must be due to their genetic similarity, is that there are also closer environmental conditions between identical twins than between fraternal twins. Identical twins may share a more similar environment, and the world may treat them much more similarly than it treats fraternal twins. The higher concordance in personality factors, then, may not be due to their genetic similarity, but to this increased social similarity of environment and learning. The Shields study controlled for this possibility, however, and yielded results indicating more concordance in MZ twins regardless of environmental similarity.

Another study by Shields produced similar findings. Evaluating psychiatric maladjustment both qualitatively and quantitatively in MZ and DZ twins aged 12 to 15, he found the concordance for identical twins to be twice that for fraternal twins. When he looked at social closeness between the twins, which may indicate that they share similar environments, he found that identical twins were indeed closer, but the degree of social closeness was not related to their concordance on the psychiatric maladjustment evaluation (Shields, 1954).

GENETIC FACTORS IN MENTAL HEALTH.   Work on the origins of mental illness has led to a great deal of speculation that there may be genetic components, because in twin studies the findings have been more positive than for studies of personality characteristics. The mental disorder most often studied is schizophrenia, a psychotic disorder in which there are severe disturbances in thought processes, hallucinations (in some cases), and a loss of contact with reality. These studies have shown that in the general population less than 1% of the people develop schizophrenia. If one takes these schizophrenics and looks at the probability of more schizophenia in their families, the results are striking. As the degree of genetic similarity increases, the probability of schizophrenia increases. The results of one such study are presented in Table 18-2. Where genetic similarity is theoretically the same, as between siblings and fraternal twins, the correlations are equal. The enormously high percentage of identical twins who both develop schizophrenia (66.6–86.2%) when one has it contrasts sharply with the correlation between fraternal twins (3.3–16.7%) if one has it.

Although the incidence of schizophrenia is greatly increased in people

TABLE 18-2   Expectancy of Schizophrenia in
Relatives of Cases of Schizophrenia[a]

Relation to Schizophrenic Patient	Percent Expectancy for Developing Schizophrenia
Step siblings	1.8
Half siblings	7.0–7.6[b]
Full siblings	11.5–14.3
Fraternal twins	3.3–16.7
Identical twins	66.6–86.2
Children	
one parent affected	16.4
both parents affected	68.1
Parents	9.3–10.3
Grandparents	3.9
Grandchildren	4.3
Nephews and nieces	3.9
Unrelated persons	0.85

[a] From Fuller and Thompson (1960).
[b] Range scores are based on several studies.

with a blood tie to a schizophrenic, not all studies show correlations as high as these. The 1971 Special Report on Schizophrenia published by The National Institute of Mental Health reports that the five major studies done since 1960 on schizophrenia in twins have found the rates to vary from 6 to 43% for MZ twins and from 5 to 12% in DZ twins. Although this is less than previously estimated, the report states that confidence in the existence of a predisposing genetic factor has increased.

Psychogenetic studies have also been conducted on the incidence of schizophrenia in children of schizophrenics. The best of these studies controls for environmental factors (growing up in a "disturbed" household). A series of studies was done in Denmark comparing two groups of adopted children (Rosenthal *et al.*, 1971). In one group, the children had been adopted from schizophrenic parents; the other group of children came from normal parents. Both the high risk and normal risk children were placed with apparently stable families, and the groups were matched for sex, age, socioeconomic status of adopting families, and age at adoption. The investigators reported that 14% of the children of schizophrenic mothers experienced psychiatric hospitalization, but only 10% of the normals experienced these psychiatric problems. They also did what was called a "schizophrenic spectrum" diagnosis and found it to apply to 32% of the high risk group compared to 18% of the normal group. Only 4% of the experimental group and none of the normals, however, were considered "clearly schizophrenic." Even when raised in an adopted family then, children of schizophrenic parents have greater vulnerability to future psychiatric disturbance.

One explanation for the mechanism by which schizophrenia is influenced genetically is that the propensity for schizophrenia is transmitted through recessive genes. Another theory more currently accepted is that there is an inherited predisposition to schizophrenia, which causes dysfunction in one or more biochemical system, which, in turn, lowers an individual's resistance to physical and mental disorders.

A great deal of study has centered around psychological events that may predispose an individual to becoming schizophrenic, and it is thought that the breakdown probably occurs as a result of stress. Attempting to integrate these environmental factors with possible genetic ones, Meehl (1962) has suggested that there may be a biological deficit, which he calls schizotaxia, underlying schizophrenia. This deficit, however, only leads to schizophrenia under certain environmental and psychological conditions. If the social-psychological setting is not destructive, schizophrenia does not develop. For example, Meehl points out that one may inherit other deciding factors, such as a tolerance for stress, which interact with schizotaxia and environment. In such a case, the parents of a schizophrenic child who are not diagnosed as schizophrenic might well show thought disorders. In Meehl's terms, these parents may be schizotaxic, but due to favorable environmental conditions they never developed full blown schizophrenia.

PERSONALITY CORRELATES OF BODY TYPE

So far we have been looking at genetic contributions to the internal state of the person, but obviously the most striking characteristics we inherit are external physical ones, such as height, physique, eye and hair color, and all the subleties that give us our unique appearance. Could it be that the major clues to personality lie right before our eyes in a person's appearance? Is there any basis for our cliches of the fat jovial person and the thin high-strung one?

The suspicion that body characteristics are correlated with personality is an old one. Hippocrates (460–377 BC) thought that humors accounted for one's personality, with a predominance of one humor determining temperament. Black bile made one melancholic and depressed, yellow bile led to irritability and short temper, excess of blood made one cheerful and sanguine, and phlegm was responsible for a phlegmatic, passive, slow person. Hippocrates was looking at bile for an easy explanation. Cesare Lombroso (1836–1909) sought to establish that one could pick out a criminal type by his slanting forehead, flat nose, and large jaw. This kind of explanation has never been supported by experimental verification.

The first real attempt to offer an all inclusive system of personality based on physical type was done by Kretchmer (1925), a German psychiatrist of the nineteenth century. He divided people into three basic types: pyknic, or short and fat; athletic, the sinewy, muscular type; and asthenic; tall and thin (Figure 18-1). Based on his clinical observations, Kretchmer concluded that pyknics are predominantly extroverted, outgoing, and sociable, and asthenics are introverted, introspective, and withdrawn. He thought athletics were aggressive, active people. Although Kretchmer's work is interesting, there are many problems with his data and approach, not the least of which is that it has not stood the test of experimental verification. Burchard (1936) attempted to follow Kretchmer's classification, but found no support for his conclusions. Of the pyknic, for example, he found that 50% were extroverts and 30% were introverts.

The person who has done the most to advance this theory of personality based on body type was Sheldon (1942) whose classifications were based on

FIGURE 18-1   The different kinds of body types commonly observed.

those of Kretchmer. Sheldon, however, included typologies of the internal organs in his classification. Sheldon divided people into endomorphs, mesomorphs, and ectomorphs. The endomorph is soft and round, with overdeveloped digestive viscera, his personality is relaxed, and he loves to eat; he is viscerotonic. The mesomorph is muscular, rectangular, and strong and his behavior is accordingly energetic and assertive; he is somatotonic. The ectomorph, with a long, fragile, body, a sensitive nervous system, and a large brain is cerebrototonic; he is restrained, fearful, introverted, and artistic. Kretchmer and Sheldon have similarly paired types of personalities, and, oddly enough, these types follow our stereotypes in daily life.

Experimentation has been no kinder to Sheldon than Kretchmer, though, for neither has had his theories validated (Tyler, 1956). There are a lot of problems with these attempts to correlate physique and personality. To start with, there is often disagreement about how a particular individual should be characterized. Sheldon devised a kind of rating scale, so that each person would receive a score on each of the dimensions, with one dimension predominating. When judgments are subjective, however, there is bound to be disagreement. Another problem is that people may change their physique with changes in diet, so that to some extent we may be classifying nutrition rather than inherent build.

The underlying assumption of these theories is that one's muscular and visceral makeup is biologically correlated with behavior. To the extent that both behavior and physique are partially dependent on hormonal functioning, this may be true. The hormones influencing each of these realms, however, must be either the same or related to each other. Unfortunately, we do not know enough about hormonal influences on behavior to make a judgment at this point. Although these theories have not fared well experimentally, it may be that our ignorance of biochemical factors in behavior has caused us to look at the wrong behavioral variables. Perhaps if we were to make our selection of behavioral traits based on our knowledge of hormonal functioning, this approach to personality based on physical characteristics would prove more fruitful.

SOCIAL-EXPERIENTIAL INFLUENCES

The existential view of life is that we never are, but are always becoming. Life is a process of change. The world is constantly impinging upon us and our responses to it determine what we are. Our interaction with the world really begins before birth, but social interaction begins when we are born. Whatever potential and propensities we are born with are played out in a social context. The world not only provides a stage on which we behave, but it actively changes our behavior. We learn to interpret events in light of past events and modify our behavior in accordance with learned consequences. The first social experiences of a child are in the context of his home. Almost all personality theorists have attributed great importance to the parent-child interaction, especially between mother and child. Presumably, a child's first experiences of the world will provide the early foundation upon which other experience will build. Freud was perhaps the greatest proponent of the view that early experiences are crucial determinants of the future. How the child will view the world will depend to some extent on how the world is portrayed to him as a child.

In looking at social interaction in the home, many researchers have isolated the acceptance-rejection dimension as the most important one. It is considered by some to be the fundamental dynamic from which all other aspects of the parent-child relation derive (Baldwin, Kallhorn, & Breese, 1945). However, exactly what aspect of this factor is important is still unclear. Naturally, if a child is accepted and loved, he will perceive the world as an accepting and friendly place; conversely, if he is resented or rejected by his parents, the world looks to be hostile.

But few parents fit these extreme attitudes. Most parents love their children and their acceptance or rejection is toward the child's behavior and not the child himself. In this situation, the relevant aspect may be the parent's consistency in his response to the child's behavior. If he is warm and loving on Mondays and harsh and rejecting on Tuesdays, the child is faced with an unpredictable authority figure who sometimes punishes and sometimes rewards him for the same action. The world may seem arbitrary to him, and he may feel that he has little control over what happens to him. The appropriateness of the parents' behavior is related to this question of consistency. If a child is always punished for transgressing a rule, and is always rewarded for good behavior, he comes to see that he can control events, and he learns to modify his behavior in accordance with what is consistently expected of him. The world is seen as a fairly stable place, and the child is able to clearly perceive his position in it.

The type of punishment parents use to control a child's behavior is also thought to influence his development. Studies have shown that when children are disciplined by psychological techniques, such as temporary withdrawal of affection and reasoning with the child, the children develop very strong consciences and tend to internally regulate their own behavior. Physical punishment or reward, however, tends to produce children who are very aggressive and who have poorly internalized consciences (Brown, 1965). Perhaps the effect of physical punishment is to teach the child that the world is a very hostile place, and his response is to lash out aggressively against it; whereas psychological control teaches the child that the effects of antisocial acts are themselves antisocial, and, if he is to receive the warmth and support that he craves, he must use these same techniques to control himself. A child imitates his parents. If his parents are aggressive toward him, chances are the child will aggress also. But if the parents use reasoning, they teach reasoning.

There are various stages in the socialization of a child, and each of these stages from infancy to early childhood has been cited as important in child development. Parents are constantly wondering if children are best breast fed or bottle fed, fed when they cry or fed on schedules, punished for toilet accidents or tolerated, and so on. Since these are the child's first encounters with discipline and frustration, one might think that the technique used would be of some importance. Thus far, however, there is little evidence that particular techniques have any relation to future adjustment or personality.

Sewell (1952) looked at five variables and attempted a correlation with personality: bottle versus breast fed, regular versus demand feeding schedules, abrupt versus gradual weaning, early versus late toilet training, and punishment versus permissiveness toward toilet accidents. He found that none of these had any relation to later personality and adjustment.

In addition to being sources of discipline and support, parents are also models for their children. Children imitate and introspect on their parents' behavior. The wide differences we see in children from different social classes is a result of this imitation and learning. Freud made the child's identification with his parents a cornerstone of psychoanalytic theory. Identification was supposed to be the product of the resolution of the Oedipus conflict. Even those who do not espouse the analytic theory emphasize the importance of the child's identification with his parents and his internalization of the parents' code of conduct. The reason we do not have to keep asking our parents what is right and wrong is that we have come to learn guidelines for our behavior, and the roots of these guidelines lie to a large extent in our early socialization.

SUMMARY

This chapter has examined some of the approaches to the question of how our biological makeup determines our personality. Animal studies have shown us that some aspects of behavior are genetic and can be inbred, e.g., aggression and emotionality. If one looks at infants, even at an early age, there are evident differences in their behavior such as activity level, perceptual sensitivity, and reactivity to stress. Even within their limited behavioral repertoire, infants display detectable differences. Some of these differences, however, may not be due to genetics. Prenatal influences have been found to exert an effect on infant behavior both before and after birth.

The largest body of information on the question of genetic contribution to personality comes from studies of individuals with identical genetic makeup, i.e., identical twins. Unfortunately, the results of these studies have been far from unequivocal. The data seem to be stronger when studying the incidence of behavioral abnormality such as schizophrenia than when looking at simple personality characteristics. We can predict concordance between twins better with respect to schizophrenia, for example, than shyness. This discrepancy, however, may reflect our lack of sophistication in the measurement of personality.

Theories relating one's personality to one's body type have not found much experimental support, although maybe our limited knowledge of biochemical factors in behavior causes to study the wrong behavioral variables.

No matter what one's genetic makeup may be, experience and learning will mold and shape the display of behavioral tendencies. Early experiences usually revolve around the parents; therefore, our concluding observations have revolved around the early socialization of the child. It is during this formative period that innate predispositions receive their first modification.

We are a long way from proving that "anatomy is destiny," but we are also far from the cry that experience is all. If the evidence for genetic contributions to personality seems meager, it may be because we have not yet learned the proper questions to ask or how to ask them.

SUGGESTED READINGS

EYSENCK, H. J. *The biological basis of personality.* Springfield, Illinois: Thomas, 1967.

SCOTT, J. P. *Aggression.* Chicago: Univ. of Chicago Press, 1958.

SHIELDS, J. *Monozygotic twins.* London & New York: Oxford Univ. Press, 1962.

19

Theory and Measurement in Personality

———————

You are dead. Your waxlike figure lies in a wooden casket, and the stench of death is overcome by the musk of flowers. Everyone walks by your body, tears rushing down their faces, and gasps of disbelief and sorrow fill the room. You were such a fantastic person, so sensitive and alive. They should have made an effort to understand, because you were so right. The burden of guilt for your death falls so heavily on their shoulders, and their eulogies will never lift that weight. Now you've shown them how unjustly they ignored your beauty and scoffed at your idealism. Now they are robbed of you, and they will know through pain all that you were.

Have frustration, alienation. and anger never found you reveling in that fantasy? Have you ever worried about your sanity when you daydream like that? Almost everyone sometimes fantasizes his own death, what the world will do, and the grief it will bring. Thoughts like these are rarely the product of craziness; more often they are the intrusion of our needs for love, understanding, and importance. Dreams and fantasies are as much a part of our personality as the way we interact with our conscious world. Freud considered the material of such dreams even more significant indicators of our psyche than our overt behavior. Such a fantasy would be laden with symbolic images in the Freudian schema, from its general theme (aggression?) to its specific contents. (Were those white lilies covering the casket, and did you say you do not remember having any arms? Could your armless condition be a symbol of your helplessness?)

This chapter deals with some of the major approaches to the study of personality, from psychodynamic theories such as Freud's, to learning theories such as that of Dollard and Miller (1950). These theories are concerned with the ways behavior, both dreams and actions, can be explained. The second part of this chapter exposes the problems of measuring of personality and uncovering and analyzing its structure.

FREUD AND THE PSYCHOANALYTIC APPROACH

Sigmund Freud has had such an overwhelming impact on twentieth-century thought that his name and many of his ideas have become household words. His concept of the unconscious directly stimulated the growth of surrealism in literature and painting, where his influence is still felt. By suggesting that man had a rich and intricate inner life in his subconscious, Freud opened a completely new avenue of approach to the mysteries of human behavior. Seemingly irrational and unexplainable events now could be interpreted in light of a theory. Indeed, one of the reasons why Freud's theory of personality is so seductive is that its assumptions explain a great deal about behavior.

Freud was a practicing Viennese psychiatrist, and his theory was derived from clinical observations. Over the roughly two decades from the publication of his first book *The interpretation of dreams* in 1900 to his death in 1939, Freud continued to revise his theoretical formulations, especially his ideas on the ego. Since his death, psychoanalytic theory has come under even more revision by his followers. The splinter groups, which have grown as offshoots of analytic theory, are only partially representative of Freud's analytic theory. Therefore, for a true understanding of analytic theory, we must look at Freud's initial principles directly.

Levels of Consciousness: Conscious, Preconscious, Unconscious

The concept that there are different levels of consciousness is an essential part of Freudian theory (Figure 19-1). In dealing with his patients, Freud was struck by the fact that there were some events of the past that his patients were able to recall very clearly; there were others that they could recall by making a concerted effort to do so, and there were still other things that they appeared to have no remembrance of whatever. In the course of analysis, this later category of events appeared to be most closely associated with the patient's current problems. From his observations, Freud attempted to explain

FIGURE 19-1   A pictorial representation of Freud's ideas on the levels of consciousness.

this phenomenon by postulating that there are different levels of consciousness, and that one need not be consciously aware of events of the past for these events to influence behavior.

There is a Freudian analogy between personality and levels of an iceberg. There is an upper layer, which we can see, a middle layer just beneath the surface, and a deep layer, which supports the iceberg and, indeed, forms the largest part of it. Those events of which we are aware or can recall with clarity are part of the conscious level of personality. Most of the details of daily living fall into this category, as well as many nonthreatening or non-anxiety-producing memories. Just beneath this conscious level is the preconscious. Included in this category are those events that we cannot recall immediately, but given some concentration they come to mind. Where one went to dinner last Saturday night might fall into this classification. It is the third level of consciousness, the unconscious, that is most important in the Freudian analysis of personality. Events residing in the unconscious are buried from awareness. It takes training to uncover those events buried in this deepest psychic layer. The unconscious is the storehouse of traumatic childhood events, inherited predispositions, and repressed conflicts. The material in the unconscious is not forgotten or dormant. It has been repressed because of its anxiety-producing nature, but its influence on behavior is all-pervasive. The unconscious constitutes personality. Much of our behavior is acting out our unconscious fantasies, motivations, and conflicts. Our decisions as to our occupation, whom we marry, and what we like are reflections of the unconscious forces shaping our behavior. Unconscious processes intrude into our lives in such seemingly irrational events as slips of the tongue, "forgotten" appointments, and "misplaced" items. Consciously we are not aware of any meaning in these trivialities, but actually such events are not arbitrary. The whole aim of psychoanalysis is to uncover these powerful influences on our behavior and to bring these motivations and related events to conscious awareness.

Id, Ego, and Superego

In addition to his analysis of personality into levels of consciousness, Freud proposed that the structure of the personality be divided into three units. He called these units the id, the ego, and the superego (Figure 19-2). All of our psychic life can be thought of as the mutual interactions of these three parts. However, one should not think of the id, ego, and superego as parts in the sense of parts of a machine, but rather as hypothetical structures, ways of conceptualizing dimensions of influence. These three aspects of the personality often clash with each other and the ensuing conflict is of great psychological importance. In his later writings, Freud placed greater emphasis on these intrapsychic conflicts and the id, ego, and superego forces than he did on the earlier concept of the importance of levels of consciousness.

Id.   Freud believed instinctual forces played an important role in behavior. Freud called the seat of these instinctual forces the id. The id is the realm from which all psychological energy is derived. Freud called life energy the

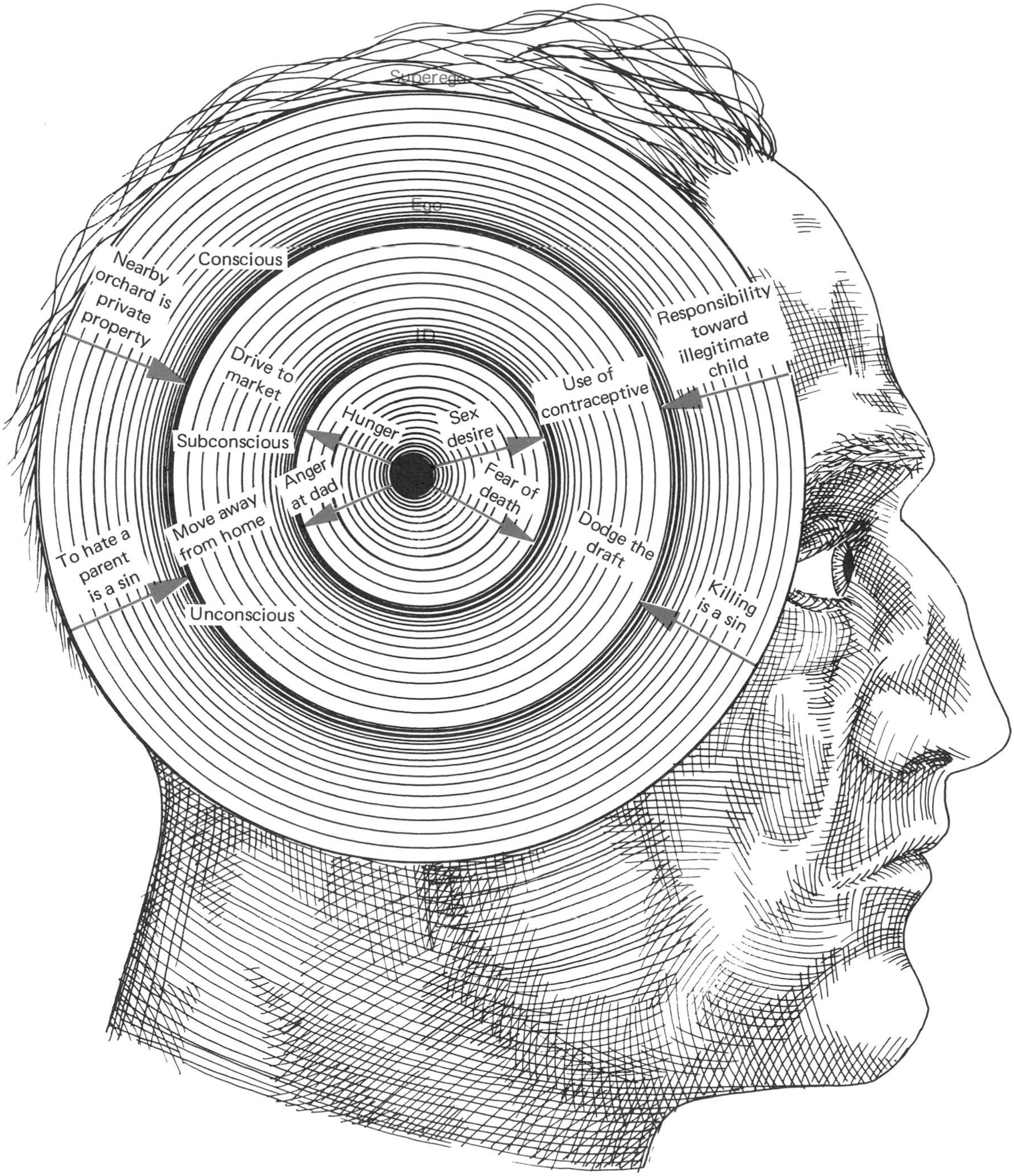

FIGURE 19-2   Freud's view of the psychodynamic process in man. The id, ego, and superego are in a constant struggle for control.

libido. The basic primary impulses of the id, sexual and aggressive in nature, are always striving for gratification. When one follows the directives of the id, this tension for gratification is reduced, and the discharge is pleasurable. It is in this sense that the id is said to follow the pleasure principle. The impulses of the id, which push for immediate gratification, are not subject to influence from the reality of the outside world. Freud called this kind of thought primary process because it occurs developmentally earlier than realistic, logical thought or secondary process thinking. Our fantasies and dreams are sometimes characterized by primary process when they disregard reality and are guided by wish-fulfillment. The impulse of the id that Freud considered most important in personality is the sexual impulse. It was Freud's overriding emphasis on sex that precipitated the break between him and many of his followers. Freud saw a great deal of symbolic sexual imagery in the dreams of many of his patients: elongated objects as penes, objects with orifices as vaginas, round objects with protuberances as the breast. His method of dream analysis was based on his interpretation of imagery, which he considered to be symbolic of repressed underlying conflict within a personality.

Freud considered the elaboration of sexuality to be of such importance in personality development that he devoted much of his writings to this topic. He considered sexuality to unfold in various psychosexual stages which he called oral, anal, phallic, and genital (see Chapter 4).

EGO.   The id, then, was Freud's formulation of the "little savage" within man, his most primitive basic self. Unfortunately for man, however, the world is not the Garden of Eden. He must deal with the restrictions of reality. The system of the personality that must accommodate to the world Freud called the ego. The ego is responsive to external reality demands; it operates on the reality principle. All of the impulses of the id cannot be satisfied; some must be denied, some delayed, and some modified. The ego is the arbiter of these demands. The id operates by the primary process; the ego operates by the secondary process. The ego must learn in the course of its development how to realistically satisfy the demands of the id, while at the same time satisfying the restrictions of the superego or internalized conscience, the third part of the personality. Psychoanalytic theorists have developed various techniques for assessing the strength of the ego. Ego strength is thought to vary among individuals, even from earliest infancy.

SUPEREGO.   We have now accounted for the impulsive and reasonable sides of man. But there is a third side, man's moral nature, the superego. The superego develops from the interactions between child and parents. It has both a positive and negative aspect, the ego ideal and conscience, respectively. As a child's behavior comes under the social control of his parents, the child is rewarded for "good" behavior, that is, behavior in accordance with their standards, and punished for "bad" behavior. To win parental approval and avoid punishment, the child conforms to these standards. Gradually, these values come to be internalized by the child, the internalized inhibitions becoming the conscience. Those values that violate the dictates of conscience produce guilt, and conversely, living up to the ego ideal engenders feelings of pride. Controls that were once external become powerful internal controls of behavior. The superego is constantly exerting pressure on the ego to inhibit the impulsive demands of the id that violate its code. The ego, then, must be a buffer between these two powerful opposing forces. One of the mechanisms by which the ego deals with the conflicts within a personality is through defense mechanisms. It must defend itself against the constant intrapsychic war that is raised within the systems of personality.

THE MECHANISMS OF DEFENSE

The opposing demands of the systems of the personality are a source of anxiety and conflict. The id impetuously demands gratification, while the superego, formed by the prohibitions of society, violently opposes instinctual gratification. This conflict generates anxiety, of which there are three kinds: moral anxiety, neurotic anxiety, and reality anxiety. Moral anxiety is the product of the guilt induced by the conscience over immoral acts or thoughts. Neurotic anxiety arises from a fear that the id will become all powerful in the personality and desires will get out of hand. Reality anxiety is a fear of real dangers in the outside world. Not all anxiety, then, is due to intrapsychic conflict, and not all anxiety must be dealt with surreptitiously. Reality anxiety can be dealt with directly, by allaying the source of fear. The anxiety from intrapsychic conflict, however, is less easily dealt with, and from it Freudians posed the mechanisms of defense.

Repression

The major defense mechanism is repression. In repression, material that is threatening to the ego is denied conscious awareness. Buried in the unconscious, it still influences behavior but the ego is saved from the tremendous conflict that its conscious awareness would elicit. Deep seated aggression, in the form of murderous impulses, for example, would elicit overpowering guilt if they were recognized, since such feelings and impulses especially toward key persons such as one's parents are socially forbidden. The ego may deal with such hatred by simply denying it access to conscious awareness. The individual is unaware of repressed material, but he is not free of its influence. The hostile impulses may, if the repression fails, eventually find some means of distorted expression in the person's behavior, but the cause of the behavior will remain hidden to his conscious self.

Projection

In projection, an unacceptable characteristic or feeling is attributed to another person, when, in fact, it belongs to the individual himself. Again, hostility is a good example. Because you cannot acknowledge that you hate the football coach's guts, you say that he hates you. Projection permits an indirect expression of the forbidden impulse because it is out in the open, while at the same time it is "safe," since the subject is not the self but another person.

Reaction Formation

Another way of dealing with a forbidden feeling or impulse is by consciously acknowledging it as its opposite. This mechanism is called reaction formation, and it is accompanied by repression of the forbidden tendency. A person who is anxious about his sexuality and strong sexual desires may act very prudish and asexual. A mother who is strongly resentful of her child and who feels very hostile toward him may act overly solicitous and loving. In this way, the forbidden feeling is denied expression and anxiety is lessened. Behaviors based on reaction formation tend to be rigid and overexaggerated, and it is in this way that we can see through their veneer of sincerity. One must realize, however, that the person is unaware of his hypocrisy. In fact, this is precisely why the defense is effective.

Regression

Regression is a process in which a person behaves in ways which are considered earlier, more primitive patterns of responding. Faced with a situation of stress, for example, a person's rational, mature behavior may break down and he may begin to act in a childlike manner. He may "not care about the facts," throw a temper tantrum, sulk, want to be held, and so forth. He may even engage in those activities that he enjoyed as a child. By going backward to an earlier stage, the person is attempting to gain security in ways that once worked for him.

A classic study of regression was done with children (Barker, Dembo, & Lewin, 1941). The researchers presented children with a set of fascinating toys and allowed the children to become absorbed in playing with them. While the children were enjoying the toys, the experimenters took some of the essential parts of the toys away from them, and observed their response to this frustrating situation. According to the authors, many of the children displayed regressive behavior, which was a year or more immature than their behavior in the nonfrustrating play situation. The child lurks in all of us, and behaviors that were once gratifying are hard to erase completely from one's repertoire of behavioral responses.

Intellectualization

A defense mechanism, which in some sense goes in the opposite direction of regression is intellectualization. Instead of allowing himself to react to anxiety, the individual attempts to overcome it by freely acknowledging the source of conflict, analyzing it in detail, and acting in a "rational" fashion. Although the person deals with it in this intellectual way, he never truly acknowledges the threatening conflict emotionally or at a gut level. He has so completely objectified the situation that it almost stands apart from himself. He wards off anxiety by making it an intellectual exercise, and never permits the truth of the situation to really seep into his skin and affect his emotions. This is one of the problems frequently encountered during the course of psychoanalysis. As the person learns more and more about the source of his problems, he may be very articulate about them, but he defends himself against anxiety by reducing his conflict to intellectual, emotionally empty terms. We may often marvel at friends who are able to discuss intimate details of their problems with such apparent ease, but perhaps the reason they do so is because they have effectively intellectualized their problems sufficiently to negate threat.

Rationalization

Another of the intellectual gyrations of defense is rationalization. In rationalization a person attempts to explain his behavior by offering a reason for it that is not completely valid. Usually the person has acted impulsively or perhaps immorally, and, rather than admit the true motivation for his behavior, even to himself, he conjures up some acceptable, reasonable explanation. The person may know that he is hunting for a justification for his behavior, but he may be completely unaware of his true motive. Rationalization is usually used to protect self-esteem.

Sublimation

Freud considered sublimation to be the highest form of defense. Because sexual impulses are constantly pressing for gratification in a world not amenable to constant sexual activity, Freud proposed that sexual energy can be dissipated if the energy is displaced or redirected onto other than sexual objects. He felt that many activities of man such as scientific and artistic achievement were, in part at least, attempts to sublimate sexual impulses into acceptable channels. Since Freud, the concept of sublimation has been broadened to include any impulse that is satisfied by substituting an acceptable object or activity for an unacceptable one. Hence, aggression may be vented through social criticism, competition, or athletics. An important product of this defense is that it effectively discharges the redirected energy, but there is some controversy among clinicians over whether or not sublimation is truly effective.

We have by no means exhaustively covered all of the possible mechanisms of defense, nor should one get the impression that these defenses are mutually exclusive. Individuals use many of the defenses of the ego, often simultaneously. According to the psychoanalytic position, most personalities function successfully because of these defense mechanisms. The pathological personality is seen as one in which the defense mechanisms have broken down and are no longer able to protect the ego from massive anxiety and conflict. Far from being destructive forces, then, the defense mechanisms are protective. The particular defense mechanisms chosen by any given individual is thought to be influenced by his previous learning experience. Different socioeconomic classes tend to use different patterns of defense, just as different behaviors are tolerated within various groups. One must remember that defenses are maintained because they are reinforced, i.e., they work. By successfully insulating the person from sources of anxiety or ameliorating that anxiety, these defenses tend to become resistant to change.

Freudian View of Man

To the Victorian society that visualized man as a rational and unemotional being, Freud's creature of libidinous and aggressive impulses and raging conflicts was a monster. Over the decades, his ideas have so filtered through society that it is hard for us to appreciate how shocking and revolutionary his view of man was. The Freudian approach to personality is an intrapsychic one. External events and particular situations play less of a role in determining behavior than do internal forces. Unconscious motives, instinctual drives, and anxiety govern behavior at a level beyond awareness. Behavior is just an outward manifestation of powerful inward events. No behavior is arbitrary to the Freudian.

The theory postulates a motivational determinism for all behavior. Intrapsychic causes and functions can be found for even the most trivial events. Slips of the tongue reflect repressed or suppressed thoughts, forgotten appointments or facts are deliberate attempts at denial, and even our doodling on notebooks may contain latent sexual symbols. The motivational chain to the initial source of a behavior may be circuitous and hidden in distortion, but to the Freudian it is there.

The roots of many unconscious motives lie in the psychosexual development of early childhood when many of the unconscious motives that are later to shape behavior are laid out. Freud placed heavy emphasis on early experience in laying the foundation of development. Certain of man's conflicts are universal ones against which all men struggle, and certain conflicts belong to each man alone. It is the state of internal conflict itself which all men share.

At the time that Freud developed his theory, little was known about learning principles (other than those of association). Since then, a whole discipline has developed around the principles governing learning behavior. Many of Freud's ideas are not incompatible with learning theory. In fact, the learning theorists' approach to personality can be integrated with Freud's giant theory of man.

THE LEARNING THEORY APPROACH

In order to make sense of the complexities of behavior, Freud looked inside the individual in his attempt to find the factors controlling personality. As psychologists began to discover the extent to which behavior is governed by external factors, experience, and learning, some theorists began to cast aspersions on the Freudian framework, alleging that it was no longer necessary to appeal to vague concepts, such as libidinal energy, id, ego, and superego. Personality is behavior, and, as behavior, it is subject to the laws of learning.

Freudianism and behavior theory became antagonistic, but this potentially explosive debate was defused by two theorists who offered one of the first attempts to reconcile Freudian analytic concepts with a learning theory approach. Dollard and Miller's (1950) publication of *Personality and psychotherapy* exposed the falsity of the assumption that Freudianism and behavior theory were of necessity antithetical. The personality theory of Dollard and Miller will be considered as an example of the way in which a learning theorist approaches the study of personality. Not all learning theorists have felt the necessity of integrating behavior principles with Freudian dynamics. Some have gone on to offer theories of personality that stand autonomously. Although theorists may differ in what experiential factors they choose to emphasize, the basic approach of all learning theorists is to look at personality as a learned phenomenon in a stimulus-response framework; it is to this extent that they are all comparable.

Dollard and Miller

Dollard and Miller effected a reconciliation between psychoanalytic concepts and behavior theory, but unlike Freud who based his theory on a strong biological base, i.e., the id instincts, these two theorists based their theory on the assumption that behavior is learned. There are four key concepts in the Dollard and Miller formulation: drive, cue, response, and reinforcement.

Drive is motivation; it is anything that impels action. Any strong stimulus, whether external or internal, may impel action, and may therefore function as drive. Hunger pangs are an example of such an internal stimulus, and the sight of a beautiful and approachable girl may be an example of an external stimulus. The stronger the stimulus, naturally, the stronger its drive function. Some drives are innate and some are learned. The innate basic drives and their stimulus counterparts, i.e., hunger, thirst, pain, fatigue, and sex, are presumably the basic motivations; they are called primary drives. For modern man in an affluent society, however, primary drives are easily satisfied. It is the operation of secondary or learned drives that most often motivates our behavior. Learned drives are acquired on the basis of primary drives and are an elaboration of them. An example of a secondary drive is fear.

One comes to fear certain objects or situations because they have been associated in the past with pain or extreme unpleasantness. An example of conditioning fear is the child who has some physical disorder and must receive painful weekly injections from a doctor. After a few visits, the doctor who was initially a neutral, nonthreatening person to the child now evokes a fear response from him. Simply the sight of the man or even the mention of his name will elicit fright. We know that fear is a drive because it can motivate behavior, and, since its reduction is reinforcing, the lessening of fear can act as a reinforcer for learning new responses. In our example, the child may devise devious ways of making himself inaccessible when it comes time to go to the doctor, and, if he is successful, the ensuing reduction of fear will reinforce these strategies. Dollard and Miller's concept of drive as a significant variable in behavior is in some ways much like the Freudian notion of innate impulses which direct behavior. These later theorists elaborated upon Freud in recognizing that some drives (or impulses) are learned, but they also acknowledged the importance of drives in motivating behavior.

The second key concept of the learning theory approach is cue. Cues are stimuli that give information about the how, when, and where of a response. Drive impels actions; cue tells you when to respond, where to respond, and which response to make. Any stimulus can serve as a cue, and it can be in any sensory mode. One of the most hideous cues known to modern man is the sound of his alarm clock in the morning. It delivers a great deal of unwanted information about where, when, and which response to make. Cues direct behavior. Many responses are acceptable in some situations and not in others; sex is fine in private but prohibited in the street. Stimuli that serve as cues for the individual enable him to make this kind of discrimination.

A strong stimulus may serve as drive; thus, stimuli can serve the dual function of being both drive and cue, if they both motivate and direct our behavior. The alarm clock in our example certainly impels us to action, and, just as unfortunately, it directs our behavior as well.

The concept of response is self-explanatory. Dollard and Miller drew upon the Hullian concept of habit hierarchy in their assertion that certain responses are more likely to occur in certain situations than are other responses. By rewarding certain responses, we are changing this hierarchy of responses.

The satisfaction of any drive, primary or secondary, is rewarding. Dollard and Miller's formulation of the drive-reducing property of reinforcement is very similar to Freud's concept of the pleasure principle. Both theories view the individual as seeking a reduction of tension set up by drives. Just as there are primary and learned drives, there are learned reinforcements. Pieces of engraved colored paper have nothing inherently rewarding about them. It is only through learning that money can act as a powerful reinforcer.

Like Freud, Dollard and Miller emphasize conflict and anxiety especially in neurotic behavior. The tendency to approach and the tendency to avoid a certain situation may on occasion be equally strong, and it is here that maximum conflict ensues. The factors contributing to the desire to engage in or avoid a given behavior may be learned. Our desire for money, for example, is learned. Our abhorence of the types of things we must do to make a lot of money is also learned. An individual may find himself in the situation of both wanting wealth (approach) and despising what he must do for it (avoidance). He finds himself in a situation of terrible conflict and anxiety. Whereas Freud concentrated on the internal clash of id and superego as the precursors of conflict, Dollard and Miller look to external experiential factors. But the learning theorists formulation can just as easily be applied to innate impulses (id) and learned prohibitions (superego). It is a very flexible theory.

Although they concentrate on learned behavior, Dollard and Miller accept unconscious factors in behavior. They have elaborated Freud's concept of unconscious repression in terms of reinforcement theory. For example, a child is punished when he behaves aggressively toward his parents. Therefore, the child soon comes to associate aggression, or even the thought of aggression, with punishment. In order to avoid punishment and the anxiety associated with it, the child behaves more docily. But, in the future, when the child sees himself begin to aggress or wish to aggress against another, he will become anxious. To forestall this anxiety, he soon learns not to even think about aggressive incidents. This "not-thinking" can be thought of as parallel to Freud's phenomenon of repression, except that, in the Freudian scheme, repressed thoughts still influence behavior, though in a disguised form. The behaviorists "not-thinking" removes both the thought and its influence on behavior.

The learning theory approach can be applied to many more Freudian concepts. Phobias, for example, can be explained on the basis of a neutral stimulus being paired with a feared or painful stimulus. Eventually the person will learn to avoid the previously neutral stimulus, because it now evokes the anxiety that was once reserved for the feared object itself. It is in this way that symptoms are learned and maintained through reinforcement. The contributions of Dollard and Miller are not confined to their success at reconciling Freudianism and behaviorism. Their emphasis on the importance of stimulus variables and reinforcement contingencies in the development and maintenance of personality greatly enriched our thinking and lessened the mysteries surrounding personality and human behavior.

TRAIT THEORIES

When we meet a person for the first time, we gain a certain impression of him, and we are likely in the future to describe him in terms of various physical and personal characteristics. We may describe his personality as affable or nasty, outgoing or withdrawn, warm or aloof. We try to capture the essence of one another by applying labels to various aspects of personality. One way in which we can approach the analysis of personality is to systematically study the individual characteristics comprising a personality. Instead of delving deep into the recesses of the psyche, as do the Freudians, or concentrating on stimulus characteristics and experiential factors, as do the learning theorists, we can simply describe an individual in the here and now. We can describe the various dimensions of his personality in terms of certain characteristics called traits.

Traits are behaviors or characteristics that distinguish two or more people from each other and are relatively enduring. The list of traits by which we can describe people is practically limitless. The aim of the trait theorist, therefore, is to reduce this superfluity of traits down to their common factors or common denominators. His aim is to emerge with a series of dimensions on which all individuals can be characterized, and which will include all the significant factors in personality. The trait theorist assumes that behavior is guided by broad traits or dispositions that manifest themselves under many different situations. Behavior then is a function of a certain number of predispositions operative under many different kinds of situations. The theorist's task is to identify each person's position on these personality dimensions by comparing him with others. Therefore, the trait theorist administers a wide variety of personality tests to many individuals and attempts to extract from this data the basic traits that form the personality.

The Methodology of Trait Theory

An essential component of trait theory is its quantitative methodology. This methodology is called psychometric because it aims to quantify individual psychological differences. One should remember that these psychometric tests have certain limitations; we can only get out of them what we put into them. It is decided beforehand which dimensions are considered significant, and test questions, which are operationally defined as measurements of these characteristics, are then devised. There is no certainty that our questions do, in fact, tap those characteristics we say they do. For instance, in asking a subject if he enjoys going to parties, it is only our assumption and not an established fact that an affirmative answer belies the trait of sociability. In addition, it is very difficult to be sure that we have measured all significant factors, since, in order for a personality factor to emerge from our battery of tests as a generalized trait, we must have programmed it into the profile. Thus, to a certain extent our conclusions are a function of our semantics and previous assumptions. In taking this approach, we are inferring underlying traits from behavior. We assume that the way in which an individual answers a question about himself is an indicator of a certain predisposition. We are not interested in the subject's test responses per se, but only in the traits they presumably reveal. His test behavior is used as an indicator of general behavior outside of the test situation.

Kinds of Traits

A trait is not an entity; it is an abstraction, a construct. We can divide traits into many different kinds according to our interests. For example, we can differentiate between physical and mental traits, individual and universal traits, and ability and preference traits. The way we choose to cluster them is our own decision. All theorists have specified kinds of traits.

Gordon Allport, a leading proponent of trait theory, has differentiated three kinds of traits: cardinal, central, and secondary. Allport (1937) believes that people have generalized dispositions that guide most of their behavior. He calls this disposition a cardinal trait. A woman who organizes her whole life around home activities and family may have a cardinal trait of domesticity. The woman who goes on for a professional degree and whose source of primary satisfaction is her work may have a cardinal trait of achievement. Central traits are less pervasive than cardinal traits, although they too influence a wide variety of behavior. Those traits that are more situation-specific and less consistently present Allport calls secondary traits. Allport classifies traits according to the generality of their influence.

Raymond B. Cattell (1946), another leading theorist, also clusters common traits, which are universal, and unique traits, which belong to a particular individual (Table 19-1). In addition, this theorist talks about surface and source traits. Surface traits are traits that are commonly found together in clusters, and source traits are the causal factors that underlie the surface manifestation. To uncover source traits, Cattell uses the technique of factor analysis. Cattell divides source traits into what he calls environmental-mold traits and constitutional traits. Both of these sources can be either general or specific, according to the range of their influence.

The obvious distinction between physical and behavioral characteristics is made by another well-known theorist, J. P. Guilford. Guilford (1959) talks about somatic traits, which are based on the physical endowment of the individual, and behavior traits.

Trait theorists take a nomethetic approach to the study of personality. This approach is comparative and attempts to understand an individual by

TABLE 19-1 Cattell's Formulation of Primary Traits
of Personality

versus

I. Cyclothymia	**Schizothymia**
outgoing	withdrawn
good-natured	embittered
adaptable	inflexible
II. Intelligence	**Mental Defect**
intelligent	stupid
painstaking	slipshod
deliberate	impulsive
III. Emotionally Mature	**Demoralized**
realistic	evasive
stable	changeable
calm	excitable
IV. Dominance	**Submissiveness**
assertive	modest
headstrong	gentle
tough	introspective
V. Surgery	**Melancholy**
cheerful	unhappy
placid	worrying
sociable	aloof
VI. Sensitive	**Tough Poise**
idealistic	cynical
imaginative	habit-bound
grateful	thankless
VII. Trained, Socialized	**Boorish**
thoughtful	unreflective
sophisticated	simple
conscientious	indolent
VIII. Positive Integration	**Immature, Dependent**
mature	irresponsible
persevering	quitting
loyal	fickle
IX. Charitable, Adventurous	**Obstructive, Withdrawn**
cooperative	obstructive
genial	cold-hearted
frank	secretive
X. Neurasthenia	**Vigorous Character**
incoherent	strong-willed
meek	assertive
unrealistic	practical
XI. Hypersensitive	**Frustration Tolerance**
demanding	adjusting
restless	calm
self-pitying	self-effacing
XII. Surgent Cyclothymia	**Paranoia**
enthusiastic	frustrated
friendly	hostile
trustful	suspicious

From Cattell (1946).

comparing him with others. The more common clinical approach is an ideo-graphic one, an in-depth study of the particular individual as unique. One must not get the impression that trait theory is just a listing of static individual characteristics. Trait theory is an approach to the study of personality that is based on the conviction that, before we can gain knowledge of the development and workings of personality, we should have a better understanding of the variables that make up personality. It is a systematic attempt to objectively define that nebulous structure we so blithely call personality. The argument is that only after we can explicitly state the significant factors in personality can we begin to investigate such issues as the effect of learning and the contribution of genetics. The first stage in this search is to uncover the characteristics of our unknown quantity; it is at a later stage that we can track down its origins.

SELF THEORY: CARL ROGERS

The personality theory of Carl Rogers (1951) has elements of other major theoretical approaches. For this reason, it serves as a good exemplar of self theory. This theory actually represents a synthesis of phenomenology, organismic theory, interpersonal theory, and self theory. Phenomenological theory states that behavior is a function of the phenomenal field of the individual. A phenomenal field is the totality of experiences of which the person is aware. What phenomenology stresses is that the important aspects of reality are not objective reality, but reality as perceived by the person. It is this aspect of a situation to which he is responding.

Organismic theory is an extension of Gestalt psychology, and emphasizes the unity, consistency, and coherence of the personality. It is the antithesis of the atomistic approach, which divides to conquer. In the organismic view, the person responds as a complete organism to the totality of his experience. He cannot be segmented to be understood. This theory makes the further assumption that there is one primary drive, the motive of self-actualization. Self-actualization means that man strives to develop all of his potential by whatever means are open to him. This is the primary motive of human behavior. The organism (person) possesses an inherent potential for growth, and, if not thwarted by a malignant environment, a healthy integrated personality will unfold.

Interpersonal theory, based on the writings of Harry Stack Sullivan (1949), holds as its major tenet that, by definition, personality does not exist except as an interpersonal dynamic. It is a hypothetical entity inferred from interpersonal behavior. Personality is organized, therefore, in terms of interpersonal events and not intrapsychic phenomena.

The self theory of Carl Rogers combines elements of these other approaches, but it is a distinct theory. From this theory, he derived his client-centered therapy for which he is most well known. The principal elements in Roger's theory are the organism, which is the total individual, the phenomenal field, or the totality of experience, and the self, which is one's conscious awareness of one's own values and perceptions. It is this last concept that forms the core of the theory. The self develops out of one's interactions with the environment, that is, learning to see the "self-as-object." Through the process of living, the self attaches positive and negative values to experiences. Experience is everything that is going on within the individual, including somatic and sensory events, and it may be conscious or unconscious. Rogers considers the conscious to be those events that are symbolized and the unsymbolized to be the unconscious. The individual exists in the center of this constantly changing world of experience. Roger's theory is phenomenological because he asserts that the individual reacts to his perceptions of reality. If we are to understand a person's behavior, we must view his personal assessments of reality as the only significant variables. The person's own internal frame of reference is the best place from which to view his behavior.

The organismic approach is evident in two of Roger's assumptions about the self. First, he regards the individual as an indivisible whole. The person reacts or behaves as an organized whole. No single dimension is responsible for his behavior. The individual exists in the context of his environment, and the totality of the physical and psychological self is in unitary interaction with the environment. Second, all behavior is a function of one basic motive, self actualization. Behavior is directed toward the actualization, maintenance, and enhancement of the self. Self-actualization is sometimes an elusive concept to grasp, but basically it means "following one's own drummer." Each of us has propensities and hidden capacities, which we have not drawn forth and expanded. Self-actualization means discovering and expanding these potentials and thereby enhancing ourselves. Rogers places the role of heredity as setting down the lines by which the individual can achieve self-actualization. One is not free to become virtually anything; there are genetic directives that influence what potentials one has to develop. Rogers does not promise that the road to self-actualization is going to be easy. To accomplish this end involves struggle and pain as one metaphorically gives birth to a unique self. Despite the pain of creation, however, each person possesses an inherent potential for growth. Why then do some individuals seem to choose self-destructive paths? The growth tendency is not some magical force coercing the person to make all the "right" decisions. The growth tendency can only operate when the alternatives are clearly perceived and symbolized.

Another of the characteristics of this actualizing self is that it strives for consistency. One thinks of oneself in a particular way, for example, honest, loving, law-abiding, beautiful, etc. We hold these hypotheses about ourselves, and we seek to confirm these assumptions in our experience. According to Rogerian theory, information that is inconsistent with our image or ourself is either distorted or denied symbolization (a concept like repression). These inconsistent experiences are perceived as threatening. As these threats become more numerous, the individual attempts to defend himself against them by becoming more and more rigid, unaccepting of possible inconsistency. Psychological maladjustment ensues when, for reasons like inconsistency, significant sensory events are denied symbolization.

Rogers was primarily concerned with developing a therapeutic technique, not a theory of personality. It was only after the formulation of his approach of client-centered therapy that Rogers saw the necessity of basing it in some assumptions of a theoretical nature about personality. Like Freud, his view of personality was shaped by his clinical experiences with patients, but the assumptions of these two men both in theory and practice differed substantially. Freud assumed that the overt content of the individual's statements were important only to the extent that they reflected the more significant latent meanings and motivations. Rogers however, believed there was a great deal of validity in what the patient reported, and he stressed the conscious factors in behavior. Unconscious motivation actually plays no part in Rogerian theory. For the Rogerian, the personality is revealed directly in the individual's self-reports and these reports are to be believed. The Rogerian does not assume that the surface reports of the patients are distortions of unconscious truths. The Rogerian believes that the self-as-object is a conscious phenomenon, and can be reported to the therapist. In order to change behavior the Rogerian does not delve into layers of psychic consciousness, but rather concentrates on changing the concept of the self reported by the patient. Since consistency is valued by the self, presumably as one changes the self concept one has changed behavior.

THE MEASUREMENT OF PERSONALITY

The area of psychological tests and measurements is an area unto itself, and its complication is beyond the scope of this introduction to psychology. Psychological tests are so widely used, however, that the student should have some idea of the nature of these measurements. They are used as part of an overall diagnostic assessment in the treatment of disturbed individuals as well as in such diverse areas as personnel placement in industry.

Objective Tests

Evaluation of personality often runs the risk of being confounded by subject-tester interaction and tester bias. That is, the prejudices of the tester interfere with objective assessment of the subject. To minimize this problem, various tests have been devised to provide a more objective measure of personality. The tests are designed to determine the individual's standing on a certain number of psychological traits. These tests often take the form of rating scales on which the rater assesses the relative amount of some traits possessed by an individual. The rater is carefully trained in both observation and rating technique. Rating scales, however, have a built in problem of their own, known as the halo effect, that is, when an individual rates high on some outstanding trait, there is a tendency to also rate him high on other traits in the same direction. Presumably the halo effect can be overcome with training.

In a personality inventory, the individual answers questions about himself. The more sophisticated of these tests use questions that are not so transparent as to be easily faked, and they incorporate in them indexes of false or inconsistent information.

One of the most common personality tests is the *Minnesota Multiphasic Personality Inventory* (MMPI). This test was designed for use in assessing the type and intensity of abnormal behavior. It was developed from the responses of many types of patients and normal individuals. From their responses to the items, scales were obtained based on which ones discriminated subjects with specific types of disturbance. The nine most widely used scales are as follows.

1. Hypochondriases (Hs). The subject reports being worried about bodily functions. This is often associated with past history of exaggerated physical complaints.

2. Hysteria (Hy). The subject reports being worried about paralysis, gastric or intestinal complaints, attacks of weakness, fainting, or even epileptic attacks.

3. Depression (D). The subject reports being in the depths of depression, discouraged, and without self-confidence.

4. Hypomania (Ma). The subject reports he is overproductive in both thought and action. Often this may go along with trouble resulting from attempting too much and from a disregard of social conventions.

5. Psychopathic deviate (Pd). The subject's responses reflect an absence

of deep emotionality. Nothing seems to matter. He may be intelligent, but likely to lie, cheat, or be addicted to drugs. Crimes may be undertaken without interest in personal gain.

6. Paranoia (Pa). The subject is suspicious, oversensitive, and has delusions of persecution.

7. Psychastenia (Pt). These responses are typical of those with phobic or compulsive behaviors. The subject may have disturbing thoughts or ideas from which he cannot escape.

8. Schizophrenia (Sc). The subjects who give responses scored as unusual and bizarre are high on this scale. Generally, these responses reflect a dissociation of the subjective life of the individual from reality.

9. Masculinity-feminity (Mf). This scale tends to differentiate masculine-feminine psychological characteristics between men and women in the normal group of subjects.

The subject is given a series of questions printed on cards, and he is to respond either "yes," "no," or "can't say" to each of the items by placing them in the appropriate part of the box. He does not give his answers verbally, as this might influence the sincerity of his replies. The test also includes a lie scale based on the number of improbable answers, indicating denial of symptoms or traits which are so common that denial indicates an evasion. There is also a false score calculated on extremely rare responses indicating faking an answer or responding invalidly.

Projective Tests

In contrast to the objective tests, which are concerned with delineating specific traits, the projective tests are concerned with global personality functioning. The common feature of all projective tests is that they consist of presenting different kinds of ambiguous stimuli, sometimes abstract, sometimes pictorial, and the patient is asked to interpret what he sees. The assumption is that the subject reveals his personality in the way he interprets the stimulus. The individual tends to impute characteristics of his own onto the stimuli, especially when they involve human figures. Thus, in a picture showing two women, a girl with strong hostility toward her domineering mother may say that the women are mother and daughter, and the mother is ruining the girl's life by forcing her to act a certain way. This same picture would be interpreted differently by someone with a warm mother-child relationship.

Two of the most common projective tests are the Rorschach and the Thematic Apperception Test (TAT). The Rorschach consists of ten very abstract inkblots onto which the patient is encouraged to project anything he wants (Figure 19-3). The TAT uses representational pictures mostly of people, alone or in interaction, as the basis for interpretation (Figure 19-4). The subject is asked to tell a story about each picture incorporating what is happening, how the people in the picture are feeling and what they are thinking, what went before the present scene, and what will be the outcome. The TAT consists of 20 pictures. Like the Rorschach, the scoring of the TAT is a very precise task requiring a great deal of training. Interpretation of this test is in broad descriptive statements, not in terms of percentiles or other statistics.

One of the advantages of projective tests is that, since there are no obvious right or wrong answers, it is very hard to fake. In addition, it is often difficult for people to admit of certain feelings in themselves, but it is less threatening to impute these feelings to others. A major disadvantage, however, is that valid interpretation is a function of a great deal of training and clinical experience.

A somewhat different projective test is the Hutt Adaptation of the Bender Gestalt Test. This test is based on stimuli used in a popular visual-motor test to detect abnormalities due to brain damage. Hutt adapted these stimuli to a projective test. The stimuli are nine line drawings. In the first phase, the patient is asked to make a freehand drawing of each stimulus. In the second phase, he is reshown the cards and asked to make any modifications he wishes in his drawings. In the last phase, he is asked to give his association to both the original and his modified drawing. The underlying assumption is that one's personality would influence the kinds of changes made in the drawings. For instance, the amount of increase or decrease in size is thought

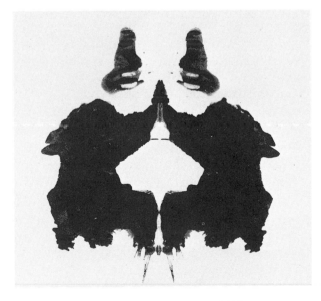

FIGURE 19-3   A Rorschach inkblot.

FIGURE 19-4   A picture used in the Thematic Apperception Test.

to be an index of an approach or withdrawal tendency, and the poles of depression and euphoric mood swing are related to the amount of change in the orientation of the figure. The adapted Bender Gestalt Test is used less frequently than other tests, and there are still some problems with validation of the test, but it provides a good example of the range of projective techniques possible.

Situation Tests

Ideally, one should judge behavior as a hidden observer in a real life situation. Since this is practically unfeasible, many psychologists have turned to what are known as situation tests of personality. In these situations, the psychologist observes the behavior of the individual in a simulated real life situation, and then assumes that the behavior he displays is characteristic of behavior in actual similar circumstances. The Office of Strategic Services used this approach during World War II. Subjects were given a task or problem, and then observed during solution of it. Leadership ability, ingenuity, and tolerance of frustration were inferred from the subjects' approach and reactions. Frequently stooges were planted to make trouble and bungle the job on which they were cooperating to provide an opportunity to observe the reaction of the subject to such a frustrating situation (Office of Strategic Services, 1948).

Although one would guess that such tests would correlate relatively highly with behavior in natural situations, there have been no comprehensive studies on this question. One of the obvious problems with these tests is that they require elaborate preparation and some standard way of scoring that has yet to be developed. If these problems could be overcome, they would probably serve as a source of valuable information unavailable through the common pencil and paper personality tests. However, the responses the tester observes are dependent on the situations he creates, and the test can only reveal those personality characteristics elicited by the test situations.

SUMMARY

Theories are generally tolerated for as long as they stimulate new ideas and are amenable to experimental verification. Theories of personality, however, have mostly escaped this judgmental process. Each theory begins with a set of assumptions leading to various predictions, but does that necessarily prove the validity of the underlying assumptions? The fact that personality encompasses intangible and unmeasurable factors has further complicated attempts to subject this area to the rigors of experimentation. The consequence of these problems has been a proliferation of theories about human behavior, but little objective evaluation of the validity of any of them.

Theorists have attempted to impose order on the seemingly chaotic behavior of man by choosing a position from which to view him. Freud delved into the recesses of man's psyche and sought an explanation of his behavior in terms of internal drives and conflicts. Psychoanalytic theory looks within to explain external behavior.

The learning theorists, such as Dollard and Miller, have chosen the environment as the best place from which to view behavior. Of their four major variables, drive, cue, response, and reinforcement, only drive suggests an inner force, and that variable is only relevant as it manifests itself in overt behavior.

Likewise, the Rogerians do not emphasize inner man or unconscious forces, but have taken a holistic approach to man as a self-actualizing being. The self emerges from interaction with the environment.

Perhaps the most experimentally based approach is that of the trait theorist. The emphasis here on the delineation of the major components of personality has been based on factor analytic studies. These studies, however, have not provided an integrated theory of the causes of or interrelations between personality variables.

The same problems that beset theory construction plague the area of measurement. Some of the major personality tests depend on assumptions that are frequently not testable. Projective tests, for example, assume that one's responses to ambiguous stimuli reflect one's own psychological conflicts and not pure imagination or creativity. These tests, however, have provided us with some tools for psychological analysis and enable us to draw distinctions between persons based on their responses. This ability to class people on psychological dimensions is an important first step in understanding the variables of human behavior.

SUGGESTED READINGS

GILLFORD, J. P. *Personality*. New York: McGraw-Hill, 1959.

HALL, C. S., & LINDZEY, G. (Eds.) *Theories of personality*. (2nd ed.) New York: Wiley, 1970.

JANIS, I. L. (Ed.) *Personality: Dynamics, development and assessment*. New York: Harcourt, 1969.

SEMEONOFF, B. *Personality assessment*. Baltimore: Penguin Books, 1966.

20

The Abnormal Personality

———————

Nothing generates more interest than "crazy" people. Our images conjured by the term "mentally ill" include the weird, bizarre, uncontrollable, and somewhat exotic picture embodied in the slang terms "off the wall" and "out of his head." In actual fact, the classification of abnormality includes far less debilitation than this total breakdown. The identification of psychological pathology, however, is far from clear and set. Professionals argue not only diagnosis but definitions of normal and abnormal.

In everyday life we constantly come across situations where the normality of someone's behavior is questioned. Most of the time these behaviors are not so radically different that deviance is clear. If someone's habit of throwing things against the wall when he is good and angry means he has a temper, does it also mean he is abnormal and needs psychological help? An example of abnormality will be seen in the following case history.

PARANOID SCHIZOPHRENIA

The case to be reported occurred in a 41-year-old command pilot with 7,500 hours, who had flown 135 combat missions in World War II and Korea. At the time of his illness, he was a chief pilot in a command headquarters. He was an excellent pilot and had consistently received superior ratings because of his conscientious and dependable performance. The overt onset of his illness was related to a period of TDY at a conference where flight procedures on a new type aircraft were being drafted. However, in retrospect, it was learned that for several weeks he had been preoccupied and upset, had sensed that he could read other people's minds by radio waves, and suspected those with whom he worked of being "queer."

While at the conference, he developed ideas of reference, believing that certain comments which his companions made, or which he heard over the radio, had hidden meanings and were directed toward him. For example, when the conferees spoke of "take-off," he did not know whether they were referring to an airplane or a woman, and suspected they were suggesting he should have an illicit sexual relationship. He developed the delusional idea that his associates were trying to "teach" him something and puzzled them several times when he confronted them with a demand that they tell him openly whatever they wanted him to learn. They became further concerned when he became increasingly upset, tearful and incoherent, and when he did not improve after several days of "rest" at his brother's home, he was admitted to the hospital.

On admission, he was suspicious of those about him, wondering whether they were dope-peddlers or communists, and he refused to talk to people who could not assure him they were cleared for top secret. He believed that he was accused of taking dope, that there were concealed microphones about the ward, and he had hallucinations consisting of voices which accused him of being "queer." He was often apprehensive and tearful, but this alternated with periods when he was inappropriately jovial. He was oriented in all spheres, and physical and neurological exams were entirely normal.

A review of the patient's past history revealed no other evidence of emotional disturbance. He was the second of four children of a strict, moralistic, financially successful farm family. He did well in school and one year of college, but always felt inadequate in comparison with his peers. He entered the Air Corps and flew 32 B-17 missions in World War II, was separated, then recalled in 1950 and flew 103 combat missions in Korea. He had been married for 18 years and had five children. He used alcohol only rarely, and there was no evidence that toxic or exogenous factors could have been implicated in his psychosis.

The patient received psychotherapy and began to improve within a few days after admission. For this reason, no drug or other somatic treatment was instituted. He continued to improve over the course of the next several weeks and seemed greatly relieved after telling of an isolated extramarital adventure during the TDY. He gradually gained insight into the unreality of his experiences and was discharged from the hospital after one month.

Following his discharge, the patient was given duties in supply and ground training which he handled without difficulty. However, he had always enjoyed flying immensely and taken pride in his outstanding proficiency, and he made repeated visits to his flight surgeon and psychiatrist to try and get back on flying status. He was referred to the School of Aerospace Medicine for evaluation and recommendation regarding return to flying status.

When seen at the School, he was found to be very well integrated, although some underlying anxiety was apparent. Despite his apparently satisfactory remission, some residuals of his previous thinking disorder were evident. He wondered at times whether he had not been partly right about the events on TDY, and whether his fellow conferees had not been playing a practical joke on him. He had recently considered going to his Wing Commanding officer to ask whether the experiences had been part of some kind of "test" of his mental stability, but had decided against this because it might create an unfavorable impression if he were being tested. He had decided that whatever had happened, it was best forgotten, and through the use of his suppressive mechanism had continued to function effectively. Because of his clear-cut history of a psychotic disorder without an underlying organic basis, as well as the evidence of a continuing minimal thinking disorder, return to flying status was not considered to be consistent with flying safety [Enders & Flinn, 1962].

NORMALITY AND ABNORMALITY

A young man feels compelled to repeatedly check the basement each day to see if there are any oily rags lying about and to check the stove to make sure the gas is turned off. He finds himself worrying that a fire will break out and his anxiety over a potential fire permeates his day. Is this man behaving strangely or abnormally? Suppose that, a week before, the man's house had actually caught fire, and, while he had escaped unharmed, the incident had so startled and terrified him that he is now experiencing a transitory period of anxiety. Although this man is reacting compulsively, we can see a "rational" reason for his behavior. Now suppose that another man is behaving just like the first one, but this second man has not had an experience with a fire. Moreover, the man is convinced that an enemy is going to set his house afire unless he keeps a close watch. In this case, the man's behavior would not be tolerated as a transitory situational reaction, but would be considered abnormal behavior. The same outward behavior can be judged as both normal and abnormal, depending on the situation. The problem of defining abnormal behavior is an enormously difficult one (Figure 20-1). There is a wide spectrum of individual differences among people not only in their personalities, but in their reactions to stressful events. Each person, culture, and subculture are willing to tolerate different behaviors as normal and brand different behaviors as deviant. Because of this lack of universality, psychologists have been hard pressed to provide a simple definition of abnormality. Most psychologists today do not view abnormal behavior as a separate and distinct way of behaving reserved only for people who are "crazy." Rather, they have come to recognize that deviant behavior is simply an extension or overexaggeration of normal behavior. We are all capable of these deviant behaviors, and in some situations some of these behaviors are displayed by the general population. Most people, however, have either learned to inhibit these deviant be-

FIGURE 20-1   Who is normal? Is it a relative judgment?

haviors or, through their social conditioning, they have not learned these behaviors at all. It is presumably due to the operation of these internal constraints that most people differ from those thought to be abnormal.

For some time now, behavioral abnormality has been viewed in terms of a medical model. The conceptualization has been that the abnormal personality was a psychological disease much like a physical disease. As a result of this medical model, such terms as mental illness, symptom, and pathological have come to dominate our vocabulary. Psychologists are now questioning the validity of this medical framework, asserting that the deviant individual is not ill in the traditional sense of the term, but is an individual responding to a stressful life circumstance. Within the framework of the client's world, as he sees it, his behavior may be understandable and rational. We must therefore view the individual not as sick, but as seeking to come to terms with a very difficult life situation. His abnormal behavior may simply be that behavior which takes him out of his stressful environment or minimizes the adversity of it.

The advent of the popularity of mind-expanding drugs has further challenged existing views of what can be considered normal patterns of thought. Some theorists are now proposing that the psychotic thought processes are not due to mental dysfunction, but are actually expansions of awareness. In his *Politics of experience* (1967), Ronald Laing, a British psychiatrist, has offered the fascinating thesis that, rather than seeing a distortion of reality, the psychotic may be exploring levels of human consciousness beyond the level at which most of us operate. It is as if some individuals are able to turn into themselves where they discover the myriad of thoughts, fears, and emotions that lie buried in the psyche. Because so few of us have made this inward journey, it is an uncharted area about which we know very little. The strange behavior of the psychotic may be his reaction to this frightening experience which he must face alone. The individual whom we view as diseased or sick may actually be embarked in a pursuit of self discovery. However, not many scientists take this view seriously.

What then do we mean by abnormal behavior? How have we resolved our dilemma? Three approaches have been taken in drawing the line between normal and abnormal: a statistical approach, a cultural approach, and the approach of personal adjustment.

The statistical approach says that any behavior that departs from the average is abnormal. This definition, however, is tautological. The problem with this definition is that at this point we do not know qualitatively or quantitatively how the average or normal person feels; hence, we do not know what behavior is significantly different from the normal to be called abnormal. We would need to know, for example, how many people live with feelings of pervasive anxiety, and we would need some way of measuring the anxiety to adopt a statistical approach to defining abnormality.

Realizing that different cultures have different standards of behavior, some people have adopted a cultural definition of normality-abnormality. From this point of view, one must judge a person's behavior from the viewpoint of his own society. Any behavior that violates the mores and customs of a particular society is deviant. Although this culture-bound definition certainly has great merit in recognizing that normality is a relative concept, it faces some of the same problems of the statistical approach.

Societies are frequently composed of subcultures, cohesive groups within a society, such as the ethnic and racial subcultures within American society who have their own set of standards. These particular standards of behavior may be at variance with the culture as a whole. Tolerance for physical aggression, for example, differs between subcultures.

Must we then have a separate definition of normality for the general society and for the subculture, and, if we do, which diagnosis characterizes the person? Do we alter his behavior to fit the demands of the society at large or the subculture from which the person comes? The cultural definition has bought us the theoretical recognition of the relativity of normality, but it still presents us with practical problems.

Judging whether or not a person is psychologically healthy by involving cultural and statistical definitions has encountered so many problems that some theorists have suggested abandoning the "objective" approaches altogether. Instead, they suggest that personal adjustment be used as a criterion of psychological stability. Only behaviors that interfere with daily functioning or produce anxiety should be considered abnormal. However, this pragmatic approach has its own set of built-in problems. Who is to be the ultimate judge of whether a behavior interferes with daily functioning? What shall we consider a well-adjusted individual so that we may use this as our standard? Must we categorize as normal the individual who denies that his neuroticism interferes with his chosen life style? Such an approach may facilitate therapeutic decisions, but, by making each person an individual case study, we have not advanced our theoretical knowledge of the psychological basis of abnormality.

The definition of mental disturbance is an aribitrary and ambiguous one about which there is still much disagreement. In addition to disagreement over a general definition, there is a lack of agreement when it comes to designating specific diagnoses. There are few if any symptom complexes that are readily identifiable and completely exclusive in their character. Indeed, there are great problems with the reliability of a diagnosis. Symptoms, for example, change over time; there is an overlap in symptoms among diagnostic categories, and patients with the same basic diagnosis may differ considerably from one to another in the manifestation of their symptoms. This confusion has led some psychologists to advocate abandoning diagnosis altogether. There are both pros and cons of this suggestion, but at present there is strong pressure to maintain the concept of diagnosis for research purposes. Of the wide range of complexes currently differentiated, two broad groups will be described: psychoneuroses and psychoses. Despite the lack of precision, these two areas can be further divided into symptom complexes with at least some highlighting characteristics. Before we leave this chapter, the reader should be cautioned that, despite the debate over classification and diagnosis, some pathological behavioral patterns can be discerned and are considered classical concepts in the study of abnormal behavior. All is not chaos, but there are controversy and possible ambiguity in the area.

THE PSYCHONEUROSES

The two most widely known groups of pathological behavior are the psychoneuroses and the psychoses. Psychoses involve a much more severe and complete personality disruption than neurotic disorders. Neurotic individuals are rarely hospitalized, and their symptoms are generally confined to certain areas of their personality. In contrast, the psychotic individual is unable to function effectively, various aspects of reality are distorted, he often requires hospitalization, and he may be injurious to himself and others. Table 20-1 lists some major factors distinguishing the psychoses.

The nucleus of the neurotic disorder is anxiety. The neurotic's behavior is an attempt to deal with this anxiety by employing strategies. As in all learning situations, a behavior is maintained if it is reinforced. Those behaviors that we consider neurotic are performing a function of the individual; they are minimizing anxiety. They are strategies for anxiety reduction, and they are there because they work. Unfortunately, however, they are also disruptive and frequently prevent the person from leading a completely satisfying and uninhibited life. The neurotic behavior may consume a great deal of energy and be fairly pervasive, or it may be relatively encapsulated and confined to a small area of the person's life.

Neurotic disorders can take many forms, and there can be as many strategies as there are people with problems. The source of the neurotic's conflicts usually stems from his previous learning experience. The individual is not born with guilt and anxiety. They are learned, just as ways of coping with the ensuing conflict are learned. There are seven common forms of psychoneuroses.

TABLE 20-1   Psychotic Disorders (Functional Psychoses)[a]

Personality disintegration with disorientation for time, place, and/or person. Hospitalization ordinarily required.

Schizophrenic reactions—a group of psychotic reactions involving withdrawal from reality, disturbances in thought processes, and emotional blunting and distortion.

1. Simple type—apathy and indifference without conspicuous delusions or hallucinations
2. Hebephrenic type—severe disorganization with silliness, mannerisms, delusions or hallucinations.
3. Catatonic type—conspicuous motor behavior with excessive motor activity and excitement or generalized inhibition and stupor.
4. Paranoid type—poorly systematized delusions; often hostility and aggression.
5. Acute undifferentiated type—sudden schizophrenic reaction which may clear up or develop into other definable type.
6. Chronic undifferentiated type—chronic, mixed symptomatology not fitting other types.
7. Schizo-affective type—admixture of schizophrenic and affective reactions.
8. Childhood type—schizophrenic reactions occurring before puberty.
9. Residual type—mild residual symptoms following more severe cases.

Paranoid reactions—persistent delusions usually without hallucinations. Behavior and emotional responses consistent with delusions. Intelligence well preserved.

1. Paranoia—well systematized delusions, generally of persecution or grandeur.
2. Paranoid state—transient paranoid delusions, not well systematized, lacking the bizarre fragmentation of the schizophrenic.

Affective reactions—exaggerations of mood with related thought disturbances.

1. Manic depressive reaction—prolonged periods of excitement or depression or mixture of alternation of the two.
2. Psychotic depressive reaction—severe depression and delusions of unworthiness.

Involutional psychotic reaction—depression in involutional period without previous psychosis.

[a] From *Abnormal psychology and modern life* by James C. Coleman. Copyright © 1964 by Scott, Foresman and Company. Reprinted by permission of the publisher.

Conversion Reaction

A woman complains that she can feel nothing in her right hand. She goes to her general practitioner, and he says he can find nothing physiologically wrong with her. Furthermore, the anesthesia the woman complains about is very strange. It is confined to her hand, and includes no part of her arm, an impossibility if her symptom were due to neural damage. The woman's symptom is not really a physical disturbance, but a psychological one. In conversion reaction or conversion hysteria, the neurotic complains of some physical ailment for which there is no apparent physiological basis. The giveaway that the person has psychologically caused the ailment is that the disturbance is often an anatomical impossibility.

Freud was the first to argue that such hysterias, very common in the nineteenth century, were due to some previous psychological trauma, which the patient was now attempting to deny by a paralysis or anesthesia of a part of his body. The area affected is generally that part of the body linked in some way with the traumatic event. In fact, many cases stem from overriding guilt over sexual feelings, and the guilt and anxiety is translated into a physical symptom. Contrary to what one might suppose, the individual is frequently not upset about his anesthesia, indicating that it is serving some psychological purpose. Conversion reactions are most often employed by persons who are very dependent and suggestible and have immature personality structures. The increased attention and sympathy which the patient receives with his ailment may actually serve to reinforce his pattern of helpless dependence. Conversion reactions most frequently take the form of tics, deafness, blindness, anesthesia, or paralysis, but, while Freud saw many such cases in nineteenth century Vienna, this form of neurotic disorder has become much less prevalent today.

Dissociative Reactions

As the name implies, a dissociative reaction is an attempt to dissociate oneself from one's own being. The person blocks off a part of his life from his conscious memory either through a brief amnesia for particular events or through an extended fugue state, a total amnesia for one's past. The individual is attempting to relinquish his old personality, which was inadequate in dealing with his problems, and assume a new and different personality, divorced from his old one. Like the conversion reaction, dissociative reactions are based on attempts to repress psychologically threatening material. The person may clothe himself in his new personality as a way of denying those aspects of his person over which he feels guilt or extreme anxiety.

Dissociative reactions are thought to arise from psychological conflict within the individual over desired but forbidden behavior. By assuming two different personalities, the person is able to satisfy both aspects of the conflict. When he is behaving under personality A he can engage in the forbidden behavior. When the guilt becomes too great, he simply switches to the other, more conforming and "innocent" personality.

Obsessive–Compulsive Reactions

Obsessive and compulsive reactions are frequently found together. Therefore, they are grouped as one pattern, although either of them may exist without the other. These two reactions, along with phobias, were formerly called psychasthenia. An obsessive reaction is the occurrence of persistent thoughts which the person may realize as absurd but cannot prevent. Everyone has experienced an obsessive thought at one time or another, e.g., not being able to stop thinking about an impending exam, or what our lover is doing at the moment, or what we should have done in some situation, but these thoughts are usually relatively transient.

When these thoughts are obsessive, the person literally cannot shut them off. Frequently, obsessive thoughts are fears of some uncontrollable impulse seizing the person. The fear may be that one is always just about to shout out some obscenity, push someone out the window, club someone over the head, or jump from a tall building. Even though the person does not really carry out these actions, he is tortured by the thoughts nonetheless, and may even feel guilt over them.

Compulsive reactions are impulses to perform actions that are also absurd, but the person feels compelled to perform them. Compulsive reactions may take any form, e.g., constantly checking to see if a door is locked, constantly washing one's hands, walking down a certain street, or refusing to step on the cracks in the sidewalk. Resisting the compulsive impulse and not performing the act usually results in tension and anxiety; performing the ritual, however, is followed by a feeling of satisfaction.

In their extreme forms, compulsive reactions may become the so-called manias: kleptomania, the compulsion to steal; pyromania, the compulsion to set fires; poriomania, the need to move from place to place. Persons who develop these obsessive–compulsive reactions typically have a personality with characteristics of meticulousness, rigidity, perfectionism, and attention to detail. The person may engage in these obsessive diversions as an unconscious strategy to take his mind off the stresses or conflicts that presumably lie at the base of his reaction.

Phobic Reaction

A phobia is an intense and irrational fear of some object or situation which objectively is not dangerous or in which the danger is not proportional to the person's fear. Phobias often accompany obsessive-compulsive reactions.

TABLE 20-2   Common Phobias[a]

---

acrophobia—high places
agoraphobia—open places
algophobia—pain
astraphobia—storms, thunder, lightening
claustrophobia—closed places
hematophobia—blood
mysophobia—contamination or germs
monophobia—being alone
nyctophobia—darkness
ochologphobia—crowds
pathophobia—disease
pyrophobia—fire
syphilophobia—syphilis
zoophobia—animals or some particular animal

---

[a] From *Abnormal psychology and modern life* by James C. Coleman. Copyright © 1964 by Scott, Foresman and Company. Reprinted by permission of the publisher.

Although there is no restriction on the types of phobias possible, the most common forms are listed in Table 20-2.

A phobia may come about through the association of some object or event with a situation in which some danger was actually present, that is, the phobia may be a product of some previous conditioning experience, or it may result from some unconscious conflict in which the feared object plays a symbolic part. If the phobia remains a small and circumscribed one, it may not interfere with the person's daily life very much. But if the phobia is either an all-encompassing one or it generalizes to more and more situations, the phobic reaction may be a particularly disruptive neurotic disorder.

Anxiety Reaction

Anxiety underlies all the neuroses; indeed, it is the precursor of all neurotic reactions. By engaging in the neurotic behavior, the individual "binds" his anxiety, that is, the anxiety is lessened through the use of defenses. In the anxiety reaction the anxiety is not bound, but is "free-floating," i.e., it is experienced directly. The person's chronic state of tension and apprehension is punctuated by attacks of acute and powerful anxiety. These attacks may last from a few seconds to a few hours; they come on suddenly, reach a peak, and then subside.

Physiologically, the person exhibits a typical fear response: his heart pounds, he perspires, he has trouble breathing, and he trembles. Psychologically, the individual is in a comparable state of alarm in which he usually has a vague but intense feeling that some terrible calamity is about to occur. Even when the anxiety neurotic is not having an acute attack, he is in a mild state of tension and apprehension. He worries constantly, has trouble making decisions for fear of making a mistake, and, once a decision is made, is preoccupied with possible error.

The anxiety neurotic is a perpetual pessimist who actually manufactures worries and problems and appears to thrive on them. Feelings of inadequacy are the wellsprings of the anxiety reaction. The individual fears that he is incapable of meeting the stresses of daily life, and he lives in a chronic state of tension. All of us feel threatened at times by our own incapacity to handle problems, but the threat is constant and overexaggerated for the anxiety neurotic. He feels threatened by stress situations that would not throw the normal person. The anxiety neurotic perceives the world as most demanding and difficult, and he sees himself as fighting a constant battle in which the odds are stacked against him.

Depressive Neuroses

The distortion of reality in the neurotic depressive reaction is a quantitative rather than a qualitative one. The individual is reacting excessively to a crisis or loss by mourning for long periods of time. He is overwhelmed with a feeling of doom, and he feels despair at his own helplessness, deficiencies, and frustrations. All the negative aspects of living become magnified out of proportion. His depression results in insomnia, apathy, boredom, and the inability to concentrate. Although life is not pleasant for him, the neurotic depressive is usually able to carry out everyday tasks. On occasion, however, the reaction may be so severe that the person ceases all activity and simply sits staring out into space. In such cases, hospitalization is typically required to guard against suicide.

In most cases, the depressive is able to recognize the initial source of his depression, but he cannot explain the reasons for his overreaction. Frequently, repressed hostility parallels the depressive reaction. Although the hostility is not conscious, it engenders feelings of guilt, perhaps because of hostile fantasies. Should something happen, the neurotic may feel as if his fantasies have come true, and he may feel instrumental in bringing about the catastrophe. The feelings of extreme guilt, though unfounded, may lead to psychological self-punishment and extreme depression.

Hypochondria

Eventually all of us encounter a hypochondriac. He has a way of making the whole world revolve around the state of his health. He dwells on every sensation, large and small, with equal fervor, constantly fearing that it presages some serious illness. His exaggeration of the slightest dysfunction places him in the situation of spending most of his life being "sick." He searches for disease so meticulously that it is as if he enjoys poor health. The hypochondriac's behavior may be a maneuver to prevent him from having to participate in a world in which he feels inadequate and fears failure. Being sick offers the perfect defense; he escapes participation but it is not his fault. Other speculations on the causes of this reaction propose that it is rooted in feelings of unworthiness and guilt. The individual may be seeking punishment and confirmation of his negative self-concept, and sickness fulfills this need.

THE PSYCHOSES

The neurotic individual has a great deal of anxiety, but his neurotic defenses help him to cope with stress, enabling him to function in society. For the most part, the neurotic has a hold on objective reality, and he is able to appropriately define himself *vis-à-vis* his world. The psychotic, however, is said to have lost contact with reality. Whereas the neurotic is aware of his irrationality and his deviance, the psychotic rarely acknowledges that his acts are in any way out of the ordinary or irrational. The emotions displayed by a psychotic individual may be inappropriate to situations; he may show a "flattened affect," i.e., very little emotion. Often hallucinations or delusions are present, distorting his perceptions of the world and himself.

The difference between neurotic and psychotic behavior may be illustrated this way: the normal sometimes says "on occasion I feel as if I were a computer"; the neurotic with his anxiety may say "on occasion I feel as if I were a computer that is breaking down, or whose wiring is faulty"; the psychotic is likely to say "I am a computer." All three individuals are expressing the same basic concerns about the threat of dehumanization of modern society, but only the normal and the neurotic maintain the analogy as analogy. They still acknowledge the reality that they are not computers; they are still able to appropriately define themselves.

A more amusing anecdote expressing the same relation notes that neurotics build castles in the air, psychotics live in them, and psychiatrists collect the rent. This seemingly facetious statement about mental disorders raises an important point about abnormal behavior. The neurotic's "castles in the air" are his defenses. These reactions are adaptive to the extent that they reduce anxiety, and they stem coherently from some set of psychological conditions and are not completely arbitrary. Likewise, the behavior of the psychotic is not arbitrary. His behavior, while inconsistent with empirical definitions of reality, may be consistent with the structure of his own world. The psychotic is reacting to the stresses of our mutual world by withdrawing into a fictional one of his own. He has built a closed system which is self-validating and internally consistent. If one is convinced that the Earth is on the verge of an invasion by Martians, it is consistent to live in fear of that event and perhaps to take appropriate precautions, like building a survival shelter or being suspicious of strangers. This psychotic behavior is inconsistent with objective probability and reality, but, given the assumptions of the psychotic's own world, it is not completely irrational or arbitrary.

The psychoses are divided into two types according to the known etiology, organic and functional. Organic psychoses are those disorders resulting directly from brain damage due to tumors, diseases of the nervous system, overdoses of certain chemicals, or circulatory impairments such as occur in senility. Functional psychoses stem from no known physical defects, but appear to be psychological in origin. Only the functional psychoses will be discussed here.

Paranoid Reactions: Paranoia and Paranoid State

Paranoia is a delusional system that is systematized, well-organized, and usually rotates around the central themes of persecution and grandeur. It usually develops slowly over a period of time, and, except for the delusions, does not cause radical changes in the person's personality. Usually the delusions center around a major theme. Delusions of persecution may concern an alleged enemy, such as a supposedly unfaithful wife or a repressive system of government, which is out to destroy the paranoid. Delusions of grandeur may center around some Messianic mission the person has been born to perform, a scientific invention he has created, or social reform that he is uniquely suited to institute. The individual insists that he is some great figure, and he spends a great deal of time trying to convince the world of this identity. A great number of these grandiose persons believe that their status was conferred by God and that their positions are a birthright. The distinguishing characteristic of the paranoid reaction is that the delusional system is well worked out, systematic, and complete. It admits no loopholes. All events are selectively perceived to support the paranoid's delusion.

Affective Reactions

The major characteristic of the affective reactions is that the person shows an extreme of mood. In psychotic depression, there is exaggerated feeling of worthlessness, futility, gloom, and morbid thoughts of impending disaster.

The person's whole world is bleak and negative. There is a slowing down of both mental and physical activity, perhaps so the person has no energy at all. In its more severe degrees, the depressive patient may refuse to move, and thus be bedridden. He often refuses to eat or talk and becomes incontinent. Disorientation regarding time and place is evident, and often the person is wracked by hallucinations and grotesque fantasies.

The contrasting affective disorder is the manic reaction. Here the individual is restless and highly excitable. He usually talks incessantly and loudly, and his behavior is boistrous, flamboyant, and possibly violent. In his frenzy of activity he may go around banging on things, giving speeches, and engaging in a dozen activities at once. His speech, often incoherent, shows a wild flight of ideas. He is often boastful, authoritarian, and dictatorial. There may be temporary delusions and hallucinations. Affective psychotics usually show either of these two dichotomous extremes, but in the manic depressive psychotic, the person alternates between these two states. The mood swings from mania to depression need not be precipitated by an external event. There may even be periods of relative normality interspersed between the extremes.

Schizophrenic Reactions

The term schizophrenia has turned out to be a grab bag classification with a great deal of symptomatic variation (Table 20-3). The accusation has

TABLE 20-3   Types of Schizophrenia[a]

1. **Simple type**—apathy and indifference without conspicuous delusions or hallucinations.
2. **Hebephrenic type**—severe disorganization with silliness, mannerisms, delusions, hallucinations.
3. **Catatonic type**—conspicuous motor behavior with excessive motor activity and excitement or generalized inhibition and stupor.
4. **Paranoid type**—poorly systematized delusions, often hostility and aggression.
5. **Acute undifferentiated type**—sudden schizophrenic reaction which may clear up or develop into other definable type.
6. **Chronic undifferentiated type**—chronic, mixed symptomatology not fitting other types.
7. **Schizo-affective type**—admixture of schizophrenic and affective reactions.
8. **Childhood type**—schizophrenic reactions occurring before puberty.
9. **Residual type**—mild residual symptoms following more severe cases.

[a] From *Abnormal psychology and modern life* by James C. Coleman. Copyright © 1964 by Scott, Foresman and Company. Reprinted by permission of the publisher.

been leveled that, when one does not know what is wrong with an obviously disturbed individual, the diagnosis of schizophrenia is arbitrarily applied. In general, the schizophrenia reaction includes a disturbance at almost every level of functioning. Although symptoms seem to vary with each patient, the basic core of symptoms stems from a withdrawal from reality. The schizophrenic lives in a world of his inner fantasies. This autism usually includes a lack of interest in other people and events of the external world. His emotions consequently are distorted and perhaps inappropriate. Shallowness of affect or extreme silliness are common. Cognitive processes are objectively impaired. A flight of ideas and a lack of coherency are evident in his speech. Delusions and hallucinations are often present. In addition, the schizophrenic often shows various anomalies of behavior such as peculiarities of movement, gesture, or expression. He may be mute or constantly giggling. He may engage in a repetitive motor act, such as constant rocking or swinging. There is often a deterioration in personal hygiene. The overall picture of the schizophrenic is one of general withdrawal and psychological degeneration.

SUMMARY

What is our tolerance for deviance? This question paraphrases the problem of defining abnormal behavior. There are many approaches to the definition of abnormality: the statistical approach, the cultural approach, and the approach of personal adjustment. None of them provides set guidelines for infallible decisions about behavior. We have pointed out the sometimes arbitrary nature of this diagnostic decision and some of the considerations that have led to theoretical positions on the subject. At one extreme is the medical model which views abnormal behavior as sick and the individual as diseased, much as in a physical disease. At the other extreme is the position that environments and not individuals are sick. The deviant individual is simply responding to a very difficult life situation. It has even been proposed that behavior that appears to be extremely abnormal is simply a reflection of new levels of consciousness, a frightening journey into the recesses of the psyche.

Despite the controversy over what comprises deviance, one can see classes of behavior that resemble each other. From these observations, classifications of behavior have emerged; we have discussed two large classes, the neuroses and the psychoses. Just as physiologists often learn about the normal functioning of the body through studies of abnormal functioning or disease, so psychologists will hopefully gain a clearer understanding of personality by studying those individuals who fall at the far ends of the continuum of human behavior.

SUGGESTED READINGS

BANDURA, A. *Principles of behavior modification.* New York: Holt, 1969.

LAING, R. D. *The politics of experience.* New York: Ballantine Books, 1967.

MEHRABIAN, A. *Tactics of social influence.* Englewood Cliffs, New Jersey: Prentice-Hall, 1970.

SZASZ, T. A. *The myth of mental illness: Foundations of a theory of personal conduct.* New York: Harper, 1961.

ULLMANN, L. F., & KRASNER, L. A. *A psychological approach to abnormal behavior.* Englewood Cliffs, New Jersey: Prentice-Hall, 1969.

21

The Treatment
of Psychological
Disorders

In the previous chapter we discussed the basis of the concept of abnormality. The identification of a problem, however, is only the first step in its solution. We must also deal with the problem of treating psychological disorders. The treatment we employ is a function of our assumptions about the causes of behavior. As you will see, there is no one right way to deal with psychological maladjustment. The treatment used by a therapist reflects his theoretical orientation to personality development.

THERAPY: THE TREATMENT OF PSYCHOLOGICAL DISORDERS

When psychological problems are mild and do not severely hamper the daily functioning of the individual, they are usually treated with benign neglect. All forms of treatment are costly and time-consuming, and usually are not undertaken lightly. Hence, many people find themselves behaving neurotically in some or many situations, but they fail to seek any remedy for their problem. Some of these individuals suffering from mild personality disorders obtain short-term therapy from social workers, marriage counselors, psychologists, and psychiatrists, and their treatment is more in the nature of counseling than therapy. Many of these people are simply suffering from some transient psychological problem, perhaps as a result of a recent stressful event, and talking out their difficulty enables them to cope with it more successfully.

Individuals with more severe personality disorders, psychotics and more severe neurotics, generally do seek professional help. The source of help comes almost exclusively from psychiatrists and psychologists. Psychiatrists are medical doctors who have done an internship in psychiatry; psychologists are also doctors, but not medical doctors. They have a Ph.D. in psychology (usually in clinical psychology), a degree that generally requires four or five years of study including an internship. Both psychiatrists and psychologists may do psychotherapy, but, since the psychologist does not have a medical degree, he cannot dispense drugs or engage in any form of organic treatment. Some people are under the erroneous impression that psychiatrists are more "qualified" to do psychotherapy, but this is simply not the case. There are many forms of treatment for the severely disturbed, and they can be classified as either medical treatment, drug treatment, or psychotherapy. Of the latter there are many orientations, but we will consider only a sample of some of the major forms.

MEDICAL THERAPIES

Medical therapy is sometimes referred to as somatotherapy, since it involves changing the individual organically. It is based on the assumption that psychological disturbance is predicated upon an organic dysfunction, so that, in order to restore normal psychological functioning, one can intervene directly into neurological processes. The most drastic of the medical therapies is psychosurgery in which an area of the brain is excised or cut.

In a lobotomy, the most anterior part of the cortex, the prefrontal area, is removed or severed from its connections with lower brain centers. When successful, these patients postoperatively are much less emotional and violent. Unfortunately, however, these patients also suffer from a loss of ambition, drive, and interest in the world. Their energy level in general seems to be reduced; the effects are not confined neatly to anxiety or destructive behavior. Since this treatment is so drastic and permanent, it is used only as a last resort, and, since the advent of drug therapy in the 1950's, it is used much less frequently.

There is also a new type of psychosurgery employing radiation on focused areas of the brain. Although it is still experimental and relatively new, the technique is superior to older forms of psychosurgery since the lesions can be focused more precisely and one can make a subcortical lesion without necessarily damaging the cortex (Kisker, 1964).

Another of the medical therapies is called shock therapy. In this technique, coma or convulsions are induced either through the administration of drugs or electric shock. In insulin shock therapy, the patient is given an injection of insulin, which lowers the blood sugar level to the point of producing coma. The person comes out of the coma either naturally or through the injection of carbohydrates, which returns the sugar level to normal. With electroshock therapy, electrodes are placed on the patient's head and a brief current is passed through the brain. These treatments are given over a period of time, and are supposedly most effectively used with depressive patients. However, with the advent of drugs, this form of treatment has become less common.

All the medical therapies are based on theories of just what goes wrong with the psychologically disturbed individual, but at the present time medical science has no firm knowledge of the causes of mental disturbance, and there are only speculations about why these treatments work when they do. Since so little is known about brain function, the use of these techniques has prompted accusations that, since their use is based on speculation rather than fact, the use of these treatments is unethical. Unfortunately, however, so little is known about therapy that expedience has replaced certainty as the criterion for therapeutic acceptability.

DRUG THERAPY

In 1952 it was discovered that reserpine was effective in calming some disturbed individuals. Since the 1950's, drugs have been used extensively as a form of treatment both in hospitals and as part of out-patient care. For patients who are hyperactive, anxious, and excessively nervous, tranquilizing drugs, sometimes called depressants, are prescribed. In the opposite cases, involving depression, withdrawal, and underactivity, stimulants or antidepressants are given. As is the case with shock therapy, the physiological effects of chemotherapy are unknown.

These drugs have been very successful in radically altering the patient's moods, but the behavioral changes are dependent upon the use of the drug. When the drug is no longer given, the patient's condition is not altered. There are also side effects of these drugs, which range from insomnia to liver damage, thus necessitating caution in their administration. As different people react differently to various drugs, one can never predict how a drug will affect a given patient; therefore, there is no drug that is a universally acceptable treatment for a specific problem.

Presumably these tranquilizers and stimulants are given not as cures for mental disturbance but as an adjunct form of therapy. The patient is made more manageable and amenable to psychotherapy. Unfortunately, however, the shortage of qualified psychotherapists in our mental hospitals results in the use of drugs exclusively for many patients. Since drugs can make the individual much less active and less destructive, they are frequently used simply for administrative ease. Hopefully, as we learn more about the possible chemical factors involved in mental disturbance, this situation can be rectified.

PSYCHOTHERAPY

In order to understand the various forms of psychotherapy, it is necessary to have a working knowledge of the personality theories upon which they are based. The reader is, therefore, advised to review the theories presented in an earlier section. There are many orientations to psychotherapy too numerous to discuss in a general chapter such as this one. Three representative forms have been chosen here, but the reader should not get the impression that this is an exclusive sampling.

Psychoanalysis

Freudian (so-called classical or orthodox) psychoanalysis is rooted in the assumption that personality disturbances are the result of childhood traumas, which "lie buried" in the unconscious. For as long as these events are repressed, the individual is a victim of unconscious motivation and conflict. The aim of psychoanalysis, therefore, is to give the individual insight into the roots of his problems and to surface these conflicts to consciousness. There are several important aspects to psychoanalytic therapy: free association, dream analysis, transference, resistance, and interpretation. It is through the interaction of these facets that therapy is achieved.

Throughout therapy, the analyst assumes the role of a nonevaluative, permissive listener who interprets, i.e., analyzes, rather than advises or teaches. The patient is encouraged to spend his session saying everything that comes into his mind, censoring as little as possible. This free stream of ideas is called free association, and it is based on the premise that thought sequences are not arbitrary, but rather reflect a relation in the ideas being expressed. The patient's unconscious associations will be inferred by the analyst through this free speech, although the person may be unaware that his ideas have any relation to one another.

Although the therapist is generally nondirective and interrupts infrequently, at appropriate moments he will lead the patient to see possible psychological implications of his statements. As the patient begins talking about significant, anxiety-arousing events, he often pauses or changes the subject or perhaps becomes emotional by crying or becoming hostile. This serves as a cue to the therapist that the patient is "resisting" and that they are walking the edge of repressed focal material. The therapist may encourage the patient to explore his various forms of resisting before getting to what it is that is being held back.

In the course of therapy, the patient is reviewing events of the past, often his childhood. Transference is the process by which the patient reacts to the therapist as though the therapist were some significiant person in his past. His feelings toward that person are vented upon the analyst, giving expression and relief to these pent-up emotions. He may expect the therapist to behave as did this other person, and he may handle him as he did in the past. A woman who perceived her father as cold and disinterested in her problems began to accuse the therapist of being indifferent, and she resorted to her old coping maneuvers of coyness and childlike behavior. This transference is considered an essential part of the analytic process.

Freud considered dreams to be a tremendous source of information about the unconscious. He integrated an intricate system of dream analysis into his analytic therapy. Patients are encouraged to remember their dreams and report them during the therapy sessions. Dream content is thought to be a function of both the events of the preceding day and repressed material symbolically expressed during the dream.

There are two levels of analysis of a dream: the manifest content and the latent content. The manifest content is what the person actually dreamed, the images themselves. The latent content is the symbolic hidden meaning of the dream. It is the latent content that is of importance. The patient is encouraged to free associate to the images in his dreams and to try to draw the meaning from them. *The interpretation of dreams* by Freud is a fascinating book and is highly recommended to anyone interested in this area.

Psychoanalysis is the longest and most time consuming of the therapies. Usually in complete psychoanalysis the patient receives treatment for three to five hourly sessions per week, and often the course of the therapy is about three to five years. Psychoanalysis has come under a great deal of criticism, not only for the time it requires but for its possible ineffectiveness. Even some former patients and analysts claim it is ineffective (Ellis, 1962). Yet for most of those desiring radical changes in personality, it is the preferred form of therapy.

Rogerian Client-Centered Therapy (

The assumption of Rogerian therapy is that, given a conducive setting, the patient will cure himself. The basic feature of client-centered therapy is the creation of a totally accepting, supportive, warm setting in which the client feels completely at ease. It is a convention in this type of therapy to refer to the therapist as a counselor and the patient as the client. These terms are consonant with Rogers' ideas of individuals being responsible for the resolutions of their own conflicts. Unlike Freudian analysts who influence the patient's conversation and offer interpretation, the Rogerian counselor does not guide his client in any way. The client completely structures his own sessions, talking when he wishes to and about any topic he prefers. His silences are not interpreted as resistance, and his discussion of apparent trivia is not considered reflective of unconscious association. Everything the client says is considered important and taken in good faith. The counselor voices his support of the client by restating, but not critically rephrasing, the client's statements. He is careful not to let voice inflection or facial expression belie anything but support.

The Rogerian emphasis on the phenomenological aspect of behavior means that an important aspect of the therapy is the adoption by the counselor of the client's own internal frame of reference. The counselor must look at the behavior not from his own point of view, but from the vantage point of the client. Rogers believed strongly in the growth tendency of every individual and in the capacity for people to "cure" themselves. It is his belief that positive changes in personality will occur if the client feels unconditionally accepted by the counselor. The client needs the counselor to support but not direct these changes.

The nondirective nature of the client-centered approach makes it appear as if anyone could assume the role of counselor, since no interpretations or guidance are necessary. This is a gravely erroneous assumption. It is very difficult to be nonevaluative and completely supportive toward another person; a whole system of "body language" and facial expressions may give away our thoughts without our being aware of this communication. Therefore, it takes a great deal of training to be an effective counselor. The individual who enters into client-centered therapy expecting to unload his problems onto a "doctor's shoulders" and have him tell him what to do do is in for a rude awakening, but, if he is willing to grant the assumptions of his potential for constructive growth, both he and the counselor will partake of the exciting process of the awakening of a new personality and a sense of personal responsibility.

Behavior Therapy

The psychodynamic approaches to therapy concentrate on global personality change achieved through insight and therapist-patient interaction. The application of learning principles to behavioral change has led to another therapeutic approach, which significantly departs from these traditional methods and their underlying assumptions of the causes of behavior. This direct application of learning principles has come to be called behavior therapy. Joseph Wolpe, a psychiatrist who became disillusioned with traditional psychotherapy, is the name most often associated with this approach, although it has been widely adopted by a number of other therapists.

Wolpe (1958), in *Psychotherapy by reciprocal inhibition*, argued that maladaptive responses are a product of learning and, as such, can be modified by learning techniques. In contrast to the psychodynamic approach, behavior therapy is not aimed at global personality reorganization, but at the elimination of specific responses; it assigns no special role to insight or therapist-patient interaction. Behavior therapy is concerned with the overt manifestation of behavior and does not assume that behavior is controlled by unconscious intrapsychic events which must first be rooted out and explored. Behavior is learned and it can be unlearned. Both classical and operant conditioning are applied to this end.

SYSTEMATIC DESENSITIZATION.   Wolpe hypothesized that, in neurotic behavior, anxiety is a conditioned response elicited by situations or stimuli that are not normally anxiety-producing. One way of altering this stimulus-response link is to establish another response in its place, one which is incompatible with anxiety. Thus, in counterconditioning, the therapist exposes the patient to anxiety-provoking stimuli while making him perform a response that is incompatible with anxiety. Relaxation is the response most often used, because it is easy to teach and can be used in a variety of situations. By repeatedly pairing stimuli with relaxation in a classical conditioning paradigm, the patient eventually relaxes to the stimulus, just as he had previously learned to be anxious to it.

The technique of systematic desensitization proceeds in a number of steps. It is a carefully controlled learning situation. These steps will be examined as they occurred in the case of the desensitization of a girl who was afraid of the dark and the man who was allegedly trying to kill her.

The first step is establishing an anxiety hierarchy. The therapist determines the areas that are producing anxiety by interviewing the patient. There may be many areas or themes, but each one is dealt with separately. For each theme, the patient is asked to rank various situations according to how much anxiety it would elicit. In our case, the girl might rank "being alone in the house at sunset" as mildly anxiety producing, and "being alone, in bed, and hearing a noise downstairs" as very anxiety producing. When a variety of situations are covered, the therapist ranks these situations in order, from the least to the most anxious, as the patient has scored them. Frequently, the therapist also gives the patient a preference scale to determine what kinds of things the patient likes, and then incorporates these things into the images he is to later build. In the case of our girl, strawberries and the Beatles ranked high as preferred items.

The second step is teaching the incompatible response, relaxation. Relaxation training involves teaching the patient to become aware of the muscles of his body and when they are tense. The patient first tenses and then relaxes a variety of muscles, concentrating on one area of the body at a time. Starting with the head, the eyes, mouth, forehead, cheeks, and progressing to the feet, the patient tenses a muscle and then relaxes it until his whole body is completely serene. With training, a patient can do this progression very rapidly, almost instantaneously at any time in any place.

During the phase of counterconditioning, the therapist helps the patient to adopt this posture of complete relaxation, and he presents to the patient, under this completely relaxed state, the anxiety hierarchy items. Usually the therapist gives the item verbally and asks the patient to imagine the situation as vividly as possible. The situations are presented strictly in order from least threatening to most threatening. If the patient feels the slightest bit anxious, he indicates this to the therapist, perhaps by raising his finger, and the therapist goes back to a less threatening situation.

The anxiety hierarchy is mastered progressively by very small steps, and moving from one position to another on the hierarchy is predicated upon there being no anxiety at the previous stage. As you can see, by imagining these scenes while completely relaxed, the patient is learning to replace his old response of anxiety with the more adaptive one of relaxation. Because of the incompatibility of these responses, this is called reciprocal inhibition.

One of the items presented to the girl afraid of the dark was to

> Imagine that you are home alone, it's around 10 o'clock, and you feel hungry so you have a huge dish of fresh strawberries, and you put on the Beatles, and you are feeling very content when suddenly you hear noises in the living room. The noises don't upset you though, because you realize that it's probably just the heating system,

or maybe the cat, and you just go on eating your strawberries before bed.

The patient was to imagine this as vividly as possible as the therapist talked. Because they had gradually built up to this stage of the hierarchy, she felt no anxiety and the therapist could proceed to the next scene. The next scene was to

> Imagine being at home alone all night. You wake up in the middle of the night, and you hear creaking noises, as you look around the room you see shadows moving on the wall. You quickly realize that it must be the wind that is responsible for the noises and even the shadows, by making the trees sway and cast the shadow in your room.

This image, unlike the previous one, did create some anxiety in the patient, and she raised her finger to indicate that she was no longer completely relaxed. The therapist simply told her to stop imagining it, and they went back to a variation of the preceding scene that she coped with successfully.

The application of systematic desensitization to this patient's fear of the dark and of the alleged man who was to kill her was successful. The entire length of therapy was about two hours a week for two months. Systematic desensitization can be used to treat any abnormal behavior in which a source of anxiety can be determined. Since the source of fear is obvious in a phobia, it is especially amenable to this kind of treatment.

CONDITIONED AVERSION.   Counterconditioning techniques are not restricted to the elimination of negative responses to stimuli. They can also be applied to changing preference or attraction to stimuli, when it is in the best long-term interests of the patient to eliminate the preference. In these cases, one aims at a conditioned aversion of the stimuli. Examples of this preference are fetishistic behavior, alcoholism, and homosexuality. It should be emphasized that the patient, not the doctor, decides to change these preferences, as this is not an evaluative process.

In conditioned aversion, the positively valued stimulus is made to occur in the presence of an unpleasant or painful stimulus. By repeated pairing, the previously positive stimulus becomes associated with the aversive stimulus and it, too, becomes aversive. Homosexuality, for instance, may be treated in the following way. The man is shown pictures of a homosexually erotic nature. Simultaneous with the pictures, he may receive an electric shock, unpleasant but not harmful in intensity. Gradually, the man learns to associate the erotic pictures with shock, and the homoeroticism takes on the unpleasant properties of the shock.

This counterconditioning often employs operant conditioning techniques as well. The homosexual patient may be treated by an anticipatory avoidance technique. If he changes the slide of the male nude within 8 seconds of its presentation, he can avoid getting one shock. If he continues to look at the slide after 8 seconds, he receives shock until he indicates by saying "no" that he wishes the slide to be withdrawn. Simultaneous with the removal of the slide and the termination of the shock, a picture of an attractive female is projected onto the screen. The male nude then becomes associated with pain (shock) and anticipation of pain and the female with reduction of anxiety and pain (removal of shock).

One study, employing this technique with 26 homosexuals, reported that 18 of these subjects had relinquished their homosexual behavior as determined by follow-ups ranging from 3 months to 2 years later. Since deviant sexual behavior is usually so resistant to change, this is a significant success (Feldman, 1966).

Alcoholism can likewise be treated by counterconditioning. In this case, the person may be given a drug that, when mixed with alcohol, causes nausea. The person is then given a drink of liquor. The alcohol acquires very aversive associations for the patient, and its old positive qualities are replaced by a new association. Of course, in the case of alcoholism, if the person is drinking to escape from some unpleasant stressful situation, one must also attempt to change his life situation so that he does not seek another source of escape.

CHANGING THE SYSTEM OF REWARDS.   We can to some extent manipulate behavior by manipulating its consequences. A behavior can be strengthened if its occurrence is followed by some rewarding event (reward training). It is also strengthened if its occurrence leads to the termination of an unpleasant event. As mothers universally know, punishment training, or following a behavior with an unpleasant consequence, leads to a reduction of that response (aversion therapy). One can change behavior by either giving or taking away a positive or negative stimulus appropriately. Behavior therapists are sharply aware of the power of this manipulation of consequences, and the first step in their analysis of behavior is a search for the consequences of the behavior they are to change. Frequently, a child's behavior is maintained inadvertently by the parents. The child who is a disciplinary problem, throwing temper tantrums and exhibiting bizarre behavior, may be rewarded for his deviance by getting attention from his parents. If it is attention that he seeks, the parents' excitement and fluster at such times only serves to reinforce the very behavior they wish to extinguish. In such cases, the therapist would prescribe set responses for the parents to make each time the child engages in the unwanted acts. They may withdraw attention for a time, or place the child in a room by himself until he displays only reasonable behavior. In any case, the child's behavior would no longer be followed by attention, but only by an unrewarding contingency. This extinction of a response through nonreinforcement is called omission training.

Omission training has been used in the treatment of schizophrenics. Ayllon (1968) reports treating a 47-year-old chronic schizophrenic by this method. The woman had become a managerial problem on her ward because of three persistent activities: stealing food, hoarding towels, and wearing piles of clothing. In addition, the woman was severely overweight, tipping the scales at 250 pounds. The staff's attempts to deal with these behaviors had all proved futile. Ayllon proceeded to subject all of these responses to behavioral control. To deal with the stealing, the woman was seated alone in the cafeteria. She was closely watched by the staff. Any instance of stealing led to her immediate removal from the cafeteria. The consequence of stealing was the withdrawal of a positive stimulus, food. Within two weeks, the stealing behavior was extinguished. Ayllon similarly dealt with the clothing problems. Before the woman could receive a meal she was weighed with her clothing on, and, if this weight exceeded a certain amount, she could not get her meal. After eleven weeks the patient had reduced her clothing so that it weighed only three pounds. The towel hoarding was dealt with somewhat differently. Towels had previously been something cherished by the patient and systematically removed by the staff. Under the behavior modification, the patient was not only permitted to keep towels but was progressively flooded with them. By the third week she was given sixty towels a day. When the patient had literally hundreds of towels in her room, she herself began to remove them and eventually the hoarding behavior was eliminated and did not reappear for a year. As you can see, Ayllon simply changed the stimulus, towels, from a positively valued one to an aversive, negative one. By changing the contingencies of behaviors, the responses are amenable to radical change, and it is this fact upon which the operant techniques of behavior modification are based.

Behavior Therapy in Perspective

Behavior therapy, or behavior modification as it is called, is a very controversial issue among therapists today, with its disciples and critics each defending opposing points of view. Advocates of behavior therapy have pointed out a number of real advantages to the approach. First of all, it is easy to learn and apply, so that its techniques can be taught to aides, social workers, teachers, and family, enabling many people to enter into the therapeutic process. Second, it takes far fewer sessions to treat a patient by this method than does traditional psychotherapy. Often the difference is not one of months but years. This offers an advantage to both therapist and patient. The therapist is able to treat many more patients; the patient is saved both time and expense. Third, by specifying more clearly the exact behavior to be changed, the effects of the therapy may be studied more empirically. Behavior therapy has introduced more scientific rigor into therapy and maintains a liason with the laboratory. Fourth, it minimizes verbal interaction between patient and therapist, and it does not rely on reflection and insight. These are advantages when dealing with less-educated and inarticulate patients.

The advocates of behavior therapy have also pointed to studies showing the efficacy of behavior therapy over more traditional psychotherapy. One study comparing the effect of behavior therapy, traditional psychotherapy (eclectic psychotherapy), and no therapy on patients suffering from stage-fright found that the group that received desensitization showed the greatest improvement with no evidence of relapse or symptom substitution two years later (Paul, 1967). The proponents of this technique report great success with its application, with one reviewer claiming a substantial reduction of symptoms in about 90% of the treated cases (Lovibund, 1966). One must exercise caution in evaluating these statistics, however, since most of the judgments of cure are made by the treating therapist, not an unbiased second party; therefore, objectivity is open to question.

Psychodynamic theorists have frequently criticized behavior modification on the grounds that "symptom substitution" is all that is really being effected. Since these theorists assume that neurotic behavior is a symptom of some underlying conflict or trauma, erasing the symptom certainly does not cure the disease. The patient will simply develop another symptom in its place. The learning theorists, of course, do not seek causes in intrapsychic events but in the experience of the person, past and present, with the world. Their assertion that symptom substitution will not occur has generally been borne out experimentally (Bergin, 1966; Grossberg, 1964; Lazarus, 1961). Once a behavior has been extinguished, they contend that it is not replaced by a new one. The problem with adequately assessing this question, however, is deciding what one means by symptom substitution and how one can clearly identify it. How long must a patient be complaint-free and how different must problems be before one can assume independence of two complaints? If someone has been desensitized to fear of sexual relations and then two years later shows up with the problem that he can't get along with his spouse, is this a new problem or is this somehow related to and possibly a distortion of the old problem of sexual anxiety? Behavior is extremely complex and questions like these are very difficult to resolve. *However*

Despite these issues, behavior modification has been of real assistance in dealing with some types of neurotic and even psychotic behavior. Within the next few years, we will probably see a widening of behavior modification techniques and a joint application of this approach and traditional psychotherapy. The pragmatic approach of the behavior therapist has much to recommend it, but, in dealing with severely and globally disturbed individuals, it is probably best applied in conjunction with a broader psychotherapy that can deal with the more subjective aspects of the behavioral disorganization, while the learning theorists attack its overt manifestations.

SUMMARY

Many treatments are commonly used with patients experiencing psychological disorders. Those who believe that most behavioral problems stem from psychological processes employ psychotherapy; those who believe in biological causes tend to use medical therapies; and those who believe that the psychological cause is immaterial and concern themselves with the resulting behavior use behavior therapy. Each method has met with successes and failures. We are a long way from completely understanding the causes and knowing the sure cures for mental illness.

SUGGESTED READINGS

HALL, C. S., & LINDZEY, G. *Theories of personality.* (1st ed.) New York: Wiley, 1957.

MISCHEL, W. *Introduction to personality.* New York: Holt, 1971.

ROGERS, C. R., & SKINNER, B. F. Some issues concerning the control of human behavior *Science,* 1956, **124,** 1057–1066.

22

Aspects of
Social
Behavior

What do Alcoholics Anonymous, encounter groups, political demonstrations, and lynch mobs have in common? All of these activities reveal the powerful behavior of groups and, although some seem detrimental while others are highly positive, they may be explained by many of the same psychological principles. If you have thought about such group phenomena, if you wonder why people are sometimes conforming, why they typically do not help one another in emergency situations, or how attitudes affect behavior and vice versa, you have been asking questions asked by social psychologists. Although we are each unique and therefore respond to these situations in somewhat different ways, there are also social and psychological constants that affect each of us similarly despite our personal differences. This is the major focus for social psychology. We begin our examination of this field with a consideration of the attitudes an individual holds and their consequences for his behavior. Since attitudes are shaped and changed by social and environmental influences, this is an important first step in understanding man as a social organism.

THEORY OF COGNITIVE DISSONANCE

Many psychologists feel that people do not merely subscribe to a random collection of attitudes, but rather possess coherent belief systems, which are internally and psychologically consistent. They suggest that all men possess a drive toward cognitive consistency that motivates belief and attitude change when inconsistency arises. One of the most elegant formulations of this idea is the cognitive dissonance theory proposed by Leon Festinger in 1957. The central assumption of this theory is that human beings cannot tolerate inconsistency. Consequently, whenever an individual perceives that inconsistency exist, he will try to eliminate or reduce it.

Suppose you believe that students should only have limited power in running the university. In fact, you believe that they may really not be well qualified to make policy decisions or to hire and fire faculty. Then one day, you are walking along campus and stop to watch a rally being held by classmates who believe just the opposite. They feel that students should have unlimited control over every aspect of university life. The rally looks interesting and you decide to stay. Quickly, however, it gets out of hand and the administration has to call the police. After a bloody confrontation everyone, including you, gets carted away to jail. According to Festinger, an individual in this situation will experience dissonance. That you have been arrested and undergone great suffering for this attitude is inconsistent with the cognition that you really do not hold the belief. Thus, dissonance exists whenever two or more cognitive elements are in a psychologically inconsistent relation.

Cognitive elements are bits of knowledge or beliefs either about the environment or about oneself or one's behavior. According to Festinger, cognitive elements can be in any one of three relationships. They can be dissonant, consonant, or irrelevant. In the above example, a consonant element with "I am against student power" would be "I refuse to go to rallies run by the nuts who think students should have total control." A dissonant element would be "I have been arrested for participating in a rally which advocates power." An irrelevant element would be "I smoke cigarettes." Since cognitive elements are linked to a person's beliefs, his behavior, or to the environment, changes in any one of these could produce changes in his cognitive structure. Consequently, one way that an individual can reduce his dissonance, i.e., bring his behavior and his beliefs into a constant relation, is by changing his behavior.

The theory suggests that, not only can behavior change follow from attitude change, but, in addition, attitude change can follow from shifts in behavior. The student in the example can actually resolve his dissonance by coming to believe that, in fact, students should have control over all aspects of the university. This belief is consonant with the cognition that he has been arrested and undergone some sacrifice on behalf of greater student power. Dissonance is reduced in this case by a change in attitude.

Magnitude of Dissonance

Dissonance theory further predicts that not all inconsistencies produce the same amount of dissonance. Rather, the magnitude of the dissonance is a function of two variables. First, the amount of dissonance an individual experiences is affected by the importance of the relevant cognitive elements. If it were not important to the student that he was arrested and thrown into jail, this occurrence would not necessarily produce a great deal of dissonance. Second, the magnitude of the dissonance is a function of the number of relevant dissonant and consonant elements. For example, in addition to the student being thrown into jail for his participation in the rally, he is put on academic probation and his parents are forced to pay a large bail bond which they deduct from his allowance for the next two years. These elements would be all dissonant with the cognition that "I really don't believe that students should have greater control over the university," thereby increasing the magnitude of the dissonance. As dissonance increases, the likelihood of attempts to reduce the dissonance also becomes greater.

Applications of Dissonance Theory

CHOICE.   Dissonance theory was initially concerned with decision making situations. Clearly, any time an individual is put in a situation where he must make a choice between two or more alternatives, he is in a potentially dissonance-producing situation. Suppose, for example, you are registering for next semester and trying to decide between two courses. One course may be very easy with little work, simple exams, and so forth. The teacher, however, has a reputation of being terribly bad. The other course has a marvelous teacher, but everyone says that the course is extremely difficult and involves extensive preparation both in examinations and field work. Each course then has both positive and negative qualities. After either course is chosen, the loss of the positive qualities of the other is dissonant with the knowledge that that course was not selected. Postdecision dissonance is greater if the two alternatives are nearly equally attractive. When there is less justification for having chosen one over the other, there is greater dissonance during the postdecision phase.

One way to reduce dissonance is by overrating the chosen alternative and, at the same time, underrating the alternative that was not chosen (Brehm & Cohen, 1962). Returning to our example, if you choose the course which has the very difficult material but the excellent teacher, the theory predicts that you would come to believe that the teacher was absolutely superb and that the material was really not so difficult. In addition, you would probably think that the rejected course had a teacher that was impossibly bad and the work load was really a little harder than you had thought. Brehm (1956) found precisely these effects when subjects were allowed to choose between two household products. Brehm's subjects rated the attractiveness of these products both before and after making their decision and he found that the chosen alternative was overrated after the choice had been made and the nonchosen alternative was underrated.

Insufficient Justification

Both of the products which Brehm offered his subjects had positive and negative qualities, but people often engage in behaviors for which there are very few positive outcomes. It is interesting to consider what happens to someone who engages in a behavior, for very little justification, which is discrepant with an attitude that he holds. To test this question, Festinger and Carlsmith (1959) asked college students to perform an exceedingly boring test as part of a psychology experiment. The task consisted of rotating blocks, which were mounted on a peg, for a full hour. The task seemed to have no specific purpose. After the task was completed, some subjects were asked by the experimenter to help him in the next part of the experiment. He mentioned that his regular assistant could not make it that day and he wondered if the subject would take his place. The experimenter then explained that the main part of the study was to determine the effects of set or expectations on the performance of the task. The subject was then told by the experimenter that he, in fact, was in the condition in which there was no set or expectation. The next subject, however, was to be in a condition in which he was to be told that the task was extremely enjoyable. This information was regularly given by the assistant who was unable to make it that day. The experimenter asked the subject if he would be willing to help with the new situation. In essence, the experimenter was asking the subject to tell a lie to another subject by telling him that the boring task was enjoyable. For doing this, the experimenter offered subjects either $20 or $1. After subjects told the lie to the next subject (almost all of them agreed to do so), they were asked to rate how enjoyable they found the task.

You may be surprised to learn that when the new temporary assistants were asked to tell a lie and given only $1, they actually found the task far more enjoyable than subjects who were given $20 for telling a lie. Festinger and Carlsmith reasoned that, for these subjects, saying the boring task was interesting, was dissonant with the fact that they were only paid $1 to do so. The dissonance was reduced by changing one of the dissonant elements, that is, they claimed that the task was actually interesting, not boring. Parenthetically, these results suggest that parents or teachers who try to bribe children with money or fancy presents may be getting them to engage in counterattitudinal behavior without producing real attitude change. It appears that the smaller the reward (as long as it is sufficient to warrant the behavior), the greater the dissonance and, thus, the more attitude change in line with the behavior.

In a similar experiment, Zimbardo (1969) tried to get subjects to engage in counterattitudinal behavior for minimal justification. Very popular or disliked sergeants asked army privates to eat fried grasshoppers. Although subjects were equally willing to agree to eat the fried grasshoppers whether asked by a highly liked or disliked sergeant, subjects who ate the grasshoppers for the negative sergeant appeared to like the grasshoppers better and expressed a greater desire to eat them in the future (Figure 22-1). Again, as the theory predicts, the cognition that "I do not like fried grasshopper" is dissonant with the cognition "I ate fried grasshoppers for a sergeant that I detest." Dissonance is reduced by changing one's attitude toward the fried grasshoppers. That is, "I like fried grasshoppers, so I am willing to eat them for a sergeant that I dislike."

Commitment

All these studies suggest that attitudes are not stable or fixed but are often in flux. They are re-evaluated in light of the individual's own behavior, the circumstances in which he finds himself, or the events in which he participates. When these elements are inconsistent, a person is likely to experience dissonance. He attempts to reduce this dissonance by changing one of his attitudes and/or behaviors. This is a dynamic, interactive situation in which the person is greatly affected by his environment and is also changing it. Brehm and Cohen (1962) have argued, in fact, that the individual must be actively involved in the process for dissonance to occur. They believe that subjects will not experience dissonance unless they perceive that they have had a choice and have committed themselves in some way to engaging in the behavior that is discrepant with their attitude. When individuals perceive that they have committed themselves freely, without external justification, Brehm (1969) has argued that even motivations as basic as hunger and thirst come under cognitive control.

Brehm was interested in testing what happens when a hungry person

FIGURE 22-1   A soldier is placed in a dissonant state by having to eat a grasshopper for a sergeant he dislikes (Zimbardo, 1965). The soldier resolves this dissonance by afterward claiming he does not mind eating grasshoppers.

voluntarily commits himself to a state of additional or prolonged deprivation. The individual is aware of the aversiveness of the tension associated with his hunger, yet he knows that he has freely chosen to be exposed further to this state. This dissonance may be reduced by actually decreasing his feelings of hunger. In other words, the cognition that he has agreed to undergo further deprivation is indeed consistent with the fact that he is really not very hungry.

Brehm asked his subjects to come to the experiment without eating breakfast or lunch in order to participate in a study examining the effects of food deprivation on intellectual and motor functioning. When they arrived at the laboratory, they were asked to rate how hungry they felt before the experiment actually began. After taking tests for about 15 minutes, the subjects were told that more testing would be needed that evening and all subjects were being asked to go without dinner as well so that the effects of greater deprivation could be studied. Half of the subjects were told that unfortunately the experimenter was unable to give them any more credit points (all subjects were offered points initially for participating in the experiment), but he would appreciate it very much if they could help. He stressed that the final decision, however, was totally up to them. These then are high choice subjects, freely committing themselves to continue without any external justification such as money or pressure for doing so. Another group of subjects was offered $5 for continuing to go without food and participating in the later part of the experiment. These are subjects for whom there is a strong external reason for continuing to go hungry a little while longer. After this manipulation, all subjects were again given ratings asking them to evaluate their hunger and, in addition, they were asked to order the number of sandwiches they would like once the experiment was completed.

The results showed that subjects who committed themselves to food deprivation for no external incentive rated themselves as much less hungry after they had made that choice. Subjects experiencing little dissonance, that is subjects who were provided with $5 in order to continue participating in the experiment, rated themselves even more hungry after they had agreed to continue. This group also ordered many more sandwiches then the high dissonance subjects. The data then support the notion that even something as fundamental as a biological drive state can be affected by dissonance in the same way as opinions or overt behavior. In Brehm's experiment, dissonance is reduced by reducing the experienced intensity of the drive state.

Clearly, there is an important interaction between cognitive events and physiological drive states that goes beyond a simple notion that we always eat when we are hungry and drink when we are thirsty. In fact, the way that we interpret and respond to internal states such as hunger or thirst or feeling states such as emotion may be greatly affected by cognitive, external, or situational events. Indeed, it seems likely that there is no one-to-one relationship between a biological drive state and the psychological interpretation of that state. As demonstrated in Brehm's experiment, subjects in both conditions were fully deprived and had rated themselves equally hungry before the commitment to continue was made. But after the choice, subjects in the high dissonance group perceived themselves as less hungry and made a behavioral commitment, i.e., ordering fewer sandwiches, to this reduced hunger.

COGNITIVE CONTROL OF MOTIVATION

In what other areas can we investigate cognitive or external control of physiological states? When else does the individual make judgments about his internal state on the basis of external events? Consider for example, emotional states like joy, fear, or anger. Several investigators have argued that there are not specific and identifiable internal bodily states associated with these emotions, but rather that cognitive or situational factors may be the major determinant of emotional states (see Chapter 4). Working within this framework, Schachter (1964) has suggested that an emotion is a function of both physiological arousal and a cognition appropriate to this arousal. Cognitions exert a steering function providing the label for the physiological arousal, but the arousal alone is not sufficient to produce the emotion.

Labeling of Emotional Arousal

To explore this assumption, subjects were asked to come to the laboratory to participate in an experiment testing the effects of a new vitamin, Suproxin, on vision (Schachter & Singer, 1962). Actually, subjects were given an injection of epinephrine, which typically produces palpitation, tremor, flushing, and accelerated breathing. Some of these subjects were fully informed about the expected effects of the epinephrine, that is, they were told that the side effects of the vitamin were palpitations, tremor, and so forth. Other subjects were misinformed about the possible side effects of the drug, for they were told that it often caused numbness, itchiness, and a slight headache. A third group of subjects was told nothing about possible side effects.

Each subject then entered a room to wait for the experiment to begin, and found another subject, presumably also waiting to participate, behaving very strangely. Sometimes this subject, who was really a confederate of the experimenter, spent his time making jokes, playing with a Hula Hoop, shooting paper airplanes, etc., that is, in general, engaging in fairly amusing and giddy kinds of behavior. In other cases, with different subjects, the confederate became extremely angry over a questionnaire which he was asked to complete, consisting of questions like "With how many men other than your father has your mother had sexual intercourse?" In summary, there were subjects who were physiologically aroused, informed as to the cause of this arousal or ignorant about the drug's real effects, and in the presence of an angry or euphoric stooge. Schachter and Singer found that, when subjects were aroused by epinephrine but had no explanation (like Suproxin is causing my stirred up feelings) for the arousal, they could be readily manipulated into the disparate emotional states of anger or euphoria depending on the stooge's behavior. The subjects interpreted their arousal in the context of the social situation and labeled it accordingly.

When aroused subjects knew that their tremor and flushing were due to the drug, they did not describe themselves as emotional. Their external information provided an acceptable label for their arousal state. Clearly, the cues from the external environment play a major role in determining how people perceive and interpret our internal states. Another group of subjects, injected with a placebo instead of epinephrine, was relatively unaffected by the antics of the stooge. Thus, subjects did need the internal cues provided by the drug to identify the fact that they were in an emotional state, but they needed the external cues of the situation, the stooge's behavior, to discriminate which emotion they were experiencing.

Reducing Emotions by Relabeling Arousal

Although this experiment relied on the artificial induction of arousal with an injection of epinephrine, it has been demonstrated that subjects who arouse themselves can be made, under certain circumstances, to behave as if their arousal were due to something else. In an experiment by Nisbett and Schachter (1966), subjects were threatened with shock to make them afraid. All subjects were given a placebo pill, which had no real physiological effects (Figure 22-2). Half the subjects, however, were told that the pill would cause tremor, palpitation, increased breathing, i.e., feelings that can be expected in people who are afraid. If the subjects can be led to blame these symptoms on the pill, rather than on their fear of shock, they may actually behave less fearfully. It was found that these subjects actually took more shock and rated it less painful than subjects who could only attribute their fear symptoms to the shock itself.

In another study, subjects who were highly aroused over the threat of impending shock behaved far less fearfully if they could attribute the arousal to an external unemotional source, e.g., some unusual set of noises (Ross, Rodin, & Zimbardo, 1969). There were increased breathing and heart rate, palpitations, and butterflies in the stomach, that is, the usual internal physiological reactions that accompany strong emotions. When given a choice between working on two puzzles, the solution of one leading to avoiding the shock and the other providing a reward and a shock, subjects who attributed their stirred-up state to the noise spent much less time working to avoid shock

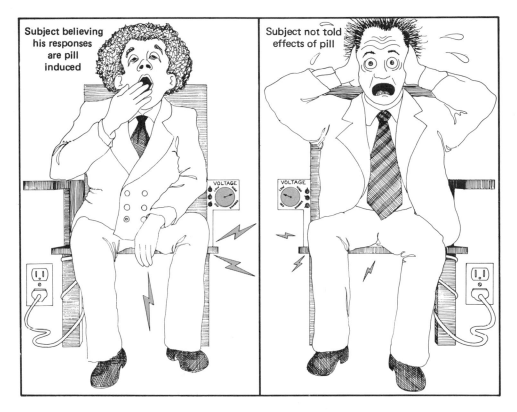

FIGURE 22-2 Subjects responded differently when threatened with shock. If the subject believed that his increased arousal was due to a pill, he was able to behave less fearfully.

than subjects who had only the anticipated shock on which to blame their aroused feelings. By the reattribution of arousal symptoms to an unemotional source, subjects actually behaved less fearfully. The clinical implications of this sort of technique were immediately recognized and it has recently been shown that insomniacs actually fell asleep faster on the nights when they believed their symptoms such as heart pounding, mind racing, etc., were caused by a pill that was, unknown to them, actually a placebo (Storms & Nisbett, 1970).

Variables Affecting Hunger and Eating

Feelings of pain and joy and anger are not specific, distinguishable physiological events, but are labeled in terms of the external, cognitive, or social situation. Clearly, if the labels applied to internal states are so malleable, perhaps inappropriate labels can also get readily assigned to a feeling state.

For example, in the occurrence of chronic obesity, it is possible that people overeat and grow fat because they have learned to call every stirred up internal state hunger or, alternatively, they may call no internal state hunger, suggesting that they get little information from their stomachs to tell them when they are physiologically in need of food. In fact, several studies have shown that the internal deprivation state has little influence on either self-report of hunger or actual eating in overweight subjects.

INTERNAL CONTROL OF EATING.   When subjects who have gone without breakfast were asked to report every 15 minutes whether or not they felt hungry, normal individuals most likely reported hunger when their stomachs were contracting. In contrast, reports of hunger in the obese bore little relation to actual stomach contraction (Stunkard & Koch, 1964). Moreover, when normal weight subjects were deprived of food for several hours, they ate far more than when they were full; by contrast, overweight subjects actually ate a little more when they were sated than when physiologically deprived (Schachter *et al.*, 1968). These results suggest that the eating behavior of the obese is not under internal physiological control. Whether or not the overweight individual eats seems unrelated to his actual state of physiological need.

EXTERNAL CONTROLS OF EATING.   What cues are the obese using to tell them when they are hungry if they are so unresponsive to the state of their gut? Actually, external food-relevant cues in the environment trigger eating in the overweight person (Figure 22-3). After all, everyone knows obese people who simply cannot walk past a candy store or bakery without being drawn inside. In experiments to test these assumptions, it was found that eating in the obese is largely determined by external factors such as the passage of time, the taste and sight of food, and the number of food cues present.

The extent of external control was never more dramatically shown than when a clock was faked to run at either twice or half its normal speed. It was found that overweight subjects were greatly influenced by the manipulation of time. They ate considerably more when they thought it was their dinner hour than when they thought it was much earlier. Normal weight subjects, knowing whether or not they were hungry by what their stomachs were telling them, were relatively unaffected in their eating by the rigged clock.

It now appears that overweight people do not eat endlessly, but rather they eat and overeat only when the environmental situation provides a number of highly compelling food stimuli. If the obese eat mainly in response to external cues, they should abstain from eating more easily than normal weight people when the environment provides no cues for eating. On Yom Kippur,

FIGURE 22-3   Fat people tend to be sensitive to external cues. An obese person eats when the clock says it is time to eat, whereas a normal will wait for internal signals.

the Jewish Day of Atonement, which is a day of fasting and prayer, external food cues are extremely sparse for those who remain in a synagogue. It was found that overweight Jews were more likely to fast than those of normal weight and that the longer the time they spent in the synagogue, the easier the fast. However, for normal weight Jews, responsive to their internal deprivation state, the painfulness of the fast was unrelated to the length of time spent in the synagogue (Goldman, Jaffa, & Schachter, 1968).

ATTRIBUTION THEORY

In a classic book in social psychology, *The psychology of interpersonal relations*, Fritz Heider, one of the fathers of modern social psychology, describes how we make attributions about the world around us. It seems that man is invariably predisposed to interpret all events in the environment "as being caused by particular parts of the relatively stable environment [Heider, 1958]." As a result, we constantly attribute causes to explain our own behavior as well as the behavior of others.

The studies on emotion and eating described earlier suggest that we do not always have direct and unmistakable knowledge about our internal physiological states. It now seems that, in identifying our own internal states, we each rely partly on the same external cues that others use to learn about our internal states. Daryl Bem (1967) has suggested that this is not only true of physiological states, but of private events like attitudes and opinions.

When we want to know what others are thinking, we rely on publicly observable external cues, especially their actions. Bem believes that we infer our own opinions from our own observable behavior as well. He has called this self-perception theory. To test the idea, Bem gave subjects a series of electric shocks and told them before each trial whether the experimenters wanted them to try to endure the shock or to escape it, although the final decision was up to the subject. Although the shocks were all of equal intensity, subjects were told they were somewhat different and asked to rate the painfulness of each shock right after receiving it. Subjects rated the shocks they escaped as more painful than the ones they endured. Bem argued that subjects were making the same inferences about themselves, viewing their behavior, that an observer who had seen them respond to the shock would make.

Inducing Beliefs in False Confessions

Bem believes that, since an individual uses his behavior and the situational circumstances motivating that behavior as information about his attitudes, he would be more likely to infer, just as an outside observer would, that, if he were paid a lot of money to say or do something, he would not necessarily believe it or have done it otherwise. If he is only paid a very small sum, however, the external reasons for the behavior are not clear; therefore, one infers he must really have wanted to do it anyway. If this sounds reminiscent of the Festinger and Carlsmith dissonance experiment, it is no accident, for Bem was trying to show that the dissonance results could be explained without postulating an underlying drive state that the individual was motivated to reduce. Bem's argument denies any motivational interpretation of the attitude change found in experiments on insufficient justification described earlier. His work does not challenge the dissonance results, however, but merely their interpretation.

An interesting application of Bem's research is in describing how people can be made not only to give false confessions but to believe them as well. In his experiment (Bem, 1965), subjects were asked simple questions about themselves and told to answer them truthfully in the presence of an amber light and to lie in the presence of a green light. Following this, all subjects were asked to read statements aloud, which Bem knew, from prior testing, that the subject disagreed with. He found that, when subjects read such statements in the presence of the amber truth light, they believed that they represented their real attitudes more than when they read the statements in the presence of the green lie light.

This suggested that saying does indeed become believing whenever someone makes statements under conditions in which he expects himself to be telling the truth. If a skillful interrogator could induce an individual to make inadvertent errors and distorted statements in the surroundings of a police station, surroundings that may act as truth signals for the average citizen, the suspect himself could actually come to believe them, especially if he can be made to confess without coercion. Although these ideas are interesting and provocative, Maslach (1971) demonstrated that individuals show much less confidence in the recall accuracy for their false statements than in the recall accuracy for their true statements. This confusion may make them more susceptible to skillful interrogation and thus lead to a possibly false confession. However, this does not necessarily mean the suspect has actually come to believe it.

Inferences about Our Attitudes from Behavior

In addition to determining what we feel by external events, we also learn what we do. In fact, we seem likely to make causal inferences about ourselves from new information about any aspect of our behavior, the behavior of others, or the general context in which it occurs. This again is the core idea in attribution theory. As an example of the attribution process, Kiesler, Nisbett, and Zanna (1969) asked Yale undergraduates to try to persuade passersby to sign a petition urging action against air pollution. With each subject when he was requested to take the petition, was another subject, who was actually a confederate, who was asked to take a petition about auto safety. When the confederate agreed to take the petition, saying that he would not mind trying to convince people about something important like auto safety that he really believed in, the real subjects seemed to increase their own beliefs on the importance of air pollution, even though they were asked when the stooge was no longer present. The stooge's reason for agreeing was apparently accepted by the subjects as the reason why they too agreed, and they consequently inferred that they felt quite strongly about air pollution. Subjects who heard a stooge agree to take the petition on auto safety because the topic seemed to be a good one for the experimenter's purpose did not increase their stand against air pollution. These subjects also appeared less motivated to work hard at gathering signatures than the subjects who had expressed stronger feelings about air pollution.

Inferences About Our Attitudes from Our Physiological Response

It might be argued that many individuals may not really know where they stand on air pollution and can, therefore, be easily manipulated into misperceiving their intentions. Or it may be that they wanted to look as committed to an important issue as the other subject had, in order to look good in the experimenter's eyes. But what if we take something that we think all subjects must know about themselves, that is, the kinds of features by which they are "turned on" in the opposite sex. Valins (1966) showed slides of nude females to male college students who were wired to dummy electrodes which were presumably measuring their heart rate (Figure 22-4). While looking at the nudes they were allowed to "overhear" their heartbeats, which sometimes increased during a particular slide. Subjects rated the nudes as more attractive when they thought their heart rate had increased and chose to take more of those photographs home with them. Clearly, external information about autonomic arousal was used by subjects in making inferences about their liking for the various photographs. Whereas Schachter showed that labeling of actual arousal was directly affected by external events, Valins demonstrated that subjects simply have to think they are aroused and the same effects occur.

Similarly, Rodin (1971) has concluded that subjects' beliefs about internal states greatly affect their behavior. Common opinion has it that women are less reliable than men in high pressure situations. Since women are likely to be depressed and upset when menstruating, Rodin reasoned that females who believe their frustration and depresssion is due to menstruation might perform better, not worse, when in an upsetting situation. It follows that if something disturbs them and they can attribute their feelings to the fact that they are menstruating, they should appear less affected by the upsetting event. Rodin found that subjects worked on a frustrating, annoying task longer when they were menstruating than when they were not, and the subjects who persevered the longest were those who complained of the most severe menstrual symptoms.

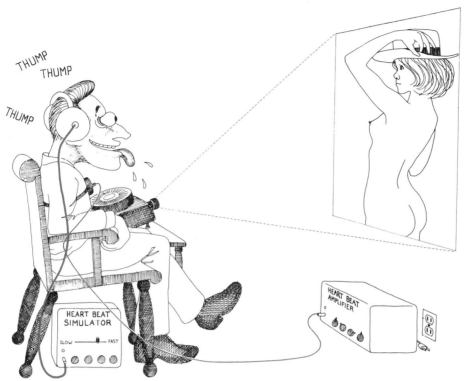

FIGURE 22-4   An experiment by Valins (1966) demonstrated how attitudes are affected by supposed physiological responses.

THEORY OF SOCIAL COMPARISON

It now seems clear that we do not have a fixed or totally independent knowledge of our attitudes and feelings nor do we have direct or infallible knowledge about the causes of our behavior. Since we so frequently turn to the external world for information about ourselves, it is no wonder that we are readily influenced by the behavior of others. In fact, Festinger (1954) has suggested that, when there is no external objective information by which to evaluate our opinions and abilities, we use social comparison, i.e., other people, to provide the necessary information. Since we try to make accurate assessments about our opinions and abilities, we are most likely to compare ourselves to people who are similar to us. A political revolutionary does not get much information by comparing his opinions with those of Ronald Reagan, just as one would not be able to accurately evaluate his tennis ability by comparing himself to Rod Laver. One especially important development of this theory, suggested by Festinger, is that, if an individual's desire for self-evaluation can be accomplished by means of social comparison, people should seek out associations with others, belong to groups, and so forth. If we do seek out other people for self-evaluation, we should be more likely to do so when we are uncertain about our opinions. In an experiment by Radloff (1961), subjects heard speeches about various issues relevant to the cost of college education and then were asked to answer the question, "What percent of the cost of their education should college students be expected to pay?" Some subjects then learned how a group of experts answered the questions while others were told nothing at all about how anyone else answered the question.

Next the experimenter told the subjects that discussion groups with other students were being formed to consider the question they just answered and asked subjects to indicate whether they wished to join. Subjects given no information about the opinions of others were far more anxious to join these groups than subjects who had the experts' ratings from which they could evaluate their own responses. If the information was labeled as representing the responses of other college students rather than experts (and thus presumably less objectively correct), subjects showed more interest in joining the subsequent discussion groups. The less opportunity subjects had to evaluate the correctness of their opinions by the information given to them, the more they wished to discuss the issues with other people.

Why People Affiliate

The desire for social comparison also leads individuals to seek out other people, when they are anxious and upset. In one experiment, subjects were told they would be in a situation involving painful electric shock and were put in a room with frightening-looking mechanical equipment (Figure 22-5). The experimenter, with an ominous-sounding name like Dr. Gregor Zilstein, asked if they had ever had a heart condition and lauded the importance of suffering for science. There was a 10-minute waiting period before beginning the experiment, which subjects would spend alone or waiting with others. After subjects made a choice of spending the time alone or with others, the actual experiment was ended and no one really received shock. It was found that, when subjects were very afraid because of the shock, they much preferred to wait with others (Schachter, 1959). Further experiments showed that they did not want to wait with just anyone, but only others who were in the same plight, thus suggesting that "misery loves miserable company." Even when they could not actually talk to one another, fearful subjects chose to be together. Gerard and Rabbie (1961) validated these results by showing that, if a person

SUBJECTS TO BE SHOCKED

DR. GREGOR ZILSTEIN'S LABORATORY

FIGURE 22-5   Misery loves company. Subjects who think they are going to be shocked prefer to wait with others who are going to be shocked.

is uncertain about the intensity of his emotional reaction, he will seek information from others to help him measure it. If he already has such information, his desire to be with others should be reduced.

These findings suggest that fearful subjects want to be together in order to evaluate their feelings through comparison with other people and also to directly reduce their anxiety. It seems, therefore, that emotions are highly subject to social influence.

SOCIAL INFLUENCE AND CONFORMITY

Is this social influence process limited to more ambiguous states like attitudes and emotions or do the responses of others affect even something so basic and seemingly absolute as visual perception? It has been shown that, when an individual is confronted with a unanimous opinion agreeing that one line is longer or shorter than another, he often goes along with the group despite what his eyes tell him is correct (Asch, 1951). Subjects in this experiment were asked to tell which of three lines on a screen in front of them matched a standard line also presented on the screen. The judgments appeared relatively easy and straightforward. For example, on the first trial the standard line was 10 inches and the comparison lines were $8\frac{3}{4}$, 10, and 8 inches. All subjects matched the second line to the standard, and the same thing occurred on the next trial. On the third trial, however, the other subjects, who were really experimental confederates, unanimously selected an incorrect line. This often happened again on subsequent trials. When the whole group selected the wrong line, 33% of the real subjects also selected that line as the correct match. Thus, even when judgments involve objective physical reality, subjects are likely to be strongly influenced by the responses of other people (Figure 22-6).

In variations on the basic experimental design, it was found that conformity can be greatly reduced by having one other subject appear to disagree with the group. Interestingly, the size of the group was not a crucial variable beyond a certain point. Further increasing the size of the unanimous group beyond three or four had little effect.

FIGURE 22-6   An experiment by Asch (1951) showed that there is tremendous social pressure to conform even when one knows that the conforming behavior is in error.

Behavioral Compliance to Social Pressure

Let us extend these dramatic findings to consider what happens when the compliance not only involves agreeing with a group, but actually requires a specific action to be taken that ordinarily would not be made. It does not necessarily follow that the individuals in the experiments who showed verbal conformity would necessarily also act in accord with the behavior of a group. Just how far-reaching are the effects of social influence?

To answer this question, Stanley Milgram (1963, 1964) tried to see whether individuals would hurt another person in order to comply with external social pressure. Milgram believed that the atrocities committed by the Nazis against the Jews in World War II were not simply attributable to a basic character flaw in the German people, but that, given the appropriate circumstances, almost everyone could be made to yield to social pressure.

Milgram's subjects believed they were participating in a learning experiment in which they had "randomly" been assigned the role of teacher. Their job was to shock the learner with increasingly severe shock for each incorrect response he made. A subject sat facing a large shock generator with 30 levers which were marked in volts from 15–450 volts and also with verbal labels from "moderate shock" to "DANGER: severe shock." The learner, a confederate of the experimenter, went to another room and answered, using a standard sequence of correct and incorrect responses which ultimately required the subject to deliver shock at the the danger level. Finally, he screamed and refused to continue. If the subject-teacher wanted to stop delivering the shock, the experimenter tried to induce him to go on claiming that he really had to continue and that the experimenter accepted all responsibility. Under these conditions, 62% of the subjects shocked the learner to the limit of the machine's capacity. Since hurting another person is closely related to matters of ethics and conscience, the obediance to authority demonstrated in this study is striking.

Further studies have shown that subjects also shocked the learner a great deal when experimental confederates, acting as other teachers, inflicted the limit of the machine's capacity. This occurs in the absence of overt urging on the part of the experimenter, suggesting the powerful effects of social influence. Unlike the Asch situation where subjects could go along with the group but secretly hold the view that another line was correct, yielding in this experiment was an unalterable and irreversible act.

It would be unfair to end discussion of Milgram's studies, however, without noting, as indeed was the case in Asch's experiments as well, that there were large individual differences in response to group pressure. Some individuals followed the group or the authority closely, while others resisted totally.

Altruistic Behavior

Since the presence of other people inflicting pain on someone can induce individuals to behave accordingly, it should be equally likely that people can also be positively influenced by one another. If, for example, we witness people helping another person, it should be expected that our own helping behavior would increase. Bryan and Test (1967) found that automobile drivers were much more likely to stop to help a girl fix her tire when they had passed, a quarter of a mile earlier, another girl with a flat tire being helped by someone. They also found that, when they set up a Salvation Army kettle at a shopping center near Princeton, a model depositing money greatly increased the likelihood that someone else would deposit money within the next 20 seconds. Thus, the presence of helping models significantly increases subsequent altruistic behavior.

It is difficult to conclusively determine from these studies whether subjects are responding to social influence or whether the model's behavior is simply making already existing social norms more salient. However, since the Salvation Army kettle and bell ringing already function as cues reminding individuals of their obligations toward charity, this explanation seems insufficient to handle the results. It would be an even more compelling demonstration of the effects of social influence to deal with situations in which people are behaving in ways antithetical to norms of social responsibility. Certainly, the Milgram study is one such instance, and another, more relevant to the issue of helping behavior, is the response of bystanders to emergencies.

Bystander Intervention

The newspapers are quick to call our attention to the large number of incidents in which witnesses to a murder, rape, or drowning do nothing to help the victim. In one of the most famous, or infamous, of these incidents a woman named Kitty Genovese in New York was attacked for almost 2 hours and finally murdered, while 38 people watched from their apartments and not one of them even called the police (Figure 22-7). Such events have been decried as indications of the apathy and alienation of our current society. Research into this question, however, has suggested that the witnesses to emergencies such as this are not apathetic and uncaring, but rather are strongly influenced by the behavior of the other people around them or their expectations about what others are doing.

According to Latané and Darley (1970), before people will act in an emergency, they must notice the event and interpret it as an emergency and

FIGURE 22-7   Who intervenes when there is trouble?

then they must decide if they should intervene and what course of action to take. At every level of this decision process, the presence of other people can have a powerful effect. When more than one person witnesses an emergency, they often watch one another for cues about what the other is thinking. Each person, seeing the inaction of the other, may judge the situation as less serious than he would if alone. And each person appears momentarily inactive to the other because each is waiting to see what the others will do. If every member of the group is trying to appear calm and at the same time is looking around at the other members to gauge their reactions, each may be led (or misled) by the others to define the situation as not critical. Until someone acts, each person only sees other nonresponding bystanders and is likely to be influenced not to act himself. This line of reasoning suggests that individuals may be less likely to intervene in an emergency if they witness it in the presence of other people than if they see it alone.

Latané and Rodin (1969) had subjects, while filling our questionnaires, overhear a woman in the next room fall, knock over some books and chairs, and moan loudly in pain. They found that, when subjects witnessed this emergency alone, 70% of them intervened. When two strangers heard the incident, only 40% of them helped, this despite the fact that, in this instance, there were twice as many potential helpers. When the subject was tested with a passive stooge who simply continued working on his questionnaire, only 7% of the subjects intervened. In all these cases, subjects who did not intervene did not believe they had behaved callously or immorally. Rather, they had simply decided that the situation was not serious.

In addition to affecting whether individuals notice the situation and how they interpret it, the presence of another individual may also alter the reward and costs for not acting. Certainly, the greater the number of people present during an emergency, the less each individual will feel personally responsible for helping or personally to blame for not acting. This potential diffusion of responsibility and blame across bystanders further decreases the likelihood that the victim will be aided when a number of people are present.

The cost and rewards for intervention and nonintervention in the real world can both be greater. One attempt has been made to study bystander behavior in a real life natural setting (Piliavin, Rodin, & Piliavin, 1969). Field studies are less frequently used than laboratory experiments, largely because of the difficulties in unraveling the complex working of real world phenomena. Conducting a field investigation of these questions, for example, required a setting that would allow the repeated staging of emergencies in the midst of reasonably large groups, which remained similar in composition from incident to incident. It was also desirable that that group retain the same composition over the course of the incident and that a sufficient amount of time be available after the emergency for good samaritans to act.

The experimenters were able to fulfill these requirements by staging emergencies during the $6\frac{1}{2}$ minute nonstop express run of a New York subway where a total of 4500 people served as the unsolicited participants in the study. The study found that when victims passed out in the subway car carrying a cane they received considerably more help than when they passed out carrying a liquor bottle wrapped in a brown bag. Overall, however, the level of helping was substantially higher than in the laboratory. Here readers may be happily amazed at the willingness of individuals to help their fellow man. When the victim was sympathetic, it did not matter whether he was black or white, that is, he got a good deal of help and was equally likely to get it from a black or white bystander. When he appeared drunk, however, black victims received more assistance from black helpers and white victims from white helpers. It may be that a drunk of another race is not only distasteful but somehow more frightening.

Mob Behavior and Deindividuation

It has often been recognized (Brown, 1954, 1965; Zimbardo, 1969) that a crowd can also cause contagion of panic, leading each person in the crowd to overreact to an emergency to the detriment of everyone's welfare. According to Brown, the presence of a crowd in a fire, for example, creates an unequal reward structure in which everyone does not have an equal likelihood of escaping. As soon as one person bolts for the door, others follow and a panic often ensues. Zimbardo suggests that the presence of a crowd increases the likelihood of spontaneous, impulsive, and typically antisocial behavior because a group serves as a model for action, and by generating physical activity and excitement it serves as a catalyst to trigger behavior in a given direction. He believes that the presence of a group also facilitates high intensity emotional behavior, e.g., things people would not do if they were alone, by enhancing feelings of anonymity and shared responsibility (Figure 22-8). This process has been called deindividuation and was first described by Festinger. When it occurs, people tend to no longer feel personally accountable for their actions. These events create the possibility for such violent and atypical behaviors as crowds stampeding the referees in an Argentinian soccer match because of an unpopular decision and the wild behavior of crowds during Mardi Gras.

As group members feel more and more anonymous, as they feel their individual identities more and more submerged in the mob, they should be more likely to behave in morally or normatively inappropriate ways. Zimbardo found that, when subjects were in groups of four wearing hoods and oversized lab coats and never called by name, they shocked another subject in a learning task almost twice as much as groups of subjects who were highly identifiable. He also found that, if he asked these subjects for assistance in testing his senior seminar in how well they learned methods of passive resistance, the hooded anonymous subjects were far more aggressive, taunting, and actually assaulting the would-be demonstrators. During the shock session which followed, these deindividuated subjects shocked the learner even more than they had prior to their encounter with the demonstrators. Since it is commonly thought that the expression of aggression leads to catharsis and the reduction of subsequent aggression, this result may seem surprising. However, it is now fairly well documented that expressing aggression in the absence of anger or frustrations increases aggressiveness whereas, when an individual is initially

FIGURE 22-8   People behave differently in mobs than when alone.

angry or frustrated, expressing aggression reduces his anger and makes it less likely that he will behave aggressively immediately afterward.

GROUP DYNAMICS

It is appropriate at this point to ask whether groups have any positive characteristics. We have been considering how the power of social influence may force inaction or violent and inappropriate action on group members. Kurt Lewin, in studying group dynamics, found group meetings and decision-making a powerful agent for attitudinal and behavioral change. He used the group interaction as a way to change housewive's attitudes toward serving initially unattractive food to their families during World War II (see page 578).

Extending this work in an industrial setting, Coch and French (1948) found that a group could be used as a means of overcoming resistance to change. Workers at a manufacturing plant showed low performance after being transferred to another job within the factory long after they had apparently learned their new job. They believed that the operators, frustrated and antagonistic toward the management because of the transfer, developed group standards against high output. When the groups actively participated in making plans for the transfer and designing the changes, the group recovered to their high level of efficiency and often went higher in productivity. When individuals were transfered with no or limited participation in the planning, the efficiency rates dropped. The experiment showed that powerful group standards were operative affecting the production rate of each member and that whether or not the group's power over its members was used to increase or decrease productivity depended on the level of participation the group had in making plans for the change.

RISKY SHIFT

In a series of studies on risk taking (Kogan & Wallach, 1967; Wallach & Kogan, 1965), subjects were each asked to act as an adviser to an individual faced with a choice between two alternatives differing in probability and attractiveness. The subject was to advise the central person what probability of success he should require before recommending the alternative that had the more desirable outcome. For example, in one situation an engineer had to decide whether to quit a good job to go to work for a company that may or may not survive. If it does survive, he is certain to make a lot of money. Subjects check the lowest probability of success that they would consider acceptable, from the chances of 1 in 10 the company will prove financially sound to the chances of 9 in 10 the company will prove financially sound. In another situation, a woman must decide whether to undergo dangerous surgery for cancer, not knowing then whether or not she has cancer but recognizing the danger of going without surgery if she is really ill.

After making these decisions alone, subjects are asked to join group discussions about these issues and arrive at a unanimous decision on each one. Most studies show a strong and pervasive tendency for groups to shift to riskier decisions, even when the decisions have consequences not only for hypothetical people but for the subjects themselves. One explanation of the risky shift phenomenon is that groups make individuals feel less responsible for their actions.

When thinking of other examples of enhanced risk taking in groups, the concept of diffusion of responsibility is often mentioned in connection with the risky action of mobs and crowds.

SUMMARY

We have seen in this chapter some of the constants of our social behavior. Our personal behavior can be greatly affected by our being present in social groups, that is, an individual's behavior can be manipulated by group influences. One cannot help but wonder how to interpret each phenomenon in terms of our traditional concepts of personal freedom.

SUGGESTED READINGS

FESTINGER, L. *A theory of cognitive dissonance*. New York: Harper, 1951.

LINDZEY, G., & ARONSON, E. (Eds.) *Handbook of social psychology*. Reading, Massachusetts: Addison-Wesley, 1968–69. 5 vols.

MILLS, J. (Ed.) *Experimental social psychology*. New York: Macmillan, 1969.

SCHACHTER, S. *Emotion, obesity, and crime*. New York: Academic Press, 1971.

ZIMBARDO, P. G., & EBBESEN, E. B. *Influencing attitudes and changing behavior*. Reading, Massachusetts: Addison-Wesley, 1969.

23

Social
Psychology and
Social Problems

———————

We live in a rapidly changing world, and these changes often breed social problems. Our cities are crowded, dirty, and noisy. Minority groups are in a state of seething discontent, and the violence so readily portrayed on television and in movies is becoming pervasive in reality. Are these problems really new? An examination will reveal that some of them, at least at the psychological level, are old, and that they can be characterized by what seem to be relatively consistent behavior patterns. Other problems, such as pollution of our environment, are new, and therefore in need of systematic examination. This chapter will analyze some of these problems in social psychological terms.

THE IMPACT OF TELEVISION VIOLENCE

P.S. 108 is a school in New York's East Harlem, a school that has established a relatively good reputation for maintaining discipline and a good learning atmosphere. In mid March, 1972, school officials reported an unusual degree of restless behavior. The children were unruly and their games had turned noticeably more violent. The conversation in the school yard dealt with rumbles, and some children were found to be carrying toy guns in their pants.

One child came to class swinging a heavy chain, and another actually pulled a knife during a fight. These types of incidents were not typical of the school. A conversation with several of the students traced the unrest to the film version of *West Side Story*, a portrayal of two warring street gangs, which had been shown a week earlier on network television (O'Connor, 1972).

What is the effect of television violence on the behavior of children and adults? A study supported by Congress and conducted under the supervision of the Surgeon General of the United States reviewed twenty-three studies on the issue and reported that "the present entertainment offerings of the television medium may be contributing, in some measure, to the aggressive behavior of many normal children [Cisin, Coffin, Janis, Klapper, Mendelsohn, Omwake, Pinderhughes, de Sola Pool, Siegel, Wallace, Watson, & Wiebe, 1972]."

Imitation Learning

Why should watching a violent act on the television screen instigate a person to "real life" violence (Figure 23-1). One possible answer is imitation. We have all learned numerous skills and responses by imitating others. Why, when, and how do we imitate another?

FIGURE 23-1   Does viewing violence on television cause aggressive behavior? Present evidence suggests that it does.

Some theorists (e.g., Miller & Dollard, 1941) have attempted to account for imitation in the traditional stimulus-response reinforcement framework. The process proposed is called "matched-dependent" learning. According to these theorists, the occurrence of behavior (a response) that matches that of a model is initially a chance affair. Appropriately matched responses will be reinforced, while unmatched responses will be ignored or punished. By this method of chance imitation, resulting in subsequent reinforcement, a person learns to imitate another. Further, he learns whom to imitate, since imitating some models leads to rewards, while the imitation of others leads to none.

A series of experiments reported by Miller and Dollard (1941) demonstrated that both rats and children can learn either to imitate or not to imitate a leader. In one experiment, each child observed a leader who obtained gumdrops from a machine by either rotating or depressing a lever. Following the leader, the subject was also given an opportunity at the machine. When the subject imitated the leader's response, he was also rewarded with a gumdrop. This sequence of leader-response and subject-response was repeated several times with the leader following a complex schedule of rotations and depressions. The subjects quickly learned to imitate the leader, but not another leader whose responses were not rewarded.

"The Miller-Dollard theory of social imitation has been severely criticized as, in effect, requiring the person to be able to make a response before he can learn it through imitation [Deutsch & Krauss, 1965]." In order to learn a response the person has to make a response (at random) that just happens to match that of the model. Further criticism (Bandura & Walters, 1963) revolves around the theory's inability to explain other kinds of imitation, like those in which there is an apparent absence of any reinforcement.

A second theory of imitation learning (Bandura & Walters, 1963) argues that novel responses can be acquired through the mere observation of another's behavior. Further, these responses can be acquired without reinforcement and often are precise imitations of the model's behavior. Although Bandura and Walters affirm that reinforcement is central in strengthening and maintaining behavioral tendencies, they do not feel that it plays a dominant role in initial acquisition of the response. Instead, Bandura suggests that "the process of response acquisition is based upon contiguity of sensory events and that instrumental conditioning and reinforcement should perhaps be regarded as response selection rather than response acquisition or response strengthening procedures [Bandura, 1962, p. 260]."

Bandura and Walters conducted a series of experiments in which they have exposed nursery school children to either an aggressive or a nonaggressive model. The models included human adults in person, human adults on film, and cartoon characters on film. The results showed that children who view models kicking, punching, and sitting on a large plastic doll responded to subsequent frustration with considerable aggression, much of which precisely imitates the behavior of the model. Equally frustrated children who have observed inhibited nonaggressive models respond with considerably less aggression to the same frustrating experience. Given the context of this discussion, i.e., television and aggression, it is noteworthy that viewing of the cartoon figures and the adults on film had the same effects as viewing the adult in person.

In further experiments, children were exposed to models who were either punished or rewarded for their aggressive behavior. The results indicated that, although the child may acquire the response by mere observation, his readiness to perform it was partly contingent on whether the model was rewarded or punished as a result of the behavior. It seems that the observation of an aggresive response for which a model is rewarded may lead to similar aggressive behavior, while the observation of a model being punished for aggressive behavior may lead to the inhibition of general aggressive tendencies and the rejection of the model as a basis for emulation.

In reviewing an additional study examining the relationship between viewing television violence and subsequent aggressive behavior, it must be remembered that a correlation between two variables does not mean that one causes the other. For example, there are three possible interpretations of a correlation between viewing television violence and subsequent aggressive behavior: (1) The viewing of the violence caused the aggressive behavior. (2) Aggressive people are prone to watch violent television programs. (3) There may be a third factor that is responsible for both aggressive behavior and television violence viewing, for example, socioeconomic status of the parents. These factors should be kept in mind when considering the results of these studies.

Lefkowitz (Lefkowitz, Eron, Walder, & Huesman, 1971) collected data on the violence levels of favorite television programs and aggressive behavior of children in the third grade, with follow-ups in the eighth grade and the thirteenth grade (one year after graduation from high school). The child's favorite programs in the third grade were reported by the mother, while the child himself reported his favorites in the eighth and thirteenth grades. Aggression was measured by peer ratings. The ratings included such questions as, "Who starts fights over nothing?" The results indicate a modest relationship between viewing television violence and aggressive behavior in the third grade (males only), and no such relationship for the same boys at grades eight and thirteen. However, among boys, a relatively high correlation was found between viewing television violence in the third grade and aggression at grade thirteen. This suggests that early viewing of television violence may lead to aggressive behavior years later.

It is evident from this study, as well as the experimental work of Bandura and Walters, that there is reason to suspect a causal relationship between viewing violence and aggression. But science is cautious, and further experimentation will be necessary before such a conclusion should be accepted.

INTERGROUP PREJUDICE AND CONFLICT

What are the factors that breed prejudice and foment riots? It would seem that these problems of intergroup prejudice and conflict are tailor-made for the social psychologist. Are prejudicial attitudes different from other kinds of attitudes? Do ethnic groups interact differently than other groups?

Roots of Prejudice

There are two essential ingredients in the definition of prejudice: (1) reference to an unfound judgment and (2) reference to a feeling or tone (Allport, 1958). When we speak of prejudice as a social problem, we are refering to "negative prejudice," an irrational, unfounded, negative evaluation of others.

Prejudice is a complex phenomenon determined by many factors, that is, it has multiple origins (Collins, 1970). There is not one all-inclusive theory of prejudice. In fact, there are many, sometimes overlapping, theories about the roots of prejudical behavior. In effect, theories are advanced to call attention to an important aspect of the problem. They do not suggest that no other factors are involved.

It is possible to distinguish between two levels of the analysis of prejudice: the societal level and the individual level (Collins, 1970). Societal explanations concern themselves with when and how prejudice develops in a given social system, whereas individual explanations are concerned with the causes of prejudice on the individual personality level. An examination of one theory from each level of analysis will allow us to gain some understanding of the complexity of the problem.

REALISTIC-GROUP-CONFLICT THEORY.   A prerequisite to the understanding of societal analyses of prejudice is familiarity with the terms "ingroup" and "outgroup." Ingroup refers to those people who identify with a certain group and are regarded from the point of view of the members as belonging to the group. Any group of people not belonging to an ingroup are considered by that group as members of an outgroup. The basic premise of realistic-group-conflict theory, a theory of the origin of prejudice that is included in what we have called societal analyses, is that "the character of the (existing relations) between ingroup and outgroup generates attitudes toward the outgroup that are consonant with these relationships [Secord & Backman, 1964]." When the goals of two groups are compatible, that is, they do not conflict and possibly even facilitate each other, positive intergroup attitudes will result. When the goals of the group are incompatible, that is, when they are mutually exclusive, negative intergroup attitudes result.

The robbers' cave experiment, a field study conducted by Sherif and his associates (Sherif, Harvey, White, Hood, and Sherif, 1961), tested realistic-group-conflict theory. Twenty-two "normal, healthy, socially well-adjusted boys" with similar middle-class backgrounds were the subjects. Although the boys were all from the same town, none of them had met prior to the experiment. Each of the boys was assigned to one of two groups. The assignment was done in a manner so that the groups would be equal in terms of physical and intellectual attributes. The two groups were then brought separately to a Boy Scout camp that was relatively isolated from outside influences.

The experiment had three stages: (1) the formation of ingroups, (2) the creation of intergroup hostility, and (3) the reduction of intergroup hostility. Stage 1 of the experiment, creating a feeling of groupness, arranged situations that would stimulate group goals with common appeal to the individuals, and which required the members of the group to work together for their attainment. Examples of these activities included arranging church services, building a rope bridge, and preparing a meal. These problems all required the cooperative effort of the group. As stage 1 progressed, the group members became friends and developed a feeling of "groupness."

Stage 2 of the experiment, creating intergroup conflict and hostility, brought the two groups into competitive contact through a series of contests. These included baseball, football, and a tug-of-war (Figure 23-2). As predicted, the researchers found that these situations produced hostile intergroup attitudes. The children name called, derogated the outgroup, and explicitly expressed the desire not to associate with the outgroup.

In the final stage of the experiment, intergroup conflict was reduced. The first attempt to reduce conflict involved bringing the two groups together in a pleasant environment, for example, eating together. It was totally unsuccessful. The next attempt at group hostility reduction was the introduction of superordinate goals, that is goals that had common appeal to the individuals and whose accomplishment require the two groups to work together. An example was a tug of war with a truck. The procedure was successful in eliminating

FIGURE 23-2   The effects of a group having a common goal are very beneficial. When put in competition, clear hostilities arise. Here the hostilities are seen in the form of verbal abuse.

the hostility between the groups. In simple terms, the introduction of interdependent goals eliminated the bases of conflict.

FRUSTRATION-AGGRESSION HYPOTHESIS.   Before considering an example of an individual-level analysis of prejudice, it will be necessary to review one of the classic theories of psychology, the frustration-aggression hypothesis. As originally formulated by Dollard and his associates (Dollard, Doob, Miller, Mowrer, & Sears, 1939), the frustration-aggression hypothesis simply stated that aggression always presupposes frustration, and that frustration is always followed by aggression. More recent research has qualified the nature of the frustration-aggression relationship. It has been demonstrated that there are situations in which aggression can occur without a frustrating stimulus (Bandura & Walters, 1963) and that, although frustration causes an "instigation to aggression," aggression will not always occur (Berkowitz, 1965). Setting these qualifications aside for the moment, it is not unreasonable to presume that, in many situations, when people are frustrated, they will aggress.

The frustration-aggression hypothesis is the basis for what has been called the scapegoat theory of prejudice. The theory "assumes that (for some people) living in organized society is inevitably a frustrating experience which produces 'free-floating aggression' [Collins, 1970, p. 264]." Dollard has described the source of these aggressive feelings as the "cultural restrictions in childhood

FIGURE 23-3   The scapegoat theory of prejudice. Instead of the aggressor expressing his frustration to the employer, he takes it out on an innocent bystander. This. in turn. leads to the formation of a prejudice.

and the limitation of daily life in adulthood [that] provide frustrations for every individual; hostility is aroused in response to these frustrations [Dollard *et al.*, 1939, p. 433]." Since fear of retaliation often prevents an individual from directing his aggression toward the source of frustration, e.g., parents and employers, he often displaces it onto some outgroup in the form of prejudice (Figure 23-3).

Miller and Bugelski (1970) conducted a field experiment that tested the two premises of the scapegoat theory: (1) that frustration arouses aggression and (2) that this aggression might be displaced onto members of an outgroup. The subjects were thirty-one young men working at a summer camp. As part of the educational program of the camp, the men were to be required to take several long and uninteresting exams that were so difficult that everyone would be bound to fail miserably. "Furthermore, the tests would be certain to run far overtime so that the young men would miss what they looked forward to as the most interesting event of the otherwise dull week: Bank night at the local theater . . . [Miller & Bugelski, 1970]." The attitudes of the young men toward both Mexicans and Japanese were measured just before they learned about the difficult test and again just after they had completed the test and missed the evening's entertainment. The results clearly indicated that outgroup members were evaluated lower after the frustrating experience than they had been beforehand. A control group given the same attitude questionnaires at equal time intervals showed no such change in evaluations. The experiment seems to lend support to the scapegoat theory.

Last, it is important to point out a major limitation of the theory. We are all frustrated at one time or another, but this does not necessarily make us all potential bigots. People obviously handle their frustrations in different ways and some have more tolerance for frustration than others. It is evident that other personality variables, such as the ability to cope with frustration, should be taken into account in any scapegoat theory analysis.

RIOTS AND THEIR CAUSES

On Saturday evening, July 22, (1967) the Detroit Police Department raided five "blind pigs." The blind pigs had their origin in prohibition days, and survived as private social clubs. Often they were after hours drinking and gambling spots.

The fifth blind pig on the raid list (was) the United Community and Civic League at the corner of 12th Street and Clairmount . . . Police expected to find two dozen patrons in the blind pig. That night, however, it was the scene of a party for several servicemen, two of whom were back from Vietnam. Instead of two dozen patrons, police found 82 . . . A few minutes after 5:00 A.M., just after the last of those arrested had been hauled away, an empty bottle smashed into the rear window of a store. Rumors circulated of excess force used by the police during the raid. A youth . . . was shouting: "We're going to have a riot!" and exhorting the crowd to vandalism [Kerner, Lindsay, Harris, Brooke, Corman, McCulloch, Abel, Thornton, Wildins, Peden, & Jenkins, 1968, pp. 84–86].

The Relative Deprivation Hypothesis

Can social psychology help us to understand and remedy the causes of riots? The results of a study (Stouffer, Suchman, DeVinney, Star, & Williams, 1949) that examined the effects of a liberal promotion system on soldiers' satisfaction and morale provides us with our first insight. Common sense would predict that soldiers would be more satisfied when promotions were rapid and widespread than when they were scarce. A liberal promotion system would allow people to move ahead faster in their careers, whereas a more conservative system could frustrate career goals. Contrary to common sense, Stouffer's comparison of Air Corpsmen, who had a liberal system of promotion, with the Military Police, whose system was piecemeal, indicated that Air Corpsmen were considerably more frustrated concerning promotions than the Military Police (Figure 23-4).

What does Stouffer's study have to do with the Detroit riots? A closer examination of both Stouffer's results and the conditions leading up to the riots that ravished American cities in the late sixties may well reveal that the underlying psychological explanations for both are the same.

REFERENCE GROUP.   Before we examine the similarities between the conditions that led to the riots and those that led to the morale problems of the Air Corpsmen, it will be necessary to understand the social psychological concept of reference group. The term "reference group" was coined by Hyman (1942) who suggested that people use groups as frameworks for their judgments. For example, in order to decide whether you are a good student, you might compare your grades to those of other students in your class. The class to which you belong gives you a frame of reference. It provides a standard that allows you to evaluate your own performance. If you receive a B on an exam and the remainder of your class receives C's, you know that you

FIGURE 23-4 Who are happier—the people in a group with a liberal promotion system or those in a group with a more stringent system?

have done a good job. On the other hand, if you receive a B and the remainder of the class receives A's, you know that your performance was not up to par. In both cases the performance was the same, but how it was evaluated depended on the standard set by your reference group.

In his study, Hyman found that he could not always accurately predict a person's subjective status, i.e., the status to which a person thinks he belongs, using factors such as income and education. However, he did find that, to a certain extent, one's subjective status depends on what groups one uses as his frame of reference. Frequently, these reference groups were not groups to which the person belonged, but rather groups to which he aspired. This finding led Hyman to distinguish between a "membership group," the group to which someone belongs, and a "reference group," the group which someone employs as a basis of comparison for self-appraisal. In some cases, the reference and membership group are the same; in others not.

Let us now return to Stouffer's morale problem. Air Corpsmen who saw many of their peers being promoted rapidly compared themselves to these peers and saw themselves as failures. This was true even though their own chance for promotion was good. Military Police seldom saw their peers move up and consequently viewed their own performance as adequate, i.e., as equal to the standard set by their reference group. It is clear that it is not the absolute level of attainment that makes for poor morale so much as "relative deprivation," the discrepancy between what one anticipates and what one attains. The relative deprivation occurs when an individual feels deprived in comparison to relevant reference groups.

The last decade has seen both statutory and social changes that have presumably paved the way for racial equality. At least, these changes have helped to form new expectancies for the American black. On television and in movies he sees that blacks can aspire to and acquire all the rewards of an affluent society: a nice house, a nice car, and a good job. These changes have given the lower-class blacks an opportunity to adopt a new reference group, the middle class. Unfortunately these expectations have seldom been met with real changes in the system that would allow their fulfillment. Jobs are still hard to get and the trappings of the middle class are still a dream. According to Pettigrew (1964), blacks in the last decade have been experiencing actual gains, but these gains are translated into psychological losses when compared with whites.

An analysis of the Detroit and Newark riots in terms of relative deprivation was attempted by Caplan and Paige (1968). Both rioters and nonrioters were asked whether things were getting better or worse in the past few years. Although they found no support for the rising expectancies notion, they did find that 39% of the rioters and 27% of the nonrioters thought that other blacks were earning more than they were and that the discrepancy was increasing. Thus, 39% of rioting blacks interviewed saw themselves as earning less than other blacks, as not meeting up to the standard set by their reference group, and as being relatively deprived. The reported consequence of these feelings were frustration and dissatisfaction that, according to the authors, led to riot behavior. Although this study does not support the previously developed argument that blacks have shifted their reference group in the last few years, it does support the relative deprivation hypothesis.

Describing the lower-class black's condition as one of relative deprivation does not really confront the problem. Although the state of relative deprivation leads to low morale, dissatisfaction, and frustration, it has yet to be demonstrated that such a state could lead to riot-type behavior. A most plausible possibility is that relative deprivation leads to a state of frustration that, under certain conditions, causes an aggressive response (Berkowitz, 1965).

PERSUASION

"Bring them back alive!" Many of you will recognize this as the slogan of the American Automobile Association. Organizations like the A.A.A., as well as business and political concerns with less altruistic motives, are constantly bombarding us with slogans and appeals. Buy my product! Attend my functions! Give to my fund! Whatever the cause, the communicator inevitably resorts to a form of psychology, a way of presenting their message so that you will comply. Sometimes the appeal is presented by a famous person; at other times you are warned of the catastrophic consequences of noncompliance. Which of these techniques are effective; and even more important, what do psychologists, not to mention advertising agents, really know about persuasion?

The Group and the Individual

Because of the shortage of popular food stuffs during World War II, the United States Government was interested in developing a program to convince consumers to eat less desirable, cheaper cuts of meat. Kurt Lewin and his students at the University of Iowa were called upon to develop techniques of changing the ingrained attitudes of American housewives. The results of his investigation have interesting implications for the persuasive process.

In a series of experiments, Lewin (1947) compared the effectiveness of lectures and group discussions followed by group decision in changing housewives' food-buying practices. Some groups of housewives attended a lecture where the lecturer advocated the desired food-buying behavior, i.e., buying visceral meats. Other groups attended a discussion group where the discussion leader made the same points as the lecturer, but also encouraged the group to participate in the discussion and asked them to reach a consensus that they would act on a decision to buy. The subjects were interviewed several weeks later in order to determine if they had changed their food-buying practices. In all experiments, the results indicated that women in the group discussion treatment had adopted the advocated behavior to a greater extent than those in the lecture treatments. Why was the group discussion more effective? Was it the discussion itself or the required group consensus?

A subsequent experiment provides a partial answer. In an experiment that attempted to induce college students to volunteer as subjects for psychology experiments, Bennet (1955) found that a greater percentage of subjects who were asked to make a decision complied to the suggestion than those not asked to make a decision. The experiment, although not conclusive, strongly suggests that the power of the group over the individual may have been mobilized by the perception of the individual that the remainder of the group favored the proposed action.

A series of other experiments clearly indicate that in cohesive groups, that is, groups whose members are strongly attracted to the group, the group's attitude strongly affects the attitude of the individual. In one experiment, Back (1951) created high and low cohesive groups. In the high cohesive group, the subjects were told about the benefits of being in a group. The low cohesive groups were given the exact opposite impressions.

Before meeting each other, the subjects were asked to write a story about a set of three pictures. They were then brought together to discuss their respective interpretation of the pictures. After discussion, the subjects were asked to write a final version of the stories. The results indicated that subjects in the high cohesive group showed both a greater tendency to attempt to influence each other during the discussion and a greater tendency to change the final version of their stories in the direction of their partners than subjects in the low cohesive groups. The experiment supports the notion of the importance of the group in the persuasive process.

Communication and Persuasion

Carl Hovland and his associates at Yale University undertook a research program designed to determine what factors affected an audience's acceptance of a persuasive message. The question that they have proposed in their book,

Communication and Persuasion (Hovland, Janis, & Kelley, 1953), is: "Who said what to whom?" In other words, what are the effects of: different communicators (Who), different kinds of communications (What), and different kinds of audiences (Whom) on the acceptance of a persuasive message? A review of several of their findings will give us an idea of the results of this massive research effort.

The effectiveness of a communication is commonly presumed to depend on who delivers it. Aspirin commercials on television are bolstered by the support of "80% of the doctors interviewed," and U.S. Government reports are authored by "a group of distinguished scientists." Does the credibility of the communicator actually affect communication acceptance? In an experiment by Hovland and Weiss (1951), subjects were presented with communications attributed to either high or low credibility sources. For example, a communication dealing with the advisability of certain drugs being sold without a doctor's prescription was either attributed to the *New England Journal of Biology and Medicine* (high credibility) or a mass circulation monthly pictorial magazine (low credibility). The subjects' opinions were obtained immediately after reading the articles and again 4 weeks later. The result of the immediate testing indicated that high credibility sources had a substantially greater effect on the audience's opinions than low credibility sources. However, when tested 4 weeks later, the positive effect of the high credibility sources tended to disappear. The low credibility sources, however, tended to begin to have an effect on opinion. This latter effect has been called the "sleeper effect."

In a further experiment, Kelman and Hovland (1953) again presented subjects with either a high or low credibility source communication. This time the experimenters reminded the subjects of the source of the communication just before the delayed attitude measurement. Subjects who were reminded of the source of communication showed the same effects that had appeared immediately following the communication. The authors concluded that the sleeper effect was caused by dissociation of the source from the communication. More simply, the source who had served as a cue for acceptance or rejection of the communication had been forgotten.

The nature of the communication should also be considered. Several years ago, the Surgeon General of the United States released a report warning of the dire effects that cigarette smoking has on health. The report was met with a sudden drop of cigarette sales, which lasted about 2 months. Within a year, cigarette sales had reached an all-time high. It seems that, contrary to common opinion, high fear communications may not be the most efficacious.

Janis and Feshbach (1953) presented subjects with a questionnaire concerning dental hygiene care. One week later, the subjects attended a 15-minute illustrated lecture on the perils of tooth decay that aroused strong, moderate, or minimal fear. (A different form of the communication was used for each level of fear.) The three talks contained the same information on tooth decay and oral hygiene, but differed in the amount of threatening material presented. A week after the communication was presented, the subjects again answered the questionnaire on their dental hygiene practices. The results indicated that the minimal fear appeal was most effective in eliciting verbal conformity to the suggestions presented in the communication.

Leventhal has reported several studies (e.g., Dabbs & Leventhal, 1966) that have suggested the opposite relationship. In a series of experiments, Leventhal has aroused differential levels of fear concerning tetanus, and has suggested in the communication that subjects get tetanus innoculations. The studies have repeatedly indicated that the high fear condition creates the greatest attitude change. In an attempt to eliminate any differences in topic or communication that might have accounted for the discrepancy between his own results and those of Janis and Feshbach, Leventhal (Leventhal & Singer, 1966) replicated the original Janis and Feshbach experiment using the same topic and communications used in the original study. The data regarding acceptance was clear-cut. Acceptance was greater in the high than in the low fear condition.

URBAN STRESS

Anybody visiting New York City for the first time becomes aware of many aspects of city life that hard core New Yorkers hardly notice. Milgram (1970) has characterized the city with its complex myriad of stimuli as overloading the individual's system. Unable to cope with all the potential inputs in his environment, the person adapts. He "tunes out" unimportant information and is aware of only those stimuli that are relevant to his normal functioning.

It is clear that in the cognitive sense of not being aware, as well as in the physiological sense of not responding, humans can adapt and "tune out" much of their environment. Unfortunately, this adaptation is not always beneficial as it might seem. We can tune out noise, but are we paying in other ways? Some recent research seems to indicate we are.

Psychological Effects of Noise

Noise has long been the cause of hearing impairments as well as a source of irritation for the urban dweller, but today, more than ever, noise is an omnipresent unwanted companion. In fact, a recent report from the United

States Environmental Protection Agency (1971) has declared that noise is an insidious form of pollution that may affect at least 80 million Americans. The report stated that "all of the factors clearly support the contention that noise can be a source of psychological distress through annoyance, disturbance of activities such as sleep and speech communications . . . (and that distress) can contribute to a list of symptoms such as nausea, irritability, general anxiety and change in mood." The impact that noise can have on psychological processes is exemplified by a noise survey in London that found a correlation between the noise in certain areas of the city and admissions to psychiatric hospitals there (McKennel & Hunt, 1966).

Glass and Singer (1972) undertook a series of experiments to demonstrate some of the adverse effects of noise. In each experiment, the subjects were tested individually. On entering the laboratory, the subject was seated in a comfortable chair. Sensors were attached to one of his hands so that the experimenter could monitor the subject's physiological responses. After a short period during which the subject relaxed and got accustomed to his surroundings, he was instructed to work on a task that involved solving arithmetic problems. He was also forewarned that, while he was working on the task, he would be hearing bursts of loud noise through a speaker directly over his head and behind him. Half the subjects heard noise that was administered on a random schedule, that is, it was administered in a way that made it impossible for the subject to know when the next burst would start. The other half of the subjects were administered the noise on a fixed schedule, which allowed them to predict when each consecutive noise burst would start.

Unlike previous studies, Glass and Singer were not primarily interested in how the subjects in the two conditions would perform on the arithmetic task that they were working on during the noise, but rather they were interested in the subjects' performance on subsequent tasks worked on after the noise exposure period had ended. One of these subsequent tasks was designed to measure the subject's tolerance for frustration. In this task, he was instructed to solve several puzzles. However, the subject did not know that many of the puzzles were unsolvable. The measure of tolerance for frustration was the amount of time the subject would spend on the unsolvable puzzles. The results indicated that subjects exposed to unpredictable noise spent less time on the unsolvable puzzles, that is, they had less tolerance for frustration, than those exposed to predictable noise or no noise. The unpredictable noise group also performed poorer on other tasks following noise exposure.

In subsequent studies, a small button was attached to the arm of the subject's chair. Half of the subjects were told that they could stop the noise if it became too stressing by merely pressing the button. But they were asked not to press the button unless it was absolutely necessary, since it would terminate the experiment. The remaining half of the subjects were not told anything about the button. Obviously, the subjects who were told that they could terminate the noise felt that they had some control over the stressing situation (although the button was never actually pushed), whereas subjects who were not told that the noise could be terminated perceived no such control. The results indicated that subjects who were exposed to unpredictable noise and given the perception of control showed appreciable improvement in frustration tolerance and postnoise task performance.

The Glass-Singer research has demonstrated two interesting and important points. (1) Cognitive (mental) factors, such as predictability and perceived control over the noise, to a great extent determine its effects. "Psychological factors, not simply physical parameters of the noise stressor, are the important elements in the production of noise aftereffects [Glass & Singer, 1972, p. 157]" (2) Exposure to high intensity noise may lead to short-term and even long-term effects in both task performance and the ability to deal with frustration.

Psychological Effects of Crowding

In Chesapeake Bay, about 14 miles from Cambridge, Maryland, lies James Island, approximately half a square mile of uninhabited land. In 1916, four or five deer were released on the island. Allowed to breed freely, the herd grew until, in 1955, there were about 280 or 300, a density of about one deer per acre. The island was called to the attention of John Christian, an ethologist with training in medical pathology. Several years earlier, Christian had proposed that increases and decreases in certain animal populations are controlled by physiological mechanisms that respond to density. According to Christian, as the number of animals in a given area increases, competition and aggressive behavior increases. This style of behavior is the cause of a continually stressing state that builds up until it triggers an endocrine mechanism that operates in the animals to regulate the population. Christian had been looking for an opportunity of this kind to test his theory.

Christian (Christian, Flyger, & Davis, 1960) continued to count heads for several years. Apparently, the population density that had been reached in 1955 was about the maximum that the species would allow. From 1955 to 1957, the population density remained at about one deer per acre. In 1958, however, 60% of the deer died and 109 deer survived. In 1959, the population further decreased to 80 deer. After 1960, the population resumed growth.

It should be noted that Christian was able to rule out food shortage as the cause of the decrease in the population. Food was abundant on the island and the dead animals that were examined showed no signs of malnutrition.

[Several well accepted theories of population control (e.g., Wynn-Edwards, 1968) had been based on the concept of food scarcity.] He was also able to rule out disease and poisoning as possible causes of the die-off.

If the animals did not die of starvation or disease, what was responsible for the sudden death of more than 190 deer in a 2-year period? In an attempt to find out, Christian collected carcasses during the years of the die-off and also shot several deer in the later years when the population had begun to grow again. Autopsies performed on 18 of the deer indicated that adrenal weight of the deer increased through 1958 when the die-off began and started to decrease after 1960 when the population had started to grow again.

The change found in the adrenal glands points to great stress in the animals during the die-off years. The adrenals play a great part in the regulation of growth, reproduction, and the level of the body defenses. The size and weight of these important glands are not fixed, but respond to stress. When an animal is under excessive stress, the adrenals will enlarge. Therefore, the increases in the size of these glands during the die-off years lend significant support to Christian's theory. The animals during those years seemed to be under considerable stress.

Is there similar evidence for humans? Certainly, overpopulation is one of the most serious problems facing the world today. Even if we were able to control population, we would still be stuck with disproportionate amounts of people living in restricted spaces. Overcrowded buses and subways, not to mention living quarters, are a way of life in the city. Yet, despite the fact that scientists in many fields are embracing ecological problems, there are only a few controlled experiments on the effects of crowding on human behavior.

Before delving further into how crowding might effect human behavior, it is important to decide exactly what constitutes crowding. An experiment by Desor (1972) of Cornell University provides us with a clue. Desor presented his subjects with scaled-down rooms and miniature human figures and asked them to place as many people as possible in the room without overcrowding them. The area of the miniature rooms was constant, but architectural features such as partitions, number of doors, and changes in dimensions were different for each room. The results indicated that the perception of being crowded depended on the architectural features of the room, even though the space in all the rooms was the same. For example, more miniature people were placed in partitioned rooms than in nonpartitioned rooms. Desor explains his findings by defining crowding as the reception of "excessive social stimulation" and not merely the lack of space.

These results are consistent with those of many researchers concerned with man's use of space (e.g., Dubos, 1966; E. T. Hall, 1966; Sommer, 1967) who view crowding largely as a matter of perception. Hall's (1966) description of the Arab who tucks his ego down inside his body, so that even when in close physical contiguity he does not feel crowded, exemplifies the cultural relativity of the concept.

For humans, crowding is relative, a matter of perception. Still, this finding does not give us a clue to how humans react under crowded conditions. Is there a biological mechanism in man similar to the one in animals that reacts unfavorably to overpopulation? And if there is, why is it not operating in countries like India and Pakistan where the crowds of humanity make our cities look like paradise? Kessler (1968) who feels that there may be such a mechanism in humans suggest that it may be overshadowed by learning.

An examination of the few human experiments investigating the effects of crowding on human behavior may give us an answer to our problem. An experimental study by Hunt and Vaizey (1966) found that children were more aggressive and destructive during free-play periods when the playroom was more densely occupied. In a series of studies, Jonathan Freedman (1970) of Columbia University investigated the effects of crowding on task performance and cooperation. Freedman placed both men and women (never in mixed groups) in both small and large rooms for 4 hours. Although he found no appreciable difference in performance on a wide variety of tasks between crowded and uncrowded subjects, he did find that men were more competitive and more aggressive in crowded situations than in uncrowded ones. Women were less affected by room size, but competed somewhat less in crowded rooms.

According to Christian, as the number of animals in a given area increases, competition and aggressive behavior increases. This style of behavior is the cause of a continually stressing state that builds up until it triggers an endocrine mechanism that operates in the animals to regulate the population. Is the competitiveness and aggression reported in the human studies of crowding the first link in this chain? The question is still unanswered.

SUMMARY

This chapter has provided a glimpse of how the social psychologist views several contemporary social problems. Several of these problems were analyzed in terms of existing psychological theory. Bandura and Walters' conception of imitation learning was discussed as a possible basis for understanding why viewing television violence would lead to subsequent viewer aggression. Reference group theory and Stouffer's concept of relative deprivation provided a conceptual framework to be used in the understanding of the causes of the riots of the late 1960's. Research and theory concerning the group's influence on an individual's attitudes and behavior, as well as research on factors affecting the efficacy of mass communicative techniques, were the basis of a discussion on the persuasion process.

A second approach, the systematic examination of a specific social problem, was also exemplified. This included correlational studies on the relationship between viewing television violence and subsequent aggressive behavior, as well as studies designed to examine human response to urban stress. Both of the approaches, analysis through existing theory and direct examination of a problem, help to provide a greater understanding of the nature of the problems and the nature of human processes.

SUGGESTED READINGS

Aronson, E. *The social animal.* New York: Viking Press, 1972.

Brown, R. *Social psychology.* New York: Free Press, 1965.

Collins, B. B. *Social psychology.* Reading, Massachusetts: Addison-Wesley, 1970.

Deutsch, M., & Krauss, R. M. *Theories in social psychology.* New York: Basic Books, 1965.

Jones, B. B., & Gerard, H. B. *Foundations of social psychology.* New York: Wiley, 1967.

VII

The Mind
of Man

24

Physical Aspects
of Mind

———————————

We have come a long way in our study of behavior in this book. It is one of the most exciting and challenging of all scientific fields and needs considerable attention in the next half century. The reasons for this are self-evident for sitting right at the top of all behavior is the mind and, with it, conscious experience. To understand mind is to understand life. Yet, what is mind? What does it mean to be conscious?

Incredibly enough, one traditional and popular way to approach this problem is to, in fact, reject the question. Behaviorists such as J. B. Watson and B. F. Skinner have been doing this for years. They say the mind cannot be demonstrated; it is an illusion. All that is observable is behavior. Therefore, they consider psychology to be the study of how environmental contingencies change the behaving organism.

The contrary tradition has, of course, a long and rich history. From the early Greeks up until Descartes, the mind was thought to exist. In more modern times, the scientific study of mind in conscious experience fell largely into the hands of Karl Lashley, and it is his students who have kept the issue alive in the behavioral sciences. As recently as 1969, R. W. Sperry put forth a comprehensive argument on the importance of understanding mind if one wants to understand behavior. In this chapter, the study of mind and conscious experience will be introduced by reviewing a series of studies on the split-brain.

CONSCIOUS EXPERIENCE

The idea of consciousness stands out alone as man's most important, most puzzling, and most abused problem. Most other human ideas pale in complexity next to this one and the long series of associated questions surrounding the nature of brain and mind. Indeed, upon studying the problem and reading the literature, one cannot help but conclude that the only subjects of greater mystery are the articles written about the problem of consciousness.

It is difficult if not impossible with our present knowledge to define explicitly what is meant by conscious experience. It is the dimension that makes humans more like dogs than computers. Since this is hardly a sophisticated or formal notion, we talk about the functions of consciousness in order to make the subject of consciousness scientifically manageable. Eating, drinking, reading, and loving are all analyzed in their separate parts. By studying these aspects of conscious activity we hope to gain some understanding of the whole idea of consciousness. In real terms, of course, how such processes relate to brain mechanisms remains unknown. Yet it is these kinds of questions that arise when considering the problems of the bisected brain in both animal and man.

Over the past ten years it has been shown that, following midline section of the cerebrum, common normal conscious unity is disrupted, leaving the split-brain patient with two minds (at least): mind left and mind right. They coexist as two completely conscious entities, in the same manner as conjoined twins are two completely separate persons. However, this view has been contested by a variety of people (Eccles, 1965; MacKay, 1966).

The Split-Brain in Animals

In many ways the split-brain phenomenon is as startling and basically mysterious today as when R. E. Myers and R. W. Sperry (Sperry, 1961, 1968) first discovered it in animals in the early fifties. Their now classic experiment demonstrated that midline sectioning of the optic chiasma, corpus callosum, and anterior commissure in the cat produced an animal who was unable, using the untrained eye, to perform a visual discrimination learned through the opposite eye. Thus, when a cat with a patch over one eye is trained and overtrained on a pattern discrimination, testing of the untrained eye finds the animal unable to perform the task. The second half-brain must learn the discrimination from the beginning. Comparison of the learning curves between the two hemispheres shows them to be nearly identical. This finding, which gave rise to the double-brain phenomenon, startled the neuropsychological community. Here for the first time in the history of experimental psychology, surgical disconnection of a brain structure resulted in a complete breakdown of communication of high-order "mental" properties between brain areas. Yet, the surgery itself in no way produced easily detectable abnormalities with respect to the everyday behavior of the organism.

Another example of this phenomenon is seen in the split-brain monkey during a visual discrimination transfer task. After split-brain surgery, which in effect disconnects the two cerebral hemispheres (see brain model), vision restricted to the right eye projects to only the right hemisphere; when visual information is restricted to the left eye, the converse is true. Typically, the animal views the visual situation through one eye, and either or both hands are free to make the response. After training and considerable overtraining on the visual pattern discrimination, the trained eye is occluded and the untrained eye is tested. What one sees on the first transfer trials is a complete naivete with respect to the test stimulus. The animal's response latencies and his examination of the stimulus panels are reminiscent of the kinds of behavior seen when the first eye was learning the discrimination. In short, the animal shows no knowledge of the problem through the untrained eye, and proceeds to learn the discrimination at the normal rate.

Of course, if such tests were run on chiasma-sectioned, callosum-intact monkeys, nearly complete transfer would be observed. Here, when a monkey is trained on a discrimination through one eye, the untrained eye can usually perform the task with little or no apparent deficit.

Brain Bisection in Man

Clearly, the issue of "double mind" in man is more dramatic than in the animals. In most of the following we will be talking about double mind as it exists in split-brain patients. Several epileptic patients were operated on in California; the aim of the surgery was to prevent the interhemispheric spread of seizures (Bogen et al., 1965). To this end, the great cerebral commissure, the corpus callosum, which spans the midline of the brain and interconnects the two half-brains, was sectioned in one operation (Figure 24-1). In addition, a second, smaller commissure, the anterior commissure, was cut.

Therapeutically, the operation has been largely successful. Behaviorally, the patients for the most part appear entirely normal, and the untrained observer would be unable to ascertain that brain surgery had ever been performed. It is only under special testing conditions that the peculiar phenomena

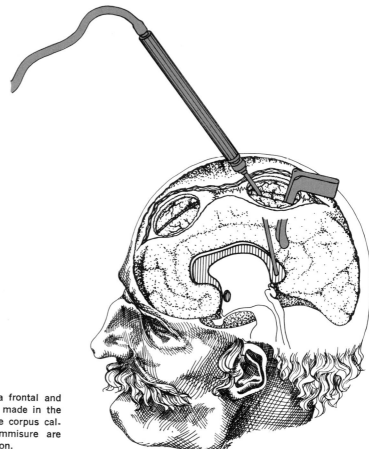

FIGURE 24-1 Both a frontal and a posterior opening are made in the split-brain operation. The corpus callosum and anterior commisure are sectioned in one operation.

reveal themselves (Gazzaniga & Sperry, 1967; Gazzaniga, 1970; Sperry, 1968). The left hemisphere, because of its intact language and speech system, can fully communicate its thoughts and ideas; it seems to be normal and conscious. It is the right hemisphere's status that is both crucial and difficult to ascertain. It does not have a speech system and thus cannot tell about its experiences through speech. This problem has been circumvented by using nonverbal response procedures (Figure 24-2). As a result, it has been possible to define many right-hemisphere functions that can go on independently and largely outside the awareness of the left hemisphere. The right hemisphere can read, learn, remember, emote, and act all by itself. It can do almost anything the left can do, with admitted limitations in the degree of its competence.

The suggestion that these kinds of observations support the idea of double consciousness, i.e., a separate set of mental controls for each hemisphere, has been challenged by Donald M. MacKay. He raises a crucial and fascinating question. All organisms have, of course, normative systems. Clearly, in split-brain man, at the physical level, basic humoral and electrotonic brainstem influences are unified and intact. MacKay wonders whether basic psychological systems such as our response priority-determining mechanism exist in duplicate in these patients. This is the system that sets the goals priorities and rank order of objectives of an organism, that is, it assigns values or response probabilities—one of the most important features of brain activity. Without this mechanism, the world would seem flat and any activity would be like any

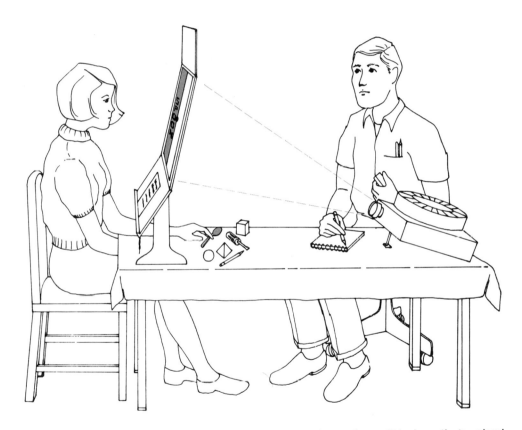

FIGURE 24-2   Using an apparatus especially designed for testing split-brain patients, visual stimuli can be presented to one or the other hemisphere exclusively. Tactual testing is also possible by allowing exploration of objects presented out of view to either hand. In testing right-hemispheric function, pictures or words are quick-flashed to the left visual field. The subjects invariably say they saw nothing or will make a guess. Yet the left hand, which sends its touch information to the right hemisphere, will be able to retrieve the object described. After the task is correctly completed, the subject will still deny knowledge of the specific aspects of the event, because the activity was carried out by the disconnected right hemisphere, which is now disconnected from the left speech hemisphere, which is the half-brain talking to the experimenter.

other. MacKay maintains that this system, which he calls the "metaorganizing system," is a basic feature of brain function and is rarely, if ever, in conflict. As a result, he maintains, it falls to us to demonstrate whether or not each half-brain has its own priority-determining system that can work independently of the other.

Bilateral Symmetry of Brain Waves

There are seemingly a lot of things going in favor of MacKay's criticism. For example, it has been recently shown that the contingent negative variation (CNV) brain wave, which appears over the parietal lobe region prior to a specific motor response, is bilaterally symmetrical, even though only one half-brain sees the triggering stimulus (Figure 24-3) (Hillyard, 1971). In this test, recordings were made on each side of the skull, while a visual discrimination was flashed to only one hemisphere. The subject was trained to make a manual response to a tone that followed the numeral one but did not follow a zero. Thus, when the one appeared the expectancy brain wave develops,

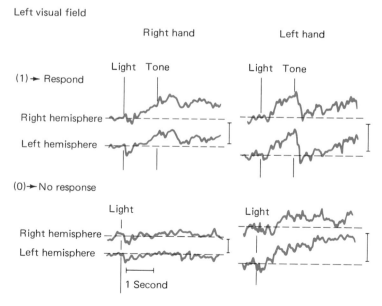

FIGURE 24-3   Computer-averaged CNV's ($N = 12$) recorded simultaneously from the scalp over the right and left hemispheres when the right or left hand was used and left visual field-right hemisphere was presented the visual discrimination task. Clearly, both hemispheres develop the expectancy wave even though only one knows what the triggering stimulus was. From Hillyard (1971).

but does not appear if a zero is flashed. When the information was presented in the left visual field, which projects to the right hemisphere, the subject responded appropriately. When subsequently asked what the stimuli were, the subjects said they did not know—that was the left hemisphere talking. Yet the physiological recordings showed that the normal expectancy wave developed in each hemisphere.

In the past, such waves were thought to have a one-to-one correspondence to basic psychological processes. Although this may still be true, the relation becomes more remote. The separated hemispheres are linked in these parameters but remarkably different in both their subjective and objective reports. The CNV seems to have psychological significance with respect to the events that trigger it, but it cannot be indexing a psychological process like attention or expectancy because the nonexpectant hemisphere also has the CNV. As a result, what initially looked like a strike for hemisphere unity now appears to be otherwise.

The MacKay question is still open. Experimentally, the question becomes whether one environmental situation can precipitate two different behavioral responses, each having a different value for each half-brain? In other words, could the same rewarding event elicit a different probability of responding in each separate hemisphere?

Reward Mechanisms and the Cerebral Hemispheres

This basic question of whether a reward can have a value x for one hemisphere and a value y for the other was recently analyzed using split brain monkeys (Johnson & Gazzaniga, 1970). During the course of studying the role of reward in learning, it became apparent that the positive stimulus of a visual discrimination, which may become a rewarding event in and of itself in one brain, simultaneously elicited neutral responses in the other half-brain.

It was shown that, when one naive hemisphere observes the errorless performance of the other on a pattern discrimination, it also learns. In other words, a half-brain need not experience errors to learn a visual discrimination.

Johnson and Gazzaniga next tried to analyze the role of reward. In brief, they taught one half-brain a new problem and then advanced the reward schedule to fixed ratio 2 (FR-2). Thus, the animal was rewarded on every other trial (Figure 24-4). On the unrewarded trials, both the trained half-brain and the naive half-brain were allowed to view the discrimination. On the rewarded trials, only the trained hemisphere saw the problem; the naive half-brain saw nothing. Could the naive half-brain learn if it only observed correct

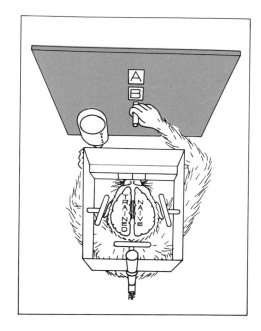

FIGURE 24-4   Split-brain monkeys observe a visual discrimination through a specially designed training apparatus, which allows for the separate or combined projection of visual information to each eye. Here, a naive hemisphere is free to observe the errorless performance of a trained hemisphere.

performance and never experienced a reward? It was assumed that, if the normative system (which assigns values or response probabilities to all events) was common to both hemispheres, the monkey would calmly and easily learn the discriminative cues even though there was no primary reward present, that is, the secondary or quasi-reward value of the stimulus ought to register instantly on the naive side.

What happened was most surprising. The naive hemisphere not only did not learn the discrimination, but on the unrewarded trials it actively interfered with the ongoing normal discriminative activity of the trained half-brain. In other words, the naive half-brain was not content to observe the performance of the trained side on these trials as it had when rewards were present. It disregarded any response tendency that might have transferred and sought its own solution to the problem. As a result, it actively intruded and interfered with behavior.

Clearly, any quasi-reward value of the discrimination per se that may have been assigned to the stimulus by the trained half-brain did not transfer and was in no way communicated to the naive half-brain. If it had, the naive half-brain would have learned easily and would not have been frustrated. Indeed, when looking at the actual behavior, it was as if two different value systems were competing for control over one response mechanism.

These animal studies are in agreement with recent testing of the split-brain patients on the effects of reward (Figure 24-5). It was shown that when feedback, the appearance of the word "right" for correct responses and "wrong" for incorrect responses, was flashed to one half-brain and a visual discrimination was presented exclusively to the other, no learning occurred in over thirty trials. In callosum-intact people, the information is immediately synthesized and learning occurs in one or two trials. Johnson went on to show, however, that if the split-brain patient was reprimanded for making an error, quick learning occurred. It is hypothesized that the reward, or feedback, no longer

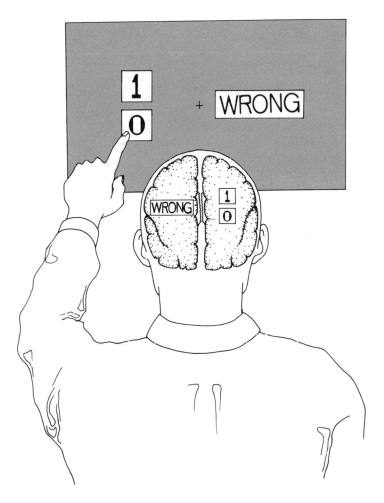

FIGURE 24-5 Split-brain subjects are unable to describe verbally from the left hemisphere visual information presented to the right hemisphere (left of fixation). Here, a discrimination is presented to the right hemisphere, while only the left receives reward information. Normals learn the problem quickly, but a split remains at chance level after 30 trials.

remained cortical. When the "wrong" light appeared the patient would now make an exclamation, sigh, and gesture disgust. On the next trials, learning occurred. Thus, when the reward took on more general affective responses, the cuing became so massive that the opposite half-brain could figure out which stimulus was producing the general negative reaction and which was not. Taken together then, it can be said that higher-order feedback information can remain isolated and separate in the split brain. Each hemisphere apparently is free to assign different or even conflicting response probabilities to the same stimulus.

LANGUAGE TRAINING

The extensive evidence collected by Gazzaniga and Sperry on the cognitive capacity of the disconnected right hemisphere in man supported the claim of the existence of double consciousness following transection of the cerebral commissures. This mute, passive cognitive system was shown to be capable of a number of mental operations, which were outlined above. One inference from this work was that if the left, dominant hemisphere should ever be damaged in a normal adult, the right side with proper training ought to be able to come to its aid. Although this idea has received little support from huge amounts of clinical data, it nonetheless seemed viable as a result of the studies on the bisected brain.

In one study (Glass, Gazzaniga, & Premack, 1973), an 84-year-old global aphasic was able to learn some basic language operations. This woman had had a major stroke involving the left speech and language center that rendered her hemiparalytic and unable to understand or produce natural language. Nonetheless, using the language scheme developed by Premack for chimpanzees (see Chapter 6), it was possible to train her to arrange correctly cut-out paper symbols that were referent to language operations (Figure 24-6).

Contrary to existing views, which hold that the left hemisphere's language center is specialized for the processing of symbolic information, the subject learned that a variety of paper symbols were each referent to a particular linguistic operation. For example, when two similar objects were placed side by side, the subject could place between them a symbol meaning "same." When the objects were different, another symbol, representing "different," would be appropriately placed. The proper use of the "same" and "different," symbols was not restricted to the items used in training but transferred freely

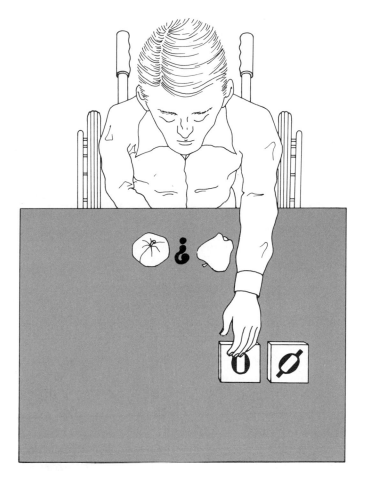

FIGURE 24-6   A stroke patient is using the artificial language system described in Chapter 6.

to nontraining items. A question symbol was introduced in the same-different construction and given the meaning of "missing element"; the subject showed her grasp of the symbol by successfully substituting for it whatever element was missing, predicate as well as object. In addition, the subject would form the negative in the injunctive mode. These observations have been extended by training six more global aphasics. Some have been brought to the level of generating simple sentences using these methods.

Although, of course, one cannot completely rule out the possibility that undamaged parts of the left hemisphere are active in carrying out these tasks, a more likely explanation is that the remaining right hemisphere is doing the work. In other words, the original split-brain data humans, which spelled out the boundary condition of mental competence on the right side, gave support to the notion that the right hemisphere, separated or not from the left hemisphere, can do many complicated and sophisticated cognitive operations.

These remarkable abilities in severely brain-damaged global aphasics demonstrate that the languageless human still possesses a conceptual system that can handle certain logical tasks. Moreover, the data suggest that there exists in the brain a conceptual system that is separate and independent from the natural language system. Indeed, it could be that this primitive conceptual system may be the primordial cognitive system of primates, from which may have come the language abilities of man. Approaching the problem of cognition in this light suggests the theoretical importance of coming to a better understanding of the brain-damaged human. With the confounding and interwoven language mechanisms put to rest, one can begin to see how the brain deals with complex logical operations in the raw.

The Sleeping Hemispheres

There is additional support for the view that the right hemisphere has tremendous cognitive powers. We have seen the intact brain at work performing perceptual tasks outside and independent of the normal language system. In some exploratory and preliminary tests carried out at Cornell Medical School, unilateral amytal testing was done on the left hemisphere of two nonaphasic brain-damaged patients subsequent to a required angiogram. Prior to injection of the anesthetic, which has the effect of putting one half-brain briefly asleep, an object was placed in the subjects's left hand, out of his view. When asked what it was, the subject responded correctly by saying "spoon." This showed that the left hand–right hemisphere somesthetic projection system was working as well as the right hemisphere–left hemisphere callosal link to the speech center. Next, the amytal was administered and the left hemisphere went out. At this time, when the patient is totally unable to use or understand language, another object was placed in the left hand. Since the right hemisphere is exclusively awake, it is free to remember the test object. The subject held it for awhile, and then it was removed. Shortly thereafter, the effects of the drug wore off and the left hemisphere woke up. A typical exchange between the experimenter (E) and subject (S) went as follows.

E: "How do you feel?"
S: "Fine."
E: "What did I put in your hand?"
S: "I don't know."

> *E:*   "Are you sure?"
> *S:*   "Yes."

Then a series of objects were shown to the subject.

> *E:*   "Which one was it?"

The left hand immediately pointed to the correct object.

It is still too early to report all the necessary qualifications on this experiment. Other patients, for example, are unable to remember anything at all. Yet, the first result suggests that, when the natural language and speech system is not functioning, perceptually stored information encoded at that time is not subsequently available to the language system upon its return to normal operation. In a way it is like the common experience of being unable to remember events earlier than the age of two or three. It is possible that the brain can remember critical events, which may later play a role in the control of behavior, but, because the remembered events occurred prior to the clear establishment of the language system, they cannot be subsequently recalled through this system.

BRAIN CODE AND THE CORPUS CALLOSUM

Experimenters in brain research assume that there is a corollary physical code to personal psychological experience. It has not been at all clear how and where one would approach this problem in the brain, but it now seems that the corpus callosum might be a good starting point. This brain structure relates the psychological, conscious experiences of one hemisphere to the other. Therefore, if insight were gained into the nature of the callosal transfer mechanism, it would be possible also to find some answers to the more general question of how the brain encodes and transmits psychological data.

The interhemispheric exchange of information in normals was first examined in this context. Obviously, in order to begin to understand the corpus callosum, it is necessary to study people in whom it is still intact. Briefly, the original idea was to use lateralized visual stimuli in combination with reaction time measures in an effort to determine the timing and transfer properties of this great commissure. By asking for a spoken response in a left hemisphere-dominant person, it was hoped that there would be a difference between the reaction time to incoming stimuli that were originally projected to the left hemisphere, as opposed to information originally projected to the right half-brain.

In one of the first studies, Filbey and Gazzaniga (1969) found that, when a simple dot was flashed to the left hemisphere, subjects responded approximately 30 milliseconds faster using speech than when it was flashed to the right hemisphere. The response was to say "yes" when the dot was present and "no" when it was absent. When a trial consisted of a simple flash, the "no" response took approximately 40 milliseconds more than when the left hemisphere was responding to a dot. This was explained by the fact that the left half-brain had to wait for a signal from the right as to whether a stimulus had appeared or not. There was no reliable difference in this task when a manual response was required.

Along with the dot experiment, the extent to which each hemisphere in normal man is capable of controlling language processing was also examined. The Posner and Mitchell (1961) "name identity versus physical identity" tasks were used. Tasks requiring verbal processing were done more quickly when the test material was first presented to the left half-brain. There were two conditions in this experiment. In the first condition, the subject was required to respond manually only to physically identical stimuli. Thus AA or aa would require a response, whereas AB, Ab, or ab would not. The results showed that there was no difference in response rate as a function of left or right visual field presentation. In other words, either hemisphere could perform this task rather easily.

In the second condition, however, the subject was instructed to respond to name identity only, i.e., whether the two adjacent letters were of the same class. Here there was a difference between the two hemispheres. When the information was presented to the right nondominant hemisphere, the response took longer than when it was flashed to the left speech hemisphere.

Can the interhemispheric exchange relation be reversed? It was thought a visual-spatial task would demonstrate right-hemisphere superiority (Gibson *et al.*, 1970). Using a simple visual pattern task that required subjects to judge which two zigzag figures were oriented in the same direction, it was found that, with a verbal response, the discrimination could be performed much more quickly when presented first to the right hemisphere. When first presented to the left hemisphere, the task takes approximately 14 milliseconds longer to perform. The interpretation is that information needing spatial analysis that is presented to the left hemisphere must first be relayed to the right hemisphere for decoding and then sent back to the left for the verbal response.

In a sense, of course, these kinds of early studies simply demonstrated that reaction time techniques are sensitive enough to be used to trace information flow in the brain; but it remains for these techniques to be used to discover properties of the callosum itself. A series of experiments requiring the interhemisphere matching of visual information quickly demonstrated that interhemisphere matches using difficult-to-see visual stimuli (subjects indicate whether two words are the same or different) are far less accurate when one word is flashed to one hemisphere and the other to the opposite than when both are flashed to the same hemisphere. If the stimuli are bright, crisp, and clear, no such differences are seen.

Perhaps the callosum is a rather limited communication channel. It is normally engaged in communicating the activities of one half-brain to the other in a still unspecified spatial-temporal neural code, and it does not easily encode weak signals presented to one hemisphere. However, even if such a code exists, it might not be recognized. Indeed, the problem of properly conceptualizing how this system might work is both the challenge and the mystery of the corpus callosum.

SUMMARY

The physical substrate of conscious experience exists in duplicate in the human brain. For reasons that are not entirely clear, the separate systems are linked together in the normal organism by the corpus callosum. Furthermore, the critical function of assigning values, or response probability, which is certainly a core activity of brain and behavior processes, involves neural systems that can maintain a mutual independence after cortical-cortical disconnection. While it has never been clear what brain areas are involved in these crucial mechanisms in behavior, many researchers have assumed that subcortical systems, which remain functionally interconnected in the cortical commissure-sectioned animal, would have been primarily involved.

Most important, the interhemispheric connections in the normal subject allow for conscious unity. In other words, we can now say that a particular brain structure, the corpus callosum, transmits information responsible for subjective experience. When it is intact, we have our normal sense of conscious unity; without it the private experiences of the right hemisphere go on outside the awareness of the left, and vice versa. As a result of these studies, we have succeeded in beginning to tie down highly complex psychological processes to specific neurological systems.

SUGGESTED READINGS

GAZZANIGA, M. S. *The bisected brain.* New York: Appleton, 1970.

MACKAY, D. M. *Freedom of action in a mechanistic universe.* London and New York: Cambridge Univ. Press, 1967.

POLANYI, M. *Personal knowledge.* Chicago, Illinois: Univ. of Chicago Press, 1957.

SPERRY, R. W. Hemisphere deconnection and unity in conscious awareness. *American Psychologist*, 1968, **27**, 723–733.

References

The numbers in brackets after each reference indicate the text pages on which that reference is cited.

ALLPORT, G. *Pattern and growth in personality*. New York: Holt, 1937. [497]

ALLPORT, G. W. *The nature of prejudice*. New York: Doubleday, 1958. [569]

ANAND, B. K., & BROBECK, J. R. Localization of a feeding center in the hypothalamus of the rat. *Proceedings of the Society for Experimental Biology and Medicine*, 1951, **77**, 323–324. [458]

ANISFELD, M., & KNAPP, M. Association, synonymity and directionality in false recognition. *Journal of Experimental Psychology*, 1968, **77**, 171. [438]

A-O.K., ESP. *Time*, July 5, 1971. [187]

ARONFREED, J. *Conduct and conscience*. New York: Academic Press, 1968. [98]

ARONSON, E., & CARLSMITH, J. M. The effect of the severity of threat on the devaluation of forbidden behavior. *Journal of Abnormal and Social Psychology*, 1963, **66**, 584–588. [81, 82]

ASCH, S. E. Effects of group pressure upon the modification and distortion of judgments. In H. Guetzkow (Ed.), *Groups, leadership, and men*. Pittsburgh, Pennsylvania: Carnegie Press, 1951. [556]

ATKINSON, R. C., & SHIFFRIN, R. M. Human memory: A proposed system and its control processes. In K. W. Spence and J. T. Spence (Eds.), *The psychology of learning and motivation: Advances in research and theory*. Vol. 2. New York: Academic Press, 1968. [413, 430, 433, 434]

ATTARDI, D., & SPERRY, R. W. Central routes taken by regenerating optic fibers. *Physiologist*, 1960, **3**, 12. [12]

ATTNEAVE, F. Some informational aspects of visual perception. *Psychological Review*, 1954, **61**, 183–193. [287, 289]

AYLLON, T., & AZRIN, N. H. *Token economy: A motivational system for therapy and rehabilitation.* New York: Appleton, 1968. [535]

AZRIN, N. H., HUTCHINSON, R. R., & SALLERY, R. D. Pain-aggression toward inanimate objects. *Journal of the Experimental Analysis of Behavior,* 1964, **7,** 223–228. [76]

BACK, L. W. Influence through social communication. *Journal of Abnormal and Social Psychology,* 1951, **46,** 9–23. [578]

BADDELY, A. The influence of acoustic and semantic similarity on long-term memory for word sequences. *Quarterly Journal of Experimental Psychology,* 1966, **18,** 302. [438]

BALDWIN, A. L., KALLHORN, J., & BREESE, S. Patterns of parent behavior. *Psychological Monographs,* 1945, **58,** (3, Whole No. 4). [479]

BANDURA, A. Social learning through imitation. In M. R. Jones (Ed.), *Nebraska symposium on motivation.* Lincoln, Nebraska: Univ. of Nebraska Press, 1962. Pp. 211–269. [97, 567]

BANDURA, A. *Principles of behavior modification.* New York: Holt, 1969. [76]

BANDURA, A., & WALTERS, R. H. *Social learning and personality development.* New York: Holt, 1963. [567, 571]

BARKER, R. G., DEMBO, T., & LEWIN, K. *Frustration and regression: An experiment with young children.* Univ. of Iowa Stud. Child Welfare, 1941. [490]

BARLOW, H., BLAKEMORE, C., & PETTIGREW, J. D. The neural mechanisms of binocular depth discrimination, *Journal of Physiology (London),* 1967, **193,** 327–342. [327]

BELMONT, J. M., & BUTTERFIELD, E. C. What the development of short-term memory is. *Human Development,* 1971, **14,** 236–248. [163, 166]

BEM, D. J. An experimental analysis of self-persuasion. *Journal of Experimental Social Psychology,* 1965, **1,** 199–218. [551]

BEM, D. J. Self-perception: An alternative interpretation of cognitive dissonance phenomena. *Psychological Review,* 1967, **74,** 183–200. [550]

BENNET, E. B. Discussion, decision commitment, and consensus in "group decision." *Human Relations,* 1955, **8,** 251–274. [578]

BERGIN, A. E. The effect of dissonant persuasive communications upon changes in a self-referring attitude. *Journal of Personality,* 1962, **30,** 423–438. [239]

BERGIN, A. E. Some implications of psychotherapy research for therapeutic practice. *Journal of Abnormal Psychology,* 1966, **71,** 235–246. [536]

BERKOWITZ, L. The concept of aggressive drive: Some additional considerations. In L. Berkowitz (Ed.), *Advances in experimental social psychology.* Vol. 2. New York: Academic Press, 1965. [571, 577]

BINET, A., & SIMON, T. Upon the necessity of establishing a scientific diagnosis of inferior states of intelligence. *Annee Psychologique,* 1905, **11,** 163–190. Translated by E. S. Kite. In H. H. Goddard (Ed.), *The development of intelligence.* Baltimore, Maryland: Williams & Wilkins, 1916. [206]

BLAKEMORE, C., & COOPER, G. F. Development of the brain depends on the visual environment. *Nature (London),* 1970, **228,** 477–478. [11, 33]

BLAKEMORE, C., & SUTTON, P. Size adaptation: A new aftereffect. *Science,* 1969, **166,** 245–247. [298]

BOGEN, J. E., FISHER, E. D., & VOGEL, P. J. Cerebral commissurotomy: A second case report. *Journal of the American Medical Association,* 1965, **194,** 1328–1329. [591]

BOWER, G. H. Organizational factors in memory. *Cognitive Psychology,* 1970, **1,** 18. [437]

BOWER, T. G. R. Discrimination of depth in premotor infants. *Psychonomic Science,* 1964, **1,** 368. [169]

BOWER, T. G. R. Stimulus variables determining space perception in infants. *Science,* 1965, **149,** 88–89. [156]

Boy with IQ of 55 is genius at Ciavo. *New York Times,* August 6, 1971. [204]

BRACKBILL, Y. Research and clinical work with children. In R. Bauer (Ed.), *Some views on Soviet psychology.* Washington, D.C.: American Psychological Association, 1962. [150]

BRAINE, M. D. S. The ontogeny of English phrase structure: The first phrase. *Language,* 1963, **39,** 1–13. [122]

BREHM, J. W. Post-decision changes in desirability of alternatives. *Journal of Abnormal and Social Psychology,* 1956, **52,** 384–389. [541]

BREHM, J. W. Modification of hunger by cognitive dissonance. In P. G. Zimbardo, (Ed.), *The cognitive control of motivation.* Glenview, Illinois: Scott, Foresman, 1969. Pp. 22–29. [542]

BREHM, J. W., & COHEN, A. R. *Explorations in cognitive dissonance.* New York: Wiley, 1962. [540, 542]

BROADBENT, D. E., & GREGORY, M. Division of attention and the decision theory of signal detection. *Proceedings of the Royal Society, Series B,* 1963, **158,** 222–231. [371]

BROWN, R. *Social psychology.* New York: Free Press, 1965. [480]

BRYAN, J. H., & TEST, M. A. Models and helping: Naturalistic studies in aiding behavior. *Journal of Personality and Social Psychology,* 1967, **6,** 400–407. [558]

BURCHARD, E. M. L. Physique and psychosis: An analysis of the postulated relationship between bodily constitution and mental disease syndrome. *Comparative Psychology Monographs,* 1936, **13,** 357. [477]

BURT, C. The genetic determination of differences in intelligence: A study of monozygotic twins reared together and apart. *British Journal of Psychology,* 1966, **57,** 137–153. [216]

CAMPBELL, F. W., & RUSHTON, W. A. H. Measurement of the scotopic pigment in the living human eye. *Journal of Physiology (London),* 1955, **130,** 131–147. [261]

CAPLAN, N. S., & PAIGE, J. M. A study of ghetto rioters. *Scientific American,* 1968, **219**(2), 15–21. [576]

CATTELL, R. B. *Description and measurement of personality.* Yonkers, New York: World Book, 1946. [497, 498]

CHOMSKY, N. *Syntactic structures.* The Hague: Mouton, 1957. [106]

CHOMSKY, N. Review of Skinner's *Verbal behavior. Language,* 1959, **35,** No. 1, 26–58. [114]

CHOMSKY, N. *Aspects of the theory of syntax.* Cambridge, Massachusetts: MIT Press, 1965. [108]

CHRISTIAN, J. J., FLYER, V., & DAVIS, D. E. Factors in the mass mortality of a herd of Sika deer, *Cervus nippon. Chesapeake Science,* 1960, **1,** 79–95. [582]

CISIN, I. H., COFFIN, T. E., JANIS, I. L., KLAPPER, J. T., MENDELSOHN, H., OMWAKE, E., PINDERHUGHES, C. A., DE SOLA POOL, I., SIEGEL, A. E., WALLACE, A. F., WATSON, A. S., & WIEBE, G. D. *Television and growing up: The impact of televised violence.* Washington D. C.: US Govt. Printing Office, 1972. [566]

COCH, L., & FRENCH, J. R. P. Overcoming resistance to change. *Human Relations,* 1948, **1,** 512–532. [563]

COLEMAN, J. C. *Abnormal personality and modern life.* (3rd ed.) Glenview, Illinois: Scott, Foresman, 1964. [518, 522]

COLLINS, A., & QUILLIAN, R. Retrieval time from semantic memory. *Journal of Verbal Learning and Verbal Behavior,* 1969, **8,** 240. [441]

COLLINS, B. E. *Social psychology.* Reading, Massachusetts: Addison-Wesley, 1970. [569, 571]

CONRAD, R. Acoustic confusions in immediate memory. *British Journal of Psychology,* 1964, **55,** 75–83. [419]

CONRAD, R., & HULL, A. Information, acoustic confusion, and memory span. *British Journal of Psychology*, 1964, **55**, 429–437. [419]

COONS, E. E. *Evolutionary aspects of motivation.* 1973, in preparation. [446]

COONS, E. E., LEVAK, M., & MILLER, N. E. Lateral hypothalamus learning of food-seeking response motivated by electrical stimulation *Science*, 1965, **150**, 1320–1321. [458]

CORNSWEET, T. N. *Visual perception.* New York: Academic Press, 1970. [261, 279]

CRUIKSHANK, R. M. The development of visual size constancy in early infancy. *Journal of Genetic Psychology*, 1941, **58**, 327–351. [155]

DABBS, J. M., JR., & LEVENTHAL, H. Effects of varying the recommendations in a fear-arousing communication. *Journal of Personality and Social Psychology*, 1966, 4, 525–531. [580]

DENES, P. V., & PINSON, E. N. *The speech chain. The physics and biology of spoken language.* Murray Hill, New Jersey: Bell Telephone Laboratories, 1963. [118, 119]

DESOR, J. A. Toward a psychological theory of crowding. *Journal of Personality and Social Psychology*, 1972, **21**, 79–83. [583]

DEUTSCH, J. A. *The structural basis of behavior.* Chicago, Illinois: Univ. of Chicago Press, 1960. [462]

DEUTSCH, M., & KRAUSS, R. M. *Theories in social psychology.* New York: Basic Books, 1965. [567]

DIMOND, S. J. *The social behavior of animals.* London: B. T. Batsford, 1970. [53]

DOLLARD, J., DOOB, L. W., MILLER, N. B., MOWRER, O. H., & SEARS, R. R. *Frustration and aggression.* New Haven, Connecticut: Yale Univ. Press, 1939. [571, 573]

DOLLARD, J., & MILLER, N. E. *Personality and psychotherapy. An analysis in terms of learning, thinking, and culture.* New York: McGraw-Hill, 1950. [483, 493]

DUBOS, R. *Man adapting.* New Haven, Connecticut: Yale Univ. Press, 1966. [583]

DUNCKNER, K. Induced motion. In W. D. Ellis (Ed.), *A sourcebook of Gestalt psychology.* New York: Harcourt, 1938. Pp. 161–172. [341]

ECCLES, J. C. *The 19th Arthur Stanley Eddington memorial lecture.* London & New York: Cambridge Univ. Press, 1965. [590]

EIBL-EIBESFELDT, I. *Ethology: The biology of behavior.* New York: Holt, 1970. [42, 47, 48]

ELLIS, A. *Reason and emotion in psychotherapy.* New York: Lyle Stuart, 1962. [529]

ENDERS, L. J., & FLINN, D. E. Clinical problems in aviation medicine, "schizophrenic reaction, paranoid type." *Aerospace Medicine*, 1962, **33**, 730–732. [510]

ESTES, W. All-or-none processes in learning and retention. *American Psychologist*, 1964, **19**, 16–25. [401]

FELDMAN, M. P. Aversion therapy for sexual deviations: A critical review. *Psychological Bulletin*, 1966, **63**, 65–79. [534]

FESTINGER, L. A theory of social comparison processes. *Human Relations*, 1954, **7**, 117–140. [553]

FESTINGER, L. *A theory of cognitive dissonance.* Stanford, California: Stanford Univ. Press, 1957. [539]

FESTINGER, L., & CARLSMITH, J. M. Cognitive consequences of forced compliance. *Journal of Abnormal and Social Psychology*, 1959, **58**, 203–210. [541]

FESTINGER, L., & FREEDMAN, J. L. Dissonance reduction and moral values. In P. Worschel & D. Byrne (Eds.), *Personality change.* New York: Wiley, 1964. [82]

FILBEY, R. A., & GAZZANIGA, M. S. Splitting the normal brain with reaction time. *Psychonomic Science*, 1969, **17**, 335–336. [602]

FLAVELL, J. H. Developmental studies of mediated memory. In H. W. Reese & L. P. Lipsitt

(Eds.), *Advances in child development and behavior.* Vol. 5. New York: Academic Press, 1970. Pp. 181–211. [165]

FONBERG, E., & DELGADO, J. M. R. Avoidance and alimentary reactions during amygdala stimulation, *Journal of Neurophysiology*, 1961, **24**, 651–664. [455]

FOX, L. Effecting the use of efficient study habits. *Journal of Mathematics*, 1962, **1**, 75–86. [95]

FREEDMAN, J. The effects of crowding on human performance. Unpublished manuscript, Columbia University, 1970. [584]

FREUD, S. *The interpretation of dreams.* London: Hogarth, 1900. [483]

FULLER, J., & THOMPSON, W. R. *Behavior genetics.* New York: Wiley, 1960. [475]

GARCIA, J., KIMELDURF, D. J., & HUNT, E. L. The use of ionizing radiation as a motivating stimulus. *Psychological Review*, 1961, **68**, 383–395. [454]

GARDNER, R. A., & GARDNER, B. G. Teaching sign language to a chimpanzee. *Science*, 1969, **165**, 664–672. [129]

GAZZANIGA, M. S. *The bisected brain.* New York: Appleton, 1970. [592]

GAZZANIGA, M. S., & SPERRY, R. W. Language after section of the cerebral commissures. *Brain*, 1967, **90**, 131–148. [592]

GEDDES, D. P. *An analysis of the Kinsey reports on sexual behavior in the human male and female.* New York: New American Library, 1954. (Mentor book). [192]

GERARD, H. B., & RABBIE, J. M. Fear and social comparison. *Journal of Abnormal and Social Psychology*, 1961, **62**, 586–592. [554]

GIBSON, A. R., FILBEY, R., & GAZZANIGA, M. S. Hemispheric differences as reflected by reaction time. *Federation Proceedings, Federation of American Societies for Experimental Biology*, 1970, **29**, 658. [602]

GIBSON, A. R., & HARRIS, C. S. The McCollough effect: Color adaptation of edge-detectors or negative afterimages? Paper read at Eastern Psychological Association, Washington, D.C., April, 1968. [299]

GIBSON, J. J. Adaptation, after-effect, and contrast in the perception of curved lines. *Journal of Experimental Psychology*, 1933, **16**, 1–31. [339]

GIBSON, J. J. *The perception of the visual world.* Boston, Massachusetts: Houghton, 1950. [305, 306, 310]

GIBSON, J. J. *The senses considered as perceptual systems.* Boston, Massachusetts: Houghton, 1966. [317]

GILINSKY, A. S. The effect of attitude upon the perception of size. *American Journal of Psychology*, 1955, **68**, 173–192. [306]

GILINSKY, A. S. Orientation-specific effects of patterns of adapting light on visual acuity. *Journal of the Optical Society of America*, 1968, **58**, 13–18. [296]

GLANZER, M., & CUNITZ, A. R. Two storage mechanisms in free recall. *Journal of Verbal Learning and Verbal Behavior*, 1966, **5**, 351–360. [417]

GLASS, D. C., & SINGER, J. E. *Urban stress: Experiments on noise and social stressors.* New York: Academic Press, 1972. [581, 582]

GLASS, A. V., GAZZANIGA, M. S., & PREMACK, D. Language training after brain damage. *Neuropsychologia*, 1973, in press. [598]

GLEASON, H. A. *An introduction to descriptive linguistics.* New York: Holt, 1961. [119]

GOLDIAMOND, I. Self-control procedures in personal behavior problems. *Psychological Reports*, **17**, 851–868, 1965. [96]

GOLDMAN, R., JAFFA, M., & SCHACHTER, S. Yom Kippur, Air France, dormitory food, and the eating behavior of obese and normal persons. *Journal of Personality and Social Psychology*, 1968, **10**, 117–123. [549]

GOTTESMAN, I. I. Heritability of personality: A demonstration. *Psychological Monographs,* 1963, **77**, (9, Whole No. 194). [473]

GREEN, D. M., & SWETS, J. A. *Signal detection theory and psychophysics.* New York: Wiley, 1966. [368]

GREGORY, R. *The eye and brain.* New York: McGraw-Hill, 1966. [332]

GROSBERG, J. M. Behavior therapy: A review. *Psychological Bulletin,* 1964, **62**, 73–88. [536]

GROSSMAN, S. P. Eating or drinking elicited by direct adrenergic or cholinergic stimulation of hypothalamus. *Science,* 1960, **132**, 301–302. [460]

GUILFORD, J. P. *Personality.* New York: McGraw-Hill, 1959. [497]

GUTHRIE, E. R., & HORTON, G. P. *Cats in a puzzle box.* New York: Holt, 1946. [346]

HAITH, M. M. Developmental changes in visual information processing and short-term memory. *Human Development,* 1971, **14**, 249–261. [160]

HALL, C. S. Temperament: A survey of animal studies. *Psychological Bulletin,* 1941, **38**, 909–943. [469]

HALL, E. T. *The hidden dimension.* Garden City, New York: Doubleday, 1966. [583, 584]

HAMILTON, C. R. Intermanual transfer of adaptation to prisms. *American Journal of Psychology,* 1964, **77**, 457–462. (a) [333]

HAMILTON, C. R. *Studies on adaptation to deflection of the visual field in split-brain monkeys and man.* (Doctoral dissertation, California Institute of Technology) Ann Arbor, Michigan: University Microfilms, 1964. No. 64-11, 398. (b) [336]

HARLOW, H. The heterosexual affectional system in monkeys. *American Psychologist,* 1962, **17**, 1–9. [71]

HARLOW, H. F. *Learning to love.* San Francisco, California: Albion, 1971. [68]

HARRIS, C. S. Perceptual adaptation to inverted, reversed, and displaced vision. *Psychological Review,* 1965, **72**, 419–444. [337]

HARRIS, C. S., & HARRIS, J. R. Rapid adaptation to right-left reversal of the visual field. Paper read at Psychonomic Society, Chicago, October 1965. [338]

HARTLINE, H. K. The neural mechanisms for vision. *Harvey Lectures,* 1942, **37**, 39. [270]

HAYES, C. *The ape in our house.* New York: Harper, 1951. [128]

HAYES, J. Memory span for several vocabularies as a function of vocabulary size. *Quarterly progress report.* Cambridge, Massachusetts: Acoustics Laboratory, MIT, 1957. [420]

HAYNES, H., WHITE, B. L., & HELD, R. Visual accommodation in human infants. *Science,* 1965, **148**, 528–530. [154]

HEBB, D. O. *The organization of behavior.* New York: Wiley, 1949. [292]

HEBB, D. O. Distinctive features of learning in the higher animal. In J. Dalafresnaye (Ed.), *Brain mechanisms and learning.* London & New York: Oxford Univ. Press, 1961. P. 37. [431, 432]

HEIDER, F. *The psychology of interpersonal relations.* New York: Wiley, 1958. [550]

HEINEMANN, E. G., TULVING, E., & NACHMIAS, J. The effect of occular or motor adjustments in apparent size. *American Journal of Psychology,* 1959, **72**, 32–45. [305]

HELD, R. Plasticity in sensory-motor systems. *Scientific American,* 1965, **213**(5), 84–94. [333, 336]

HELD, R., & HEIN, A. Movement produced stimulation in the development of visually guided behavior. *Journal of Comparative and Physiological Psychology,* 1963, **56**, 872–876. [335]

HELLYER, S. Frequency of stimulus presentation, and short-term decrement in recall. *Journal of Experimental Psychology,* 1962, **64**, 650. [431]

HESS, E. H. Imprinting in animals. *Scientific American,* 1958, **198**, 81–86. [60, 61]

HESS, E. H. Imprinting. *Science,* 1959, **130**, 133–141. [59]

HILLYARD, S. A. The psychological specificity of the contingent negative variation and late evoked potential. *Electroencephalography and Clinical Neurophysiology*, 1971, **31**, 302–303. [594]

HIRSCH, H. V. B., & SPINELLI, D. N. Modification of the distribution of receptive field orientation in cats by selective visual exposure during development. *Experimental Brain Research*, 1971, **12**, 509–527. [34]

HOCHBERG, J. E., & McALLISTER, E. A quantitative approach to figural "goodness." *Journal of Experimental Psychology*, 1953, **46**, 361–364. [287, 288]

HOCHBERG, J., TRIEBEL, W., & SEAMON, G. Color adaptation under conditions of homogenous stimulation (Ganzfeld). *Journal of Experimental Psychology*, 1951, **41**, 153–159. [278]

HOHMANN, G. W. Some effects of spinal cord lesions on experienced emotional feelings. *Psychophysiology*, 1966, **3**, 143–156. [78]

HOLWAY, A. H., & BORING, E. G. Determinants of apparent visual size with distance variant. *American Journal of Psychology*, 1941, **54**, 21–37. [303]

HOMME, L. E. Perspectives in psychology. XXIV. Control of coverants: The operants of the mind. *Psychological Record*, 1965, **15**, 501–511. [96]

HOVLAND, C. I., JANIS, I. L., & KELLEY, H. H. *Communication and persuasion*. New Haven, Connecticut: Yale Univ. Press, 1953. [579]

HOVLAND, C. I., & WEISS, W. The influence of source credibility on communication effectiveness. *Public Opinion Quarterly*, 1951, **15**, 635–650. [579]

HUBEL, D. H., & WIESEL, T. N. Receptive fields, binocular interaction and functional architecture in the cat's visual cortex. *Journal of Physiology (London)*, 1962, **160**, 106. [31, 295]

HULL, C. *Principles of behavior*. New York: Appleton, 1943. [391]

HUNT, C., & VAIZEY, M. J. Differential effects of group density on social behavior. *Nature (London)*, 1966, **209**, 1371–1372. [584]

HYMAN, H. H. The psychology of status. *Archives of Psychology*, 1942, **269**, 5–92. [574]

INHELDER, B. Some aspects of Piaget's genetic approach to cognition. *Monographs of the Society for Research in Child Development*, 1962, **27**(2), 19–34. [142, 148]

INHELDER, B., & PIAGET, J. *The growth of logical thinking from childhood to adolescence*. New York: Basic Books, 1958. [148, 149]

INHELDER, B., & PIAGET, J. *The early growth of logic in the child*. New York: Norton, 1964. [172, 174, 175]

JAMES, W. *Principles of psychology*. New York: Holt, 1890. [77]

JANIS, I. L., & FESHBACH, S. Effects of fear-arousing communication. *Journal of Abnormal Social Psychology*, 1953, **48**, 78–92. [579]

JANIS, I. L., MAHL, G. F., KAGAN, J., & HOLT, R. R. *Personality. Dynamics, development, and assessment*. New York: Harcourt, 1969. [470]

JENSEN, A. R. How much can we boost IQ and scholastic achievement? *Harvard Educational Review*, 1969, **39**, 1–123. [207, 213–215]

JOHNSON, B., & BECK, L. F. The development of space perception: Stereoscopic vision in preschool children. *Journal of Genetic Psychology*, 1941, **58**, 247–254. [157]

JOHNSON, J. D., & GAZZANIGA, M. S. Interhemispheric imitation in split-brain monkeys. *Experimental Neurology*, 1970, **27**, 206–212. [595]

KAMIN, L. Heredity, intelligence, politics, and psychology. Seminar, Columbia University, 1972. [213]

KAUFMAN, L., BACON, J., & BURROSO, F. Stereopsis without image segregation. *Vision Research*, 1972, in press. [266]

KAUFMAN, L., CYRULNIK, I. KAPLOWITX, J., MELMICK, K., & STOFF, D. The complementerity of apparent and real motion. *Psychologische Forschung*, 1971, **34**, 343–348. [346]

KAUFMAN, L., & ROCK, I. The moon illusion. *Scientific American*, 1962, **207**, 120–130. [330]

KELLOGG, W. N. *The ape and the child*. New York: McGraw-Hill, 1933. [127]

KELMAN, H. C. Human use of human subjects: The problem of deception in psychobiological experiments. *Psychological Bulletin*, 1967, **67**, 1–11. [239, 240]

KELMAN, H. C., & HOVLAND, C. I. "Reinstatement" of the communicator in delayed measurement of opinion change. *Journal of Abnormal Social Psychology*, 1953, **48**, 327–335. [579]

KENNEDY, G. C. The hypothalamic control of food intake in rats. *Proceedings of the Royal Society, Series B*, 1950, **137**, 535–548. [456]

KERNER, O., LINDSAY, J. V., HARRIS, F. R., BROOKE, E. W., CORMAN, J. C., McCULLOCH, W. M., ABEL, I. W., THORNTON, C. B., WILDINS, R., PEDEN, K. G., & JENKINS, H. *Report of the national advisory commission on civil disorders*. New York: Bantam Books, 1968. [575]

KESSLER, A. Social behavior and population dynamics: Evolutionary dynamics. In D. C. Glass (Ed.), *Biology and behavior: Genetics*. New York: Rockefeller Univ. Press, 1968. [584]

KIESLER, C. A., NISBETT, R. E., & ZANNA, M. P. On inferring one's beliefs from one's behavior. *Journal of Personality and Social Psychology*, 1969, **11**, 321–327. [551]

KINSEY, A. C., POMEROY, W. B., & MARTIN, C. E. *Sexual behavior in the human male*. Philadelphia, Pennsylvania: Saunders, 1948. [197, 198]

KINSEY, A. C., POMEROY, W. B., MARTIN, C. E., & GEBHARD, P. H. *Sexual behavior in the human female*. Philadelphia, Pennsylvania: Saunders, 1953. [192, 194, 195]

KISKER, G. W. *The disorganized personality*. New York: McGraw-Hill, 1964. [527]

KLEITMAN, N. Patterns of dreaming. *Scientific American*, 1960, **203**, 82–88. [227]

KNOBLOCH, H., RIDER, R. V., HARPER, P., & PASAMANICK, B. Neuropsychiatric sequelae of prematurity: A longitudinal study. *Journal of the American Medical Association*, 1956, **161**, 581–585. [471]

KOFFKA, K. *The growth of the mind*. New York: Harcourt, 1928. [282]

KOGAN, N., & WALLACH, M. A. Risk taking as a function of the situation, the person, and the group. In G. Mandler (Ed.), *New directions in psychology*. Vol. III. New York: Holt, 1967. [563]

KOHLER, I. Experiments with goggles. *Scientific American*, 1962, **206**, 62–72. [333]

KÖHLER, W. *The mentality of apes*. London: Routledge and Kegan Paul, 1925 (2nd ed., 1927). Paperback available from Vintage Books, New York, 1959. [59]

KRETSCHMER, E. *Physique and character*. New York: Harcourt, 1925. [477]

KRIECKHAUS, E. E. Innate recognition aids rate in sodium regulation. *I.C.P.P.*, 1970, **73**, 117–122. [453]

LAING, R. D. *The politics of experience*. New York: Ballantine, 1967. [512]

LASHLEY, K. S. The problem of serial order in behavior. In L. A. Jeffress (Ed.), *Cerebral mechanisms in behavior: The Hixon symposium*. New York: Wiley, 1951. [105]

LATANÉ, B., & DARLEY, J. M. *The unresponsive bystander: Why doesn't he help?* New York: Appleton, 1970. [558]

LATANÉ, B., & RODIN, J. A lady in distress: Inhibiting effects of friends and strangers on bystander intervention. *Journal of Experimental Social Psychology*, 1969, **5**, 189–202. [560]

LAZARUS, A. A. Group therapy of phobic disorders by systematic desensitization. *Journal of Abnormal and Social Psychology*, 1961, **63**, 504–510. [536]

LEEPER, R. W. A study of a neglected portion of the field of learning: The development of sensory organization. *Journal of Genetic Psychology*, 1935, **46**, 41–75. [291]

LEFKOWITZ, M., ERON, L., WALDER, L., & HUESMAN, L. R. Television violence and child aggression: A follow-up study. In G. A. Comstock and E. A. Rubinstein (Eds.), *Television and social behavior*. Vol. 3. *Television and adolescent aggressiveness*. Washington, D.C.: US Govt. Printing Office, 1971. [568]

LEIBOWITZ, S. E. Hypothalamic beta-adrenergic "Satiety System antagonizes an alpha-adrenergic 'hunger' system in the rat." *Nature (London)*, 1970, **226**, 963. [460]

LEVENTHAL, H., & SINGER, R. P. Affect arousal and positioning of recommendations in persuasive communications. *Journal of Personality and Social Psychology*, 1966, **4**, 137–146. [580]

LEVINE, S., & MULLINS, R. F., JR. Hormonal influences on brain organization in infant rats. *Science*, 1966, **152**, 1585–1591. [67]

LEWIN, K. Group decision and social change. In T. M. Newcomb & E. L. Hartley (Eds.), *Readings in social psychology*. New York: Holt, 1947. Pp. 330–444. [577]

LEYHAUSEN, P. Ver Naltensstudien bei Katzen. *Zeitschrift für Tierpsychologie*, 1956, **2**. [55]

LEYER, K. Tiefenwahrnehmung in den Entwicklungsphasen. *Zeitschrift für Psychologie*, 1939, **146**, 229–279. [157]

LINDZEY, G., LYKKEN, D. T., & WINSTON, H. P. Infantile trauma, genetic factors, and adult temperament. *Journal of Abnormal and Social Psychology*, 1960, **61**, 7–14. [470]

LORENZ, K. *On aggression*. London: Methuen, 1963. [76]

LOVEJOY, E. P. Analysis of the overlearning reversal effect. *Psychological Review*, 1966, **73**, 87–103. [404]

LOVIBUND, S. H. The current status of behavior therapy. *Canadian Psychologist*, 1966, **7a**, 93–101. [536]

MACFARLANE, D. A. The role of kinesthesis in maze learning. *University of California Publications in Psychology*, 1930, **4**, 277–305. [395]

MACKAY, D. M. In J. C. Eccles (Ed.), *Brain and conscious experience*. Berlin & New York: Springer-Verlag, 1966. [590]

MANDLER, G. From association to structure. *Psychological Review*, 1962, **69**, 415–427. [170]

MANDLER, G. Organization and memory. In K. W. Spence and J. T. Spence (Eds.), *The psychology of learning and motivation: Advances in research and theory*. Vol. 1. New York: Academic Press, 1967. [436, 437]

MASLACH, C. The truth about false confessions. *Journal of Personality and Social Psychology*, 1971, **20**, 141–146. [551]

McCOLLOUGH, C. Color adaptation of edge-detectors in the human visual system. *Science*, 1965, **149**, 1115–1116. [297]

McDOUGAL, W. *An outline of psychology*. London: Methuen, 1923. [44]

McKENNEL, A. C., & HUNT, E. A. *Noise annoyance in central London*. London: Government Social Survey, 1966. [581]

MEEHL, P. E. Schizotaxia, schizotype, schizophrenia. *American Psychologist*, 1962, **17**, 827–838. [476]

MEEHL, P. E. On the circularity of the law of effect. *Psychological Bulletin*, 1950, **47**, 52–75. [399]

MELZACK, R. Effects of early experience on behavior: Experimental and conceptual considerations. In *Psychopathology of perception*. New York: Grune & Stratton, 1965. Pp. 271–299. [73]

MILGRAM, S. Behavioral study of obedience. *Journal of Abnormal and Social Psychology,* 1963, **67,** 371–378. [240, 557]

MILGRAM, S. Group pressure and action against a person. *Journal of Abnormal and Social Psychology,* 1964, **69,** 137–143. [557]

MILGRAM, S. The experience of living in cities. *Science,* 1970, **13,** 1461–1468. [580]

MILLER, G. A. The magical number seven plus or minus two: Some limits on our capacity for storing information. *Psychological Review,* 1956, **63,** 81–97. [422]

MILLER, G. A. Some psychological studies of grammar. *American Psychologist,* 1962, **17,** 748–762. [110]

MILLER, N. E., & BUGELSKI, R. The influence of frustration imposed by the in-group on attitudes expressed toward out-groups. In R. I. Evans & R. M. Rozelle (Eds.), *Social psychology in life.* Boston, Massachusetts: Allyn & Bacon, 1970. [573]

MILLER N. E., & DOLLARD, J. *Social learning and imitation.* New Haven, Connecticut: Yale Univ. Press, 1941. [567]

MILLS, J. Changes in moral attitudes following temptation. *Journal of Personality,* 1958, **26,** 517–531. [83]

MISCHEL, W. Theory and research on the antecedents of self imposed delay and reward. In B. A. Maher (Ed.), *Progress in Experimental Personality Research.* Vol. 3. New York: Academic Press, 1966. Pp. 85–132. [95]

MORAY, N. Attention in dichotic listening: Affective cues and the influence of instructions. *Quarterly Journal of Experimental Psychology,* 1959, **11,** 56–60. [419]

MULDER, M., & STEMERDING, A. Threat, attraction to group, and need for strong leadership. *Human Relations,* 1963, **16,** 317–334. [239]

MUNN, N. L. *The evolution and growth of human behavior.* Boston: Massachusetts: Houghton, 1965. [163]

MURDOCK, B. B., JR. Recent developments in short term memory. *British Journal of Psychology,* 1967, **58,** 421–433. [424]

National Institute of Mental Health. *Special report: Schizophrenia.* Prepared by L. R. Mosher and D. Feinsilver, Rockville, Maryland, 1971. [475]

NEISER, U. *Cognitive psychology.* New York: Appleton, 1967. [412]

NELSON, T. O. Savings and forgetting in long-term memory. *Journal of Verbal Learning and Verbal Behavior,* 1971, **10,** 568. [438]

NELSON, T. O., & FEHLING, W. On the nature of semantic savings for items forgotten from long-term memory. Unpublished manuscript, 1972. [438, 439]

NELSON, T. O., & ROTHBART, A. Acoustic savings in long-term memory. *Journal of Experimental Psychology,* 1972, in press. [438, 439]

NEWMAN, H. H., FREEMAN, R. N., & HOLZINGER, K. J. *Twins: A study of heredity and environment.* Chicago, Illinois: Univ. of Chicago Press, 1937. [472]

NISBETT, R. E., & SCHACHTER, S. The cognitive manipulation of pain. *Journal of Experimental Social Psychology,* 1966, **2,** 227–236. [546]

NORMAN, D. A. *Memory and attention.* New York: Wiley, 1969. [158]

O'CONNOR, J. J. Was 'West Side Story' bad for East Harlem? *New York Times,* 1972. [566]

Office of Strategic Services. *Assessment of men: Selection of personnel for office of strategic services.* New York: Holt, 1948. [506]

OLDS, J. Self-stimulation of the brain. *Science* **127,** 1958, 315–324. [461]

OLDS, J., & MILNER, P. *Journal of the Comparative and Physiological Psychology,* 1954, **49,** 281. [461]

OLVER, R. R., & HORNSBY, J. R. On equivalence. In J. S. Bruner, R. R. Olver, & P. M. Greenfield (Eds.), *Studies in cognitive growth*. New York: Wiley, 1966. Pp. 68–85. [171–173]

ONO, H. Apparent distance as a function of familiar size. *Journal of Experimental Psychology*, 1969, **79**, 109–115. [307]

PAIVIO, A. Imagery and deep structure in the recall of English nominalizations. *Journal of Verbal Learning and Verbal Behavior*, 1971, **10**, 1–12. [114]

PAPOUŠEK, H. Experimental studies of appetitional behavior in human newborns and infants. In H. W. Stevenson, E. Hess, & H. L. Rheingold (Eds.), *Early behavior: comparative and developmental approaches*. New York: Wiley, 1967. Pp. 249–278. [150]

PAUL, G. L. Insight vs. desensitization two years after termination. *Journal of Consulting Psychology*, 1967, **31**, 333–348. [536]

PEARSON, K. On the inheritance of mental and moral characteristics in man, and its comparison with the inheritance of physical character. *Journal of The Royal Anthropological Institute*, 1903, **33**, 179–237. [210, 472]

PENFIELD, W., & ROBERTS, L. Speech and brain mechanisms. Princeton, New Jersey: Princeton Univ. Press, 1959. [136]

PETERSON, L. R., & PETERSON, M. J. Short-term retention of individual verbal items. *Journal of Experimental Psychology*, 1959, **58**, 193–198. [424]

PETTIGREW, T. F. *A profile of the Negro American*. Princeton, New Jersey: Van Nostrand-Reinhold, 1964. [576]

PFAFFMAN, C., & BARE, J. K. Gustatory nerve discharges in normal and adrenalectomized rats. *Journal of Comparative and Physiological Psychology*, 1950, **43**, 320–324. [454]

PFUNGST, O. *Clever Hans*. New York: Holt, 1965. [223]

PIAGET, J. *The origins of intelligence in children*. New York: International Universities Press, 1952. [151, 178]

PIAGET, J. *Play, dreams, and imitation in childhood*. New York: Norton, 1962. [170, 177]

PILIAVIN, I. M., RODIN, J., & PILIAVIN, J. A. Good samaritanism: An underground phenomenon. *Journal of Personality and Social Psychology*, 1969, **13**, 289–299 [560]

POLLACK, I. The information of elementary auditory displays. *Journal of The Acoustical Society of America*, 1954, **26**, 155–158. [420]

POSNER, M. Short-term memory systems in human information processing. *Acta Psychologica, Amsterdam*, 1967, **27**, 267–284. [438]

POSNER, M. I., & MITCHELL, R. F. Chronometric analysis of classification. *Psychological Review*, 1967, **74**, 392–409. [438]

POSTMAN, L., & PHILLIPS, L. W. Short term temporal changes in free recall. *Quarterly Journal of Experimental Psychology*, 1965, **17**, 132–138. [417]

PREMACK, D. Reinforcement theory. In D. Levine (Ed.), *Nebraska Symposium on Motivation*. Vol. 13. Lincoln, Nebraska: Univ. of Nebraska Press, 1965. Pp. 129–148. [399, 400]

PREMACK, D. Language in chimpanzee? *Science*, 1971, **172**, 808–822. [130]

RACHLIN, H., & HERRNSTEIN, R. On the law of effect. *Journal of the Experimental Analysis of Behavior*, 1970, **13**, 243–266. [391]

RATLIFF, F. *Mach bands*. San Francisco, California: Holden-Day, 1965. [271]

REICHARD, S., SCHNEIDER, M., & RAPAPORT, D. The development of concept formation in children. *American Journal of Orthopsychiatry*, 1944, **14**, 156–162. [171]

REITMAN, J. Mechanisms of forgetting in short-term memory. *Cognitive Psychology* 1971, **2**, 185–195. [426]

REYNOLDS, G. S. Behavioral contrast. *Journal of the Experimental Analysis of Behavior*, 1961, **4**, 57–71. [405]

RICCIUTI, H. N. Object grouping and selective ordering behavior in infants 12 to 24 months old. *Merrill-Palmer Quarterly*, 1965, **11**, 129–148. [169]

RHEINGOLD, H. L., GEWIRTZ, J. L., & ROSS, H. W. Social conditioning of vocalizations in the infant. *Journal of Comparative and Physiological Psychology*, 1959, **52**, 68–73. [152]

RIESEN, A. H. Effects of early deprivation of photic stimulation. In S. Osher & R. Cooke (Eds.), *The biosocial basis of mental retardation*. Baltimore, Maryland: Johns Hopkins Press, 1965. [294]

ROCK, I., & EBENHOLTZ, S. The relational determination of perceived size. *Psychological Review*, 1957, **66**, 387–401. [305]

ROCK, I., & EBENHOLTZ, S. Stroboscopic movement based on change of phenomenal location rather than retinal location. *American Journal of Psychology* 1962, **75**, 193–207. [305, 343]

ROCK, I., & HARRIS, C. S. Vision and touch. *Scientific American*, 1967, **216**(5), 96–104. [337, 339]

RODIN, J. Diminished frustration in females through menstruation attribution. Unpublished manuscript, 1971. [552]

ROGERS, C. R. *Client-centered therapy*. Boston, Massachusetts: Houghton, 1951. [499]

ROSENTHAL, R. On the social psychology of the psychological experiment: The experimenters hypothesis as unintended determinant of experimental results. *American Scientist*, 1963, **51**, 268–283. [237]

ROSENTHAL, R., & JACOBSON, L. *Pygmalion in the classroom: Teacher expectancy and pupil's intellectual development*. New York: Holt, 1968. [238]

ROSENTHAL, R. *et al.* Danish collaborative adoptee study. Cited in *NIMH Special report: Schizophrenia*. Prepared by L. R. Mosher and D. Feinsilver, Rockville, Maryland, 1971. [475]

ROSS, L., RODIN, J., & ZIMBARDO, P. G. Toward an attribution therapy: The reduction of fear through induced cognitive-emotional misattribution. *Journal of Personality and Social Psychology*, 1969, **12**, 279–288. [546]

RUNDUS, D. Analysis of rehearsal processes in free recall. *Journal of Experimental Psychology*, 1971, **89**, 63. [432, 433, 435]

RUNDUS, D., LOFTUS, G., & ATKINSON, R. Immediate free recall and three-week delayed recognition. *Journal of Verbal Learning and Verbal Behavior*, 1970, **9**, 684. [434]

RUSHTON, W. A. H. Visual pigments in man. *Scientific American*, 1962, **207**, 120–132. [262]

SARASON, I. G. *Personality: An objective approach*. New York: Wiley, 1966. [471]

SCHACHTER, S. *Psychology of affiliation*. Stanford, California: Stanford Univ. Press, 1959. [554]

SCHACHTER, S. The interaction of cognitive and physiological determinants of emotional state. In P. H. Leiderman & D. Shapiro (Eds.), *Psychobiological approaches to social behavior*. Stanford, California: Univ. of California Press, 1964. [545]

SCHACHTER, S. *Emotion, obesity, and crime*. New York: Academic Press, 1971. [79]

SCHACHTER, S., GOLDMAN, R., & GORDON, A. The effects of fear, food deprivation, and obesity on eating. *Journal of Personality and Social Psychology*, 1968, **10**, 91–97. [548]

SCHACHTER, S., & SINGER, J. E. Cognitive, social, and physiological determinants of emotional state. *Psychological Review*, 1962, **69**, 379–399. [545]

SCOTT, J. P. *Aggression*. Chicago, Illinois: Univ. of Chicago Press, 1958. [469]

SEARS, R. R. Relation of early socialization experiences to aggression in middle childhood. *Journal of Abnormal and Social Psychology*, 1961, **63**, 466–492. [77]

SECORD, P. F., & BACKMAN, C. W. *Social psychology*. New York: McGraw-Hill, 1964. [570]

SEKULER, R. W., & GANZ, L. Aftereffect of seen motion with a stabilized retinal image. *Science*, 1963, **139**, 419–420. [296, 341]

SEWELL, W. H. Infant training and the personality of the child. *American Journal of Sociology*, 1952, **58**, 150–159. [480]

SHEINGOLD, K. A developmental study of short-term visual storage. Unpublished doctoral dissertation, Harvard University, 1971. [160–161]

SHELDON, W. H. *The varieties of temperament: A psychology of constitutional differences.* New York: Harper, 1942. [477]

SHERIF, M., HARVEY, O. J., WHITE, B. J., HOOD, W. R., & SHERIF, C. W. *Intergroup conflict and cooperation: The robbers' cave experiment.* Norman, Oklahoma: University Book Exchange, 1961. [570]

SHIELDS, J. Personality differences and neurotic traits in normal twin school children. A study in psychiatric genetics. *Eugenics Review*, 1954, **45**, 213–246. [474]

SHIELDS, J. *Monozygotic twins.* London & New York: Oxford Univ. Press, 1962. [473]

SHIRLEY, M. M. A behavior syndrome characterizing prematurely born children. *Child Development*, 1939, **10**, 115–128. [472]

SIQUELAND, E. R., & LIPSITT, L. P. Conditioned headturning in human newborns. *Journal of Experimental Child Psychology*, 1966, **3**, 356–376. [151]

SKINNER, B. F. *Science and human behavior.* New York: Macmillan, 1953. [84, 87]

SKINNER, B. F. *Verbal behavior.* New York: Appleton, 1957. [102]

SMITH, O. W., & SMITH, P. C. Developmental studies of spatial judgments by children and adults. *Perceptual and Motor Skills*, 1966, **22**, 3–73. [157]

SOMMER, R. Small group ecology. *Psychological Bulletin*, 1967, **67**, 1145–1152. [583]

SONTAG, L. W. War and fetal maternal relationships. *Marriage and Family Living*, 1944, **6**, 1–5. [471]

SPENCE, K. W. The nature of discrimination learning in animals. *Psychological Review*, 1936, **43**, 427–449. [404]

SPERLING, G. The information available in brief visual presentations. *Psychological Monographs*, 1960, **74** (Whole No. 11). [411]

SPERLING, G. A., & SPEELMAN, R. G. Acoustic similarity and auditory short-term memory experiments and a model. In D. A. Norman (Ed.), *Models of human memory.* New York: Academic Press, 1970.

SPERRY, R. W. Cerebral organization and behavior. *Science*, 1961, **133**, 1749–1756. [590]

SPERRY, R. W. Hemisphere deconnection and unity in conscious experience. *American Psychologist*, 1968, **23**, 723–733. [590, 592]

SPERRY, R. W. A modified concept of consciousness. *Psychological Review*, 1969, **26**, 532–536. [589]

SPITZ, R. A. The smiling response: A contribution to the ontogenesis of social relations. *Genetic Psychology Monographs*, 1946, **34**, 57–125. [41]

STERNBERG, S. High-speed scanning in human memory. *Science*, 1966, **153**, 652–654. [427]

STEVENS, S. S. On the operation known as judgment. *American Scientist*, 1966, **54**, 385–401. [364]

STORMS, M. D., & NISBETT, R. E. Insomnia and the attribution process. *Journal of Personality and Social Psychology*, 1970, **16**, 319–328. [547]

STOUFFER, S. A., SUCHMAN, E. A., DEVINNEY, L. C., STAR, S. A., & WILLIAMS, R. N. *The American Soldier.* Vol. 1. *Adjustment during army life.* Princeton, New Jersey: Princeton Univ. Press, 1949. [574]

STRATTON, G. M. Some preliminary experiments on vision without inversion of the retinal image. *Psychological Review*, 1896, **3**, 611–617. [332]

STRATTON, G. M. Vision without inversion of the retinal image. *Psychological Review*, 1897, **4**, 341–360, 463–481. [332]

STUART, R. B. Behavioral control of overeating. *Behaviour Research and Therapy*, 1967, **5**, 357–365. [93]

STUNKARD, A. J., & KOCH, C. The interpretation of gastric motility. I. Apparent bias in the reports of hunger by obese persons. *Archives of General Psychiatry*, 1964, **11**, 74–82. [548]

SULLIVAN, H. S. The theory of anxiety and the nature of psychotherapy. *Psychiatry*, 1949, **12**, 3–13. [499]

SUTHERLAND, N. S. The learning of discrimination by animals. *Endeavour*, 1964, **23**, 140–152. [404]

SWETS, J. A. Is there a sensory threshold? *Science*, 1961, **134**, 168–177. [368]

TANNER, W. P., JR., & SWETS, J. A. A decision-making theory of visual detection. *Psychological Review*, 1954, **61**, 401–409. [368]

TEITELBAUM, P. Sensory control of hypothalamic hyperphagia. *Journal of Comparative and Physiological Psychology*, 1955, **48**, 156–163. [457]

TEITELBAUM, P., & EPSTEIN, A. N. The lateral hypothalamic syndrome: Recovery of feeding and drinking after lateral hypothalamic lesions. *Psychological Review*, 1962, **69**, 74–90. [459]

TERRACE, H. S. Discrimination learning without errors. *Journal of the Experimental Analysis of Behavior*, 1963, **6**, 1–27. [406]

THORNDIKE, E. L. *Animal intelligence*. New York: Macmillian, 1911. [570]

THORPE, W. H. *Bird song*. London & New York: Cambridge Univ. Press, 1961. [57]

TINBERGEN, N. *The study of instinct*. London & New York: Oxford Univ. Press, 1951. [46, 49–51]

TINKLEPAUGH, O. L. An experimental study of representative factors in monkeys. *Journal of Comparative Psychology*, 1928, **8**, 197–236. [395]

TOLMAN, E. C., & HONZIK, C. H. Introduction and removal of reward, and maze performance in rats. *University of California Publications in Psychology*, 1930, **4**, 257–275. [376, 377]

TOLMAN, E. C., RITCHIE, B. F., & KALISH, D. Studies in spatial learning. II. Place learning versus response learning. *Journal of Experimental Psychology*, 1946, **36**, 221–229. [395, 396]

TULVING, E. Theoretical issues in free recall. In T. Dixon & D. Horton (Eds.), *Verbal behavior and general behavior theory*. Englewood Cliffs, New Jersey: Prentice-Hall, 1968. [436, 437]

TULVING, E., & PEARLSTONE, Z. Availability vs. accessibility of information in memory for words. *Journal of Verbal Learning and Verbal Behavior*, 1966, **5**, 381. [436]

TYLER, L. E. *The psychology of human differences*. New York: Appleton, 1956. [478]

United States Environmental Protection Agency. *The report to the president and congress on noise*. Washington, D.C.: US Govt. Printing Office, 1971. [581]

VALENSTEIN, E. S., & COX, V. C. Influence of hunger, thirst and previous experience in the test chamber. *Journal of Comparative Physiological Psychology*, 1970, **70**, 189. [460]

VALINS, S. Cognitive effects of false heart-rate feedback. *Journal of Personality and Social Psychology*, 1966, **4**, 400–408. [552, 553]

VON BÉKÉSY, G. *Experiments in hearing*. New York: McGraw-Hill, 1960. [355]

VON HELMHOLTZ, H. *Treatise on physiological optics.* (Translated and edited by J. P. C. Southall.) Vol. 3. New York: Dover, 1962. [312]

VON HOLST, E. Relations between the central nervous system and the peripheral organs. *British Journal of Animal Behaviour*, 1954, **2**, 89–94. [336]

VURPILLOT, E. Judging visual similarity: The development of scanning strategies and their relation to differentiation. *Journal of Experimental Child Psychology*, 1968, **6**, 632–650. [162]

WALLACH, H. Brightness constancy and the nature of achromatic colors. *Journal of Experimental Psychology*, 1948, **38**, 310–324. [276]

WALLACH, H., & O'CONNELL, D. N. *Journal of Experimental Psychology*, 1953, **45**, 205–218. [317]

WALLACH, M. A., & KOGAN, N. The roles of information, discussion, and consensus in group risk taking. *Journal of Experimental Social Psychology*, 1965, **1**, 1–19. [563]

WATSON, J. B. *Behaviourism.* Chicago, Illinois: Univ. of Chicago Press, 1924. [139]

WATSON, J. B., & RAYNER, R. Conditioned emotional reaction. *Journal of Experimental Psychology*, 1920, **3**, 1–14. [74]

WAUGH, N. C., & NORMAN, D. A. Primary memory. *Psychological Reviews*, 1965, **72**, 89–104. [413]

WEISBERG, P. Social and nonsocial conditioning of infant vocalizations. *Child Development*, 1963, **34**, 377–388. [152]

WEISS, P. *Principles of development: A text in experimental embryology.* New York: Hafner, 1969. [53]

WERNER, H. *Comparative psychology of mental development.* Chicago, Illinois: Follett, 1948. [177]

WERTHEIMER, M. Psychomotor coordination of auditory and visual space at birth. *Science*, 1961, **134**, 1692. [343]

WHITE, B. L. Informal education during the first months of life. In R. D. Hess & R. M. Bear (Eds.), *Early education.* Chicago, Illinois: Aldine, 1968. Pp. 143–169. [154]

WHITE, B. L., CASTLE, P. W., & HELD, R. Observations on the development of visually-directed reaching. *Child Development*, 1964, **35**, 349–364. [151]

WICKLEGREN, L. W. Convergence in the human newborn. *Journal of Experimental Child Psychology*, 1967, **5**, 74–85. [154]

WOLPE, J. *Psychotherapy by reciprocal inhibition.* Stanford, California: Stanford Univ. Press, 1958. [531]

WRIGHT, W. D. *Researches on normal and defective colour vision.* St. Louis, Missouri: Mosby, 1947. [265]

WYNNE-EDWARDS, V. C. Population control and social selection in animals. In D. C. Glass (Ed.), *Biology and behavior: Genetics.* New York: Rockefeller Univ. Press, 1968. [583]

YOUNISS, J., & FURTH, H. G. The influence of transitivity on learning in hearing and deaf children. *Child Development*, 1965, **36**, 533–538. [178]

ZEIGLER, H. P., & LEIBOWITZ, H. Apparent visual size as a function of distance for children and adults. *American Journal of Psychology*, 1957, **70**, 106–109. [157]

ZIEGARNIC, B. On finished and unfinished tasks. In W. D. Ellis (Ed.), *A source book of Gestalt psychology.* London: Routledge & Kegan Paul, 1955. [221]

ZIMBARDO, P. G. Reported in P. G. Zimbardo & E. B. Ebbesen. *Influencing attitudes and changing behavior.* Reading, Massachusetts: Addison-Wesley, 1969. [542, 561]

Index

Numbers in *italics* indicate the pages on which figures appear.

Human Brain Model
Assembly Instructions

Items needed:
Two large (22″ × 28″) sheets of thin poster board
Rubber cement or paper glue
Single edge razor blade or X-acto knife
Scissors
Paper tape
Tacks
Small board (4″ × 5″ or larger)

Carefully remove all brain model pages from the book binding. Lay out and glue or cement the pages on the poster board. Carefully cut out all the individual pieces, notching the tabs a little more than indicated. Stack the pieces in order not to lose any. Using a single edge razor blade or an X-acto knife, cut all the slots, making sure to cut all the way through the entire length of the slot (better a little too much than not enough, but do not get carried away). Fold any pieces on dotted lines if so indicated. Arrange the pieces before you so that all are visible. The pieces are identified by their distinctive tab, slot, or tack numbers.

Take the rectangular stand piece with tack numbers and place it on a small piece of wood. Tack it to the wood with tacks 1–4. Take the piece containing tab 1 and place it in slot 1, slipping the cerebellum through slot zero and the splenium in the slot above it. Align tack positions 5–16 on the piece containing slot zero with those on the board and tack it down. Continue assembling tabs and slots in order: first numbers, then letters, and finally Roman numerals.

It would be best to tape each letter tab and slot combination on the back side as they are assembled. Once the Roman numerals are completed, the finished cortex can be split apart slightly on the midline and slid over the stand. After careful assembly, this brain model becomes a welcome study aid.

A great deal more can be learned about the structure and function of the brain from this model by studying it as it is assembled. Look over each piece as you add it to the others and see how its structures correspond to those of the surrounding pieces. Cross sections of the right cortex (tabs 21–29) are unlabeled, providing an easy method to test any anatomical knowledge gained by studying the labeled cross sections of the left cortex (tabs 11–19). Functions are mapped on the outer left cortex. However, these should not be taken too literally. Although there is good reason to believe that the left hemisphere is usually dominant for language and speech, the brain areas responsible for such functions as creative thought are not really known.

For enthusiasts of anatomy, structures indicated on the brain model are indexed below by pieces on which they appear. Again, distinctive tab (T), slot (S), or tack (t) numbers are used to identify individual pieces; thus T19 refers to the most frontal cross section of the left cortex, i.e., the once containing Tab 19.

Amygdala—T16

Angular Gyrus—see Outer Left Cortex (OLC)

Anterior Commissure—T1, T10, T17

Anterior Paraolfactory Sulcus—Ts

Aqueduct—T9

Auditory Radiation—T15

Brachium Conjunctivum—S7, T7, T8, T9, T13, T14

Brachium Pontis—S6

Calcarine Sulcus—see OLC, T13

Caudate Nucleus—T12, T14, T15, T16, T17, T18

Central Sulcus—see OLC, T16

Cerebellum—T1, T6

Chorioid Plexus—T11

Cingulate Cortex—Ts

Cingulate Sulcus—Ts

Collateral Sulcus—see OLC, T13

Corpus Callosum—Ts, T1, T10, T11, T14, T15, T16, T17, T18, T19

Cranial Nerves

   III Oculomotor—T9

   IV Trochlear—S8, T8

   V Trigeminal—T7

   VI Abducens—T6

   VII Facial—T6

   VIII Vestibular—T6

   VIII Ventral Cochlear—T5

   IX Glossopharyngeal—T4

   X Vagus—T3

   XI Accessory—T2

   XII Hypoglossal—T3

Cuneatus—T3

Cuneus Lobule—Ts

Dentate Nucleus—T6

Dorsal Ramus—t6

Fimbria Hippocampi—T10

Fornix (Fx)—T10, T11, T14, T15, T16, T17

Frontal Cortex—T12, T18, T19

Fusiform Gyrus—see OLC

Gracilis—T3

Hippocampal Gyrus—see OLC

Hippocampal Sulcus—see OLC

Hippocampus—T14, T15

Hypothalamus—T17

Inferior Colliculus—S9, T9

Inferior Frontal Gyrus—see OLC

Inferior Frontal Sulcus—see OLC

Inferior Olive—T3, T4, T5

Inferior Parietal Lobule—see OLC

Inferior Temporal Gyrus—see OLC

Inferior Temporal Sulcus—see OLC

Infundibulum—T9

Insula—T11, T16, T17

Internal Capsule—T11, T17

Lateral Fissure—T11, T15, T16, T17

Lateral Geniculate—S9, T9

Lateral Occipital Lobe—see OLC

Lateral Olfactory Stria—T10

Lateral Sulcus—see OLC

Lateral Ventrical (L.V.)—T11, T13, T14, T15, T16, T17, T18, T19

Lemniscal Tegmentum (Lem. Teg.)—T14

Mammilary Body—T9, T10, T16

Marginal Sulcus—Ts

Medial Geniculate—S9, T9, T14

Medial Olfactory Stria—T10

Medulla Oblongata—T1

Middle Frontal Gyrus—see OLC

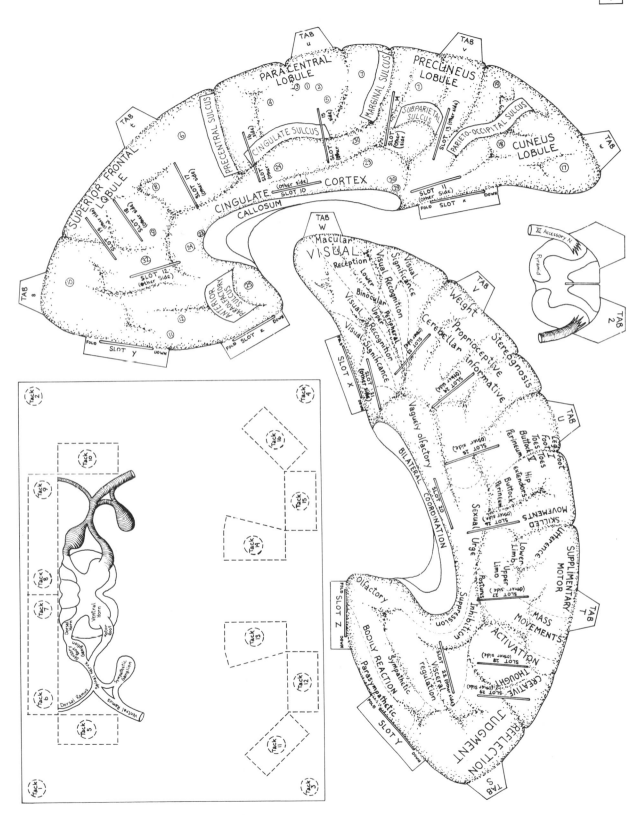

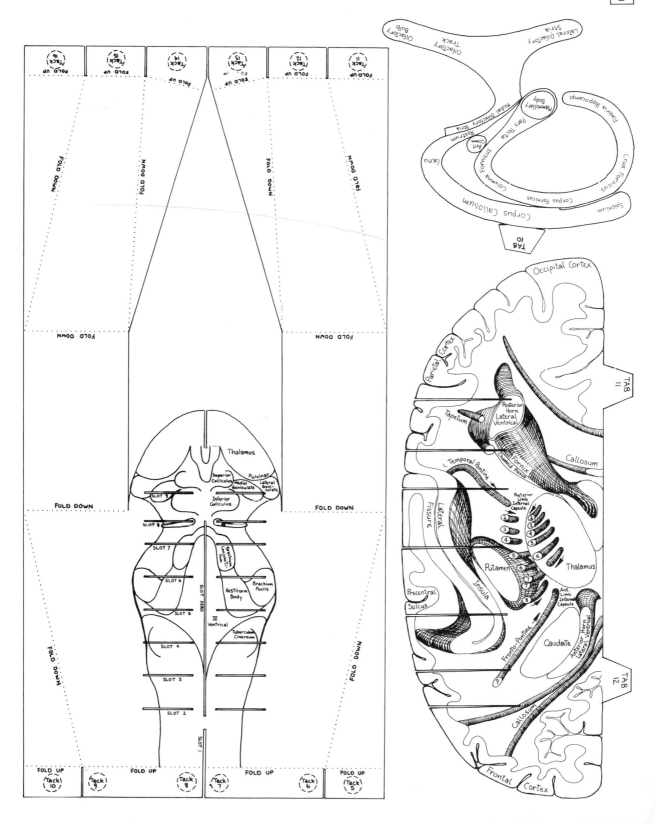

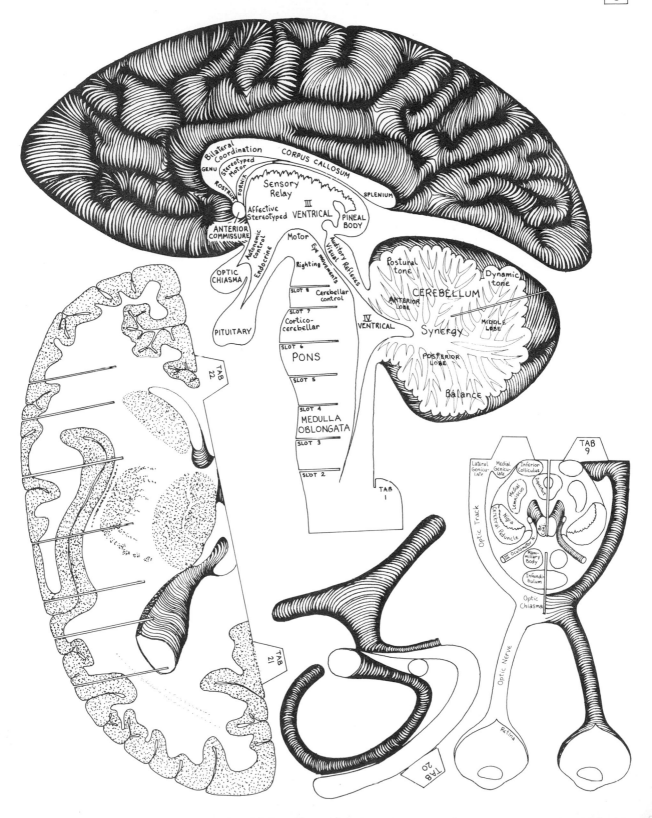

Bilateral Coordination

CORPUS CALLOSUM

GENU

Stereotyped Motor

ROSTRUM

FORNIX

Sensory Relay

SPLENIUM

Affective Stereotyped

III VENTRICAL

PINEAL BODY

ANTERIOR COMMISSURE

Autonomic Control

Motor

Righting

Auditory Reflexes

Visual

Eye Movements

Endocrine

OPTIC CHIASMA

SLOT 8

Cerebellar Control

SLOT 7

Cortico-cerebellar

PITUITARY

SLOT 6

PONS

SLOT 5

SLOT 4

MEDULLA OBLONGATA

SLOT 3

SLOT 2

TAB I

Postural tone

CEREBELLUM

ANTERIOR LOBE

Dynamic tone

MIDDLE LOBE

IV VENTRICAL

Synergy

POSTERIOR LOBE

Balance

TAB 22

TAB 21

TAB 20

TAB 9

Lateral Geniculate

Medial Geniculate

Inferior Colliculus

Medial Lemniscus

Nigra

Cerebral Peduncle

Red Nucleus

III Oculomotor

Mammillary Body

Infundibulum

Optic Chiasma

Optic Track

Optic Nerve

Retina

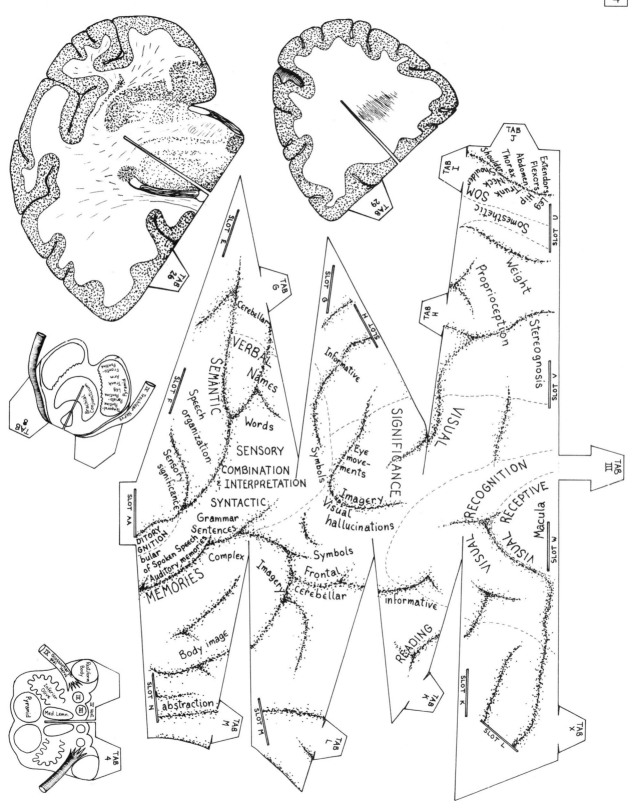

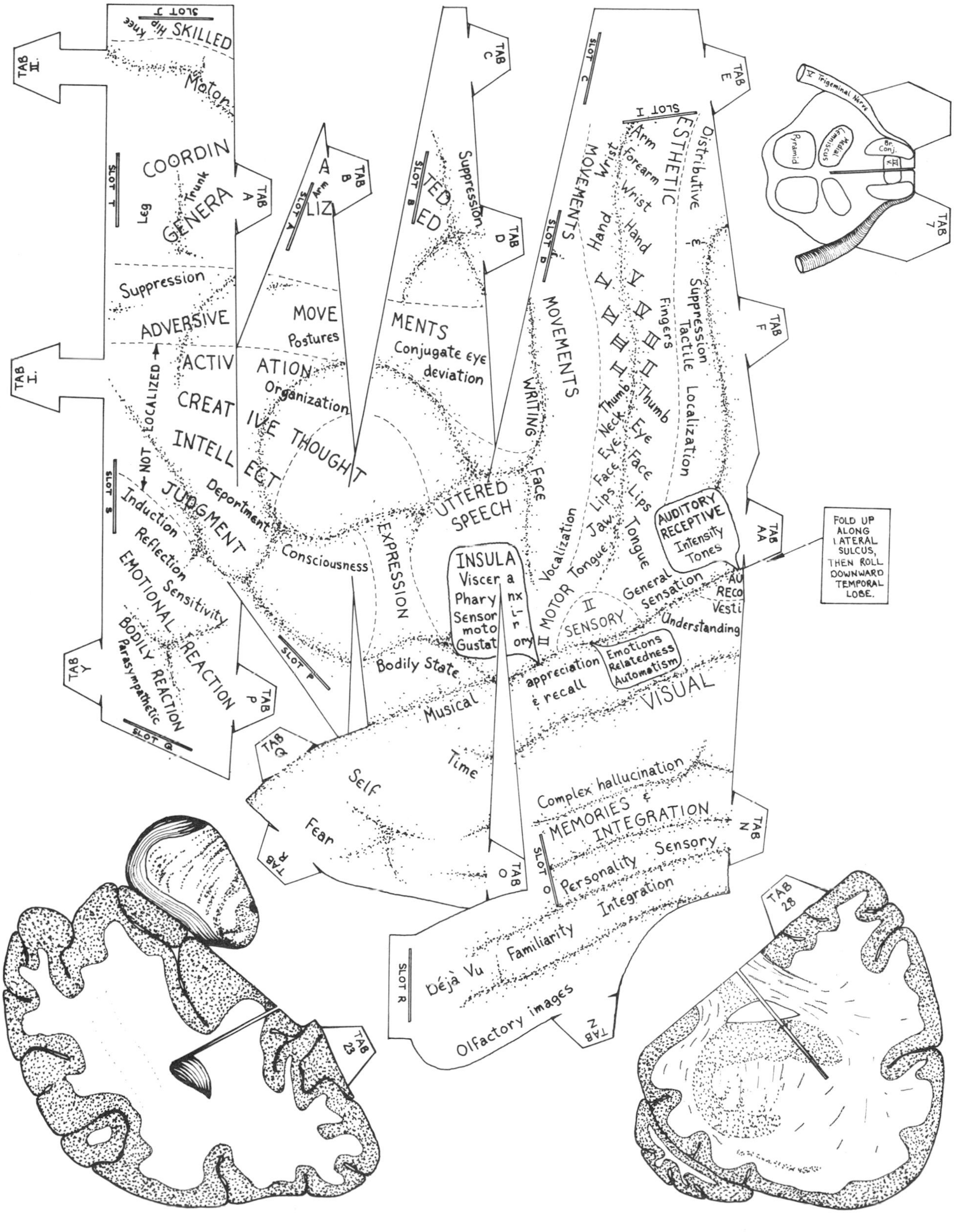
SLOT J
Hip
Knee
SKILLED
Motor
TAB II.
TAB I.
SLOT T
COORDIN
Leg
Trunk
GENERA
TAB A
A
LIZ
Arm
SLOT Y
TAB B
SLOT B
TED
ED
Suppression
TAB C
TAB D
SLOT C
SLOT D
SLOT I
TAB E
ESTHETIC
Distributive
MOVEMENTS
Arm
Forearm
Wrist
Wrist
Hand
Hand
Suppression
ADVERSIVE
MOVE
Postures
MENTS
Conjugate eye
deviation
MOVEMENTS
Fingers
Suppression
Tactile Localization
TAB F
NOT LOCALIZED
ACTIV
ATION
Organization
CREAT
IVE THOUGHT
INTELL
ECT
JUDGMENT
Deportment
WRITING
Thumb
Neck
Eye
Face
Lips
Jaw
Tongue
Thumb
Eye
Face
Lips
Tongue
SLOT S
Induction
Reflection
Sensitivity
EMOTIONAL
REACTION
BODILY REACTION
Parasympathetic
TAB Y
TAB P
SLOT Q
SLOT P
Consciousness
EXPRESSION
UTTERED SPEECH
Face
Vocalization
MOTOR
INSULA
Viscer a
Phary nx
Sensor
moto
Gustat ory
II
SENSORY
General sensation
AUDITORY RECEPTIVE
Intensity
Tones
TAB AA
AU
RECO
Vesti
Understanding
Emotions
Relatedness
Automatism
FOLD UP ALONG LATERAL SULCUS, THEN ROLL DOWNWARD TEMPORAL LOBE.
Bodily State
appreciation
& recall
Musical
VISUAL
TAB Q
Self
Time
Complex hallucination
MEMORIES &
INTEGRATION
TAB N
Fear
TAB R
TAB O
SLOT O
Personality
Sensory
Integration
SLOT R
Déjà Vu
Familiarity
Olfactory images
TAB N
V Trigeminal Nerve
Pyramid
Medial Lemniscus
Br. Conj.
TAB 7
TAB 23
TAB 28

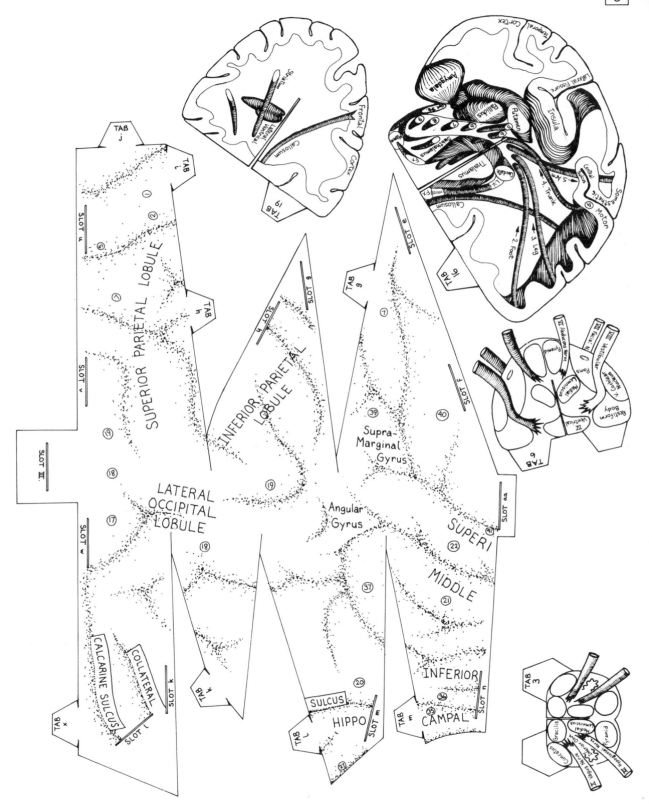

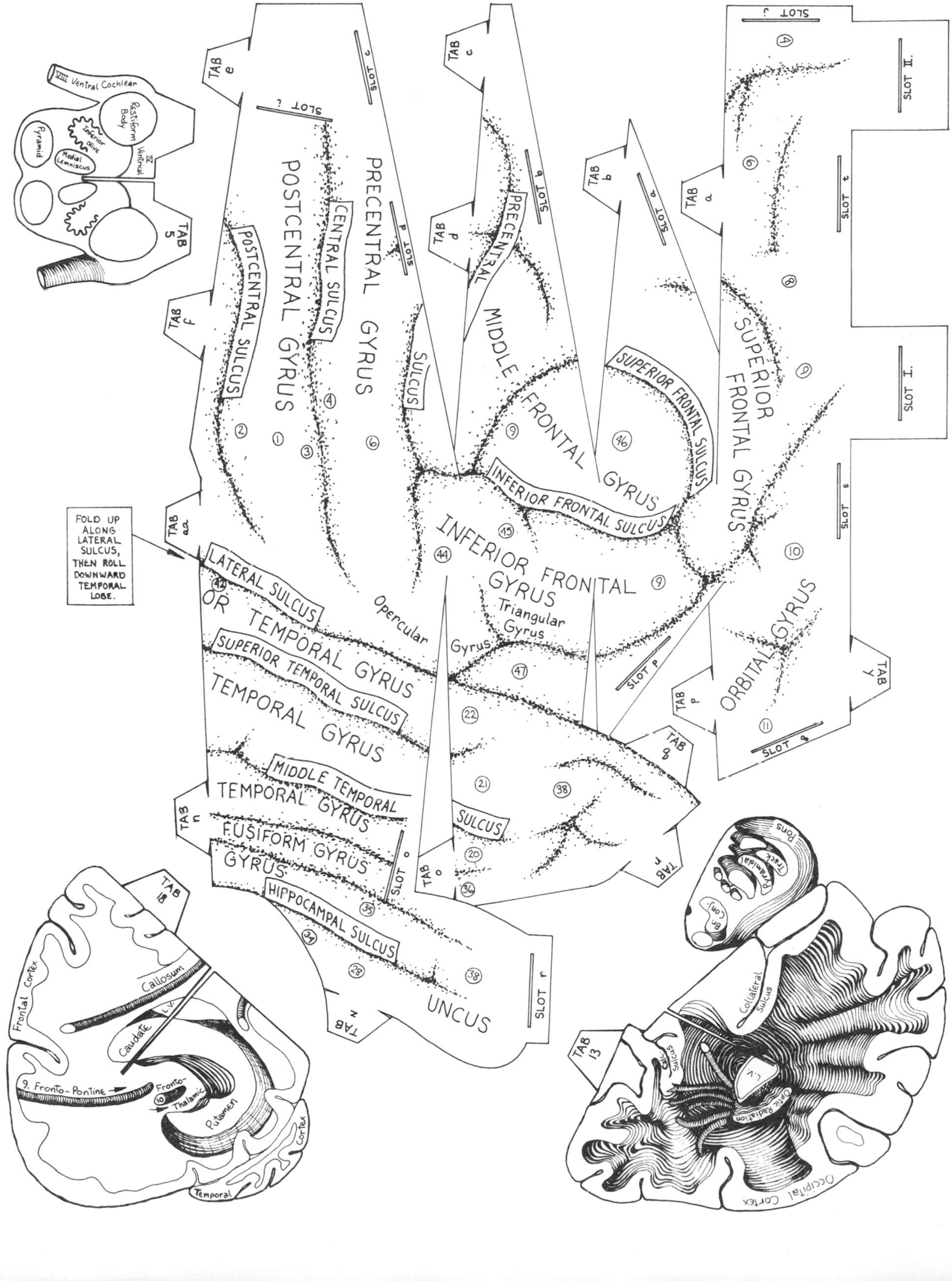
VIII Ventral Cochlear
Restiform Body
Inferior olive
Pyramid
Medial Lemniscus
IX Ventral
TAB 5
TAB e
SLOT i
SLOT c
TAB c
SLOT j
SLOT II
SLOT b
TAB b
SLOT a
TAB a
SLOT t
TAB d
SLOT d
POSTCENTRAL SULCUS
POSTCENTRAL GYRUS
CENTRAL SULCUS
PRECENTRAL GYRUS
PRECENTRAL SULCUS
MIDDLE FRONTAL GYRUS
SUPERIOR FRONTAL SULCUS
SUPERIOR FRONTAL GYRUS
TAB f
SLOT I
INFERIOR FRONTAL SULCUS
INFERIOR FRONTAL GYRUS
Triangular Gyrus
Opercular Gyrus
FOLD UP ALONG LATERAL SULCUS, THEN ROLL DOWNWARD TEMPORAL LOBE.
TAB aa
LATERAL SULCUS
SLOT s
OR TEMPORAL GYRUS
SUPERIOR TEMPORAL SULCUS
TEMPORAL GYRUS
ORBITAL GYRUS
TAB y
TAB p
SLOT p
TAB g
SLOT q
MIDDLE TEMPORAL SULCUS
TEMPORAL GYRUS
TAB n
FUSIFORM GYRUS
GYRUS
SLOT o
TAB o
TAB r
HIPPOCAMPAL SULCUS
UNCUS
SLOT r
TAB N
TAB 18
Frontal Cortex
Callosum
L.V.
Caudate
9. Fronto-Pontine
10 Fronto-Thalamic
Putamen
Temporal
Cortex
Pons
Pyramidal Tract
Br. Conj.
Collateral Sulcus
TAB 13
Calc. Sulcus
L.V.
Optic Radiation
Occipital Cortex

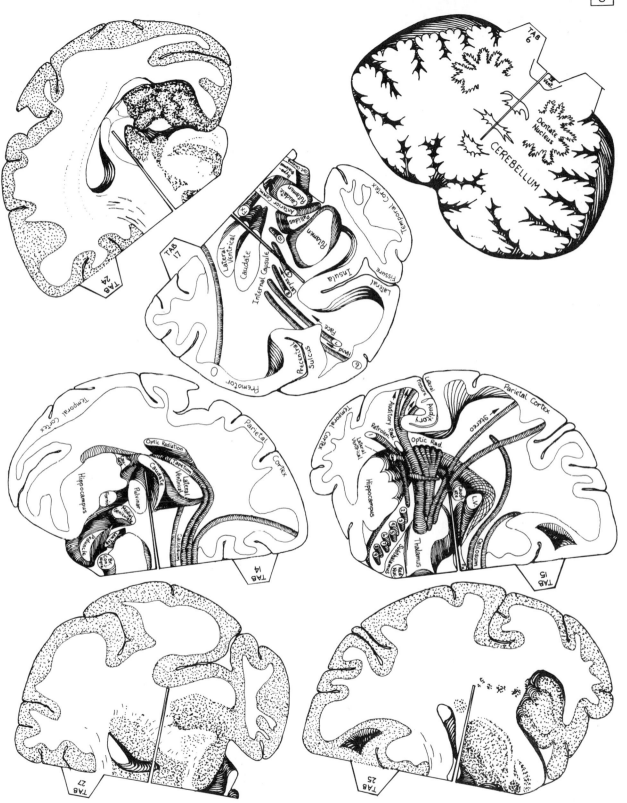